Anderson Guide to Enjoying Greenwich, Connecticut

The Anderson Guide is user-friendly and loaded with information. It answers questions about Greenwich we didn't know we had. Since buying our first copy in 1998, we have relied on The Anderson Guide for everything from researching preschools to finding the best fried chicken in town.
—Heather Picchione

I've lived in Cos Cob since 1990 and find your restaurant ratings to be very accurate. Also, you have lots of new information on places of local interest that I wasn't aware of. Thanks for producing this great reference guide.
—Ruth Schlosser

I have been a lifelong resident and now have my own home in Greenwich. The Anderson Guide is indispensable.
—Sandra Walker

The Anderson Guide is a treasure trove of information about Greenwich. Solid Gold and five stars!!!!!!
—Joan Roome

The Guide just keeps getting better and better.
—Livvy Floren

I am thrilled with the new edition of the Guide. It is the book I reach for instead of the telephone directory. Every area resident who dines out, whether frequently or infrequently, will find this helpful, informative book a necessity. The reviews are right on. I truly appreciate all of the effort that goes into it.
—Linda Taylor

Anderson Guide to Enjoying Greenwich, CT

Written by
Carolyn Anderson &
Anderson Associates, Ltd.
www.greenwichliving.com
164 Mason Street, Greenwich, CT 06830
203.629.4519

Illustrations by
Vanessa Y. Chow

Published by
Ickus Guides, Avocet Press Inc
3 Moison Rd N, Blauvelt, NY 10913
www.avocetpress.com

ISBN 978-0-9677346-7-5

Cover Photos Credit:
Blue and Lola on the Collins' boat, Photo by John Collins
Stephanie Zeeve, Cheerleader, Photo by Chris Gennarelli
Meghan Lynch, CT State Swim Champion, Photo by Chi Chi Ubina
Jerry and Carolyn Anderson, Photo by Philip Kuperberg

Printed in the United States of America

Anderson Guide to
ENJOYING GREENWICH
Connecticut
An insider's favorite places

Tenth Edition

Anderson Associates
Greenwich Real Estate Specialists

with illustrations and maps
by Vanessa Y. Chow.

Avocet Press Inc

WHAT KIND OF GUIDE IS THIS?

The Guide is a list of local resources...simply that. It is not a book of advertisements. No place mentioned in the Guide had any idea that it would be included. We never accept favors as a result of including someone. Establishments and programs are listed because we like them. Although the Guide is about Enjoying Greenwich, you will note many selections are outside of Greenwich's town limits. These easy to reach places complement our many in-town resources.

Initially, many years ago, our first Guide was prepared for our real estate clients. Then the calls came in- their friends needed a copy. The owner of a local bookstore saw it and said we must publish it. That is where it started. Our initial reason for writing it has not changed. We know finding favorite spots takes a while. We have lived in Greenwich for many years and we hope the resources in the Guide will help everyone moving into town feel right at home.

The new edition has over 240 restaurant reviews. Jerry and Carolyn anonymously visit each one at least twice before writing the review. We are looking at the whole experience- food, ambience and service. If the restaurant is disappointing in too many ways, we do not include it. Restaurant reviewing is a professional responsibility. We have a great deal to do with a restaurant's success or failure. We have extensive food and restaurant experience. Carolyn is the author of the Complete Book of Homemade Ice Cream and several other cookbooks. For a number of years we owned and operated a small vineyard. Tasting foods and wines and knowing how they are prepared is greatly helpful in reviewing. Carolyn is a professional member of the American Society of Interior Designers. Before devoting full time to real estate, she designed restaurants. Many people remember the popular restaurant, Morgan, open for many years in Greenwich which she designed. Knowing the requirements of good restaurant design is helpful in reviewing. We love discovering new "finds." We hope our readers of the Guide will enjoy them too.

We are grateful to so many residents for their support and enthusiastic appreciation of the Guide. We hope you will find this edition useful, too! The Greenwich Library keeps copies at their information desk to help people with questions. The Historical Society has copies of our past editions in their archives. We are pleased to be documenting our town's many events, restaurants, shops and tips about the Greenwich way of life.

Please let us know what you think of this Guide or of the restaurants, stores or services we reviewed. We love your comments and suggestions! Please send your comments to Carolyn@GreenwichLiving.net or call Carolyn at 203.629.4519 x 118.

Sincerely,

Carolyn   Jerry   Amy   Monica

With a special thanks to Katie Bookser, John Collins Jr. and Philip Kuperberg for tireless editing.

Greenwich Guide Website

Because stores and restaurants change so frequently, we will post changes and new reviews on the Anderson Associates Facebook page.

Disclaimer

The purpose of this Guide is to educate and entertain. Every effort has been made to make this guide accurate; however, it should not be relied upon as the ultimate source of information about Greenwich or about any resource mentioned in the Guide.

There may be mistakes both typographical and in content. We have done our best to lead you to spots we hope you will like. This is by no means a complete guide to every resource in Greenwich. Unfortunately, even the best are not always perfect. If you have tried one of our favorites and are disappointed, if we have missed your favorite, or if we have made a mistake in a description, please email us.

A note about "Hours"

The hours and days of operation are intended as a guide, but they should not be considered definitive. Establishments change their hours as business dictates. In addition, many change their hours for winter and summer and during holidays. Finally, just about every establishment takes a vacation.

.

CONTENTS

CONTENTS

CONTENTS

CONTENTS

CONTENTS

CONTENTS

CONTENTS

GREENWICH

Greenwich is recognized as the best town in Connecticut—one of the best places to live and raise your family in the United States. If you are looking for a beautiful town with safety, amenities, top-rated public and private schools, convenient access to New York City and a home that will be a great investment—you will love Greenwich.
For government contacts, see GOVERNMENT.

- Median age: 43
- Median household income: $127,201
- Average residential sales price: $2,128,194
- Median residential sales price: $1,315,556
- Assessed value of all residences: $24.4 billion
- Population 2014: 62,256 (2000 census 61,101)
- Number of households: 22,249 (70% are single family homes)
- 48 square miles
- 1,500 acres of public parks
- Greenwich is 25% green, it has 8,000 acres of protected land, 32 miles of shoreline, 20 parks, 4 beaches, a municipal golf course and 150 miles of riding trails.
- 40 houses of worship
- 9 yacht clubs, 9 country clubs, 11 garden clubs and 1 tennis club
- 98 special interest organizations
- 38 languages spoken in the high school
- 17% of public school students come from non-English speaking homes
- Public School Budget $140,973,644 (2013-2014)
- Per pupil expenditure $17,909 (average class size 19.5)
- 91% of faculty have a masters degree or higher
- Surveys show Greenwich has one of the top high schools in the US
- 10 Private and Parochial Schools
- Greenwich Library ranked #2 in New England
- Bruce Museum ranked in the top 10% of US Museums
- Rated safest community in Connecticut
- Ranked #1 in Robb Report's 10-best places to live in the US
- Town of Greenwich budget: $395,688,483 (2014-15)
- Town of Greenwich capital budget: $39,400,000 (2014-15)
- Town of Greenwich Mill Rate: 10.969, an increase of 02.75%

Information based on data from the Town website, CERC Town Profile, Greenwich Multiple Listing Service, and the Town's Budget presentation to the RTM.

GREENWICH

For more information on Greenwich check:
* Greenwich Association of Realtors www.GreenwichRealtors.com
* Census Bureau www.census.gov
* Town web site www.GreenwichCT.org
* Connecticut Economic Research Center
  www.cerc.com/TownProfiles/list.asp
* Community Answers www.greenwichlibrary.org/commanswers.htm
* Greenwich Chamber www.greenwichchamber.com/greenwichave.asp

Greenwich Rated Best Place to Live

Time and again, Greenwich is rated as Connecticut's number one place to live. Greenwich is the premier town along what is called the Connecticut Gold Coast. The town's unique beauty has been preserved by very careful town planning and zoning. Like Beverly Hills, Greenwich has the rare distinction of being one of those recognizable names. But unlike Beverly Hills, which is a 5.7 square mile enclave, Greenwich extends over 50 square miles with rolling hills, woodlands, meadows and 32 miles of gorgeous shoreline bordering the Long Island Sound. Greenwich is not isolated—it is a real community and a wonderful place to raise a family.

Although Greenwich conjures up thoughts of stately country homes and waterfront estates reserved for the select few, Greenwich is much, much more. As you will discover, Greenwich offers diversity, not only in real estate and architecture, but also in residents. Greenwich is home to a cosmopolitan group of executives and a great variety of professionals, full-time moms, artists, writers, diplomats, actors, and sports figures. And a few couch potatoes as well.

In addition to being rated tops by Connecticut Magazine, the Robb Report rated Greenwich one of the 10-best places to live in the USA. Greenwich has a vast array of attractions. Whether you look at the picturesque shopping areas, the personal service provided by its mix of elegant shops, its fantastic library (the most used in Connecticut), its ultra modern hospital or its fifty fabulous restaurants, Greenwich has it all. The *New York Times* declared that Greenwich has more Very Good and Excellent restaurants per capita than any other community in Connecticut. One of the many unique things about Greenwich can be found on Greenwich Avenue every day between the hours of 9 am and 6 pm: the police officers at the street corners directing traffic. These officers help to preserve the feeling of a small town and, of course, also help keep the town's crime rate low.

Quality of Life

Greenwich is still 25% green. It has 32 miles of coastline, with its main beaches at Greenwich Point (147 acres), Byram Beach and the two Town owned islands (Captain's Island & Island Beach). Greenwich has 8,000 acres of protected land, over 1,000 acres of town parks, 35 town tennis courts (not including the YWCA Courts), an indoor ice rink, 14 public marinas and a 158-acre, 18-hole golf course (open only to residents). Music lovers enjoy the Greenwich Symphony and the Bruce Museum is rated one of the best museums in Connecticut. *See PARKS and CULTURE for more information.*

Education

Greenwich public schools (eleven elementary, three middle and one high school) continually draw high ratings. 40% of the graduates go to the "Most Competitive Colleges." The school budget is approximately $141 million dollars. The average class size is 20 and 91% of the teachers have masters degrees. In addition, Greenwich has thirty independent pre-schools and ten excellent private and parochial day schools. *For details, see SCHOOLS.*

Fire Department

15 Havemeyer Place. Non-emergency phone: 203.622.3950
To report a fire dial 911
www.greenwichct.org/FireDept/FireDept.asp
The Greenwich Fire Department consists of uniformed career firefighters and volunteer firefighters who work together to preserve life and protect property in Greenwich.

Our fire department responds to over 4,000 emergency calls per year, ranging from minor fire alarm activations to structure fires, motor vehicle accidents, and even hazardous materials incidents. The Fire Department operates out of 8 fire houses within Greenwich (and Banksville, New York) with the help of nearly 100 uniformed career firefighters, and over 150 well-trained and dedicated volunteers.

See NUMBERS YOU SHOULD KNOW for a complete list of fire stations and their telephone numbers.

Police Department

11 Bruce Place
Non-emergency phone: 203.622.8000, emergency number: 911
www.greenwichct.org/PoliceDept/PoliceDept.asp
The Greenwich Police Department is a group of helpful, kind and competent professionals. They are charged with the protection of life and property, the preservation of public peace, the prevention and detection of crime, the apprehension of offenders and the enforcement of state and local laws and ordinances, as well as the countless calls for service that the Police Department handles on a daily basis. The Department offers a ten-week Citizen Police Academy program, allowing residents the opportunity to get a behind the scenes look at police operations.
www.greenwichct.org/PoliceDept/pdCitizensPoliceAcademy.asp

Crime

Greenwich is rated the safest community in Connecticut and one of the safest in the country—and it's no wonder: with 14 police cars on the road at all times, traffic downtown directed by police officers, and with a force of 155 dedicated police officers, the average response time to a call is often less than 4 minutes.

Greenwich Library

www.greenwichlibrary.org
The Greenwich Library is a special treasure used by young and old alike. In a typical year the library loans 675,000 customers an average of 4.5 books per minute. It is no wonder the library has been rated the best in the country. The library received a $25,000,000 bequest from Clementine Peterson. Based on this bequest and funds raised by the Friends of Greenwich Library, Architect Cesar Pelli designed the 31,000 square foot addition as well as renovations to the original building. In addition to the Main Branch, the library has marvelous branches in Cos Cob and Byram. Old Greenwich has its own superb independent library, Perrot. *For more information on our wonderful libraries see LIBRARIES AND BOOKS.*

GREENWICH

Greenwich Hospital
5 Perryridge Road, 203.863.3000
www.greenhosp.org
The 160-bed Greenwich hospital is an affiliate of Yale University School of Medicine. It is a world-class hospital, providing the town with excellent health care. Patients from all over Fairfield and Westchester seek treatment at Greenwich Hospital. The hospital has a state of the art cancer center (Bendheim) as well as a $129,000,000 expansion to make it a high tech diagnostic and healing center without the austere look, normal delays and "red tape" often associated with hospitals. With the $98,000,000 expansion "The Watson Pavillion," Greenwich residents have a completely new hospital with the best of services and amenities. For more information on the Hospital and other medical services, see **HEALTH.**

Greenwich Town Hall
101 Field Point Road, 622.7700
Call this number for any town department or go to www.greenwichct.org
Note: See GOVERNMENT for a complete list of meeting rooms and departments with their hours of operation.
Note: Post Offices and Zip Codes are listed under their own heading.
Note: See www.GreenwichLiving.com to explore Greenwich Neighborhoods.

Location
Greenwich is in the southwest corner of Connecticut, conveniently close to a big city, while being situated in the comfort and security of the country. Greenwich has an excellent transportation system and is just minutes from Westchester Airport, which makes trips to nearby cities such as Boston or Washington convenient. Greenwich is only 29 miles from Times Square (43 minutes by one of the 78 trains that operate daily between New York City and Greenwich). There are 4 train stations conveniently located throughout the town. U.S. Route 1, the historic Post Road, is the main commercial artery. Locally, it is named Putnam Avenue. In addition, Interstate 95 and the Merritt Parkway traverse Greenwich, giving it excellent regional accessibility. It takes about 10 minutes to drive to Stamford, about 60 minutes to Danbury and approximately 15 minutes to White Plains. Limousines provide easy and quick access to New York City's international airports: La Guardia Airport is about a 45-minute drive, Kennedy Airport is about a 60-minute drive. The Merritt Parkway, built in 1935 for cars only, was placed on the National Register of Historic Places in 1993.

GREENWICH

Population

The population of Greenwich grew until about 1970. Since 1970, the resident population has been more or less stable. This has been accompanied by the construction or conversion of more dwellings to house the same number of people. In 1950, the population of 40,835 lived in 10,524 households, with an average of 3.9 persons in each. In 1990, the population of 58,441 persons lived in 23,515 households, with an average of 2.5 persons. In 2000 the population was 61,101. Presently the population is 62,256 living in 22,249 households with an average of 2.8 persons. 70% of Greenwich homes are for single families, mostly detached, one to a lot. The town's residential zones provide a wide variety of housing types, from small condominiums to single family homes of more than 10,000 square feet on 4 acres or more. Greenwich is divided into several strictly enforced zoning areas. In or near town, the density is high as a result of condominiums and apartments. Further from the center of town, the zoning changes to 1 acre per family, then to 2 acres per family and north of the Merritt Parkway it is a minimum of 4 acres per family. The population of the town continues to be diverse. One sixth of all public school students, with 38 different first languages, are learning English as a second language.

Jobs and Income

Greenwich is a job center where 35,278 people are employed. More people now come to work in Greenwich than go to work elsewhere. As a result of the many offices moving to the suburbs, Greenwich has become a net provider of jobs during the past twenty-five years. At the same time the median household income in Greenwich has been growing steadily. In 1979 it was $30,278. Ten years later, in 1989, it was $65,072. Today it is over $127,201.

Taxes

The Town of Greenwich operates on a "pay as you go" basis and does not carry long term debt (except for sewer bonds). This allows Greenwich to keep property taxes low while maintaining a budget of $395,688,483. Real estate taxes are based on assessments limited by statute to 70% of market value, at present 10.969 (up 02.75 from last year) per thousand of assessed value (mill rate). There are no separate school taxes. There are no separate County taxes. There is a personal property tax on cars equal to the mill rate. There is no town income tax. The state has an income tax of 3 to 6.7%, depending on your tax bracket.

Trends

Greenwich is in the largest metropolitan area of the United States, and is fortunate in its location, natural features, and historic development. Within the New York metropolitan area, Greenwich is the most desirable place to live. The migration of business and jobs from New York City to White Plains, Greenwich and Stamford has increased the demand for housing here. Greenwich intends to keep its place as the premier town to live in. To maintain control of its future, Greenwich has developed a Plan of Conservation and Development (POCD). This plan, filled with maps and information on the town, is very influential in preserving the town's goals. It can be purchased from the Planning & Zoning Commission at Town Hall, 203.622.7700 or on-line at www.greenwichct.org/government/departments/planning_and_zoning/ plan_of_conservation_development_pocd.

Greenwich has a Geographic Information System (GIS) which allows the town and residents to access information such as property boundaries, assessments and building lines. The GIS map request form is online at www.greenwichct.org/grAllFormsList.asp

Government

www.GreenwichCT.org

Unlike many towns and cities, there is a great feeling of community here. Greenwich is run primarily by volunteers, not politicians. The town is governed by a Board of Selectmen (one full-time and two part-time) who are elected every two years. Although town departments are staffed by paid professionals, except for the Selectmen, all town boards (such as the Board of Estimate and Taxation, which serves as the town's comp-troller) and the Representative Town Meeting, are made up of unpaid citizen volunteers. In addition to the volunteers in government offices, Greenwich depends on many residents who serve in unofficial capacities. The volunteer network supports and supplements the work of town departments and gives the town its unparalleled cultural and social values.

GREENWICH

Representative Town Meeting (RTM)

www.greenwichct.org/rtm

Greenwich still retains the traditional New England Representative Town Meeting. The RTM consists of 230 members selected by the voters in the town's 12 districts. It is larger than the State's House and Senate combined. Candidates run on a non-partisan basis and serve without compensation. The RTM serves as the town's legislative body and most issues of importance, including appointments, labor contracts, town expenditures over $5,000, town ordinances and the town budget, must be approved by the RTM. Any town issue may be brought before the RTM by a petition of twenty registered voters. Because many of the RTM members are quite successful in business and other careers, the town is run efficiently, honestly, conservatively and in the interest of its citizens. RTM meetings are held at night about once every month. RTM meetings are open to everyone and are a good source of information about the town. The League of Women Voters (203.352.4700) is very active and is a great way to get involved. They publish an informative guide on Greenwich Government, "People Make it Happen."

History

Greenwich is the tenth-oldest town in Connecticut. Named after Greenwich, England, the town began as a temporary trading post founded by Captain Adrian Block in 1614. Greenwich was settled in 1640 when it was purchased from the Indians as part of the New Haven Colony, with allegiance to England. The settlers grew restless under the Puritan influence and, in 1642, withdrew their allegiance to England and transferred it to the more liberal Dutch. At this time, the Cos Cob section of Greenwich was occupied by the Siwanoy Indians and a toll gate was set up between them and the central part of Greenwich, called Horseneck. In 4 years the town was forced back under the domination of the New Haven Colony. Greenwich supported the British during the French and Indian War, but during the Revolution the town was sacked several times by the King's troops. The advent of the New Haven Railroad in 1848 began the transformation of Greenwich into a residential community. This period saw many wealthy New Yorkers, including Boss Tweed, building summer homes. In the twenties, the town began to grow rapidly and land values began to soar. By 1928, Greenwich led the nation in per capita wealth. In 1933 the town had grown so large that it had to abandon open town meetings and adopted the Representative Town Meeting (RTM). Although the population growth has abated (because of the scarcity of buildable land) the property values have continued to climb.

Areas and Villages

Greenwich is made up of a number of small villages and neighborhoods, each with its own character and charm. The largest of these are Byram, Banksville, Back Country, Central, Cos Cob, Mianus, Old Greenwich, Glenville, and Riverside. All parts of Greenwich share the same government, school system, property tax rate and access to public facilities.

Main Streets

The central street connecting the main part of Greenwich with the Riverside, Cos Cob, and Old Greenwich sections is Putnam Avenue (a.k.a. Post Road, US 1). It runs essentially east to west through the town (of course out-of-town maps show US-1 running North/South from Stamford to Port Chester). Greenwich Avenue, the main shopping street, is the dividing line between East and West Putnam Avenue. Sound Beach Avenue on the eastern end of Putnam Avenue is the main shopping street for Old Greenwich and runs to Greenwich Point Beach (Tod's Point).

Organizations Dedicated to Preserving Greenwich History

Children of the American Revolution
Mary Bush Society, Putnam Cottage, 243 East Putnam Avenue
www.nscar.org, www.connecticutcar.org

Daughters of the American Revolution
Putnam Hill Chapter, 243 East Putnam Avenue, 203.869.9697
www.ctdar.org/Chapters/Putnam_Hill.htm

Greenwich Library Oral History Project
www.glohistory.org

Historic District Commission
www.greenwichct.org/historicdistComm/HistoricDistComm.asp

Historical Society of the Town of Greenwich
39 Strickland Road, Cos Cob, 203.869.6899
www.hstg.org

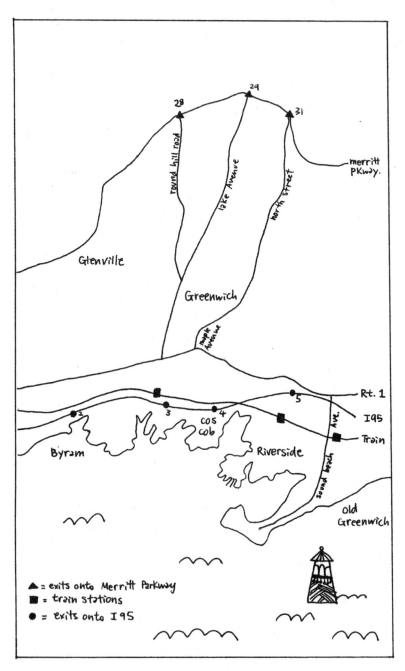

CENTRAL GREENWICH MAP

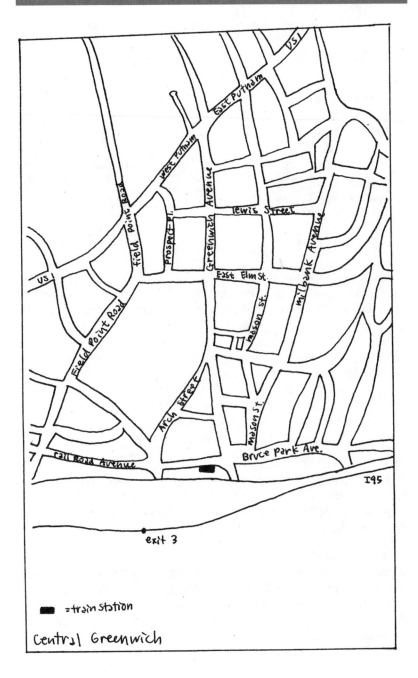

Central Greenwich

AUTOMOBILES

See TRAVEL for airports, trains, taxis, buses, limousines and travel agencies.
See FITNESS & SPORTS for Auto Racing.

Sections:
General Car Information
Automobile Dealers
Body Shops and Customizing
Car Wash, Detailing
Driver's License (Car Registration & Driving Instruction)
Parking
Rentals (Car, Truck, Bus)
Vehicle Emissions Inspections

GENERAL CAR INFORMATION

Commuting Information
Local commuters can untangle their morning commutes by consulting *News 12* on Cable or Channel 3 or by the following commuter transportation websites:
MetroPool: www.metropool.com
The site offers news and information on commuting in and around Fairfield and Westchester counties.
Greenwich Traffic Cams: www.ct.gov/dot (click on traffic cams)
Commuters can search for car pool partners on www.nuride.com
For Parking Permits at the Greenwich Station see
www.greenwichct.org/Parking/psParkingPermits.asp

Charging Stations
To find electrical vehicle charging stations, go to AAA.com/TripTik and enter an address or point of interest. Then click on the EV charging icon. AAA has a mobile app to find charging stations. See AAA.com/Mobile to download the app.

Police Directing Traffic
We still have the privilege of having police direct traffic on Greenwich Avenue. They are always helpful and friendly. When you can't find something, they are a great source of information. However, be warned, pedestrians and drivers alike are expected to pay attention. Follow their crossing instructions or face humiliation. Street crossings are allowed only when traffic is stopped in all directions.

AUTOMOBILES

AUTOMOBILE DEALERS

- **Acura**, 343 West Putnam Avenue, 203.625.8200
- **Aston Martin**, (Miller Motor Cars), 342 West Putnam Ave, 203.629.4726
- **Audi**, 181 West Putnam Avenue, 203.661.1800
- **Bentley**, (Miller Motor Cars), 342 West Putnam Ave, 203.629.3890
- **BMW** 355 West Putnam Avenue, 203.413.1900
- **Bugatti**, (Miller Motor Cars), 342 West Putnam Ave, 203.629.3890
- **Cadillac**, 144 Railroad Avenue, 203.625.6300
- **Carriage House Motor Cars**, 25 Railroad Ave, 203.661.6669
- **Ferrari** (Miller Motor Cars), 342 West Putnam Ave, 203.629.3890
- **Honda**, 289 Mason Street, 203.622.0600
- **Infiniti**, 315 Milbank Ave, 203.869.2600
- **Jeep-Chrysler-Dodge**, 631 West Putnam Avenue, 203.531.0505
- **Lexus**, 19 Railroad Avenue, 203.869.6700
- **Maserati** (Miller Motor Cars), 342 West Putnam Avenue, 203.629.3890
- **McLaren** (Miller Motor Cars), 342 West Putnam Avenue, 203.629.3890
- **Mercedes-Benz**, 261 West Putnam Avenue, 203.869.2850
- **Pagani** (Miller Motor Cars), 342 West Putnam Avenue, 203.629.3890
- **Porsche**, 241 West Putnam Avenue, 203.869.8900
- **Rolls Royce**, 275 West Putnam Avenue, 203.661.4430
- **Saab**, 144 Railroad Avenue, 203.413.1344
- **Toyota**, 75 East Putnam Avenue, 203.661.5055
- **Volkswagen**, 200 West Putnam Avenue, 203.869.4600

BODY SHOPS AND CUSTOMIZING

AfterFX Customs (Custom Alarm, Radio, Sunroof)
20 Crescent Street, Stamford CT, 203.975.1188
If you are envious of your friends' GPS, Satellite Radio, back-up camera and sensors, you don't have to trade in your car. Instead, have it upgraded.
Hours: Weekdays 8:30am-5pm, Saturday 10am-3pm.

East Coast Auto Spa (Window Tinting, Pin-Stripping)
69 Cottage Street, Portchester NY, 914.937.0300
www.EastcoastWindowTinting.net
This shop has been in business for a long time.

AUTOMOBILES

Grover Cunningham Auto Body Shop
74 North Water Street, Byram CT, 203.531.8468
This family owned business has been operating for 100 years. Bruce Cunningham, the grandson of the founder, now runs the business.

Island Park Auto Body
29 New Broad Street, Port Chester NY, 914.937.7336
The shop that many car dealers often use. We find them reliable.

CAR WASH AND DETAILING

Classic Shine Auto Fitness Center
67 Church Street, Greenwich CT, 203.629.8077
www.classicshine.com
This car detailing firm does not often advertise, but has been in business for many, many years. They operate primarily on the strength of recommendations.
Hours: Monday-Saturday by appointment.

Old Greenwich Car Wash and Lube
1429 East Putnam Avenue *(at the Mobil station),* Old Greenwich CT, (203) 637-7903
When you are in a hurry and just want a quick machine wash.

Splash Car Wash
• 73 East Putnam Avenue, Cos Cob CT, 203.625.0809
• 625 West Putnam Avenue, Byram CT, 203.531.4497
www.splashcarwashes.com
Both locations do hand washes and interior cleaning. The Byram location also has an express (machine) lane. Mark Curtis and Chris Fisher, both lifelong Greenwich residents, developed the concept of washing cars in line on conveyor by hand. In 1994, they opened their first hand wash in Greenwich and called it Splash. Now with 16 locations, they wash more than 1,000,000 cars a year. They can hand wash your car in 15 minutes or less.
Hours: Monday-Saturday 8am-6pm (Friday to 7pm), Sunday 9am-5pm.

AUTOMOBILES

DRIVERS LICENSE AND CAR REGISTRATION

AAA / CT Motor Club

1101 High Ridge Road, Stamford CT, 203.388.2189

www.aaa.com

The place to get your international driver's license or other help for a trip. This is the easiest place for members to renew their driver's license. Vehicle registration and new licenses can only be obtained at the DMV. Hours: Weekdays 9am-5pm, Saturday 9am-1pm.

Department of Motor Vehicles Bureau (DMV)

540 Main Avenue (Route 7), Norwalk, CT, 800.842.8222, 860.263.5700, www.ct.gov/dmv

New residents must obtain a Connecticut driver's license within sixty days, even if they hold a valid license from another state. Vehicles must also be registered within sixty days after the owner has established residency. The car must pass an inspection before being registered. This is also the place for learner's permits, name changes, license plate cancellations and a variety of registration and title services. Before going, be sure to check the website for current requirements and hours.

Directions: I 95 N to exit 15, Rte 7 N; follow Rte 7 expressway to end, R and straight into the DMV.

Driver's License Renewals

CT Licenses can be renewed at the AAA offices in Stamford or at DMV in Norwalk.

Green Light Driver's Education

444 East Putnam Avenue, Cos Cob, CT 203.861.1188

http://www.freshgreenlight.com/Greenwich-Driving-School.html

Driver education for teens and adults. Check their website for requirements.

Tom's Driving School

1212 East Putnam Avenue, Riverside, 203.869.7240

www.tomsdrivingschoolct.com

Since 1951, Greenwich residents have been learning to drive in this driver's education program. They have both car and motorcycle instruction.

AUTOMOBILES

PARKING

www.greenwichct.org/Parking/Parking.asp
For permit renewals and payment of parking tickets on-line.

www.greenwichct.org/Parking/psMunicipalParkingLots.asp
Municipal Parking lot map, parking permits and Electronic Smart Cards for parking meters.

Parking App

The Town uses the free Parkmobile app in many Greenwich locations including Town Hall, Island Beach, Horseneck and Soundview parking lots. You can park all day at the train station for $5. There is a $0.35 user fee. For more information call the Parking Services Department at 203.618.3060.

Parking Meters

Parking meters in Greenwich are not expensive, but parking tickets are. You must pay for parking Monday-Saturday, 9am-5pm. Meters are being converted from direct pay to credit card payment booths or for Smart Cards. In the meantime, meters will accept quarters. On Sundays and holidays, parking is free. Old Greenwich is still free of parking meters.

PARKING PERMITS

Train Station Parking

Call 203.622.7730, for details about train station parking permits and the location of municipal lots, or go to www.greenwichct.org/Parking/psParkingPermits.asp
Railroad station parking permits are limited in number and as soon as you know you will need one, put your name on their waiting list.

Senior Center Parking

Call the Senior Center, 203.862.6720, for parking permits in front of the Center.

Smart Cards

Smart Cards are re-loadable and can be purchased and funds added/re-loaded at the Town of Greenwich Parking Services Office, Town Hall ground floor. They are available in $10-$20-$50 increments.
Hours: Weekdays 8:30am-4pm.

AUTOMOBILES

RENTALS

BUS RENTALS:
J&R Tours
80 Edison Avenue, Mount Vernon NY, 800.444.5786
www.JandRtours.com

CAR RENTALS

Enterprise Rent a Car
15 Edgewood Ave (Just off West Putnam Avenue, next to McDonald's)
203.622.1611 www.Enterprise.com
They often have the lowest rates, but charge for mileage.
Hours: Weekdays, 7:30am-6pm, Saturday, 9am-1pm.

Hertz Rent a Car
1 Station Place, Stamford CT, 203.324.3131
www.Hertz.com
At the Stamford Metro Center.

Zip Car
866.494.7227, www.zipcar.com
Members (from $6 a month) can rent cars by the hour or the day. Reserve
your car online or through their mobile app. Westchester Airport and
Purchase College are the closest zip locations at the present time. Of
course, Zip Car locations are all over Manhattan and at most major airports.

TRUCK RENTALS

City Truck Rentals (Penske)
45 Cedar Street, Stamford CT, 203.359.2181
www.gopenske.com
When you need a large, well maintained truck, call them first.

U Haul
25 Jefferson Street, Stamford, 203.324.3869
www.uhaul.com
U Haul rents everything from a van to a large truck. They also have a
large stock of boxes and other moving supplies. Their vans are well kept
and are great for local moves. Their best trucks are saved for long distance runs. Don't expect customer service to be a high priority.

VEHICLE EMISSION INSPECTIONS

Car Inspections
888.828.8399
www.ctemissions.com
Cars must be inspected every two years. The following local stations are certified. These stations do inspections on a first-come, first-serve basis. Call for inspection hours.

Mobile Lube Express
1429 East Putnam Avenue, Old Greenwich CT, 203.637.7903

Shell of Greenwich
83 East Putnam Avenue, Greenwich CT, 203.661.8871

TIP: THE JOB SEARCH

If you are looking for a job or an employee, check out the Job Board. This free public bulletin board is run by Community Answers for people from the ages of 17 to 55. It can be viewed in the window of Community Answers during Library hours. Postings can be phoned in at 203.622.7979 or posted in person weekdays from 9am to 5pm at the central Greenwich Library. For older job seekers, check out USE (Utilizing Senior Energy) at the Greenwich Senior Center, (203.629.8032). Younger job seekers should go to The Student Employment Service at the Greenwich High School (203.625.8008) until June and to Community Answers during the summer.

Black Forest (Bakery)
52 Lewis Street, 203.629.9330
www.BlackForestPastryShop.com
German-style bakery. Don't miss the black forest cake and chocolate mousse bombe, summer fruit tarts, delicious wedding cakes and coffee cakes. A nice place to stop in, have a pastry and a coffee. We love their melt-away pastry. Hours: Monday-Saturday 7:30am-6pm, Sunday 8am-1pm.
Size: seats 6

Cassone Bakery (Bakery Outlet)
202 South Regent Street, Port Chester NY, 914.939.1568
www.JJCassone.com
People in the know come to this bakery outlet early in the morning for their pastries. Everyone likes their breads, which they have in all varieties and sizes. The service is very pleasant and helpful. Bring cash. They do not accept credit cards or checks.
Hours: Weekdays 6am-8pm, Saturday & Sunday 6am-7pm.

City Limits Diner (Bakery)
135 Harvard Avenue (at La Quinta), Stamford CT, 203.348.7000
The restaurant review is in RESTAURANTS. Pastry Chef Tracy Kamperdyk-Assue, makes everything in-house. Take a look at the display counter just inside the diner. You will be amazed at the fancy cake creations. They even do wedding cakes. Don't forget to pick up some of their delicious pastries.
Hours: Open every day 6am-10pm (Friday & Saturday 11pm).

Crumbs Bake Shop (Bakery)
48 West Putnam Avenue, Greenwich CT, 203.618.9500
www.Crumbs.com
Crumbs, a mini chain with 48 stores, went into bankruptcy. It was purchased out of bankruptcy by Marcus Lemonis star of CNBC show "The Profit." Besides cupcakes and coffee, they have pastries, donuts, muffins, scones, brownies, cakes, croissants, pies and tarts. Lemonis has added a new product, the Baissant (a cross between a bagel and a croissant). It isn't bad but our favorite is the Blackout. Their giant cupcakes and miniatures are popular for parties.
Hours: Monday-Thursday 7am-7:30pm, Friday 7am-9pm, Saturday 8am-8pm, Sunday 9am-6pm.
Size: seats: 2

BAKERIES

Di Mare Pastry Shop (Bakery)
1263 East Putnam Avenue (Riverside Commons Shop Center), Riverside CT, 203.637.4781
www.DimarePastryShop.net
A hot spot to order your child's birthday cake with a large selection of themes & characters for decoration (computerized and handmade.) This bakery is often selected as the best bakery in Fairfield County.
Hours: Monday-Saturday 8am-6:30pm, Sunday 8am-3 pm (July & August and most holidays 8am-1pm).

Dunkin' Donuts (Bakery)
375 East Putnam Avenue, Cos Cob CT, 203.869.7454
(This location also sells Baskin-Robbins ice cream.)
271 West Putnam Avenue, Greenwich CT, 203.869.5791
184 Sound Beach Avenue, Old Greenwich CT, 203.990.0157
www.DunkinDonuts.com
Founded in 1950 in Quincy, MA, the company has about 10,000 locations. Although it originally focused on baked goods, more than half of its business today is coffee, although they still have more than 1,000 varieties of donuts.
Hours: Cos Cob, Monday-Sunday 5am-11pm; Greenwich and Old Greenwich locations close earlier.
Size: Cos Cob seats 16, Greenwich seats 6, Old Greenwich seats 12.

(The) Kneaded Bread (Bakery)
181 North Main Street, Port Chester NY, 914.937.9489
www.KneadedBread.com
A first-rate bread bakery. Every day they bake over 17 varieties of crusty, European-style breads. Be sure to try their chocolate or raisin walnut bread. They also have Danish, scones, cookies, pies, muffins, salads, soups, Focaccia and sandwiches. Stop in for a good coffee and sandwich. On Sunday mornings, lines form early for their freshly made sticky buns, croissants and cinnamon donuts. This is good stuff!! Be sure to order holiday breads (Thursday) in advance.
Hours: Weekdays 7am-5pm, Saturday 8am-4pm, Sunday 8am-2pm.
Size: seats 50.

Le Pain Quotidien Bakery (Bakery, Restaurant)

382 Greenwich Avenue, Greenwich CT, 203.404.7533

www.LePainQuotidien.com

The restaurant review is in RESTAURANTS. If you are in a hurry and can't sit down, you can get good coffee, muffins, pastries and bread to take out. We really like their very French, myriad of layers, croissants baked in their kitchen. The rest of the bakery items come from their NYC bakery. They also have good quiche ready to go.

Hours: Weekdays 7am-7pm, Saturday & Sunday 8am-7pm

Neri Bakery Outlet Store (Bakery Outlet)

31-37 Pearl Street, Port Chester NY, 914.939.3311, 3235

www.nerisbakery.com/retail-product-list.aspx

At a beautiful wedding, we discovered this resource for delicious wedding cakes at reasonable prices. Be sure to check out their frosted donuts, pies, cakes, cookies, breads and pastries. They make unique holiday pastries. Bring cash. They do not accept credit cards or checks.

Hours: Monday-Saturday 7am-7:30 pm, Sunday 7am-5pm.

Panera Bread (Bakery, Restaurant)

10 Westchester Avenue, Port Chester NY, 914.939.0079

www.PaneraBread.com/enu/bakery

Located at the movie complex in Port Chester, Panera Bread is a combination bakery and fast food café. There are over 1,500 locations in the US. Fresh dough for their artisan and specialty breads is delivered to the store every day from NJ. Their selection of pastries and cookies is enough to satisfy almost anyone's cravings. If you dare, you can get nutrition information on their website.

Hours: Sunday-Wednesday 7am-8pm, Thursday 7am-9pm, Friday & Saturday 7am-10pm.

Size: seats 100.

BAKERIES

SoNo Baking Company & Café (Bakery, Restaurant)
101 South Water St., South Norwalk CT, 203.847.7666
www.SoNoBaking.com
A dear friend and food writer first introduced us to this place, saying "it's full of delicious pastries, cakes, cookies and breads." Come early for the best selection and watch the bakery in action. Where else can you get a terrific whole wheat croissant? Soups and sandwiches are good here, too. Its not surprising, the owner is John Barricelli, Senior Food Editor for Martha Stewart Living.
Hours: Monday-Thursday & Sunday 7am-3pm, Friday & Saturday 7am-5pm. (The hours change with the seasons.)
Size: seats 26.

St. Moritz (Bakery)
383 Greenwich Avenue, Greenwich CT, 203.869.2818
www.StMoritzPastryShop.com
What would the Avenue be like without St. Moritz? For over 60 years this family owned shop has been filled with luscious, rich pastries, chocolate mousse and cakes. Be sure to try the Sarah Bernhardt cookies. Everything is made on the premises.
Hours: Monday-Saturday 7am-5:30pm.

Sweet Lisa's Exquisite Cakes (Bakery)
3 Field Road, Cos Cob CT, 203.869.9545
www.SweetLisas.com
Wonderful cakes, pastries and designer cookies by special order only. They usually require seven days notice. Their website has lots of pictures of their creations. Their exquisite cookies make perfect party favors.
Hours: Tuesday-Friday 9am-5pm, Saturday 9am-3pm.

Sweet Pea's Baking Company (Bakery)
212 Sound Beach Avenue, Old Greenwich CT, 203.990.0008
Rafael and Katja Pita opened a bakery with freshly roasted coffee and breads coming out of the oven every two hours. The pastries are international, including one of Rafael's favorites-Brazilian Cheese Balls.
Hours: Monday-Wednesday 7am-4pm, Thursday-Saturday 7am-5pm, Sunday 8am-3pm.

BAKERIES

Upper Crust Bagel Company (Bakery, Deli)
197 Sound Beach Avenue, Old Greenwich CT, 203.698.0079
www.UpperCrustBagel.com
Our favorite bagels! They have 15 varieties of bagels, tasty old-fashioned kettle-boiled and hearth-baked ones, as well as 12 gourmet spreads. They also have good sandwiches, salads and coffees. This is a neighborhood place, with lots of notices posted about coming events.
Hours: Weekdays 6am-4pm, Saturday 7am-4pm, Sunday 7am-3pm.
Size: seats 20

Versailles (Bakery, Restaurant)
315 Greenwich Avenue, Greenwich CT, 203.661.6634
www.VersaillesGreenwich.com
The restaurant review is in RESTAURANTS. This very French bistro, now owned and run by Mark and Evelyne Penvenne of Meli-Melo fame, has a front counter full of pastries that will make your day worth living. Their showcase of treats reminds us of delightful Paris patisseries. Try their operas and éclairs. The right place to order a take-out quiche. All of their bakery items are made locally.
Hours: Monday-Saturday 7am-10pm, Sunday 8am-10pm.

TIP: TOWN PARTY
www.GreenwichTownParty.com
Live music, kids' activities, food trucks and more. This is such a popular event, residents buy their tickets as early as December for this May party. You can buy tickets anytime on-line or at Town Hall in May. Proof of residency or employment is required to purchase tickets.

BOOKS & LIBRARIES

Sections
    Book Sales and Donations
    Book Stores
    Libraries
    Literary Organizations

BOOK SALES AND DONATIONS

Book Exchange
At the Greenwich Recycling Center, Holly Hill Lane, 203.622.0550
This is fun you cannot miss. Residents drop off unwanted books. A volunteer librarian organizes the books by topic and author. Free books are available on all subjects. Just follow the rules: keep the shelves neat, 10 books per family, enjoy your reading!
Donation and exchange hours: Friday and Saturday, 7 am-noon.

Byram Shubert Book Sale
The Friends of the Byram Shubert Library conduct a not-to-be-missed sale twice a year. Last year over 200 people donated books, CDs, DVDs, and artwork. Proceeds help support the expansion and programs of the library. For more information or to schedule a pickup of your donation, call Lisa Johnson, Sale Chair, 203.570.8527 or the Library at 203.531.0426.

Darien Book Aid Plan
1926 Post Road, 203.655.2777
http://DBA.Darien.org
This worthy group has been sorting and shipping donated books to countries around the world since 1949. They are particularly interested in children's story books, books in braille, grammar texts, teenage literature and books on medicine, agriculture and gardening. The lobby is open for donations 24 hours a day. Check the website for the types of books they are seeking and for the workshop hours.

Ferguson Library Used Books
Corner of Broad & Bedford Streets, Stamford CT, 203.964.1000
www.fergusonlibrary.org
We discovered this source for used books over a cup of Starbucks Coffee (Starbucks is next door). The coffee house opens directly into the "Friend's Book Shop." The library receives books and book collections from a wide area. The sale of these used books benefits the Ferguson Library.

BOOKS & LIBRARIES

Pequot Library Book Sale
720 Pequot Ave., Southport section of Fairfield CT, 203.259.0346
www.pequotlibrary.org
Known as the best book sale in New England, book lovers will find this worth the trip. Held in July, usually the third week, this annual book sale takes place under huge tents. Check their website for times.

St. Paul's Fair for All
St. Paul's Episcopal Church, 200 Riverside Avenue, 203.637.2447
Every year, on the Friday and Saturday following Memorial Day, your whole family will enjoy the St. Paul's fair with rides, games and food plus a whole hall filled with used books. Proceeds support their outreach mission.

BOOK STORES

Barnes & Noble (Books)
Stamford Town Center, 100 Greyrock Place & Tresser Blvd, 203.323.1248
www.bn.com
B&N has 658 stores. This 40,000 sf store is the largest in Connecticut. It also sells magazines, newspapers, DVDs, CDs, graphic novels, gifts, games, and music. Barnes & Noble began to publish books during the 1980s by re-issuing out-of-print titles.
Hours: Monday-Saturday 9am 10pm (Friday & Saturday to 11pm), Sunday 9am-9pm.

Diane's Books (Books)
8A Grigg Street, 203.869.1515
www.dianesbooks.com
A family-owned bookstore specializing in family books for all ages. You will find a huge selection, including a wealth of children's books, an excellent travel book section and, best of all, a knowledgeable, resourceful sales staff. This is a must-visit bookstore. You will enjoy their newsletter filled with book suggestions and be sure to check their website for their calendar of author events.
Hours: Monday-Saturday 9am-5pm.

BOOKS & LIBRARIES

Carol Davenport (Antiquarian Bookseller)
5 Oval Avenue, Riverside, 203.637.4160
www.davenportbooks.com
E-mail: info@davenportbooks.com
She specializes in modern first editions, art & photography, signed books, and scarce non-fiction titles. She issues catalogs in her areas of specialty. She offers bibliographic services, including appraisals, and collection development services for individuals and institutions.

(A) Timeless Journey (Comic Book Store)
2 Eighth Street, Stamford CT, 203.353.1720
www.ATimelssJourney.com
New comics, back issues, graphic novels, cards and collectibles. Paul Salerno, who has been in business for 25 years, has one of the few surviving comic book stores.
Hours: Tuesday-Saturday 11am-6pm (Wednesday 7pm), Sunday 12pm-4pm.

TIP: GREENWICH LIBRARY DATABASES
The Greenwich Library subscribes to over 60 databases which can be accessed free of charge to Library card holders. Almost all of these databases can be accessed from your computer. To find a database of interest, like the Antiques Reference Database, call the Greenwich Library Reference Desk at 203.622.7900 or go to:
www.greenwichlibrary.org

BOOKS & LIBRARIES

LIBRARIES

Book Clubs

The Libraries often sponsor book clubs, such as the Thursday Evening Book Club which meets on the first Thursday of each month at the Cos Cob Library at 7:30pm year round. All are welcome. Call 203.622.6883.

Greenwich Library Card Guidelines

Library cards are free to Greenwich residents and are valid for 3 years. Greenwich Residents must show a photo ID with a current Greenwich address or 2 items that include your name and current Greenwich address.

Greenwich Library

www.greenwichlibrary.org
The Greenwich Library is a special treasure used by young and old alike. In a typical year the Library loans 675,000 customers an average of 4.5 books per minute. It is no wonder the library has been rated the best in the country. The library received a $25,000,000 bequest from Clementine Peterson. Based on this bequest and funds raised by the Friends of Greenwich Library, Architect Cesar Pelli designed the 31,000 square-foot addition as well as renovations to the original building. The Byram Shubert branch is beautifully renovated and doubled in size. We have a wonderful new Cos Cob Library. These branches provide convenient neighborhood locations and serve as community centers. The library provides a large number of programs which are noted in other sections of this guide. Use the website to check a book's availability or phone 203.622.7910 to reserve items, and ask to have your reserved materials sent to one of the branches. Membership in the library is free. There is no limit to the number of books you can check out. In addition to books, the library has over 30 data bases which can be used free of charge. If you use your library number, most can be accessed from your home computer.

> **TIP: DOWNLOAD BOOKS FROM THE GREENWICH LIBRARY**
>
> The Library provides downloadable audio books to Library card holders. To download a book, go to http://overdrive.greenwichlibrary.org You will need to install the free media software and have your Library card number handy.

- Greenwich Library (Main Library)
101 West Putnam Avenue, 203.622.7900
Hours: weekdays 9am-9pm (July & August 5pm),
Saturday 9am-5pm, Sunday 1pm-5pm (September-June).

- Byram Shubert Library (Branch)
21 Mead Avenue, Byram CT, 203.531.0426
Hours: Monday, Wednesday, Friday & Saturday 9am-5pm, Tuesday 10am-6pm, Thursday 12pm-8pm, closed Sunday.
The renovation doubled the Library's space to 10,000 sf.

- Cos Cob Library (Branch)
5 Sinawoy Road, Cos Cob CT, 203.622.6883
Cos Cob is a new library, perfect for family enjoyment. While the youngest ones enjoy playing or reading in the children's corner, older ones can read favorite books or search the Internet. The dynamic staff organizes events for both children and adults. It is an important part of Cos Cob community life.
Hours: Monday 12pm-8pm, Tuesday-Saturday 9am-5pm, Closed Sunday.

Perrot Library of Old Greenwich
(Independent Library)
90 Sound Beach Avenue, Old Greenwich CT, 203.637.1066
Children's Library, 203.637.8802
www.perrotlibrary.org
The Perrot Memorial Library is a non-profit institution independent of the Greenwich Library. It is open to all residents of Greenwich, although it principally serves the residents of Old Greenwich, Riverside and North Mianus. Perrot has a beautiful ($3.3 million), 7,000 square foot Children's Library.
Hours: Monday, Wednesday, Friday, 9 am-6 pm; Tuesday & Thursday, 9 am-8 pm; Saturday, 9 am-5 pm; Sunday, 1 pm-5 pm (closed Sundays in the Summer).

TIP: GREENWICH LIBRARY ORAL HISTORY

If you want to learn about the Town, from the first-hand experiences of residents, you will love the oral history series available in the Library. Volunteers have compiled 850 interviews into 138 books. Books are also for sale at the Oral History office www.glohistory.org

BOOKS & LIBRARIES

LITERARY ORGANIZATIONS

American Pen Women (Greenwich Branch)
www.penwomen.org
Greenwich Pen Women is a non-profit organization of professional artists, writers, and composers.

Friends of Byram Schubert Library
A volunteer organization founded in 1953 to support the Byram Shubert Library. They sponsor cultural programs and events for children and adults. Membership is $25. To join please see the staff at the library or e-mail byramshubertlibraryfriends@gmail.com

Friends of Cos Cob Library
coscobfriends@greenwichlibrary.org
A volunteer organization founded in 1972 to support the Cos Cob Library. They sponsor cultural programs, art shows, and special events for children and adults. Membership is $10 for Seniors and $20 for families plus other levels of membership are available.

Friends of Greenwich Library
The Library is maintained by the Town but all capital improvements are funded by contributions from the Friends. Any donation to the Greenwich Library makes you a "Friend." To receive the Keep Posted newsletter with book reviews and program events be sure to give them your e-mail.

Greenwich Reads Together
www.Greenwichreadstogether.org
There is a lot to love about Greenwich, and this makes the list! A few years ago, Gail Wilson suggested we choose a book, encourage the whole town to read it and then host book discussions. The Town responded- and now over 20 organizations are involved. Everyone all over town is discussing the book. If you want to catch up, read: *The Book Thief* by Marcus Zusak, *Zeitoun* by Dave Eggers, *When the Emperor Was Divine* by Julie Otsuka and *The Boys in the Boat* by Daniel Brown.

Literary Matters
16 Highmeadow Road, Old Greenwich CT
www.LiteraryMatters.net
Esther Bushell recommends great books to read and holds events to meet the author. Her recommendations and insights are excellent. Be sure to subscribe to her email newsletter.

CHARITABLE & SERVICE ORGANIZATIONS

AmeriCares
88 Hamilton Avenue, Stamford CT 203.658.9500
www.americares.org

American Legion (Greenwich)
Greenwich Post 29
248 Glenville Road, Greenwich CT, 203.531.0109
www.legion.org

Greenwich Jaycees
PO Box 232, Greenwich CT 06836
www.greenwichjaycees.org

Greenwich Kiwanis Club
PO Box 183, Greenwich CT 06836
www.greenwichkiwanis.org

Greenwich World Hunger
PO Box 7444, Greenwich CT 06836
www.greenwichworldhunger.com

Junior League of Greenwich
231 East Putnam Avenue, Greenwich CT, 203.869.1979
www.jlgreenwich.org

Knights of Columbus
37 West Putnam Avenue, Greenwich CT, 203.622.1939
www.kofc.org/un/eb/en/officers/fac.html

TIP: THE ENCHANTED FOREST
Each year in early November, the Junior League organizes a magical display of beautifully decorated Christmas trees and gingerbread houses, all donated by Greenwich organizations and individuals. The auction of these items helps support the good works of the Junior League. www.jlgreenwich.org This is a fun event for the whole family. Call 203.869.1979 for details.

CHARITABLE & SERVICE ORGANIZATIONS

Lions Club of Greenwich
PO Box 1044 Greenwich CT 06836 1044
www.lionsclubs.org

Lions Club of Old Greenwich
PO Box 215, Old Greenwich CT 06870
www.lionsclubs.org

Lions Club of Western Greenwich
www.lionsclubs.org
Jack Nearing, President, 203.531.9668

P.E.O. Sisterhood, Greenwich Chapter
www.peointernational.org

Rotary Club of Greenwich
PO Box 1375 Greenwich CT 06836
www.greenwichrotary.org

United Way of Greenwich
1 Lafayette Court, Greenwich CT, 203.869.2221
www.unitedway greenwich.com

Veterans of Foreign Wars
Cos Cob Post 10112
PO Box 8, Cos Cob CT 06807
www.vfw.org

Veterans of Foreign Wars
Greenwich Post 1792
PO Box 128, Greenwich CT 06836
www.vfw.org

Volunteers on Call
P.O. Box 4434 Greenwich CT 06831, juliana@volunteersoncall.org
www.volunteersoncall.org

Woman's Club of Greenwich
89 Maple Avenue, Greenwich CT, 203.869.2046
www.womansclubofgreenwich.org

CHILD ENRICHMENT

For other Children related activities see the sections CHILDREN or BOOKS & LIBRARIES.
For nursery, pre-schools and other public/private schools see SCHOOLS.
For children and adult sports see SPORTS.

SECTIONS
Art
Chess
Cooking
Computers
Dance & Etiquette
Extracurricular Kids' Programs
Languages
Music & Acting
Reading
Tutors

ART

Bruce Museum
1 Museum Drive, Greenwich CT, 203.869.0376 x 325
www.brucemuseum.org
Art classes offered throughout the year, including during school holidays.

Lakeside Pottery
543 Newfield Avenue, Stamford CT, 203.323.2222
www.lakesidepottery.com
Children's pottery program for ages 8-13. They also offer summer and winter camps and birthday parties. Many adult classes offered, too.

(The) Greenwich Arts Council
299 Greenwich Avenue, Greenwich CT, 203.862.6750
http://www.greenwichartscouncil.org/
Children's after-school art programs.

(The) Greenwich Art Society
299 Greenwich Avenue, Greenwich CT, 203.629.1533
www.greenwichartsociety.com
Art workshops often including cartoon drawing, pastels, clay, paper collage and sculpture after school. Adult art classes also available.

CHILD ENRICHMENT

CHESS

National Scholastic Chess Foundation (NSCF)
171 East Post Road, White Plains, NY, 914.683.5322
www.nscfchess.org
If your child enjoys games and problem-solving, chess lessons from these experts will open up a wonderful world. Classes are held at the Boys and Girls Club, 4 Horseneck Lane, Greenwich. Classes offered for grades K-6, cost is about $150 for 5 weeks, usually on Saturday afternoons.

Youth Chess
Chess is offered in many after school programs, at town libraries and at the YMCA.
The Greenwich YMCA Youth Chess Club is for players of all levels. It is taught by National Master Rich Jackson.

COOKING

Aux Delices
23 Acosta Street, Stamford CT, 326.4540 x 108
www.AuxDelicesFoods.com
This wonderful gourmet food shop offers a variety of cooking classes for children and adults at their Stamford location. Birthday parties are offered at home or in their shop.

Kids 'r' Cookin
914.937.2012
www.KidsRcookin.com
Restauranteur Bandy Acciavatti offers cooking courses and birthday parties for kids.

COMPUTERS

Cyber Discoveries
877.376.0048
Greenwich, CT — call for location.
www.Cyberdiscoveries.com
Computer classes for ages 3 -6 and 7-15.
See also computer camps in CHILDREN, Summer Camps.

CHILD ENRICHMENT

DANCE & ETIQUETTE

Allegra Dance Studio
37 West Putnam Avenue, Greenwich CT, 203.629.9162
http://allegradancegreenwich.com/
Claudia Devita is a popular Greenwich dance teacher. Ages 3 to adult; classes in jazz, ballet, tap, hip-hop and ballroom dancing.

Ballet Des Enfances
Shop Rite Center, 2000 West Main Street, Stamford CT, 203.973.0144
www.balletdesenfants.net
Ballet studio offering classes for 2-6 year olds and up.

Barclay Ballroom Dancing for Young Children
397 Round Hill Road, Greenwich CT
Lois Thomson, Director, 908.232.8370
Friday evening classes, starting in September, are held at the Round Hill Community Center. The one-hour classes teach ballroom dancing and social etiquette to children in grades 4, 5, & 6.

(The) Chinese Language School (Mandarin & Chinese Dance)
P.O. Box 515, Riverside CT, 866.301.4906
www.chineselanguageschool.org
Chinese Folk Dance classes. This is the only full-time professional school of Chinese dance in the country. Classes are held at Eastern Middle School. They have an extensive program teaching Mandarin Chinese.

Dance Adventure
36 Sherwood Place, Greenwich CT, 203.625.0930
www.danceadventure.com
Programs for parent and child, 12 months to 2.5 years;
pre-ballet and pre-tap for ages 3-5; ballet, tap & jazz for kindergarten to teens.

TIP: KIDS' PROGRAMS AT PURCHASE COLLEGE
The Performing Arts Center www.artscenter.org at Purchase College, in addition to their superb adult concert series, has a series of sensational performances designed for children. For pre-k to grade 12. For more information about Arts-in-Education, call 914.251.6232.

CHILD ENRICHMENT

Greenwich Ballet Academy
914.305.4377
www.GreenwichBalletacademy.org
They hold classes at the Greenwich Arts Council and The Greenwich Ballet Academy Studios in Port Chester. Their mission is to nurture young dancers ages 9-21 toward a career in classical ballet and contemporary dance. Early Prep for children ages 2-5. See their website for more information. http://greenwichballetacademy.org/gba-early-prep-ballet-program-for-children-2014/

Greenwich Ballet Workshop
Felicity Foote, 339 Round Hill Road, Greenwich CT, 203.869.9373
Dedicated children (up to age 18) are coached to look their very best on stage.

Greenwich Dance Studio
YWCA, 259 East Putnam Avenue, Greenwich, CT 203.990.0370
2000 West Main Street, Stamford, CT 203.990.0370
www.GreenwichDanceStudio.com
http://greenwichdancestudiopetite.com/
Ballet, jazz, hip hop, creative movement classes for children ages 3 years and up. Greenwich Dance Petite Studio located just across the border in Stamford offers classes for children ages 1-9.

Lynn Academy of Irish Dance
42 Magee Ave 2nd Floor (2 Studios), Stamford CT, 203.323.0550
www.LynnAcademy.com
Irish dance instruction for children and adults.

Mayfair Ballroom Dancing for Young Children
Call the Brunswick School 203.625.5800
www.brunswickschool.org
Mayfair is sponsored by the Brunswick Parents Association, but is open to all children in Greenwich. Like Barclay, they teach ballroom dancing and etiquette to children in grades 5 and 6. Friday classes start in September, 5th grade 4:30-5:45pm; 6th grade 6:15pm-7:30pm, and are usually taught at Brunswick. For girls, there may be a waiting list. There's always room for boys.

CHILD ENRICHMENT

New Dance
914.690.9300
www.newdance.net
This studio offers a variety of classes to boys and girls including ballet, tap, hip hop, jazz and cheerleading. Visit the website for class offerings and locations.

YWCA Children's Dance
259 East Putnam Avenue, Greenwich CT, 203.869.6501
www.ywcaGreenwich.org
Pre Ballet for ages 3-4, Beginning Ballet ages 5-6, Ballet l ages 7-9, Ballet ll
ages 10-18, Beginning Pointe ages 11-13. Now offering Jazz and Hip Hop for ages 6-13.

EXTRACURRICULAR KIDS' PROGRAMS

College for Kids
Norwalk Community College, Richards Avenue, Norwalk CT, 203.857.7080
www.ncc.commnet.edu
Unique courses for children grades K-10, such as spooky science, web design, undersea art, manners and chess.

ZANIAC
644 West Putnam Avenue (above CVS), Greenwich CT, 203.919.9264
www.ZaniacLearning.com/greenwich
Year round programs for kids K-8th grade; learn math, computer programing, minecraft, logo robotics, chess, typing and more.

TIP: KITE FLYING FESTIVAL (Go Fly A Kite!)
www.greenwicharts.org
Every April, at Tod's Point, children of all ages have fun at the Kite Flying Festival. It is sponsored by the Greenwich Arts Council and the Town of Greenwich Department of Parks and Recreation. Participants are encouraged to bring kites of all shapes and sizes, made of paper, plastic or fabric.

CHILD ENRICHMENT

LANGUAGES

Alliance Française
299 Greenwich Avenue, Greenwich CT, 203.629.1340
www.afgreenwich.org
Classes for beginners, intermediate and advanced are given in the French Center for children ages 3-13 years and teens. "Mommy and Me" lets 2 year olds learn with their mothers. On Tuesdays, French classes are offered for native French-speaking children who are enrolled in English-speaking schools.

(The) Chinese Language School of Connecticut
Eastern Middle School, 51 Hendrie Avenue, Riverside CT, 866.301.4906
www.chineselanguageschool.org
This school operates from September to June. Classes are held Sundays at Eastern Middle School, 51 Hendrie Avenue, Riverside, CT and weekdays at the Second Congregational Church, Room 19, 139 East Putnam Avenue, Greenwich, CT. This non-profit organization is dedicated to teaching Mandarin Chinese as a second language to children. They also teach dance.

Evrika Learning Center
Stamford CT, 203.975.1134
www.evrikacenter.com
Saturday and summer Russian language school. Russian classes for ages 2 to 15 incorporate games, poems and puzzles.

French-American School
Larchmont NY, 914.250.0469
Mamaroneck NY, 914.250.0451
Scarsdale NY, Campuses 914.250.0522
www.Fasny.org
Adult and children's classes in French, Mandarin Chinese, Russian, Spanish, Arabic and Italian. With a knowledge of basic French, children grades 1-3 can enjoy cooking, juggling and circus arts, as well as model airplane making and a variety of sports.

CHILD ENRICHMENT

German School
(Rippowam Middle School) 381 High Ridge Road, Stamford CT, 203.792.2795
www.germanschoolct.org, www.dsny.org
Saturday morning German language and cultural instruction for novice to native speakers. Available for children pre-school through high school. They also have an adult program. Closed during the summer. Classes begin in September.

Greenwich Reform Synagogue (Flexible Hebrew Instruction)
www.grs.org/learning
Private Hebrew instruction for students in grades 3-7 on weekday afternoons of your choice.

India Cultural Center of Greenwich
www.iccGreenwich.org
They offer classes in Hindi for ages 2 to 12. They also offer classes in Bharatanatyam.

Linguakids
2 East Avenue, Larchmont NY, 203.426.7004, 914.833.0781
www.linguakids.com
Classes in French, Spanish, and Chinese for children ages 6 months and up.

(The) Language Exchange
203 East Putnam Avenue (Mill Pond Shop Cntr), Cos Cob CT, 203.422.2024
www.ForeignLanguageExchange.com
Adult and children's classes in Spanish, French, Dutch, German, Mandarin Chinese, Italian & Russian. Children's classes for ages 3 to 13. They offer total immersion camps for students in Elementary, Middle and High School.

Little Language League
22 Purdy Avenue, 2nd Floor, Rye NY, 914.921.9075
http://www.languageleague.com
Little Language League offers foreign language courses for ages 6 months and up.

CHILD ENRICHMENT

Mencius Mandarin Chinese Preschool

First United Methodist Church, 2nd Floor, 59 East Putnam Avenue, Greenwich CT, 203.540.5770

www.menciusmandarin.com

English-Mandarin Chinese bilingual preschool for children ages 2 to 5 years old. No prior knowledge of Mandarin Chinese is required.

MUSIC AND ACTING

BeMused Productions

508 Warburton Avenue, Suite #3, Yonkers NY 10701

http://www.bemusedproductions.com/

Weekend workshops, 2 hour rehearsals for children ages 4 through teens, culminating with a show. The director is great with kids and BeMused is very fair priced.

Connecticut School of Music

Kenneth Kuo, 299 Greenwich Avenue (3rd Floor), Greenwich CT, 203.302.9968

www.CTSchoolOfMusic.com

Private lessons for piano, violin/viola, cello, guitar, flute, bass, music theory & composition, voice, ear training as well as ensemble programs. They rent instruments.

Curtain Call, Inc.

1349 Newfield Avenue, Stamford CT 06905, 203.329.8207

www.curtaincallinc.com

Acting workshops and camps for kids, teens, and adults of all abilities.

Greenwich Music & Fraioli School of Music

1200 East Putnam Avenue, Riverside CT, 203.637.1119, 203.869.3615

www.greenwichmusic.com

This is a music store and a school. They offer instruction in voice and many instruments. They even have a class about how to be a rock star.

CHILD ENRICHMENT

Greenwich Performing Arts Studio
261 East Putnam Avenue, Cos Cob CT, 203.273.7827
www.GreenwichPerformingArts.com
Private lessons and group classes teach children to act, sing & dance. Under adult supervision, students can write and perform their own original musicals and standard shows. Classes include acting, tap and creative drama, musical theater, ballet, jazz, improv, on camera classes and voice classes.

Greenwich Suzuki Academy
Lessons: Christ Church, 254 East Putnam Avenue, Greenwich CT, 203.561.6176
Mailing address: 15 E. Putnam Ave, #176, Greenwich CT 06830
www.greenwichsuzukiacademy.org
The Suzuki method of teaching violin, viola, flute and cello is available for children ages 3-18. It is taught in private and group classes. Parent training is available as well as instruction in beginning orchestra, jazz theory, improvisation, and chamber music.

Kinder Musik
Old Greenwich Music Studio
23 Clark Street, Old Greenwich CT, 203.637.0461
www.OGMstudio.kindermusik.net
Pre-instrumental programs for infants to 8 years. A delightful way to encourage a child's love of music.

Mary Ann Hall's Music For Children
YWCA, 259 East Putnam Avenue, Greenwich CT, 203.854.9797
www.musicforchildren.net
A song, dance, and instrument program for children from birth to age 10. Advanced musical theater program for ages 10-14.

Music Conservatory of Westchester
216 Central Avenue, White Plains NY, 914.761.3900
www.musicconservatory.org
High quality, individual instrumental instruction for children in violin, Suzuki violin, piano, guitar and woodwinds, provided by the Music Conservatory of Westchester. Music theory lessons also available.

(The) Music Source
203.698.0444

www.themusicsource.org

This is a good resource for sheet music, including every Broadway play in print. A large selection of music, supplies and gifts for all instruments. They used to have a Greenwich store but they now operate online only.

Music Together of Fairfield County
76 Walbin Court, Fairfield, CT, 203.256.1656

www.CTMusicToGether.com

Fun, informal family music-making classes for babies to 5 year olds. They hold classes in Greenwich.

Riverside School of Music
401 East Putnam Ave, Cos Cob CT, 203.661.9501

www.atelierconstantinpopescu.com

They sell instruments and give private lessons for violin, viola, cello, piano, guitar & voice for children 2 and up. They are great with kids. Open just about every day.

Studio of Victoria Baker
15 Putnam Green, Greenwich CT, 203.531.7499

Victoria Baker, an opera singer and columnist for the Greenwich Post, gives private voice and piano lessons.

Vinny Nobile
24 Grand Street, Greenwich CT, 914.980.3082

www.linkedin.com/in/vinnynobie

Vinny will come to your home for private lessons in trumpet, trombone or piano.

Young Artists Philharmonic
PO Box 3301, Ridgeway Station, Stamford CT, 203.532.1278

www.syap.org

For over 40 years, this highly sophisticated regional youth symphony orchestra has inspired youth and entertained adults.

CHILD ENRICHMENT

READING

Pre-School Stories
Stories are read to pre-schoolers in the mornings most weekdays. During the summer, stories may be read in a nearby park.
www.greenwichlibrary.org
- Byram Shubert Library, 21 Mead Avenue, Byram CT, 203.531.0426
- Cos Cob Library, 5 Sinowoy Road, Cos Cob CT, 203.622.6883
- Greenwich Library, 101 West Putnam Avenue, Greenwich CT, 203.622.7900
- Perrot Library, 90 Sound Beach Avenue, Old Greenwich CT, 203.637.1066

Young Critics Club
Perrot Library, 90 Sound Beach Avenue, Old Greenwich CT, 203.637.8802
www.PerrotLibrary.org
Children in grades 6-8 who love to read and talk about books, gather on Friday afternoons with Kate McClelland and Mary Clark for a guided discussion. By application only. It is often over booked. The Young Young Critics Club, grades 4 and 5, meets alternate Tuesday afternoons.

TUTORS

Community Answers Tutors Notebook
Community Answers at the Greenwich Library, 101 West Putnam Avenue, Greenwich CT, 203.622.7979 www.communityanswers.org
They maintain a notebook of resumes and flyers of local tutors, as well as the current Greenwich Public Schools tutors.

Kumon Learning Center
CVS Building, 132 East Putnam Avenue, Cos Cob CT, cell:914.433.1116
www.Kumon.com, http://www.Kumon.com, http://center.ikumon.com/showpage.aspx?url=91381
Kumon concentrates on math and reading skills for grades K through 12.

Stand By Me
Greenwich High School, 10 Hillside Road, Greenwich CT, 203.625.8007
www.greenwichschools.org/page.cfm?p=5524
A program designed to give underachieving ninth grade students a chance to have a senior stand by them.

CHILD ENRICHMENT

Sylvan Learning Centers
180 South Broadway, White Plains NY, 914.948.4116
http://tutoring.sylvanlearning.com/whiteplains/Index.cfm
Their tutors tailor individualized learning plans to improve skills, habits and attitudes. Instruction is available in math, reading, writing, study skills, homework help and test preparation.

Tutoring Club
69 High Ridge Road, Stamford CT, 203.323.1929
http://stamfordct.tutoringclub.com/localinfo.asp
www.TutoringClub.com
Individualized instruction from professional tutors to bring each student to the desired academic level as quickly as possible.

Tutoring Match
Director: Henry Lane, 205 Sunset Ave, Fairfield CT, 203.366.3396
www.TutoringMatch.com
Tutoring assistance in just about any subject for students of all ages. Tutors come to your home.

TIP: TOUCH A TRUCK
The Junior League of Greenwich www.jlgreenwich.org holds an annual spring fund raiser, usually in early June, called Touch A Truck. This is lots of fun for children (and adults) who love to climb on interesting equipment such as construction vehicles, public safety equipment, Humvees and other assorted vehicles. For information call the Touch A Truck hotline at 203.977.0770 or the Junior League office at 203.869.1979.

CHILDREN

Greenwich is an ideal place to raise children. We have a top-rated school system, ranked among the best in the country. Children nurtured in Greenwich have unique opportunities to develop their skills and to grow into happy, healthy, mature individuals. For an excellent book on Children, go to www.cga.ct.gov/coc/playbook_home.htm and download the 90-page playbook.

There are many web sites for children's activities. You might try these:
www.westport.macaronikid.com
www.gigsalad.com/Variety/Children-Kids-Entertainment/CT/Greenwich
www.familydaysout.com/kids-things-to-do-usa/greenwich/ct
www.greenwichmag.com
www.myconnecticutkids.com

For nursery, pre-schools and other public/private schools see SCHOOLS.
For more information on beaches and Greenwich parks see PARKS.
Child Safety providers are in SERVICES.
See SPORTS for Adult and Youth activities.
See section TEENS for more ideas.
CHILD ENRICHMENT is a separate Section.

SECTIONS:

Babysitting
Before and After School Programs
Childcare
Fairs, Festivals & Carnivals
Family Outings
Parties at Home
Parties Away from Home
Playgrounds
Scouting
Sports
Summer Camp Information
Summer Camp Programs
Support Services for Children

CHILDREN

BABYSITTING

Babysitting Training
Red Cross, 99 Indian Field Road, Greenwich CT, 203.869.8444.
http://www.redcross.org/ct/greenwich
The Red Cross sponsors a comprehensive all-day babysitting course which is open to 11-15 year olds and offered 2 to 3 times a month. Call 1-800-Red-Cross for details on when courses are offered in Greenwich.

Child Care and Parenting Services
Greenwich Library, 101 Putnam Avenue, Greenwich CT, 203.622.7900.
A wonderful pamphlet compiled by Community Answers and Greenwich Early Childhood Council is available at the Community Answers desk.

Child Care Infoline
800.505.1000
www.ChildCareInfoLine.org
They provide information on licensed daycare, summer camps and nursery school programs throughout Connecticut.

Kid's Night Out
YMCA, 50 East Putnam Avenue, Greenwich CT, 203.869.1630
www.gwymca.org
A few evenings a month, parents of children in grades K-6 can enjoy an evening out, while their children enjoy an inexpensive, fun, safe night of activities, including gym games, swimming, movies, popcorn and board games.

(The) Sitting Service
Kristen Calve, owner.
30 Old Kings Highway South, Darien CT, 203.655.9783
www.TheSittingService.com
Office hours are 9am-1pm, weekdays. This state-registered babysitting, pet-sitting and house-sitting referral service has been in Fairfield County for over 20 years. Yearly membership is $265 + tax per family plus an hourly rate.

Student Employment Service
Greenwich High School, Greenwich CT, 203.625.8008
www.ghs-ses.org
Hours during the school year: Weekdays, 11:30am-2pm.
In summer, the service is run through Community Answers, 203.622.7979.

CHILDREN

Utilize Senior Energy (USE)
Senior Center, 299 Greenwich Avenue, Greenwich CT, 203.629.8032
http://utilizeseniorenergy.org/
Hours: weekdays 9:30am-12:30pm. Employment referral service for people 50 years and over.

BEFORE AND AFTER SCHOOL PROGRAMS
For nursery, pre-schools and other public/private schools see SCHOOLS.
Elementary School Programs
The following elementary schools have on-site, before and after-school childcare programs for students enrolled in that school.
- Cos Cob School, 203.869.4670
- Glenville School, 203.531.9287
- Hamilton Avenue School, 203.869.1685 (2nd grade scholars)
- International School at Dundee 203.637.3800
- Julian Curtiss School, 203.869.1896
- New Lebanon School, 203.531.9139
- North Mianus School, 203.637.9730
- North Street School, 203.869.6756
- Old Greenwich School, 203.637.0150
- Parkway School, 203.869.7466
- Riverside School, 203.637.1440

BANC
Byram Archibald Neighborhood Center After School Program
289 Delavan Avenue, Greenwich CT, 203.531.1522
Ages: 5 -13 yrs. Four days per week. Follows public school calendar.

Girls Inc.
PO Box 793, Greenwich CT, 203.536.3322
www.girlsincswct.org, www.girlsinc.org
Girls, ages 6 -18. Hours 3:15pm-5:45pm. An excellent five day-a-week, informal education program for girls. The focus is on science, math and technology.

Greenwich Boys and Girls Club
4 Horseneck Lane, Greenwich CT, 203.869.3224
www.bgcg.org
Co-ed, Ages: 6 and up, Hours: 3pm-6:30pm. On school holidays, the program starts at 8am. Summer hours are 8am-6pm.

CHILDREN

Kaleidoscope YWCA
259 East Putnam Avenue, Greenwich CT, 203.869.6501 x 251
www.ywcaGreenwich.org
Co-ed, Ages: K-grade 5, Hours: 2:30 pm to 6 pm. Follows the public school schedule, including early release days. Social, educational and recreational enrichment. Transportation is provided from all Greenwich schools. Kaleidoscope also provides childcare services during school closings for holidays and vacations.

Sundial at the Mead School
1095 Riverbank Road, Stamford CT, 203.595.9500
www.MeadSchool.org
The after-school program is for children from 4 years old through 4th grade. The programs are based on the interest of the child, such as fitness, soccer, science, archery, tennis, and chess. This program runs Monday and Wednesday 3:30pm-5:30pm and Fridays 12:15pm-3:30pm.

YMCA After School Program
203.869.3381
www.gwymca.org
They run after-school childcare programs at Hamilton Avenue, New Lebanon, and North Mianus Schools.

Zaniac After School Programs
644 West Putnam Avenue, Suite 201, Greenwich CT, 203.918.9264
www.zaniaclearning.com/greenwich

CHILDCARE

Children's Day School
449 Pemberwick Road, Greenwich CT, 203.532.1190
8 Riverside Avenue, Riverside CT, 203.637.1122
www.ChildrensDaySchool.net
All day daycare and pre-school for children ages 6 weeks-6 years, Hours: 7:30am-6 pm.
Director: Sara Champion

CHILDREN

Family Centers
Joan Warburg Early Childhood Center
20 Bridge Street, 203.629.2822, Children ages 6 weeks-2 years, hours: 7:30pm-6pm.
Arch Street PreSchool,
40 Arch Street, Greenwich CT, 203.869.4848, for children 3-5 years.
www.familycenters.org
203.869.4848 bilingual, 203.629.2822

Gateway School
2 Chapel Street, Greenwich CT, 203.531.8430
www.familycenters.org
Children ages 2-5. Full-day, year-round childcare; need-based tuition. Director: Danielle Bridey, 203.869.4848
Hours: 7:30am-6pm.

Little Angels Play Group
Greenwich Catholic School
471 North Street, Greenwich CT, 203.869.4000 x 109
www.GreenwichCatholicSchool.org
• Children ages 3-4; hours: weekdays, 8:30pm-11:30pm, Tuesday-Thursday 12pm-3pm.
• Pre K program, ages 4-5, hours: 8:30am-12pm; extended day options.

Little Friends
25 Valley Drive, Greenwich CT, 203.861.6549
Year-round child care for up to 150 children, ages 6 weeks-5 years; hours: 6:30am-6:30pm. Early drop off, 6:30am; late pick up, 6:30pm.
Also 2, 3 and 5 day programs, either half or full day.

YMCA Child Care
2 Saint Roch Avenue, Byram CT, 203.869.3381
Children ages 6 weeks to 5 years. All day, year round childcare. Hours: 7am-6pm.

YWCA Playroom and Playroom Plus
259 East Putnam Avenue, Greenwich CT, 203.869.6501 x 221
Children ages 15 months-3 years. Professional on-site childcare services, either for parents attending Y classes or pursuing off-site activities. Morning or afternoon sessions available.

FAIRS, FESTIVALS & CARNIVALS

Many of the town's elementary schools and churches hold fairs as fundraisers:

- Cos Cob School Fair (early May)
  300 East Putnam Avenue, 203.869.4670
- North Mianus School Pow Wow (early May)
  309 Palmer Hill Road, 203.637.9730
- Renaissance Festival (early June)
  International School of Dundee, 55 Florence Road, Riverside
  Sword fights, horseback jousting and live chess, 203.637.3800
- St. Catherine's Carnival (middle August)
  4 Riverside Avenue, 203.637.3661
- St. Paul's Episcopal Church Fair (late May)
  200 Riverside Avenue, 203.637.2447
- St. Roch Feast (early August)
  10 Saint Roch Avenue, Greenwich CT, 203.869.4176

United Way Oktober Fest
The Loading Dock, Stamford CT
(October), 203.869.2221
www.UnitedWay-Greenwich.com

Scarecrow Festival
Mill Pond Park, Strickland Road, Cos Cob CT
Hosted by the Bush-Holly House (203.869.6899), this fun-filled October day includes live entertainment, lots of food vendors, scarecrow contests, horse-drawn wagon rides, hay maze, art projects, three-legged races and much more.

The Junior League of Greenwich
203.869.1979
www.jlgreenwich.org
The Junior League hosts several popular fund-raising events throughout the year including:
- Touch a Truck (early June)
Held at the Greenwich Town Hall lot and fields. Children have a chance to climb onto backhoes, dump trucks, and emergency vehicles. Tattoos (temporary) and musicians make it festive, too.
- The Enchanted Forest (November)
Held at the Hyatt in Old Greenwich, the Enchanted Forest is a two-day event which features over 100 decorated trees, wreaths and gingerbread houses and photos with Santa.

CHILDREN

FAMILY OUTINGS

Although there is some duplication, adult-oriented museums are listed in CULTURE under Museums.

American Museum of Natural History
Central Park West at 79th Street, New York, NY, 212.769.5100
www.amnh.org
This museum is terrific for kids, with lots of special exhibits, programs and workshops.
Hours: Open daily from 10am-5:45pm

Audubon Center Greenwich
613 Riversville Road, Greenwich CT, 203.869.5272
http://greenwich.audubon.org/
Founded in 1942, this 285-acre sanctuary has 7 miles of trails and a superb learning and exhibit center, with a terrific nature store. You will want to stay.
Hours: Open year- round except for major holidays, 10am-5pm.

Bridgeport Bluefish
Harbor Yard, 500 Main Street, Bridgeport CT, 203.345.4800
www.bridgeportbluefish.com
Professional Minor League Baseball in the Atlantic League. Verify hours and ticket availability before you go.
Hours: May to September, Monday-Saturday 7pm; Sunday 1pm.

Bridgeport Sound Tigers
600 Main Street, Arena at Harbor Yard, Bridgeport CT, 203.334.4625
www.soundtigers.com
Ice Hockey, New York Islanders "farm" team. They begin playing their 40 home game season in October.

Bronx Zoo
Fordham Road at Bronx River Parkway, Bronx, NY, 718.367.1010
www.bronxzoo.com
World class zoo with terrific rides and exhibits. Easy to find. Free admission every Wednesday. You can purchase tickets on-line.
Hours: Weekdays 10 am-5 pm, weekends and holidays 10am-5:30pm, November-March 10am-4:30pm.

CHILDREN

Bruce Museum
1 Museum Drive, Greenwich CT, 203.869.0376
www.brucemuseum.org
Impressive rotating exhibits and many programs for adults and children. They have a terrific gift shop with a large selection of books. The Museum has been accredited by the American Association of Museums as being in the top 10 percent of US museums. The Museum sponsors 2 fairs in Bruce Park every year; the mid-May Craft Fair and the Columbus Day Arts Festival have juried artists from around the country and draw visitors from all over the area. During the summer, visit the Seaside Center at Tod's Point for daily activities such as animal feeding and arts and crafts activities. Visit the website for a full schedule of summer events.
Hours: Tuesday-Saturday 10am-5pm, Sunday 1pm-5pm. Closed on major holidays.

Bush Holley House Museum
39 Strickland Road, Cos Cob CT, 203.869.6899
www.hstg.org
Home of the Historical Society, this is the place to learn about Greenwich history. They also have a good library and a shop with books on Greenwich history, as well as reproductions of 19th-century children's toys and books. While you are there, pick up a list of their informative programs.
Hours: March-December: Wednesday-Sunday 12pm-4pm;
January-February: Saturday & Sunday 12pm-4pm.

Dinosaur State Park
400 West Street, Rocky Hill CT, 860.529.8423
www.dinosaurstatepark.org
Dinosaurs fascinate us all. With over 2,000 tracks, this is one of the best sites in North America. Make your own castings right on the site.

Discovery Museum
4450 Park Avenue, Bridgeport CT, 203.372.3521
www.discoverymuseum.org
Hands-on art and science exhibits for children of all ages and their parents. A special section for pre-schoolers with dozens of attractions based on principles of early childhood development. Families who know about the Discovery Museum go there regularly.
Hours: Tuesday-Sunday 10am-5pm. Open Monday in summer.

CHILDREN

Essex Steam Train & Riverboat

One Railroad Avenue, Essex CT, 860.767.0103, 800.377.3987
www.essexsteamtrain.com
Take a trip back in history through the scenic Connecticut River Valley.
Passengers board the 1920 steam train at the Essex station for a one
hour ride. At Deep River Landing the train meets the river boat for a one
hour cruise. The North Cove Express offers brunch, lunch and dinner
during a 2 hour excursion. Call for reservations on the Dinner Train.
Pre-schoolers won't want to miss the Thomas the Tank Engine ride, a 25-
minute ride with Thomas held on 3 weekends in late April and early
May.

Flanders Nature Center-Maple Sugaring

5 Church Hill (at Flanders Road), Woodbury CT, 203.263.3711
www.flandersnaturecenter.org, www.woodburyct.org
Spend an afternoon at a sugarhouse and learn how to make pure maple
syrup and then taste it. During a good season, there is sugaring in Connecticut for 6 or 7 weeks. In an off year, the season could be only a
couple of weekends, so be sure to call before you go. The Flanders Nature
Center is 1½ to 2 hours from Greenwich. Woodbury is a well-preserved
colonial town with a number of antique shops and some good restaurants. The syrup operation is open to the public. Demonstrations are
given on weekends from 3pm to 5pm from late February through March.

Franklin Mineral Museum

Sterling Hill Mine
30 Plant Street, Ogdensburg NJ, 973.209.7212
www.sterlinghill.org, www.sterlinghillminingmuseum.org
About 2.5 hours from Greenwich is a world-famous collection of fluores-
cent rocks, many from the Sterling Mine. The Sterling Hill mine operated
from about 1761 to 1986. For the tour of the mine wear sturdy boots and
bring a jacket (it's 56° even in the summer). Tours take about 3 hours.
Not appropriate for children under six.
Museum Hours: Open everyday, April through November
Tour Hours: Call for hours.

CHILDREN

TIP: STAMFORD PARADE
A spectacular parade is put on every November in Stamford with huge balloons and fun for everyone. For information call 203.348.5285 or visit www.Stamford-downtown.com

IMAX Theater

At the Maritime Aquarium, 10 North Water Street, Norwalk CT, 203.852.0700
www.maritimeaquarium.org
With a screen that is 6 stories high and 8 stories wide and a 24,000 watt sound system, the experience is truly amazing.
Hours: Open daily at 10am; September-June until 5pm;
July-Labor Day, until 6pm.

Lake Compounce Family Theme Park

186 Enterprise Dr, Bristol CT, 860.583.3300
www.lakecompounce.com, www.hauntedGraveyard.com
The best wooden roller coaster in the world is about 1½ hours north of Greenwich built on the side of a mountain. It is simply "awesome." All rides in the Circus World Children's Area and some rides in Splash Harbor are designed for young children. Children must be 42" to 54" tall depending upon the ride. Adults may accompany children on some rides. In October, the "Haunted Graveyard" can be lots of fun.

Legoland Discovery Center

39 Fitzgerald Street, Yonkers NY, 866.243.0770
www.legolanddiscoverycenter.com/westchester
Soft play area, rides, games, 4D movies and, of course, lots of Lego. It is designed for children ages 3 to 10. Tickets are $18 for kids 3 and up. Legoland is a chain of Lego-themed parks owned and operated by the British company Merlin Entertainments.

Maritime Aquarium

10 North Water Street, Norwalk CT, 203.852.0700
www.MaritimeAquarium.org
Interactive exhibits often include a Shark Touch Pool. Cited as one of the 10 Great Aquariums to visit.
Hours: Open daily, September-June 10am-5pm;
July-Labor Day 10am-6pm.

67

CHILDREN

Mystic Seaport and Museum
Mystic CT, Visitor Information: 888.973.2767
www.mysticseaport.org
Mystic is a two-hour drive. The Mystic Seaport Museum has a world-renowned waterfront collection of ships and crafts telling the story of America and the sea. Mystic also has a good aquarium, with exciting special exhibits. While in the Mystic area, stop by Stonington, which is about 5 miles east on US-1. Stonington is a 19th century fishing village which has kept its charm and has become a center for antique shops. Don't forget Mystic Pizza, which inspired the movie. There is one in Mystic, 860.536.3700 and one in North Stonington, 860.599.3111.
Hours: Open every day except December 25th; ships & exhibits 9am-5pm, Museum grounds 9am-6pm.

Philipsburg Manor
Sleepy Hollow NY, 914.631.8200, 914.366.6900
www.HudsonValley.org
An 18th-century working farm, with water-powered grist mill and livestock. Tours are conducted by interpreters in period costumes.
Hours: May-November, Wednesday through Sunday, 10 am-5 pm. Also open on holiday Mondays.

PICK YOUR OWN FRUITS & VEGETABLES
(Also See HOME DELIVERY AND FARMS.)
Picking your own fruit and vegetables has become a popular pastime in Connecticut. There are 9 farms in Fairfield County offering urbanites the opportunity to pick their own produce.
For more detailed information call 860.713.2500 or 1 800.861.9939
www.state.ct.us/doag
Some you might consider are:

• Bishop's Orchards
1355 Boston Post Road (I-95, exit 57), Guilford CT, 203.458.7425, 203.453.2338
www.bishopsorchards.com
They have a great many varieties of fruit to pick, including over 20 varieties of apples, 9 kinds of blueberries, 12 of peaches, 3 of pears, 8 of strawberries and 2 varieties of raspberries. This orchard is definitely worth the trip.
Market hours: From June through October, Monday-Saturday 8am- 7pm, Sunday 9am-6pm.

CHILDREN

- Eden Farms
947 Stillwater Road, Stamford CT, 203.325.3445
www.edenfarms.biz
A nursery and greenhouse open 7 days a week, just minutes from Greenwich, Eden Farms has seasonal celebrations: Easter Bunnies, Halloween Hayrides, Pumpkin Patch, Haunted House and Santa visits. Call to check events and times before going.

- Jones Family Farm
606 Walnut Tree Hill Road & Route 110, Shelton CT, 203.929.8425
www.jonesfamilyfarms.com
This pick-your-own farm began in the 1940s. They have strawberries in June, followed by blueberries in July and August, and pumpkins in the autumn. Hayrides are offered in October, and in December you can cut your own Christmas tree.
Hours: Best to call, hours change seasonally.

- Silverman's Farm
451 Sport Hill Road (exit 46 off the Merritt Parkway), Easton CT, 203.261.3306
www.silvermansfarm.com
Peaches in July, apples in August. Three-acre animal farm for youngsters.
Hours: Open Daily, 9am-5pm. Closed on major holidays. Call for hours in January or in case of bad weather.

- White Silo Farm
32 Route 37 East, Sherman CT, 860.355.0271
www.whitesilowinery.com
Strawberries, asparagus, raspberries, blackberries and rhubarb.

Playland Park
Playland Parkway, Rye NY, 914.813.7010
www.ryeplayland.org
Recently renovated amusement park, just 15 minutes away. A wide variety of rides for older kids from Go Karts to Zombie Castle and Old Mill. Kiddyland has 20 of Playland's 50 rides. Playland also has a beach, swimming pool, lake cruises, ice casino, miniature golf and sightseeing cruises on Long Island Sound and firework shows during the summer.
Hours: Open May to mid-September. The ice rink is open from October to April. Call for hours.

CHILDREN

Revolutionary War Battle
Putnam Cottage, 243 East Putnam Avenue, Greenwich CT, 203.869.9697
www.PutnamCottage.org
Originally a tavern serving travelers along the Post Road, it is now a museum owned by the Daughters of the American Revolution. Each year on the last Sunday in February (1pm-3pm), the Putnam Hill Revolutionary War battle is recreated. A definite must-see for adults and children alike.

Renaissance Faire
Route 17A, Sterling Forest, Tuxedo NY, 845.351.5171
www.renfair.com
Over 300 actors, in costume, mingle with the visitors (who can also don costumes) in a mock 16th century village. A wonderful way to enjoy a day of improvisation and learning.
Hours: August to mid-September weekends only, 10 am-7 pm.

Six Flags Great Adventure
Route 537, Jackson NJ, 732.928.1821
www.sixflags.com/parks/greatadventure
The park is a 2½ hour drive from Greenwich. But if you like roller coasters, it is worth a trip. This large amusement park has rides for every age. The Nitro and Medusa roller coasters (2 of their 13) are well known by coaster aficionados. Six Flags Wild Safari is the world's largest drive-thru Safari outside Africa. Hurricane Harbor has water rides. Be sure to call for hours of operation before you go.

Stamford Museum & Nature Center
39 Scofieldtown Road (corner of High Ridge Rd), Stamford CT, 203.322.1646
www.stamfordmuseum.org
118-acres, with a 10-acre working farm, pond life exhibit, boardwalks, natural history exhibits, planetarium and observatory. If your child hasn't grown up on a farm, this is the perfect place to learn about farming and farm animals.
Hours: Open year round except for major holidays, Monday-Saturday 9am-5pm, Sunday 11am-5pm; Planetarium shows Sunday at 3pm; Observatory, Friday 8pm-10pm.

CHILDREN

Stepping Stones Museum for Children
303 West Avenue (Mathews Park), Norwalk CT, 203.899.0606
www.steppingstonesMuseum.org
Excellent interactive museum for kids under 10.
Hours: Memorial Day through Labor Day: Monday – Sunday, 10am – 5pm;
Labor Day through Memorial Day: Tuesday – Sunday, 10am – 5pm

United States Military Academy
West Point, NY, 845.938.2638
www.usma.edu
Visitors now need a military ID to enter the grounds of the academy, except for the visitor's center and military museum. One-hour guided tours are available but photo IDs are required.
Hours: Guided tours: Daily 9am-4:45pm. Closed Thanksgiving, Christmas and New Year's Day.

PARTIES AT HOME
Open Greenwich photo albums and you'll see pictures of fabulous parties. Many of the best parties are hosted by imaginative parents at home. See ENTERTAINING for tents, caterers, party supply shops and other useful party information.
See Children's Parties in CATERERS for Frozen Yogurt Catering and see FOOD TRUCKS for a list of trucks to make any party a success.

Amazing Animal Balloons
914.774.2200, balloonfun25@gmail.com
www.amazinganimalballoons.com
We agree, Scott Kazan does an amazing job of making incredible balloon creations. He has great rapport with children.

Arcade-2-Go
81 Bungay Road, Seymour CT, 203.881.8111, 866.362.6873
www.mobileamusements.info
A trailer load of video games. 18 kids can play at once.

Aux Delices
23 Acosta Street, Stamford CT, 203.326.4540 x 108
www.AuxDelicesFoods.com
Fun, hands-on cooking parties can be held in their Stamford location or at your home.

Dave's Cast of Characters
914.235.7100
www.davescast.com
They specialize in professional entertainment, from full-costumed characters to carnival rides and inflatables.

Fairytale Beginnings
203.585.3711
www.fairytale-beginnings.com
Much to our surprise, Tinkerbell has zipped into our office! How did she find us and why is she here?? Could it be true? Yes! It is our very own Office Manager, Katie Bookser! We are delighted to discover that on weekends, you can find Katie portraying all of the beloved princesses while entertaining children of all ages. Her company, Fairytale Beginnings, brings joy and smiles to birthdays and special events all over Greenwich!! You must view her website today! Be sure to reserve early, her parties are very popular.

Fire Trucks
Check with your local firehouse. Many will bring a truck over to your house in exchange for a donation. The fire department's non-emergency phone is 203.622.3950. The non-emergency numbers for all of the local fire companies are in NUMBERS YOU SHOULD KNOW.

Franc-O-Fun
807 Ridgefield Road, Wilton CT, 203.762.5645
www.Franc-o-fun.com
A unique, fun, delicious French party with a Madeline doll theme. Children learn to make two French tarts (apple and chocolate), play with dolls (and bears for the boys) while having a song time and lesson in French. Each child will receive a chef hat and un sac de surprises which will include Belgian chocolate, French stickers, pencil and coloring sheet.

Gofer's Ice Cream Stand
522 East Putnam Avenue, Greenwich CT, 203.661.9080
www.goferIceCream.com, www.IceCreamPartyBox.com
You can order a order a box of ice cream and toppings or you can have a complete catered party with staff and a deluxe cart.

CHILDREN

Graham Clarke
43 Butler Hill Road, Somers NY, 914.669.5843
www.grahamclarke.com
Graham is well known by many a Greenwich child. He sings silly songs with his guitars and the kids go crazy!

Life Guard for Swim Parties
203.496.3225, cjdel6@aol.com
Cindy Del Vecchio, a CPR / First Aid certified Swim instructor charges $60-80 per hour for pool parties.

Mad Science of Fairfield County
1404 Barnum Avenue, Flr. 2, Stratford CT, 203.381.9754
www.madscience.org/connecticut
Interactive experiments for children ages 5 to 12, combining science with entertainment. Party programs are tailored to the age group and can include chemical magic, vortex generators, indoor fireworks, or model rocket launchings.

Parties by Lisa
914.648.9197
www.partybyLisa.com
Face painting, balloons, clowns, craft parties, jugglers and more.

Peez Out Productions (DJ for Kids or Adults)
Contact Matthew Kiger, 917.715.4190
www.peezout.com
A complete music production company.

Pied Piper Pony Rides
203.431.8322, 914.763.6925
www.piedpiperponyrides.com
You may want to invite one of their gentle ponies and friendly staff members to your party. The children will have a good time and the pony droppings will be removed. Closes for the winter.

Princess Tea Parties by Eileen
203.532.0547
Dress-up parties with tea sandwiches and entertainment to charm little girls in your home.

CHILDREN

Science Parties
11 Tubbs Spring Court, Weston CT, 203.227.8112, 800.311.9993
www.sciencemadefunct.net
Hands-on interactive parties where each child is involved with every experiment. Children ages 5-11 have lots of science fun making edible gummy drops or volcanoes and launching rockets. Parties are age-appropriate. They also do after-school programs in elementary schools.

Super Fun Inflatables
203.794.1400
www.Superfuninflatables.com
Super Fun Inflatables rents a large selection of children's entertainment equipment.

PARTIES AWAY FROM HOME

AMF Bowling Centers
701 Connecticut Avenue, Norwalk, 203.838.7501
47 Tarrytown Road, White Plains NY 914.948.2677
www.amfcenters.com
Bowling parties have been a hit for generations.

Audubon Center
613 Riversville Road, Greenwich, 203.869.5272
http://greenwich.audubon.org/special-events-rentals
Holding a party at the Audubon is a wonderful way to foster a love of nature. Highly trained guides will lead nature walks. You can rent space in the gorgeous center for a party.

Bartlett Arboretum & Gardens
151 Brookdale Road, Stamford CT, 203.322.6971
www.bartlettarboretum.org
Nature-Based Birthday Parties for children aged 3-12. Saturdays at either 10am or 1pm, June to December.

Boys and Girls Club of Greenwich
4 Horseneck Lane, Greenwich CT, 203.869.3224
www.bgcg.org
This newly renovated building has a large gym for multi-sport activities led by friendly staff and a party room nearby for the kids to do arts/crafts, bouncy castle, etc. Another option is to have an ice skating party. Charlie really enjoyed his party here.

CHILDREN

Chelsea Piers Birthday Parties
1 Blachley Road, Stamford CT, 203.989.1004, parties@chelseapiersCT.com
www.chelseapiersct.com/birthday/index.cfm
Children's birthday party packages include dynamic coaching and world-class facilities as well as balloons, paper goods and candles. Packages are also available that include pizza, beverages, cake and catering services. Choose from 12 sport specific activities such as dodgeball or batting cages to adventure parties on trampolines or rock climbing. There are also age-appropriate games for children ages 1 to 5 years.

Chocopologie Birthday Parties
133 Washington Street, Norwalk CT, 203.854.4754
www.knipschildt.com/
What could be better than wearing a chef's hat, watching chocolate being made and then eating super sundaes and chocolate treats? Children get all the fun.

Darlene's Heavenly Desires Ice Cream Parties
185 Sound Beach Avenue, Old Greenwich CT, 203.698.9441
www.darlenesheavenlydesires.com
Children age 4 and up love ice cream sundaes, decorating Cone People and all of the fun games.

Dance Adventure
36 Sherwood Place, Greenwich CT, 203.625.0930
www.danceadventure.com
They offer sweet theme parties for young girls.

Dorothy Hamill Skating Rink
Sherman Avenue, Greenwich CT, 203.531.8560
Call about renting the facility for a fun party.

Dynamic Martial Arts
202 Field Point Road, Greenwich CT, 203.629.4666
www.GreenwichKarate.com
A party where children can learn karate. Ages 4 and above.
Hours: Saturday parties, 12pm-1:30pm.

CHILDREN

Fun for Kids (Laser Tag)
370 West Main Street, Stamford CT, 203.326.5656
www.fun4kidsArcade.com
Though the location seems a bit seedy, once inside this arcade makes for a super party. Choose a soft play theme for young kids under 8 or go for the laser tag for the older ones.

Grand Prix (Go Karting, Bowling, Arcade)
333 North Bedford Road, Mount Kisco NY, 914.241.3131
www.GPNY.com
For Go Karts children should be 7 years old or 4-feet tall. For bowling parties you only need to be old enough to walk. Custom catering and private party spaces.

Great Play
2000 W. Main Street (Shop Rite Center), Stamford CT, 203.978.1333
www.greatplay.com
Customized 90-minute parties right on the border of Greenwich. Choose from Field Day (age 3 -10), Fun and Games (ages 1-6) and Multi Sport (ages 4 -10).

Eastern and Western Greenwich Civic Center Gymnasiums
Call Frank Gabriele at Parks & Recreation for details call 203.532.1259

Greenwich Skatepark
100 Arch Street, Roger Sherman Baldwin Park, Greenwich CT, 203.496.9876
www.greenwichct.org/ParksAndRec/prSkatePark.asp
The Greenwich Skatepark offers birthday parties on Saturday and Sunday mornings 10am-12pm. The fee is $100 which includes 10 children. Lessons are available for $25 per instructor. Bring a cake and pizza and have fun!

Kids U
633 Hope Street, Stamford CT, 203.358.9500
www.kidsu.com
The gym parties include an hour of soft free play then the kids march into the gym for supervised activities and pizza.

CHILDREN

Liberty Paint Ball
1 Thunder Ridge Road, Patterson NY, 845.878.6300
www.LibertyPaintBall-NY.com
350 acres of varied terrain, just north and west of Danbury CT. They are open all year. Friends tell us they rate it 5 stars. They suggest the beginner bring a group of about 20 participants and rent equipment there. Parties for kids ages 10-17 require a group of 15. Players 18 and over must have a minimum of 20 players. Don't forget to wear protective clothing, including gloves and boots rather than sneakers.

My Gym
7 Hyde Street, Stamford CT, 203.327.3496
www.my-gym.com
2 hours of non-stop fun. Games, gymnastics, puppets, rides and songs you can customize to your child's liking.

My Three Sons (Laser Tag)
62 Wall Street, Norwalk CT, 203.838.3013
www.mythreesonsfun.com
Like Fun For Kids, this is a popular place for laser tag parties.

Nimble Thimble
21 Putnam Avenue, Port Chester NY, 914.934.2934
Choose a project for your age group; for instance, make a fabric covered bulletin board or a vest. Parents can bring cake and ice cream. Ages 5 and up.

Norwalk Aquarium
10 North Water Street, Norwalk CT, 203.852.0700 x 2206
www.maritimeaquarium.org
Everyone loves this aquarium and having a party here combines fun and education.

PEZ Factory
35 Prindle Hill Road, Orange CT, 203.298.0201
www.pez.com/visit_us/
A staff member hosts your party with goodie bags, pizza and soft drinks. The guest of honor will be able to make a special batch of PEZ candy. Packages start for 15 guests and can be tailored to accommodate larger parties. Each party lasts 90 minutes.
Hours: Monday-Saturday: 10am-6pm, Sunday: Noon- 5pm

CHILDREN

Shaolin Studios
397 Putnam Avenue, Cos Cob CT, 203.661.5501
www.sdsskungfu.com
A karate studio where Alex had a great birthday party.

Slot Car Raceways
342 Sawmill River Road, Elmsford NY, 914.592.5375
www.flatoutfun.com
For 38 years the del Rosario family has entertained children and their parents with 62" slot car racing. Ages 4 to 99.

Soarin' Indoors
422 North Main Street, Manchester CT, 860.645.1595
www.SoarIndoors.com
About 1½ hours away is a 12,000 sf indoor aerial adventure, with a low course and a high course with rope bridges, cargo nets and zip lines. Children who can reach their arms up to a height of 5 feet (while standing flat on the floor) can take part.
Hours: Monday, Wednesday-Saturday 10am-8pm, Sunday, 11am-6pm.

Sports Center of Connecticut (Laser Tag)
784 River Road (Route 110) Shelton CT, 203.929.6500
http://www.sportscenterct.com/
About 50 minutes north of Greenwich, is a golf driving range, 18 hole mini-golf course, jungle themed Laser Tag arena, bowling, game zone arcade and baseball/softball batting cages.

Stepping Stones Museum
Matthews Park, 303 West Avenue, Norwalk CT, 203.899.0606 x 228
www.steppingstonesmuseum.org
Parties for up to 20 children ages 4 and up. After the guided tour, they have a special party room with cake and crafts.

YMCA
50 East Putnam Avenue, Greenwich CT, 203.869.1630
www.gwymca.org
Rent the gym or pool for your party with cake and presents in the party room. The Y can even provide a clown or magician. All ages.
Hours: Monday-Frdiay 5am to 10pm, Saturday 6:30am to 7pm, Sunday 8am-5pm (summer hours may be shorter).

CHILDREN

YWCA
259 East Putnam Avenue, Greenwich CT, 203.869.6501 x 235
www.ywcagreenwich.org
Rent a party room and/or hire one of their special instructors to teach the children activities such as soccer, swimming, gymnastics or climbing their rock wall. Parents provide the refreshments. Parties for all ages.
Hours: Parties are held during regular Y hours: weekdays 6:30am-10pm, Saturday 7:30am to 5pm (summer Saturday hours are shorter).

Zaniac Birthday Parties
644 West Putnam Avenue, Suite 201, Greenwich CT, 203.918.9264
www.zaniaclearning.com/greenwich
Birthday celebrations for Pre K to 8th grade. Create a biome, program a robot or build a video game.

PLAYGROUNDS
Town playgrounds are open from 9am-4pm. From late June through early August, the Greenwich Department of Parks and Recreation conducts supervised activities at the playgrounds for children ages 7-15. There are a number of small playgrounds scattered throughout the town (Binney Park, Bible Street Park, Christiano Park, Eastern and Western Greenwich Civic Centers, Island Beach and Loughlin Avenue Park), some are worth a trip even if you don't live in that area. Here are our favorites.
See the section PARKS for more information.

Bruce Park
60 acres, across from the Bruce Museum on Museum Drive. One of Greenwich's prettiest parks, with excellent play equipment.

Byram Park
30 acres, located on Ritch Avenue and Byram Shore Road in Byram. The park has an attractive beach area and the town's only public fresh water pool. How can you go wrong? (The playground is tucked behind the Byram Shore Boat Club.)

Greenwich Common
16 acres, located adjacent to Greenwich Avenue, with an entrance on Greenwich Avenue next to the Havemeyer Building (Board of Education). This is a wonderful place to rest during a busy shopping day and let your children play. The Common has a small but attractive playground area.

CHILDREN

Island Beach
See PARKS for information on ferry operation and beach passes.

Public Elementary Schools
These playgrounds are well-kept and extensive. They are available to residents during the weekends and summer when school is not in session. *For more information on the location of the elementary schools, see the Public Elementary School section under SCHOOLS.*

Western Greenwich Civic Center
10 acres, located on the corner of Glenville Road and Pemberwick Road. This playground is a favorite with kids.

SCOUTING

Adventure Guides
YMCA, 50 East Putnam Avenue, Greenwich CT, 203.869.1630
www.gwymca.org
Outings and camp-outs for fathers and their 5 to 10 year old children.

Boy Scouts of America
Greenwich Council #67, 63 Mason Street, Greenwich CT, 203.869.8424
www.GreenwichScouting.org or www.GreenwichBSA.com
This is the headquarters of the local chapter of the non-profit organization dedicated to instilling ethical values in young people. The Scouts are fortunate to own the Seton Reservation, a large preserve located at 363 Riversville Road. It serves as the site for the Cub Scout day camp as well as many other scouting outdoor programs. Call to check on a troop near you. The chapter sponsors the following programs. Programs open to boys: Tiger Cubs, age 6; Cub Scouts, ages 7-10; Boy Scouts, ages 11-18. Programs open to boys and girls: Explorers, ages 14-20 (specialties: aviation, scuba, emergency rescue.)
The Greenwich office has a small store for uniforms. A larger selection is available at the Darien Sports Shop (1127 Post Road, Darien, CT, 203.655.2575), and the Connecticut Yankee Council #72, Boy Scouts of America (in Norwalk CT, exit 40A on the Merritt Parkway, 362 Main Avenue, 203.847.2445).
Hours: Greenwich Scouts office: weekdays 8:30am-4:30pm.

CHILDREN

Girl Scout Council of Southwestern Connecticut
529 Danbury Road, Wilton CT, 800.882.5561, 203.762.5557
http://www.gsofct.org/
This is the headquarters of the local chapter of the non-profit organization dedicated to addressing girls' interests and their future contemporary roles as women. Programs: Daisies, kindergarten; Brownies, grades 1-3;
Junior Girl Scouts, grades 4-6; Cadettes, grades 7-9;
Seniors, grades 9-12. Uniforms are available from the Darien Sports Shop, 1127 Post Road, Darien CT, 203.655.2575.
Hours: Weekdays 9am-5:30pm, Thursday until 8:30pm.

SPORTS

For Uniforms and Equipment see STORES.
For Adult and Junior Sports see SPORTS.
If an activity (such as Tennis, Golf, Go Karting, Horseback Riding, Skiing or Karate), can be for both adults and children, the review is in SPORTS.

AMF Bowling Centers
See SPORTS and the section Parties Away From Home.

Arena Gymnastics
911 Hope Street (Riverbend Center), Stamford CT, 203.357.8167
www.arenagymnastics-ct.com
They offer coed preschool programs for ages 1 1/2-5 yrs, after school programs for girls ages 5 & up, after school programs for boys ages 5-10, competitive programs for girls at all Levels. This school comes highly recommended for more serious gymnasts.

Bobby Valentine Sports Academy (Baseball, Softball, Track)
72 Camp Avenue, Stamford CT, 203.968.2872
www.BobbyVAcademy.com
This facility in the Springdale section of Stamford is a state of the art baseball and softball training center. They are the home of Parisi Speed Classes which help young athletes improve their performance.

CHILDREN

Boys and Girls Club of Greenwich (Skating, Ice Hockey, Basketball, Football, Swimming, Ping Pong, Chess)
4 Horseneck Lane, Greenwich CT, 203.869.3224
www.BGCG.org
They have an extensive hockey program, including co-ed Broomball, girls ice hockey clinics and Mite Development Hockey League. A good place for private lessons: learning to skate & figure skating. They have girls and boys basketball, punt-pass-Kick football. They are the home of the Barracudas swim team and Kids in Sports. Kids in Sports (212-744-4900). www.kidsinsports.com runs sports programs for children 12 months to 12 years old. They have a number of outdoor activities, including a wiffle ball traveling team, canoeing, biking and swimming http://bgcg.org/imagineadventures

Chelsea Piers Connecticut

1 Blachley Road, Stamford CT, Membership: 203.989.1200
Children's programs 203.989.1100, www.ChelseapiersCT.com/youth
This 460,000 sf facility has a large number of children's programs: The little athletes programs are for children 4 months to 5 years, the youth sports programs are for ages 5-17. Some of their facilities are: two ice skating rinks for hockey and figure skating, an Olympic-size pool and a 6,000 sf splash zone with slides and water play area, a 15,000 sf gymnastics training center, baseball and softball training with batting cages, an adventure center with trampolines, rock wall and open play, 11 singles squash courts and 1 doubles court, a 100-yard indoor turf-field for soccer, lacrosse, football, field hockey, softball & baseball; hardwood courts for basketball and volleyball; 7 indoor tennis courts and 2 mini-courts; 7,000 sf high level athletic training center and more. They host single sports and multi-sports camps, birthday parties and are a licensed childcare and preschool center for children ages 3 months to 5 years.

(The) Cliffs (Climbing)
See SPORTS.

Cos Cob Athletic Club (T-Ball, Football, Cheerleading)
79 Cos Cob Avenue, Cos Cob CT, 201.437.2893
Contact: Heidi and Tom Pastore, 203.637.7767
A community organization sponsoring spring coed T-Ball for beginners in grades K-2 (T-Ball uses a batting tee) and The Cos Cob Crushers football teams (elementary and middle school football teams for ages 8 -13). The Crushers have cheerleaders in the fall.

CHILDREN

(Greenwich) Department of Parks and Recreation Programs
2nd floor, Town Hall, 101 Field Point Road, Greenwich CT, 203.622.7814
www.greenwichct.org/ParksAndRec/ParksandRec.asp
Office Hours: Weekdays 8am-4pm.
The Department sponsors a multitude of sports programs. Always go to their website or visit them at Town Hall to see what they are currently sponsoring. Below are some of their programs.
• Indoor baseball clinics January-March for children ages 7 to 13
• Co-ed spring outdoor clinics for Small Fry age 7 and Midget for age 8
• Doyle Baseball School for ages 7-12 during school vacation in April
• July & August co-ed baseball league for ages 9-12
• Indoor softball clinics for girls ages 10 to 15
• Co-ed baseball clinics, K to 6th grade
• Girls' baseball clinics, K to 6th grade
• Girls' Middle School baseball clinics, 6th through 8th grade
• Indoor lacrosse clinics.
• Co-ed introductory, non-contact Lacrosse clinics (ages 7 & 8, 9 & 10)
• Field hockey programs.
• Co-Ed volleyball games from elementary to adult
• Co-Ed indoor soccer for children k-6th grade

(The) Dolphins (Swim Team)
YWCA of Greenwich, 259 East Putnam Avenue, Greenwich CT, 203.869.6501
www.greenwichdolphins.com
In addition to the high school swim team, the town has several superior competition swim teams, like the Dolphins. The Dolphins are for serious swimmers. Kids start early: swim practice is every day, with meets held on most Sundays. All that is required to join is parental consent and the ability not to sink. Some children start as early as four.

Dorothy Hamill Skating Rink (Skating, Hockey)
Sue Merz Way off Sherman Avenue, Greenwich CT, 203.531.8560
Off Season: 203.622.7830
www.greenwichct.org/ParksAndRec/prSkating.asp
See SPORTS

CHILDREN

Doyle Baseball Academy (Baseball)
203.622.7830, Rick Siebert: 865.560.8765
www.doylebaseball.com
rick.siebert@doylebaseball.com
Hosted by Greenwich Department of Parks and Recreation in April at the Eastern Greenwich Civic Center. Groups are divided by age: 6-8, 9-10 & 11 -12.

Eastern Greenwich Civic Center
(aka Old Greenwich-Riverside Community Center)
90 Harding Road, Old Greenwich, 203.637.3659
www.greenwichct.org/ParksAndRec/prFacilityPrograms.asp#eastern
Old Greenwich-Riverside Community Center, 203.637.3659
www.myogrcc.org
Together they sponsor a variety of basketball, baseball and softball teams as well as instruction programs for girls and boys from kindergarten through 8th grade. Among their activities are indoor golf, indoor soccer, adult pick-up basketball for 18 and over, roller skating and yoga. OGCC sponsors a number of basketball programs for young children through adults: youth basketball for boys and girls in the 3rd and 4th grades; boys' basketball and girls' basketball for 5th to 8th graders as well as a number of summer tennis, baseball & soccer camps. The Old Greenwich-Riverside Soccer Association provides a comprehensive soccer program for over 700 youngsters who just wish to play for fun, as well as for those who wish to compete. The Van Williams Academy of Martial Arts teaches here.

Great Play (Children's Fitness and Sport Skills)
2000 West Main Street (Shop Rite Center), Stamford CT, (Stamford/Old Greenwich border), 203.978.1333
www.greatplay.com
A unique gym that offers fun classes to help kids develop motor skills, fitness and coordination.

Greenwich Babe Ruth League (Baseball)
Greenwich Department of Parks & Recreation Hotline: 203.618.7659
www.greenwichbaberuth.org
Non-profit organization sponsoring baseball. The Bambino division is for children 10-12; Junior division is for ages 13-15; Senior division is for ages 16-18. Teams play from late May through mid-July. Registration starts in February at Town Hall.

CHILDREN

Greenwich Basketball Association
www.GreenwichBasketball.org
Now in its 20th season, the Association was founded by a group of Greenwich fathers. It provides a townwide instructional and competitive co-ed basketball program for 5th-10th graders, designed to encourage and stimulate each child to build basketball skills. All skill levels are welcome and everyone is guaranteed to play at least half of each game. Registration and evaluations start in October. Use the website to register.

Greenwich Blues Youth Ice Hockey Association
PO Box 1107, Greenwich, CT 06836
Contact: see website for contacts and telephone numbers.
www.greenwichblues.com
Non-profit organization sponsoring competitive travel teams for boys and girls: Mites, under age 9; Squirts, 9-11; Peewees, 11-13; Bantam, 13-15. Dorothy Hamill Rink is their home rink. Season is from September through March, tryouts are in early September. For information send an email to greenwichbluespresident@gmail.com
 or greenwichblueshockeydirector@gmail.com

Greenwich Community Sailing
PO Box 195, Old Greenwich CT, 203.698.0599
www.GreenwichSailing.com
See SPORTS.

Greenwich Basketball
Old Greenwich Civic Center, 90 Harding Road, 201.652.4477
www.GreenwichBasketball.com
Basketball Leagues and camps for grades K-5. Check the website for locations and times.

Greenwich Kids Triathlon
www.greenwichkidstri.com
The triathlon consists of a swim, bike and run, at the Greenwich High School campus. It is for 7-10 and 11-12 year olds.

Greenwich Lacrosse
201.652.4477
www.GreenwichLacrosse.com
Leagues and camps for grades k-7 are offered at locations such as the Carmel Academy 270 Lake Avenue and other locations in Greenwich.

CHILDREN

Greenwich Soccer Association
Mailing Address: 88 Knapp Street, Stamford CT, 06907
Register Online at www.greenwichtravelsoccer.com
Girls' and boys' travel soccer teams for ages 7 to 11. They play travel teams from other Fairfield County towns on Sunday afternoons. Tryouts are required and usually begin in November for the spring season.

Greenwich Soccer Club
PO Box 383, Cos Cob CT 06807, 203.661.2620
www.greenwichsoccer.com
The GSC is a townwide recreational program open to every boy and girl, ages 6-14, who either resides in or attends school in town. In the fall, over 1,700 boys and girls participate on Saturdays (coached by some 350 parent volunteers) with mid-week clinics taught by professional instructors. There are separate leagues for the boys and girls. The GSC is a privately funded, non-profit community service organization founded in 1976.

Greenwich Skateboard Park
Roger Sherman Baldwin Park, Arch Street, Greenwich CT, 203.496.9876
www.greenwichct.org/ParksAndRec/prSkatePark.asp
The 7,754 sf skate park was a gift of the Junior League of Greenwich. The maximum number of skaters is 40. Check website for day pass costs. Greenwich residents may apply for annual membership at the Parks and Recreation office in Town Hall weekdays from 8am-4pm. The Department of Parks and Recreation conducts clinics in basic techniques, safety and etiquette for children ages 6- 14. Check the town website for information on clinics, camps and birthday parties.
Hours: The usual skate park hours are weekdays 3pm-7pm, weekends noon-7pm. Hours vary depending upon when schools are in session.

Greenwich Youth Cheerleading League (GYCL)
www.gycl.org
GYCL operates as an entity alongside the GYFL and is open to girls and boys 3rd to 8th grade throughout town. Sign-ups are in May. The season runs from late August to November.

CHILDREN

Greenwich Youth Football League (GYFL)
www.gyfl.net
Town wide instructional/competitive tackle football league for children ages 8-13. Registration takes place in May. First-timers sign up at Town Hall Department of Parks and Recreation. Spaces fill quickly. The season runs from late August to November. Practices are held 2-3 times a week. Games are on Sunday mornings. Each team has three levels: Bantam, 3rd & 4th graders; Junior, 5th & 6th graders; Senior, 7th & 8th graders. See Greenwich Youth Cheerleaders (GYCL) above. These are the teams:
1. Mavericks (Glenville) www.GlenvilleMavericks.com
2. Banc Raiders (Byram) www.bancgreenwich.org
3. Crushers(Cos Cob)
4. Bulldogs (North Mianus) www.nmbulldogsfootball.com
5. Gators (Riverside) www.gatorfootball.ws
6. Putnam Generals (Old Greenwich) www.putnamgeneralsfootball.com

Greenwich Youth Lacrosse
www.GreenwichYouthLacrosse.org
www.facebook.com/greenwichyouthlacrosse
A non-profit organization sponsoring lacrosse teams. House League for boys and girls in grades 1-6; Travel teams for boys and girls in grades 3-4 and 5-6. Boys travel teams for grades 7-8. Registration is usually in March.

Greenwich Youth Water Polo League
See website for email addresses.
www.GreenwichWaterPolo.com
Founded by the coaches of the Greenwich High School water polo team, the GHS has one of the strongest programs on the Eastern seaboard. This league is for boys and girls ages 5 to 15 who want to learn to play water polo. They have a House League (teaching) and a Travel League (competitive).

In-Line Roller Hockey (Roller Skating)
Eastern Greenwich Civic Center (aka Old Greenwich Riverside Community Center), 90 Harding Road, Old Greenwich CT, 203.637.3659
Adult pickup roller hockey as well as spring and summer instruction and games for boys and girls ages 6-14. Call for times and details.

Jack Rabbits Gymnastics
Round Hill Community House, 397 Round Hill Road, Greenwich CT, 203.622.0004
www.jackrabbitsgym.com
Jack Rabbits has classes for kids ages 1- 9 years; it is a great way to wear your children out!

Liberty Paintball
(Thunder Ridge Ski Area) 1 Thunder Ridge Road, Patterson NY, 845.878.6300
www.libertypaintball-ny.com
See SPORTS.

Longshore Sailing School
260 Compo Road South, Westport CT, 203.226.4646
www.longshoresailingschool.com
See SPORTS.

(The) Marlins (Swim Team)
YMCA Greenwich CT, 203.869.1630
www.macombmarlins.com
Run at the YMCA, this swim team competes with the Dolphins. The Marlins is a year-round swim club that starts at age 6. They compete in USA sanction swim meets and the Connecticut Summer Swim League. Register online.

My Gym
7 Hyde Street, Stamford CT, 203.327.3496
www.my-gym.com
Gymnastics and movement classes for children ages 3 months to 13 years.

Nike Adult Sports Schools and Junior Camps
800.645.3226
www.ussportscamps.com
Nike sponsors a great number of adult and junior sports camps: tennis, golf, volleyball hockey, soccer, lacrosse, softball, baseball, rugby, water polo and more.

Outward Bound (Adventure Trips)
www.outwardbound.org
See SPORTS

CHILDREN

Spirit Zone Too (Tumbling & Cheerleading)
22 Mill Street, Byram CT, 203.531.9663
www.CTSpirit.com
SZT has programs for athletes of all ages and abilities. Clinics for cheer and tumbling as well as for competitive cheer and dance.

Sports Center of Connecticut
784 River Road (Route 110) Shelton CT, 203.929.6500
www.sportscenterct.com
See SPORTS.

Western Greenwich Civic Center
(aka. Bendheim Greenwich Civic Center)
449 Pemberwick Road, Glenville CT, 203.532.1259
www.greenwichct.org/ParksAndRec/prFacilityPrograms.asp
The Center has programs for a variety of activities such as weight lifting, fitness and exercise, roller skating, basketball, indoor soccer, youth and adult ballet, indoor field hockey, fencing (See Greenwich Fencing), Tennis for Tots, kendo, guitar lessons, theater and dance classes, karate classes, coed volleyball, little language league, chess club, boot camp and sports clinics for children. They are also the site of a child care / children's day school.

Windy Hill Figure Skating Club
www.windyhillsc.com
Non-profit skating club affiliated with the US Figure Skating Association. Membership is open to all figure skaters who have progressed beyond "Basic 6." Home ice is the Dorothy Hamill Rink.

YMCA (aka Greenwich Family Y)
50 East Putnam Avenue, Greenwich CT, 203.869.1630
www.gwymca.org, www.greenwichymca.org
See SPORTS

YWCA
259 East Putnam Avenue, Greenwich CT, 203.869.6501
Adrianne Singer, President and CEO
www.YWCAGreenwich.org
See SPORTS

CHILDREN

SUMMER CAMP INFORMATION

No need to travel to New Hampshire or Maine, the Greenwich area has all sorts of camps.

American Camping Association
New England Section, 781.541-6080
www.acanewengland.org
A national non-profit educational organization that accredits children's summer camps. Call to get a copy of their directory.

Community Answers
203.622.7979
www.greenwichlibrary.org/commanswers.htm
Call for a copy of their Summer Resource Guide.

Summer Camp Website
www.MySummerCamps.com
877.777.7738
Used by many Greenwich Residents, it lists over 15,000 camps.

Summer Camp Fair
Greenwich High School, Greenwich CT, 203.625.8000
www.greenwich.k12.ct.us/ghs/ghs.htm
Known as "Summerfare," this event is sponsored by the Greenwich High School PTA and draws hundreds of camps from around the USA. The fair is usually held in February.

Summer Camp Expo
Greenwich Academy, Greenwich CT, 203.625.8900
www.greenwichacademy.org
Their Summer Opportunity Fair is usually held at the end of January.

TIP: SCARECROW FESTIVAL
Every year in October, the Mill Pond Park on Strickland Road is taken over by scarecrows waiting to be judged. Activities include pumpkin painting, scarecrow making, games, crafts and lots of fun for everyone. For information on the event contact the Greenwich Chamber of Commerce, 203.869.3500.

CHILDREN

SUMMER CAMP PROGRAMS

Check SPORTS for summer camp ideas. Many, such as Mead Farm and Getner Farm or Downunder Kayaking, have summer camps.
Tip: Packages Plus-N-More, 215 East Putnam Avenue (Mill Pond Shopping Center), Cos Cob, 203.625.8130. They will pack and ship your child's camping gear.

Allegra Summer Stock Performing Arts Camps
37 West Putnam Avenue, Greenwich CT, 203.629.9162
http://allegradancegreenwich.com/
Drama, theater, jazz, tap and other fantastic art programs.

Arch Street Teen Center
100 Arch Street, Greenwich CT, 629.5744
www.archstreet.org
Hands-on arts and crafts, graphic design, film and radio production for kids entering grades 7-12.

Art Scampers
www.fpcg.org
First Presbyterian Church, 37 Lafayette Place, 203.869.7782
Summer day camp for ages 2.5-6. They Focus on art, music & drama.

Audubon Summer Children's Programs
Audubon Center, 613 Riversville Road, 203.869.5272
http://greenwich.audubon.org
The Audubon Summer Nature Day Camp offers themes for children entering K to 5th grade and for older children. Outstanding teens training in ecological research for grades 6 to 8.

Banksville Community House Summer Camp
12 Banksville Road, Greenwich CT, 203.622.9597
http://thebch.org/
A perfect camp for those living in the Banksville area, featuring summer fun activities such as archery and swimming.

Bible Camps
• St. Paul Evangelical Lutheran Church, 203.531.8466
• Greenwich Baptist Church, 203.869.2807
• Stanwich Congregational Church, 203.661.6509

91

CHILDREN

Greenwich Boys and Girls Club
4 Horseneck Lane, Greenwich CT, 203.869.3224
www.bgcg.org
Open to members ages 6-12. Located at the Clubhouse on Horseneck Lane. Activities include: swimming, gym, field sports, computers, crafts, and educational programs. Clubhouse campers will stay energized all summer with a healthy breakfast and lunch at the Clubhouse. Also see Camp Simmons.

Boy Scouts of America
Greenwich Council, 63 Mason Street, Greenwich CT, 203.869.8424
http://greenwichscouting.org/
The Seton Reservation at 363 Riversville Road is a great treasure. Day camp is available for boys in grades 1 to 4 with no prior Scouting experience. The camp does a good job of teaching outdoor sports such as swimming, archery, canoeing and fishing.

Brunswick School Summer Sports Camps
100 Maher Avenue, Greenwich CT, 203.625.5800, 203.625.5822
www.brunswickschool.org
Summer camps for boys ages 7-13 in many different sports, as well as co-ed summer play camps for ages 3-5.

Bush-Holley Summer Camps
39 Strickland Road, Cos Cob CT, 203.552.5329, 203.869.6899
www.Hstg.org
Summer History + Art Camp: 2-week sessions focusing on history and art. Co-ed, for grades 1-7.

Camp Pelican
471 North Street, Greenwich CT, winter: 203.622.6654, summer: 203.869.4243
www.pelicandaycamp.com
Established in 1965, this day camp provides instruction in a variety of outdoor and indoor activities. The camp begins in June and ends in August. Sessions are 4 to 7 weeks. Co-ed ages 3-13. Capacity 500. The camp is located on the campus of Greenwich Catholic School.

CHILDREN

Camp Simmons
744 Lake Avenue, Greenwich CT, 203.869.0176, 203.869.3224
www.BGCG.org
Run by the Boys and Girls Club of Greenwich. Two-month session includes canoeing, swimming, field sports, archery, and nature hikes. Camp for ages 6-12.

Cardinal Baseball Camp
Directed by former Greenwich High Varsity Coach, Mike Mora, 203.869.3736
www.cardinalbaseballcamp.com
For players ages 6-13, from 9am-12pm; 4-week and 2-week sessions begin in July at Eastern Middle School.

Children's Day School
www.childrensdayschool.net/
449 Pemberwick Road, Greenwich CT, 203.532.1190
8 Riverside Avenue, Riverside CT, 203.637.1122
Ages 3-7. Art, cooking, creative movement and music.

Chelsea Piers Summer Sports Camps
1 Blachley Road, Stamford CT, 203.989.1004
This 400,000 sf sports complex has age appropriate camps (Little Athletes 3-6 years), (5-12 years and 13+), (Girls leadership ages 14-18) for gymnastics, ice hockey, ice skating, lacrosse, soccer, squash, swimming, tennis, volleyball and basketball. They offer full-day and half-day programs, single-sport or multi-sport.

Computer Camps

Imagination Computer Camps
877.248.0206 www.computercamps.com
Email: camp@computercamps.com
For the kid who can think of nothing but computers. Like-minded children come from all over the world to learn programming, computer graphics and rocketry. The closest camp is at Fairfield University.

iD tech Camps
888.709.8324 www.internalDrive.com
Princeton, Columbia, Vassar and Sacred Heart all have programs for children ages 7-17 from beginner to advanced.

CHILDREN

Creative Summer Camp at The Mead School
1095 Riverbank Road, Stamford 203.595.9500 x 63
www.meadschool.org
For boys and girls ages 6½ to 16 interested in dance, painting, design, drawing and more. Emphasis is on creativity, under the guidance of professional artists.

Department of Parks and Recreation
203.622.7830
There is a great variety of town-sponsored co-ed camps, such as Kamp Kairphree (ages 5 to 12), the Music and Art Program (children who have completed 3rd grade to 8th graders, who have had at least one year of study with an instrument) and Future Stars Tennis Camp (ages 6-14), offers Greenwich Adventurers, Skatepark Ramp Camps, and Filmmakers camp. Don't forget to ask for their program bulletin.
• Baseball programs
• Co-ed T Ball for 5 & 6 year olds
• Small Fry Baseball 7-9 year olds. There is also a completely separate baseball summer program, as well as other sports such as soccer and swimming.

ESF Sports Camp
Held at the Greenwich Academy, 200 North Maple Avenue, 203.869.4444
http://www.esfcamps.com/greenwich/
Open to boys and girls.
• Mini Camp (Art, Water Play, Music) age 3
Day Camp (Crafts, Sports, Music) ages 4-8
• Sports Camp (8 Sports), ages 6-14
• Senior Camp (Sports, Arts & Adventures), ages 9-15
• Tennis Camp (full or half-day), ages 6 to 15. Full or half day for beginner, intermediate and advanced players.

FASSP Summer Squash Camp
Sportsplex, 49 Brown House Road, Stamford CT, 203.536.0066
www.sportsplex-ct.com
Programs designed for all levels from beginner to Advanced players.

Field Club Squash Camp
276 Lake Avenue, Greenwich CT, 203.869.1309
A private club that offers a weekly Junior Summer Squash Camp, sometimes open to the public. The camp instructors are some of the best players in the world.

CHILDREN

First Church Day Camp
First Congregational Church, 108 Sound Beach Avenue, Old Greenwich CT, 203.637.5430
www.fccog.org
Co-ed day camp for ages 3 to 5. Beach activities, games, music and sports.

Future Stars Sports Camps
Armonk Tennis Club, 546 Bedford Rd, Armonk NY, 914.273.8124, 273.8500
www.fscamps.com
In its 30th year, this camp allows boys and girls, ages 6-16, to focus on a sport of their choice: tennis, soccer, lacrosse, basketball, baseball, softball, even computer, circus arts and magic. Programs run 9 am-4 pm at SUNY Purchase College and some Greenwich locations.

Gan Israel Camp
270 Lake Avenue, Greenwich CT, 203.869.5486
www.campgan.com
Run by Chabad Lubavitch of Greenwich, provides traditional camp activities for ages 18 months-3 years, and 4 to 13 years. Co-ed. July.

Greenwich Academy Sports Camps
200 North Maple Avenue, 203.625.8900
http://www.greenwichacademy.org/page.cfm?p=543

Greenwich Country Day School Summer Camps
Old Church Road, 863.5600 x 5504
http://www.gcdscamp.org/
Summer day camps for ages 3-13. Now in its 50th year, they have many programs for each age group, including swimming, tennis, arts, crafts, computers, woodworking and sailing.

Greenwich Public Schools Summer Program
203.531.7977
www.greenwichschools.org
Enrichment and review courses for all students from pre-K to grade 12. Held at multiple locations, see the website for details.

Greenwich Racquet Club
1 River Road, Cos Cob CT, contact: Ricardo Leon 203.661.0606
www.GreenwichRacquetClub.com
Tennis and sports camp for children ages 4-7 and 8-16.

Greenwich Crew
49 River Road, Cos Cob, 203.661.4033
www.GreenwichWaterClub.com
Rowing for ages 12 to 18.

Greenwich Skate Park Summer Ramp Camp
100 South Arch Street, Greenwich CT, 203.622.7821, 203.622.7830,
203.496.9876
www.greenwichct.org/ParksAndRec/prRecPrograms.asp
Ages 6-14.

Italian Center Summer Camps
1620 Newfield Avenue, Stamford CT, 203.322.6941
www.ItalianCenter.org
Half day and full day camps for kids 3 years-6th grade. The active program is designed to aid children in mastering the skills to build confidence.
Camp activities which vary from day to day and throughout the summer include: swimming, gym, dance, music, tennis, arts & crafts, nature, ballfield sports, softball, touch football, soccer and fitness.

Kamp Kairphree
Greenwich Department of Parks and Recreation, 203.622.7814
www.greenwichct.org/ParksAndRec/ParksandRec.asp
A happy camp for 5-12 year olds.

Manhattanville College
2900 Purchase Street, Purchase, NY, 914.323.5214
www.mville.edu
The college (914.694.2200) provides a summer writing workshop for young people in grades 4-11, and hosts a number of sports camps, including soccer, basketball and tennis.

Nike Camps
800.645.3226
http://www.ussportscamps.com/
Nike runs a number of swim, volleyball, golf and tennis camps for boys and girls ages 10 to 18.

CHILDREN

Pre School Summer Camp
139 East Putnam Avenue (Second Congregational Church), Greenwich CT, 203.869.8388
www.ThePreSchoolGreenwich.com
An independent, non-sectarian preschool camp for children ages 2 to 5. Activities center around arts and crafts, music and drama, water play, gardening and sports.

Purchase College
735 Anderson Hill Road, Purchase NY, 914.251.6500
www.Purchase.edu
The State University of New York (SUNY) at Purchase offers a number of Summer Youth Programs in the Arts (art, music, and acting) for ages 6-17. They have early drop-off and extended-day options.

Robin Hood Camp
Herrick Road, Brooksville ME, 831.659.9143 (winter), 207.359.8313 (summer)
www.robinhoodcamp.com
One of the best all around camps in the USA. It has a strong Greenwich connection. I'm proud to count myself as an alumnus.

Saint Paul's Summer Camp
200 Riverside Avenue, Riverside CT, 203.637.3503
Camp for children 3-6; art, dance, sports, music, water play & nature.

Sandpiper's Beach Camp
203.637.3659
www.ogrcc.com
Sponsored by the Old Greenwich Riverside Community Center for children ages 3-10. OGRCC also offers many sports camps.

Shady Lane Farm
69 Stone Hill Road, Bedford NY, 914.962.3674
www.ShadyLaneFarmNY.com
Summer camp teaches kids 5-13 the basics of riding and horsemanship. Hours: Tuesday-Sunday 9am-5pm.

CHILDREN

Silvermine School of Art
New Canaan CT, 203.966.6668 ext. 2
www.silvermineart.org
Creative summer camp for the artistically inclined, ages 5-17. Learn painting, drawing, photography and sculpture on an attractive 4-acre campus.

Sound Waters Camp
Cove Island Park, 1281 Cove Road, Stamford CT, 203.323.1978
www.soundwaters.org/camp
Nature Discovery Grades K-5, Sea Stars Grades K-1, Bluefish Grades 2-3, Sharks Grades 4-5
Small Boat Sailing Grades 4-8, Opti Sailing Grades 4-6, Pixel Sailing Grades 5-8.

Westchester Circus Arts
www.westchestercircusarts.com/camp/
YMCA Tappan Hill Early Learning Center
50 Ichabod Lane, Tarrytown NY, 914.275.5711
Year-round circus arts training. They offer daily classes and 2-week summer day camps in July for ages 5-18, where campers learn to climb the silks, hang on a trapeze, walk a tightrope and make human pyramids.

Whitby School Summer Camp:
www.whitbyschool.org
969 Lake Avenue, 203.869.8464
They have many summer programs for children in grades 1-6.

Windswept Farm (aka Mead Farm)
107 June Road, Stamford CT, 203.322.4984
www.meadfarm.com
Co-ed ages 5-17. Weekly horseback riding, horse care, grooming, show prep and games. No previous riding experience necessary.

YMCA
50 East Putnam Avenue, 203.869.1630
www.gwymca.org
Summer Fun Clubs: 2-week co-ed sessions begin at the end of June. They include field trips, sports, and environmental education.

CHILDREN

YWCA
259 East Putnam Avenue, 203.869.6501, ext. 225
www.ywcagreenwich.org, www.ywcagreenwich.org/schools-camps/
childrens-camps/
• Camp Ta Yi To is a co-ed camp for grades K to 5; includes swimming and tennis.
• Pre-school Camp, ages 15 months-2 years; songs, stories, play.
• Pre-school Camp, ages 3-5: gymnastics, swimming, cooking.
• Dance Camp, ages 10-16: ballet, jazz, choreography, hip hop.
• Girls' Circle Camp-grades 6-8

SUPPORT SERVICES FOR CHILDREN

ABILIS Greenwich
50 Glenville Street, Glenville CT, 203.531.1880
www.abilis.us
Family support services and after-school programs for families of children with special needs.

Child Guidance Center of Southern Connecticut
196 Greyrock Place, Stamford CT, 203.324.6127, 203.983.5294;
Greenwich CT, 203.983.5294, 24-hour crisis line 203.323.9797
www.childguidancect.org
Professionally-staffed mental health center for children and adolescents. Individual, group and family therapy, parent guidance, 24-hour crisis services, and community education programs.

Community Answers
203.622.7979
www.communityanswers.org
Information on parent education programs, support groups, crisis programs, counseling services, nannies, au pair and babysitting services.

Family Centers
40 Arch Street, Greenwich CT, 203.869.4848
20 Bridge Street, Greenwich CT, 203.629.2822
www.familycenters.org
This United Way human service agency offers a multitude of helpful programs such as the Den for Grieving Kids and individual or family counseling.

CHILDREN

Family Health
Greenwich Department of Health, Greenwich CT, 203.622.6488, 203.622.7836
www.greenwichct.org/HealthDept/HealthDept.asp
Prenatal and postpartum home visits, well child clinics (birth to age 5), immunization and hypertension screening clinic (5 years to adult); school health services; early childhood/day care licenses.

Kids in Crisis
1 Salem Street, Cos Cob CT, 203.327.5437
www.kidsincrisis.org
Crisis intervention counseling and short term shelter. Ages Newborn to 17 years.

La Leche League
St Paul's Lutheran Church, 286 Delavan Avenue, Greenwich CT, 203.613.6656, 203.532.9819
http://www.lllct.org/greenwich
Support groups and information on breast feeding.

Parents' Exchange
25 Valley Drive, Greenwich Health at Greenwich Hospital, Greenwich CT, 203.863.3794
http://www.greenhosp.org/tender-beginnings-programs
Weekly discussion groups led by child development specialists. A good environment to stimulate and provide parents with opportunities to exchange ideas. Parents are grouped by their child's age from infants to adolescents. Babysitting is available.

Parent to Parent Network
50 Glenville Street, Greenwich CT, 203.629.1880 x 300
Information network for families with children who have special needs.

Tender Beginnings
At Greenwich Hospital, Greenwich CT, 203.863.3794
http://www.greenhosp.org/tender-beginnings-programs
Expectant parent classes, Lamaze classes, baby care and breastfeeding classes, nutrition, prenatal exercise, newborn parenting groups, grandparenting, baby food preparation, babysitting, sibling classes.

CLUBS

Garden Clubs are listed in the section FLOWERS & GARDENS.
Information about clubs and organizations is also available from
Community Answers www.greenwichlibrary.org/commanswers.htm
See GREENWICH for organizations preserving Greenwich History.
See also CHARITABLE AND SERVICE ORGANIZATIONS.

SECTIONS
Country Clubs
Newcomers' Clubs
Skating Clubs
Yacht Clubs

COUNTRY CLUBS

Greenwich has a number of yacht and country clubs. Costs to join a club vary from about $12,000 to $40,000 for the initiation fee with annual dues ranging from approximately $6,000 to more than $10,000. Country clubs with golf courses are typically the most expensive. Clubs with dining rooms usually require a quarterly food minimum. In addition, clubs may have assessments for capital improvements. Membership in most private clubs requires a proposer and several seconders or sponsors. Proposers are usually required to have no business connection with the proposed member. The more members you know, the easier it is to join. Clubs which serve a particular area, such as Belle Haven or Milbrook, often give preference to area residents. The waiting period to join a club can be several years.

Bailiwick Club of Greenwich
(Swimming, Paddle Tennis and Tennis)
12 Duncan Drive, Greenwich CT, 203.531.7591 (summer)
www.bailiwickclub.com

Burning Tree Country Club
(Dining, Golf, Swimming, Tennis, Paddle Tennis)
120 Perkins Road, Greenwich CT, 203.869.9004
www.burningtreecc.org

Fairview Country Club
(Dining, Golf, Tennis, Paddle Tennis, Swimming)
1241 King Street, Greenwich CT, 203.531.6200
www.fairviewcountryclub.org

CLUBS

Field Club
(Dining, Tennis [grass & composition], Squash, Paddle Tennis, Swimming)
276 Lake Avenue, Greenwich CT, 203.869.1300
www.fcofgreenwich.com

Greenwich Country Club
(Dining, Golf, Tennis, Squash, Paddle Tennis, Swimming, Skeet)
19 Doubling Road, Greenwich CT, 203.869.1000
www.greenwichcountryclub.org

Greenwich Polo Club
Field Location: 1 Hurlingham Drive (Upper North Street at Conyers Farm)
Office: 80 Field Point Road, Greenwich CT, 203.561.5821
www.GreenwichPoloClub.com
Greenwich has a world-class polo facility. Most summer Sundays you can watch a good polo match in a beautiful setting. Matches begin at 3 pm, the gates open at 1 pm. General admission is $40 per car. Attire is "Garden Party Chic." The Greenwich Polo Club also offers individual and group polo lessons. Lessons include the use of a polo pony, all tack, polo mallets and balls. Call their office to get a copy of their magazine "Greenwich Polo."

Innis Arden Golf Club
(Dining, Golf, Tennis, Paddle Tennis, Swimming)
120 Tomac Avenue, Old Greenwich CT, 203.637.6900
www.innisardengolfclub.com

Italian Center of Stamford
(Indoor and Outdoor Pools, Gym, Tennis, Paddle Tennis, Miniature Golf)
1620 Newfield Avenue, Stamford CT, 203.322.6941
www.italiancenter.org
Situated on 28 acres in a country club setting, the center is a unique type of club with membership open to everyone.

Milbrook Club
(Dining, Golf, Swimming, Paddle Tennis, Tennis)
61 Woodside Drive, Greenwich CT, 203.869.4540
www.milbrookclub.com

CLUBS

Round Hill Club
(Dining, Golf, Swimming, Tennis, Skeet)
33 Round Hill Club Road, Greenwich CT, 203.869.2350
www.RhClub.org

Stanwich Club
(Dining, Golf, Swimming, Tennis, Paddle Tennis)
888 North Street, 203.869.0555
www.Stanwich.com

Tamarack Country Club
(Dining, Golf, Swimming, Tennis)
55 Locust Road, 203.531.7300
www.tamarackcountryclub.com

NEWCOMERS' CLUBS

Old Greenwich Riverside Newcomers' Club
PO Box 256, Old Greenwich CT, 06870
www.greenwichnewcomers.com
The Club is 48 years old and hosts a great variety of functions, from wine tastings to museum trips. There are events for everyone, and they welcome new and established residents of Greenwich and surrounding areas. Be sure to ask for their excellent newsletter.

SKATING CLUBS

Greenwich Skating Club (Figure Skating & Hockey)
Cardinal Road, Greenwich CT, 203.622.9583
www.GreenwichSkatingClub.org
The Skating Club, set inconspicuously off Fairfield Road, has an outdoor rink and offers a strong skating program for children. Because of its small membership, it is one of the more difficult clubs to join. See the website for admissions information.

CLUBS

YACHT CLUBS

As one might expect for a town on the water, Greenwich has a number of excellent yacht and boating clubs. Many yacht clubs have long waiting lists (some as long as 12 years). Like the country clubs, most are private.

Belle Haven Club
(Dining, Boating, Tennis, Swimming)
100 Harbor Drive, Greenwich CT, 203.861.5353
www.bellehavenclub.com

Byram Shore Boat Club
Byram Park, Greenwich CT, 203.531.9858 (Clubhouse)
www.byramshore.org
Mooring/docking adjacent to town park and beach.

Cos Cob Yacht Club
PO Box 155, Riverside CT 06878, 203.661.5946
Social club for people interested in boating. Membership is by invitation.

Greenwich Boat & Yacht Club
(Club House, Mooring/Docking and Picnic Areas)
Grass Island, Greenwich CT, 203.622.9558
PO Box 40 Greenwich CT 06830
www.gbyc.org
Membership is open to all interested residents of the town.

Greenwich Water Club
(Dining, Crew, Boating, Swimming, Gym)
49 River Road, Cos Cob CT, 203.601.4033
www.GreenwichWaterClub.com
The Club has a full working marina with a 250 slip capacity, onsite repair service, fueling dock, visiting slip privileges, winter storage facilities, and a ship's store. They teach safe boating as well as other boating classes.

Indian Harbor Yacht Club
(Dining and Boating Facilities including Mooring/Docking)
710 Steamboat Road, Greenwich CT, 203.869.2484
www.indianharboryc.com

CLUBS

Mianus River Boat & Yacht Club
98 Strickland Road, Cos Cob CT, 203.869.4689
www.mrbyc.com
Boat and yacht club open to any Greenwich resident. Meets the first Monday of the month usually at 7:30 pm at the clubhouse.

Old Greenwich Yacht Club
(Club House, Kayak, Sailing, Cruising, Fishing)
Greenwich Point (aka Tods Point), Old Greenwich CT, 203.637.3074
www.ogyc.org
Open to all residents with beach cards. Membership costs are reasonable. It has deep water moorings as well as Mercury sailboats for member use. The club provides sailing lessons on weekends and trophy races during the summer.

Riverside Yacht Club
(Dining, Swimming, Beach, Tennis and Boating)
102 Club Road, Riverside CT, 203.637.1706
www.riversideyc.org

Rocky Point Club
(Clubhouse, Mooring, Salt Water Pool)
Rocky Point Road, Old Greenwich CT, 203.637.2397 (summer only)
PO Box 359
www.Rockypointclub.com

TIP: HOW TO GET ON A TOWN BOARD OR COMMISSION

There are a number of independent boards and commissions www.greenwichct.org/town_hall.asp#agencies that are completely volunteer and yet have great power in how the Town runs. The Board of Selectmen interviews candidates and recommends their appointment to the Representative Town Meeting (RTM). The Appointments Committee of the RTM and one or more of the other RTM standing committees will interview the candidate. The nomination is then brought to the RTM for a vote. If you are interested in serving on one of these boards you can nominate yourself of talk to a member of the Selectman's Nomination Advisory Committee (SNAC) by going to www.greenwichct.org/government/committees/selectmens_nominations_advisory_committee/

COFFEE, TEA, JUICE & SMOOTHIES

CFCF (Coffee)
118 Greenwich Avenue, Greenwich CT, 203.661.8300
With a coffee roaster as the center piece, this stylish modern glass, brick, chrome shop is comfortable and the just-roasted coffee is very good. Stop in and have a treat from "Balthazar" in Manhattan or a sandwich. If you are wondering, CFCF stands for Coffee Coffee.
Hours: Monday-Saturday 6am-7:30pm, Sunday 6:30am-7:30pm.
Size: Seats 28.

Dunkin Donuts (Coffee)
• 271 West Putnam Avenue, Greenwich CT, 203.869.5791
• 375 East Putnam Avenue, Cos Cob CT, 203.869.7454
184 Sound Beach Avenue, Old Greenwich CT, 203.990.0157
Founded in 1950 in Quincy MA, the company has about 10,000 locations. It originally focused on baked goods. More than half of its business is coffee, although they have more than 1,000 varieties of donuts.
Hours: Cos Cob, Monday-Sunday 5am-11pm; Greenwich and Old Greenwich locations close earlier.
Size: Cos Cob seats 16, Greenwich seats 6, Old Greenwich seats 12

(The) Drawing Room (Coffee & Tea)
5 Suburban Avenue, Cos Cob CT, 203.661.3737 www.thedrawingroom.cc
Tucked around the corner from the Post Road, near the Cos Cob Library is the perfect place for light lunch and/or afternoon tea. This small, cheerfully-decorated tea room serves tea, hot chocolate, coffee, finger sandwiches, scones and desserts. The staff are tea experts who can help you make delightful tea choices. Having tea and browsing through the adjoining art gallery make this a fun and civilized break in the day.
Hours: Breakfast, Monday-Saturday 8am-1pm; Lunch, 11pm-5pm (Official tea time is considered to be 11am-4pm); Grand Afternoon Tea, $26.
Size: Seats 15 inside and 16 outside. No reservations.

Fairway (Coffee)
699 Canal Street, Stamford CT, 203.388.9815 www.FairwayMarket.com
This 50,000 sf grocery store has a huge selection of fresh products. They have a coffee center where they roast their beans (worth the trip just for the beans). A coffee expert, in a recent lecture, named Fairway as her top choice.
Hours: Grocery open daily 8am-10pm (closes early on many holidays).

green & tonic (Juice and Smoothies)
- 7 Strickland Road, Cos Cob CT, 203.869.1376
- 85 Railroad Avenue, Greenwich CT, 855.464.2638

www.GreenAndTonic.com

If you think healthy food can't be tasty, you need to stop at this small eatery, owned by Greenwich resident Jeffrey Pandolfino, former owner of Plum Pure Foods. Vegans and everyone else will love their cold-pressed juices, smoothies, raw prepared foods, salads, soups, sandwiches and side dishes. You must try our favorite smoothie "Ultimate Warrior." The restaurant is reviewed in the RESTAURANT section.

Hours: Weekdays 7am-7pm, Saturday 8am-5pm, Sunday 9am-5 pm.

Size: Cos Cob seats 16

Juice Press (Juice & Smoothies)

360 Greenwich Avenue, Greenwich CT   www.juicepress.com

Cold pressed juice, smoothies, raw foods and soups. This 24 location chain was founded in 2010 by Marcus Anteb. Everything is organic, most items are kosher and vegan.

Hours: Every day 7am-7pm.

Size: no seating; Delivery: to Greenwich area.

Meli-Melo (Juice Bar, Restaurant)

362 Greenwich Avenue, Greenwich CT, 203.629.6153

www.melimelogreenwich.com

A popular, always-crowded restaurant, with French casual foods. See review in RESTAURANTS. They have an amazing selection of fresh-squeezed juices. The fruit sorbets are excellent as are their pastries.

Hours: Weekdays 7am-10pm, Saturday & Sunday 8am-10pm. No reservations. Size: Seats 60.

Robeks (Smoothies)

132 East Putnam Avenue, Cos Cob CT, 203.769.5870   www.robeks.com

California smoothies have come to Greenwich. Robeks is a franchise chain started in 1966. It has 140 locations in 16 states (90 of the locations are in California). They offer a huge assortment of smoothies. Healthy eating is their theme. We like the nutritional information they provide on each product. Take-out only.

Hours: Weekdays 6:30am-9pm, Saturday 8am-9pm; Sunday 9am-7:30pm. (They open later and close earlier in the fall & winter.)

COFFEE, TEA, JUICE & SMOOTHIES

Starbucks (Coffee)
• 301 Greenwich Avenue, 203.661.3042
• 60 East Putnam Avenue (Whole Foods Shopping Center), 203.629.0432
• 147 East Putnam Avenue, Cos Cob, 203.661.1543
• 1253 East Putnam Avenue (Riverside Shopping Cntr), 203.698.1790
www.starbucks.com
One of the few places you can get your coffee made with soy milk, or just about any other way. During the summer, their Vivanos (a sort of smoothie) are great.
Greenwich Avenue Hours: Monday-Thursday 5:30am-10pm, Friday 5:30am-11pm, Saturday 6am-11pm, Sunday 6am-11pm; other locations may close earlier. Size: seats 20

Tropical Smoothie Café (Smoothies)
410 Greenwich Avenue, Greenwich CT, 203.340.9430
www.tropicalsmoothiecafegreenwich.com
A great variety of smoothies-24 oz smoothies for adults and 12 oz ones for kids. We like having the calorie information for each smoothie. See review in Quick and Casual.
Hours: Weekdays, 7am-10pm, Saturday 8am-12am, Sunday 9am-10pm.
Size: seats 12.

Willoughby's (Coffee and Tea)
550 East Main Street, Branford CT, 800.388.8400 or 203.481.1700
www.willoughbyscoffee.com
www.RoastMasters.com
If you are seeking the best coffee and tea, this shop will interest you. They are proud of their coffee sources and roasting process. They offer un-roasted coffee beans as well as home coffee-roasting machines and every kind of coffee item through their partner store, Roast Masters. Because there is no close location, you may wish to order online.

CONTINUING EDUCATION-ADULTS

There are many language schools and other continuing education resources in and around town. The following are some of our favorites. For additional information on art, dance or music instruction, see the appropriate section under CULTURE.
For Sports Instruction, see FITNESS & SPORTS.
For Children's Education see CHILDREN.
For reading and research see BOOKS & LIBRARIES.

Index

Art Training
Greenwich Arts Council
Greenwich Art Society Art Classes
Silvermine Guild Art Center
Westchester Art Workshop (@Westchester Community College)

Computer Training
Diane McKeever
Greenwich Continuing Education
Norwalk Community College
Find computer courses designed for seniors in the SENIORS section.
For computer repairs see SERVICES.

Cooking Courses
Aux Delices Cooking School
Chocopologie Cooking School
Cucina Casalinga
Greenwich Continuing Education
Institute of Culinary Education
Lauren Groveman's Kitchen
Ronnie Fein School of Creative Cooking
Shaw Guides
Williams-Sonoma Cooking Classes

Dancing Skills
Arthur Murray Grand Ballroom of Greenwich
Fred Astaire Dance Studio

Gardening Education
For Gardening Clubs see FLOWERS AND GARDENS.
Garden Education Center

CONTINUING EDUCATION-ADULTS

General Adult Education
Archaeological Associates of Greenwich
Astronomical Society of Greenwich
Fairfield University
Greenwich Continuing Education
Lifetime Learners Institute
Manhattanville College
Norwalk Community College
Shaw Guides
Stamford Adult Education
SUNY Purchase
UCONN Stamford
Westchester Community College
World Affairs Forum

Language Training
Alliance Française
Chinese Language School
French-American School
Greenwich Continuing Education

Music Training
Anthony Aibel
Greenwich Arts Council
Fraioli School of Music (Greenwich Music)
Riverside School of Music
Robert Marullo Piano Lessons

Woodworking Skills
Wood Workers' Club

TIP: PLAN OF CONSERVATION AND DEVELOPMENT
The Greenwich Plan of Conservation and Development (POCD) took
several years to develop and will be the Town's governing document
for the next ten years.
www.greenwichct.org/PlanningZoning/PlanningZoning.asp
It is well worth reading.

CONTINUING EDUCATION-ADULTS

Alliance Française
299 Greenwich Avenue (2nd floor Greenwich Arts Center), Greenwich CT,
203.629.1340
www.afgreenwich.org
An ideal way to learn or refresh your French.

Anthony Aibel (Music & Drama Coach)
203 992 1081, 917.226.9803
www.anthonyaibel.com
Private music and voice lessons as well as song writing. Anthony is listed
in the Juilliard private teacher directory, www.Juillard.edu. He teaches
adults, teens and kids.

Archaeological Associates of Greenwich
33 Byram Drive, Greenwich CT, 203.661.4654
http://people.brandeis.edu/~jbernard/brucemuseum/lectures.html
They have a wonderful program of lectures by distinguished archaeological speakers at the Bruce Museum and act as a clearinghouse for
archaeological education programs in the Greenwich area. Membership
is open to all.

Arthur Murray Grand Ballroom of Greenwich
6 Lewis Street, Greenwich CT, 203.485.9422, 203.769.1800
www.arthurmurraygreenwich.com
Learn the latest dances with experienced instructors.

Astronomical Society of Greenwich
Bruce Museum, 1 Museum Drive, Greenwich CT, 203.413.6762
www.seocom.com/asg
Meetings cover general astronomical discussions and related
information,and usually include a special speaker. Weather permitting,
observatory public nights are the 2nd & 4th Tuesdays. The Bowman
Observatory is at the Julian Curtiss Elementary School, 180 East Elm
Street, Greenwich CT.

CONTINUING EDUCATION-ADULTS

Aux Delices Cooking School
23 Acosta Street, Stamford CT, 203.326.4540 x 108
Debra Ponzek, well-known for her delicious Aux Delices foods, chef instructor Lynn Manheim, and pastry chef Cyril Chaminade have a series of hard-to-resist cooking classes, such as: Easy Asian Cooking, Tapas, Cooking with Kids, Cooking for the Jewish Holidays, Spa Cooking and For Chocolate Lovers Only. Usually, classes are for up to 20 people and cost $75 per person.

Chinese Language School
Eastern Middle School, Riverside CT
www.chineselanguageschool.org/register
In addition to their many children's programs for learning Mandarin Chinese, they offer Adult 1 and Adult 2 classes, both one hour on Sundays at the Eastern Middle School.

Chocopologie Cooking School
133 Washington Street, Norwalk CT, 203.854.4754
www.knipschildt.com
Fritz Knipschildt, named one of the best chocolatiers in the world by Gourmet Magazine, shares his secrets for making chocolate truffles.

Cucina Casalinga
Wilton CT, 203.762.0768   www.cucinacasalinga.com
Sally Maraventano has been teaching homestyle Italian cooking for over 15 years. She has daytime, evening, and weekend classes and can accommodate groups as large as 15 students. Classes cost about $150 per person (which includes dinner).

Diane McKeever, CPP
www.dianemckeever.com
Diane for years has helped groups and individuals of all levels with their computer skills. She is a CPP (Certified Patient Person) and she deserves this title! Diane has two sides-quality software training and social media marketing services. Her book, 100 Amazing Computer Tips, is available on Amazon.

Fairfield University

Fairfield, CT, 203.254.4000   www.fairfield.edu
Fairfield is a major university with a 200 acre campus and great offerings in almost every conceivable subject. Definitely worth a call to get their catalog. They have over 1,000 continuing education students.

Fred Astaire Dance Studio

36 Sherwood Place, Greenwich CT, 203.340.2760
www.dance-greenwich.com
Have fun learning the the basics or venture into dances such as the Merengue or Salsa.

Fraioli School of Music @ Greenwich Music

1200 East Putnam Avenue, Riverside CT, 203.637.1119
www.greenwichmusic.com
Their store is filled with sheet music and instruments. They have a large selection of guitars & drums and a helpful staff. A full line of instruments is available for rent: a great way to discover if that instrument is right for you or your child. They have a music school (Fraioli School of Music) next door where they give lessons for the instruments they carry. Hours: Weekdays, 11am -6pm, Saturday 10am -5pm

French American School

Larchmont, Mamaroneck and Scarsdale Campuses, 914.250.0000
www.Fasny.org
Bilingual classes for pre-school to 12th grade.

Garden Education Center

Montgomery Pinetum, Bible Street, Cos Cob CT, 203.869.9242
www.gecgreenwich.org
The Center's new horticulture buildings provide classrooms and workrooms for a variety of excellent programs and lectures. Founded in 1957, the center is not only a strong educational facility, but also provides a good framework for new residents to make friends. They are closed during the summer.

TIP: TOUR GREENWICH GARDENS

Each year in June, the Garden Education Center: www.gecgreenwich.org organizes a tour of some of Greenwich's most special, private gardens. Call 203.869.9242 for details.

Greenwich Arts Council

299 Greenwich Avenue, 203.862.6750   www.greenwichartscouncil.org
GAC is a good resource for classes in art, music, yoga and dance. They
provide studios, exhibition and performance space for individual artists
and groups. GAC leases space to Alliance Francaise, CT School of Music,
Friendship Ambassadors Foundation, Greenwich Art Society, Greenwich
Choral Society and Greenwich Symphony Orchestra.

Greenwich Art Society Art Classes

299 Greenwich Avenue, 203.629.1533   www.GreenwichArtSociety.org
A delightful place to study painting, drawing, botanical illustration, sculpture or monotype.

Greenwich Continuing Education

Greenwich High School, 203.625.7474, 203.625.7475
www.GreenwichACE.com
This amazing program offers a wide range of courses taught at the high
school in the evening by interesting teachers. It is always priced right.
Registration is in January and August/September. Some 6000 students
per year participate in 250 online and traditional non-credit courses each
year. Be sure to check their catalog; you are bound to see several courses
you can't resist.

Institute of Culinary Education

50 West 23rd Street, New York NY, 800.522.4610, 212.847.0700
www.iceculinary.com
Although this school is in New York City, it has from time to time conducted courses in the Greenwich area. Founded by Peter Kump in 1975, it
has established a large Greenwich following. Hands on courses and workshops from 5 to 25 hours. The emphasis is on techniques of fine cooking.
The average class size is 12 for hands on instruction and 30 for demonstrations. The school has a staff of 45 who operate from a large facility
with 9 kitchens. Hands on classes range from $85 to $605.

Lauren Groveman's Kitchen

55 Prospect Avenue, Larchmont NY, 914.834.1372
www.laurengroveman.com
Established in 1990, the school provides 5 session participation courses
as well as individual classes for adults and young people. The emphasis
is on techniques and the preparation of comfort foods, breads and appetizers. The average class size is 6. Cost is $450 for a five session course
and $100 for a specialty course.

CONTINUING EDUCATION-ADULTS

Lifetime Learners Institute
Norwalk Community College, 188 Richards Avenue, Norwalk CT, 203.857.3330
www.LifeTimeLearners.org
A fabulous organization, affiliated with the Elderhostel Institute Network. It is an independent continuing education program within NCC. To join you must be over 50 and want to continue learning. Members can choose from over 40 courses.

Manhattanville College
2900 Purchase Street, Purchase NY, 914.694.2200
www.mville.edu
A local college with an attractive campus and good course offerings.

Norwalk Community College
188 Richards Avenue,Norwalk CT, 203.857.7080
www.ncc.commnet.edu (Click on Extended Studies)
A surprisingly large selection (more than 300 courses) of adult education courses on a variety of subjects. Nice, modern facilities.

(The) Riverside School of Music
403 East Putnam Avenue, Riverside CT, 203.661.9501
www.atelierconstantinpopescu.com
Excellent instructors in a variety of string instruments.

Robert Marullo Piano Lessons
203.869.4943
This popular, talented piano teacher at Greenwich Academy also gives private lessons. We strongly recommend him for lessons as wells as piano repairs and tuning.

Ronnie Fein School of Creative Cooking
32 Heming Way, Stamford, 203.322.7114
Year round cooking workshops with an emphasis on ingredients, techniques and menus for American, baking/pastry, children, French, healthy/vegetarian & Italian. She also has children's classes or will tailor a course to fit your needs. Workshops are usually 4 people and cost $250 per session. She has been teaching cooking and writing food stories for the Greenwich Time for over 20 years.

CONTINUING EDUCATION-ADULTS

Shaw Guides
www.shawguides.com
A database of career and recreational cooking schools, wine courses, golf & tennis schools & camps, high performance programs, writers conferences, photography, film & video workshops & schools, art & craft workshops, language vacations, cultural travel programs, and artists' and writers' residencies & retreats.

Silvermine Guild Art Center
New Canaan, CT, 203.966.9700, 203.966.6668   www.silvermineart.org
Excellent art instruction for adults and youngsters alike in famed art site. They have year-round classes for everyone age 2 to 102. They offer classes in creative writing, digital imaging, drawing, jewelry, painting, photography, printmaking, sculpture, silver smithing and more.

Stamford Adult Education
Adult Learning Center, 369 Washington Blvd., 203.977.4209
www.stamfordadulted.com
Check their website for their large number of enrichment classes.

SUNY Purchase
735 Anderson Hill Road, Purchase, NY, 914.251.6500 www.purchase.edu
Purchase College is a part of the State University of New York. It has beautiful grounds and striking modern buildings. Check out their adult education offerings.

UCONN Stamford
Connecticut Information Technology Institute
One University Place, Stamford, 203.251.8400
www.stamford.uconn.edu
Close by, in Stamford, is an exciting new facility where the University of Connecticut offers undergraduate programs plus professional and technical continuing education courses.

Westchester Community College
www.Sunywcc.edu
• Main campus: 75 Grasslands Road, Valhalla NY, 914.606.6600 offers a wide variety of continuing education classes.
• Art workshop: 196 Central Avenue (Westchester County Center), White Plains NY, 914.606.7500 has classes in fine arts, photography, computer arts and crafts.

Williams Sonoma Cooking Classes

- Stamford Town Center, Stamford, CT, 203.961.0977
- The Westchester Mall, 125 Westchester Avenue, White Plains, NY 914.644.8360

www.WilliamsSonoma.com

Classes in this popular store are held on Wednesday evenings from 6pm to 9pm. Be sure to call for a reservation. Classes are demonstration only, for 12 to 15 people and cost $50 per person. They teach courses such as: Elegant Holiday Dinners Made Easy, The Antipasto Table, Hors d'oeuvres and First Courses.

Woodworkers Club

215 Westport Avenue, Norwalk CT, 203.847.9663

www.woodworkersclubnorwalk.com

Classes are in their 5,000 square foot shop, next to their store. They teach beginner and intermediate levels. Learn to build bookshelves, build a mortise and tenon bench or turn a spindle.

World Affairs Forum

800 Summer Street, Suite 340, Stamford CT, 203.356.0340

www.WorldAffairsForum.org

A non profit, non partisan organization whose mission is to expand understanding of global affairs and America's role in the world. Join this group and get the inside views from experts at their breakfast or dinner meetings.

TIP: PUTNAM'S RIDE RE-ENACTED

In February, the Putnam Hill Chapter of the DAR re-enacts General Putnam's 1779 ride. Men are in official Revolutionary attire with muskets, and conduct Revolutionary War drills and skirmishes. General Putnam's ride is featured on the seal of the Town. What better way to learn history! The location is Putnam Cottage, 243 East Putnam Avenue. For details call 203.869.9697 or visit www.PutnamCottage.org

CULTURE

Greenwich has a full appreciation of the arts. Note the peaceful expressions on the faces in the audience of the Greenwich Symphony, or the joyful chatter of a family in the Bruce Museum, or the smiles surrounding the Grace Notes, and you may discover how many of our high powered, busiest residents relax and refresh themselves.
Libraries are described under BOOKS & LIBRARIES.
See also Family Outings in CHILDREN.

Sections in Culture

Art
Films and Movie Theaters in Greenwich
Movie Theaters Nearby
Movie Rentals
Museums
Music
Theater
Tickets
Tours and Special Events

ART

Art galleries and framers are listed under STORES
For art education see CONTINUING EDUCATION or CHILDREN

Art Society of Old Greenwich

PO Box 103, Greenwich CT, 06830
www.artsocietyofoldgreenwich.com
An organization of amateur and professional artists with membership open to everyone. We always enjoy their Sound Beach Avenue sidewalk art show in the Fall.

Brant Foundation Art Study Center

941 North Street, Greenwich CT 06830
www.brantfoundation.org, www.brantfoundation.tumblr.com, www.facebook.com/pages/The Brant Foundation Art Study Center/ 166562330051562
An appointment only gallery in Conyers Farm. The 1902 stone barn houses Peter Brant's collection of contemporary works by more than 25 artists, from Andy Warhol and Jeff Koons to Cindy Sherman and Keith Haring. The gallery is open from late May through February. Reservations may be made by email. thebrantfoundation@gmail.com

CULTURE

Greenwich Arts Council (GAC)
Bendheim Gallery
299 Greenwich Avenue, Greenwich CT, 203.862.6750
www.greenwichartscouncil.org
Established in 1973, the GAC provides year round, high quality arts programs, educational outreach programs and gallery exhibits. Housed in the landmark Greenwich Arts Center building, the GAC is home to The Bendheim Gallery, and offers affordable performance, meeting, exhibition and office space, art studios and a large dance studio. It is also home to the Choral Society, Symphony and the Art Society, as well as the Alliance Francaise and Friendship Ambassadors Foundation (a United Nations affiliated cultural organization). The GAC maintains a talent bank of all types of music, theater, dance and art teachers and publishes an informative newsletter. The Bendheim Gallery is available to rent for private functions. Every April at Tod's Point they sponsor "Go Fly A Kite!"

Flinn Gallery
Greenwich Library, Second Floor, 101 West Putnam Avenue, 203.622.7947
www.FlinnGallery.com
The Flinn Gallery of the Greenwich Library is run by volunteers, who select, curate and install exhibitions and hold receptions. They put on 6 exhibitions a year. These exhibits generally run for 6 weeks and are scheduled between September and June.

Greenwich Art Society
299 Greenwich Avenue, Greenwich CT, 203.629.1533
www.GreenwichArtSociety.org
The Art Society was founded in 1912 by the Cos Cob Colony of Artists. Today it has more than 350 artists from Fairfield and Westchester counties. Many of these talented artists are from Greenwich. The society has art classes for adults and children. It holds 3 juried exhibitions and a non-juried members exhibition every year. While walking along Greenwich Avenue, stop in the Greenwich Art Center to see the latest show.

TIP: ART FOR LOAN
Located on the second floor of the Greenwich Library and sponsored by the Friends of the Library, you will discover 250 prints you can borrow to decorate your walls.

119

CULTURE

FILM AND MOVIE THEATERS IN GREENWICH

Criterion Cinemas at Greenwich Plaza 3
2 Railroad Avenue, Greenwich CT, 203.869.4030
www.bowtiecinemas.com/plaza 3.htm
Greenwich's remaining commercial movie house. Use it or lose it. You can buy your tickets online, rather than standing in line. General Admission $11.50, Children (11 and under) $8.50, Seniors (62 & over) $10.

Focus on French Cinema
Alliance Francaise, 203.629.1340
www.FocusOnFrenchCinema.org
Held at Pepsico Theater, Performing Arts Center, Purchase College and at the Greenwich Bow Tie (Criterion) theater, this annual event is organized by Alliance Francaise of Greenwich. Last year over 2,000 people attended. All films are in French with English subtitles. This exciting film festival, held at the end of March or early April, includes films not usually available in the US and gives a unique insight into the French film industry. Not only do you get to see great films, but the audience has the opportunity to meet actors and directors.

Greenwich Classic Film Series
914.725.0999
www.GreenwichClassicFilmSeries.com
Now in its 50th season and with over 500 members, it has two 6 film series. Movies from the 30s through the 70s with lectures by guest film critics are shown at the Greenwich Movie Theater, Monday evenings at 7 pm. Membership is $140 for a 6 film series. Join their mailing list by sending your e mail address.

Greenwich Library Friday Films
101 West Putnam Avenue, 203.622.7910
www.greenwichlibrary.org/About the Library/Greenwich Library Friends/ FriendsFridayFilms.aspx
On most Friday nights at 8pm (doors open at 7:40pm) in the Cole Auditorium, the Library shows award winning US and foreign films. Admission is free. Call or use the web site to get a schedule and verify that a film is being shown.

CULTURE

MOVIE THEATERS NEARBY GREENWICH

AMC Loews 14
40 Westchester Avenue, (Waterfront Place) Port Chester NY, 914.510.1000
www.amcentertainment.com/PortChester
Lots of free parking and 14 screens in the Waterfront complex.

Avon Art Films (Classic Films)
272 Bedford Street, Stamford CT, 203.967.3660
www.AvonTheater.org
The Avon Theater is a fully-restored classic movie theater. Built in 1939, the Avon was run by Crown Theaters until it closed in 1998. In 2001 it was purchased by a private investor from Greenwich. The theater was fully restored and reopened January, 2004 and shows independent, art and foreign films as well as Hollywood classics.

Bow Tie Cinemas Landmark 9
5 Landmark Square (Broad Street), Stamford CT, 203.324.3100
www.bowtiecinemas.com/landmark 9.html

Bow Tie Cinemas Majestic 6
118 Summer Street, Stamford CT, 203.323.1690
www.bowtiecinemas.com/majestic 6.html
This theater in Stamford is right in the heart of the restaurant district.

Garden Cinemas
26 Isaac Street, Norwalk CT, 203.838.4504
www.ghcinemas.com
A mix of current and foreign movies. The theater has lots of leg room.

IMAX Theater
At the Norwalk Aquarium, 10 North Water Street, SoNo, 203.852.0700
www.maritimeaquarium.org
The screen is 6 stories high and 8 stories wide and the visual effects are stunning. See full description under CHILDREN, FAMILY OUTINGS.

State Cinema
990 Hope Street, Stamford, 203.325.0250
www.ghcinemas.com
One of the least expensive theaters in the area. A good place to take a group of children and your best bet for avoiding long lines.

CULTURE

MOVIE RENTALS

Greenwich Library

101 West Putnam Avenue, Greenwich CT, 203.622.7900

www.greenwichlibrary.org

The Library has an extensive collection of CDs, Video Tapes and DVDs. Use the website to reserve availability or phone 203.622.7910 to reserve items. Ask to have your reserved materials sent to the branch near you. With your library card, you can stream and download thousands of movies, TV shows and music albums to your phone, tablet or computer. There is a free Hoopla app for your phone.

Redbox (Movie and Video Game Rentals)

Pickup location: 161 West Putnam Avenue (Stop & Shop), Greenwich CT. www.Redbox.com , 866.733.2693

Reserve your movie on line and pick it up when it's convenient.

MUSEUMS

Children oriented museums are listed in CHILDREN under Family Outings.

Aldrich Contemporary Art Museum

258 Main Street, Ridgefield CT, 203.438.4519

www.AldrichArt.org

This museum is devoted to innovative contemporary art. The art collection is in a 25,000 sf space, which includes a 100-seat performance area and an education center. The museum has a 2-acre outdoor exhibition space.

TIP: SCULPTURES IN GREENWICH

Greenwich has 30 outdoor sculptures. Some are tucked away in parks, some are in public buildings. Have fun on a sculpture hunt. Stop in the Greenwich Arts Council (second floor of 299 Greenwich Avenue) and ask for the map of sculpture locations.

CULTURE

Bruce Museum

1 Museum Drive, Greenwich CT, 203.869.0376

www.BruceMuseum.org

This year the Bruce attracted over 100,000 visitors to their exciting exhibitions making the Bruce one of the most popular museums in Connecticut. In addition, the Bruce sponsored over 50 lectures and gave educational programs to over 18,000 children. Under the leadership of Peter Sutton, the Museum has been able to attract major art exhibits. No wonder the Bruce is placed in the top 10% of US museums. The Museum sponsors two fairs in Bruce Park every year. The mid May Craft Fair and the Columbus Day Arts Festival have juried artists from around the country and draw visitors from all over the area. When you become a member (which you should), you will be informed about their wonderful events. There are a number of organizations affiliated with the Bruce.

Archaeology Associates of Greenwich

Astronomical Society of Greenwich, 203.413.6762

Connecticut Ceramics Study Circle, www.CTceramicscircle.org

Greenwich Antiques Society, www.GreenwichAntiques.org

Forum for World Affairs, 203.356.0340, www.worldaffairsforum.org

Seaside Center at Greenwich Point, open in July and August,
Wednesday-Sunday, 10am-4pm.

Museum Hours: Tuesday-Sunday 10am-5pm, Last admission 4.30pm.

Bush Holley House Museum

39 Strickland Road, Cos Cob CT, 203.869.6899

www.GreenwichHistory.org

Home of the Historical Society, this is the place to learn about Greenwich history. They have a good library and a shop with books on Greenwich history, as well as reproductions of 19th century children's toys and books. The museum showcases 8 period rooms from the late 1890's when it was a boarding house for the Cos Cob art colony. Be sure to take the guided tour. While you are there, pick up a list of the wonderful programs and events sponsored by the Greenwich Historical Society.

Hours: , 12pm 4pm: January-February, open Saturday & Sunday, March-December, open Wednesday-Sunday.

Donald M. Kendall Sculpture Gardens
At Pepsico, 700 Anderson Hill Road, Purchase NY, 914.253.2000
www.sirpepsi.com/pepsi1.htm
One of the world's finest sculpture gardens is located right next to Greenwich. The collection includes forty pieces by such 20th century artists as Noguchi, Moore, Nevelson, and Calder. The sculptures are set on 168 carefully landscaped acres. Pick up a map at the visitors' parking lot. There are some picnic tables.
Hours: Open every day from dawn to dusk, except for Saturdays in August.

Historical Society of the Town of Greenwich
39 Strickland Road, Cos Cob CT, 203.869.6899; Archives ext. 23
www.hstg.org
Their mission is to collect, preserve and disseminate the history of Greenwich. The society conducts a wide variety of adult and children's educational programs, exhibitions and workshops. Their extensive archives are open to anyone wanting to research town history. We sincerely appreciate this organization's dedication to preserving our community's historical roots.

Katonah Museum of Art
Route 22 at Jay Street, Katonah NY, 914.232.9555
www.katonahmuseum.org
The Museum offers an extensive range of activities to engage visitors of all ages. Exhibitions present art from the past to the present. The Museum's Learning Center is an interactive exhibition space in which children can experience the fun of artistic exploration. Call for hours.

Kykuit
For GPS use 381 North Broadway, Sleepy Hollow NY, 914.631.8200 Weekdays, 914.631.3992 on weekends.
www.hudsonvalley.org
John D. Rockefeller's home, Kykuit, has remarkable architecture, gardens and art as well as spectacular scenery. Home to four generations of Rockefellers, this is the Hudson Valley's most exceptional house and gardens. Tours include Nelson A. Rockefeller's extraordinary collection of 20th century sculpture as well as the Coach Barn with its antique carriages and autos. A garden and sculpture tour is offered most weekdays.
Hours: Open early May-early November. Call before going.

CULTURE

Lockwood Mathews Mansion Museum
295 West Avenue (Mathews Park), Norwalk CT, 203.838.9799
www.lockwoodmathewsmansion.com
A National Historic Landmark since 1971, the Lockwood Mathews Mansion Museum is one of the earliest and most significant Second Empire Style country homes in the USA.

Lyndhurst
Lyndhurst is located 2 miles south of the Tappan Zee Bridge on Route 9 in Tarrytown NY, 914.631.4481   www.lyndhurst.org
The home of Jay Gould, it is one of the great domestic landmarks of America. A visit to this Gothic Revival mansion and its 67 acre park is a must for all who are interested in 19th century architecture, decorative arts, and landscape design.
Hours: mid April to October, open Tuesday-Sunday 10am 5pm: November to mid-April, open weekends 10am-4pm.

Neuberger Museum
735 Anderson Hill Road, Purchase, NY, 914.251.6100
www.neuberger.org
The museum is located on the 500 acre campus of the State University of New York (SUNY) at Purchase. It has 25,000 sq. ft. of gallery space, a café, a store and an interactive learning center. It houses a notable collection of modern art.
Hours: Tuesday-Sunday 12pm-5pm. Their hours seem to change frequently, call before you go.

NY Botanical Gardens
Bronx River Parkway at Fordham Road, Bronx NY, 718.817.8700
www.nybg.org
They are considered the best botanical garden in the country.
Hours: During the warmer weather, Tuesday Sunday 10am 6pm (check their website for winter hours).

Philip Johnson Glass House
Visitor Center, 199 Elm Street, New Canaan CT, 866.811.4111
www.TheGlassHouse.org
Tickets may be purchased online to view the Glass House and other structures on the 47-acre campus run by the National Trust for Historic Preservation. The tour is limited to 10 people and includes a half mile walking tour across the site. Children ages 10 and up are welcomed.
Open: May 1st-October 1st

CULTURE

Putnam Cottage (Knapp's Tavern)
243 East Putnam Avenue, Greenwich CT, 203.869.9697
www.putnamcottage.org
Originally a tavern serving travelers along the Post Road, it is now a museum owned by the DAR. Each year on the last Sunday in February (1 3 pm) the Putnam Hill Revolutionary War battle is recreated. A definite must see for adults and children alike.
Hours: April to November, Sundays 1pm-4pm.

Storm King Art Center
Old Pleasant Hill Road, Mountainville NY, 845.534.3115
www.stormking.org
Take a walk or picnic in this leading outdoor sculpture museum with 120 masterworks set in a stunning 400 acre landscaped park. Great place to take the kids for a picnic.
Hours: April-November, Wednesday-Sunday 10am-4:30pm.

Union Church of Pocantico Hills
555 Bedford Road, North Tarrytown NY, 914.631.8200, 2069
www.hudsonvalley.org/historic sites/union church pocantico hills
Stained glass windows created by Henri Matisse (1869 1954) and Marc Chagall (1887 1985).
Hours: April October, open daily (except Tuesday) 11am-5pm, Saturdays 10am-5pm, Sundays 2pm-5pm.

Washington Irving's Sunnyside Home
639 Bedford Road, Pocantico Hills NY, 914.631.8200
www.hudsonvalley.org/historic sites/washington irvings sunnyside
Tour the home and grounds of one of the USA's great authors: Legend of Sleepy Hollow. While there, you should also visit Philipsburg Manor, Montgomery Place and Van Cortlandt Manor.

Weir Farm
735 Nod Hill Road, Wilton CT, 203.834.1896
www.nps.gov/wefa
This is the country's only national park dedicated to American painting. The property today includes 16 buildings on 60 acres of land. The Weir home and studio have been authentically restored. Julian Alden Weir (1852 1919) helped pioneer the development of American Impressionism.

MUSIC

Caramoor Center for Music and Arts

149 Girdle Ridge Road, Katonah NY, 914.232.1252

www.caramoor.com

About 20-minutes North of Greenwich, Caramoor has wonderful music programs. It should be on everyone's "must do" list. For evening performances, it is fashionable to bring a fancy picnic supper and eat on one of the lawns before the show. Caramoor has 100 acres of parklands and formal gardens. Most performances are under an open-sided tent. Mosquitoes are sparse but bringing some bug spray in the summer can't hurt. The main season is June through August although Caramoor provides fall, winter and spring indoor programs on a more limited schedule.

Chamber Players

For more information call 203 637 4725

www.greenwichsymphony.org/chamber players greenwich symphony

Musicians selected from the Greenwich Symphony Orchestra present concerts each year; usually 4 pm on Sunday afternoons at Round Hill Community Church and 8 pm Monday evenings at the Bruce Museum. A wine and cheese reception at each concert is a wonderful way for the audience to become acquainted with the musicians.

Connecticut Ballet

203.964.1211 www.ConnecticutBallet.com

Local performances are held at the Palace Theater in Stamford CT.

Curiosity Concerts

www.curiosityconcerts.org

Sponsored by the Greenwich Arts Council, these free classical music concerts for children and their families are held at different locations in Greenwich. All concerts are less than one hour. Advance registration is required. These programs are popular, so be sure to reserve early.

TIP: GREENWICH POPS CONCERT

For a lovely evening, pack a picnic and head to the Roger Sherman Baldwin Park for one of the Pops concerts sponsored by the Greenwich Arts Council www.greenwicharts.org and the Department of Parks & Recreation. The park opens for picnics at 6 pm and the concerts start at 7:30 pm. Call the Arts Council at 203.862.6750 for details.

CULTURE

Fairfield County Chorale
Reserve your tickets online
www.fairfieldcountychorale.org
Founded in 1963, the Chorale's repertoire consists of more than 100 classic works by composers from the 16th through the 20th century. Most performances are held at the Norwalk Concert Hall, 125 East Avenue, Norwalk CT.

Gateway Classical Music Society
1117 East Putnam Avenue #314, Riverside CT, 203.618.9444
www.GateWayClassical.org
Their goal is to foster excitement, appreciation and popularity for classical music. Ida Angland, a Greenwich resident, is the conductor and artistic director.

Grace Notes
Contact them by email through their website.
www.TheGraceNotes.com
A women's "a cappella" singing group that has been entertaining Greenwich audiences for over thirty years. Whether you are listening to or singing with this group, it is always a rewarding experience.

Greenwich Choral Society
299 Greenwich Avenue, 3rd floor, 203.622.5136
www.GreenwichChoralSociety.org
Founded in 1925, the Society's 30 singers perform throughout the area primarily during the winter months. Their annual Christmas concert held at Christ Church is a very popular event.

Greenwich Symphony Orchestra
203.869.2664
www.greenwichsymphony.org
This 90 member professional orchestra is in its 58th season. They play consistently excellent music at low ticket prices. Ask for a CD of their music highlights. Concerts are Saturday evenings and Sunday afternoons at Greenwich High School. Be sure to attend pre concert lectures.

Melody Men
www.greenwichrma.org/activities 2/melody men/
The Melody Men are musical members of the Retired Men's Association. They have fun singing together and bring cheer to Greenwich residents.

CULTURE

Palladium Musicum
For information contact Marie Williams, President, 203.661.6856
www.PalladiumMusicum.org
They offer several classical music events (vocal and instrumental) each
season. Performances often combine music and lectures.

Town Concerts and other summer events
Greenwich Department of Parks and Recreation, 203.622.7830
www.greenwichct.org/parksandrec/ParksAndRec.asp
During July and August the Department of Parks and Recreation arranges
free Tuesday afternoon and Wednesday evening concerts. Call or visit
the website for locations and times.

THEATER

Acting Company of Greenwich
Call 203.629.2094 for information, 203.863.1919 for reservations
www.actgreenwich.org
This local amateur theater group, with good acting and good fun, welcomes actors and audiences for its annual series of plays held in the
auditorium of the First Congregational Church in Old Greenwich. They
also teach improvisation classes.

Connecticut Playmakers
First Congregational Church, 108 Sound Beach Avenue, Old Greenwich
Contact: 203.249.5419
www.ctplaymakers.org
Sponsored by the Greenwich Center for the Arts and the First Congregational Church, Old Greenwich, they provide free, live theater open to adult
participants from age 16. In addition to their major productions, the
monthly meetings include dramatic presentations. The Playmakers Young
People's Theater puts on a musical each summer. This is an enjoyable
way for young people to meet each other and learn about the theater.

TIP: SoNo ARTS CELEBRATION
In early August South Norwalk has an exciting art festival with over
150 juried artists as well as an interesting mix of performances on
five stages. The festival runs from 10 am to midnight and is appropriate for children as well as adults. Visit www.sonoarts.org

---

CULTURE

Curtain Call Theaters
Sterling Farms Theater Complex, 1349 Newfield Ave, Stamford CT, 203.329.8207
Call the Box Office for details: 203.461.6358
www.curtaincallinc.com
Curtain Call uses two theaters at this location. "The Kweskin Theater" presents full run productions such as "The Odd Couple" and "Arsenic and Old Lace." "The Dressing Room" has cabaret style seating. Bring your own food and enjoy charming dramas and musicals, such as "The Fantastics." Evening performances start at 8pm, Matinees at 2pm. For the aspiring actor, Curtain Call offers a full line of educational workshops in the performing arts, ages 5 through adult.

Emelin Theater
153 Library Lane, Mamaroneck NY, 914.698.0098
www.emelin.org
Emelin is the oldest continuously-operating performing arts theater in Westchester County. The Emelin holds a variety of terrific events: speakers, cabaret, jazz, classical music, musical theater, children's theater and more. Call for a catalog or get on their mailing list

Fairfield Theater Company
70 Sanford Street, Fairfield CT (directly in front of the Metro North train station), 203.319.1404, Box office: 203.259.1036
www.FairfieldTheatre.org
The Fairfield Theater Company was founded in 2000. Their mission is to bring the best of New York's Off and Off Off Broadway directly to Fairfield. This is professional theater from NYC, brought intact, and delivered to our backyard.

Festival Theater
1850 Elm Street, Stratford CT
www.stratfordfestival.com
This Connecticut Shakespeare theater is hoping to re-open. Check their website for information.

Goodspeed Opera House

6 Main Street, East Haddam CT, 860.873.8668

www.goodspeed.org

The restored 19th century Goodspeed Opera House is now devoted to musicals. April through December season, Goodspeed produces 3 musicals. At the nearby Norma Terris Theatre in Chester, Connecticut, Goodspeed develops new musicals. The Connecticut River Valley is less than 2 hours away and has a great variety of family attractions.

Long Wharf Theater

222 Sargent Drive, New Haven CT, Box office: 203.787.4282

www.longwharf.org

Professional theater which produces traditional plays as well as plays by new playwrights. Over the last 40 years, Long Wharf has presented numerous world premieres, American premieres and transfers to Broadway.

(The) New Paradigm Theatre

www.nptheatre.org

A professional nonprofit using the power of theatre to develop leaders, assist other nonprofits, and promote local businesses. Their unique mentoring program gives all age groups the opportunity to learn about and experience the world of theatre. They feature custom built shows with Broadway stars. A highlight is their annual "Broadway Holiday Show." Katie enjoys her private vocal lessons with Kristin Huffman.

Off-Beat Players

Arch Street Teen Center, 100 Arch Street, Greenwich CT, 203.629.5477

http://www.offbeatplayers.org

A Summer theater company of teens and young adults, with and without disabilities. They welcome any enthusiastic actor who wants to grow professionally and personally. Check the website for show schedule and ticket information.

Palace Theater

61 Atlantic Street, Stamford CT, 203.358.2305, Box Office 203.325.4466

www.stamfordcenterforthearts.org

The Palace, along with the Rich Forum, is part of the Stamford Center for the Arts. The Palace is a 1,584 seat vaudeville theater that was acclaimed as "Connecticut's most magnificent" when it opened in 1927.

CULTURE

TIP: ART TO THE AVENUE

www.greenwichartscouncil.org/Art-to-the-Avenue.html
If you want to enjoy Greenwich Avenue at its best, do not miss a stroll down the Avenue on the opening night of this festival. The Greenwich Arts Council sponsors this event in early May. Over 150 artists, retailers and restaurants take part. Call 203.862.6750 for details.

Play with Your Food
299 Greenwich Avenue (Greenwich Arts Council), Greenwich CT, 203.293.8729   www.PlayWithYourFood.org
A winter series of noon time theater. All shows are noon to 1:30pm and include lunch and professional readings of one act plays for $45. Can there be a better way to spend your lunch time? Call well in advance to reserve.
Box Office Hours: January-March, Weekdays 10am-4pm.

Pound Ridge Theater Group
Conant Hall, 257 Westchester Avenue (Route 137), Pound Ridge NY, 914.764.1902.   Www.poundridgetheatre.org
Off Broadway style productions of dramas, musicals and comedies. Playgoers should try our favorite local restaurant, North Star. See its review in the Restaurant Section.

Shakespeare on the Sound
203.299.1300
www.shakespeareonthesound.org
In June and July, Shakespeare on the Sound produces an annual free outdoor Shakespeare festival in Connecticut, with performances in public parks. Recently, performances have been in Rowayton. Don't miss this event! Although the concerts are free, for a small fee you can reserve seats in the first rows. They also offer free lectures for adults or children before the performances. See their website for details.

Shubert Theater
247 College Street, New Haven CT, Box Office: 203.562.5666
For tickets order online, at the box office or through Ticketmaster @ 800.745.3000   www.capa.com/newhaven
This not for profit theater is considered the crown jewel of downtown New Haven. Some shows come directly from Broadway.

CULTURE

Summer Theater of New Canaan
Box office 203.966.4634
www.stonc.org
What fun to have this regional theater so near by! It produces professionally-staged family musicals and Shakespearian productions during the summer. Shakespeare is performed in the outdoor walled garden at Waveny Park in New Canaan, CT. Musicals and other performances are held in the Saxe Middle School Theater, South Avenue, New Canaan.

SUNY Performing Arts Center
745 Anderson Hill Road, Purchase NY, box office: 914.251.6200
www.artscenter.org
The Performing Arts Center at the State University of New York at Purchase, just a few minutes from Greenwich, has wonderful music and dance performances, as well as plays. They have a number of summer offerings although the main season is September to May.

Westport Country Playhouse
25 Powers Court, Westport CT, 203.227.4177
www.westportplayhouse.org
A 6 play summer season starting in June. Very professional. The theater recently underwent $17 million renovation. Only a 20 minute trip.

Yale University Repertory Theater
1120 Chapel St., PO Box 1257, New Haven, CT, 203.432.1234
www.yale.edu/yalerep
It is an hour's drive, but it's well worth it. Often as good as Broadway, but with much less hassle, better seats and lower prices. You can park right next to the theater for free. Subscribers can get front row seats.

TICKETS

All Shows (Formerly the Concert Connection)
555 Theodore Fremd Avenue, Suite B304, Rye NY, 203.869.0060
www.allShows.com
Ticket broker to major sports, music, theater and family entertainment events. They can get you those high-demand tickets you want, but often at a steep markup. If you can wait to the last minute you will often get a deal, sometimes even below cost. A good place to sell tickets you can't use.

133

CULTURE

TOURS & SPECIAL EVENTS

Calendars of Events
Community Answers has a good online Events Calendar.
www.greenwichlibrary.org/commanswers.htm

Art to the Avenue
Greenwich Arts Council, 203.862.6750
www.greenwichartscouncil.org/Art to the Avenue.html
If you want to enjoy Greenwich Avenue at its best, do not miss a stroll down the Avenue on the opening night of this festival. The Greenwich Arts Council sponsors this event in early May. Over 150 artists and retailers take part.

Bruce Museum Outdoor Crafts Festival
www.brucemuseum.org/events
This show of exceptionally fine crafts is held annually one week prior to Memorial Day weekend in May.

Bruce Museum Outdoor Arts Festival
www.brucemuseum.org/events
Held annually on Columbus Day weekend in October. This show features fine arts only, no crafts.

Connecticut Art Trail
www.ArtTrail.org
Visit 15 world class museums and historic sites throughout Connecticut and explore interesting towns.

Connecticut Wine Trail
www.ctwine.com
Visit 25 wineries.

Old Greenwich Sidewalk Art Show
www.artsocietyofoldgreenwich.com
We always enjoy the Sound Beach Avenue sidewalk art show held on a Saturday and Sunday in September by the Old Greenwich Art Society.

Putnam Hill Revolutionary Battle
Putnam Cottage, 243 East Putnam Avenue, Greenwich CT, 203.869.9697
www.putnamcottage.org
Each year on the last Sunday in February the Putnam Hill Revolutionary War battle is re-enacted outside of the Putnam Cottage.

DELICATESSENS

Alpen Pantry
23 Arcadia Road, Old Greenwich CT, 203.637.3818
www.alpenpantry.com
Renowned for their terrific sandwiches. The "Stilton" (Ham, Swiss, Turkey, blue cheese dressing on Russian black bread) is delicious.
Hours: Weekdays 9am-5pm, Saturday 9am-3pm.
Seating: Take-out only   Delivery: No

Aux Delices (French)
• 3 West Elm Street, Greenwich CT, 203.622.6644
• 1075 East Putnam Avenue, Riverside CT, 203.698.1066
www.AuxDelicesFoods.com
Provencal-style food with an American twist prepared under the direction of talented Chef Debra Ponzek. Delicious gourmet take-away food. They have a weekday home delivery service and will deliver your order even when you are not home, packaged to keep the food at the proper temperature.
Greenwich Hours: Weekdays 7am-6:30pm, Saturday 8am-6:30pm, Sunday 8am-4pm.
Riverside Hours: Weekdays 7am-6:30pm, Saturday 7am-6:30pm, Sunday 7:30am-5pm
Seating: Both locations have a few tables (grab one for a quick breakfast or late lunch).
Delivery: Yes

Balducci's (Deli, Grocery, Wine)
1050 East Putnam Avenue, Riverside CT, 203.637.7600
www.Balduccis.com
A sophisticated gourmet deli and country shop for fruits, vegetables and unique foods. It is owned by King's Grocery. Balducci's carries imported and American cheeses and a nice selection of flavorful soups. Their wine store carries a large selection of American and international wines.
Hours: Monday-Saturday 9am-8pm, Sunday 10am-5pm.
Delivery: No

Cardillo's Deli
77 Valley Drive, Cos Cob CT, 203.661.3354
Cardillo's, an Italian Deli and a small convenience-style grocery store, open for breakfast, lunch and dinner.
Hours: Weekdays 6am-5pm, Saturday 6am-4 pm, Sunday 7am-3pm.
Seating: 15   Delivery: Yes (Free with $10 minimum order)

DELICATESSENS

Castle View Deli

2 Morgan Avenue, Greenwich CT, 203.531.5353

Castle View was started by former Greenwich resident, Louis Spiro-a graduate of The Culinary Institute of America-who prides himself on making dishes from scratch. We like the roast beef (with herb cheese & horseradish spread) and the turkey and Münster (with cole slaw & Thousand Island dressing).

Hours: Weekdays 6:30am-3pm, Saturday 6:30am-2pm.

Seating: 10   Delivery: No

Corbo's Corner Deli

- 1380 E. Putnam Avenue, Old Greenwich CT, 203.354.4675
- 59 E. Putnam Avenue, Cos Cob CT, 203.869.8500
- 479 W. Putnam Avenue, Greenwich CT, 203.629.4987

www.CorbosDeli.com

Whatever section of town you are in, you're near a Corbo's. Two Greenwich residents, Matt Watson and Jon Czarnecki, named it after Jon's grandfather. With music playing, there is a youthful, happy atmosphere. Egg and cheese sandwiches are tossed with skill to the many high school students. We like the Bruin, the Dude Ranch and the Cardinal.

Old Greenwich Hours: Weekdays 6am-4pm, Saturday 7am-3pm; Cos Cob Hours: Weekdays 8am-4pm, Saturday 8am-4pm, Sunday 8am-3pm; Greenwich Hours: Weekdays 6am-4pm, Saturday 7am-3pm.

Seating: 20 (Cos Cob location).

Delivery: Yes (Old Greenwich location only).

Firehouse Deli

265 Mill Street, Greenwich CT, 203.531.0002   www.FireHouseDeli.com

Located across the street from the fire station, this family-run business has attracted crowds since 1996. A fireman's favorite. The wedges are huge. We like the Cousin Vinny, Untouchable, Lethal Weapon and the Chipotle Chicken. Don't let the crowds keep you away. This is a swift, friendly place.

Hours: Monday-Saturday 6am-5pm, Sunday 7am-3pm

Seating: No   Delivery: Yes

DELICATESSENS

Fjord Fisheries
158 East Putnam Avenue, Cos Cob CT, 203.661.5006
www.FjordFisheries.com
This market has an abundance of fresh fish plus a delicatessen and sandwich shop. If you were to ask "where is the best fish and chips?", you would probably be directed here. We also think their Crab Cake Po'boy, Salmon Club and Tuna sandwiches are outstanding. Fjord is a great place for sliced smoked salmon or salmon tartare. If you are in a hurry, place your order in advance. We love their freshly prepared sushi. Try their mango rice paper spring roll and tuna tataki and you will be singing their praises too.
Hours: Monday-Saturday 8am-7pm, Sunday 9am-6pm.
Delivery: Yes

Garelick & Herbs
48 West Putnam Avenue, Greenwich CT, 203.661.7373
www.GarelickAndHerbs.com
A sophisticated deli with so many first-rate, ready-to-serve dishes, it's hard to choose.
Hours: Weekdays 7am-6:30pm, Saturday 8am-6pm,
Sunday 9am-5:30pm.   Seating: 12 Delivery: No

G*Ville Deli
17 Glenville Street, Greenwich CT, 203.202.9737
www.gvilledeli.com
The G*Ville Deli is family run. They opened in February 2012. Some of our favorites are: The Civic Center, The Maverick and Hold the Meat. Their sweet potato fries are good too! Be sure to check out the daily specials!
Hours: Weekdays 6:30am-4pm, Saturday 6:30am-2pm,
Sunday 7am-12pm. Seating: No Delivery: No

North Water Deli Plus
39 North Water Street, Greenwich CT, 203.531.4500
A cheerful place with hanging flower baskets and a menu featuring Peruvian and Colombian food-not your usual deli. We recommend the Peruvian Rotisserie Chicken.
Hours: Everyday 7am-7pm.
Seating: 15   Delivery: Yes (Free with $15 minimum order)

DELICATESSENS

Olive Branch Café
26 Railroad Avenue, Greenwich CT, 203.622.9099
www.OliveBranchToGo.com
The Olive Branch, right next to the Greenwich Train Station, has a wide menu selection. We usually choose one of their salads-chicken with grapes, Asian salad or curry chicken. Their Mona Lisa Panini, the Chalet sandwich and soups are good.
Hours: Weekdays 6:30am-4pm, Saturday 8am-3pm.
Seating: 20 Delivery: Yes (free with $20 minimum order)

Paesano's Deli
146 Mason Street, Greenwich CT, 203.625.0040
In 30 years, this popular Deli has made lots of sandwiches. We like their smoked turkey with mozzarella and chipotle mayo presata. The talented Barresi family also own Doppio.
Hours: Weekdays 7am-5pm, Saturday 8am-4pm.
Seating: 8 (inside), a few tables outside. Delivery: Yes, free

Pasta Vera's Delicatessen
48 Greenwich Avenue, Greenwich CT, 203.661.9705
www.PastaVera.com
This popular, casual restaurant is noted for its homemade pastas. In the front of the restaurant is a deli area with a variety of fresh, ready-to-go selections. The seafood salad is scrumptious. The restaurant is reviewed in RESTAURANTS.
Hours: Monday-Saturday 11:30am-10pm, Sunday 4pm-9pm; Open most holidays. Seating: Deli is take-out only

Pemberwick Xchange Delicatessen
83 Pemberwick Road, Greenwich CT, 203.531.7110
The "Xchange" has been a family business for 80 years. They serve hot deli sandwiches and daily specials. On Mondays they have hot dogs cooked in beer.
Hours: Weekdays 6am-3pm, Saturday 7am-2pm.
Seating: 15 Delivery: No

DELICATESSENS

Plum Pure Foods
236 East Putnam Avenue, Cos Cob CT, 203.869.7586
www.PlumPureFoods.com
Plum takes pride in using natural products grown locally. They have something for everyone: soups, sandwiches and hot entrees.
Hours: Weekdays 7:30am-3pm, Saturday 8am-5pm.
Delivery: No   Seating: 6

Rinaldi's Deli
70 Orchard Street, Cos Cob CT, 203.622.8315
www.RinaldisDeliAndGrill.net
Rinaldi's Deli, owned by 2 sisters, has been in business in Cos Cob for 10 years. They have hot plates, grilled food and cold sandwiches to go. We like The Bruin, The Beast and the #7.
Hours: Weekdays 5am-5:30pm, Saturday 5am-4pm. Open Sunday for Catering Only.
Seating: No   Delivery: No

Villa Nuova
551 East Putnam Avenue, Cos Cob CT, 203.422.0174
www.VillaNuovaCT.com
Villa Nuova is a great place for homemade Italian food-21 varieties of raviolis and fresh pasta. A good place to pick up a loaf of Arthur Avenue bread and eggplant and chicken francese. Cos Cob Crusher is tops.
Hours: Monday-Thursday 8:30am-5:30pm, Friday and Saturday 8:30am-4:30pm, Sunday 11am-2pm.   Seating: 8
Delivery: Yes ($50 minimum order; 10% surcharge for all deliveries, plus $5 fuel charge).

TIP: WHERE TO GET FRESH ITALIAN SAUCES
- Pomodoro, 203.698.7779
- Pasta Nostra, 203.854.9700
- Villa Italia, 203.348.7742
- Pizza Post, 203.661.0909
- Bella Nonna, 203.992.1888

Combine one of these fresh sauces with some fresh pasta from places like Tarry Market, 914.253.5680, Pasta Vera, 203.661.9705 or Villa Nuova, 203.422.0174 and everyone at your table will applaud your culinary brilliance.

ENTERTAINING

Party information specific to Children is listed in CHILDREN.
For wine, see FOOD AND BEVERAGES.
To practice your dancing, see Adult CONTINUING EDUCATION.
Cakes are listed under Bakeries in FOOD AND BEVERAGES.
Florists and Nurseries are listed in FLOWERS AND GARDENS.

Sections in Entertaining
   Caterers: Adult Parties & Children's Parties
   Entertainment
   Invitations
   Parking
   Party Goods
   Party Planners
   Party Rentals

CATERERS

The caterers listed below have quality food. They usually arrive on time and are dependable. As a result, they are often in high demand. Reserve early. However, remember, no one person or group is always perfect. Your best bet for a perfect event every time is to choose a group and stick with them. Regulars always get good service. Many restaurants also want to cater your events.

CATERING AN ADULT PARTY

Abigail Kirsch Culinary Productions
71 West 23rd Street, Suite 1611, Manhattan NY, 212.696.4076
www.AbigailKirsch.com
Caterer of choice for many Greenwich residents when they are having a large party. Dear friends used Abigail for both daughters' weddings. Their website has a number of exclusive and non-exclusive locations to host larger events.

Aux Delices Gourmet Food Shop & Catering
23 Acosta Street, Stamford CT, 203.326.4540 x101
www.AuxDelicesFoods.com
Debra Ponzek and her acclaimed Aux Delices are well known for excellent food. They will cater or plan events of all types and sizes or simply provide home delivery of a terrific meal just for your family. In our Tasting Contest, Aux Delices received the highest overall score.

Barcelona Catering

18 West Putnam Avenue, Greenwich CT, 203.952.3355

www.barcelonawinebar.com/catering.htm

You know their tapas are good, so call Kim Fox about catering your next function. If you don't want tapas, they will do complete menus.

Burke Catering

16 Sound Beach Avenue, Old Greenwich CT, 203.698.2875

www.burkecatering.com

Burke, with its emphasis on healthy food, was selected by the YWCA to operate its Skylight Café. Burke recently catered the Round Hill Community Church Harvest Supper.

Captain John's

99 Commerce Street, Norwalk, CT, 203.866.4343

www.CaptainJohns.com

For 33 years, Captain John's has been providing classic New England clambakes, barbeques and picnic parties. They will plan and arrange everything or just provide you with a traveling clambake.

(The) Cooking Fairy

914.548.9379   www.TheFairyCook.com

Joanna Wallis, a Greenwich resident and professional chef, prepares and delivers meals to suit your family's needs. Choose a plan-2 times or several times a week.

Fairway Catering

699 Canal Street, Stamford CT, 203.388.9850

http://www.fairwaymarket.com/catering

You may not think of a grocery store catering an event, but the catering manager, Diane Russo, the past owner/chef of Mary & Martha catering, knows how to make her clients happy. We use them and they do a great job. Rebecca Martin is head of the kosher kitchen at Fairway. She offers catering for Seder feasts. Fairway delivers, but you will need to have your own wait staff.

ENTERTAINING

Festivities Events
203.847.7774   www.festivitiesevents.com
For 28 years, Chef Nicole Straight has been catering private parties or providing busy families with weekly menus of fresh seasonal foods from local farms. In 2007 and 2008 Festivities was awarded "Best Wedding Caterer" by The Knot.com. The minimum order is $ 375.00 plus an 18% service charge which includes sales tax and delivery expenses. All orders require one week advance notice.

Food Design
28 Old Field Point Road, Greenwich CT, 203.622.0725
www.FoodDesignCatering.com
Caterer for the Red Cross's annual Red & White Ball as well as for some of our local celebrities.

Fjord Fisheries
158 East Putnam Avenue, Cos Cob CT, 203.325.0248
www.FjordCatering.com
If you are invited to a clambake or lobster party, Fjord is often the provider. They are a full-service caterer. Their website has a number of suggested menus.

Garelick and Herbs
48 West Putnam Avenue, Greenwich, 203.661.7373
www.garelickandherbscatering.com
This gourmet delicatessen caters everything from a light lunch to fancy dinners. They will also provide staff for your events.

Great Performances
304 Hudson Street, New York City, 212.727.2424
www.greatperformances.com
We recently went to a Greenwich party where they were serving fabulous hors d'oeuvres, entrees and desserts. They are good at large functions and have their own list of exclusive locations.

Greenwich Harbor Cruises
500 Steamboat Road, Greenwich CT, 201.918.1590 (Captain Jonathan Wilkes) www.GreenwichHarborCruises.com
Cruises for 2-4 hours, for birthdays, class reunions, sightseeing or weddings. Catering and entertainment are available.

Happiness Is

1069 North Street, Greenwich (near Banksville), 203.861.4020
www.HappinessEvents.com
When Joan was recuperating from an injury, her daughter gave her a gift of Tuesday night dinners delivered from Happiness Is. On Saturday she received an email with three menus choices. She loved it. We were equally impressed with the Ladies Luncheon we ordered.

Libby Coverly Cooke Catering

49 Brownhouse Road (Sportsplex Health Club), Stamford, CT 203.536.9600   www.LibbyCookeCatering.com
Known for her fabulous presentations, she is equally competent with an intimate dinner party or a grand affair. If you want to try her food, order a take-out (48-hours in advance).

Marcia Selden

65 Research Drive, Stamford CT, 203.353.8000   www.MarciaSelden.com
For 25 years, Marcia and daughter Robin and son Jeff have been orchestrating small and large parties in Greenwich.

On The Marc Events

Research Park, Stamford CT, 203.274.6808   www.onthemarcevents.com
Chef Marc Weber started in 2007 as a personal chef doing parties for 12 to 20 people. Since then he has expanded to handle an event completely.

Raphael Palmero

Westchester NY, 203.629-2930   www.pasioncatering.com
Raphael Palmero, owner of Sonora, specializes in Nuevo Latino Tapas.

Plum Pure Foods

236 East Putnam Avenue, Cos Cob, 203.869.7586
www.PlumPureFoods.com
Plum provides delicious takeout foods made primarily from natural products grown locally. They are exceptional caterers. Plum scored at the top during our 2005 Catering Contest.

Royal Tea Company

Trumbull CT, 203.452.1006   www.RoyalTeaCompany.net
Listed in Connecticut Magazine's Best of Connecticut, their teas are perfect for bridal and baby showers, birthdays and holiday parties. Every one loves their tea sandwiches and scones.

Sugar Bee Catering
50 Iselin Terrace, Larchmont NY, 914.834.3410
www.SugarBeeCatering.com
When I asked my dear friend Mary, "who is your favorite caterer?", she immediately said "Sugar Bee!"

Truffles Catering
- 201 Irving Avenue, Port Chester NY, 914.935.0901
- 157 North Water Street, Greenwich CT
www.trufflescateringltd.com
We attended a party catered by Truffles and loved Patricia Raitanen's creations. They will cater large and small events, from finger foods to full buffets to prepared complete meals.

Victoria's Wood Fired Pizza Catering
8 Canterbury Court, Danbury CT, 203.994.2359
http://www.victoriaswoodfiredpizza.com/w/Home.html
Bruce Lyon, a delightful person and a graduate of the Culinary Institute, has a full service mobile catering truck. See your Neapolitan-style pizza baked fresh, before your eyes.

Watson's Catering
1 Glenville Road, Glenville CT, 203.532.0132
www.WatsonsCatering.com
You will want to have a cocktail or dinner party just to have Sue Scully's delicious food. Although large parties are her forte, she handles intimate parties equally well. An excellent choice! She is a real favorite of ours!

CATERING A CHILDREN'S PARTY
Food Trucks and frozen yogurt are often a good choice.

Victoria's Wood Fired Pizza Catering
8 Canterbury Court, Danbury CT, 203.994.2359
www.victoriaswoodfiredpizza.com/w/Home.html
Bruce Lyon, a delightful person and a graduate of the Culinary Institute, has a full service mobile catering truck. See your Neapolitan style pizza baked fresh, before your eyes.

Pinkberry Yogurt Catering
369 Greenwich Avenue, Greenwich CT, 203.863.2000
www.pinkberry.com/frozenyogurtcatering

ENTERTAINMENT (Adult Parties)

For children's Parties seen CHILDREN-Parties at Home.
For musicians see CULTURE.

David Ferst
914.649.4246
www.Magicdave.net
Slight of Hand artist for private parties, corporate events and even magic lessons. We love him.

James Daniel
125 Bedford Street, Stamford CT, 203.969.2400
www.JamesDaniel.com
A reliable source for music, entertainment or event lighting.

PM Amusements
36 Bush Avenue, Port Chester NY, 914.937.1188
www.PMAmusements.com
This is the ultimate party fun source. If you want to turn your backyard into an amusement park or just rent a cotton candy machine, they have it all. Ask about sumo wrestling, a velcro wall, miniature golf, karaoke, clowns, inflatable rides, or perhaps an Abe Lincoln or Mick Jagger look-a-like/impersonator. They have a great catalog.

INVITATIONS

The following invitation sources are described in STORES.
j papers, 100 Bruce Park Avenue, 203.769.5104
Papyrus, 268 Greenwich Avenue, 203.869.1888
Saint Clair, 96 Greenwich Avenue, 203.661.2927

Grace Connell
Westport CT, 203.557.9017
www.GraceConnellDesigns.com
Grace designs creative menus, envelopes, invitations and table numbers using hand-inked calligraphy.

PARKING SERVICES

Advanced Parking Concepts
Verona NJ, 203.353.1415
www.AdvancedParkingConcepts.com
They are totally professional, impeccably groomed and knowledgeable about Greenwich.

Off-Duty Policeman
To hire an off-duty officer for services such as directing traffic at a party, call 203.622.8016 or call the main number 203.622.8000 and select the extension.

Parking Productions
25 Walnut Avenue, Suite 4, Clark NJ, 203.629.0003
www.ParkingProductions.com
We are impressed by their ability to effortlessly take care of a large number of cars in a short period of time. Valet parking at its best. John Dent will also arrange curbside greeters, guest transportation and coordinate self parking.

PARTY GOODS
The following Party Goods sources are reviewed in STORES.
   East Putnam Variety, 26 Greenwich Avenue, 203.869.8789
   Party Paper and Things, 403 East Putnam Avenue, 203.661.1355
   Party City Locations:
         Kohl's Shopping Center, 535 Boston Post Road, Port Chester
         914.939.6900
         Ridgeway Shopping Center, 2255 Summer Street, Stamford
         203.964.4961

TIP: GREAT CHEFS
In March the Greenwich Hospital sponsors a benefit featuring more than 50 of the area's finest restaurants and catering companies.
Be sure to reserve in advance for this popular event.
For details or to purchase tickets call 203. 863.3865
or email GHFoundation@greenwichospital.org.

ENTERTAINING

PARTY PLANNERS

Hollywood Pop Gallery
24 Field Point Road, Greenwich CT, 203.622.4057
www.hollywoodpop.com
A global event production company. They will create and coordinate every element of your event from amazing decorations to cutting-edge entertainment. If you want your party to be remembered decades later, just give them a call. They put together about 200 adult and 1,000 children's parties a year.

PARTY RENTALS (Tents, Tables, Equipment)

Northeast Tent Productions
55 Poplar Street, Stamford CT, 203.961.8100
www.NorthEastTent.com
You will be impressed with the variety of tent styles and lighting possibilities.

Smith Party Rentals
133 Mason Street, Greenwich CT, 203.869.9315
www.SmithPartyRentals.com
For years this has been the leading party rental source in town. They are still the source for just about everything possible for adult and children's parties. If they don't have it, you probably don't need it.

Sperry Tents Greenwich
203.930.4021
www.SperryTentsCT.com
Elegant sailcloth and clear top tents.

Stamford Tent and Party Rental
84 Lenox Avenue, Stamford CT, 203.324.6222
www.StamfordTent.com
A good local resource for almost any type of tented party. Check the website for helpful tent sizing advice.

FITNESS

This section covers improving your strength or flexibility. For all other activities including walking, climbing and running see the sections SPORTS or PARKS.

If you need a chiropractor or physical therapy to recover from an excess of activity see HEALTH.

For child-focused activities see CHILDREN.

To exercise your mind see CONTINUING EDUCATION, CULTURE or BOOKS AND LIBRARIES.

FITNESS INDEX

Exercise Studios
Combine Training
CrossFit
Go Figure Exercise Studio
Pure Barre
Thompson Exercise
Elite Health Services

Gyms
Clay Health Club & Spa
Chelsea Piers
Equinox
Fitness Edge
Greenwich 24/7 Fitness
Italian Center
JCC
Life Time Fitness
New York Sports Club
Peak Physique
Sportsplex
Greenwich Civic Centers
YMCA
YWCA

Pilates Studios
Core Pilates
Greenwich Pilates Center
GXB Yoga & Pilates

Spinning Studios
Soul Cycle

Yoga Studios
Be Shri Yoga
GXB Yoga & Pilates
Kaia Yoga
Mantra Mind Body
Yoga Center

FITNESS

A Yoga Brief

According to the American Yoga Association there are more than 100 different types of yoga. Some studios combine different types of yoga. Some of the more common styles are:

• Anusara (or Ashtanga)

A structured, but physically demanding form done in complete silence.

• Bikram (Hot Yoga)

A workout practiced in 95F-105F heat. It is usually a 90-minute workout of 26 poses.

• Lyengar

This emphasizes correct alignment of all parts of the body. Unlike other forms it uses props such as chairs and stools.

• Hatha

The best known and easiest to learn. It is the foundation of most styles.

• Kripalu

A branch of Hatha which encourages practitioners to listen to their bodies through holding poses for longer times.

• Kundalini

This yoga works on breathing more so than other yogas. It also incorporates chanting and meditation.

• Power

Another athletic style. Pace is the key here with no pausing between movements.

• Vinyasa (also called Flow)

Vinyasa means breath-synchronized. Classes can range from gentle to athletic and some classes have the heat turned up.

FITNESS RESOURCES

Be Shri Yoga (Flow Yoga)

1345 East Putnam Avenue (2nd floor), Old Greenwich CT, 203.219.1715
www.BeShriYoga.com

They have total beginner classes, gentle yoga and flow yoga for intermediate and advanced practitioners. The hours below are approximate as there are a number of sessions in between which you sign up for on their website.

Class Start Hours: Monday 7am-6pm, Tuesday 9:30am-7pm, Wednesday 7am-7pm, Thursday 9:30am-7:30pm, Friday 8:15-9:30pm, Saturday & Sunday 9am.

FITNESS

Chelsea Piers Adult Fitness (Gym)
One Blachley Road, Stamford CT, 203.989.1000
www.ChelseaPiersCT.com/fitness
As you might imagine, this 460,000 sf facility, in addition to its many youth sports programs, has a large number of adult personal trainers and fitness classes, some of which are aqua zumba, boot camp, cardio tennis, gymnastics, rock climbing, squash fitness and parkour. They also have a masters swim program, triathlon training and endurance racing. Some classes are members only.

Clay Health Club & Spa (Gym)
11 Riverdale Avenue, Port Chester NY, 914.937.5000
www.insideclay.com/greenwich
Right on the Greenwich border is a luxurious 25,000 sf club with steam and sauna, cardio and strength training equipment. They have 5 dedicated training studios: group exercise, pilates, yoga, spin and golf performance training. They also have lounges, a café and valet parking.
Hours: Monday-Thursday 5:30am-10pm, Friday 5:30am-9pm, Saturday and Sunday 7am-7pm.

Combine Training (Fitness)
469 West Putnam Avenue, Greenwich CT, 203.717.1700
www.CombineTrainingCT.com
Adult and youth Triathlon (swim, bike, run) training. The head coach is Craig Vitale, a Greenwich resident and Ironman / Triathlon All American.

Core Pilates
6 West Greenwich Avenue, Greenwich CT, 203.914.4433
www.CorepilatesStudio.com
They use pilates to help strengthen tennis and golf players. They are helpful to breast cancer survivors and individuals with hip and knee replacements.
Hours: Individual and group classes are by appointment. They operate 7 days a week from 7am-7:30pm.

CrossFit 06830
1374 East Putnam Avenue, Greenwich CT, 203.990.0479
www.Crossfit06830.com
In a 4,000 sf studio you can get individual or group workouts for beginners to advanced. Jay Higgins uses a variety of conditioning techniques to achieve strength and agility. He guarantees you will not get bored.
Hours: Call to set up a free trial lesson.

FITNESS

EHS-Elite Health Services (Physical Therapy & Personal Training)
1445 East Putnam Avenue (2nd floor) Old Greenwich CT, 203.983.5748
www.EliteHealthServices.com
A group of highly-trained physical therapists and trainers. Besides doing functional manual therapy, they do personal, triathlon, golf and other sport performance training in their spacious, well-appointed studio or at your home. Tara Gibson, DPT, is enthusiastically determined to put me back on the ski slopes!
Hours: Monday-Thursday 7am-7pm, Friday 7am-5pm,
Saturday 9am-1pm

Equinox (Gym)
16 Old Track Road, Greenwich CT, 203.863.0070
www.equinox.com
They have four fitness studios, a spa, juice bar and fitness floors for physical training. Classes include yoga, studio cycling, pilates, personal training, isometrics, ballet strengthening, kickboxing and martial arts. Equinox operates four separate fitness brands: Equinox fitness, PURE Yoga, Blink Fitness and Soul Cycle.
Hours: Monday-Thursday 5am-10pm, Friday 5am-9pm, Saturday 7am-8pm, Sunday 7am-7pm.

Fitness Edge (Gym)
1333 East Putnam Avenue, Riverside CT, 203.637.3906
www.theedgefitnessclubs.com/Greenwich
One of 10 locations in CT, this is a popular place to work out. Lots of machines and classes, including one-on-one personal training. Dozens of classes per week including functional training, zumba, spinning, yoga and pilates. The Kids program is a plus. Children exercise while you are working out.
Hours: Monday-Thursday 5am-10pm, Friday 5am-9pm,
Saturday 7am-6pm, Sunday 7am-5pm.

Go Figure Exercise Studio (Multi-Discipline Exercise)
141 West Putnam Avenue, Greenwich CT, 203.625.7616
www.gofigurestudio.com
One of 10 studios. The Figure Method Barre class combines the principles of ballet, yoga, Pilates and orthopedic exercises to give you great posture, flexibility and lean muscles. This studio believes in using a holistic approach to exercise to create a method that is gentle, yet challenging.
Hours: Call to book a class.

FITNESS

Greenwich 24/7 Fitness (Gym)
209 Bruce Park Avenue, Greenwich CT, 203.661.5017
www.bruceparkfitness.com
A 24 hour fully-automated facility, with personal trainers, yoga, cardio boxing (box physique) and massage. Use their trainers or bring your own. Hours: 24/7.

Greenwich Continuing Education
Havemeyer Building, 290 Greenwich Avenue, 203.625.7474, 7475,
www.greenwichace.org
Most classes are held at the Greenwich High School. They usually offer beginning and advanced yoga courses as well as tai chi ch'uan classes.

Greenwich Pilates Center (Pilates & Gyrotonics)
309 Greenwich Avenue (second floor), Room 204, 203.869.3900
With over ten years' teaching experience, Edvins Puris personalizes every client's workout, ranging from elite athletes to post-physical therapy rehabilitation. It is an exclusive one-on-one studio experience. Edvins offers Pilates combined with Gyrotonics.

GXB Yoga & Pilates (Yoga & Pilates)
469 West Putnam Avenue, Greenwich CT, 914.826.6627
www.GXBYogaPilates.com
Genevieve X. Boulanger is skillful, dedicated and enthusiastic. She is certified in pilates and yoga, and can combine the two to help her private clients. I feel very fortunate to be one of her clients.
Hours: Call for the schedule of classes or to arrange a private lesson.

Italian Center
1620 Newfield Ave, Stamford CT, 203.322.6941
www.ItalianCenter.Org
Set on 26 acres, with 3 outdoor pools and an indoor pool and spa, a 2-level fitness center with circuit training, treadmills, step masters, Xtrainers, free weights, weight resistance machines, body sculpting, yoga, aquatics and more. Personal training or group lessons.
See a complete description in SPORTS.
Hours: Weekdays 5am-9:30pm, Saturday & Sunday 7:30am-6pm. Outdoor pool hours during the summer are generally 11am-6pm.

FITNESS

JCC
1035 Newfield Avenue, Stamford CT, 203.322.7900
www.StamfordJCC.org
Group fitness classes and private fitness classes: yoga, cycling, pilates, barre, boot camp, boxing, aquatics and more. Lots of programs for children. See a complete description in SPORTS.
Hours: Monday-Thursday 5:30am-10pm, Friday 5:30am-6pm, Saturday 7:30am-9pm, Sunday 7:30am-6pm. The JCC is closed on most Jewish Holidays.

Kaia Yoga (Yoga)
328 Pemberwick Road @ The Mill, Glenville CT, 203.532.0660
www.Kaiayoga.com
They practice a variety of styles for asanas (postures), pranayama (breath exercises), meditation and yoga nidre (deep relaxation) and "HOT" or basic vinyasa yoga at the Greenwich Water Club, 49 River Road, Cos Cob, CT. You don't need to be a Water Club member to participate.
Hours: Call for class times or check their website.

Life Time Fitness (Gym)
1 Westchester Park Drive, Harrison NY, 914.290.5100
www.LifeTimeFitness.com
Life Time is a chain of luxury, mega-fitness centers. It has long hours and good security. This 206,000 sf facility has indoor and outdoor pools, state-of-the-art fitness equipment, and instruction in pilates, yoga, squash, tennis, weight loss and much more. They have a Kids' Academy for ages 3 months to 11 years.
Hours: 4am-12pm every day.

Mantra Mind Body (Aerial Yoga)
1455 East Putnam Avenue, Old Greenwich CT, 203.990.0500
www.MantraMindBody.com, www.youtube.com/user/MantraMindBody
Carla Zilka teaches a variety yoga styles including aerial yoga.
Hours: Check website for hours and to register for a class.

FITNESS

New York Sports Club (Gym)
6 Liberty Way, Greenwich CT, 203.869.1253
www.MySportsClubs.com
There are over 120 NYSC clubs in New York, New Jersey and Connecticut. In addition to a 6,000 sf state-of-the-art fitness center, the aerobics and spinning studios offer classes 7 days a week. Medically-based health and wellness programs include nutrition, massage, personal training and a Medicare certified physical therapy department. Childcare available.
Hours: Weekdays 5:30am-10pm, Saturday 7am-5pm,
Sunday 8am-5pm.

Peak Physique (Fitness)
50 Holly Hill Lane, Greenwich CT, 203.625.9595
www.peakphysique.biz
If you are not down to the weight you want for your beach vacation, sign up for their bikini boot camp. In one month (5-day a week program of diet and exercise) they promise to have you ready for the beach. Dom Novak, the owner of Peak Physique, is a well-regarded trainer keeping many Greenwich residents fit year round.
Hours: Open 7 days a week from 7am to about 7pm.

Punch Fitness
321 Greenwich Avenue, Greenwich CT, 203.992.1916
www.PunchFitnessCenter.com
Kick boxing for fitness and as a martial art. Started by Mr. Da Costa, a former Portuguese national kickboxing champion. They train adults as well as children as young as 5. Training can be one-on-one or in a class. Their website has the class hours and instructor where you can book your lesson. They will give you a free 30-minute introductory lesson.
Hours: Weekdays 5:45pm-9:30pm, Saturday & Sunday 7am-1pm.

Pure Barre (Fitness)
280 Railroad Avenue, Greenwich CT, 203.489.3500 www.PureBarre.com
A high energy, low impact exercise class that utilizes the ballet barre to do isometric movements. Someone described it as an intense workout combining ballet, pilates and yoga. Classes are usually 55 minutes.
Hours: They are open every day. Consult the website for their hours.

FITNESS

Soul Cycle (Spinning)
266 Mason Street, Greenwich CT, 203.653.7685
www.soul-cycle.com (Set your region to "Connecticut")
Soulcycle is a Manhattan-based chain of health clubs using stationary bicycles. They have more than 30 locations. In the Greenwich location they have 60 bikes. Classes are 45 minutes and are designed for fat burning and strengthening. Soul Cycle is owned by Equinox and is one of its four fitness brands.   Hours: Every day from about 7am to about 5pm.

Sportsplex (Fitness, Squash, Swimming, Racquetball)
49 Brownhouse Road, Stamford CT, 203.358.0066
www.Sportsplex-CT.com
On the border of Stamford and Old Greenwich is a complete training facility for adults and children. Morning programs for pre-schoolers and after school programs for ages 6-8. Supervised nursery for children. In addition to machines and spinning, they have an Olympic-length pool, four squash courts and one racquetball court. Swimming and squash lessons are available. The aerobics center has a specially designed exercise floor, a variety of exercise programs and, of course, they have zumba. Call for an enthusiastic tour.
Club Hours: Monday-Thursday 5am-10pm; Friday 5am-9pm; Saturday & Sunday 7am-6 pm.
Nursery Hours: Monday-Thursday 8:30am-12pm, Monday 6pm-8:30pm, Thursday 5pm-7:30pm, Friday 8:30am-1pm, Saturday 8am-12:30 pm, Sunday 8:30am-12pm (No evening hours during the summer.)

Thompson Exercise
Grand Slam Tennis Center, Bedford NY, 914.234.9206
www.Grandslamtennisclub.com
Thompson Method classes work on stretching, strength and stamina (including combinations). Associates who attend the school love it. Classes are held at the Ivan Lendl Grand Slam Tennis Club. Bill believes that anyone, no matter what age or ability, has the potential to achieve a high level of fitness and well being.
Hours: Schedule is on the Grand Slam website. Classes start at 8am.

FITNESS

Greenwich Civic Centers
Western (Bendheim) Greenwich Civic Center
449 Pemberwick Road, Glenville CT, 203.532.1259
Eastern Greenwich Civic Center
90 Harding Road, Old Greenwich CT, 203.637.4583
www.greenwichct.org/ParksAndRec/prFacilityPrograms.asp
Weights, boot camp, dance exercise and zumba.
See a complete description in SPORTS.

Yoga Center (Hatha & Asanas Yoga)
125 Greenwich Avenue, Greenwich CT, 203.661.0092
www.yogacentergreenwich.com
In the heart of Greenwich, this popular studio for yoga is run by a mother
and daughter team, Toni Goodrich and Heather Trzuskowski. You will
find a variety of classes at this center, including hot yoga.
Hours: Check website for class schedule.

YMCA (a.k.a. Greenwich Family Y)
50 East Putnam Avenue, Greenwich CT, 203.869.1630
www.gwymca.org, www.greenwichymca.org
Personal Training and Small Group Training: aerobics, boxing, interval
training, boot camp, Brazilian fitness, yoga, pilates, studio cycling, aquatic
fitness, massage therapy and more.
See a complete description in SPORTS.

YWCA
259 East Putnam Avenue, Greenwich CT, 203.869.6501
www.YWCAGreenwich.org
State-of-the-art fitness center for adults 14 and over with an array of
equipment; group lessons using kettlebells, kickboxing, mat pilates, spinning and moderately paced aerobics for seniors. Personal trainers, aquatics, massage therapy and Reiki therapy. Lots of programs like gymnastics for children.
See a complete description in SPORTS.

FLOWERS & GARDENS

The Greenwich Department of Parks has a green thumb and together with the talents of garden club volunteers (who you will see gardening on many of the town's intersections) make Greenwich so beautiful. See PARKS for more information.

SECTIONS
Gardening Education
Garden Clubs
Florists and Nurseries are described in the STORES.

GARDENING EDUCATION

Garden Education Center
Montgomery Pinetum, 130 Bible Street, Cos Cob CT, 203.869.9242
www.gecgreenwich.org
The Center's horticulture buildings provide classrooms and workrooms for a variety of programs and lectures. Founded in 1957, the center is not only a strong educational facility, but also provides a good framework for new residents to make friends. The quality of their programs is amazing. If you are interested in gardening, these programs should not be missed. Call and get on the list for their newsletter.
Hours: Weekdays 9am-4pm. Closed during the summer.
Greenhouse Hours: Monday, Wednesday, Thursday and Friday 10am-2pm. Closed in July and August.

New York Botanical Gardens
Bronx, NY, 718.817.8700
www.nybg.org
Greenwich garden enthusiasts know their way to the NY Botanical Gardens. The gardens have recently undergone a $25 million renovation and are considered the best in the country.
Hours: Tuesday-Sunday 10 am-6 pm. (Winter until 5pm) Wednesdays are free.

FLOWERS & GARDENS

FLORISTS and NURSERIES

The following Florists and Nurseries are described in STORES:

- Cos Cob Farms, 61 East Putnam Avenue, Cos Cob CT, 203.629.2267
- Greenwich Hospital Gift Shop Flowers, 203.863.3371
- Greenwich Orchids, 106 Mason Street, Greenwich CT, 203.661.5544
- Mark Mariani's Garden Center, 45 Bedford Rd, Armonk NY, 914.273.3083
- McArdle-MacMillen, 48 Arch Street, Greenwich CT, 203.661.5600
- Sam Bridge Nursery, 437 North Street, Greenwich CT, 203.869.3418
- Shanti Bithi Nursery, 3047 High Ridge Road, Stamford CT, 203.329.0768
- Tulips Greenwich, 91 Lake Avenue, Greenwich CT, 203.661.3154

GARDEN CLUBS

Garden Club of Old Greenwich

www.gardencluboffoldgreenwich.org

They care about keeping the Old Greenwich area beautiful and work on many civic projects. They share their talents and knowledge through horticulture programs designed for the young and the elderly. Membership is by invitation.

Green Fingers Garden Club

www.greenfingersgc.org

An active club, responsible for the biennial "Preview of Spring," a major flower show usually held at Christ Church in early March. The club sponsors many wonderful civic projects such as the renovation of the area around the ferry boat landing. Membership is by invitation.

Greenwich Daffodil Society

GreenwichDaffodilSociety@gmail.com

In the Spring, daffodils burst into bloom all over town. If you love daffodils you will love membership in this group. The group sponsors the annual Connecticut Daffodil Show at Christ Church.

Greenwich Garden Club

www.GreenwichGardenClub.org

Founded in 1914, they promote interest in horticulture, flower arranging, and conservation. They have an amazing list of civic improvement projects-making our Town beautiful! Membership is by invitation.

FLOWERS & GARDENS

Greenwich Green & Clean

www.greenwichgreenandclean.org

113 Pemberwick Road, 203.531.0006

When someone says, "Wow, Greenwich is so clean and pretty!" tell them about this dedicated group of volunteers, working hard to keep it that way. Founded in 1986, when the town was going through some drastic budget cutting, this group formed and took action. Now working in partnership with the town, they are the inspiration for the pretty flowering baskets along the Avenue and the flowers on many of the traffic islands. Join this group and take part in the fall and spring Town Clean Up. Take a bag, join your neighbors and have fun in this well-organized effort to clean our streets and parks.

Greenwich Woman's Club Gardeners

89 Maple Avenue, 203.869.2046

The Woman's Club, a greatly enjoyed, highly-respected philanthropic service organization in our town has a special branch of women devoted to gardening, horticultural education and projects to enhance the beauty of our town. New members to the Woman's Club and to this special branch of Gardeners are welcomed.

Hortulus

PO Box 4666, Greenwich CT, 06831

www.hortulus.org

This garden club, founded in 1930, is dedicated to furthering a knowledge and love of gardening. Membership is by invitation.

Knollwood Garden Club

PO Box 1666, Greenwich 06836

Contact: Em Toohey 203.661.7988

This garden club, founded in 1955, maintains and supports the Seaside Garden at Greenwich Point and they provide garden therapy at Nathaniel Witherell. Membership is by invitation.

Riverside Garden Club

PO Box 108, Old Greenwich, 06870

www.Riversidegardenclubct.org

This local club is a member of the National Council of State Garden Clubs and is a charter member of the Federated Garden Clubs of America. Members have a wonderful time together as they work on horticultural education programs and on projects to enhance the beauty of Greenwich. New members are heartily welcomed.

FOOD TRUCKS

Food trucks are often used to cater an event or party.

Caffé Bon (Food Truck)
Town Hall Parking Lot, Greenwich CT, 203.536.0524
www.facebook.com/caffebon
The green, flowered truck is a town favorite. Maria Pietrobon, a Riverside resident and mother of two, has created an upscale food truck. Her ingredients are very fresh, healthy foods. Expect really good paninis. She bakes her own muffins and biscotti; her Tuscan bread and focaccia are from the Tarry Market. She cares about having the best coffee and even has a cappuccino machine.
Hours: Hours and locations vary. Check her Facebook page for weekly schedule updates.

Dom's Weiner Wagon (Food Truck)
Board of Ed. parking lot on Greenwich Ave, Greenwich CT, 203.536.6046
Dominick Pisano Jr, specializes in hot dogs, but he also has soups and sandwiches.
Hours: Weekdays 11am-3:30pm or so.

Frank's Franks (Food Truck)
In the Garden Center, 1294 King Street, Greenwich CT, 203.223.5560
www.franksfranks.com
Frank DeNicola, a generous volunteer and an elected member of the Representative Town Meeting (RTM), is also famous for his food truck. The chili dogs, cheese steaks and cheese fries are favorites. Every day there are specials, some prepared by a Mexican chef and others by a Peruvian chef.
Hours: Open everyday (except major holidays), Monday-Saturday 7am-4pm, Sunday 7am-3pm.

Good Baker (Food Truck)
Baker@followThatCupCake.com
www.followthatcupcake.com
This terrific cupcake truck (we love the chocolate one) can sometimes be found around 17 East Putnam Avenue. Yes, he has gluten free and vegan cupcakes as well. But most of his business come from private events-think children's party.

FOOD TRUCKS

Hutchy's Hot Dogs (Food Truck)
East Putnam Avenue next to Walgreens, Old Greenwich CT, 203.561.6241
Hot dogs, steak sandwiches and Gorgonzola salads are popular. The truffle
French fries are his customers' favorite.
Hours: Weekdays, 11am-3pm.

LobsterCraft (Food Truck)
cell: 203-856.2635
www.LobsterCraft.com   www.facebook.com/LobsterCraft
This truck is often parked in the lot of 500 West Putnam Avenue on
Thursdays and on Fridays outside the Greenwich Library at 101 West
Putnam Avenue. if you happen to see it, you will surely enjoy their lobster sandwiches and lobster bisque. Recently Lobster Craft opened a small
restaurant on the Rowayton Darien border at 284 Tokeneke Road, Darien
CT, 203.655.5400. They are open Tuesday-Saturday 11am-7pm, Sunday
12pm-7pm.

Mama's Kitchen (Food Truck)
101 West Putnam Avenue (in front of the Greenwich Library)
914.230.6774
A mother-daughter team, Clara and Maria Fonseca, are proud of their
soups, omelets and pancakes. They have a large variety of sandwiches,
as well as salads and burgers.
Hours: Weekdays 7:30am-3:30pm.

Melt Mobile (Food Truck)
Town Hall on Fridays; 500 West Putnam Avenue on Wednesdays,
203.609.1422
www.MeltMobile.com, www.Facebook.com/Meltmobile
Darlene Andersen serves gourmet grilled cheese sandwiches, such as the
Montecristo with ham & turkey, the insanewich with bacon & tomatoes,
the philly melt and the mexi-melt. Monica simply can't pass this truck
without stopping for a sandwich!
Hours: approximately 11:45-2pm. To know her exact hours and locations, like her on Facebook.

Tandoori Express (Food Truck)
Arch Street area, Greenwich CT, 203.637.4110
www.TandooriCT.com
If you don't have time to dine in their Port Chester restaurant, you can
enjoy their food (cooked in their restaurant) on the go.
Hours: Weekdays 11am-8pm.

GOVERNMENT

For an explanation of how the town operates see, GREENWICH.

SECTIONS
Town Government
State Government
Federal Government
Local Political Organizations and Advocacy Groups

TOWN GOVERNMENT

First Selectman
Peter Tesei, 203.622.7710
www.greenwichct.org/FirstSelectman/Selectman.asp

Board of Selectmen
John Toner 203.622..7714
Drew Marzullo, 203.622.7706
www.greenwichct.org/FirstSelectman/fsBoardSelectmen.asp

Board of Estimate and Taxation (BET)
Chair, Michael Mason, 203.622.7720
www.greenwichct.org/government/boards/board_of_estimate_taxation

Representative Town Meeting (RTM)
Moderator, Thomas J. Byrne, 203.637.4307
Moderator Pro Tempore, Joan E. Caldwell, 203.869.2553
For a list of your district representatives,
www.greenwichct.org/search.asp?mode=2
For details on the Town Meeting and how to become a member see www.greenwichct.org/government/rtm/ The RTM's website is http://rtm.greenwich.org It is a good place to find members, committees, committee membership, Districts and RTM rules.

TIP: LOCAL GOVERNMENT IN ACTION
The best way to understand how our Town can be run so efficiently by the largest legislature in Connecticut–the RTM or Representative Town Meeting –is to attend some of their meetings. Meetings are open to the public and are held in the beginning of most months at the Central Middle School auditorium. Ask the Town Clerk (203.622.7700) for a schedule of their meetings and for an agenda, "The Call," or find it on the website at www.greenwichct.org Guests always sit in the last rows.

GOVERNMENT

Town Hall
101 Field Point Road, Greenwich CT, 06830
203.622.7700 (All Departments) www.GreenwichCT.org
www.greenwichct.org/town_departments.asp
For online forms, permits and applications: www.greenwichct.org/forms

- Meeting Rooms:
  1st Floor: Town Hall Meeting Room, Mazza & Gisborne
  2nd Floor: Cone Meeting Room
  3rd Floor: Hayton & Evaristo Meeting Rooms

NOTE: Government office hours tend to change frequently, so be sure to check the hours before you go.

- Assessor's Office, 203.622.7885
  1st floor, 8am - 4pm.

- Beach Card Office, 203.622.7814
  1st floor, generally 8am - 3:45pm, April through November 15th.
See Beaches in PARKS & RECREATION for information on obtaining a beach card.

- Building Department, 203.622.7754
  2nd floor, Winter Hours: Monday, Wednesday & Friday 8am - 12pm,
  Tuesday & Thursday 8am-2:30pm; Summer hours: (Memorial Day - Labor Day) Monday, Wednesday & Friday, 7:30am - 12pm,
  Tuesday & Thursday 7:30am - 2:30pm.

- Conservation Commission, 203.622.6461
  2nd floor, 8am - 3:30 pm.
  Call ahead to make an appointment to meet with a staff member.

- Geographic Information Department (Information Technology),
  203.622.6448
  Basement, 9am - 4pm; print out on site or pick up large map on
  Friday. www.greenwichct.org/forms

- Health (Septic) Department, 203.622.6488
  3rd floor, 8am - 4pm.

- Highway Division(Public Works), 203.622.7766
  2nd floor, 8am - 4pm.

- Parks & Recreation Department, 203.622.7814
  2nd floor, 8:15am - 3:45pm.

GOVERNMENT

- Planning & Zoning Department, 203.622.7894
  2nd floor, 8am - 3:30pm.
  To meet with a planner, 9am - 12pm (weekdays except Wednesday).

- Probate Court, 203.622.7879
  1st floor, 8am - 4pm (closes at noon on Fridays in July & August).

- Public Works (Sewer) Department, 203.618.3001, 203.622.7760
  2nd floor, 8am - 4pm.

- Selectman's Office, 203.622.7710
  1st floor, 8:30am - 4pm, Call for appointment.

- Social Services Department, 203.622.3800
  3rd floor, 8:30am - 5pm, after hours by appointment.

- Tax Collector, 203.622.7891
  1st floor, 8:30am - 3:30pm.

- Town Clerk, 203.622.7897
  1st floor, 8am - 4pm.

- Voter Registration, 203.622.7889
  1st floor, Monday-Friday 8am-4pm.
  www.greenwichct.org/forms

- Wetlands, 203.622.7736
  2nd floor, 8am - 3:30pm.
  To meet with a compliance officer, weekdays 9am - noon.
  Call ahead for an appointment.

First Selectman's Special Committees
www.greenwichct.org/FirstSelectman/fsSpecialCommittees.asp

Town Boards and Commissions and Committees
www.greenwichct.org/town_hall.asp#commissions
Most boards and commissions are run by volunteers. If you are interested in sharing your talents by serving on a committee or commission, contact a member of the Selectman's Nomination Advisory Committee (SNAC), http://www.greenwichct.org/government/committees/selectmens_nominations_advisory_committee/
or self-nominate yourself by filling out the nomination form at www.greenwichct.org/grAllFormsList.asp

GOVERNMENT

STATE GOVERNMENT

Governor
• Dannel Malloy (Democrat), 800.406.1527, www.CT.Gov/Malloy

State Senate
• State Senator L. Scott Frantz (Republican Minority Whip) 800.842.1421
   District 36, Representing: Greenwich, New Canaan, Stamford
   Www.SenatorFrantz.cga.ct.gov

State Representatives
• State Representative Livvy Floren (Republican), 800.842.1423
   Representing the 149 Assembly District (Greenwich)
   www.repfloren.com

• State Representative Mike Bocchino (Republican),
   Representing the 150 Assembly District (Greenwich)

• State Representative Fred Camillo (Republican) 800.842.1423
   Representing the 151 Assembly District (Greenwich)
   www.repfredcamillo.com

GOVERNMENT

FEDERAL GOVERNMENT
- US Senator, Richard Blumenthal (Democrat), 202.224.2823
  www.blumenthal.senate.gov
- US Senator, Christopher Murphy (Democrat), 202.224.4041
  www.murphy.senate.gov
- US Congressman for the 4th District Jim Himes (Democrat)
  866.453.0028
  www.himes.house.gov/index.html

LOCAL POLITICAL ORGANIZATIONS AND ADVOCACY GROUPS

(Greenwich) Democratic Town Committee
PO Box 126, Greenwich CT, 06836
www.greenwichdemocrats.com

League of Women Voters
PO Box 604, Greenwich CT 06836, 203.352.4700
www.lwvg.org
A non-partisan organization you should join and a good place to go for complete information about our elected officials. They encourage informed and active participation in government through education and advocacy. Membership is open to men and women. Some of their publications include:
- People Make It Happen: A Guide to Greenwich Government
- How to Make it Happen: Facts for Greenwich Voters
- The RTM Directory
- How to Run for Greenwich Office

Republican Club of Cos Cob
Promotes the Republican party and holds an annual clambake.

(Greenwich) Republican Town Committee
P.O. Box 4030, Greenwich CT 06831
http://www.greenwichrtc.com

Note: Farmers Markets, Pick-your-Own and Home Delivery are in a separate section HOME DELIVERY AND FARMS. DELICATESSENS have their own section.

A & P Fresh (Grocery)

160 West Putnam Avenue, Greenwich CT, 203.622.0374
www.APFreshOnline.com
A good general purpose grocery. 2009 was its 150th anniversary. A&P has gone from about 16,000 stores in 1930 to 301 stores in 2014. Once called "The Food Emporium" this store has been restructured to compete with stores like Whole Foods.
Hours: Monday-Saturday 7am-10pm, Sunday 7am-9pm.

Augustine's Farm (Fruit & Vegetables)

1332 King Street, Greenwich CT, 203.532.9611
For more than 50 years Kathy and John Augustin have been providing Greenwich residents with fresh corn, tomatoes, apples, pumpkins, honey, eggs and cider. Its great fun to stop here, load up on fresh vegetables and buy beautiful plants and flowers. This is the perfect place to buy your Christmas tree or holiday wreath.
Hours: Open every day 9am-5pm during the season; during the winter Kathy is in the greenhouse weekdays 10am-2pm.

Balducci's (Grocery, Deli, Wine)

1050 East Putnam Avenue, Riverside CT, 203.637.7600
www.Balduccis.com
A sophisticated gourmet deli and country shop for fruits, vegetables and unique foods. It is owned by King's Grocery. Balducci's carries imported and American cheeses and a nice selection of flavorful soups. Their wine store carries a large selection of American and international wines.
Hours: Monday-Saturday 9am-8pm, Sunday 10am-5pm.

Bon Ton (Seafood)

100 Bruce Park Avenue, Greenwich CT, 203.869.0462
www.bontonfishmarket.com
In Greenwich since 1902, this is a reliable fish store. They have high-quality fish as well as prepared seafood specialties, including poached and smoked salmon platters, and a full line of Russian caviar. Linda loves their crab cakes. Right next to Greenwich Prime Meats, it's a handy location with ample parking.
Hours: Monday-Saturday 8am-6pm, Sunday 10am-3pm.

GROCERIES & SPECIALTY FOODS

Citarella (Grocery)
600 West Putnam Avenue, Greenwich CT,   www.citarella.com
This seven location high-end grocery chain is owned by Joe Gurrera. They feature fresh seafood and aged prime meats as well as prepared food and epicurean groceries, such as truffles and caviar. However, you can also find fresh produce and ingredients you would find in a general purpose grocery.

Bukovina (Russian Grocery)
301 Hope Street, Stamford CT, 203.978.0408
The local source for Russian and Ukrainian food.
Hours: Monday-Saturday 10am-8pm.

Cos Cob Farms (Fruit & Vegetables)
61 East Putnam Avenue, Cos Cob CT, 203.629.2267
In the season, flowers surround the shop. Open the door and you are greeted by the friendly owner and a wide selection of fresh fruit, vegetables and flowers at reasonable prices. A good place to put together a gift basket of fruit.
Hours: Monday-Saturday 8am-7pm, Sunday 9am-6pm.

Costco (Grocery & Department Store)
1 Westchester Avenue, Port Chester NY, 914.935.3103
www.Costco.com
Costco is the 5th largest retailer in the US, with just under 500 locations. You have to buy a membership to shop at this international chain, but that hasn't kept this megastore, a.k.a. warehouse, from being a Greenwich hit. The bottom floor is electronics, the second floor is primarily groceries. As one young boy explained to his sister, "this is the everything store." Costco focuses on selling products at low prices, usually bulk-packaged. Kirkland Signature is Costco's store brand. Yearly membership is $55. Purchases made on their website do not require a membership; but a 5% surcharge is added to purchases made by non-members.
Hours: Weekdays 10am-8:30pm, Saturday 9:30am-7pm,
Sunday 10am-6pm; closed most major holidays.

GROCERIES & SPECIALTY FOODS

DeCicco's Family Market (Grocery)
17 Maple Avenue, Armonk NY, 914.499.1100
www.deciccos.com
A diverse selection of food for serious home chefs, as well as a large deli and cheese section. They have a huge selection of beer.
Hours: Monday-Saturday 7:30am-8:30, Sunday 8am-7:30pm.

Edible Arrangements
384 West Putnam Avenue, Greenwich CT, 203.625.5555
www.EdibleArrangements.com
The company has over 1,000 locations. Some are company owned, most, like this one, are franchised. They sell creative fresh fruit baskets that look like a bouquet of flowers, as well as gift boxes of chocolate dipped fruit.
Hours: Weekdays 9am-7pm, Saturday 8am-5pm, Sunday 9am-2pm.

Fairway (Grocery)
699 Canal Street, Stamford CT, 203.388.9815
www.FairwayMarket.com, www.FairwayWines.com
This 50,000 sf store has a huge selection of fresh products (fish, fruit, meat, vegetables) as well as just about anything one could want in everyday groceries-all at competitive prices. They have a coffee center where they roast their beans (worth the trip just for the beans), a very large cheese area, dozens of olive oils, and a good deli section. Their wine store is next door. The 80-seat café is a good place to try their delicatessen foods.
Hours: Grocery open everyday 8am-10pm (closes early on many holidays);
Wine shop open Monday-Saturday 9am-9pm, Sunday 10am-5pm.
Café open every day 8am-8pm.

Fjord Fisheries (Seafood)
158 East Putnam Avenue, Cos Cob CT, 203.661.5006
www.FjordFisheries.com
This market has an abundance of fresh fish plus a delicatessen and sandwich shop. If you were to ask "where is the best fish and chips?", you would probably be directed here. We also think their Crab Cake Po'boy, Salmon Club and Tuna sandwiches are outstanding. Fjord is a great place for sliced smoked salmon or salmon tartare. If you are in a hurry, place your order in advance. We love their freshly prepared sushi.
Hours: Monday-Saturday 8am-7pm, Sunday 9am-6pm.

GROCERIES & SPECIALTY FOODS

Fuji Mart (Japanese Grocery)
1212 East Putnam Avenue, Riverside CT, 203.698.2107
An authentic Japanese grocery, very well-stocked with most everything
you will need, all in a very small space. A nice selection of fresh ingredients plus frozen foods and sushi. Buy a bag of frozen gyoza.
Hours: Weekdays 9:30am-6:30pm (Monday 6pm), Saturday & Sunday
10am-6:30pm.

Greenwich Cheese Company (Cheese)
154 East Putnam Avenue, Cos Cob CT, 203.340.9227
www.greenwichcheese.com
Laura Downey and Chris Palumbo, owners of the Fairfield Cheese Company, opened this 1,200 sf shop offering more than 100 cheeses including American artisanal cheese and local cheeses. A great place to learn
about cheese.
Hours: Monday-Saturday 10am-7pm.

Greenwich Prime Meats (Meat)
100 Bruce Park Avenue, Greenwich CT, 203.861.6328
A shop run by former members of famed Manero's butcher shop. They
are located next to the Bon Ton fish store. Terrific meats (even Kobe
steaks) and friendly advice along with Manero's special take-out treats:
Gorgonzola salad, garlic bread, fried onions, steak fries and steak sandwiches. Easy parking behind the store. Free delivery in the local area.
Hours: Monday-Saturday 9am-6pm, Sunday 9am-5pm.

Kaas & Co (Dutch Foods)
83 Washington Street, (South) Norwalk CT, 203.838.6161
www.KaasnCo.com
Gift items predominate, but you can find a small selection of Dutch and
Indonesian foods and spices.
Hours: Monday-Saturday 11am-5pm.

Kam Sen Foods (Asian Foods)
22 Barker Avenue (in White Plains Mall), White Plains NY, 914.428.4500
www.KamSenFoods.com
Located on the lower level of the Mall is a huge Asian grocery. They
specialize in Chinese and Korean foods, but they also carry a selection of
Filipino and Japanese items. They are stocked with a vast variety of meat,
fish and vegetables. The Bakery carries Hong Kong style pastries and
cakes. The housewares section has great woks.
Open everyday 10am-7:45pm.

GROCERIES & SPECIALTY FOODS

Kings Food Market (Grocery)
26 Arcadia Rd, Old Greenwich CT, 203.637.1701
www.KingsFoodMarkets.com
This popular store is a meeting place for neighbors. They offer a mix of traditional and upmarket grocery items, with an emphasis on local and organic products and good service. This store has a large deli section. In 2009 King's acquired Balducci's.
Hours: Monday-Saturday 7am-9pm, Sunday 7am-8pm.

Lobster Bin (Seafood)
204 Field Point Road, Greenwich CT, 203.661.6559
www.LobsterBin.com
Since 1975 we have loved their seafood and helpful advice. Daily, Jon Tung buys fresh fish from the Fulton Fish Market. We like their sushi. Every holiday we celebrate with their poached salmon. Many of our local restaurants get their seafood here. Located just off Railroad Avenue, with easy parking. You will recognize the shop by the lobster on top.
Hours: Monday-Saturday 8am-6pm, Sunday 10am-2pm.

Mt. Kisco Smokehouse (Seafood)
146 Mason Street, Greenwich, CT   www.mtkiscosmokehouse.com
This successful, family-owned Westchester enterprise, sells only smoked seafood. They smoke all their fish in Mt. Kisco and deliver it daily to Greenwich.
Hours: Monday-Saturday 9am-5.30pm, Sunday 9am-12.30pm.

Olivette (Olive Oil & Balsamic Vinegars)
1084 Post Road, Darien CT, 203.621.0643
www.OlivetteCT.com
This is the first store of this kind in Connecticut. There are over 200 stores in the US, mainly on the West Coast. We are wowed with the freshness of the 30 olive oils and the deliciousness of the 25 aged and flavored balsamic vinegars. This store is actually a tasting room. When you have made your selection, you fill the size bottle you wish. They have terrific gift packages. Hours: Monday-Saturday 11am-6pm.

Patel Brothers (Indian Food)
330 Connecticut Avenue, Norwalk CT, 203.939.1777
www.PatelBros.com
This 10,000 sf store is an amazing Indian grocery-wonderful spices, canned goods and fresh vegetables rarely seen in traditional US groceries. This family-owned store is one of 35 and we are certainly glad there is one near Greenwich. Open everyday 10am-8:30pm.

Penzey's Spices (Spices)
197 Westport Avenue, Norwalk CT, 203.849.9085
www.Penzeys.com
Oh, what a wonderful smell! Penzey's is a store devoted just to spices and herbs-over 250 choices. Fresh spices make all the difference. This store, one of over 60 in the US, is just past Stew Leonard's. Their large selection of spices, their blends and extracts -as well as pretty wooden boxed sets- make much-appreciated gifts.
Hours: Monday-Saturday 10am-6pm, Sunday 11am-5pm.

(The) Round Hill Store (Grocery)
Corner of Old Mill and Round Hill Road, Greenwich CT, 203.629.1083
This small country store, which opened in 1801, still provides milk, eggs and staples for the surrounding area. Try one of their delicious turkey sandwiches. Most of their customers are people who work in the backcountry or live nearby.
Hours: Weekdays 6am-6:30pm, Saturday 7am-5pm, Sunday 8am-4pm.

Scarpelli's Market (Sausage)
45 Bible Street, Cos Cob CT, 203.869.2771
Mac Scarpelli is still making the same wonderful sausage his parents, Maria and Peter, made when they opened the store in 1920. Mac makes amazingly delicious sausage (sweet, hot, extra hot). Stop in here and you will have one more reason why you love living in Greenwich. Many local restaurants pick-up their sausage here.
Open everyday 9am-1pm.

Stew Leonard's (Grocery)

100 Westport Avenue, Norwalk CT, 203.847.7214

www.StewLeonards.com

Famous throughout the metropolitan area and worth the trip. This huge food store has been called the Disneyland of grocery stores by the New York Times. Bring your children.

Hours: Everyday 7am-11pm (butcher closes at 8pm); Closed Dec 25

Stop & Shop (Grocery)

• Super Stop & Shop, 15 Waterfront Place, Port Chester NY, 914.937.7318
• 161 West Putnam Avenue, Greenwich CT, 203.625.0622
• 11 Glenville Road, Glenville CT, 203.531.0541

www.StopAndShop.com

With 380 stores, Stop & Shop is the largest New England food retailer. You can order food delivered by placing your order through www.PeaPod.com.

Hours: Greenwich everyday 7am-11pm (Sunday 10pm); Glenville everyday 7am-9pm.

Tarry Market (Italian Grocery and Deli)

179 North Main Street, Port Chester NY, 914.253.5680

www.TarryMarket.com

Started in 2010, this is a great place to get fresh Italian ingredients, such as: black fettuccini, sauces, breads, olive oils and cheese, even steaks from the Donley Farm. Whether you are cooking from scratch or wanting items ready to serve, you will find it here. They offer Italian culture and cooking classes for children and adults. Next door, Tarry Wine is a small shop featuring Italian wines.

Hours: Monday-Saturday 8am-8pm, Sunday 8am-6pm.

Size: Seats 24.

Trader Joe's (Grocery)

1041 High Ridge Road, Stamford CT, 203.321.8440

www.TraderJoes.com

Trader Joe fans will be glad to know there is a store not far from Greenwich. This 13,000 sf grocery sells healthy food at good prices. Private labeling helps keep their costs down. Try one of their soups or frozen dinners.

Open everyday 8am-9pm.

Village Prime Meats (Meat)
475 Main Street, Armonk NY, 914.273.5222
An old-fashioned butcher shop. It is worth the trip when you want something special. Where else can you get rabbit, game birds, Peking or Muscovy duck or just that special cut of meat you need? They also have a number of unique food products, such as white or black truffle oil and a large number of fresh pates.
Hours: Weekdays 8am-6pm, Saturday 8am-5:30pm.

Whole Foods (Grocery)
• 90 East Putnam Avenue, Greenwich CT, 203.661.0631
• 575 Boston Post Road (Kohl's Shop Cntr), Port Chester NY, 914.708.1985
www.WholeFoods.com
This organic grocery store has an abundance of fruit, vegetables and cheese, plus a first-class deli. When you shop here you are bound to meet your friends buying their Sunday bagels, fresh fish, vitamins (in the next door shop), and other staples. It is great to have an expert available in each food area to happily give you advice about selections. Their fresh sushi is prepared by Genji's sushi chefs. Large platters should be ordered 24-hours in advance. The 48,000 sf Port Chester store is considerably larger than the Greenwich store. It has a large prepared foods area and seats for 50. Open everyday except Dec 25 Greenwich 7am-10pm; Port Chester 8am-10pm.

GROOMING

Barbers
Benford Barber Shop at The Palm
Classic Barber
Generations Barber Parlor
Graham's Kids' Cuts of Greenwich
(The) Haircut Place
Kennedy's
Palm Barber Shop

Spas
Celia B. Skin Care
Empy's Day Spa
Noelle Spa for Beauty and Wellness
Serenity Spa
Spa at the Delamar Hotel

Hairdressers
Christopher Noland Salon &
  Beauty Spa
Coppola Tambascio Salon
Do's Blow Dry Bar
Enzo Ricco Bene Salon
Frederic Fekkai
GlamBlow
Greenwich Salon
Hopscotch
Noelle Spa for Beauty and Wellness
Panache Hair Salon
Partners Salon and Spa
Salon 221
Salon Moda Enzo
Warren Tricomi Salon

Nail Salons
Coco Nail Spa
Cozy Nail & Spa
Dream Nails
Empy's Day Spa
Hilltop Nails
Nail Boutique
Tiffany Nails
Tip Top Nails

Benford Barber Shop at The Palm
20 Church Street, Greenwich CT, 203.661.7383
This out-of-the way barber tucked in the back of the Palm Barber Shop is used by many of Greenwich's prominent residents. Haircuts are by appointment.
Hours: Wednesday-Saturday 8am-5pm. Prices: Haircut $21 and up

Celia B. Skin Care
http://www.celiabskincare.com/
181 Greenwich Avenue (2nd Floor) Greenwich CT, 203.861.6850
Celia offers a wonderful menu of facials. A very plesant experience.
Hours: By appointment. Prices: Women's Facial $130.

175

GROOMING

Christopher Noland Salon & Beauty Spa
124 Greenwich Avenue, 2nd floor, Greenwich CT, 203.622.4247
www.ChristopherNoland.com
Expert cutting, coloring and styling, massage therapy, facials, manicures, pedicures and waxing. Greenwich Magazine and Serendipity Magazine readers constantly vote this salon the Best. They make every client feel special.
Hours: Monday, Wednesday & Friday 8am-6pm, Tuesday & Thursday 8am-7pm. Prices: Women's cuts $110 and up, Men's cuts $75 and up, Child's cuts $55 and up.

Classic Barber
396 Greenwich Avenue (upstairs), Greenwich CT, 203.869.3600
www.classicbarbergreenwich.com
The Merollas have relocated from the longtime Subway barbershop to start their own shop. A modern atmosphere with flat-screen TVs and an airplane chair for children.
Hours: Monday-Saturday 8am-5pm (Thursday to 6pm) & by appointment. Prices: Haircut $29.

Coco Nail Spa
1263 East Putnam Avenue, Riverside CT, 203.698.2220 www.cocospa.com
They offer everything from manicures/pedicures, waxing to Spa packages that range from $125-$500.
Hours: Monday-Saturday 9:30am-7pm, Sunday 10am-6pm.
Prices: Manicure $12; Pedicure $25.

Coppola Tambascio Salon
20 North Water Street, Byram CT, 203.531.0766
www.coppolatambasciosalon.com
Charming salon with friendly, welcoming, accommodating professionals. Thanks, Bobby, for your great hair cuts!
Hours: Tuesday-Friday 10am-6pm. Saturday 9am-5pm.
Prices: Women's cuts $55 to $70, Men's cuts $20 to $40, Children's cuts $15 to $30.

Cozy Nail & Spa
103 Greenwich Avenue (behind CVS), Greenwich CT, 203.622.3023
A local favorite. The services are reasonable and they give the best back rubs. Hours: Monday-Saturday 9:30am-7:30pm. Prices: Manicure $10, Pedicure $25.

GROOMING

Do's Blow Dry Bar
25 Lewis Street, Greenwich CT, 203.489.3200
www.doshair.com
Wash, blow, style is all they do. Quick and convenient. In July 2014, Christopher Noland bought the company.
Hours: Monday & Wednesday 9am-7pm, Tuesday, Thursday & Friday 9am-8pm, Sunday 9:30-5pm. Prices: Shampoo and Blow Dry $40

Dream Nails
280 Railroad Avenue, Greenwich CT, 203.629.6888 / 6398
Reasonably priced nail salon.
Hours: Weekdays 9:30am-7:30pm, Saturday 9:30am-7pm, Sunday 10am-6 pm. Prices: Manicure $9; Pedicure $23.

Empy's Day Spa
143 West Putnam Avenue (Stop & Shop Plaza), Greenwich CT, 203.661.6625
Haircuts, facials, waxing, manicures and pedicures by a friendly staff in a low key atmosphere.
Hours: Weekdays 9am-6pm Saturday 8:30am- 4:30pm. By appointment or walk-in.
Prices: Women's cut $45 and up, Facials $125 and up, Manicure $18, Pedicure $38.

Enzo Ricco Bene Salon
1800 East Putnam Avenue (at the Hyatt), Old Greenwich CT, 203.698.4141
This attractive salon located off the lobby of the Hyatt Regency Hotel offers a pleasant and talented staff of colorists and stylists. For the easiest access use the free valet parking.
Hours: Monday 9am-5pm, Tuesday, Wednesday & Friday 8am-6pm, Thursday 8am-8pm, Saturday 8am-4:30pm.
Prices: Women's cut $90-$125; Facials $100 and up.

Frederic Fekkai
2 Lewis Court, Greenwich CT, 203.861.6700
www.Fekkai.com
Highly trained stylists offering "luxury, pampering services."
Hours: Monday, Tuesday, Wednesday & Saturday 8:00 am -6 pm, Thursday & Friday 8am -7pm. Prices: Women's cut from $135-$250.

GROOMING

Generations Barber Parlor
3 Boulder Avenue, Old Greenwich CT, 203.637.8266
www.GenerationsParlor.com
The name says generations and clearly the High School generation is finding this a favorite spot. They are open 7-days a week, setting them apart from traditional barber hours.
Hours: Monday 10:30am-8pm, Tuesday-Friday 8am-8pm, Saturday 8am-5pm, Sunday 9am-3pm.
Prices: Men's cut $27, Boy's cut $27, Women's cut $70, Girl's cut $40.

GlamBlow
18 Lewis Street, Greenwich CT, 203.622.0018
www.glam-blow.com
Convenient stop for a shampoo and blow dry.
Hours: Monday, Wednesday, Thursday & Saturday 9am-6pm, Tuesday & Friday 9am-7pm, Sunday 10am-4pm.
Prices: Blow dry $38.

Graham's Kids' Cuts of Greenwich
60 Greenwich Avenue, Greenwich CT, 203.983.6800
Unique children's hair salon in the back of a toy store. Appointments for haircuts are recommended.
Hours: Tuesday- Saturday 10am-5pm. Prices: Haircut $36.

Greenwich Salon
144 Mason Street, Greenwich CT, 203.661.4093
Popular full service salon-styling, cuts, manicures, pedicures, and waxing.
Hours: Monday- Saturday 8:30am-5pm, Thursday until 7pm.
Prices: Women's cut $55 and up, Men's cut $40 and up, children under 13 $40 and up. Manicure $20, Pedicure $54 for one hour, Bikini waxing $38, Brazilian waxing $45.

(The) Hair Cut Place
259 Sound Beach Avenue, Old Greenwich CT, 203.637.1313
An Old Greenwich institution formerly called Off Center Barber Shop. Kids love haircuts in the plane or police car. Appointments are available, walk-ins welcomed.
Hours: Monday-Saturday 8am-5pm, (Wednesday and Friday until 7pm).
Prices: Haircut for Men & Children $25, Women's cut $30 and up.

Hilltop Nails
235 Glenville Road, Glenville CT, 203.532.8000
Several of our associates treat themselves to the services here, including the manicure/pedicure combination package. Walk-ins are accepted.
Hours: Monday-Saturday 9:30am-7pm, Sunday 10am-6pm.
Prices: Manicure $12 and up, Pedicure $27 and up.

Hopscotch
10 Railroad Ave, Greenwich CT, 203.661.0107
www.HopscotchSalon.com
A cutting-edge high-tech salon with very nice owners catering to a fashionable clientele. People come from New York City to go here. Frequent winner of Greenwich Magazine's "Best Women's Salon."
Hours: Weekdays 8:30am-6pm (Tuesday & Thursday until 8pm), Saturday 8:30am-5:30pm, Sunday 10am-4pm.
Prices: Women's cut $65 and up; Men's cut $45 and up; Child's cut $45 and up. Facials $85-and up.

Kennedy's
116 East Putnam Avenue, Greenwich CT, 203.769.5729
http://www.kennedysbarberclub.com/
They encourage membership in their "Club" which offers perks, various special services and monthly billing.
Hours: Tuesday-Thursday 10am-7pm, Friday & Saturday 9am-6pm, Sunday 10am-4pm. Prices: Men's cut $65, Boy's cut $35.

Nail Boutique
522 East Putnam Avenue, Greenwich CT, 203.422.5512
Centrally located salon near I-95 exit 4, next to the Pizza Post. This salon is staffed by friendly, capable women.
Hours: Monday-Saturday 9:30am-7pm. Prices: Manicure $9; Pedicure $20.

Noelle Spa for Beauty and Wellness
1100 High Ridge Road, Stamford CT, 203.322.3445 www.Noelle.com
Complete day spa with talented hair colorists and stylists. They have a great variety of services from make-up, bridal, hand & foot, massages, body treatment, esthetic, teeth whitening, healing therapies & yoga. Spa for men.
Hours: Tuesday, Thursday & Friday 8am-8:30pm, Wednesday 9:15am-8:30pm. Saturday 8am-6pm, Sunday 10am-3pm.
Prices: Women's cut $55 and up, Men's cut $45 and up, Women's Facials $100-$120.

GROOMING

Palm Barber Shop
20 Church Street, Greenwich CT, 203.869.0292
Tony gives good cuts for youth and adults.
Hours: Monday-Saturday 7:30am-6pm. Prices: Haircut $20.

Panache Hair Salon
182 Sound Beach Avenue, Old Greenwich CT, 203.637.2777
Since 1985, this recently redecorated salon is a favorite "in spot" for mothers and daughters-and fathers too. Owner Dora Faugno has a staff of talented hairdressers who work magic with every client-cutting, styling and coloring and simply making everyone feel and look beautiful. Thank you, Alison, for your great haircuts!!
Hours: Tuesday-Saturday 9am-5pm. Later hours on Thursday.
Prices: Women's cut $80, Men's cut $45, Child's cut $25 and up.

Partners Salon and Spa
1200 East Putnam Avenue, Riverside CT, 203.637.0478
Full salon and spa services with excellent staff. Valet Parking.
Hours: Tuesday & Thursday 9am-7pm, Wednesday & Friday 9am-5pm, Saturday 8am-5pm.
Prices: Women's cut $95 and up, Men's cut $70 and up, Child's cut $50, Women's Facial $95 and up.

Salon 221
221 East Putnam Avenue (2nd floor Mill Pond Shop Cntr), Cos Cob CT, 203.661.8838
Full service salon with custom hair color and precision cuts. Lynn, a client for a decade, would follow Joe anywhere.
Hours: Tuesday & Wednesday 9:30am-5pm, Thursday & Friday 9:30am-7pm, Saturday 9am-5pm.
Prices: Women's cut $85, Men's cut $50, Child's cut (under 10 years) $35.

Salon Moda Enzo
522 East Putnam Avenue, Greenwich CT, 203.552.0680
This relaxed full-service hair salon is conveniently located next to the Pizza Post.
Hours: Tuesday-Friday 9am-5pm, Saturday 8am-4pm.
Prices: Women's cut $65 and up, Men and Boy's cut $35, Girl's cut $45.

GROOMING

Serenity Spa
49 Greenwich Avenue, Greenwich CT, 203.629.9000
www.SerenitySpaNow.com
Experience the essential indulgence of nurturing skin care services and all natural facial products in a serene environment.
Hours: Monday 9am-5pm, Tuesday & Thursday 9am-7pm, Wednesday & Friday 9am-6pm, Saturday 9am-5pm.
Prices: Women's Facials $100 and up.

Spa at the Delamar Hotel
500 Steamboat Road, Greenwich CT, 203.413.3520
www.spaatdelamar.com
Located on the second floor of the hotel, this luxury day spa offers an extensive selection of massages, facials and body treatments.
Hours: Daily 9:30am-6:30pm
Prices: Massage $65 and up, Facials $95 and up.

Tiffany Nails
349 Greenwich Avenue, Greenwich CT, 203.661.3838
Walk-ins only.
Hours: Monday Saturday 9:30am-7pm, Sunday 10am-5:30pm.
Price: Manicure $12, Pedicure $27.

Tip Top Nails
1 Havemeyer Lane, Old Greenwich CT, 203.698.3320
By appointment or walk in.
Hours: Monday-Saturday 9:30am-7pm, Sunday 10am-5:30pm.
Price: Manicure $10, Pedicure $25.

Warren Tricomi Salon
1 East Putnam Avenue, Greenwich CT, 203.863.9300
www.WarrenTricomi.com
Popular, NYC-style salon-but friendlier. Excellent talent, particularly the colorists. Tamara is one of the best, and perhaps most expensive, make-up artists and eyebrow shapers in the area. Great stop for bridal parties. Free parking.
Hours: Monday 8am-5pm, Tuesday, Wednesday & Saturday 8am-6pm, Thursday & Friday 8pm-7pm.
Prices: Women's cut $121-$351, Child's cut $83, Men's cut $83.

HEALTH

HEALTH INDEX
See FITNESS for Yoga, Pilates, Personal Trainers and Exercise Classes.
See SENIORS for Senior Housing and Home Care.
See STORES for Glasses and Contact Lens.

Addiction Recovery Programs
Greenwich Al-Anon, 888.825.2666
Greenwich Alcoholics Anonymous, 203.869.5221
Greenwich Hospital Addiction Recovery Program, 203.863.4673
Silver Hill Hospital, 203.966.3561

Domestic Abuse
211 Infoline
YWCA Domestic Abuse Service, 203.869.6501 ext 175
YWCA 24-Hour Domestic Abuse Hotline: 203.622.0003

Drugstores (Pharmacies)
CVS Pharmacies (including their 24-Hr pharmacies)
CVS Minute Clinic
Finch Pharmacy
Greenwich Pharmacy
Grannick's Pharmacy
North Street Pharmacy
Walgreens 24-Hr Pharmacy

Emergencies
Dial 911
Access Ambulance
CVS Minute Clinic (walk-in-clinic)
Doctors Express Urgent Care (walk-in-clinic)
Fire Fly (after hours Pediatrics)
Greenwich Convenient Medical Center (walk-in-clinic)
Greenwich Emergency Medical Service (GEMS)
Greenwich Hospital Emergency Room

Exercise Equipment
Gym Source
Relax the Back

Glasses and Contact Lens
See STORES

Understanding Eye Doctor Designations

• Optometrists are considered the general practitioners of eye healthcare. They can prescribe eyeglasses and contact lenses to correct nearsightedness, farsightedness and astigmatism. This doctor also identifies various eye conditions, such as retinal diseases, glaucoma and cataracts, and treats these disorders with non-surgical methods. Upon completion of optometry school, candidates graduate from an accredited college of optometry and hold the Doctor of Optometry (O.D.) degree.

• Ophthalmologists are medical doctors (M.D.) or Doctors of Osteopathic Medicine (D.O.). who have completed a college degree, medical school, and an additional four years of post-graduate training in ophthalmology.

Health Information

211 Infoline
Castle Connolly Top Doctors
Greenwich Hospital Consumer Health Reference Center
Greenwich Library Health Information Center
Greenwich Hospital Health Extensions
Physician Referral Service
Planned Parenthood
Tick Testing Laboratory

Health and Wellness Organizations

American Red Cross
Breast Cancer Alliance
Greenwich Hospital Auxiliary

Hearing Aids

Solomon-Shotland Audiology

Hospitals and Clinics

Advanced Radiology Consultants (mammogram walk-in clinic)
Burke Rehabilitation Hospital
Doctor's Express Urgent Care (walk-in-clinic)
Greenwich Convenient Medical Center (walk-in clinic)
Greenwich Hospital
Physician Referral Service
Silver Hill Hospital
Westchester Medical Center
Yale New Haven Hospital

HEALTH

Medical Supplies and Equipment
Grannick's Pharmacy
Liberty Rehab and Patient Aid Center
Relax the Back

Physical Therapy and Chiropractors
Buirsky's Integrated Therapies (Chiropractor)
Burke Rehabilitation Hospital
Elite Health Services (EHS)
Greenwich Physical Therapy
Greenwich Rolfing (Chiropractor)
Greenwich Sports Medicine (Chiropractor)
New England Physical Care (Chiropractor)
ONS Physical Therapy
Peak Wellness
Performance Physical Therapy
Sam Schwartz (Chiropractor)
Snowball Integrated Medical Center (Pain Management)
Tully Health Center (Physical Therapy)

Senior Housing
See SENIORS for Senior Housing and Home Care.

Shoe Orthotics
Stride Custom Orthotics

Vitamins
GNC
Vitamin Shoppe
Whole Body

HEALTH RESOURCES

211 Infoline
Dial 211 or 800.505.2000 or www.infoline.org
United Way's free, confidential, 24-hour a day information on a variety of subjects such as pre-natal care, legal assistance, AIDS testing, crisis intervention and emergency assistance. Assistance is provided by trained call specialists.

Access Ambulance (Medical Transportation for Non-Emergencies)
64 Magee Avenue, Stamford CT, 203.637.2351
www.NelsonAmbulance.com, www.CTAmbulance.com
Private, for-profit, emergency and non-emergency ambulance service owned by Nelson Ambulance Service. They provide transportation between patients' homes and medical facilities such as hospitals, nursing homes, and cancer centers. Check with them about your insurance coverage.

Advanced Radiology Consultants
1325 Washington Boulevard, Stamford CT, 203.356.9729
www.adrad.com
They will schedule appointments, but also accept walk-in mammograms. Hours: Weekdays 8:30am-5pm.

American Red Cross
Greenwich Chapter, 99 Indian Field Road, Greenwich CT, 203.869.8444
www.redcross.org/ct/greenwich
The Greenwich Red Cross is now part of the Metro New York North Chapter.

Dr. Birsky's Integrated Therapies (Chiropractor, Kinesiologist)
528 Post Road, Darien CT, 203.655.8828
A Titleist Golf Fitness Pro, Dr. Bursky uses an eclectic mix of healing techniques for sports rehabilitation. He is strongly recommended by friends for injuries such as tennis elbow or golf elbow.

Breast Cancer Alliance
48 Maple Avenue, Greenwich CT, 203.861.0014
www.breastcanceralliance.org
Go For Pink!

HEALTH RESOURCES

Burke Rehabilitation Hospital (Hospital)
785 Mamaroneck Avenue, White Plains NY, 914.597.2500
www.burke.org
A nearby 60-acre private, not-for-profit, facility specializing in inpatient
and outpatient multi-disciplinary physical rehabilitation and research.
They have a national reputation for their programs tailored to lessen
disability and dependence resulting from disease or injury.

Castle Connolly Top Doctors
42 West 24th Street, New York NY, 212.367.8400
www.castleconnolly.com
The source of information used by Greenwich and Connecticut Magazines' survey of Top Doctors.

CVS (Pharmacy)
www.cvs.com
• 122 East Putnam Road, Cos Cob CT, 203.422.2129.
  Drive-Thru pharmacy.
  Pharmacy Hours: Weekdays 8am-8pm, Saturday & Sunday 8am-6pm.
• 225 Sound Beach Avenue, Old Greenwich CT, 203.698.1457
  Pharmacy 203.698.1457. Pharmacy Hours: Weekdays 8am-9pm,
  Saturday & Sunday 8am-6pm.
• 1239 East Putnam Ave (Thru Way Shopping Center), Riverside CT,
  203.698.4006. 24-Hour Pharmacy
• 644 West Putnam Avenue, Greenwich CT, 203.422.2022.
  24-Hour Pharmacy and Drive-Thru Pharmacy.

CVS Minute Clinic (Walk-in-Clinic)
1239 East Putnam Avenue, Riverside CT, 866.389.2727
www.MinuteClinic.com
Nurse Practitioners and Physician Assistants give flu shots, vaccinations,
treat minor wounds, as well as writing prescriptions for common family
illnesses. They also do routine lab tests for diabetes, cholesterol and high
blood pressure.
Clinic hours: Tuesday-Friday 8:30am-7:30pm, Saturday 9am-5:30pm,
Sunday 10am-5:30pm. (Note: they are required to take a one hour lunch
break.)

Doctors Express Urgent Care (Walk-in-Clinic)
3000 Summer Street (Corner of Long and High Ridge), Stamford CT, 203.969.2000
www.DoctorsExpressStamford.com
No appointment is necessary. This is a walk-in-clinic with board-certified doctors. They do physicals, flu shots, immunizations and are prepared to help with just about anything except life-threatening illnesses or injuries. They accept most insurance. They were named 2014 Business of the Year.
Hours: Weekdays 8am-8pm, Saturday & Sunday 8am-5pm. Open most holidays.

EHS-Elite Health Services
(Physical Therapy & Personal Training)
1445 East Putnam Avenue (2nd floor) Old Greenwich CT, 203.983.5748
www.EliteHealthServices.com
A group of highly- trained physical therapists and trainers. Besides doing functional manual therapy, they do personal, Triathlon, Golf and other sport performance training. Tara Gibson, DPT, is enthusiastically determined to put me back on the ski slopes!
Hours: Monday-Thursday 7am-7pm, Friday 7am-5pm, Saturday 9am-1pm

Finch Pharmacy (Pharmacy)
3 Riversville Road, Glenville CT, 203.531.8494
www.finchpharmacy.com
Friendly pharmacy in the heart of Glenville, where people know you and care about your needs.
Hours: Weekdays 8am-6pm, Saturday, 9am-6pm.

Fire Fly (After Hours Pediatrics Urgent Care)
1011 High Ridge Road, Stamford CT, 203.968.1900
www.FireFlyPediatrics.com
Board certified pediatricians will help you with no appointment necessary. The visit records will be sent to your pediatrician. Most medical coverage is accepted.
Hours: Open 365 days a year, Weekdays 4pm-11pm, Saturday & Sunday & Holidays. Call before you go.

GNC (General Nutrition Centers)

1237 East Putnam Avenue (Riverside Commons), Riverside CT, 203.637.4262 www.gnc.com
They typically stock a wide range of weight loss, bodybuilding and nutritional supplements as well as health and fitness books, magazines, vitamins, natural remedies, and health and beauty products. GNC has over 6,000 stores in the US and is the largest US retailer of nutritional supplements.
Hours: Weekdays 10am-8pm, Saturday 10am-7pm, Sunday 10am-6pm.

Grannick's Pharmacy (Pharmacy)

277 Greenwich Avenue, Greenwich CT, 203.869.3492
www.grannickspharmacy.com
A family business that has been helping their customers since 1942. Like the chain stores you can call in your prescription for refill. Unlike the chain stores they deliver. They sell and rent some medical equipment.
Pharmacy Hours: Monday-Saturday 9am-6pm.

Greenwich Convenient Medical Center (Walk-In-Clinic)

1200 East Putnam Avenue, Riverside CT, 203.698.1419
www.greenwichconvenientmedicalcarecenter.com
Walk-in clinic run by Dr. Robert Gabriel; no appointment is required. Quick and efficient service for immunizations, minor injuries and routine illnesses. Payment required at the time of service. No insurance is accepted.
Hours: Weekdays 8am-6pm, Saturday 9am-5pm, Sunday 10am-4pm.

Greenwich Emergency Medical Service (GEMS)

111 East Putnam Avenue, Greenwich CT, Call: 911 or 203.637.7505 (general information)
www.GreenwichEMS.org
GEMS is a non-profit, town-supported Emergency Service. GEMS also provides programs in CPR and basic first aid. GEMS ambulances have the latest equipment and well-trained Emergency Medical Technicians and paramedics. Once you call 911, their computer-aided dispatch system allows them to reach 75% of patients within 5 minutes and 95% with 8 minutes. Greenwich is lucky to have such a coordinated ambulance organization. Hours: 24-hours a day, 7 days a week.

HEALTH RESOURCES

Greenwich Hospital
5 Perryridge Road, Greenwich CT, 203.863.3000
Greenwich Hospital Emergency Room: 203.863.3637
www.greenhosp.org
Greenwich Hospital is a 160-bed, non-profit, community teaching hospital, affiliated with Yale-New Haven Hospital. Since 1996, the Hospital has been completely rebuilt and it is a model for health care. The cost of the entire project (including the Helmsley Building and the Watson Pavilion) was $220,000,000, of which $138,000,000 came from private community donations. The rooms have been carefully designed to make the patient feel comfortable. As a result, many feel it's more like staying at a fine hotel than a hospital. Even the intensive care unit has woodland views and amazing amenities. Word is spreading fast that this is the most comfortable place to have your baby. Greenwich Hospital is ranked first in Connecticut in patient satisfaction and was named in the "Top 100 Most Wired Hospitals."

Greenwich Hospital Auxiliary
Greenwich Hospital, 5 Perryridge Road, Greenwich CT
Auxiliary office: 203.863.3220, Volunteer Office: 203.863.3222

Greenwich Hospital Consumer Health Reference Center
5 Perryridge Road, Greenwich CT, 203.863.3285
Public Hours: Weekdays 9am-4pm.

Greenwich Library Health Information Center
Greenwich Library, 101 West Putnam Avenue, Greenwich CT, 203.622.7900
www.GreenwichLibrary.org
Everyone in Greenwich can be a well-informed healthcare consumer. Greenwich Library has an extensive health information center with 18 subscription databases. Most databases are available through the library's website by entering your library card number. In addition the Center has over 100 authoritative reference materials, 40 journals, 5,000 circulating books, more than 300 videos and a large collection of audio books. A specially trained librarian is on duty to assist with healthcare research. The library also has speakers on current health topics. If you give them your email address, they will keep you posted.

HEALTH RESOURCES

Greenwich Hospital Health Extensions (Health Information)
Community Wellness Programs @ Greenwich Hospital
www.greenhosp.org
The Greenwich Hospital publishes an extensive schedule and description of the community's many wellness programs. The extent of the programs is amazing. Call Public Relations, 203.863.3126, to get a program bulletin or a subscription to their Health Extensions newsletter.

Greenwich Pharmacy
116 Greenwich Avenue, Greenwich CT, 203.661.2721
www.GreenwichRX.com
A local, independent, family pharmacy. They compete with big chains by offering lots of helpful personal service. Phone in your prescription and they will deliver it to your door. Why be just a number when you can deal with someone who knows and cares about you?
Hours: Open every day 9am-7pm.

Greenwich Physical Therapy Center (Physical Therapy)
1171 East Putnam Avenue, Riverside CT, 203.637.1700
www.GreenwichPhysicalTherapy.com
An independent (non-physician owned) physical therapy center specializing in orthopedic and sports-related injuries. Everyone raves about Scott Gelbs and his team.
Hours: Monday, Wednesday, Friday, 8am-4pm,
Tuesday & Thursday 9am-7pm.

TIP: LYME DISEASE
Ticks, unfortunately, also live in Greenwich—even some carrying Lyme Disease. If you remove a tick you might want to take it "Dead or Alive" to the Department of Health in Town Hall. They will test it for the Lyme Disease bacteria. For information on Lyme disease, call the Greenwich Lyme Disease Task Force at 203.969.1333 or visit www.cdc.gov/lyme

Greenwich Rolfing (Chiropractor)
296 Sound Beach Avenue, Old Greenwich CT, 203.698.2965
www.GreenwichRolfing.com
www.greenwichrolfing.com/craigswanonrolfingvideo.html
Rolfing is the commonly used name for the system of Structural Integration soft tissue manipulation (originally called Postural Release) developed by Dr. Ida Rolf. Rolfing is a system of soft tissue manipulation that makes clients stand straighter, gain height, and move better. Mark Swan is very helpful.
Hours: Weekdays 7am to 8pm, Saturday & Sunday 7am to 5pm.

Greenwich Sports Medicine (Chiropractor)
7 Riversville Road, 3rd floor, Greenwich CT, 203.531.3131
www.GreenwichSportsMedicine.com
www.FitAndFunctional.com
Dr. Gil Chimes is a sports chiropractor who specializes in Active Release Techniques (ART) to help athletes recover from injuries. ART breaks up scar tissue, eliminates pain and increases range of motion. Their treatments can incorporate acupuncture, chiropractic, exercise therapy, weight loss and nutritional counseling.
Hours: Monday & Wednesday, 8am-7pm, Tuesday & Thursday 8am-1:15pm, Friday 8am-5:45 pm, Saturday 9am-12pm.

Gym Source (Exercise Equipment)
20 Railroad Avenue, Greenwich CT, 203.622.5069
www.GymSource.com
With 31 stores, they are the largest US distributor of fitness equipment. They seem to carry everything from sophisticated equipment to TheraBands.
Hours: Monday-Saturday 10am-6pm (Thursday until 8pm), Sunday 11am-5pm.

Liberty Rehab and Patient Aid Center (Home Medical Equipment)
65 Stillwater Avenue, Stamford CT, 203.327.5250
www.libertyrehab.net
This nearby medical equipment shop has items to rent as well as buy. You will appreciate their prices.
Hours: Weekdays 8:30am-5pm.

HEALTH RESOURCES

North Street Pharmacy (Pharmacy)
1061 North Street, Banksville CT, 203.869.2130
www.northstreetpharmacy.com
In a world where change is the norm, it is wonderful to be greeted by
Paul Fiscella and his wife who have run this neighborhood pharmacy for
over 20 years.
Pharmacy Hours: Weekdays 9am-6pm, Saturday 10am-5pm.

New England Physical Care (Chiropractor)
161 East Avenue, Suite 102, Norwalk CT, 203.313.3844
www.Nephysical.com
The pros at the Field Club swear by Dr. Brian Nathanson's Graston and
Fascial Manipulation therapy.
Hours: By appointment.

ONS Physical Therapy & Sports Rehabilitation (Physical Therapy)
6 Greenwich Office Park, Greenwich CT, 203.869.3470
www.ONSPhysicalTherapy.com
Owned and supervised by ONS (the Orthopaedic & Neurological Surgery
Specialists). The therapists are positive, encouraging and friendly.
Hours: Weekdays 6:30am-7:30pm, Saturday 7am-12pm.

Peak Wellness (Physical Therapy, Weight Loss, Sports Medicine)
195 Field Point Road, Greenwich CT, 203.625.9608
www.PeakWellness.com
They have a second location in Beverly Hills, CA. They provide a combination of traditional and alternative approaches to medical care. Their
services include dietary guidance, including weight loss, sports medicine
& physical therapy. They offer private, VIP medical services.
Hours: Weekdays 9am-5pm.

Performance (Physical Therapy, Hand Therapy, Fitness)
35 River Road, Cos Cob CT, 203.422.0679
www.CtPerformancePT.com
Todd Wilkowski has been the rehabilitation consultant for the New York
Rangers. His specialty is working with adolescent sports injuries.
Hours: Weekdays 6am-8pm, Saturday 8am-2pm.

HEALTH RESOURCES

Physician Referral Service (Health Information)
Greenwich CT, 203.863.3627
Sponsored by Greenwich Hospital, this service is available 24 / 7. They will find the doctor with the qualifications you are looking for and will even make your first appointment.

Planned Parenthood
1039 East Main Street, Stamford CT, 203.327.2722
www.PlannedParenthood.org

Relax the Back (Health, Furniture)
367 Greenwich Avenue, Greenwich CT, 203.629.2225
www.relaxtheback.com
For people seeking relief and prevention of back and neck pain, they offer attractive posture and back support products and self-care solutions. Many products are exclusive to the store. Started in 1984 by an osteopath, there are now 121 stores.
Hours: Monday-Saturday 10am-6pm, Sunday 12pm-4:30pm.

Dr. Sam Schwartz (Chiropractor)
492 Northridge, Rye Brook NY, 914.939.0558
www.drsamuelschwartz.com
Dr. Sam has boundless energy and great comprehension of each individual's needs. In addition to his years in Chiropractic, he has a 14 year background as a Registered Respiratory Therapist. He spends every minute of each visit personally with each patient.
Hours: Weekdays 8am-6pm, Saturday 8am-12pm.

Silver Hill Hospital (Substance Abuse)
208 Valley Road, New Canaan, CT 866.542.4455, 203.966.3561
www.silverhillhospital.org
A private, not-for-profit, full-service psychiatric and substance abuse hospital, providing inpatient, outpatient, partial hospital programs and transitional care. Their DBT program provides treatment for people with a history of impulsive behaviors, including suicide attempts. Anonymity is important. Many celebrities have quietly restored their health here.

Snowball Integrated Medical Center (Pain Management)
2015 West Main Street, Suite 100, Stamford CT, 203.863.4588
www.SnowballMD.com
Dr. Halina Snowball applies non-surgical traditional and non-traditional approaches (such as Acupuncture, EPAT & PRP) to treat the cause of pain. She has two sports massage therapists and physical trainers.

Solomon-Shotland Audiology (Hearing Aids)
Julie O'Shea, Au.D, FAAA
Debra Skorney, MS, FAA, Patricia Martucci, MS, FAA
at the Burke Rehabilitation Hospital
785 Mamaroneck Avenue, White Plains NY, 914.949.0034, 914.290.6635
www.hearing-care.org
If you or someone you know is having some difficulty with their hearing, head straight to this audiologist. They are very competent and caring. They provide comprehensive diagnostic hearing testing for all ages. They work with the latest technologies from a number of the best hearing aid companies, including Lyric's invisible, non-surgical hearing aid.
Office Hours: Monday-Thursday 8:30am-5pm, Friday 8:30am-3pm.

Stride Custom Orthotics (Orthotics)
80 Turnpike Drive, Middlebury CT 203.758.8307, 800.787.7879
www.StrideOrthotics.com
Their only business is orthotics. You can make an appointment at the factory (Middlebury is about 1 hr.) or arrange a local fitting with one of their certified representatives.

Tick Testing Laboratory
Greenwich Department of Health @ Town Hall
101 Field Point Rd, Greenwich CT, 203.622.7843
www.GreenwichCT.org
Place the tick, dead or alive, in a small plastic bag and bring to the lab in Town Hall. They will test it for lyme disease bacteria.
Laboratory Hours: Weekdays 8am-3pm.

Tully Health Center and Fitness Institute (Physical Therapy)
32 Strawberry Hill Court, Stamford CT, 203.355.4567
www.TheHealthAndFitnessInstitute.com
A modern 250,000 sf healing facility for those who have suffered from illness or injury. The Tully Center is part of the Stamford Health System. They offer, among many other programs, a number of sophisticated massage therapies and water therapies.

(The) Vitamin Shoppe (Vitamins)
- 535 Post Road, Port Chester, NY, 914.939.5189
- 1003 High Ridge Road, Stamford CT, 203.609.0147
www.vitaminshoppe.com
A 500 store national chain with a good website and a large selection of products (over 20,000 different vitamins & supplements).
Hours: Monday-Saturday 9am-9pm, Sunday 11am-6pm.

Walgreen's (Pharmacy)
1333 East Putnam Avenue, Old Greenwich CT, 203.637.1496
www.walgreens.com
In addition to normal drugstore items, they carry a large variety of general grocery foods, staples and snacks. Walk-in clinic for flu shots.
Pharmacy Hours: Open 24-hours, every day.

Westchester Medical Center (Hospital)
100 Woods Road, Valhalla NY, 914.493.7000
www.wcmc.com
Connected with the New York Medical College, their Trauma Center and Children's Hospital are renowned.

Whole Body @ Whole Foods (Vitamins)
90 East Putnam Avenue (Whole Foods Shop Cntr), Greenwich CT, 203.661.0631
www.wholefoodsmarket.com/stores/greenwich
Products to promote health and wellness, such as: vitamins, herbal teas, cosmetics, hair care and homeopathic remedies.
Hours: Open daily 7am-10pm.

Yale-New Haven Hospital (Hospital)
20 York Street, New Haven CT, 203.688.2000
www.ynhh.org
This private, not-for-profit hospital, is the teaching hospital for Yale University School of Medicine. It is considered one of the premier hospitals in the area. Greenwich Hospital is affiliated with this hospital.

YWCA Domestic Abuse Service (Domestic Abuse)
259 East Putnam Avenue, Greenwich CT, 203.869.6501 ext 175
24-Hour Domestic Abuse Hotline: 203.622.0003
www.ywca.org
Free, professional and confidential crisis intervention for anyone experiencing violence in their life. They provide counseling & emergency shelter. When you call or see them, you can count on it being private.
Hours: Monday-Thursday 9am-5pm, Friday 9am-4pm & by appointment

TIP: TEDDY BEAR CLINIC
Once a year (usually in September or October), the Greenwich Hospital invites young children and their teddy bears to learn about surgery, ambulances and health check-ups. Each teddy bear is given its own ID bracelet. Call 203.863.3627.

Augustine's Farm (Fruit & Vegetables)

1332 King Street, Greenwich CT, 203.532.9611

For more than 50 years, our dear friends, Kathy and John Augustin have been providing Greenwich residents with fresh corn, tomatoes, apples, pumpkins, honey, eggs and cider. The Town of Greenwich proclaimed August 15th as Farmer John Day. Great fun to stop here, load up on fresh vegetables and know you are supporting Greenwich's last farm. This is the perfect place to buy your Christmas tree, holiday wreath and winter firewood.

Hours: Open every day, 9am-5pm during the growing season; during the winter, ring the greenhouse bell Weekdays 10am-2pm.

Bishop's Orchards (Pick-Your-Own)

1355 Boston Post Road (I-95, exit 57), Guilford CT, 203.458.7425, 203.453.2338 www.BishopsOrchards.com

They have many fruits to pick, including over twenty varieties of apples, nine kinds of blueberries, twelve of peaches, three of pears, eight of strawberries and two varieties of raspberries. This orchard is definitely worth a family trip.

Hours: From June through October, Monday-Saturday 8am-7pm, Sunday 9am-6pm. Their Winery and Bakery is open year round.

Blue Jay Orchards (Pick-Your-Own)

125 Plumtrees Road, Bethel CT, 203.748.0119

www.BlueJayOrchardsCT.com

Pick apples on this 140 acre farm to make your own pies or stop in their bakery for one of their 4 types of apple pie. The donuts, raw honey and cider are popular too.

Hours: Open 7 days a week from August to Thanksgiving 10am-5:30pm.

Connecticut Farm Fresh Express (Home Delivery)

24 Mt. Parnassus Road, East Haddam CT, 860.873.8760
 (cell:860.917.7627) www.CTfarmFreshStore.com

My neighbor discovered this outstanding source for fresh local produce. Deb Marsden started her service in 2008. She supplies produce from about 50 farms to towns in Fairfield County. No need to sign up for automatic deliveries. Simply choose on her website what you want delivered to your home. My neighbor loves the awesome carrots from the Tobacco Farm, all products from Two Guys from Woodbridge, and the Beltane goat yogurt (the fresh chevre is delicious too).

HOME DELIVERY & FARMS

Fresh Direct (Home Delivery)
23-30 Borden Avenue, Long Island City NY, 212.796.8002
www.FreshDirect.com
An online grocer with low prices, Fresh Direct provides next day delivery of fresh food (vegetables, meat, seafood, dairy) from local farms and fisheries. They also have over 600 choices of ready-to-heat meals.

Greenwich Farmer's Market
Horseneck Parking Lot (across from the Boys & Girls Club), Greenwich CT
From mid-May to late-October, farmers come to Greenwich, set up stands and sell their produce. It is usually picked the day it is sold and couldn't be fresher. At some of the stalls you can also find homemade items such as breads, jellies and cheese. To be sure of the opening and closing dates, contact the Greenwich Market Manager Judith Waldeyer, "the Jam Lady." 203-380-0580 or Jamlady@sbcglobal.net, www.Theherbbasketllc.net
Hours: Mid-May to Mid-October, Saturday 9:30am-1pm.

Jones Family Farm (Pick-your-own)
120 Beardsley Road, Shelton CT, 203.929.8425
www.JonesFamilyFarms.com
This pick-your-own farm began in the 1940s. They have strawberries in June, followed by blueberries in July and August, and pumpkins in the autumn. In December, you can cut your own Christmas tree. They even have hay rides in October.
Hours: Best to call, hours change seasonally. Closed Sunday & Monday. The Winery tasting room is open Friday-Saturday 11am-5pm.

Lyman Orchards (Pick-Your-Own)
32 Reeds Gap Road, Middlefield CT, 860.349.6015
www.LymanOrchards.com
All kinds of fun here-wagon rides around the grounds, picking fruit and even playing golf. Plus, the corn fields are turned into a maze, with 2-miles of pathways. The maze is changed every year. Visitors are warned, "hundreds of ways to get lost, but only one way out."
Hours: Open 7 days a week: Sept/Oct 9am-7pm; (Rest of year 9am-6pm).

HOME DELIVERY & FARMS

Marcus Dairy (Home Delivery)
Danbury, CT, 800.243.2511
www.MarcusDairy.com
Do you get milk delivered? Apparently 6,000 customers do. Isn't it wonderful that we can still have milk boxes and milk delivery! In addition they deliver products such as juice, eggs, yogurt, cottage cheese, sour cream, butter and ice cream. The minimum weekly order is $8.00; the minimum order period is two months.

Mike's Organic (Home Delivery)
203.832.3000
www.MikesOrganicDelivery.com
Mike Geller, a Greenwich native, started in 2010 to deliver organic and free range food (such as: raw honey, eggs, vegetables, chicken and pork) from about 15 farms. He serves Greenwich and neighboring towns. You can sign up on the website for the summer season of June-October with delivery of what's fresh every week or just order when you want it from the web site.
Hours: Weekdays 9am-5pm.

Old Greenwich Farmers Market
Presbyterian Church, 38 West End Avenue, Old Greenwich CT
www.oldgreenwichfarmersmarket.com
A non-profit venture with the Greenwich Department of Parks and Recreation. In the summer, they are located at the Old Greenwich Elementary School and in the Fall, at the Presbyterian Church in Old Greenwich.
Hours: The market runs Wednesday afternoons July through October, 4pm-7pm.

PeaPod (Home Delivery)
800-573-2763
www.Peapod.com
Peapod was founded in 1989. It delivers groceries from Stop & Shop. Browse the store aisles, pick what you want to buy (or review previous orders) and Peapod will deliver it.

HOME DELIVERY & FARMS

White Silo Farm (Winery & Pick-your-Own)
32 Route 37 East, Sherman CT, 860.355.0271
www.WhiteSiloWinery.com
This is a combination farm and winery. In the season you can pick your own strawberries, asparagus, raspberries, blackberries and rhubarb. Tour the old barn where the wine is made and have a taste. Call ahead if you would like to have a gourmet box lunch ready for you.
Hours: Winery, May-December, Friday-Sunday & Holidays 11am-6pm; Pick-Your-Own farm is in season September & October, every day 10am-6pm.

Websites about Organic Farms you might find interesting:
www.LocalHarvest.org
www.BuyCTgrown.com
www.WholesomeWave.org
www.CitySeed.org

HOTELS & INNS

For other Travel Information see TRAVEL.
For Connecticut Vacation Information see NUMBERS YOU SHOULD KNOW.

SECTIONS
Greenwich Area Hotels and Inns
Inns Worth a Trip

GREENWICH AREA HOTELS AND INNS

Delamar Greenwich Harbor

500 Steamboat Road, Greenwich CT, 203.661.9800, 866.335.2627
www.thedelamar.com
An 83-room Mediterranean-style luxury hotel with wonderful harbor views, just minutes from the Greenwich train station and Greenwich Avenue. Yachts can safely dock at their 600-foot private dock. This is a pet-friendly hotel. High-speed internet is available.
Rates: $259 to $1,700.

Doral Arrowwood

975 Anderson Hill Road, Rye Brook NY, 914.939.5500
www.doralarrowwood.com
Just on the border of Greenwich is a 373-room resort hotel, with golf, tennis, squash and swimming. A great place for a conference.
Rates: $149 -$229. Weekend packages with golf are $289 per night.

Homestead Inn

420 Field Point Road, Greenwich CT, 203.869.7500
www.homesteadinn.com
Exceptionally attractive country inn, with 22 lovely rooms/suites and superb food. See the restaurant review under Thomas Henkelmann in RESTAURANTS. Some rooms have wireless internet connections. A great choice.
Rates: $280-$495

Hyatt Regency

1800 East Putnam Avenue, Old Greenwich CT, 203.637.1234
www.greenwich.hyatt.com
This 374 room luxury hotel has an elegant interior with excellent food. Greenwich residents often check into this hotel for a weekend of pampering. The hotel also has a very nice health club and high speed internet access.
Rates: $149-$1,000

JHouse

1114 East Putnam Ave, Riverside CT, 203.698.6980
www.JhouseGreenwich.com
This is an 85-room high-tech luxury hotel. Techies love JHouse but if you are not comfortable with automatic toilets or using an iPad to adjust your room's bed, temperature and lighting, to close your blinds and order room service, this may not be the hotel for you. The JHouse is pet-friendly. It has a very active bar and a quality restaurant (See Eleven 14 Kitchen review in RESTAURANTS). Of course, Wi-Fi is fast and free. The pool is outside and open only during the summer.
Rates: standard rooms $179-$200, suites $299-$300, pets (100 lbs or less) $40.

Rye Town Hilton

699 Westchester Avenue, Rye Brook NY, 914.939.6300
www.hilton.com
Situated on 45 acres just next to Greenwich, this large hotel with a pleasant restaurant hosts many conventions. Pets allowed.
Rates: $149-$650

Sheraton Stamford Hotel

700 East Main Street, Stamford CT, 203.358.8400
www.HiStamford.com
Recently renovated for $20,000,000. This 380-room hotel has a health club, indoor lap pool and lots of meeting rooms.
Rates: $269-$309, suites $400.

Stanton House Inn

76 North Maple Avenue, Greenwich CT, 203.869.2110
http://www.stantonhouseinn.com/
Located in Central Greenwich, within walking distance of the shops and restaurants, this turn-of-the-century home, converted into a 24-room bed-and-breakfast with a swimming pool, is a welcoming first stop for many new residents. Internet access in some rooms. No restaurant, but a hot breakfast is served daily.
Rates: $169-$265

Stamford Suites
720 Bedford Street, Stamford CT, 203.359.7300, 866.394.4365
www.stamfordsuites.com
An extended-stay hotel with 45 furnished suites for nightly or longer term residence. Each unit contains a bedroom, living room, bathroom and a full-size kitchen. Complimentary Wifi internet access. Renovated in 1998.
Rates: Daily $125-$229, Seven-day rate: $149, 30-day rate: $119

INNS WORTH A TRIP

Bee and Thistle Inn (New London County)
100 Lyme Street, Old Lyme, CT, 860.434.1667
www.beeandthistleInn.com
About 1½ hours from Greenwich (close to the Clinton Crossing clothing outlets and Connecticut casinos) is one of the great old inns in Connecticut. Often written up as the most romantic. As an added plus, it has good, artfully simple American food. At a recent party, one of our guests arrived very late. The staff cheerfully allowed us to enjoy the evening with no hint of the inconvenience of the late hour.
Rates: $160-$320.
Directions: I-95N to exit 70 CT-156, L on Ferry, L on Lyme.

Copper Beech Inn (Middlesex County)
46 Main Street, Ivoryton, CT
www.copperbeechinn.com
860.767.0330, 888.809.2056
Gracious inn with 13 guest rooms and excellent food in a charming New England town, about 1½ hours from Greenwich. High on our list, this inn fits the perfect image of what a New England inn should be. The inn is best suited for adults unless the children have very nice manners.
Rates: $150- $375 per night. January through March, the dining room is closed Tuesday as well as Monday evenings.

Mayflower Inn & Spa (Litchfield County)
118 Woodbury Road, Route 47, Washington, CT 860.868.9466
www.mayflowerinn.com
Set on 58 acres of lovely grounds, this 30-room Inn is a perfect place to rest and refresh. Enjoy fine dining, walks in the garden, and antiquing in nearby shops and, of course, the spa. The Inn is about 1½ hours from Greenwich.
Rates: $400 to $1,800.

Mohonk Mountain House
1000 Mountain Rest Road, New Paltz NY, 844.236.0980
www.mohonk.com, www.mohonkfamilyreunions.com
Travel and Leisure magazine rated it as one of the top resorts in the world. They have activities for all age ranges. Many Greenwich families hold their reunions here.
Rates: Doubles range from $700 to $1,000, all meals and activities are included.

Woodstock Inn
14 The Green, Woodstock Vermont, 888.338.2745, 802.457.1100
www.woodstockinn.com
www.suicide6.com
www.woodstockvt.com
The Woodstock Inn is a lovely, historic Inn in a beautiful, charming town. The Inn, owned by the Rockefellers, has 142 guest rooms, a golf course, Suicide Six Ski Area, and a health spa. It has indoor and outdoor pools and tennis courts. You can't go wrong here whether you come in the winter or summer.
Rates: Doubles $250-$434, Suites $380-$664 suite. Off-season rates lower. Packages available. 2-night minimum.

ICE CREAM, FROZEN YOGURT & CHOCOLATE

(including Gelato, Sorbet & Candy)

Ada's Variety Shop (Candy)

112 Riverside Avenue (Corner of Chapel Lane & Riverside Ave), Riverside CT 203.637.0305

An old-fashioned candy store loved by children and their children. Family members vow to continue the tradition.

Baskin Robbins@ Dunkin Donuts (Ice Cream)

375 East Putnam Avenue, Cos Cob CT, 203.869.7454

www.BaskinRobbins.com

Started by Burt Baskin and Irv Robbins in 1953, it is the largest chain of ice cream stores with 5,800 locations. In 1967 Baskin Robbins (aka 31) was purchased by the parent of Dunkin Donuts. On Tuesdays, buy one Sundae and get one free.

Hours: Everyday 5am-11pm.

Size: seats 16.

Bridgewater Chocolates (Chocolates)

559 Federal Road, Brookfield CT, 203.775.2286

www.bridgewaterchocolate.com

Bridgewater won the chocolate truffle contest. Their factory store is only an hour away-a short drive for chocolate addicts. If you can wait for your chocolate fix, you can order online.

Hours: Weekdays 9am-6pm, Saturday 10am-4pm.

Carvel (Ice Cream)

604 North Main Street, Port Chester NY, 914.939.1487

www.Carvel.com

Located just on the border of Greenwich and Port Chester on US-1, this good standby for ice cream cakes and cones is open seven days a week. If you like hot fudge sundaes, the way we do, Wednesday is your day. You can get two for the price of one.

Hours: Sunday-Thursday, 10am-10pm; Friday & Saturday, 10am-11pm.

ICE CREAM, FROZEN YOGURT & CHOCOLATE

Chocopologie (Chocolate)
133 Washington Street, South Norwalk CT, 203.854.4754
www.knipschildt.net, www.facebook.com/ChocopologieNorwalk
If chocolate is your passion, as it is ours, the small Norwalk restaurant in the front of a Knipschildt's chocolate factory is a must. Not only can you watch chocolate treats being made, you can dine too. A fun place to eat or simply stop by for dessert or to bring home some luscious chocolates.

Cold Stone Creamery (Ice Cream)
1109 High Ridge Road (High Ridge Center), Stamford CT, 203.487.7400
www.ColdStoneCreamery.com
Who doesn't have fun while eating ice cream? This franchise has a formula for success: there are 1,400 franchises in the United States. You choose all your favorite sweet treats (from nuts to gummy bears) and they mix them in the ice cream.
Hours: Sunday-Thursday 12pm-10pm, Friday & Saturday 12pm-11pm.
Size: seats 14.

Darlene's Heavenly Desires (Ice Cream, Gelato, Chocolates)
185 Sound Beach Avenue, Old Greenwich CT, 203.698.9441
www.darlenesheavenlydesires.com
In summer, you will see happy people licking cones outside this shop filled with delicious Belgian chocolates, Bindi gelato, Coney Island custard and Weight Watchers ice cream. After eating a cone, you'll decide to take some home.
Hours: Monday-Saturday 10am-7:30pm, Sunday 11:30am-7:30pm. Their hours may change with the season.
Size: seats 9.

Deborah Ann's Homemade Chocolates (Chocolate)
381 Main Street, Ridgefield CT, 203.438.0065
www.DeborahAnns.com
About 45 minutes away, their truffles are a wonderful reason for visiting this pretty town. Of course, you can also order online.
Hours: Sunday-Thursday 10am-9pm, Friday & Saturday 10 am-10pm. Their hours seem to change frequently, check before going.

ICE CREAM, FROZEN YOGURT & CHOCOLATE

Godiva (Chocolate)
Town Center (100 Greyrock Place) Stamford CT, 203.357.8110.
www.godiva.com
Godiva, a Turkish-owned company, operates more than 450 shops world-wide and is available in over 10,000 specialty retailers.
Hours: Monday-Saturday 10am-9pm, Sunday 11am-6pm.

GOFER (Ice Cream & Gelato)
522 East Putnam Avenue, Cos Cob CT, 203.661.9080
551 East Putnam Avenue, Riverside CT, 203.990.0094
www.GoForIceCream.com, www.IceCreamPartyBox.com
Good hard and soft ice cream. We are fans of their Razzle. For a party they will bring an ice cream cart to you.
Cos Cob Hours: Winter: Sunday-Thursday 12:30pm-9:30pm, Friday and Saturday 12:30pm-10pm; Open later in the summer. Riverside is closed in the winter.
Size: Cos Cob seats 16.

La Fenice Gelateria (Gelato)
315 Greenwich Avenue, Greenwich CT, 203.992.1030
www.LaFeniceGelato.com
It is easy to support our local shops when they are making gelato as good as this. There are so many flavors to try, you will need to visit frequently.
Hours: Sunday-Friday 9am-9pm, Saturday 9am-10:30pm (hours may change with the seasons).

Longford's (Ice Cream)
146 Sound Beach Avenue, Old Greenwich CT, 203.637.0480
www.Longfordsicecream.com
Oh yummy, one of our favorite ice creams is now available in Old Greenwich! This high-quality ice cream is made daily at their factory in Port Chester. For 18 years, Tom Banca was dipping up Baskin Robbins ice cream in this same location. He switched to Longford's. Their Tahitian Vanilla was one of the top two ice creams in our Ice Cream Tasting Competition. If you ask, you will discover many fine restaurants and country clubs get their ice cream from Longford's.
Hours: Sunday-Thursday 12pm-9pm (Friday & Saturday 10pm); during the winter they may close.

ICE CREAM, FROZEN YOGURT & CHOCOLATE

Munson's Chocolates (Chocolates)
Main Store & Factory, 174 Hop River Road, Bolton CT, 860.649.4332
www.MunsonsChocolates.com
Their chocolates came in third in our Truffle Tasting. They have lots of CT locations, none close to Greenwich. Ordering on their website is your best bet.

Pinkberry (Frozen Yogurt)
369 Greenwich Avenue, Greenwich CT, 203.863.2000
www.pinkberry.com
The first Pinkberry opened in California in 2005. Now there are over 100 franchises. Jamie Karson, the owner of the Greenwich franchise, also owns Pinkberry in Fairfield. Pinkberry is an experience. Yes, it's yogurt and that has health benefits but it's not just that. It's also about dipping up fun that makes it the "go to" place. Did we want original, pomegranate, coconut, chocolate, blood orange or mango? What did we want for toppings? There were more toppings than we could count. Charlie Zeeve says "it's Great!"
Hours: Monday-Thursday 12pm-9pm, Friday 12pm-10:30pm, Saturday 11:30am-10:30pm, Sunday 11:30am-9pm. Their hours may change with the seasons. Size: seats 16

Rosie's (Frozen Yogurt)
• 207 East Putnam Avenue (Mill Pond Shop Cntr), Cos Cob CT, 203.622.5040
• 235 Sound Beach Avenue, Old Greenwich, CT
www.rosiesfrozenyogurt.com
Trendy and good for you too. The vibrant walls, acrylic chairs and cheerful young staff make this a fun place. Come in, sample one of their 16 yummy flavors, then serve yourself and make your own concoction with one of their 30 toppings. You pay by the weight.
Hours: Sunday-Thursday 11:30am-9pm, Friday & Saturday 11:30am - 10pm. Their hours change with the season. Size: seats 16

Yogurt City (Frozen Yogurt)
401 Greenwich Avenue, Greenwich CT, 860.992.8270 www.yogurtcity.com
This hidden upstairs frozen yogurt parlor is a pleasant place to relax and enjoy one of their 16 flavors. This location is one of 75.
Hours: Every day 12 pm-10pm. Size: seats 28.

MEDIA

MAGAZINES

atHome Magazine
203.222.0600
www.athomefc.com
A Moffly Media magazine, published 5 times a year. The magazine is filled with design inspiration, information and decorating trends in Fairfield County.

Connecticut Cottages & Gardens
203.227.1400
www.CTCandG.com
A high-quality magazine with pretty photos and good articles. Even if you just use it for a coffee table book, you will love it.

Connecticut Magazine
855.235.9032
www.connecticutmag.com
This comprehensive, attractive magazine always has well-researched articles on the best of Connecticut. Subscribe! They do a great job of rating everything from golf courses to towns to the top doctors.

Farifield County Look
203.869.0077
www.fairfieldcountylook.com
The magazine is published twice a year by Elaine and ChiChi Ubina. It is filled with photographs of Greenwich charity events. A delightful way to see pictures of your friends in party settings. Between the issues you should subscribe to the online magazine.

Greenwich Country Capitalists
www.westonmagazinegroup.com
A quarterly magazine delivered to households and businesses. It covers general topics geared toward the luxury market.

Greenwich Magazine
203.222.0600
www.greenwichmag.com
Sophisticated articles on topics of interest for everyone. A valuable source of information about Greenwich and Greenwich residents. A subscription to Greenwich Magazine is essential. The Mofflys also publish the leading magazines for Westport, Stamford and New Caanan/Darien.

Serendipity
203.588.1363
www.SerendipitySocial.com
Serendipity is a must-have lifestyle magazine covering Fairfield and Westchester counties. It's filled with articles on style, food & wine, health, fitness, home and garden. Serendipity sponsors many events including the popular "Wine and Food Festival."

Westchester Magazine
914.345.0601
www.westchestermagazine.com
This magazine focuses on Westchester and Fairfield counties. It often has articles on Greenwich. It is a helpful resource for discovering events and resources you will want to take advantage of in our neighboring towns.

NEWS ONLINE

Of course all of the Greenwich Newspapers have well-developed websites. In addition, there are several online digital news sites.

Fairfield County Insider
www.ilovefcinsider.com
Fairfield County events and news. They have a nice Fairfield county calendar.

Greenwich Daily Voice
www.Greenwich.dailyvoice.com
News from Greenwich and surrounding towns.

MEDIA

Greenwich Free Press
www.greenwichfreepress.com
If you sign-up for their newsletter, you will receive local news every morning every day of the week. You will like this site, it's just local news.

Greenwich Restaurant and Store Updates
For new restaurant reviews, store updates and closings, go to Anderson Associates' Facebook page: www.facebook.com/RealEstateGreenwichCT

Greenwich Patch
www.patch.com/connecticut/greenwich
A mix of local and national news. They also list the Greenwich open houses.

Hamlet Hub
Http://news.hamlethub.com/coscob
http://news.hamlethub.com/greenwich
http://news.hamlethub.com/oldgreenwich
https://twitter.com/oldgreenwichhub
Their focus is very local news.

HAN Radio
www.hanradio.com
Pod casts of news, sports and entertainment in Southwestern CT.

It's Relevant
http://greenwich.itsrelevant.com
Local video news stories online. Their website site allows you to browse their thousands of videos.

WAG
www.wagmag.com/tag/greenwich
A digital lifestyle magazine covering New York and Connecticut.

NEWSPAPERS

See SERVICES for newspaper delivery information.

Fairfield County Business Journal
914.694.3600
www.fairfieldcountybusinessjournal.com
This weekly newspaper tracks trends and developments that impact local businesses. If you are thinking of opening a business or simply want to know the commercial news, this paper is just the ticket.

Greenwich Post E-Edition
10 Corbin Drive, Darien CT, 203.861.9191
www.greenwich-post.com
The Greenwich Post is a lively electronic newspaper covering the Town. The paper is filled with excellent articles, updates, editorials and summaries of what is happening in Greenwich. They have extensive calendars of local and regional activities, and many special publications, including Home Magazine and 100 Things to Do. Check their website for "Things to Do" or to sign up for daily email alerts.

Greenwich Time
1455 East Putnam Avenue, Old Greenwich, 203.625.4410
www.greenwichtime.com
Greenwich is lucky to have a daily newspaper. If we were judging a national competition for the best daily local newspaper, Greenwich Time would win the top award. The Letters from Readers section is a good barometer of Town concerns. To understand what is happening in Greenwich, you must read this paper.

MEDIA

RADIO AND TELEVISION

Bloomberg News AM 1130, xm Channel 129/Sirius Channel 130
www.Bloomberg.com
Good national, international and financial news.

Cable Channel 12-Connecticut News
www.news12.com/CT

Continuous news, weather and traffic reports.
• CBS AM 880, www.NewsRadio88.com
• WINS AM 1010, www.1010wins.com

Greenwich Community Television
www.cpbi.org
Connecticut Public Television has Connecticut-based documentaries as
well as sports coverage of Connecticut teams.
• Channel 79 (Cablevision) Channel 24 (FIOS) is our local community
access station. It broadcasts "Greenwich Weekly Video Magazine" Wednesdays at 10:30 pm and Fridays at 9:30 am. RTM meetings are shown live.
The meeting calendar is shown between broadcasts or go to
www.greenwichct.org/channel79
• Channel 78 (Cable Vision) is the Greenwich Educational Access Channel.

Greenwich Radio AM 1490
71 Lewis Street, Greenwich, 203.869.1490
www.wgch.com
Tune in between 6am & 10am for an update on Greenwich happenings,
including school closings. Their interviews with Greenwich people making the news are essential to understanding town issues. "Ask the First
Selectman" airs Fridays at 9am.

Public Radio
Great in-depth coverage of national and international events without
(much) commercial interruption.
• Connecticut Public Radio FM 88.5, www.cpbi.org/radio
• National Public Radio AM 820 & FM 93.9, www.npr.org

NUMBERS & WEBSITES YOU SHOULD KNOW

See GOVERNMENT for Local, State and Federal Numbers.

Sections
  Useful Numbers and websites
  Open 24 Hours

USEFUL NUMBERS
For a complete list of useful Greenwich Department numbers, see: GOVERNMENT

Ambulance - Greenwich Police
911 Emergency, 203.622.8000 (non-emergency), 203.637.7505 (office)
See GEMS below.

Aquarion (formerly The Connecticut American Water Company)
203.445.7310 (customer service)
800.732.9678 (customer service - outside greater Bridgeport)
www.aquarion.com

AT&T
From AT&T coverage area, dial 611 for repairs; from out-of-state, dial 800.331.0500 (customer service)
www.snet.com, www.sbc.com, www.att.com

Cablevision of Connecticut
203.870.2584 (customer service), 203.870.2492 (sales)
www.cablevision.com www.optimum.com

Community Answers
101 West Putnam Avenue, Greenwich CT, 203.622.7979
www.greenwichlibrary.org/commanswers.htm
Funded by the United Way and private donations, this volunteer group is located in the Greenwich Library. Ask them anything about Greenwich (all calls are confidential). Their website is a storehouse of valuable information.
• Community Calendar provides a Community Calendar of all Greenwich events. It comes out every three months. Be sure to call and ask for it.
• Useful Article Reprints: Stop by and pick up articles which might be helpful, such as: Childcare and Parenting Services, Summer Camp and Programs in Greenwich.
Hours: Weekdays 9am-3pm.

214

Connecticut Natural Gas
203.869.6900 (customer service)
203. 869.6913 (repair & emergency)
www.cngcorp.com

Connecticut Vacation Planning
888.288.4748
Coastal Fairfield County Tourist Information
at 800.866.7925 or 203.853.7770
www.CTVisit.com, www.visitfairfieldcountyct.com

Domestic Abuse
211 Infoline
YWCA Domestic Abuse Service 203.622.0003
Calls are completely confidential.

Federal Express
800.463.3339, 800.GO.FEDEX   www.fedex.com

FedEx/Kinkos
48 West Putnam Avenue, 203.863.0099

GEMS (Greenwich Emergency Medical Service)
911 for emergency ambulance
203.637.7505 (office)

Greenwich Fire Department
911 Emergency
203.622.3950 (non-emergency)
- Amogerone Fire Company (Havemeyer Place), 203.249.2421
  or 203.622.8087   www.amogerone.com
- Byram Fire Company, 203.532.9752 or 203.622.3973
- Cos Cob Fire Company, 203.622.3972 or 203.622.1506
- Glenville Fire Company, 203.532.9606 or 203.622.3974
- Old Greenwich Fire Company, 203.637.1806 or 203.622.3975
  www.sbvfd.com
- Round Hill Volunteer Fire Company, 203.869.7185
- Banksville Independent Fire Company, 914.234.7104
  www.banksvillefire.org
- Back Country Fire Company, 203.661.2452

NUMBERS & WEBSITES YOU SHOULD KNOW

Greenwich Hospital
203.863.3000
www.greenwichhospital.org/
See complete description in HEALTH.

Greenwich Police
911 Emergency, 203.622.8000 (complaints and information)
www.greenwichct.org/policeDept/PoliceDept.asp

Greenwich Public Schools
203.625.7400
www.GreenwichSchools.org, www.greenwich.k12.ct.us
See complete description and other numbers in SCHOOLS.

Suburban Propane
55 Old Field Point Rd, Greenwich CT, 203.869.4226
www.suburbanpropane.com

Northeast Utilities/Eversource
800.286.5000
www.nu.com
Residents whose power has been turned off by Eversource should call
the Town of Greenwich Building Inspection Division at 203.622.7754.

Post Offices
For Post Office numbers & hours and Zip Codes see POST OFFICES.

Poison Control Center
800.222.1222
http://poisoncontrol.uchc.edu

Telemarketing (NO CALL List)
CT Department of Consumer Protection
800.842.2649
www.state.ct.us/dcp/nocall.htm

UPS
15 East Putnam Ave, Greenwich CT, 203.622.1114
www.ups.com/tracking/tracking.html

NUMBERS & WEBSITES YOU SHOULD KNOW

USE (Senior Center Job Placement Service)
203.629.8031
Utilize Senior Energy, run by volunteers, is a good resource for everything from office help to painters to babysitters.
Hours: weekdays, 9:30 am - 12:30 pm

Verizon Land Line Help
800.837.4966
www.Verizon.com

Verizon Internet and TV (FIOS)
888.625.8111
www.verizonfios.com
Verizon is offering FIOS, a fiber optic service competing with Cablevision.

OPEN 24 HOURS

24-Hour Pharmacies
See HEALTH for details.
• Walgreen's, 1333 East Putnam Avenue, Old Greenwich, 203.637.1496
• CVS, 1239 East Putnam Ave, Riverside, 203.698.4006

24-Hour Gas Station
Shell, 401 West Putnam Avenue, Greenwich CT, 203.661.2485

Veterinarian Referral & Emergency Center
123 West Cedar Street, Norwalk CT, 203.854.9960
www.vcavrec.com
If your vet is not available, this is a wonderful emergency room for your pet. During normal hours, appointments must be made for specialists.
Hours: 24 hours a day, 7 days a week.

PARKS & BEACHES

Greenwich extends over 47 square miles with rolling hills, woodlands, meadows and 32 miles of gorgeous shoreline bordering the Long Island Sound. Greenwich's main beaches are at Greenwich Point (147 acres), Byram Beach and the 2 city-owned islands (Captain's Island & Island Beach). Greenwich has 8,000 acres of protected land, over 1,000 acres of town parks, 35 town tennis courts (not including the YWCA Courts), an indoor ice rink (open only to residents), 4 public marinas and a 158-acre, 18-hole golf course (open only to residents).

The Parks and Recreation office is on the second floor of Town Hall. Hours are Weekdays, 8am to4 pm. Outside their door are good handouts on upcoming opportunities. For information call 203.622.7814 or visit the website www.greenwichct.org/ParksAndRec/ParksandRec.asp. The website has a complete list of Greenwich Parks.

For Playgrounds see CHILDREN.

SECTIONS
Beaches
Civic Centers
Parks & Nature Preserves
Public Marinas
Specialized Parks
Organizations Devoted to Our Parks, Rivers and Green Space

TIP: SAND SCULPTURE
www.greenwicharts.org
Every year in July at Tod's Point Beach, The Greenwich Arts Council and the Town of Greenwich Department of Parks and Recreation sponsor a Sand Blast! There is no specific theme for sand sculptures beyond the enjoyment of creating art in the sand.

PARKS & BEACHES

BEACHES

Greenwich beaches are open to residents and non-residents. You must have a beach pass before entering the beach. Passes are strictly enforced. Apply early and be sure to have it when you enter. Passes are required from May 1st to October 31st. Dogs are allowed on a leash from December 1st to March 31st. No charge is required from the middle of November to the middle of April.

Beach Cards and Passes

The Beach Card Office (203.622.7817) is located on First Floor of Town Hall. It is open weekdays 8am to 3:45pm from March through December. Proof of residency is required for a Beach Card. The Town will accept: moving documents, lease papers, a drivers license, phone or electric bills. Beach cards cost $31 for adults, $6 for children ages 5 to 15, and are free for seniors and toddlers. Daily admission passes for non-residents cost $6 per person and $25 per vehicle per day. Passes can be purchased at Eastern Civic Center or Town Hall. The Town also requires residents to obtain a seasonal parking sticker for each car or pay $25 for daily parking. Parking stickers can be obtained free with a copy of a current vehicle registration indicating that the car is on the Greenwich tax rolls. If the car is not on the tax rolls, the sticker costs Greenwich Residents $125 per season.

Byram Beach

203.861.3170
This beach on Byram Shore Road has a swimming pool, 3 tennis courts, a picnic area, wiffle ball diamond and playground.

Cruise to Nowhere

Department of Parks and Recreation 203.622.7814.
The Cruise is popular and tickets often sell out. For $15 a person you can cruise around the Islands of Greenwich.

Ferry Information

Ticket office, 203.661.5957
The ferry service from the Arch Street dock to Great Captain's Island or Island Beach varies according to the tides and time of the year. Service begins in the middle of June and lasts until the middle of September. For fees & schedule go to:
www.greenwichct.org/ParksAndRec/prFerryService.asp

PARKS & BEACHES

Captain's Island
It is rustic with no concession stand, so bring a picnic lunch. Camp sites available with permits. Tickets for overnight camping are available at Town Hall, Weekdays, 8am-4pm. Take a ferry from the Arch Street dock to this 17-acre island with beach and picnic area. Several morning and afternoon ferries are available depending upon the day and date.

Greenwich Point (Tod's Point)
Entrance at the south end of Shore Road in Old Greenwich. This 147-acre beach, with concession stand, has jogging, hiking and biking trails, lots of picnic facilities and wind surfing. Dogs on a leash are normally allowed in the winter.

Island Beach (Little Captain's Island)
203.661.5957
Take a ferry from the Arch Street dock to this 4-acre island with beaches, picnic area and concession stand.
Hours: weekdays, every hour 10am-7pm through mid-August; 10am-6pm through mid-September, weekends every half-hour.

Calf Island
A 28-acre island off Byram Shore, purchased from the YMCA for $6 million by the Stewart B. McKinney National Wildlife Refuge. It has beaches, trails, woods and wetlands. A fun place to explore, but you will need a boat to get there.

CIVIC CENTERS
The Civic centers are the sites for many sporting events and public events such as antique shows. Call for their latest catalog of events.

Eastern Greenwich Civic Center
(aka: Greenwich Civic Center or Old Greenwich-Riverside Civic Center)
90 Harding Road, Old Greenwich, 203.637.4583
www.greenwichct.org/ParksAndRec/prFacilityPrograms.asp
The center is 14 acres and operates weekdays from 8am-10pm, Saturday from 9am-10pm, and Sunday from 9am-9pm. The center has a basketball court, 2-tennis courts with lights, a baseball diamond and playground. The center is used extensively for a wide variety of activities such as roller skating, men's basketball, soccer, tennis for tots, Old Greenwich Art society painters and Halloween Happenings.

PARKS & BEACHES

Western Greenwich Civic Center
(aka Bendheim Western Civic Center)
449 Pemberwick Road, Glenville CT, 203.532.1259
www.greenwichct.org/ParksAndRec/prFacilityPrograms.asp
The newly renovated center on 9.97 acres, is the pride of the Town. From 1997 the Glenville Community led by the 9th district of the RTM and other concerned citizens started a fundraising campaign to refurbish the Civic Center. After the group raised approximately 3.5 million dollars, the Town of Greenwich matched the gift and work began in June of 2005. The new building features a state-of-the-art Daycare Center, a new gym/ auditorium, a dance, exercise studio, weight room and meeting rooms. Call for a program guide.

PARKS & NATURE PRESERVES

Greenwich, in addition to its beaches and 32 miles of coastline, has 8,000 acres of protected land, with over 1,000 acres of Town parks. The parks and nature preserves listed below are some of the more popular of the twenty parks in Greenwich. For a complete list of Greenwich parks, see http://www.greenwichct.org/ParksAndRec/prFacilitiesIndex.asp

Audubon Center
613 Riversville Road, 203.869.5272
http://greenwich.audubon.org
285 acres with well-kept trails, a great place to walk.

Babcock Preserve
North Street, 203.622.7814
297 acres located two miles north of the Merritt Parkway. Well-marked running, hiking, and cross-country ski trails.

Binney Park
Sound Beach Avenue, Old Greenwich, 203.622.7824
The park is 22 landscaped acres with a beautiful pond, 4 tennis courts, a playground, baseball diamond and pond skating. A favorite place for wedding photos. The park is the site of a variety of community activities including band concerts, July fireworks and the model sailboat regatta.

Bruce Park
Bruce Park Drive and Indian Field Road, Greenwich CT, 203.622.7824
Athletic fields, bowling green, fitness trail, picnic area, tennis courts and an exciting playground.

PARKS & BEACHES

Christiano Park
25 Lyon Avenue (off Holly Hill Lane), Greenwich CT
A 5-acre park with Pickle Ball, a baseball diamond, tennis, cricket pitch, children's play area and home to the Greenwich Pigeon Club.

Mianus River Park
Cognewaugh Road, 203.622.7824
http://www.friendsofmianusriverpark.org
391 acres owned by Greenwich and Stamford. Trout fishing, wooded hills and steep cliffs with miles of hiking trails. Take Valley Road to Cognewaugh; the entrance is on Cognewaugh Road about three miles on the right. (There is no sign.)

Montgomery Pinetum
Bible Street, Cos Cob
Armed with a map and tree guide from the Garden Center, you will have fun exploring this beautiful 91-acre wilderness. To reach Montgomery Park and Pinetum, go north on Orchard Street from the Post Road in Cos Cob. Bear right onto Bible Street and continue .7 mile. The entrance is on the west side directly opposite Clover Place.

Pomerance-Tuchman Preserve
This 118-acre tract adjacent to the Montgomery Pinetum lies between Orchard and Bible Streets in Cos Cob. The Town purchased the property for $35 million. Along with the Pinetum and Bible Street playing fields, this tract gives the Town a corridor of 227 acres of pristine woodlands.

Sabine Farm Field
A field along Round Hill Road was purchased in 2001 for $2.9 million by the Greenwich Land Trust. However, all of the money came from private donations, raised primarily through the efforts of a local resident, Edward Bragg.

Treetops
In 2002 the Town of Greenwich and 3 land trusts raised $11.5 million dollars to purchase 110 acres bordering the Mianus River. This tract forms the southern boundary of the 220 acre Mianus River Park. Inspired by David Ogilvy, residents from Town officials to school children united to make this possible.

PUBLIC MARINAS

4 marinas are available to Town residents, from April 15th through November 15th each year. Launching ramps are available at all Marinas. Winter storage is available at all marinas from September 1-June 1. A mooring requires 2 permits, a use facilities permit issued by the Department of Parks and Recreation (2nd Floor Town Hall) 203.618.7651 and a mooring permit issued by the Harbormaster.

Harbor Management Commission

www.greenwichct.org/government/commissions/harbor_management_commission
This 7-person commission proposes fees for mooring or anchorage and controls local waterways and harbors.

Harbormaster

www.greenwichct.org/government/harbormaster
The Harbor Master is charged with the general care and supervision of the harbors and navigable waterways subject to the Harbor Management Commission and the transportation commissioner's direction. They are responsible for the safe and efficient operation of such harbors and navigable waterways.

Town Boating Information:
http://www.greenwichct.org/Government/Departments/Parks_and_Recreation/Boating_and_Marinas/

Town's mooring and anchoring rules:
http://www.greenwichct.org/Public_Documents/GreenwichCT_FirstSelect/committees/coastal/docs/

(The) Byram Marina in Byram Park

It has 300 slips for vessels up to 23' overall in length with beam widths up to 9'. The marina has outwater mooring space for approximately 100 vessels up to 36' overall length and drafts up to 7'. There is some rack storage for kayaks and canoes. The Byram Dockmaster's office is 203.532.9019. Located in Byram Park just south of exit 2 of I-95 on Ritch Avenue.

(The) Cos Cob Marina

River Road, Cos Cob
The Cos Cob Marina has approximately 300 slips for vessels up to 23' overall length with beam widths up to 9'. There is also limited rack storage for kayaks and canoes. The Dockmaster's office can be reached at 203.618.9698. Located on River Road just south of the I-95 overpass.

(The) Grass Island Marina
Shore Road
Grass Island has 150 slips for boats up to 23' in length with beam widths of up to 9' (a few can accommodate boats up to 36' in length). There is out-water mooring space for approximately 75 vessels up to 36' overall length and drafts up to 5'. Grass Island has some rack storage for kayaks and canoes. Grass Island has tie-up space for visitors. There is no charge during the day. The overnight charge is based on vessel size. The Grass Island Dockmaster, 203.618.9695, is located off Shore Road in central Greenwich just south of I-95.

(The) Greenwich Point Marina
Greenwich Point Park. There are out-water mooring for about 250 boats up to 36 feet long and up to 7' drafts. There is rack storage for about 250 canoes, kayaks, and other small boats. Greenwich Point Dockmaster's office, 203.698.7792, is located at Greenwich Point Park in Old Greenwich.

SPECIALIZED PARKS

Dog Park
The Greenwich Dog Park is located on 3/4 acre at Grass Island.
The park is open from sunrise to sunset. For your dog to have a good experience, for the first visit go during a quiet time, usually weekdays between 9am-11am. The rules are posted on the fence. Children under 10 are not permitted. Owners must remain in the fenced area with their dog while the dog is off leash. Aggressive dogs are not allowed and owners are responsible for the behavior of their dog.

Dorothy Hamill Skating Rink
Skating Rink Road off Sherman Avenue in Byram, 203.531.8560
www.greenwichct.org/ParksAndRec/prFacilityPrograms.asp
Set on 18 acres, this large skating facility has been a joy to Greenwich skaters for over 34 years. All kinds of programs are available, such as: hockey clinics, Town-wide figure skating competition and general skating. Its normal hours of operation are 6am-12am, from September to Mid-March. Sessions are open to Greenwich residents. Guests are admitted when accompanied by a Greenwich resident and proof of residency is required. During the off season the rink is covered with indoor turf for lacrosse and soccer.

PARKS & BEACHES

Griffith E Harris Golf Course
1300 King Street, General Information: 203.531.7200
Reservations: 203.531.8253, Pro Shop: 203.531.7261
www.greenwichct.org/ParksAndRec/prGolfCourse.asp
This 18-hole, Robert Trent Jones-designed course, is the Town's only municipal golf course and the only non-private golf course in the Town. Use of the course is open to all Town of Greenwich residents who become members. Members are permitted to bring guests with them to play at the course. All guests are required to be accompanied by a member to play.

Skate Park
Roger Sherman Baldwin Park, Arch Street, 203.496.9876
www.greenwichct.org/ParksAndRec/prSkatePark.asp
The Greenwich Skate Park is a supervised facility for youths 6 years of age and over to skateboard and inline skate. The area is supervised whenever the park is open. Full protective gear is required. Children 6 to 9 years of age must be accompanied by an adult (18 years or older) during the time they are in the park. The facility provides a friendly and supportive environment for beginners to experts. Private and semi-private lessons are offered during regular skate park hours. They offer beginning techniques as well as tricks. The park is open 3:30pm to ½ hour before sunset February 29 to November 1. Weekends and holidays 12:30pm to ½ hour before sunset. Off- peak hours are between November 2 and November 30. Check the schedule. It is closed December to March.

Tennis and Paddle Courts
For information, call Frank Gabriele at 622.7821.
www.greenwichct.org/ParksAndRec/prTennis.asp
Tennis courts are located all over Town. There are also two paddle courts and a pickleball court. Tennis passes are required from May through December 1st. Applications for tennis passes are available at Town Hall or online with proof of Greenwich residency required. The Town offers instruction and holds an annual Town-wide tournament.

ORGANIZATIONS DEVOTED TO OUR PARKS, WATER & GREEN SPACE

We are all grateful to the Garden Clubs. They give generously of their time and money to keep Greenwich beautiful. *Garden Clubs are listed in the section FLOWERS AND GARDENS.*

Audubon Society of Greenwich
613 Riversville Road, 203.869.5272
http://greenwich.audubon.org/
Michelle Frankel, Center Director

Board of Parks and Recreation
www.greenwichct.org/ParksAndRec/prBoardofParksandRec.asp
The nine member board is nominated by the Board of Selectmen and appointed by the Representative Town Meeting (RTM). They advise the First Selectman and help coordinate department activity.

Bruce Park Association
Tom Cahill, President, 203.622.9177
A homeowners' group focusing on maintaining the integrity of Bruce Park.

Calf Island Conservancy
www.calfisland.org
Calf Island Conservancy works in partnership with the U.S. Fish and Wildlife Service to promote beneficial public uses and habitat enhancement on Calf Island.

Friends of Grass Island
Sylvester Pecora, Sr., Chairman
Jo Conboy, Secretary, 203.661.6343

Friends of Greenwich Point
PO Box 711, Old Greenwich CT, 06870
www.friendsofgreenwichpoint.org

Greenwich Conservation Commission
Denise Savageau, Director, 203.622.6461
www.greenwichct.org/ConservationCommission/ConservationCommission.asp
The Commission is an advisory board to assist the Town with planning and management of its natural resources.

PARKS & BEACHES

Greenwich Green & Clean
113 Pemberwick Road, Greenwich, 203.531.0006
www.greenwichgreenandclean.org
Since their founding in 1986, they have been committed to developing partnerships with companies and volunteers to beautify the public spaces we all share.

Greenwich Land Trust
132 East Putnam Avenue, Suite D, Cos Cob CT, 203.629.2151
PO Box 1152, Greenwich 06836-1152
www.gltrust.org
Greenwich and its residents are committed to expanding the Town's large amount of green space. Funding comes from a variety of sources, including the Town, the State, the Federal Government (www.tpl.org), the Greenwich Land Trust and private donations.

Greenwich Point Conservancy
www.greenwichpoint.org
Chris Franco, President, 203.637.4851, 203.637.6806

Greenwich Recycling Advisory Board (GRAB) Services
Greenwich Town Hall, Department of Public Works
Sally Davies, Chair, 203.629.2876

Greenwich Tree Conservancy
www.GreenwichTreeConservancy.org
They preserve and add to the tree and forest resources in Greenwich. One tree will absorb the CO_2 from four cars every year.

Plan of Conservation and Development (POCD)
www.greenwichct.org/Public_Documents/GreenwichCT_LandUse/pocd/index
This is the Town's 10-year plan.

Planning and Zoning Department (P&Z)
www.greenwichct.org/PlanningZoning/PlanningZoning.asp
The Town Department responsible for developing and enforcing Greenwich zoning regulations.

PARKS & BEACHES

Planning and Zoning Commission
www.greenwichct.org/PlanningZoning/pzCommission.asp
The Commission is composed of five regular members and three alternates who are nominated by the Board of Selectmen and appointed by the Representative Town Meeting (RTM). They prepare long-range plans, based on the POCD, for future development and make recommendations for the most desirable use of the land within the Town. They also regulate and review municipal improvement projects and subdivisions of land.

RTM Parks and Recreation Committee
http://www.greenwichct.org/Government/RTM/
RTM_Meeting_Information/Committees/Parks_Recreation_Committee/
The twelve-member Representative Town Meeting (RTM) committee is made up of one representative of each of the Town's voting districts. They advise the RTM on issues involving our parks.

RTM Land Use Committee
The twelve-member Representative Town Meeting (RTM) committee is made up of one representative of each of the Town's voting districts. They advise the RTM on issues involving land use.

Shellfish Commission
www.greenwichct.org/Shellfish/Shellfish.asp
The Commission provides recreational shellfishing for the inhabitants of Greenwich by overseeing the shellfish beds.

Trout Unlimited (Mianus Chapter)
Mianus Chapter TU, PO Box 475, Wilton CT, 06897
www.mianustu.org
703.522.0200 National Headquarters (Arlington VA)
Tony Hill, President, 203.854.4788
The Mianus Chapter is comprised of more than 500 anglers from Greenwich to Ridgefield, Connecticut, dedicated to preserving and protecting the rivers and streams of lower Fairfield County.

TIP: TOWN PERMITS AND PASSES
Permits and passes for many Greenwich activities can be applied for on the Town's website,
www.greenwichct.org/ParksAndRec/ParksAndRec.asp
http://www.greenwichct.org/Parking/Parking.asp

PETS

INDEX TO PETS

Pets, popular in Greenwich, bring great cheer to their owners and often assume the role of "Head of the Household." Over 3,000 dogs are masters of homes in Greenwich. If you hear someone calling Maggie, Max, Buddy, Sam, Lola, Molly, Harry or Jake, chances are it isn't a child being summoned.

PETS

Pet Care (Pet Walkers, Sitters and Kennels)
Best Friends Pet Resort & Salon
Canine Athletic Club
Doggie Grandparents
North Wind Kennels
Pet Sitters
Poop Patrol
Purrfect Paws Pet Services

Pet Photographers and Portraits
Amanda Jones
Ashley Weymouth
Christine Morgan/Teter
Geoff Tischman

Pet Stores
The following pet stores are described in STORES:
- Aquaria, 1064 East Putnam Avenue, Riverside CT, 203.344.1572
- House of Fins, 99 Bruce Park Avenue, Greenwich CT, 203.661.8131
- Pet Pantry, 290 Railroad Avenue, Greenwich CT, 203.869.6444
- Choice Pet Supply, 80 East Putnam Avenue, Greenwich CT, 203.869.4999

Pet Training
Dog Training by Anna Farrelly
Dog Training by Chris Onthank
Dog Training by Ken Berenson
Dog Training by Sarah Hodgson
Dog Training by Simply Sarah
Dog Training by Susan Kaminsky
Good Dog Foundation
Invisible Fencing (Canine Fence & E-Fence)

Stray Cats
Project SaveACat, 203.661.6855
PAWS (Pet Animal Welfare Society) Norwalk CT, 203.854.1798
SCAT (Southern Connecticut Animal Trust) Stamford CT, 860.535.0205

PETS

Veterinarians and Pet Hospitals
Animal Eye Clinic
Cornell University Veterinary Specialties (24 Hr), 203.595.2777
Good Shepherd Mobile Vet
Just Cats Hospital
Veterinary Oncology & Hematology Center
Veterinarian Referral & Emergency Center (24 Hr), 203.854.9960

Wildlife Rescue
All About Bats
Wild Wings
Wildlife in Crisis

LISTING OF PET RESOURCES

Adopt-A-Dog
Shelter: 23 Cox Avenue, Armonk NY, 203.629.9494 or 914.273.1674
www.adoptadog.org
Since 1981, this unique, local, not-for-profit animal agency has helped over 7,000 homeless dogs find loving families. If you have a soft spot in your heart for animals, consider adopting or becoming a foster "parent." You are always welcome to call or visit their kennels. They hold the annual October show, "Puttin' on the Dog."
Shelter Hours: weekdays 11am-5pm, weekends 11am-3pm.

Adopt a Seeing Eye Dog
http://www.seeingeye.org/aboutUs/?M_ID=129
Adopt a well-trained dog. Some dogs are just too friendly to make the grade as a seeing eye dog.

All About Bats
www.aabats.com
Humane wildlife removal and control.

Amanda Jones (Pet Photographer)

North Adams MA, 877.251.2390

www.amandajones.com

One of our nation's top animal photographers, grew up in Greenwich. Mention Amanda Jones to a dog enthusiast and you will hear how beautiful her work is. Amanda books shooting tours in advance. Check her website for a schedule. Greenwich is on most of her tours.

Animal Eye Clinic

at the Veterinarian Referral & Emergency Center

123 West Cedar Street, Norwalk, CT, 203.855.1533

www.AnimalEyeClinic.net

People from all over the area bring their pets here for eye problems.

Hours: Monday & Tuesday 8am-5pm, Wednesday & Thursday 1am-8pm, Friday 8am to 1pm.

Animal Shelter (aka Dog Pound)

393 North Street (next to North Street Elementary), Greenwich CT, 203.622.8299 www.petfinder.com/shelters/CT289.html

Greenwich is happy with its North Street 3,400 sf. animal shelter built with $900,000 of private donations. There are 12 kennels, a separate space for cats and an adoption room for people to meet pets. The Shelter is a Town of Greenwich Police Department service that handles dead or sick animals as well as stray dogs or cats. Clearly, animals lost in Greenwich receive tender loving care.

Hours: weekdays 8am-3pm, weekends until 2pm.

Ashley Weymouth (Fiber Animal Portraits)

www.AshleysFiberArt.com

Using wool from sheep, alpaca and goats, Ashley will create a wonderful image of your pet that will always make you smile.

Barks and Bubbles Grooming

60 Pemberwick Road, Greenwich CT, 203.531.7787

http://barksandbubblegrooming.com/index.htm

Chip likes to be groomed here. We think it is especially kind that owner, Patricia Gabriele, gives a discount for adopted dogs.

Best Friends Pet Resort & Salon
528 Main Avenue, Norwalk CT, 203.849.1010
www.bestfriendspetcare.com
Doggy day camp with 4-legged playmates (assuming your pet can pass the interview process). Longer stays are available. Joya loves their grooming salon.
Hours: weekdays 7 am-7 pm, Saturday, 8 am-5 pm, Sunday, 11 am-5 pm.

Bow Wow Barber Mobile Dog Groomers
40 Duke Drive, Stamford CT, 203.968.6214
Calls will be returned in the evening. They are on the road during the day.

Canine Athletic Club (Pet Care)
117 Weaver Street, Greenwich, CT, 203.587.1155
Kristin's Mobile: 203.561.9541
www.k9athletic.com
Perhaps your dog would like to belong to the Lunch Bunch. According to one of our pet friends, he is picked up every day, lunches with several of his dog buddies, and then returns home, ready for his afternoon nap. Kristin Leggio and Keith Fernim provide dog walking, exercise, and socialization service as well as in-home pet care services. If you are too busy to take your dog to the vet, they'll do that too.

Canine Company Mobile Pet Spa
877.692.5698
www.caninecompany.com/mobilespa.aspx
The Canine Company, known for their Invisible Fence, will come to your home with an extensive spa package (including shampoo, massage and even de-skunking) for your dog.

Christine Morgan/Teter (Pet Portraits)
36 Indian Road, Port Chester NY, 914.937.4944
Christine is an award-winning artist who will create watercolor portraits of your pet.

Connecticut Humane Society
455 Post Road East, Westport CT, 203.227.4137
www.cthumane.org
Although the Greenwich Animal Shelter and adopt a dog have pets to adopt, the Humane Society is the major area resource. They have many hopeful dogs, cats and even rabbits and fish waiting to meet you. They maintain a lost and found file and will come to your home to remove injured or sick wild animals or birds.
Hours: Monday-Saturday 9:30am-5:30pm, Sunday 11am-4pm.

Connecticut Pet Guide
http://www.ctpetguide.com/
Pet resources from around Connecticut.

Dog License & Connecticut Canine Laws
All dogs six months or over must be licensed and wear collar and tag at all times. Licenses are issued by the Town Clerk's office (203.622.7897) in Town Hall (8am-4pm). Make checks payable to: Town Clerk of Greenwich. All dogs must be vaccinated against rabies and owners must submit a certificate to the Town Clerk when licensing their dog. Dog licenses expire on June 30 each year. To get a license request and information on licensing go to www.greenwichct.org/TownClerk/TownClerk.asp or directly to: http://greenwichct.virtualtownhall.net/Public_Documents/GreenwichCT_TownClerk/tcDogLicense.pdf

Dog Park
Dogs are allowed in all town parks with a leash except for Byram Beach and Greenwich Point. From December 1st to March 31st, dogs are allowed at Greenwich Point. Call Parks and Recreation 203.622.7830.
The first (and only) Greenwich Dog Park is located on 3/4 acre at Grass Island. The park is open from sunrise to sunset. For your dog to have a good experience, for the first visit go during a quiet time, usually weekdays between 9am-11am. The rules are posted on the fence. Children under 10 are not permitted and the owners must remain in the fenced area with their dog while the dog is off leash. Aggressive dogs are not allowed and owners are responsible for the behavior of their dog.

Dog Training by Anna Farrelly
Gone to the Dogs, Norwalk CT, 203.858.0380, gonetothedogsct@aol.com
www.facebook.com/pages/GONE-TO-THE-DOGS/
130791903605621?v=info
Anna teaches small group classes as well as private dog training. She strives to make training fun for the dog and the owner.

Dog Training by Chris Onthank
15 Cross Street, Norwalk CT, 203.838.7729
www.DoggoneSmart.com
Training, boarding, grooming, swimming at his 15,000 sf "Dog Gone Smart Canine Center." His staff focus on training. They use the "clicker" method.

Dog Training by Ken Berenson
914.699.4982
www.kenberenson.com
Ken holds dog (and owner) training sessions at the Round Hill Community House, 397 Round Hill Road. These are excellent classes, conducted by Ken Berenson's Canine Services. For more information call Ken. "Ken is a highly qualified educator of humans and, for that reason, an effective educator of dogs." Ken also gives private lessons.

Dog Training by Sarah Hodgson
Sarah Hodgson
27 E Mountain Road, Katonah NY, 914.241.1111
www.WhenDogsTalk.com
Author of several dog training books, Sarah gives group and private lessons.

Dog Training by Susan Kaminsky
Norwalk CT, Cell: 203.434.2884
www.TheCountryDog.com
She is a Certified Professional Dog Trainer (CPDT-KA) by the Certification Council for Professional Dog Trainers and a professional member of the Association of Pet Dog Trainers. She does one-on-one in home training based on the rewards method.

Doggie Grandparents
47 Wake Robin Lane, Stamford CT, 203.595.0176
Assuming your pet can pass the initial screening, Francine Garb will let your dog roam her house, sleep on her bed and generally have a great time. Our dogs can't wait to go.

PETS

Friends of Animals
777 Post Road, Suite 205, Darien CT, 203.656.1522
Priscilla Feral, President
www.FriendsOfAnimals.org
An international, non-profit, organization founded in 1957 which is dedicated to increasing awareness of animal rights and to preventing abuse of animals. It provides the names of local veterinarians who do low cost spaying and neutering.
Hours: weekdays 9 am-5 pm.

Geoffrey Tischman
Tischman Pet Photography, Rye NY, 917.292.6647
www.tischmanpets.com
Geoffrey takes charming, relaxed photos of pets and owners. He is often commissioned to do the ASPCA photos in NYC.

(The) Good Dog Foundation
Brooklyn NY, 888.859.9992
www.TheGoodDogFoundation.org
This foundation, part of a nationwide group, operates training sessions in Greenwich for people willing to bring their animals to visit local patients. The dogs ease depression in the elderly and calm hyperactivity in children.

Good Shepherd Mobile Vet
Darien CT, 203.505.1911 (John), 203.803.5038 (Meredith)
Dr. John Gallagher and Dr. Meredith Re are both graduates of Cornell Veterinary School. They will come to your home on your schedule. Their van is equipped for almost any needed service.

Greenwich Kennel Club
Community Center, 54 Bible Street, Cos Cob CT, 203.426.1173,
 203.426.2881 www.GreenwichKC.org
The GKC is a non-profit organization whose membership is comprised of area dog enthusiasts with interests in conformation, obedience and performance events. The GKC holds an annual all breed dog show every June. If you are not sure whether you want to bring a beagle or vizsla into your home, attend this show. It is a wonderful way to meet them all, as well as to find a suitable breeder.

Greyhound Adoption
Pups Without Partners, Penny Zwart adoption coordinator,
Bridgeport CT,   203.576.1976. www.pupswithoutpartners.org
If this listing saves one of these dogs, we will be so grateful.

Home Again
www.HomeAgain.com
Ask your vet to implant a microchip, so a lost pet can be easy to find.

Invisible Fencing
• Canine Fence (Invisible Fence and Canine Training)
  493 Danbury Road, Wilton CT, 203.834.2423
  www.caninefence.com
  Hours: Monday-Saturday, 7am-6:30pm.
• E-Fence
  329 Longmeadow Road, Orange CT, 203.795.3283
www.efence1.com
If you see small white flags around the perimeter of a Greenwich yard,
most likely it is one of the "Invisible Fences." This is a safe way to keep
your dog in your yard. Also works to keep your pet out of designated
rooms in your home. Gus and Tipsy like their E-Fence.

Just Cats Hospital
1029 East Main Street, Stamford CT, 203.327.7220
http://www.justcatsonline.com/
They provide excellent medical services, boarding, grooming and TLC,
just for cats.
Hours: weekdays, 7:30 am-8 pm (Friday 6 pm); Saturday, 8 am-5 pm.

North Wind Kennels
Route 22, Bedford NY, 914.234.3771
www.northwindkennelsny.com
If you would like to leave your dog or cat where Glenn Close and Chevy
Chase are said to leave theirs, go no further. Jake Feinberg's kennel has
four "doggie suites" and can house 225 dogs and 45 cats. Unfortunately,
our experience was less than satisfactory.
Hours: Monday-Saturday, 9:30 am-5:30 pm. On Sunday or off-hours,
their machine doesn't take messages.

Pawlor Fur Dogs Mobile Grooming
203.539.1184
Carmen Montanez and Anthony Colon, a brother and sister team, do a very nice job even with frisky pets.

Pet Sitters
When in need, try www.petsitters.org or www.petsit.com. These are national organizations that usually have reliable sitters. However, it is wise to ask for references and to make sure they are insured and bonded.

Pet Stores
The following pet stores are described in the STORE Section:
- Aquaria, 1064 East Putnam Avenue, Riverside CT, 203.344.1572
- House of Fins, 99 Bruce Park Avenue, Greenwich CT, 203.661.8131
- Pet Pantry, 290 Railroad Avenue, Greenwich CT, 203.869.6444
- Choice Pet Supply, 80 East Putnam Avenue, Greenwich CT, 203.869.4999

Poop Patrol
39 Chapel Street, Greenwich CT, 203.531.6661
www.PoopPatrolCT.com
Poop Patrol scoops and removes dog waste from yards, commercial properties and kennels.

Purrfect Paws Pet Services
Ginger Szucs, Cold Ridge Road, Stamford CT, 914.506.0555
www.PurrfectPawsinc.com
Dog walking, cat visits, emergency vet visits and boarding. Nothing is delegated, all services are provided by Ginger.

Puttin' On The Dog (Annual Dog Show)
Roger Sherman Baldwin Park, held in the fall.
Run by Adopt-a-Dog, 849 Lake Avenue, 203.629.9494
www.adoptadog.org
This show is a great place to show off your dog, learn about dogs, or adopt a new friend. Always a hit with children of all ages.

Sherlock Bones
800.942.6637   www.sherlockbones.com
Since 1975 this California pet detective has helped recover missing pets around the USA.

Snip Doggy Dog
237 Sound Beach Avenue, Old Greenwich CT, 203.990.0770
www.SnipDoggyDog.com
They have locations in Fairfield and Westport as well as Old Greenwich. Dogs are scheduled to be in and out in 90 minutes: groomed, toenails clipped and smelling clean.

Stray Cats
• Project SaveACat, 203.661.6855
• PAWS (Pet Animal Welfare Society) Norwalk CT, 203.854.1798
• SCAT (Southern Connecticut Animal Trust) Stamford CT, 860.535.0205
www.adoptatscat.org
If you know of a stray cat that needs to be captured or you would like to adopt a cat, call these volunteer organizations.

Veterinary Oncology & Hematology Center
129 Glover Avenue, Norwalk CT, 203.838.6626
www.OnCoVet.com
Specialists in the diagnosis and treatment of cancer in animals. Their appointments are on time and they are particularly nice to you and your pet.

TIP: DOG VOLUNTEERS NEEDED
Adopt-a-Dog shelters and places abandoned dogs and cats in loving homes. They need volunteers to help with functions such as fundraising, dog walking, public relations and animal care. If you have a warm place in your heart for these sweet creatures, call 203.629.9494 for information or www.adoptadog.org

PETS

Veterinarian Referral & Emergency Center
123 West Cedar Street, Norwalk CT, 203.854.9960
www.vcavrec.com
If your vet is not available, this is a wonderful emergency room for your pet. During normal hours, appointments must be made for specialists.
Hours: 24 hours a day, 7 days a week.

Wild Wings
Old Greenwich CT, 203.637.9822, 203.967.2121, Wildlife Hotline: 203.389.4411
Alison Taintor and Meredith Sampson are state and federally licensed wildlife rehabilitators who operate a wildlife rescue and rehabilitation center in Old Greenwich and Stamford. They will respond to oil spill emergencies that affect wildlife.
Hours: They are on call 24 hours a day, 7 days a week for emergencies.
For general information, call weekdays, 9 am-5 pm.

Wildlife in Crisis
Weston CT, 203.544.9913
www.WildlifeInCrisis.com
If you happen to have an injured cormorant (as the Greenwich Police Department did recently) and perhaps any other wild animal who needs help, this group is willing to rehabilitate and save the animal or bird.

PHOTOGRAPHY

Framers are described in STORES.
Passport photos are described in TRAVEL.
The following camera stores are described in STORES.
- Camera Wholesalers, 1034 High Ridge Road, Stamford CT, 203.357.0467
- Images, 202 Sound Beach Avenue, Old Greenwich CT, 203.637.4193

PHOTOGRAPHERS
All photographers require an appointment.

Action Arts
242 Sound Beach Ave, Old Greenwich CT, 203.637.2685
Portrait, family photos and passport photos.

Amanda Jones
North Adams MA, 877.251.2390
www.AmandaJones.com
One of our nation's top animal photographers grew up in Greenwich. Mention Amanda Jones to a dog enthusiast and you will hear how beautiful her work is. Amanda books shooting tours in advance. Check her website for a schedule. Greenwich is on most of her tours.

Annie Watson
Greenwich CT, 203.485.0565
www.AnnieWatson.com
A photographer with an artist's eye.

Ben Larrabee
26 Fairview Avenue, Darien CT, 203.656.3807
www.BenLarrabee.com
Ben is a graduate of RISD and Yale University. His pictures are in museums in New York and Boston.

Bob Capazzo
31 East Elm Street, Greenwich CT, 203.273.0139
www.bcapazzo.smugmug.com
Bob likes to photograph people and events and he has a wonderful way of helping people relax and look their best. He has done many Greenwich Magazine covers.

PHOTOGRAPHY

Classic Kids
54 Greenwich Avenue, Greenwich CT, 203.622.2358
www.ClassicKidsPhotography.com
Charlie and Stephanie had a wonderful time having Kathleen Miller take their photographs here. They are very popular with Greenwich residents.

Clever Photos
917.345.9953
www.CleverPhotos.com
Many Greenwich residents use Cynthia Ever for their family and holiday photos.

Elaine & ChiChi Ubiña
203.869.0077
www.FairfieldCountyLook.com
The Ubiñas are local favorites-taking wonderful pictures at both private and non-profit events. With permission, the photos are on their website-a great way for everyone attending and for those who could not be there, to see their friends in party settings. If you are planning a party be sure to reserve as early as you can.

Glenville Photo & Image Center of Greenwich
25 Glen Ridge Road (Glenville Shopping Plaza) Glenville CT, 203.532.1211
www.imagesbychuan.com
Chuan Ding is a portrait photographer and everyone enjoys going to her photography shop. She will retouch or restore old or damaged photos, digitize photos, slides or negatives, transfer old movies to DVDs and take passport photos.

Jack Dog Studio
109 Greenwich Avenue, 2nd Floor, Greenwich CT, 203.487.6100
www.JackDogStudio.com, www.facebook.com/Jack.Dog.Studio
Family photography- babies and seniors too!

Jeffrey Shaw Portrait Photography
888 Main Street, #427 NYC, 212.865.0480
www.jeffreyShaw.com
He moved his studio from Greenwich to Manhattan, but he still does a lot of Greenwich work. You will treasure his photographs of your family.

PHOTOGRAPHY

Images (Photographic Services)
202 Sound Beach Avenue, Old Greenwich CT, 203.637.4193
www.imagescenter.com
In addition to framing your photographs, they restore damaged photographs by removing scratches, tears and stains, enhance photographs to reduce redeye or correct color and brightness, and, of course, enlarge, crop or add a border. No negative is required. See the Review in STORES.

Venture Portraits
48 West Putnam Avenue, Greenwich CT, 203.861.9100
www.venturephotography.com
They specialize in unique family action photos. The pictures are processed and framed in England. Check the prices before you have a session.

TIP: CONCOURS OF ELEGANCE
To exhibit a concours-quality car, apply on line at:
www.greenwichconcours.com
The Concours takes place in the Roger Sherman Baldwin Park the weekend after Memorial Day. This exciting event for all ages features an exhibit of outstanding motorcars from the last decade of the 19th century through the late 1970s. Car lovers in Greenwich have enjoyed this event for over 10 years. It is one of the most prestigious Concours events in the country, attracting over 10,000 spectators.

PIZZA

Many restaurants, like Arrosto, Capriccio, Centro, Eleven14 Kitchen, Pomodoro, Tarry Lodge, Terra, Villa Italia and Zaza sell pizzas. This section covers places that sell primarily pizzas. In a few instances, a pizza parlor is more of a sit down location and is covered here and in RESTAURANTS.

Arcuri's (Pizza)

226 East Putnam Avenue, Cos Cob CT, 203.869.6999
www.arcurispizza.com
Extensive selection of specialty pizzas. In the Anderson Pizza Contest they came in only 7 votes behind the winner. Philip loves it. He has a pizza here almost every day. They are well-known for their bountiful, hard-to-beat salads. We would skip the burgers. They deliver.
Hours: Open Sunday-Thursday 11am-10pm,
Saturday & Sunday 11am-11pm.   Size: seats about 20.

California Pizza Kitchen (Pizza)

230 Tresser Blvd @ The Stamford Town Center, Stamford CT, 203.406.0530
www.CPK.com, www.CPKtakeout.com
One of six featured restaurants at the Town Center. Started in Beverly Hills CA in 1985, the chain has over 230 locations. They are known for innovative pizzas, such as BBQ Chicken, BLT, Thai Chicken, and Jamaican Jerk Chicken. Bigger and more stylish than the normal pizza parlor, it is a good choice when shopping at the Mall with kids. The Children's menu-an activity book-has lots of kid-friendly foods to keep them happy while you enjoy a salad or Neapolitan (thin crust) pizza.
Hours: Open Monday-Saturday 11am-10 pm, Sunday 11am-9 pm.
Size: seats 50.

Coals (Pizza)

35 North Main Street, Port Chester NY, 914.305.3220
www.CoalsPizza.com
This casual, minimally-decorated pizza place is becoming a hot spot for pizza and beer lovers. They serve very good pizzas on ultra thin crusts. You should start with the deep fried brussels sprout appetizer, have a pizza and end with the nutella pizza.
Hours: Open Lunch, Friday 11:30am-3pm, Saturday noon-3pm; Dinner, Monday-Thursday 5pm-9:30pm, Friday & Saturday 5pm-10:30pm, Sunday 1pm-9pm.
Prices: Pizzas $11-$14; wine by the Glass $7-$10.   Size: Seats 32

PIZZA

Domino's (Pizza)
142 East Putnam Avenue, Cos Cob CT, 203.661.2202
www.Domins.com, www.mypizza.com
Domino's (originally DomNicks) was founded in 1960. It has more than 10,000 locations and is second in size only to Pizza Hut. In 2009 responding to the Domino's brand coming in last, the company has been working on reinventing its pizza and product offerings, such as gluten free crusts. They are one of the few companies that will deliver late.
Hours: Open everyday 10am-1am. Open all Holidays
Size: seats for 4, primarily take-out or delivery.

Doppio (Pizza)
41 East Elm Street, Greenwich CT, 203.340.9470   www.EatDoppio.com
Sleekly modern, with black tables and a friendly staff, Doppio is the venture of Louis and Joseph Barresi. Doppio means two. The name was chosen to emphasize their specialities: pizza and gelato. Their pizza has Philip's stamp of approval. His favorite is the pesto. Ours is the four cheese. However the menu goes beyond pizzas with a large selection of small plates, Panini and salads. Bring your own wine from the shop next door.   Hours: Open everyday noon-10pm.   Size: seats 36

Express Pizza (Pizza)
160 Hamilton Avenue, Byram CT, 203.622.1693
www.EspressPizzaOnline.com
We discovered this friendly, small neighborhood pizzeria when it won the 2003 Town competition for the best pizza. We still love their pizza. Try their homemade soup or ravioli. They also have a deli next door (Greco's Bella Cucina). They deliver to most of Greenwich.
Hours: Open everyday 10am-10pm. Size: seats for 14.

Frank's (Italian)
23 Putnam Avenue (just across the CT border), Port Chester NY, 914.939.8299   www.FranksPizza23.info
Popular for take-out and dining: pizza, pasta and sandwiches. Food is served with cloth napkins on stylish plates with friendly service. We are wowed by the quality and variety of their freshly prepared entrees, especially the garlic balls, eggplant parmigiana and the fettuccine Alfredo.
Hours: Monday-Thursday & Saturday 10:30am to 10pm, Friday 10:30am-10:30pm, Sunday 4pm-9pm (Lunch served until 3 pm).
Prices: Pizzas (10") $10-$13, Lunch entrees $12-$15; Dinner entrees $15-$25.   Size: seats 60.

PIZZA

Gravina (Pizza)
1 Strickland Road, Cos Cob, Ct, 203.340.9400 www.gravinact.com
In this immaculate, family owned, friendly restaurant you will find a variety of pizza, sandwiches and salads. Our favorite is the puff pastry (Pizza Rustica). Hours: Monday-Saturday 11am-9pm. Size: Seats 14.

Glenville Pizza (Pizza)
243 Glenville Road, Glenville CT, 203.532.1691
Glenville residents, as well as people all over town (including our son), love Glenville Pizza. It is one of the few places serving by the slice. They were one point from winning the town pizza contest. No deliveries. Only large pizzas. No credit cards, but they will accept a local check. An ATM is available inside. Hours: Open everyday 10am-10pm. Size: Seats 26.

Pizza Post (Pizza)
522 East Putnam Avenue, Cos Cob CT, 203.661.0909
www.ThePizzaPost.com
A local favorite since 1972. Winner of our town-wide pizza contest. We think of them for pizza, but they also have a large number of entrees. They sell their sauces. No deliveries.
Hours: Open Sunday-Thursday 11am-10pm,
Friday & Saturday 11am-11pm. Size: seats 34.

Planet Pizza (Pizza)
28 Railroad Avenue, Greenwich CT, 203.622.0999
www.planetPizza.com
A small 9-store chain serving traditional New York City-style pizza, calzones, subs, salads, wraps, pasta and entrees right next to the theater and train station. Clean, well-lighted dining area.
They deliver. Hours: Open everyday 10am-10:30pm. Size: seats 30.

Re Napoli (Pizza)
216 Sound Beach Avenue, Old Greenwich CT, 203.698.9300
www.ReNapoli.com
They make three styles of pizza, Napoletana, New York and Romana. All fired at different temperatures-some gas fired and some wood fired. Jacalyn likes the white. Nick likes the Cal Italia. Both are great choices. They deliver to Old Greenwich, Riverside and Cos Cob.
Hours: Open Sunday-Thursday 11am-10pm, Friday & Saturday 11am-11pm. Size: seats 16

PIZZA

Riverside Square Pizza (Pizza)
1072 East Putnam Avenue, Riverside CT, 203.637.1000
www.riversidesquarepizza.com
Partners with Frank's.
Hours: Open Monday-Saturday 11am-9pm. Closed Sunday.
Size: Take out or Delivery only.

Sound Beach Pizza Grill (Pizza)
178 Sound Beach Avenue, Old Greenwich CT, 203.637.1085
Bare bones decor and service. Extensive selection of specialty pizzas.
They came in second in the Anderson Pizza Competition, only 4 votes
behind the winner. If you are not ordering pizza, try a chicken dish, but
skip the hamburgers. They deliver to most of Greenwich.
Hours: Open Monday-Saturday 7am-9pm, Sunday 8am-9pm.
Size: seats 30.

Strada 18 (Pizza)
122 Washington Street, (South) Norwalk CT, 203.853.4546
www.strada18.com
Just around the corner from the aquarium is our go-to-place. They have
an extensive wine list and tons of thin crust pizza possibilities. They are
good. Equally good are the desserts. They make all their desserts including the gelatos and sorbets. The decor and the service are very informal
as are the guests. If you are in a hurry you should tell them, service can
be slow.
Hours: Open Sunday-Thursday 11am-10pm, Friday & Saturday 11am-
11pm. Size: seats 54.

POST OFFICES & ZIP CODES

For shipping services other than the Post office see Delivery Services in SERVICES.

Premium Forwarding Service

www.usps.com/premiumforwarding
If you want all of your mail (including magazines) forwarded to you at a temporary address (two weeks to one year), for $17 a week plus an enrollment fee of $16, the post office will package your mail and send it to you once a week.

Greenwich Post Offices

www.usps.com
There are six post offices and five zip codes in Town. The window service hours are different for each office. Mail for Greenwich zip codes is usually sent to Stamford to be sorted. The only post office with bins for all Greenwich zip codes is in Old Greenwich. Post Office hours are continuing to shrink, don't expect them to stay open late on April 15th.

Greenwich Post Office [Zip: 06830]
44 Amogerone Crossway, 203.869.3737
Hours: weekdays 9am-5pm; Saturday, 9am-12:30pm.

Greenwich Post Office [Zip: 06831]
29 Valley Drive, 203.625.3168
Hours: weekdays 9am-5:30pm, Saturday 9am-2pm.

Glenville Post Office [Zip: 06831]
25 Glen Ridge Plaza, 203.531.4146
Hours: weekdays 9am-4pm, Saturday 9am-12pm.

Cos Cob Post Office [Zip: 06807]
152 East Putnam Avenue, 203.869.1470
Hours: weekdays 9am -4:30pm, Saturday 9:30am -12:30pm.

Riverside Post Office [Zip: 06878]
1273 East Putnam Avenue, 203.637.9332
Hours: weekdays 8:30am -5pm, Saturday 9am -12:30pm.

Old Greenwich Post Office [Zip: 06870]
36 Arcadia Road, 203.637.1405
Hours: weekdays 9am -5pm, Saturday 9am -12pm.

QUICK & CASUAL EATERIES

Bobby Qs Pit Stop (Quick & Casual BBQ)
1340 East Putnam Avenue, Old Greenwich CT, 203.990.0606
www.BobbyQsPitStop.com
Bob LeRose, owner of Bobby Q's in Westport and Bar Q in Stamford has brought his BBQ to Greenwich. The Pit Stop is just that, wood walls and diner-style stools. Food is served on paper with plastic forks. A good place for a quick BBQ fix, chili or hamburger. You can buy their BBQ sauces. Hours: Open Monday-Sunday 11am-9pm. Size: seats 15.

Boston Market (Quick & Casual)
1345 East Putnam Avenue, Old Greenwich CT, 203.637.4088
www.BostonMarket.com
Homestyle cooking in a fast-food setting. Boston Market, originally called Boston Chicken, was founded in 1985 and has about 530 company-owned stores. Because of rapid expansion, it went bankrupt in 1998 and was purchased by McDonalds Corp.
Hours: Open Monday-Saturday 11am-10pm, Sunday 11am-9pm. Size: seats 20.

Bruckner's (Quick & Casual)
1 Grigg Street, 203.422.6300 www.bruckners.com
Just off the Avenue, this friendly, small restaurant has quick service and tasty, healthy wraps and soups. It is the "in" place for a good takeout. We dash in here all the time. A few tables are also available. The owner/chef Richard Fertig has an impressive ability to spice his food just right. They have excellent vegetarian/vegan food.
Hours: Open Monday-Thursday 8am-4pm, Friday 8am-3pm, Saturday 10am-3pm. Size: seats 12.

Buffalo Wild Wings (Quick & Casual)
44 Westchester Avenue (The Water Front), Port Chester NY, 914.690.9453
208 Summer Street, Stamford CT, 203.324.9453
www.BuffaloWildWings.com
A sports bar chain located at the movie theater complex. Buffalo Wild Wings (commonly referred to as B-Dubs, BWW, B2W or BW3) has 625 locations. It is best-known for buffalo-style chicken wings and its 15 signature sauces.
Hours: Open everyday, Sunday-Thursday 11am-12am, Friday & Saturday 11am-1am. Size: seats 200.

QUICK & CASUAL EATERIES

Burgers, Shakes & Fries (Quick & Casual)
302 Delavan Avenue, Byram CT, 203.531.7433
www.BurgersShakesnFries.com
Winner of the Anderson competition for the best burger in town, this small, corner burger place, will bring back happy childhood memories. In the tasting contest everyone felt the burger was cooked just right. They liked it being served on toast. Many feel "the french fries and onion rings are divine." The reasonable prices will also please you.
Hours: Open Monday-Thursday 11:30am-8pm, Friday & Saturday 11:30am-9:30pm, Sunday 12pm-3pm.
Prices: Cash only Size: seats 20, mostly take-out.

Cafe Brazil (Quick & Casual Brazilian)
41 North Main Street, Port Chester NY, 914.939.1139
A small, informal eatery. It is a help-yourself buffet. You pay by the pound, but count on good value. Have fun discovering Brazilian dishes. Don't miss the barbecued meat or Brazil's national dish (Feijoada) a black bean stew of beans and pork. The flan and coconut balls are yummy. If you don't know what to choose, the staff is sweet and helpful.
Hours: Open everyday 6am-8pm.
Size: seats 20 inside and about the same outside.

Chicken Joe's (Quick & Casual)
www.OriginalChickenJoes.com, www.ChickenJoesOfGreenwich.com
• 231 East Putnam Avenue, Cos Cob CT, 203.861.0075
  Open Weekdays 6am-5pm, Saturday 6am-4pm, Sunday 8am-3pm.
  Stools for 4
• 364 West Putnam Avenue, Greenwich CT, 203.625.3322
  Open Monday-Saturday 9am-10pm, Sunday 10am-8pm.
  Stools for 12
Great fried chicken, chicken bits, french fries, potato cones and onion rings. When you are hankering for grandma's fried chicken, head here. Toddlers, teens and adults love it. They have a good selection of wraps, salads and specialty sandwiches. The Greenwich location has pizzas, too. Primarily take-out.

QUICK & CASUAL EATERIES

Chipotle Mexican Grill (Quick & Casual Mexican)
- 49 Greenwich Avenue, Greenwich CT, 203.625.5391
- 1233 East Putnam Avenue, Riverside, CT

www.Chipotle.com

Chipotle has over 1,200 company-owned locations. They take pride in serving organic ingredients. Their menu consists of five items: burritos, fajitas, burrito bowls, tacos, and salads. The surroundings are sleek and modern, with a Mayan touch. We like it.

Hours: Open everyday 11am-10pm. Size: seats 30

Così (Quick & Casual)
129 West Putnam Road, Greenwich CT, 203.861.2373

www.GetCosi.com

Pronounced "Cozy," a restaurant popular in Manhattan has found its niche in Greenwich. Kids love the S'mores desserts. Lots of room to sit down, good pizzas, soup, salad and sandwiches. There are more than 140 Così restaurants in the US. The name comes from the opera Così fan tutte which was a favorite of the original owner.

Hours: Open Weekdays 6am-10pm, Saturday & Sunday 7am-10pm. Size: seats 58.

Dougie's (Quick & Casual)
604 North Main Street, Port Chester NY, 914.939.0022

www.best-hamburger.com

This old-fashioned shop is located just on the border of Greenwich and Port Chester on US-1, next door to Carvel. When you crave a steak wedge with chili, this is a place to go. On Wednesday, you can get two hot dogs for the price of one, then for dessert go next door to Carvel and get two hot fudge sundaes for the price of one.

Hours: Open Monday, Tuesday, Thursday & Friday 5am-4pm, Wednesday 5am-5pm, Saturday 6am-4pm, Sunday 7am-4pm.
Size: seats 20 inside and 8 outside.

Elton's Café (Quick & Casual American)
Greenwich Library, Lower Level
101 West Putnam Avenue, Greenwich CT, 203.622.7929

www.facebook.com/pages/Eltons-Cafe/114169312031322

A cheerful, casual, cash-only spot for a cup of homemade soup and a sandwich. Step up to the counter to order and while you are are waiting, it's fun to browse the used books for sale (2 paperbacks for 25 cents, hardcovers for 50 cents).

Hours: Open Weekdays 9am-5pm, Saturday 9am-3pm. Size: seats 30.

QUICK & CASUAL EATERIES

Eatalian (Quick & Casual Italian)
342 Greenwich Avenue, Greenwich CT, 203.717.1212
Sometimes, no matter how much you want to like a restaurant, you just can't. This stylish, ultra modern eatery seems to be focused on take-out. Even the food delivered to tables is in carry-out containers.
Hours: Open Monday-Saturday 11am-5:30pm. Closed Sunday.
Prices: Lunch selections $12, salads and sandwiches $8. Size: seats 22.

El Charrito (Quick & Casual Mexican)
7 Apache Place, Riverside CT, 203.990.0200
www.ELcharritoLLC.com
Carlos and Alexandra Terron got their start by serving food from their truck in Stamford, before opening their off-the-beaten-path spot. El Charrito is one street in from the intersection of Sheephill Road and the Post Road. They were rated 25th out of 50 best tacos in USA by www.thedailymeal.com. We like their chicken enchiladas with green mole and their roughly chopped guacamole. We still prefer Tomatillo's tacos, although we haven't tried all of El Charrito's 21 tacos including: pig tummy, cow tongue and pig ear.
Hours: Open Monday-Saturday 9am-9pm. Closed Sunday.
Take-out or Delivery anywhere in Greenwich ($20 minimum purchase)

Garden Catering (Quick & Casual)
www.GardenCatering.net
• 185 Sound Beach Avenue, Old Greenwich CT, 203.698.2900
• 177 Hamilton Avenue, Byram CT, 203.422.2555
• 140 Midland Avenue, Port Chester NY, 914.934.7810 or 7852
• Catering office: 203.637.7966
Their fried chicken and chicken nuggets have made them famous. If you like fried chicken, don't miss this takeout.
Sound Beach Hours: Open Weekdays 6am-7pm, Saturday 6am-6pm; Sunday 6am-5pm. (Seasonal; stays open later in the Spring.)
Size: Primarily take-out.

green & tonic (Quick & Casual Vegan/Vegetarian)
- 7 Strickland Road, Cos Cob CT, 203.869.1376
- 85 Railroad Avenue, Greenwich CT, 855.464.2638

www.GreenAndTonic.com

If you think healthy food can't be tasty, you need to stop in this small eatery. The owner is Greenwich resident, Jeffrey Pandolfino, former owner of Plum Pure Foods. Vegans and everyone else will love their cold-pressed juices, smoothies, raw prepared foods, salads, soups, sandwiches and side dishes. You must try our favorite smoothie "Ultimate Warrior."

Hours: Open Weekdays 7am-7pm, Saturday 8am-5pm, Sunday 9am-5pm.

Prices: soups $6, wraps $8, salads $10, juices and smoothies $7-$8.

Size: Cos Cob seats 16.

Greenwich Pasta House (Quick & Casual)
Armonk NY, 203.992.8220

www.GreenwichPastaHouse.com

Greenwich Pasta House is part of the Mazzarulli Group. They also own Three Little Pigs BBQ, Westchester BBQ and Opus 465 as well as several other restaurants. The Pasta House has a huge menu but unfortunately we can not recommend it or their other ventures. We wish their food was as good as their marketing.

Hours: Saturday-Sunday 10am-8pm. Prices: Entrees $14-$22.

Size: Delivery only ($3 Delivery charge).

Greenwich Salad Company (Quick & Casual)
375 Greenwich Avenue, Greenwich CT, 203.869.6200

Bright, light, contemporary spot with a flower on each table. Stand in line to order one of their creations or design your own from their large selection of greens and toppings. Village Bagels are available all day (as long as their supply lasts).

Hours: Open Weekdays 7am-8pm, Saturday & Sunday 8am-5pm.

Prices: salads & wraps $7-$11; kids' menu $5-$8.

Size: seats 34.

QUICK & CASUAL EATERIES

Joey B's Famous Chile Hub (Quick & Casual)
118 River Road Extension, Cos Cob CT, 203.661.0573
www.sites.google.com/site/joeybschilihub
www.facebook.com/TheNewJoeyBs
We are not surprised at the popularity of this hot dog and hamburger, counter and stool restaurant. It's a magnet for children. Adults like their breakfasts as well as their chili and Scarpelli melts. (Scarpelli sausage is made in Cos Cob.) Joey B also does a lot of take-out business.
Prices: Lunch $5-$9, Kids $6.50.
Hours: Open Monday 6am-3pm, Tuesday-Friday 6am-8pm, Saturday 7am-3pm, Sunday 7am-2pm. Size: seats 14.

Layla's Falafel (Quick & Casual Middle Eastern)
• 245 Main Street, Stamford CT, 203.316.9041
• 936 High Ridge Road, Stamford CT, 203.461.8004
www.laylasfalafel.com
Repeatedly voted the best Middle Eastern food in Fairfield County, these two small, "Plain-Jane" eateries are cooking up Lebanese and other Middle Eastern favorites. Many of the dishes are vegetarian. Have a falafel (fritters made from ground chickpeas and spices), chicken shawafal or a signature salad and you will be coming back often.
Hours: Open everyday 11am-9pm. (Hours seasonal.)
Prices: (salads, falafel platters, grilled entrees) $10-$17.
Size: Main Street seats 30; High Ridge seats 20.

Leafline Salad Co (Quick & Casual)
41 Greenwich Avenue, Greenwich CT, 203.413.9900
www.LeafLineSalad.com, www.pickleboxsandwich.com
Whether you are health-conscious or calorie counting, this is a pleasant place to eat salad. Unlike the open grocery store salad bar, cheerful servers dip up the salads behind a partition-even carefully keeping nuts in separate containers. We like that they have the calorie count for each item. They are generous with the greens and they have a bunch of tasty dressings. Wraps and juices are available too. Barn scenes and a plant wall stir memories of Grandmother's farm garden. If you want a sandwich with your salad, try one of The Pickle Box Sandwich Company's specialties.
Hours: Open Weekdays 11am-8pm, Saturday & Sunday 11am-5pm.
Prices: Salads $9-$11; kids $6; free delivery and online ordering.
Size: seats 30.

QUICK & CASUAL EATERIES

Lobster Craft (Quick & Casual)
284 Tokeneke Road, Darien CT, 203.856.2635 www.lobstercraft.com
"Callooh! Callay!" He chortled in his joy." When I can't find the lobster truck in Greenwich, I can drive to this tiny, charmingly decorated spot and have a hot buttered lobster roll.
Hours: Tuesday-Sunday 11am-7pm (Thursday-Saturday until 8pm)
Prices: lobster rolls $17-$19. Size: 8 bar stools.

McDonald's (Quick & Casual)
• 268 West Putnam Avenue, Greenwich CT, 203.629.9068
• 1207 East Putnam Avenue, Riverside CT, 203.637.8598
Started in 1940, it is the world's largest hamburger fast food restaurant with 31,000 locations. Besides hamburgers, chicken sandwiches and french fries, McDonald's sells salads, wraps and smoothies. They are also trying to compete with Starbucks by offering high quality coffees.
Hours: West Putnam location open everyday 5am-1am. Riverside location open 24 hours. Size: seats 50 (Greenwich location).

Ole Mole (Quick & Casual Mexican)
1030 High Ridge Road (Shopping Center), Stamford CT, 203.461.9962
www.olemole.net
When you are in the mood for fresh, healthy Mexican cuisine, think Ole Mole. This unimposing Stamford location is bare bones and primarily for take-out. Quick friendly service and great food. Be sure to try the Sopa de Tortilla, Ole Mole salad, enchiladas suizas or the mole poblano.
Hours: Open everyday 11:30am-9pm.
Prices: Entrees $14-$18, burritos, tacos and quesadillas $7-$12. No wine is served. Size: seats 12 inside, 10 outside. No reservations.

Olive Branch Café (Quick & Casual, Deli)
26 Railroad Avenue, Greenwich CT, 203.622.9099
www.OliveBranchToGo.com
The Olive Branch, right next to the Greenwich Train Station, has a wide menu selection. We usually choose one of their salads – chicken with grapes, Asian salad or curry chicken. Their Mona Lisa Panini, the Chalet sandwich and soups are good.
Hours: Monday – Friday 6:30am – 4pm, Saturday 8am – 3pm.
Seating: 20   Delivery: Yes (free with $20 minimum order)

QUICK & CASUAL EATERIES

Panera Bread (Quick & Casual)
10 Westchester Avenue, Port Chester NY, 914.939.0079
www.Panerabread.com
Located at the movie complex in Port Chester, their soups, salads and sandwiches are a delight. Order at the counter, then have a seat in the large airy dining space and wait for your name to be called. We wish they had shorter lines, although the wait does afford time to decide what to order. Panera has 1,500 locations. It was one of the first companies to voluntarily post calorie information. Health magazine named Panera North America's healthiest fast food restaurant. Their website has a calorie/nutrition counter.
Hours: Open Monday-Thursday 7am-9pm, Friday & Saturday 7am-10pm, Sunday 7am-8pm.
Size: seats 100.

Pickle Box Sandwich Company (Quick and Casual)
41 Greenwich Avenue, Greenwich CT, 203.413.9910
www.pickleboxsandwich.com
Inside the Leafline Salad Co is a sandwich shop.

Steam (Quick & Casual Asian)
374 Greenwich Avenue, Greenwich CT, 203.992.1500, 1502
www.Steam374.com
Steam is a good name for the eclectic items on the menu of this bright spot on the Avenue. The specials are on a large blackboard. The service is friendly and helpful. Buns and all kinds of noodles are available. Our favorites are the small plates: steamed chicken dumplings, Vietnamese summer rolls, Thai Crab Cakes and Peking Duck Spring Rolls. We are not enamored with the large plates.
Hours: Open Monday-Thursday 11am-10pm, Friday & Saturday 11am-11pm, Sunday noon-10pm.
Prices: Lunch $9-$10; Dinner $7-$15;
Size: Seats 18; Reservations only for groups of 4 or larger; lots of takeout. They only deliver to Greenwich Avenue.

QUICK & CASUAL EATERIES

Subway Sandwich (Quick & Casual)

- (Top of Avenue) 28 Greenwich Avenue, Greenwich CT, 203.622.1515
- (Bottom of Avenue) 401 Greenwich Avenue, Greenwich CT, 203.422.2218
- 469 West Putnam Avenue, Greenwich CT, 203.769.1326

www.subway.com

Here's the place for those famous sandwiches made with bread freshly baked on the premises. Our favorite is the sweet onion chicken teriyaki on honey oat. Subway started in 1965 in Bridgeport, CT. It now has almost 38,000 locations.

Hours: 28 Greenwich Avenue open Weekdays 8am-9pm, Saturday 9am-8pm, Sunday noon-7pm. 401 Greenwich Avenue open Weekdays 8am-8pm, Saturday 9am-8pm, Sunday 10am-5pm. West Putnam location open Weekdays 7:30am-10pm, Saturday 9am-10pm, Sunday 10am-9pm.

Size: take-out only, except West Putnam Avenue which seats 16.

Taco Bell (Quick & Casual)

1371 East Putnam Avenue, Old Greenwich, 203.698.2290

www.TacoBell.com

Started in 1962 by Glen Bell, they serve a variety of Tex-Mex foods including tacos, burritos, quesadillas and nachos in about 6,000 locations.

Hours: Open Sunday-Wednesday 7am-midnight, Thursday-Saturday 7am-1am. Size: seats 20

Texas Chili (Quick & Casual)

36 Broad Street, Port Chester NY, 914.937.0840

www.TexasChiliRestaurant.com

www.facebook.com/TexasChiliRest

A real hole-in-the wall, with great chili served with a smile. This spin-off from Pat's Hubba Hubba has three locations: Port Chester, Mamaroneck and New Rochelle. We've been addicted to their secret hot chili recipe for years. If you are up late and want to warm your taste buds, go here and order a double steak chili cheese wedge.

Hours: Open everyday 6am-4am.

Prices: Cash Only: Hot dogs, burgers and wedges $2-$7.

Size: Seats 18: two tables of 4 and stools at the counter.

Three Little Pigs BBQ (Quick & Casual)

See Greenwich Pasta House for the Review.

Tomatillo Taco Joint (Quick & Casual Mexican)

65 East Putnam Avenue, Cos Cob CT, 203.869.0928

www.tomatillotacojoint.com

Moe Gad has created another winner-Tomatillo Taco Joint. It has a bright and simple decor. At Tomatillo be prepared at the counter to make your choices: soft or crispy tortillas; fillings of chicken, beef, fish or pork, and toppings and garnishes of all kinds. You can even have a vegetarian, guacamole taco. We keep returning for a plate of three soft tortillas filled with hacked chicken and topped with shredded cheese, chopped tomatoes and spicy hot sauce. Theodore, age 5, loves the Churros for dessert.

Hours: Open Monday 11am-8pm, Tuesday-Friday 11am-9pm, Saturday noon-9pm, Sunday noon-8pm.

Prices: Tacos $3 each.

Size: seats 18.

Tropical Smoothie Café (Quick & Casual)

410 Greenwich Avenue, Greenwich CT, 203.340.9430

www.tropicalsmoothiecafegreenwich.com

A great variety of smoothies-24 oz smoothies for adults and 12 oz ones for kids. But this is not just a smoothie place, the wraps, noodle dishes and salads are tasty too.

Hours: Weekdays, 7am-10pm, Saturday 8am-12am, Sunday 9am-10pm.

Size: seats 12.

Upper Crust Bagel Company (Quick & Casual)

197 Sound Beach Avenue, Old Greenwich CT, 203.698.0079

www.UpperCrustBagel.com

A good place to sit down and chat while having a deli sandwich and a fruit smoothie. They have tasty old-fashioned kettle-boiled and hearth-baked bagels, as well as gourmet spreads and coffees. We think they make the best bagels in Fairfield County.

Hours: Open Weekdays 6am-4pm, Saturday 7am-4pm, Sunday 7am-3pm.

Size: Seats 20.

QUICK & CASUAL EATERIES

Wendy's (Quick & Casual)
420 West Putnam Avenue, 203.869.9885
www.Wendys.com
Wendy's, formerly known as Wendy's Old Fashioned Hamburgers, was founded by Dave Thomas in 1969. With almost 7,000 locations, it is the 3rd largest hamburger chain behind McDonalds and Burger King. This fast food burger place has a drive-through.
Hours: Open everyday 10am-1am.
Size: seats 74.

Westchester BBQ (Quick & Casual)
See Greenwich Pasta House for the Review.

Yangtze Riverside (Quick & Casual Chinese)
1074 East Putnam Avenue, Riverside CT, 203.698.0800/0808
This friendly take-out place has fed Greenwich residents for years. This is one of the few places you can order Peking Duck without advance notice.
Hours: Open Sunday-Thursday 11am-10pm, Friday & Saturday 11am-4pm.
Size: Take out only, Free delivery for orders over $20.

TIP: HOMEMADE BBQ SAUCE
Many BBQ places such as Dinosaur BBQ and Bobby's Pit Stop sell their BBQ sauces. Both have won awards for their sauces from www.TheHotPepper.com

REAL ESTATE

Buyer Agency

On June 1, 1997, Connecticut mandated that Realtors represent either the buyer or the seller, but not both (unless dual or designated agency is disclosed and agreed to by both parties) in the same transaction. Buyers like being represented by their own Realtor because their Realtor can tell them what they think a house is worth and provide excellent guidance through the real estate process. This extra protection costs the buyer nothing because the buyer's Realtor is still paid by the seller. In the first meeting, the buyer signs a representation agreement with their Realtor much the way a seller signs a listing agreement with their Realtor.

Greenwich Association of Realtors (GAR)

40 East Elm Street, Greenwich CT, 203.869.0240
Executive Vice President, Theresa Hatton
www.greenwichrealtors.com

When many other towns gave up their local boards, Greenwich did not. Greenwich has an outstanding organization devoted to local real estate. This service is funded by the over 800 active Realtors in town and is extremely helpful to homeowners and buyers. Member Realtors follow a strict code of ethics. The Association is governed by a 9-member board elected by their peers. You can use the Association site to search for Realtors by firm or by name. The Association is the home of the Greenwich MLS.

Greenwich Multiple Listing Service (MLS)

It is important to understand how Greenwich real estate works. Unlike New York City and many other locations, Greenwich Realtors share their listings. In Greenwich all properties, with rare exceptions, are multiple-listed with the Greenwich MLS. To buy property in Greenwich, you need to select one Realtor you like and trust. You will have access through your Realtor to the entire market.

Greenwich Property Owners Association (GPOA)

www.GreenwichPropertyOwners.com

This is a not-for-profit organization established by Greenwich residents to keep homeowners informed about Town Hall decisions. Please join, it's a great way to know what may be impacting your property's value. It's also a great way to make your voice heard.

RELIGION

Sections
Houses of Worship
Religious Organizations

HOUSES OF WORSHIP

Albertson Memorial Church of Spiritualism
293 Sound Beach Avenue, Old Greenwich CT, 203.637.4615
www.AlbertsonChurch.org

Anglican Church of the Advent
(Anglican-Episcopal)
Meeting at North Congregational Church, 606 Riversville Road, Greenwich CT.
Rectory, 5 Webb Avenue, Greenwich CT, 203.861.2432
www.ChurchOfTheAdvent.org

Annunciation Greek Orthodox Church
1230 Newfield Avenue, Stamford CT, 203.322.2093
www.annunciationofstamford.org

Bethel AME Church
42 Lake Avenue, Greenwich CT, 203.661.3099

Christ Church of Greenwich
254 East Putnam Avenue, Greenwich CT, 203.869.6600
www.christchurchgreenwich.org/

Church of Jesus Christ of Latter Day Saints
834 Stillwater Road, Stamford CT, 203.324.9575
www.lds.org

Diamond Hill United Methodist Church
521 East Putnam Avenue, Greenwich CT, 203.869.2395
www.diamondhillumc.com/

Dingletown Community Church
(Nondenominational Protestant)
Stanwich Road and Barnstable Lane, Greenwich CT, 203.629.5923
www.Dingletown.org

RELIGION

First Baptist Church
10 Northfield Street, Greenwich CT, 203.869.7988
www.firstbaptistchurchgreenwich.org/

First Church of Christ, Scientist
Church: 11 Park Place, Greenwich CT, 203.869.1555
Reading Room: 333 Greenwich Avenue, Greenwich CT, 203.869.2503
www.ChristianScienceCT.org/greenwich

First Church of Round Hill
(Interdenominational)
464 Round Hill Road, Greenwich CT, 203.629.3876
www.FirstChurchOfRoundhill.org

First Congregational Church
108 Sound Beach Avenue, Old Greenwich CT, 203.637.1791
www.fccog.org

First Lutheran Church
38 Field Point Road, Greenwich CT, 203.869.0032
www.1stLutheranGCT.org

First Presbyterian Church
One West Putnam Avenue, Greenwich cT, 203.869.8686
www.fpcg.org

First United Methodist Church
59 East Putnam Avenue, Greenwich CT, 203.629.9584
http://fumcgreenwich.com/

Grace Church of Greenwich
(Presbyterian Church in America)
Meets at Woman's Club of Greenwich,
89 Maple Avenue, Greenwich CT, 203.861.7555
www.GraceChurchGreenwich.com

Greek Orthodox Church of the Archangels
1527 Bedford Street, Stamford CT, 203.348.4216
www.archangels.ct.goarch.org

Greenwich Baptist Church
10 Indian Rock Lane, Greenwich CT, 203.869.2807
www.GreenwichBaptist.org

RELIGION

Greenwich Reform Synagogue
1037 East Putnam Avenue, 2nd Floor, Greenwich CT, 203.629.0018
www.grs.org

Harvest Time Assembly of God
1338 King Street, Greenwich CT, 203.531.7778
www.HTChurch.com

Japanese Gospel Church
(Protestant Evangelical Christian Church for Japanese speakers)
Meeting at St. Paul Evangelical Lutheran Church
286 Delavan Avenue, Byram CT, 203.531.6450
www.jgclmi.com

North Greenwich Congregational Church
606 Riversville Road, Greenwich CT, 203.869.7763
www.NorthGreenwichChurch.org

Presbyterian Church of Old Greenwich
38 West End Avenue, Old Greenwich CT, 203.637.3669
www.pcogonline.org

Quaker Religious Society of Friends
317 New Canaan Road, Wilton, CT, 203.762.5669
www.wiltonfriends.org

Round Hill Community Church
(Independent & Non-denominational Christian)
395 Round Hill Road, Greenwich CT, 203.869.1091
www.roundhillcommunitychurch.org

Sacred Heart Roman Catholic Church
95 Henry Street, Byram CT, 203.531.8730 (Rectory)

St. Agnes Roman Catholic Church
247 Stanwich Road, Greenwich CT, 203.869.5396 (Rectory)
www.Stagnesrc.org

St. Barnabas Episcopal Church
954 Lake Avenue, Greenwich CT, 203.661.5526
www.stbarnabasgreenwich.org

RELIGION

St. Catherine of Siena Roman Catholic Church
4 Riverside Avenue, Riverside CT, 203.637.3661
www.stcath.org

St Mary's Holy Assumption
(Russian Orthodox)
141 Den Road, Stamford CT, 203.329.9933
www.stmaryofstamford.org

St. Mary Roman Catholic Church
178 Greenwich Avenue, Greenwich CT, 203.869.9393 (Rectory)
www.StMaryParishGreenwich.org

St. Michael the Archangel Roman Catholic Church
469 North Street, Greenwich CT, 203.869.5421 (Rectory)
http://www.stmichaelgreenwich.com/

St. Paul Evangelical Lutheran Church
286 Delavan Avenue, 203.531.8466
www.stpaulsbyram.org

St. Paul Roman Catholic Church
84 Sherwood Avenue, Greenwich CT, 203.531.8741
www.StPaulGreenwich.org

St. Paul's Episcopal Church
200 Riverside Avenue, Riverside CT, 203.637.2447
www.stpaulsriverside.org

St. Roch Roman Catholic Church
10 St. Roch Avenue, Byram CT, 203.869.4176
http://www.strochchurch.com/

St. Saviour's Episcopal Church
350 Sound Beach Avenue, Old Greenwich CT, 203.637.2262
www.SaintSaviours.org

St. Timothy Chapel
1034 North Street, Banksville NY, 203.661.5196

Second Congregational Church
139 East Putnam Avenue, Greenwich CT, 203.869.9311
www.2cc.org

RELIGION

Stanwich Congregational Church
202 Taconic Road, Greenwich CT, 203.661.4420
www.stanwichchurch.org

Temple Sholom
300 East Putnam Avenue, Greenwich CT, 203.869.7191
www.TempleSholom.com

Trinity Church
15 Sherwood Place, Greenwich CT, 203.618.0808
www.trinitychurchonline.org

Unitarian Universalist Society
20 Forest Street, Stamford CT, 203.348.0708
www.uusis.org

RELIGIOUS ORGANIZATIONS

Chabad Lubavitch of Greenwich
75 Mason Street, Greenwich CT, 203.629.9059
www.ChabadGreenwich.org

Chavurat Deevray Torah
49 Arcadia Road, Old Greenwich CT, 203.637.9478
Reform/Conservative Jewish Study Group
http://www.chavurah.org/default.htm

Greenwich Center for Hope and Renewal
237 Taconic Road, Greenwich CT, 203.340.9816
www.HopeAndRenewal.org
Private and confidential services such as: counseling, interventions, renewal groups, seminars, and professional training.

Greenwich Chaplaincy Services
70 Parsonage Road, Greenwich CT, 203.618.4236
A non-profit supported by local churches and synagogues. They provide pastoral and spiritual care to the residents of nursing homes and assisted living facilities.
www.greenwichchaplaincy.org

RELIGION

Greenwich Leadership Forum
www.GreenwichLeadershipForum.org
Lectures on faith and ethics in the workplace.

Hadassah, Greenwich Chapter
Temple Sholom, 300 East Putnam Avenue, Greenwich CT, 203.869.7191
http://www.templesholom.com/

Interfaith Council of Southwestern Connecticut
(formerly the Council of Churches and Synagogues)
203.348.2800
www.interfaithcouncil.org

Philoptochos
www.philoptochos.org
Despina Fassuliotis, 203.661.5991

Soto Zen Buddhism
@ First Congregational Church, Old Greenwich CT, 914.772.1974
http://www.twiningvines.org

UJA Federation of Greenwich
1 Holly Hill Lane, Greenwich CT, 203.552.1818
Pamela Ehrenkranz, Executive Director
www.UJAFedGreenwich.org

Young Life of Greenwich
(Nondenominational Christian organization for teenagers)
203.340.2123
www.greenwich.younglife.org

RESTAURANTS-OUR FAVORITES

We are just like you. Some restaurants appeal to us more than others. Not all of the restaurants often considered the "Best" are on our list.

American
Cos Cobber
Ginger Man
Green & Tonic (Quick & Casual)
Putnam Restaurant
Rye Grill & Bar

New American
American Bounty
   (Culinary Institute of America)
Farmer's Table
Harvest
Hudson Grille
Mama's Boy
Match
Olio
Rebecca's
School House
(The) Spread
Xaviar's
X20

Asian
Asiana Cafe
Penang Grill

Bagels (Quick & Casual)
Upper Crust Bagel Company

Bakeries
(Reviewed in Bakeries)
Black Forest
(The) Kneaded Bread
St. Moritz
Versailles

Barbeque
Bar-B-Q
Bobby Qs Pit Stop (Quick & Casual)
Dinosaur Bar-B-Q

Brunch on Sunday
Windfield's @ the Hyatt
L'Escale

Chinese
Ching's Table
Hunan Gourmet
Oriental Gourmet

Cuban
Dolce Cubano

Delicatessens
(Reviewed in Delicatessen Section)
Aux Délices
Balducci's
Fjord Fisheries
Garelick & Herbs
Pasta Vera

Diner
City Limits Diner

Food Truck
Lobster Craft

RESTAURANTS-OUR FAVORITES

French
(La) Panètiere
(Le) Penquin
Bernard's
Bocuse
    (Culinary Institute of America)
(Le) Fat Poodle
Crémaillère
Meli-Melo
Versailles

Greek
Eos
Estia
Famous Greek Kitchen

Hamburgers
Burgers, Shakes & Fries
Sundown Saloon
Texas Chili (Quick & Casual)
Westchester Burger Company
    (Rye Brook location)

Indian
Coromandel
Mumbai Times
Tawa
Thali

Italian
Campagna @ The Bedford Post
Caterina de Medici (Culinary Institute of America)
Centro
Golden View Firenze
Pasta Nostra
Pasta Vera
Tarry Lodge
Terra
Villa Italia
Valbella

Japanese
Kira Sushi
Sushi Nanase

Latin American
Brasitas (Norwalk location)
Sonora
Paloma
Valencia Luncheria

Mexican
Bartaco (Port Chester location)
Ole Mole
Tequila Mockingbird
Tomatillo Taco Joint
    (Quick & Casual)

Middle Eastern
(The) Fez
Tabouli Grill

Pizza
California Pizza Kitchen
Coals
Glenville Pizza
Pizza Post
Re Napoli
Strada 18

Pub
Little Pub
McShanes
Port Chester Hall
Zaza

Quick & Casual Fast Food
Bruckner's
Chicken Joe's
Garden Catering

RESTAURANTS-OUR FAVORITES

Seafood
Coast
Elm Street Oyster House
F.I.S.H.
Gus's Franklin Park Restaurant
Mediterraneo (Greenwich location)
Rowayton Seafood Company

Southwestern
Boxcar Cantina
Truck

Spanish
Barcelona (Greenwich location)
La Paella

Steak (Also see Barbeque)
Blackstones
Hibachi Steak at Abis
Washington Prime

Tea
(The) Drawing Room

Thai
Little Thai Kitchen

TIP: CHOWDER COOKOFF
Want to find the best bowl of New England clam chowder? Every year, in early June, chefs in Norwalk, CT compete in the annual "Splash! Clam Chowder Cook-Off." Check their website www.norwalk.ws or www.seaport.org for the annual winner and their recipe. Better yet, for a $5 donation you can attend the festival, taste the soups and place a vote for the best. Call the Norwalk Seaport Association 203.838.9444 for details.

Restaurants are divided into several sections, to make finding the one you want easier. This Index is for the more formal sit down restaurants. The less formal restaurants are in their own section, Quick & Casual Eateries. Pizza Parlors, Delicatessens and Food Trucks also have their own sections.

Family Friendly

Abis
Asiana
Bar-B-Q
Beach House Café
Beehive
Bella Nonna
Boatyard BBQ & Grill
Boxcar Cantina
California Pizza Kitchen
Capriccio
Centro Ristorante
(The) Cheesecake Factory
Ching's Table
City Limits Diner
Coromandel
Chocopologie
Cobble Stone
(The) Cos Cobber
Crab Shell
Doral Arrowwood Atrium (Sunday Brunch)
Edo
Frank's
Famous Greek Kitchen
Gates
Glory Days
Gus's Franklin Park Restaurant
Hunan Gourmet
IHOP
Kazu
Kona Grill
Long Ridge Tavern
Meli-Melo
Mumbai Times

Old Mill Saloon and Smokehouse
Oriental Gourmet
P.F. Chang's China Bistro
Panda Pavilion 3
Pasta Vera
Piero's
Plan B Burger
Pomodoro
Plaza Restaurant
Putnam
Q Restaurant
Rizzuto
Rye Bar and Grill
Sundown Saloon
Tequila Mockingbird
Truck
Westchester Burger (Rye Brook)
Winfields @ the Hyatt

Hot Spot

Bartaco
Barcelona
Crab Shack @ the Crab Shell
Dolce Cubano
Eleven14 Kitchen
Little Pub
Sundown Saloon
ZAZA Gastrobar

RESTAURANT INDEX-CATEGORY

Kosher
613

Late Night
Bar-B-Q
Barcelona
Bartaco
Cobble Stone
Dinosaur Bar-B-Que
Glory Days
Harlan Publick
MacKenzie's Grill Room
McShanes
Tigin

Open Most Holidays
Abis
California Pizza Kitchen
(The) Cheesecake Factory
Glory Days
IHOP
L'Escale
Mediterraneo Restaurant
Pasta Vera
Putnam Restaurant

Pubs and Gastro Pubs
Cobble Stone
Ginger Man
Little Pub
MacDuffs Public House
MacKenzie's Grill Room
McShanes
Port Chester Hall
Rye House
Sign of the Whale
World of Beer
Tigin
Zaza

Romantic
Bedford Post
Bernard's
(La) Crémaillère
(La) Panètiere
Thomas Henkelmann (at the Homestead Inn)
Valbella
Xaviar's

Vegetarian
Back 40 Kitchen
green & tonic (vegan) in Quick & Casual
Lime
Navaratna

RESTAURANT INDEX-CUISINE

American
613
Back 40 Kitchen
Beach House Café
Beehive
California Pizza Kitchen
(The) Cheesecake Factory
City Limits Diner
Chocopologie
Cobble Stone
(The) Cos Cobber
Doral Arrowwood Atrium (Brunch)
(The) Drawing Room
Garden Café (at Greenwich Hospital)
Gates
Ginger Man
IHOP
Kona Grill
Le Pain Quotidien
Lime
Long Ridge Tavern
Meetinghouse
Moderne Barn
Plan B Burger Bar
Plaza Restaurant
Purdy's
Putnam Restaurant
Rye Grill & Bar
Sundown Saloon
Two Door
Westchester Burger Company
Winfields @ the Hyatt

American New
Bedford Post (@ The Barn)
Blue Hill at Stone Barns
Char
Crew Restaurant
American Bounty (See Culinary Institute)
Eleven14 Kitchen
Elm Restaurant
Farmer's Table
Harlan Publick
Harlan Social
Harvest
Hudson Grille
Inn at Pound Ridge
Mama's Boy
Match
Napa & Company
Olio
Hudson Grille
Rebecca's
Restaurant North
School House Restaurant
South End
(The) Spread
Washington Prime
Xaviar's
X20

RESTAURANT INDEX-CUISINE

Asian & Asian Fusion
(Chinese, Japanese & Thai are listed separately)
Asian Bistro
Asiana Café
Bambou
Ching's Table
Euro Asian
Penang Grill
Tengda Asian Bistro

British
MacDuffs Public House

Barbeque
Bar-B-Q
Boatyard BBQ & Seafood
Dinosaur Bar-B-Que
Opus 465
   (aka Wild Westchester BBQ)
   (aka Three Little Pigs BBQ)
Q Restaurant

Cajun
Rye Road House

Chinese
Ching's Table
Hunan Gourmet
Oriental Gourmet
P.F. Chang's China Bistro
Panda Pavilion 3

Cuban
Dolce Cubano

French
Barrique
Bernard's
Bocuse (See Culinary Institute)
Boulevard 18
(La) Bretagne
(La) Crémaillère
(Le) Fat Poodle
L'Escale
Meli-Melo
(La) Panètiere
(Le) Penguin
Thomas Henkelmann (at the Homestead Inn)
Versailles

Greek
Eos
Estia
Famous Greek Kitchen
Glory Days (Diner)

Indian
Coromandel
Mumbai Times
Navaratna
Tandoori
Tawa
Thali

Irish
McShanes
Tigin

RESTAURANT INDEX-CUISINE

Italian
Albas
Applausi Osteria
Aria
Arrosto
Aurora
Bar Rosso
Bedford Post (Campagna)
Bella Nonna
Café Silvium
California Pizza KItchen
Capriccio
Cava Wine Bar & Restaurant
Centro Ristorante
Columbus Park Trattoria
Coals (Pizza)
Caterina de Medici (See Culinary Institute)
Doppio
Fairways
Frank's
Golden View Firenze
Il Sogno
Louie's
Madonia
Marianacci's
Mediterraneo Restaurant
Morello Bistro
Nessa
Pasquale Ristorante
Pasta Nostra
Pasta Vera
Piero's

Polpo
Pomodoro
Quattro Pazzi
Rizzuto's
Siena
Strada 18
Tarry Lodge
Terra Ristorante Italiano
Trattoria632
Valbella
Villa Italia
Zanni

Japanese
Abis
Bambou
Edo
Kazu
Kira Sushi
Kona Grill
Sushi Nanase
Sushi Soba
Tengda

Latin American & Nuevo Latino
(Mexican listed separately)
Acuario (Peruvian)
Basso
Brasitas
Copacabana (Brazilian Steak House)
Paloma
Sonora
Valencia Luncheria

RESTAURANT INDEX-CUISINE

Mexican
Casa Volla
Maryann's Mexican Restaurant
Rio Border
Tequila Mockingbird

Middle Eastern
(The) Fez (Moroccan)
Tabouli Grill

Portuguese
Douro

Seafood
Boatyard Barbecue and Seafood
Coast
Crab Shell
Elm Street Oyster House
F.I.S.H.
Gus's Franklin Park Restaurant
L'Escale
Mediterraneo Restaurant
Morgans Fish House
Rowayton Seafood Company
SoNo Seaport Seafood

South American
(see Latin American)

Southwestern
Boxcar Cantina
Old Mill Saloon and Smokehouse
Truck

Spanish
(also see Tapas & Tacos)
Barcelona
(La) Paella

Steak
(BBQ listed separately as are Japanese Steakhouses)
Abis
Blackstones
(The) Capital Grille
Copacabana
  (Brazilian Churrascaria)
Edo
Frankie and Johnie's
Gabriele's Italian Steakhouse
Outback
Washington Prime

Swiss
Melting Pot

Tapas & Tacos
Bartaco
Barcelona
Casa Volla
Dolce Cubano

Thai
Little Buddha
Little Thai Kitchen
Thai Basil

RESTAURANTS BY NEIGHBORHOOD

Armonk NY
Beehive
Moderne Barn
Opus 465
Restaurant North
Zanni

Banksville NY
(La) Crémaillère

Bedford NY
Bedford Post
Meetinghouse
Truck

Byram CT
Char
Little Thai Kitchen
Famous Greek Kitchen

Cos Cob CT
Coast
(The) Cos Cobber
(The) Drawing Room
green & tonic (Quick & Casual)
Little Pub
Louie's
Mumbai Times

Darien CT
Coromandel
Melting Pot

Glenville CT
Bambou
Centro Ristorante
Rebecca's

Greenwich CT (Center)
Abis
Asiana Cafe
Back 40 Kitchen
Barcelona
Bella Nonna
Blackstones
Boxcar Cantina
Crew Restaurant
Doppio
Douro
Elm Street Oyster House
Fairways
Gabriele's Italian Steak House
Garden Café (at Greenwich Hospital)
Ginger Man
Glory Days
Golden View Firenze
Hunan Gourmet
Kira Sushi
L'Escale
MacDuffs Public House
Mediterraneo Restaurant
Meli-Melo
Morello Bistro
(Le) Pain Quotidien
Panda Pavilion 3
Pasta Vera
Penang Grill
(Le) Penguin
Plaza Restaurant
Polpo
Putnam Restaurant
Sundown Saloon
Tengda Asian Bistro
...CONTINUED...

277

Greenwich CT (Center)...

Terra Ristorante Italiano
Thai Basil
Thomas Henkelmann (at the Homestead Inn)
Two Door
Versailles

Harrison NY

Gus's Franklin Park Restaurant

Hyde Park NY

(See Culinary Institute)
American Bounty
Bocuse
Caterina de Medici

New Canaan CT

Boulevard 18
Cava Wine Bar & Restaurant
Ching's Table
Elm Restaurant
Farmer's Table
Gates
South End
Tequila Mockingbird
Thali

Norwalk CT

Barcelona
Basso
Brasitas
Chocopologie
Coromandel
Estia
Harlan Publick
Kazu
Lime
Match
Mama's Boy
Mediterraneo
Old Mill Saloon & Steakhouse
(La) Paella
Pasta Nostra
Rio Border
SoNo Seaport Seafood
(The) Spread
Strada 18
Valencia Luncheria
Washington Prime

Old Greenwich CT

Applausi Osteria
Beach House Café
(Le) Fat Poodle
Oriental Gourmet
Sushi Soba
Winfields @ the Hyatt

Piermont NY

Xaviar's

RESTAURANTS BY NEIGHBORHOOD

Port Chester NY
Albas
Acuario
Arrosto
Bartaco
Coals
Copacabana
Edo
Euro Asian
Frank's
Il Sogno Ristorante
Marianacci's
Maryann's Mexican Restaurant
McShanes
Nessa
Pasquale Ristorante
Piero's
Port Chester Hall
Q Restaurant
Rye House
Sonora
Tandoori
Tarry Lodge

Pound Ridge NY
(The) Inn at Pound Ridge

Purchase NY
Cobble Stone
Trattoria632

Ridgefield CT
Bernard's

Riverside CT
Eleven14 Kitchen
Pomodoro
Valbella

Rowayton CT
Rowayton Seafood Company

Rye Brook NY
Doral Arrowwood Atrium
Westchester Burger Company

Rye NY
Aurora
Frankie & Johnnie's
Morgans Fish House
(La) Panètiere
Ruby's Oyster Bar & Bistro
Rye Grill & Bar
Rye Road House

Salem NY
Purdy's Farmer & the Fish (South Salem)

RESTAURANTS BY NEIGHBORHOOD

Stamford CT
613
Asian Bistro
Aria
Bar-B-Q
Bar Rosso
Barrique Bistro
Bartaco
Barcelona
Boatyard BBQ & Grill
Brasitas
(La) Bretagne
Café Silvium
California Pizza Kitchen
(The) Capital Grille
Capriccio
Casa Volla
Cask Republic
City Limits Diner
Columbus Park Trattoria
Coromandel
Crab Shell
Dinosaur Bar-B-Que
Dolce Cubano
Eos
(The) Fez
F.I.S.H.
Harlan Social
Hudson Grille
IHOP
Kona Grill
Little Buddha
Long Ridge Tavern
Madonia
Maryann's Mexican Restaurant
Napa & Company

Navaratna
Olio
Paloma
P.F. Chang's China Bistro
Plan B Burger Bar
Quattro Pazzi
Rizzuto's
Siena
Sign of the Whale
Tabouli Grill
Tawa
Tengda Asian Bistro
Tigin
Villa Italia
World of Beer
ZAZA Gastrobar

Tarrytown NY
Blue Hill at Stone Barns

White Plains NY
Cheesecake Factory
Outback
P.F. Chang's China Bistro
Sushi Nanase
Westchester Burger Company

Wilton CT
School House Restaurant

Yonkers NY
X20

RESTAURANTS

Restaurants are divided into several sections, to make finding the one you want easier. Reviews in this section are for the more formal sit down restaurants. The less formal restaurants are in their own section, Quick & Casual Eateries. Pizza Parlors, Delicatessens and Food Trucks also have their own sections.

613 (formerly Kosh) (American, Kosher)
108 Prospect Street, Stamford CT, 203.614.8777
www.613restaurant.com
Part Deli, part informal lunch spot, part elegant dinner restaurant, part sports bar, 613 (for the number of commandments) has good Kosher food. The soft modern decor is attractive and sound- proofed to make conversations easy. The wait staff are very helpful. And, of course, having its own parking lot is a plus in Stamford.
Hours: Lunch, Sunday-Thursday 12pm-4pm;
Dinner, Monday-Thursday 4pm-9pm, Sunday 4pm-10pm.
Prices: Lunch entrees, $9-$15; Dinner entrees, $17-$35;
glass of wine $10-$13. Size: seats 130 in five areas.

Abis (Japanese)
381 Greenwich Avenue, Greenwich CT, 203.862.9100
www.abisjapanese.com
A restaurant with two personalities—the one side is traditional Japanese cuisine, the other is an Hibachi steakhouse. In the steakhouse, youngsters have a wonderful time watching their hibachi meals being prepared. The traditional menu is full of familiar choices. We are fans of their Japanese noodle dishes such as Udon or Soba. For lunch be sure to try the box lunch.
Hours: Lunch, Sunday-Thursday 11:30am-2:30pm, Saturday 12pm-2:30pm; Dinner, Monday-Thursday 5:30pm-9:30pm, Friday & Saturday 5:30pm-10:30pm, Sunday 5:30pm-9pm. Open most holidays, including Christmas and New Year's for dinner. Closed Thanksgiving. (The dinner menu is served all day Saturday & Sunday.)
Prices: Lunch, entrees $9-$14; Dinner, entrees $15-$27; Hibachi $19-$37; Hibachi children's menu $15-$19; glass of wine $7-$10.
Size: Hibachi side has 10 cook tables, each seating 8; the traditional area seats 74.

RESTAURANTS

Albas (Italian)
400 North Main Street, Port Chester NY, 914.937.2236
www.albasrestaurant.com
Where else is one greeted by a valet in a tux? This bright, large, upscale restaurant features consistently good Northern Italian food. We can't resist starting with the delicious Caesar salad and ending with Zabaglione. They are both made at your table; it's like having a private cooking lesson. The waiters, though less formally attired than the valet, are swift and professional. We find this restaurant a nice mix of refined and comfortable. You can expect a pleasant evening.
Hours: Lunch, Weekdays 11:30am-3pm; Dinner, Monday-Thursday 5:30pm-10pm, Friday 5:30pm-10:30pm, Saturday 5:30pm-11:00pm; Closed Sunday except for private parties of 50-200.
Prices: Lunch entrees $18-$33; Dinner entrees $21-$39; glass of wine $10. Size: seats 150.

American Bounty (New American)
See review under Culinary Institute.

Applausi Osteria (Italian)
199 Sound Beach Avenue, Old Greenwich CT, 203.637.4447
www.OsteriaApplausi.com
One of the three successful Marchetti-Tarantino family restaurants is located right in the heart of Old Greenwich. They own Columbus Park in Stamford and Tarantino's in Westport. Applausi, sparsely decorated, sometimes noisy, is a popular spot. You will find lots of interesting pasta choices. We like to share some of the pastas to begin, followed by one their specialties like the lemon rainbow trout or the rib-eye steak.
Hours: Lunch, Weekdays 12pm-2:30pm; Dinner, Sunday 5pm-9pm (except in the summer), Monday-Thursday 5:30pm-10pm, Friday & Saturday 5:30pm-10:30pm.
Prices: Lunch entrees $13-$20, wine by glass $8; Dinner entrees $18-$34, wine by glass $10-$15. Size: seats 55.

RESTAURANTS

Acuario (Peruvian)
163 North Main Street, Port Chester NY, 914.937.2338
www.acuariorestaurant.com
If you like ceviche, you will find 10 varieties on their menu. Not dressy, but certainly not your local dive. Even though there is a wide selection of Peruvian seafood and other entrees, we tend to skip the entrees and order the generous sized Ceviche, followed by their good flan. We especially like the Pescado Ceviche. If you order an entree, try the Pescado Saltado. The Peruvian soft drinks must be an acquired taste.
Hours: Lunch, every day 12pm-3pm; Dinner, Monday-Wednesday 5pm-10pm, Thursday-Saturday 5pm-11pm, Sunday 5pm-9pm.
Prices: Lunch $8-$12; Dinner entrees $10-$22.
Size: seats 45.

Aria (Italian)
1033 Washington Boulevard, Stamford CT, 203.324.2742
Located close to the cluster of Stamford dining spots is a small, attractive Tuscan restaurant with its own parking lot. Tables are arranged around a large wine cabinet (with an oversized chandelier). Conversations are easy. The staff is helpful. The lentil soup, butternut squash soup and Tortelloni de la Zia, are quite special.
Hours: Lunch, Weekdays 12pm-3pm; Dinner, Monday-Thursday 5pm-10:30pm, Friday & Saturday 5pm-11pm.
Prices: Lunch, (salads, wraps, pasta) $15-$30; Dinner, entrees $15-$35; glass of wine $9-$25.
Size: seats 60, party area seats 10.

Arrosto (Italian)
25 South Regent Street, Port Chester NY, 914.939.2727
www.ArrostoRestaurant.com
This large restaurant, designed around a pizza oven, gives us a number of ups and downs. The appetizers like the Arancini (rice balls) and the Crostino (Sheep's Milk Ricotta and Honey) are delicious. The entrees are just OK. Accept the drawbacks and choose this place for drinks, appetizers & pizzas and have fun with friends.
Hours: Dinner, Tuesday-Thursday 5pm-10pm, Friday & Saturday 5pm-11pm, Sunday 3pm-9pm. Closed Monday.
Prices: pizzas & entrees $14-$36, Tuesday-Thursday prix fixe specials $25-$30; glass of wine $9-$12; Sunday is family-style, fixed price $19, bottle of wine ½ price.
Size: seats 230.

RESTAURANTS

Asian Bistro (Asian)
121 Towne Street (Harbor Point Area), Stamford CT, 203.998.7333
www.StamfordAsianBistro.com
This darkish, blue and gold night club-style spot is not just for drinks. It has enjoyable food like the black pepper tuna. Primarily Japanese, Chinese and Thai food are on a large menu with lots of pictures to help you choose. The staff is friendly and the presentation is artistic.
Hours: Lunch, Monday-Saturday 11am-3:30pm, Sunday 12pm-3:30pm; Dinner, Sunday-Thursday 3:30pm-10pm, Friday & Sat 3:30pm-11pm.
Prices: Lunch $10-$17, Dinner $13-$15 (dinner menu served all day Sunday); glass of wine $8-$13.   Size: seats 60.

Asiana Cafe (Asian)
130 East Putnam Avenue, Greenwich CT, 203.622.6833
www.asianacafe.com
Ready for a savory twist on Pan Asian food? Like their cousin, Penang Grill, don't expect their dishes (Vietnamese, Chinese, Thai and Japanese) to be like you have had in other restaurants. The Szechuan spicy beef is oh-so-good. The helpings are generous and the service attentive. The atmosphere is minimalist modern. In the summer you can dine outside.
Hours: Monday-Thursday 11am-10pm, Friday & Saturday 11am-11pm, Sunday 12pm-10pm. Lunch menu ends at 3:30pm except Sunday, when dinner menu is served all day. Closed most major holidays.
Prices: Lunch $8-$14; Dinner $15-$30; glass of wine $9-$10.
Size: seats 140 inside, about 32 outside.

Aurora (Italian)
60 Purchase Street, Rye NY, 914.921.2333
www.zhospitalitygroup.com/aurora
Aurora is popular in Rye. The food is good, the service is attentive, the restaurant is attractive and dressy. Parking is easy in the lot behind. Diners dressed in very casual attire enjoy it-despite the noise. Come early to miss the noise–be sure to make a reservation. Aurora is part of the Z Hospitality Group's 6 restaurants, which include Terra and Mediterraneo in Greenwich. If you are nearby this could be a good choice, but is it worth a trip? Hours: Lunch, Monday-Saturday 12pm-2:30pm; Dinner, Monday-Thursday 5pm-10pm, Friday & Saturday 5:30pm-10:30pm, Sunday 5pm-9:30pm. Prices: Lunch, pizzas $13-$17, entrees $16-$34, express lunch, 2-course $18, 3-course $23; Dinner, entrees $18-$34; glass of wine $10-$18, ½ price bottle Tuesday evenings.   Size: seats 75.

Back 40 Kitchen (Vegetarian / Vegan)

107 Greenwich Avenue (Rear) upstairs next to CVS, Greenwich CT, 203.992.1800

www.OrganicPlanetCT.com

It is good news when a popular restaurant reappears. Julien Jarry has restarted this organic, primarily vegetarian/vegan restaurant. The menu lists the items that are vegan, vegetarian or Gluten-Free. We think it is even better than before, because much of the produce comes from their own farm-some picked that morning. The space is light and attractive with an open kitchen. The staff are attentive and anxious to please.

Hours: Open Monday-Thursday 11:30am-9pm;
Friday & Saturday 11:30am-10pm. Closed Sunday.

Prices: Lunch, (salads, sandwiches, wraps, entrees) $10-$18; Dinner, (salads, burgers, entrees) $13-$34; glass of wine $7-$11.   Size: seats 44.

Bambou (Japanese, Asian)

328 Pemberwick Road (at the Mill), Glenville CT, 203.531.3322

www.BambouRestaurant.com

Tucked inside the Mill is a unique Japanese restaurant-a treat for the eye and the palette. The entrees are presented with an artistic flair. The red and black decor is New York edgy, but dining is comfortable here. We recommend the mango jicama salad and sweet potato tempura roll.

Hours: Lunch, Weekdays 12pm-3pm; Dinner, Monday-Thursday 5pm-10pm, Friday & Saturday 5pm-11pm, Sunday 5pm- 9:30pm.

Prices: Lunch, $9-$17; Dinner, entrees $16-$27; glass of wine $8-$10.
Size: seats 36 in front room, 28 in back room & 40 outside.

Bartaco (Tacos)

• 1 Willett Avenue, Port Chester NY, 914.937.8226
• 222 Summer Street, Stamford CT, 203.323.8226

www.Bartaco.com

If you are yearning to dine in an informal, rustic island restaurant, the Byram River front café will make you happy. The restaurant is centered around a large bar- a popular hot spot. In the summer it is open to the terrace. The owners of Barcelona restaurant have taken the concept of tapas and applied it to tacos. For your first visit order a tray, which includes a great number of tastes including their good guacamole.

Hours: Open Sunday-Thursday 11:30am-11pm,
Friday & Saturday 11:30am-midnight.

Prices: $7 for 3 tacos, plates $6-$13, Trays $22-$33,
Glass of wine, $7-$10.   Size: seats 120 inside, 24 outside.

RESTAURANTS

Barcelona (Spanish, Tapas)

- 18 West Putnam Avenue, Greenwich CT, 203.983.6400
- 63 North Main Street, South Norwalk CT, 203.899.0088
- 222 Summer Street, Stamford CT, 203.348.4800

www.barcelonawinebar.com

We first enjoyed this authentic tapas restaurant near the SoNo theaters in Norwalk. It's still there, so have fun in Norwalk, Stamford, Greenwich or in one of their 16 other restaurants. The Greenwich bar is lively. There is an excellent wine list, with over 30 wines by the glass. We love the tapas. Try the mouth-watering gambas, the empanadas & scallops. For dessert be sure to try the crepas. The service is friendly and attentive.

Greenwich Hours: Open Monday-Thursday 5pm-1am, Friday & Saturday 5pm-2am, Sunday 4pm-1am (the late night menu is the lunch menu). Closed on major holidays.

Greenwich Prices: Lunch & late night, sandwiches & tapas $4-$10; Dinner, entrees, $17-$27, tapas $4-$12; glass of wine $6-$12 (Sunday ½ price wine bottles, pig roast $29).

Greenwich Size: seats 110, private room seats 50.

Bar-B-Q (Barbeque)

261 Main Street, Stamford CT, 203.316.0278

www.BarQStamford.com

They are located in an alley behind the Black Bear (261 Main Street). The barn wood siding and cow print wall paper set the scene for this fun spot. This a place for "grazing." The menu is full of interesting southwestern choices. Choose several. They will appear on a tray and everyone shares. The service is sweet and attentive. Some of the "home runs" are the pulled pork, beef brisket and the Mac & Cheese.

Hours: Open Sunday-Wednesday 11am-10pm,
Thursday-Saturday 11am-11pm.

Prices: small plates $4-$8; glass of wine $8-$12.

Size: seats 32 outside and 90 inside.

RESTAURANTS

Bar Rosso (Italian)
30 Spring Street, Stamford CT, 203.388.8640
www.barrossoct.com
Originally a collaboration between Napa's owner and the chef from Harvest Supper in New Canaan, the restaurant was sold to Giovanni Gentile, owner of Capriccio. With owners like this, you have high expectations-unfortunately we are disappointed. A large bar dominates the contemporary space, and maybe that is what it is best at- drinks and pizza.
Hours: Lunch, Weekdays, 11:30am 4pm; Dinner, Sunday-Thursday 5pm-10pm, Friday & Saturday 5pm-11pm.
Prices: Lunch special $20; Dinner, small plates $7-$16, entrees $16-$34; glass of wine $8-$18.   Size: seats 50 on the main floor; upstairs additional room for parties or overflow.

Barrique Bistro and Wine Bar (French)
188 Bedford Street, Stamford CT, 203.357.9526
www.barriquestamford.com
No longer "classic French" like the former restaurant, Chez Jean-Pierre, Barrique is a café with informal French "Mediterranean" food. To keep up with the times, there are 7 salads and 17 small plates to go with their 16 entrees and 46 choices of glass of wine. We like the restyling of the restaurant, making it open and bright. From start to finish, the staff cares about their diners.
Hours: Lunch, Everyday 12pm-3pm; Dinner 3pm-10 pm.
Prices: Lunch, small plates and sandwiches $10-$16, entrees $14-$23, price fixed $20; Dinner, small plates $9-$16, entrees $17-$30; glass of wine $10-$19.   Size: seats 44 in the front room, 36 in the bar room.

Basso Café (Mediterranean/Latin American)
124 New Canaan Avenue, Norwalk CT, 203.354.6566
www.bassobistrocafe.com
This small, off-the-beaten-path restaurant benefits from having an award-winning chef, Renato Donzelli. The food is interesting and varied. It's tempting to make a meal out of the many good appetizers. The chef's popularity has made it a destination, but the simply decorated restaurant is cramped and noisy.
Hours: Lunch, Tuesday-Saturday 11am-2:30pm; Dinner, Tuesday-Sunday 5pm-10pm.
Prices: Lunch entrees $14-$24; Dinner entrees $23-$42; BYOB, corking fee $10.   Size: seats 46.

287

RESTAURANTS

Beach House Café (American)

220 Sound Beach Avenue, Old Greenwich CT, 203.637.0367
www.beachhousecafe.com
The decor is light, bright, cheerful and comfortable. The service is attentive and friendly. A large portion of the restaurant is devoted to a bar populated by a sophisticated, youthful crowd. Food is served continuously from noon on, making it a good choice for a late lunch or early dinner. As you might expect in a beach house café, there are a large number of tasty fish choices as well as sandwiches and salads.
Hours: Lunch, Sunday 11am-5pm, Monday-Saturday, 11:30am-5pm; Dinner, Sunday & Monday 5pm-9pm, Tuesday-Thursday 5pm-9:30pm, Friday & Saturday 5pm-10pm. The bar is open later.
Prices: Lunch, $12-$18, Dinner, $12-$27; glass of wine $8-$11.
Size: seats 80.

Bedford Post (New Italian)

954 Old Post Road, Bedford NY, 914.234.7800
www.bedfordpostinn.com
www.campagna-Bedford.com
In a beautiful country setting, with first-class rustic design, the Post is divided into two restaurants, the barn and Campagna. The Barn serves casual food in a casual atmosphere from a limited menu. The food is toothsome and the staff attentive. Campagna is simple but delightfully elegant. The service is gracious. We are fans of chef Michael White's pastas and inventive dishes. Ask for a table near the window in the spring or in the winter near the fireplace in the library. The post has 8 lovely guest rooms ranging from $400 to $550 a night.
Hours for The Barn Café: Brunch, Saturday & Sunday 9am-2:30 pm; Lunch, Weekdays 8am-2:30pm; Dinner, Monday & Tuesday 5pm-9pm.
Hours for Campagna: Wednesday-Friday 5:30pm-9pm, Saturday & Sunday 5:30pm-10pm.
Barn Prices: Lunch $15-$19; Dinner $19-$29.
Campagna prices: Dinner, entrees $20-$41; glass of wine $13-$26.
Size: Barn seats 48; Campagna seats 80 in front room & 40 in the library.

Beehive (American)

30 Old Route 22, Armonk NY, 914.765.0688

www.Beehive-restaurant.com

For those in Northwest Greenwich, Armonk is only 15 minutes away. The large menu with generous servings of very good American, Greek & Italian dishes makes this casual place popular. Their pastry chef turns out creative concoctions, like baklava sundaes and white chocolate banana cream pie. The space is large, bright and inviting.

Hours: Open Monday-Thursday 8am-9pm, Friday & Saturday 10am-9pm, Sunday 8am-8pm.

Prices: Dinner: Small plates, sandwiches, wraps & burgers $9-$15, entrees $18-$32; Children's menu $8-$15; Glass of wine $8-$9.

Size: seats 80.

Bella Nonna (Italian)

280 Railroad Avenue, Greenwich CT, 203.992.1888

www.BellaNonnaGreenwich.com

Cos Cobbers cried when a bank replaced this popular, 15-year-old restaurant. We were pleased it reopened in this pretty, simply-decorated space. The friendly, family-oriented service and the menu with many choices (Pizza, Panini, Pasta, Salads, Entrees) make this a nice spot for easy eating out.

Hours: Open Monday-Thursday 11am-9pm, Friday & Saturday 11am-10pm, Sunday 4pm-9pm.

Prices: Lunch, $7-$17; Dinner, $10-$20; Children's menu (12 & under) $8; glass of wine $8.   Size: seats 46.

Bernard's (French)

20 West Lane, Ridgefield CT, 203.438.8282

www.BernardsRidgefield.com

This attractive inn-style dining spot is certainly worth the trip for special occasions (romantic dinner) or when the fall leaves are glorious. While Chef/Owner Bernard Bouissou works his culinary magic, his wife, Sarah, greets and charms their guests. The menu varies with the season. On one occasion there was a large selection of truffle dishes and game meats. The service is attentive, but not always as polished as one would expect.

Hours: Sunday Brunch, 12pm-2:30pm; Lunch, Tuesday-Saturday, 12pm-2:30; Dinner, Tuesday-Thursday & Sunday 5pm-9pm, Friday & Saturday 5pm-10pm.

Prices: Brunch $35; Lunch entrees $18-$30; Dinner entrees $28-$48, 7-course tasting menu $90; glass of wine $9-$12.   Size: seats 80.

RESTAURANTS

Blacktones (Steakhouse)

28 West Putnam Avenue, Greenwich CT, 203.661.8700
www.BlackstonesGreenwich.com
Chic, sophisticated decor-just the right balance of light and dark. The steak is top of the line and you are bound to find your favorite cut. Beef tenderloin medallions are really good. There are a variety of sauces available, but if they are not on the menu, ask for them. It is not all about steak; the menu has many fish entrees as well. This is their third restaurant and you expect them to have it all together. Unfortunately, they are understaffed and the service is likely to break down as the restaurant fills.
Hours: Open Sunday-Thursday 11:30am-10pm,
Friday & Saturday 11:30am-11pm.
Prices: Lunch, entrees $16-$30, sandwiches $16-$20, 3-course menu $25; Dinner, entrees $24-$49; bar menu $12-$20; sides $6-$8; glass of wine $10-$14   Size: seats 80.

Blue Hill at Stone Barns (New American)

630 Bedford Road, Pocantico Hills, Tarrytown NY, 914.366.9600
www.BlueHillStoneBarns.com; www.BlueHillFarm.com
Worth the trip. This unique restaurant was converted from a stone barn once owned by the Rockefellers. It is surrounded by a working farm which provides many of the ingredients, which are picked fresh each day. Because the service and setting are so elegant, most people overlook the fact they are being served weeds. This may be akin to a restaurant version of the Emperor's New Clothes. You need to make a reservation. Arrive early so you can take a walk around the pretty grounds. The dress code is business casual (jackets and ties are preferred).
Hours: Closed Monday & Tuesday; Dinner Wednesday-Saturday 5pm-10pm, Sunday 1pm-10pm. Reservations can be made every day from 9am-5pm. Reservations can be made up to 2 months in advance.
Prices: (only tasting menus are available), Dinner, 5 course tasting $108, 8 course $148, 12 course $208;glass of wine $10-$26.
Size: seats 75 in the main dining room, 64 in the private dining room.

RESTAURANTS

(The) Boatyard @ Smokey Joe's BBQ (Barbeque, Seafood)
1308 East Main Street (US 1, exit 9 off I-95.), Stamford CT, 203.406.0605
www.SmokeyJoesRibs.com,
Smokey Joe's has reinvented itself as a white table cloth BBQ and sea-food restaurant. Very friendly service and good seafood. They still have authentic Texas-style BBQ. Order their beef brisket and pulled pork, with a side of collard greens and sweet potato fries.
Hours: Open Monday-Saturday 11:30am-10pm (11pm Friday & Satur-day), Sunday 11:30am-9pm. Lunch is served until 4pm.
Prices: Lunch $8-$25; Dinner $14-$30; little skippers $5-$8; glass of wine $7-10. Size: seats 50 inside, 20 outside. Downstairs is for parties.

Bocuse (French)
See review under Culinary Institute.

Boulevard 18 (French)
62 Main St, New Canaan CT, 203.594.9900   www.boulevard18.com
Mary told me I must have the chopped salad, escargot and steak frites in her favorite spot. We find this charming, casual bistro fun. In addition to Mary's favorites you should add to the list "Devils on Horseback" and grilled octopus. Like the restaurant, the service is informal, but charm-ing. Parking is across the street behind town hall.
Hours: Open Sunday-Thursday 5pm-9pm, Friday & Saturday 5pm-10pm.
Prices: burgers $9-$16, entrees $22-$29; glass of wine $9-$16.
Size: seats 44.

Boxcar Cantina (Southwestern)
44 Old Field Point Road, Greenwich CT, 203.661.4774
www.boxcarcantina.com
Popular, informal, and child- friendly, this restaurant is an incredible hit in town. It was conceived as an homage to all of the Route 66 Cantinas of the Southwest, serving a mix of high-quality, ultra-fresh Mexican and Southwestern food. We are hooked on their posole soup and Mexican pizza. Choose one of the festive margaritas. Cheers to the Farrells!
Hours: Lunch, Weekdays 11:30am-3pm; Dinner, Monday-Thursday 5:30pm-9:30pm, Friday & Saturday 5:30pm-10:30pm; Sunday, 4:30pm-9pm. Reservations are accepted only for parties of 6 or more. On Friday and Saturday nights, be sure to arrive early.
Prices: Lunch entrees [salads, quesadillas, tacos, burritos, burgers] $10-$15; Dinner entrees $14-$22; glass of wine $10-$13; minimum order $100 for delivery; the once complimentary chips and salsa are now $4.
Size: seats 94.

RESTAURANTS

Brasitas (New Latin American)

• 954 East Main Street, Stamford CT, 203.323.3176 (iffy neighborhood)
• 430 Main Avenue, Norwalk CT, 203.354.7329
www.Brasitas.com

Brasitas serves award winning "Nuevo Latino" cuisine. Connecticut Magazine Readers Choice awarded both Brasitas locations as the best Latin American in Fairfield County. Whether you order the coconut shrimp or fried red snapper, you are sure to be happy. The Stamford location is funky and thriving even though it is in an iffy part of Stamford. The Norwalk location, our favorite, is a bright, fun spot with flair. You must make a reservation at either location.

Prices: Lunch, entrees $10-$16; Dinner, entrees $24-$28;
glass of wine, $9-$14.

Norwalk Hours: Open Tuesday-Thursday 12pm-10pm,
Friday & Saturday 12pm-11pm, Sunday & Monday 12pm-9pm.

Size: Stamford location seats 55-60; Norwalk seats 50 with a private room for up to 35.

(La) Bretagne (French)

2010 West Main Street (US-1 just across the Greenwich border), Stamford CT, 203.324.9539
www.labretagnerestaurant.com

They have been in business for more than thirty years. The traditional French menu has probably had the same selections for this same period. The interior is dimly lit and eating here is like taking a step back in time. The staff is attentive and formally attired. They make many dishes table side. This restaurant may be a choice for entertaining older relatives.

Hours: Lunch, Tuesday-Saturday 12pm-2:30pm; Dinner, Tuesday-Sunday 6pm-9:30pm. Closed Monday.

Prices: Lunch, entrees $17-$22, 2-course fixed price $24;
Dinner, entrees $24-$42; glass of wine $10.

Size: Main area seats 60, adjoining room also seats 60.

RESTAURANTS

Café Silvium (Italian)
371 Shippan Avenue, Stamford CT, 203.324.1651 www.cafeSilvium.com
This is a modest-appearing restaurant, in a commercial district. It is easy to pass by, but don't let the appearance throw you off. Inside, you will discover a thriving restaurant filled with people enjoying southern Italian food. The service is friendly and portions are generous. Our favorite is Scaloppine al Gorgonzola. They accept reservations on the weekend for parties of 5 or more.
Hours: Lunch, Weekdays 11:30am-2:30pm; Dinner, Monday-Thursday 5pm-10pm, Friday & Saturday 5pm-11pm.
Prices: Lunch, entrees $14-$18; Dinner, entrees $17-$22; glass of wine $7-$9.   Size: seats 60.

California Pizza Kitchen (Pizza)
Stamford Town Center, 230 Tresser Blvd, Stamford CT, 203.406.0530
www.CPK.com, www.CPKtakeout.com
One of 6 featured restaurants at the Town Center. Started in Beverly Hills CA in 1985, the chain has over 230 locations. The chain is known for its innovative pizzas, such as BBQ Chicken, BLT, Thai Chicken, and Jamaican Jerk Chicken. Bigger and more stylish than the normal pizza parlor, it is a good choice when shopping at the Mall with kids. The Children's menu-an activity book-has lots of kid-friendly foods to keep them happy while enjoying a salad or Neapolitan (thin crust) pizza. Skip dessert.
Hours: Monday-Saturday, 11am-10 pm, Sunday 11am-9 pm.
Prices: Pizzas $11-$14, Salads $10-$15; Children's Menu $6.
Size: seats 50.

(The) Capital Grille (Steak)
Stamford Town Center, 230 Tresser Blvd, Stamford CT, 203.967.0000
www.TheCapitalGrille.com
They strive for excellent service-remembering your name, preferences and even assigning you the same waiter, if you wish. The tender, cooked "just right" steak, the mahogany clubby atmosphere and valet parking make this an easy place to entertain. It has a huge wine list, as well as wine lockers for frequent visitors to rent for their private supply.
Hours: Lunch, Weekdays 11:30am-3pm, but the bar stays open; Dinner, Monday-Thursday 5pm-10pm, Friday & Saturday 5pm-11pm, Sunday 4pm-9pm.
Prices: Lunch, entrees $19-$31; Dinner, entrees $34-$49, sides $9-$12; glass of wine $7-$15, half bottle of wine $25-$175, Captain's wine list, bottle $55-$795.   Size: seats 200, including three private dining rooms.

Capriccio (Italian)
189 Bedford Street, Stamford CT, 203.356.9819
www.Capriccio-cafe.com
A popular, casual café. In summer, tables are spread out across the sidewalk filled with happy diners. This is a happening place! They have terrific desserts, including gelato to die for. Our favorite is the hazelnut.
Hours: open every day, Sunday -Thursday 11am-11pm, Friday & Saturday 11am-midnight.
Prices: (Panini, Piadine, Pizza, Pasta, entrees) $8-$18; glass of wine $7-$9.   Size: Inside seats 24 on each side, plus outside seating for 120 in the summer.

Casa Volla (Mexican)
866 East Main Street, Stamford CT, 203.348.0622
www.CasaVillaRestaurant.com
This is a bright, tidy, hole-in-the wall restaurant with warm chips, good salsa and guacamole. The tacos (Adobada and Tacos al Pastor) top our list of must-haves. Skip the entrees. Try fried ripe plantains for dessert.
Hours: Open Sunday-Thursday 11am-10pm, Friday & Saturday 11am-11pm.
Prices: Tacos $3 each, entrees $9-$17.   Size: seats 40 inside, 20 outside.

Cask Republic (Gastropub)
191 Summer Street, Stamford CT, 203.348.2275
www.CaskRepublic.com
With a strong track record behind him, Burns (Skal restaurant group, owner of the Ginger Man and New Haven Cask Republic), knew how to design an attractive gastropub: light, bright with craftsman-style wood paneling and plenty of space between tables. There are many choices for diners who want to mingle or not: high tables, booths, tables for 2 or 4. The beers (over 60 on tap and over 80 bottled) are the feature, but we think you will find the food good as well.
Hours: Lunch, Monday-Wednesday 11:45am-10pm, Thursday-Saturday 11:45am-11pm, Sunday 11:45am-9pm.
Prices: Lunch, bites, sandwiches, burgers, salads $8-$16; Dinner, small plates and pizzas $7-$18, entrees $14-$25; glass of wine $8-$15; beer $7-$19. Size: 165 (main room 115, event room 50).

Caterina de Medici (Italian)
See Culinary Institute for Review.

RESTAURANTS

Cava Wine Bar & Restaurant (Italian)
2 Forest Street, New Canaan CT, 203.966.6946
www.CavaWineBar.com
Entering this just-below street level, brick-faced space you have the feeling of dining in a private wine cellar (albeit a large one.) The place to go for relaxing, unwinding, and having a glass of wine and a good meal.
Hours: Open Monday-Thursday 12pm-10pm, Friday & Saturday 11:30am-11pm, Sunday 5pm-9pm.
Prices: Lunch, (Pizza, salads, pasta, panini) $12-$18, 2-course price fixed $15; Dinner, entrees $17-$30; glass of wine $7-$14.   Size: seats 60.

Centro Ristorante (Italian)
323 Pemberwick Road (at The Mill), Glenville CT, 203.531.5514
www.centroRistorante.com
Bright, cheery, and popular, with an unpretentious atmosphere. Just right when you hunger for pizzas or homemade pastas and a glass of wine from their extensive list. In the summer, request the outdoor patio overlooking the waterfall and order their Ravioli Centro or chicken-pear salad. Some of our friends go just for the desserts. Child-friendly with crayons and a kid's menu. We wouldn't recommend their burgers.
Hours: Open Monday-Thursday 11:30am-10pm, Friday & Saturday 11:30am-10:30pm, Sunday 4:30pm-9pm.
Prices: Lunch $9-$14; Dinner entrees $17-$22; kids menu $4-$9; glass of wine $8-$11.   Size: seats 120 inside & 50 on the patio.

Char (New American)
2 South Water Street, Byram CT, 203.900.1100   www.char.com
Not everything on the menu sparkles, but order the edamame dumplings and the Bucatini lamb bolognese with lemon gremolata and the years of mediocrity in this corner restaurant will be swept away. The new owner, who also owns Dolphin and Café Hudson in Yonkers, was on a mission to fill this very large restaurant with happy diners and he has succeeded. Be sure to make a reservation. The makeover-barn wood, with out-of-place fancy chandeliers, is a bit dark. The many creative dishes and welcoming (unpolished) energetic staff keep us wanting to return. The large parking lot makes parking easy.
Hours: Lunch, Weekdays 11:45am-2:45pm; Dinner, Monday-Thursday 5pm-10pm, Friday & Saturday 5pm-11pm, Sunday 4pm-9pm.
Prices: Lunch entrees $12-$23; Dinner $22-$28; glass of wine $8-$15.
Size: seats 240 (100 main dining room, 40 in the bar area, 100 down stairs).

(The) Cheesecake Factory (American)

Westchester Mall, One Maple Avenue, White Plains NY, 914.683.5253
www.thecheesecakefactory.com
With over 160 restaurants across the US, you've likely had a CF experience and know that a 20-40 minute wait to be seated is standard (beepers are assigned.) With a 14-page menu, expect to find something to please everyone. Plan to share, because the portions are big. Appetizers are large enough for a meal. We like the avocado eggrolls and the sweet corn tamale cakes. The decor is elaborate Cleopatra. The service is quick and attentive. You can buy one of their 30 cheesecakes in the bakery. We wish we liked them. Amazingly, there is no children's menu.
Hours: Open Monday-Thursday 11am-11:30pm, Friday & Saturday 11:30am-midnight, Sunday 10pm-11pm.
Prices: Lunch specials ($10-$14) end at 5pm; Dinner, small plates $5-$7, (burgers, pizzas, entrees) $11-$30; glass of wine $8-$13.
Size: seats 390.

Ching's Table (Asian Fusion, Chinese)

64 Main Street, New Canaan CT, 203.972.8550
www.ChingsRestaurant.com
This is a popular New Canaan restaurant. The service is attentive and the food equally good. It was rated the best Chinese restaurant in the country by Chinese Restaurant News. We like the wonton seaweed soup, Vietnamese salad, Pad Thai with shrimp, lemon grass chicken, glazed ginger duck and wok beef tenderloin. On busy nights, consider takeouts if you can't get a reservation.
Hours: Lunch, Sunday-Saturday 11:30am-3pm; Dinner, Sunday-Thursday 3pm-10pm, Friday & Saturday 3pm-11pm
Prices: Lunch, Fixed price menu $11, entrees, $10-$13; Dinner, entrees, $16-$22 (on Sunday the dinner menu is served all day); glass of wine $8-$13.   Size: seats 60.

TIP: CONNECTICUT IS A WINE-DOGGY-BAG-STATE

Public Act No. 03-228 and 04-33 allow a restaurant, café or hotel dining room patron to remove one unsealed bottle of wine for off-premises consumption provided the patron has purchased a full-course meal and consumed a portion of the wine with such meal. The bottle that is removed must be securely sealed and placed in a bag by restaurant personnel. www.vinodoggybag.com/statelaws.html New York is also a Wine-Doggy-Bag State.

City Limits Diner (American)
135 Harvard Avenue (at La Quinta), Stamford CT, 203.348.7000
www.citylimitsdiner.com
"A restaurant, disguised as a diner." This large restaurant, with its diner-style decor, serves upscale casual and comfort food. Their bread, pastries and ice cream are made in-house. Try their fish soup, chicken-corn quesadilla or curry chicken wrap and Valrhona chocolate pudding. If you are looking for a good early morning breakfast (orange-lemon waffles or corned beef hash) or a late-night meal, head here. They have been rated one of the best breakfasts in Fairfield County.
Hours: Open every day: Breakfast menu starts at 7am and runs all day; Lunch menu 11am-4pm; Dinner, Sunday-Thursday 4pm-10pm, Friday & Saturday 4pm-11pm.
Prices: Breakfast $8-$17; Lunch entrees $15-$21;
Dinner entrees $15-$23; Children's menu $4-$13; glass of wine $8-$10.
Size: seats 160 in the main area; private room seats 100.

Chocopologie (American)
133 Washington Street, South Norwalk CT, 203.854.4754
www.knipschildt.com
If chocolate is your passion, as it is ours, the small Norwalk restaurant in the front of a Knipschildt's chocolate factory is a must. When our tasting experts, Matthew and Cameron, gave it thumbs up, we knew this restaurant was destined for success. The menu includes soups, salads, quiches, omelets, as well as a variety of savory crepes and, of course, great hot chocolate and divine chocolate desserts. Try their crepe with strawberries in green peppercorn jus and "chocolate love" for dessert or stop by to bring home some luscious chocolates.
Hours: Open Wednesday 11am-9pm, Thursday 11am-10pm,
Friday & Saturday 11am-midnight, Sunday 10:30am-5pm.
Closed Monday & Tuesday.
Prices: entrees $9-$17, desserts $6-$17, kids menu $8, glass of wine $8-$9. Size: seats for 20 in front, plus 14 bar stools which allow you to see the factory while you eat.

RESTAURANTS

Coals (Pizza)
35 North Main Street, Port Chester NY, 914.305.3220
www.CoalsPizza.com
This casual, minimally-decorated pizza place is a hot spot for pizzas. They serve very good pizzas on ultra thin crusts. You should start with the deep-fried brussels sprouts appetizer, have a pizza and end with the nutella pizza.
Hours: Lunch, Friday 11:30am-3pm, Saturday 12pm-3pm; Sunday 1pm-3pm; Dinner, Monday-Thursday 5pm-9:30pm, Friday & Saturday 5pm-10:30pm, Sunday 3pm-9pm.
Prices: Pizzas $11-$14; glass of wine $7-$10.   Size: Seats 32.

Coast (Seafood)
203 East Putnam Avenue, Cos Cob CT, 203.869.2339
www.coastseafoodrestaurant.com
Nuage has for some time been transitioning from Asian-Fusion to seafood. Now renamed "Coast" it's clear. The space is dimly lit with remnants of the Asian design. We like that the dishes retain Asian touches. Try the sea bass or the scallops. Inside can be noisy when the restaurant is busy, so you may want to reserve a table outside when it is warm.
Hours: Lunch, Monday-Saturday, 11:30am-3pm; Dinner, Monday-Thursday 5pm-10pm, Friday & Saturday 5pm-10:45pm, Sunday 5pm-9:30pm.
Prices: Lunch, entrees $13-$22, Prix Fixe menu (2 courses + dessert) $22; Dinner, entrees $18-$89 (most are $25-$35, with sides extra), 5-course tasting menu $65, 7-course menu $85; glass of wine $8-$18.
Size: seats 46 inside, 12 outside.

Columbus Park Trattoria (Italian)
205 Main Street (Washington Blvd), Stamford CT, 203.967.9191
www.ColumbusParkTrattoria.com
The owners of this restaurant (Marchetti-Tarantino) own the Osteria Applausi in Old Greenwich. As you might expect, they have perfected good service and good pasta. A fall specialty, Pumpkin Ravioli, is totally terrific! Though the restaurant is attractive, the tables are close so you may be rubbing shoulders with your neighbor. Parking may be a challenge. The Columbus Park area is a mecca for restaurants.
Prices: Lunch entrees $15-$19, lunch special $19; Dinner entrees $23-$40; glass of wine $9-$18.
Hours: Lunch, Weekdays, 12pm-2:30pm; Dinner, Monday-Thursday 5pm-10pm, Friday & Saturday 5pm-11pm. Closed Sunday.
Size: Downstairs seats 40; private dining room upstairs seats 65.

RESTAURANTS

Cobble Stone (American)
620 Anderson Hill Road, Purchase NY, 914.253.9678
www.thecobblestonerestaurant.com
Open since 1933, this informal, pub-style restaurant is more than just a college hang-out. It is fun for any age. It has been owned and run by five generations of the same family. Try the onion soup or one of their many hamburgers. For dessert, have their Oreo cookie madness. On SUNY performance evenings you may need to reserve.
Hours: Sunday brunch 11:30am-3pm; Lunch, Monday-Saturday 11:30am-5pm, Sunday, 3pm-5pm; Dinner, Sunday-Saturday 5pm-10pm; Late night menu until midnight.
Prices: Brunch, $8-$12; Lunch, burgers and sandwiches $8-$13; Dinner burgers and sandwiches $8-$10, entrees $14-$19; children's menu $6; glass of wine $5-$6.   Size: seats 80.

Copacabana (Brazilian Steak House)
29 North Main Street, Port Chester NY, 914.939.6894
www.copacabanaportchester.com
This steak house-called a churrascaria-is all about meat. You can choose from 12 cuts of meat. It is based on a Brazilian tradition of serving meat right off the cooking skewer and carving it individually at each table (Rodizio). The salad bar has lots of choices to accompany the meat. Upscale in appearance with a helpful staff, this makes a fun night out with carnivore friends. They often have live music on Friday & Saturday nights. Check their website for "Events."
Hours: Open Tuesday-Thursday 12pm-10pm,
Friday & Saturday 12pm-11pm, Sunday 12 pm-9:30pm. Closed Monday.
Prices: Lunch buffet $20 per person; Dinner $38 per person; glass of wine $8-$9; Saturday & Sunday, dinner menu only.
Size: seats up to 200.

TIP: BEST OF THE GOLD COAST
In July Greenwich Magazine holds their Best of the Gold Coast tasting party, featuring the 200 plus winners. A great event to taste and meet the chefs of area restaurants and wine suppliers. For information call 203.222.0600 or visit www.bestofgoldcoastct.com

Coromandel (Indian)

- 68 Broad Street (corner of Summer), Stamford CT, 203.964.1010
- 25-11 Old Kings Hwy N (Good Wives Shopping Cntr), Darien CT, 203.662.1213
- 86 Washington Street, South Norwalk CT, 203.852.1213

www.coromandelcuisine.com

Hungry for Indian cuisine? Want to know where connoisseurs of fine Indian food dine? Want to be able to have a conversation? This restaurant, with its specialities from many regions and its attentive staff, will capture you. The Stamford location is one of six restaurants named after "Coromandel," the southeast coast of the Indian Peninsula. Many consider Stamford the best location. But Coromandel fans, Faith and Darius, prefer the more intimate Darien location.

Stamford Hours: Lunch, Weekdays 12pm-2:30pm, Saturday & Sunday 12pm-3pm; Dinner, Sunday-Thursday 5pm-10pm, Friday & Saturday 5pm-10:30pm.

Stamford Prices: Lunch buffet, week days $11, weekends $15; Dinner, entrees $15-$24; glass of wine $9-$11.

Stamford Size: seats 80, party room for 120 upstairs.

(The) Cos Cobber (American)

31 East Putnam Avenue, Cos Cob CT, 203.992.1333

www.TheCosCobber.com

This is a casual, come as you are, Cos Cob eatery. One feels at ease in this bright, attractive space. The short menu is composed of well-prepared, tried and true family favorites. John likes their pork chops, Amy likes their calamari. Many people come for the hamburgers.

Hours: Breakfast, Weekdays 8am-11am; Brunch, Saturday & Sunday 8am-1pm; Lunch Weekdays, 11am-5pm, Saturday & Sunday 1pm-5pm; Dinner Everyday 5pm-close.

Prices: Lunch entrees $10-$17; Dinner entrees $14-$30 ($2 to split an entree); glass of wine $8-$11. Size: seats 36.

RESTAURANTS

Crab Shell (Seafood)

46 Southfield Avenue, Stamford CT, 203.967.7229
www.crabshell.com
Casual seafood in a nautical setting. During the summer evenings, especially the weekends, it is a meeting ground for the 30 to 50-something crowd. From May to September the restaurant expands onto a huge outdoor deck-The Crab Shack-which can accommodate 200. The Crab Shack has its own late night menu and a live band most weekends. The band schedule is on their website.
Hours: Open Monday-Thursday 11am-9pm, Saturday & Sunday 11am-10pm. Closed Sundays, November to February.
Prices: Lunch (salads, sandwiches, casual entrees) $13-$19; Dinner, entrees $21-$37; children (under 12) $11; glass of wine $7-$10.
Size: seats 125.

(La) Crémaillère (French)

46 Bedford/Banksville Road, Banksville NY, 914.234.9647
www.cremaillere.com
A restaurant for celebrations since 1947. The same family has owned it since 1962. They also owned La Caravelle in NYC. Many Greenwich couples have become engaged in this restaurant. Enjoy their fine wines and very good, traditional French food in a dressy, romantic setting. Pleasant, semi-attentive service. Jackets and ties are expected at dinner. They make all of the stocks from scratch so their sauces are superb. Mussel soup and quenelles are a must.
Hours: Lunch, Thursday-Sunday 12pm-2:30pm; Dinner, Tuesday-Sunday 6pm-9pm. Closed Monday.
Prices: Lunch is prix-fixed at $29; Dinner entrees, $30-$43, 5-course tasting menu $85; glass of wine $13.
Size: seats 70; private dining rooms for 12-45.

RESTAURANTS

Crew Restaurant (New American)
280 Railroad Avenue, Greenwich CT, 203.340.9433
www.Crew280.com
This restaurant is one you love to discover. The tangerine walls, wood paneling and 18 small tables covered in white cloths give it a cozy atmosphere. Diners are greeted warmly. Hot pita and a yummy dip arrive with the menu. Every entree is available in a small plate. It is fun to share small plates like the "screaming shrimp" and the day boat scallops. Three small plates are ample for a party of two. The menu, which changes with the season, is a mix of nationalities, which they call "global American."
Hours: Lunch, Tuesday-Saturday 12pm-3pm; Dinner, Monday-Thursday 5pm-9:30pm, Friday & Saturday 5pm-10pm. Closed Sunday.
Prices: Prix Fixe lunch menu, $20; Entrees, $16-$30 as a large plate and $11-$16 as a small plates; glass of wine $8-$11.
Size: seats 36.

Culinary Institute of America Restaurants
1946 Campus Drive, Hyde Park NY, 845.471.6608
www.ciachef.edu
• American Bounty (New American)
• Caterina de Medici (Italian)
• Bocuse (French)
Treat yourself to a superb dining experience, just 1.5 hours north of Greenwich. The food, ambiance and service are all top notch. The school has high goals and the restaurants are staffed with students striving for perfection. We recommend lunch for your first visit. The trip is scenic. The campus on the Hudson is very attractive and large. We hope a lot of these chefs are attracted to the Greenwich area. Reservations well in advance are a must, even if you are going for lunch. The dress code is business casual. No jeans or sneakers. The Craig Claiborne Book and cookware store is located on the first floor of Roth Hall. You may also want to coordinate your visit with a tour of the Roosevelt home or Vanderbilt mansion.
Hours: American Bounty and Bocuse open Lunch, Tuesday-Saturday 11am-2:30pm; Dinner, Tuesday-Saturday 6pm-8:30pm. Medici open Lunch, Weekdays 11am-2:30pm; Dinner, Weekdays 6pm-8:30pm.
Prices: Lunch, entrees $18-$29, pre-fixe (Tues, Wed, Friday) $20; Dinner, entrees $24-$29, pre-fixe $30; glass of wine $6-$12 (some restaurants also provide 3 oz wine servings).
Directions: About 1.5 hours north on I-684 & Route 9 N.

RESTAURANTS

Dinosaur Bar-B-Que (BBQ)

845 Canal Street, Stamford CT, 203.517.3272
www.dinosaurbarbque.com, www.dinoBBQ.com
Dinosaur with only 6 locations, was overwhelmingly voted the best barbecue in the country on the Good Morning America show. We haven't eaten in every BBQ, but this one certainly is a winner. We like their innovative twists to wonderfully cooked meats. The sides are really good too, like the fried green tomatoes and the BBQ beans. The staff is well-trained, everyone is friendly and hoping you will have a good time. Servers wear jeans and the setting is renovated industrial.
Hours: Monday-Thursday 11:30am-11pm,
Friday & Saturday 11:30am-midnight, Sunday 11:30am-10pm.
Prices: $10-$25   Size: seats 200 inside, 50 outside.

Dolce Cubano (Cuban)

78 Southfield Avenue, Stamford CT (Stamford Landing), 203.817.0700
www.dolcecubano.com
Driving through a warehouse area, you may wonder where you are going. The setting is dramatic-direct waterfront with views of boats in the harbor. The red leather and white marble interior is strikingly attractive (only the chandeliers are a hoot). Two sides of the restaurant are glass. A large bar dominates the center of the restaurant. Tapas, some Cuban, some Italian, are featured. Don't miss the Goat Cheese, the Empanadas, the Gnocchi or the Truffle Sprouts. The servers are skilled and friendly.
Hours: Open Sunday-Thursday 11:30am-10pm, Friday & Saturday 11:30am-11pm.
Prices: Lunch, tapas $8-$15, entrees $14-$25; Dinner, tapas $9-$15, entrees $16-$30; glass of wine $7-$16. Size: seats 160 + 40 at the bar.

Doppio (Italian, Pizza)

41 East Elm Street, Greenwich CT 203.340.9470   www.EatDoppio.com
Sleekly modern, with black tables and a friendly staff, Doppio is the venture of the Barresi family. Doppio means two. The name was chosen to emphasize their specialities-pizza and gelato. Their pizza has Philip's stamp of approval. His favorite is the pesto. Ours is the four cheese. However, the menu goes beyond pizzas with a large selection of small plates, Panini and salads. Bring your own wine from the shop next door.
Hours: Open every day; Lunch 12pm- 3pm; Wine & Coffee 3pm-5pm; Dinner 5pm-10pm.
Prices: Pizza $13-$23, small plates $10 -$18, entrees $16-$23.
Size: seats 36.

RESTAURANTS

Doral Arrowwood Atrium (Sunday Brunch)
975 Anderson Hill Road, Rye Brook NY, 914.935.6600 (914.939.5500)
www.DoralArrowWood.com
The Atrium is a large restaurant in a resort hotel. One side is all windows looking over the lovely golf course, the other side, for Sunday brunch, is a banquet of foods. With such great variety, there is something for all tastes. Live music plays in the background, as a magician tours the tables showing young and old a good time. Large groups are easily accommodated.
Hours: Sunday Brunch 11:30am-2:20pm; Atrium open every day, 6:30am-10:15pm. Prices: Brunch, Adults $39, Children $15.   Size: seats 300.

Douro (Portuguese)
363 Greenwich Avenue, Greenwich CT, 203.869.7622
www.DouroRestaurantBar.com
Greenwich's first Portuguese restaurant. Dimly lit with a simple decor. The bar dominates this long, narrow restaurant. Rui Correia, the chef and owner, creates tasty, delicately-flavored food. Lots of small plates and paellas. The service is kind.
Hours: Lunch, Weekdays 11:30am-4pm; Brunch, Saturday & Sunday 11:30am-4pm; Dinner, Monday-Thursday 4pm-10pm, Friday & Saturday 4pm-10:30pm, Sunday 4pm-9pm.
Prices: Lunch, entrees $15-$25, price fixed 2-course menu $20; Dinner, entrees $16-$32; glass of wine $10-$14.
Size: 20 at the bar, tables for 40.

(The) Drawing Room (Tea & Sandwiches)
5 Suburban Avenue, Cos Cob CT, 203.661.3737
www.thedrawingroom.cc
Tucked around the corner from the Post Road, near the Cos Cob Library is the perfect place for light lunch and/or afternoon tea. This small, cheerfully-decorated tea room serves tea, hot chocolate, coffee, finger sandwiches, scones and desserts. The staff are tea experts who can help you make delightful tea choices. Having tea and browsing through the adjoining art gallery make this a fun and civilized break in the day.
Hours: Open Monday-Saturday 8am-5pm.
Prices: Lunch entrees, $8-$13, Grand Afternoon Tea, $26.
Size: seats 15 inside and 16 outside. No reservations.

Edo (Japanese Steak House)

140 Midland Avenue (shopping center next to Home Depot), Port Chester NY, 914.937.3333   www.edohibachi.com/

Just across from Home Depot, in a nondescript shopping strip, is a surprisingly attractive hibachi steak house. The cooking process, done in front of you, is very dramatic- perhaps too theatrical. If you are thinking of hosting a children's party around a hibachi table, you will have lots of room and accommodating service. You and the children will enjoy the food and the show.

Hours: Dinner, Monday-Thursday 5:30pm-10pm, Friday 5:30 pm-11pm, Saturday 5pm-11pm, Sunday 4pm-9pm.

Prices: Complete Hibachi dinners $16-$32, children's menu $8-$15.

Size: 11 hibachi tables each seating 8.

Eleven14 Kitchen (New American)

J House, 1114 East Putnam Avenue, Riverside CT, 203.698.6999 www.eleven14kitchen.com

Entering the swish, modern J House Hotel sets the mood for dining in this contemporary open room. The menu is heavily weighted with items that go well with drinks (14 appetizers, 5 pizzas and 10 main courses). Executive Chef Kwaku-Dongo's food is fresh and pleasing. We especially like the tuna steak and the goat cheese peppercorn gelato.

Hours: Open every day, 7:30am-10pm.

Prices: Lunch $15-$32; Dinner $16-$45; glass of wine $10-$18.

Size: seats 90 inside, 20 outside (next to the bar area).

Elm Restaurant (New American)

73 Elm Street, New Canaan CT, 203.920.4994   www.elmrestaurant.com

Chef, owner Brian Lewis is passionate about his food and hospitality. Dining here is a treat. Chef Lewis's creations -like crunchy quinoa on tuna or chestnut soup-are delicious. The restaurant is soft contemporary, with an open kitchen and dining areas divided. The servers are quick and efficient, though somewhat impersonal.

Hours: Lunch, Wednesday-Friday 11:30am-2:30pm; Brunch, Saturday & Sunday 11:30am-2:30pm; Dinner, Tuesday-Saturday 5:30pm-10pm, Sunday 5pm-8pm. Closed Monday.

Prices: Sunday Brunch $9-$16, children's menu $8; Dinner, entrees $28-$36, 5-course tasting menu $75; Sunday evening chef's choice menu $35; glass of wine $10-$16.   Size: seats 86.

RESTAURANTS

Elm Street Oyster House (Seafood)
11 West Elm Street, Greenwich CT, 203.629.5795
www.elmstreetoysterhouse.com
This is one of our favorites. Their raw bar and chowders are hard to beat. You will like the creative recipes and yummy desserts. Try their wasabi sesame-crusted tuna or the lobster paella. The pan fried oysters are top-rate for an appetizer. This is a small, bright, lively restaurant with good service. It is a great place to meet after work and to stay for dinner.
Hours: Open Monday-Thursday 11:30am-10pm, Friday & Saturday 11:30am-11pm, Sunday 11:30am-9pm.
Prices: Same menu lunch & dinner, entrees $27-$35; sandwiches $16-$21; glass of wine $10-$18.   Size: seats 42.

Eos (Greek)
490 Summer Street, Stamford CT, 203.569.6250 www.eosgreekcuisine.com
Our dear Greek friends, Roula and Evans, discovered this bright white, small restaurant. "You must try it, their Moussaka is better than mine." We have eaten their home cooking, so this restaurant had to be good. We recommend skipping the main courses and sharing plates of appetizers, such as Moussaka, Pastitsio and Kolokythakia. Top this off with Baklava. While our Greek friends complement the mixing of traditional with a flair for fresh and modern, we complement the tastiness.
Hours: Open Monday-Thursday 11:30am-10 pm;
Friday and Saturday 11:30am-11pm; Sunday 12pm-9 pm.
Prices: Lunch entrees, $14-$32, Wraps, $ 10-$14, Mezedes (appetizers), $6 to $16; Dinner Entrees, $20-$39, Mezedes, $6 to $22;
glass of wine $7-$12.   Size: seats 40.

Estia (Greek)
88 Washington Street, (South) Norwalk CT, 203.596.0101
www.estiagreekrestaurant.com
Eating the red snapper in lemon sauce and the Pastitsio reminds us of our favorite Athens restaurants. The kataiksio appetizer is so good, we can't wait to return. In an area where finding Greek wines isn't easy, it's wonderful to find such a fine selection. The high-tech wine list on an iPad gives lots of detail about the wine. Expect a pleasant evening in this brick-walled, white table cloth restaurant.
Hours: Lunch, Tuesday-Sunday 11:30am-3pm;
Dinner, Tuesday-Thursday 5pm-10pm, Friday 5pm-11pm,
Saturday 3pm-11pm, Sunday 3pm-10pm.Prices: Lunch $15-$26;
Dinner entrees $15-$26; glass of wine $7-$9   Size: seats 48.

RESTAURANTS

Euro Asian (Asian)

30 Westchester Avenue (@ The Waterfront), Port Chester NY, 914.937.3680
www.AsianBistroNY.com
Next to the movie theater, designed to look grand and with friendly service, is a Japanese / Chinese / Thai restaurant. Maybe the menu with its huge number of choices too many, from too many cuisines is its failing.
Hours: Open Monday-Thursday 11am-10pm, Friday 11am-11pm, Saturday 12:30pm-11pm, Sunday 12:30pm-10pm.
Prices: Lunch, $11-$15; Dinner, (sushi & entrees) $15-$28; glass of wine $8-$11. Size: seats 140.

Fairways @ The Griff (Italian)

1323 King Street, Greenwich CT, 203.531.1138
www.FairwaysAtTheGriff.com
This casual restaurant, leased from the Town, is a golfer's hot spot. For Lunch, Don highly recommends the cheeseburger club and the homemade muffins. In the evening the food is Italian. Monica recommends the chicken parmigiana and the cannoli.
Hours: Open Sunday-Wednesday 6:30am-6pm, Thursday-Saturday 6:30am-8pm. Hours seasonal with the Golf Course.
Prices: Lunch, $8-$11; Dinner, $14-$23; glass of wine $6.
Size: 40 inside, 60 outside.

Famous Greek Kitchen (Greek)

10 North Water Street, Byram CT, 203.531.6887, 203.531.4019
www.FamousGreekKitchen.com
A new generation has transformed the 33 year old "Famous Pizza & Souvlaki" into a contemporary Greek Taverna, with bold white upholstery and grey walls. John Karipide's son Steve, a Culinary Institute graduate, has taken over the kitchen. We return regularly for salmon wrapped in phyllo, Greek platters, fish specials and, Oh yes-the baklava. The whole family is there, greeting and serving and making their guests feel happy.
Hours: Open Monday-Saturday 7am-10pm, Sunday 7am-9pm.
Prices: Entrees $15-$24, Children's menu $8; glass of wine $6-$10.
Size: seats 80.

Farmer's Table (New American)

12 Forest Street, New Canaan CT, 203.594.7890

If you are tempted to leave city life and live on a farm, this will be just like your farm kitchen (assuming you are a talented chef and cook with flair like Robert Ubaldo). In this unassuming space, the open kitchen is about as large as the dining area. In the season, ingredients come straight from the owner's farm. The welcoming servers and exceptionally tasty food make this one of our go-to places. Don't consider arriving without a reservation.

Hours: Dinner, Open Monday-Wednesday 5pm-9pm, Thursday-Saturday 5pm-10pm. Closed Sunday.

Prices: Dinner entrees $20-$30; glass of wine $9-$14.   Size: seats 50.

(Le) Fat Poodle (Global French)

20 Arcadia Road, Old Greenwich CT, 203.717.1515

www.LeFatPoodle.com

This lively restaurant owned by Anshu Vidyarthi and Antoine Blech (owners of Le Penguin) is all about flavor, fun and feeling happy. The papered tables and quiet tones in this iconic Arcadia building are backdrop to the fat poodle on the wall beckoning you to relax and have a good time. Staff greet and treat you as very special guests. Foods such as fondue, Pu-Pu platter (a favorite of Lu and Jack) steak frites, angel hair diablo and banana splits are very tasty indeed.

Hours: Lunch, Weekdays 11:30am-3pm; Dinner, Monday-Thursday and Sunday 5pm-10pm, Friday and Saturday to 11pm.

Prices: Dinner entrees $22-$32; glass of wine $9-$16. Size: seats 60.

(The) Fez (Moroccan)

227 Summer Street, Stamford CT, 203.324.3391   www.TheFez1.com

Opening the door, you know you are in a one-of-a-kind place. The walls are bright red like the traditional Fez hat. The setting is just right for the uniquely-flavored food. The hummus with Fez chips is as good as it gets. The eggplant soup and kabobs are also very good. The greeter and servers are friendly and enthusiastic about their cuisine. Live music starts around 7:30pm on most evenings, but doesn't get loud until about 9pm.

Hours: Lunch, Weekdays 12pm-3pm; Dinner, Sunday-Thursday 5pm-10pm, Friday & Saturday 5pm-11pm.

Prices: Lunch (small plates, pitas & wraps) $9-$16; Dinner, small plates $8-$16, large $18-$28; glass of wine $7-$10.   Size: seats 44.

RESTAURANTS

F.I.S.H. (Seafood)
245 Bedford Street, Stamford CT, 203.724.9300 www.fishstamford.com
Fish is a long, narrow restaurant with an appealing, starkly modern look and good service. Once called "Boca," the owners have changed the restaurant's concept and name to F.I.S.H. Fresh Innovative Seafood House. Their specialty is "Naked Fish" which allows you to create your own dish without having to cook. First, you choose your fish, then decide if it should be pan-seared, grilled or blackened; then you choose from a variety of sauces. We will keep returning. Even though we would like to try new combinations, we will be hard put not to have the same ones we like so well.
Hours: Open Monday-Thursday 11:30am-10pm, Friday & Saturday 11:30am-11pm, Sunday 11:30am-9pm.
Prices: Brunch, $12-$25; Lunch (salads, sandwiches) $9-$17, naked fish $17-$19; Dinner, $20-$29; glass of wine $7-$13.   Size: seats 50.

Frank's (Italian)
23 Putnam Avenue (just across the CT border), Port Chester NY, 914.939.8299   www.FranksPizza23.info
This popular pizza, pasta, sandwich take-out is also a popular dining spot. Although the setting is informal, your food is served with cloth napkins and on stylish plates. The service is friendly. We are wowed by the quality and variety of their freshly prepared entrees. We especially like the garlic balls, eggplant parmigiana and the fettuccine Alfredo.
Hours: Open Monday-Thursday & Saturday 10:30am-10pm, Friday 10:30am-10:30pm, Sunday 4pm-9pm (Lunch served until 3 pm).
Prices: Pizzas (10") $10-$13, Lunch entrees $12-$15; Dinner entrees $15-$25.   Size: seats 60.

Frankie & Johnnie's (Steak)
77 Purchase St, Rye NY, 914.925.3900   www.FrankieAndJohnnies.com
They opened as a speakeasy in New York City in 1926 and have been a fixture in Rye for years. The slightly dark, wood-paneled "steakhouse decor" is rather charming and elegant. The service is professional and kind. If you are in Rye and want a steak, this could be a good place to go. But, we have better in Greenwich and we don't feel it's worth the trip.
Hours: Open Tuesday-Thursday 11:30am-10pm, Friday 11:30am-midnight, Saturday 5pm-midnight, Sunday 5pm-9:30pm.
Prices: Dinner, entrees $23-$60, Tuesday-Friday lunch price ,fixed $22, Sunday dinner price fixed $40; glass of wine $12-$20.
Size: Seats 120, on two levels.

RESTAURANTS

Gabriele's Italian Steakhouse (Steak)
35 Church Street, Greenwich CT, 203.622.4223
www.gabrielesofgreenwich.com
A glamorous steakhouse with attentive service (most of the time), where celebrities like to dine. The wood-paneled bar room is a popular gathering spot. Its innovative cuisine comes off well with the appetizers and pastas. The steaks are good but are they great? Often full, so be sure you reserve. Expect a high noise level.
Hours: Lunch, Friday 12pm-3:00pm; Dinner, Weekdays 4:30pm-11pm, Saturday 5pm-11pm, Sunday 4pm-11pm.
Prices: Dinner entrees $23-$63; glass of wine $9-$20.
Size: seats 120 in the main area, with 3 smaller rooms: wine room, bar area, the rotunda.

Garden Café at Greenwich Hospital (American)
5 Perryridge Road, 1st Floor, Watson Pavilion, Greenwich CT, 203.863.3228
The hospital's garden café is a pretty dining room and a nice place to lunch, whether you are visiting someone or not. Enjoy the garden views through floor-to-ceiling windows and, in good weather, dine on the trellised bluestone terrace. Enjoy a healthy and delicious salad or sandwich. The menu lists calories and sodium content. This addition was donated by the Victor Borge family.
Hours: Open Weekdays 8am-3:30pm.
Prices: Lunch, (sandwiches, salads & other entrees) $7-$10.
Size: seats 75.

Gates (American)
10 Forest Street, New Canaan CT, 203.966.8666
www.culinarymenus.com/gates.htm
An informal standby for over thirty years. On a back street, this large, gaily decorated, cheerful restaurant, is a popular place to have lunch if you are shopping in New Canaan. Service is good-humored and youthful. The menu is strong on burgers, salads and wraps as well as some more sophisticated entrees.
Hours: Sunday Brunch, 10:30am-3:30pm; Lunch, Monday-Saturday 11:30am-3:30pm; Dinner, Monday-Thursday 5pm-9:30pm, Friday & Saturday 5pm-10:30pm, Sunday 4:30pm-9pm.
Prices: Lunch $10-$17; Dinner $12-$22; children's menu $6-$9; glass of wine $8-$11. Size: seats 120.

RESTAURANTS

Ginger Man (American, Pub)
64 Greenwich Avenue, Greenwich CT, 203.861.6400
www.gingermangreenwich.com
A lively burger / beer place in a classic, upscale tavern atmosphere, with dimly lit rooms, a long wood bar and vintage Greenwich photos. Twenty-three beers on tap and sixty bottled beers. The oversize burgers on English muffins require a large bite. In the fall and winter they often have beer dinners (5-courses with 5 beers and talks about the brewery).
Hours: Monday-Thursday, 11:45am-10pm; Friday & Saturday 11:45am-11 pm, Sunday 11:45am-9 pm.
Prices: Lunch & Dinner: Sandwiches and burgers $12-$19; entrees $18-$33; Glass of wine $7-$11; Drafts $7-$10; 5-course beer dinners $75.
Size: Downstairs 100, upstairs 55 (upstairs is available only Thursday, Friday & Saturday nights).

Glory Days (Diner)
69 East Putnam Avenue, Greenwich CT, 203.661.9067
www.GloryDaysDiner.com
A welcoming diner, with a celebrity-studded clientele - open since 1923. Completely rebuilt in 2002 with a sleek new look. Nick, the friendly owner, has operated the restaurant for over 20 years. He keeps prices low and serves hearty portions. This is what a diner is supposed to be. Everyone has their favorites - we particularly like their Greek salad and baklava. It is a popular late-night meeting place for students.
Hours: Open Sunday-Thursday 6am-1am; Friday & Saturday open 24 hours;   No reservations.
Prices: $9-$17;(complete dinner entrees $15-$22). Size: seats 35.

Golden View Firenze (Italian, Mediterranean)
249 Railroad Avenue, Greenwich CT, 203.817.0920
http://gvfct.com
A whole new concept of food has landed in the former China White. This bright, light, modern space is now Italian. We like it, despite the noise. Food, wine and very accommodating service are the focus. We especially like their ravioli with four cheeses, the black bass Sicilian style and the green peppercorn steak.
Hours: Lunch, Monday-Saturday 11:30am-3pm; Dinner, Monday-Saturday 5:30pm-10:30pm, Sunday 5pm-8:30pm.
Prices: Entrees $18-36; glass of wine $8-$18. Size: seats 36.

RESTAURANTS

Gus's Franklin Park Restaurant (Seafood)

126 Halstead Avenue, Harrison NY, 914.835.9804

www.GusSeaFood.com

For those old enough to remember, a mix of Manero's and the Clam Box. this 85-year old, casual restaurant, now run by Gus's grandson, is the perfect place to put on a bib and have a lobster. Pictures of celebrities line the wall and friendly servers bring generous helpings. The Gorgonzola salad and onion rings are so good you will even eat the batter flakes in the basket. Broiled (not boiled) lobster is the popular choice. With their own seafood store next door, you know the fish will be fresh.

Hours: Lunch everyday 11:30am-3pm; Dinner, Sunday-Thursday 4:30pm-9:30pm, Friday & Saturday 5pm-10:30pm. (No reservations, but call when you are leaving for the restaurant to put your name on the wait list).

Prices: Lunch (sandwiches, burgers, fish) $10-$19, 1 lb lobster $19; Dinner entrees $16-$32, lobster at market (prices on the blackboard); glass of wine $8-$15.   Size: seats 50.

Harlan Publick (New American)

127 Washington Street, (@SoNo Ironworks), Norwalk CT, 203, 831,0727

www.harlanpublick.com

Following Chef Stephen Lewandowski's success with Harlan Social in Stamford, he brought the same vibe to Norwalk. Both restaurants are names after his son, Harlan. The exaggerated industrial setting plus the simple but creative food, makes this a fun place to hang out. A parking garage is just next door.

Hours: Wednesday, Thursday & Friday 3pm-11pm, Saturday 5pm-11pm, Sunday 11am-11pm. The bar is open later.   Prices: Entrees $15-$28; wine by the glass $9-$15.

Size: Seats 40 in the main dining room, 20 in the party room and as many as can fit in the bar area.

TIP: GREEK FESTIVAL

In October every year, the Church of the Archangels, (Bedford & Third Streets, Stamford CT) has a festival with authentic Greek food. To find out the exact date or request a take out, call 203.348.4216 or visit www.archangels.ct.goarch.org

RESTAURANTS

Harlan Social (New American)

The Lockworks, 121 Towne Street, Stamford CT, 203.883.8000
www.HarlanSocial.com
If you can't find Towne Street on your GPS, enter 699 Canal Street. This chic, stark modern bar / restaurant created by celebrated Chef Lewandowski is fun. The main restaurant is airy with lots of windows and an open kitchen. The surroundings and the friendly wait staff make this a comfortable place to dine. The Harlan Burger is tops. Whatever you order, save room for the warm cinnamon donuts.
Prices: Lunch entrees $14-$24; Dinner entrees $14-$37; glass of wine $8-$17.
Hours: Brunch Saturday & Sunday 11am-4pm; Lunch, Tuesday-Friday 11:30am-4pm; Dinner, Tuesday-Thursday 5:30pm-10pm, Friday & Sunday 5pm-11pm, Sunday 4pm-10pm.
Size: seats 120 inside, 30 at the bar, 36 outside.

Harvest (New American)

372 Greenwich Avenue, Greenwich CT, 203.869.4080
www.Harvestwinebar.com
The owners of Cava, Scena and 55 created a restaurant to entice Avenue strollers. They succeeded in making a welcoming, at-ease place for casual dining. The attractive decor is informal rustic without tablecloths. Don't be misled that it's all about the wine, the food is good too. The menu has something for everyone. Mike and Katie love the calamari, seafood pan roast and wood-grilled salmon.
Hours: Lunch, daily 11am-3pm; Dinner, Sunday-Thursday 5pm-10pm, Friday & Saturday 5pm-11pm.
Prices: Lunch, entrees $15-$25, prix fixe 2-course lunch (Brunch) $19; Dinner, entrees $18-$36; glass of wine $8-$19.
Size: Seats 90.

Homestead Inn
(see Thomas Henkelmann)

RESTAURANTS

Hudson Grille (New American)
128 Bedford Street, Stamford CT, 203.883.8600
www.HudsonGrilleCT.com
Hudson is a gigantic, intentionally dim, gastropub. The dark wood, mirrors, wine racks and prominant bar set the scene for a hot spot. The attraction is the good food, good service and good drinks. Many of the appetizers are not only delicious, but large enough for a meal. The Hudson Pizza, onion soup, mac'n'cheese, and blackened tuna are all outstanding. You can park in the lot on Spring Street behind the restaurant & have your ticket validated.
Hours: Open Monday-Thursday 11:30am-10:30pm, Friday & Saturday 11:30am-10:30pm, Sunday 11:30am-9pm.
Prices: Lunch (Salads, Burgers, Entrees) $8-$23; Dinner (Burgers & Entrees) $15-$34: glass of wine $10-$15.
Size: seats 160.

Hunan Gourmet (Chinese)
68 East Putnam Avenue (Whole Foods Plaza), Greenwich CT, 203.869.1940
www.greenwichhunan.com
A dimly-lit Chinese restaurant with white tablecloths and a dressy flair. A good place to have a conversation. Just thinking about their shredded pork with dried bean curd or sea bass with ginger makes us hungry. The staff is especially nice to children, making it a popular family place.
Hours: Open Sunday-Thursday 11:30am-9:30pm, Friday & Saturday 11:30am-10:30pm.
Prices: Lunch specials $8-$10; Dinner, entrees $11-$23.
Size: seats 100.

IHOP (American)
2410 Summer Street, Stamford CT, 203.324.9819   www.ihop.com
As you probably know, IHOP, a.k.a. International House of Pancakes, is the place for chocolate pancakes and every imaginable breakfast treat. They also have sandwiches, crepes, burgers, salads and hearty dinners (like country fried steak).
Hours: Open everyday 7am-10pm.
Prices: Senior menu (55 & over) $5-$7,
Kids menu (under 12) $4-$5, breakfast $7-$15.

RESTAURANTS

Il Sogno Ristorante (Italian)
316 Boston Post Road, Port Chester NY, 914.937.7200
www.ilsognony.com
Not where you would expect-in the midst of tire stores and fast foods-there is an attractive, NYC-style Italian restaurant run by a Manhattan chef. The wait staff is professional. While making your choices, you will be given a delicious potato croquette and vegetable dip for your bread. Whether you order branzino or pasta, save room for the zabaglione for dessert.
Hours: Lunch, everyday 12pm-3pm;
Dinner, Monday-Thursday 5pm-10pm,
Friday & Saturday 5pm-11pm, Sunday 5pm-9pm.
Prices: Lunch & Dinner are the same, entrees $16-$24;
glass of wine $10.
Size: seats 85 in the main dining room and 45 upstairs.

(The) Inn at Pound Ridge (New American)
158 Westchester Avenue, Pound Ridge, NY 914.764.1400
www.theInnAtPoundridge.com
A lovely transformation has taken place at the Inn. It is now owned by famed chef Jean-Georges Vongerichten, a Waccabuc resident. We like the modern rustic setting with its light walls and many windows. The informally-dressed servers are competent and gracious. We find the farm-to-table, seasonal menu to be pleasant, but not outstanding. However, the tuna tartare and the hake rate high marks. When you call for a reservation, ask for a booth on the lower (garden) level. It is easier to have a conversation there.
Hours: Lunch, Weekdays 11:30am -3:00pm, Brunch Saturday & Sunday 11am-3pm; Dinner, Monday-Thursday & Sunday 5pm-10:30pm, Friday & Saturday 5pm-11pm. Be sure to reserve 3-4 weeks in advance for Friday & Saturday.
Prices: Brunch (sandwiches, pasta, pizza, entrees) $18-$38; Dinner, entrees $20-$38; glass of wine $9-$28
Size: seats 110 upstairs and 120 downstairs.

RESTAURANTS

Kazu (Japanese)

64 North Main Street, (South) Norwalk CT, 203.866.7492

www.kazusono.com

Very near the Norwalk movies, so if you are in the area, order the movie box, it has a tasty sampling of their Japanese specialties. The sushi and teriyaki are good choices. We like the mix on the menu of traditional Japanese and creative Asian dishes.

Hours: Lunch, Weekdays 11:30am-2:30pm; Dinner, Monday-Thursday 5pm-10pm, Friday & Saturday 5pm-11pm, Sunday 4pm-9:30pm.

Prices: Lunch, $11-$13; Dinner, entrees $17-$22, movie bento box $20, kid's bento box $11; glass of wine $8-$17.

Size: seats 100.

Kira Sushi (Japanese)

4 Lewis Court, Greenwich CT, 203.422.2990

www.KiraSushiGreenwich.com

This hidden restaurant, just off Greenwich Avenue, is worth finding. The decor is attractive and soothing. We always order the avocado salad, seafood miso or the yellowtail jalapeno followed by the beef teriyaki or chicken tempura. As you might expect, the sushi and their special rolls, such as the iridescent Kira Wasabi roll, get high marks.

Hours: Open Sunday-Thursday 11:30am-10pm, Friday & Saturday 11:30am-11pm, Sunday 11:30am-10pm (Lunch ends at 3:30pm).

Prices: Lunch $10-$19; Dinner $14-$29; glass of wine $8-10.

Size: seats 40.

Kona Grill (American, Japanese)

230 Tresser Blvd. (Stamford Town Center), Stamford CT, 203.324.5700

www.KonaGrill.com

18 Kona Grills are located in 12 states. Sushi was their original specialty. Now the menu has sandwiches, pizzas and traditional American fare while still maintaining a strong sushi bar. The large bar area is popular with the 20 & 30 something crowd during happy hour. It's fun to watch the fish in the spectacular 2,000 gallon fish tank. If you are not going for happy hour appetizers or sushi, we recommend the Macadamia nut chicken and the chili glazed salmon.

Hours: Open every day 11am-11pm.

Prices: Dinner entrees, $18-$30; Children's menu $3-$5; Glass of wine, $7-$13; During happy hour, drinks are generally, $4-$7 & appetizer, pizzas and selected sushi are half price (on Wednesdays bottles of wine are ½ price).   Size: seats 305.

RESTAURANTS

L'Escale (French, Mediterranean)
500 Steamboat Road, Greenwich CT, 203.661.4600
www.lescalerestaurant.com
L'Escale, French for "port of call," evokes good memories of dining along the French Riviera and it's on our Greenwich waterfront! In the summer, the terrace is the perfect spot to dine. This bright, airy restaurant has nicely-spaced tables and attentive service encouraging diners to have good conversations and a good time. Whether you are in the mood for a Salade Nicoise or one of their many seafood entrees, you will enjoy it. Be sure to try one of pastry chef Wendy Laurent's creations.
Prices: Breakfast $12-$21; Brunch entrees $14-$21;
Lunch entrees $22-$39, sandwiches $14-$16; Dinner entrees $22-$39; glass of wine $10-$18
Hours: Breakfast, everyday 7am-10am; Lunch, Monday-Saturday 11:30am-2:30pm, Sunday Brunch 11:30am-3pm; Dinner, Sunday-Thursday 5:30pm-10pm, Friday & Saturday 5:30pm-11pm.)
Size: seats 100 inside; terrace seats 40.

Lime (Vegetarian)
168 Main Avenue, Norwalk CT, 203.846.9240
www.LimeRestaurant.com
A neo-hippie restaurant in an "out-of-the-way" section of Norwalk. They serve vegetarian dishes as well as fish and meat. Despite consistently being named the best vegetarian restaurant for the last 15 years, we find the food inconsistent. Dishes we like are the tofu in orange sauce and salmon burger.
Hours: Open everyday, Lunch, Monday-Saturday 11am-4pm; Dinner Monday-Saturday, 5pm-10pm, Sunday 4:30-9:30
Prices: Lunch $9-$13; Dinner entrees $18-$26; glass of wine $7-$9.
Size: seats 40.

Little Buddha (Thai)
2270 Summer Street, Stamford CT, 203.356.9166
www.littlebuddhact.com
This small restaurant with tables surrounding the open kitchen needs updating. We still go here because the servers are friendly and we like their Thai and Hakka Chinese Dishes.
Hours: Lunch, Weekdays 11am-4pm, Saturday & Sunday 12pm-4pm; Dinner every day 4pm-10pm.
Prices: Lunch, $8-$13; Dinner, $12-$20; No alcohol is served, so bring your own, no corkage fee.   Size: seats 18.

317

Little Pub (Gastropub)

531 East Putnam Avenue, Cos Cob CT, 203.717.1147

www.littlePub.com

Daneen and Doug Grabe own the Little Pub in Ridgefield and Wilton, so it's no surprise their Greenwich Little Pub is a hit. The decor is charmingly done in old barn wood. The waiters casually dressed in jeans make everyone feel at ease. There are about 60 beers on the menu and the "pub food" is first rate. One of our favorites, the "queso funtimbo," is made with local Scarpelli sausage. The lively bar draws so many that the parking has valet service.

Hours: Open every day from 11:30am-10pm or later; no reservations, so arrive before 7:15 to be sure of getting a table.

Prices: small plates, sandwiches & wraps, burgers $10-$13; entrees (Pub favorites) $13-$19; beer $5-$20; glass of wine $10-$16.

Size: seats 50 in the main seating area.

Little Thai Kitchen (Thai)

21 St. Rochs Avenue, Byram CT, 203.622.2972

www.LittleThaiKitchen.com

A tiny jewel of a place, serving some of the best Thai cuisine outside of Bangkok, is tucked away on St. Rochs. If you don't like your food spicy, you will have to tell them. We love their Nau Nam tok (beef salad), Mee Grob (Thai crispy noodles), Pad Thai noodles as well as their curries, particularly the Thai Massaman and Thai green curry. The Thai iced tea must be an acquired taste.

Hours: Open Monday-Thursday 11am-9:30pm, Friday 11am-10pm, Saturday 12pm-10pm, Sunday 12pm-9pm.

Prices: Lunch entrees, $9-$13; Dinner entrees, $15-$21; (Dinner menu is served all day Sunday); No alcohol is served, so bring your own, the corkage fee is $3.   Size: seats 26.

Long Ridge Tavern (American)

2635 Long Ridge Road, Stamford CT, 203.329.7818
www.LongRidgeTavern.com
Dating from the 1880s, this charming country restaurant gives you a sense of stepping back into history. If you are looking for tavern fare such as chicken pot pie, Yankee pot roast or bread pudding, you won't be disappointed. They have live entertainment on Friday & Saturday evenings. Check their website for details. Brunch makes a good multi-generational spot.
Hours: Sunday Brunch, 11am-3pm; Lunch, Monday-Saturday 12pm-3:00pm; Dinner, Sunday-Thursday 5pm-9pm, Friday & Saturday 5pm-10pm.
Prices: Brunch Buffet $25; Lunch (tavern fare & Sandwiches) $13-$16; Dinner entrees $17-$30, pre fixe 3-course meal $27; children's menu $10; glass of wine $8-$10.
Size: Main dining room seats 80, private rooms seat 16, 40 and 65, outside terrace seats 40.

Louie's (Italian)

136 River Road Extension, Cos Cob CT, 203.422.2177
www.louiesrestaurantbar.com
For years this place has been a casual restaurant serving comfort food. Many remember it as the Mianus River Tavern, then Augies, then Bull Dog. Now Ron Rosa, owner of Polpo, has transformed it into a southern Italian restaurant with white table cloths and valet parking. The ambiance is still old tavern with a moose head above the fireplace. We find the food uneven. We applaud having specials with prices on a blackboard.
Hours: Lunch, everyday 11:30am-3:30pm; Dinner, Monday-Saturday 3:30pm-11pm; Sunday 3:30pm-10pm.
Prices: Luncheon (limited menu mainly sandwiches) $14-$18; Dinner entrees $19-$28; glass of wine $8-$11.
Size: seats 80.

MacDuffs Public House (Pub-British/Scottish)

99 Railroad Avenue, Greenwich CT, 203.422.0563
www.MacDuffsPub.com

When you are yearning for Scotch eggs, bangers and mash, or fish and chips, this pub-style restaurant, across from the movie theater and train station, is your best bet. It's a great place to relax after the movies, have a beer, sliders and spicy nachos. The service is pleasant. Expect it to be dimly lit-even at noon you may need a flashlight to read the menu. It is especially full of cheers during World Cup soccer matches.

Hours: Lunch everyday, 11:30am-4pm; Dinner, Tuesday-Saturday 4pm-10pm, Sunday-Monday 4pm-9pm.

Prices: Lunch entrees $10-$18, Dinner entrees $15-$25; glass of wine $9. Size: seats 26.

TIP: MAPLE SUGAR FESTIVAL

The festival is usually held in early March at the Stamford Museum & Nature Center. See how trees are tapped and sap is turned into maple syrup, then come away with a your own fresh maple syrup. For information contact the Museum at 203.322.1646 or visit www.stamfordMuseum.org

RESTAURANTS

Madonia (Italian)

1297 Long Ridge Road, Stamford CT, 203.322.8870

www.madoniaRestaurant.com

The space is attractive with a lovely outside dining terrace and valet parking. Stamford Magazine gave Madonia accolades, so our expectations were high. Unfortunately, we found the food average and the service haphazard. To top it off, it was very noisy. We suggest eating outside or in the private room.

Hours: Sunday Brunch, 11:30am-3pm; Lunch, Tuesday-Saturday 11:30am-5pm; Dinner, Tuesday-Saturday 5pm-10pm, Sunday 3pm-9pm. Closed Monday.

Prices: Brunch $10-$21; Lunch entrees $10-$21; Dinner entrees $17-$27, Glass of wine $8-$13.

Size: Front room seats 80, rear room seats 60, outside seats 20, private room for 6 to 12.

Mama's Boy (New American, Southern)

19 North Water Street, Norwalk CT, 203.956.7171

www.MamasBoyCT.com

Mama's Boy can cook! We like their "out-of-the-box" southern dishes like the BLT salad with delicious fried green tomatoes, corn bread with pepper jelly, and grits with shrimp. Their blood orange margarita is a real hoot. And what a nice staff, attentive and accommodating. "Mama's Boy Southern Table & Refuge" is located in an imaginatively re-decorated garage near the Norwalk Aquarium. The bar area is active, so it's best to ask for space in the back room if you want to have a conversation.

Hours: Sunday brunch 10:30am-5pm; Lunch, Friday & Saturday 11:30am-3pm; Dinner, Tuesday-Thursday 5pm-10pm, Friday & Saturday 5:30pm-10:30pm.

Prices: Lunch, plates and sandwiches $10-$14; Dinner, entrees $21-$34; Kids menu $8; glass of wine $8-$10.   Size: seats 85.

RESTAURANTS

Marianacci's (Italian)
24 Sherman Street, Port Chester NY, 914.939.3450
www.marianaccis.com
For over 60 years, this family-owned restaurant has been serving southern Italian food on pretty plates, in a refined and quiet atmosphere. Here except on Fridays, when there is live music, you can easily have a conversation while enjoying dishes such as our favorite, red snapper in orange sauce. You are not likely to pass this restaurant while driving through Port Chester, so knowing about it is part of the fun.
Hours: Lunch, Weekdays 12pm-2pm; Dinner, Monday-Thursday 5pm-9pm, Friday & Saturday 5pm-10pm; Closed Sunday except for private parties.
Prices: Lunch entrees $17-$29; Dinner entrees 18-$32; glass of wine $10.
Size: seats 120.

Maryann's Mexican Restaurant (Mexican)
• 23½ North Main Street, Port Chester NY, 914.939.8700
• 184 Summer Street, Stamford CT, 203.323.8900
www.maryannsmexican.com
We like Mexican food, but this one is not our favorite. The service is pleasant, but rather unprofessional. The menu has a huge selection and the portions are generous. Unfortunately, the food is mediocre. We like the margaritas.
Hours: Lunch, Tuesday-Sunday 11am-4pm; Dinner, Sunday-Thursday 4pm-10pm, Friday & Saturday 4pm-11pm.
Prices: Lunch entrees $11- $15; Dinner entrees $12- $19; kids menu $6-$8; glass of wine $7-8; Happy Hour Margaritas $5. No personal checks.
Size: 100 inside, 30 outside.

Match (New American)
98 Washington Street, (South) Norwalk CT, 203.852.1088
www.matchsono.com
With its high ceilings, brick walls, white table cloths and nice lighting, Match has a trendy, relaxed, happy atmosphere. As a result of Chef Matthew Storch's innovative creations, this restaurant continues to be popular. Connecticut Magazine readers have voted Match the Best Restaurant in Fairfield County. We agree, it is one of the best. Be sure to reserve.
Hours: Lunch, Wednesday-Friday 11:30am-2pm; Dinner, Sunday-Thursday 5pm-10pm, Friday & Saturday 5pm-11pm.
Prices: Dinner entrees, $20-$38; glass of wine $8-$14.   Size: seats 40.

RESTAURANTS

McShanes (Irish Gastropub)

123 North Main Street, Port Chester NY, 914.937.7800

www.mcshanesportchester.com

This welcoming, well-designed pub is cool and spacious with dark paneling. Big screen TVs can be seen from any angle. A large bar dominates the center of the restaurant. It's a good place to cheer on your favorite team while having a hamburger or fish & chips and enjoying one of their 38 beers.

Hours: Lunch 12pm-3pm; Dinner 3pm-11pm; Late night menu 11pm-3am.

Prices: Brunch $11-$16; Lunch $10-$14; Dinner, entrees $15-$22, Burgers & Salads $10-$15; Children's menu $7; glass of wine $7-$10.

Size: seats 130 including chairs around the large bar.

Mediterraneo Restaurant (Italian, Seafood)

366 Greenwich Avenue, Greenwich CT, 203.629.4747

www.mediterraneoofgreenwich.com

Lively, bustling, welcoming, attractively-decorated in a nautical theme. Lots of people order their pizzas, but the kitchen turns out really good seafood dishes. Try the Halibut (dinner menu). The terrace provides an interesting perspective on life along Greenwich Avenue and also allows you to have a conversation. Inside, the tables in the back are the quieter ones. Don't expect a quick Lunch. Popular Terra has the same ownership.

Hours: Lunch, Weekdays 12pm-2:30pm, Saturday & Sunday 12pm-3pm; Midday menu, Weekdays 2:30pm-5pm, Saturday & Sunday 3pm-5pm; Dinner, Monday-Thursday 5:30pm-10pm, Friday & Saturday 5:30pm-10:30pm, Sunday 5pm-9:30pm; Sunday brunch 12pm-3pm.

Prices: Lunch, pizza & pasta $14-$24, entrees $16-$30; Dinner, pizza and pasta, $15-$25, entrees $24-$36; glass of wine $8-$16.

Size: seats 40 in the front and about 30 in the back; a few tables on the outside terrace in the summer.

RESTAURANTS

Mediterraneo (Italian, Seafood)
353 Main Avenue (inside Hotel Zero), Norwalk CT, 203.229.0000
www.MediterraneoOfNorwalk.com
We are fans of the Greenwich Mediterraneo. When we discovered The Hospitality Group had opened another Mediterraneo in the Hotel Zero Degrees in Norwalk, we had to try it. It has a similar menu, with just about the same prices, in a wow setting. There is big open kitchen in this stark contemporary, comfortable space. The restaurant overlooks a woods with a river running through it (as well as a train). In the summer (4pm-sunset) the rooftop deck serves oysters and cocktails. A place to enjoy the view.
Hours: Lunch, Weekdays 12pm-2:30pm, Saturday 12pm-3pm; Midday menu, Weekdays 2:30pm-5pm, Saturday 3pm-5pm; Dinner, Monday-Thursday 5:30pm-10pm, Friday & Saturday 5:30pm-10:30pm, Sunday 5pm-9:30pm.
Prices: Lunch, entrees $15-$34, express lunch 2-course $18, 3-course $21; Dinner, entrees $18-$36 (sides are extra); glass of wine $9-$18, Tuesday evening bottles of wine are 50% off.
Size: seats 130.

Meli-Melo (French Restaurant, Bakery, Sorbet, Juice Bar)
• 362 Greenwich Avenue, Greenwich CT, 203.629.6153
• Catering: 374½ Greenwich Avenue, 203.422.5001
www.melimelogreenwich.com
A popular, always-crowded restaurant with French casual foods such as the yummy croque monsieur. They have over 20 soups (our favorite is the onion soup) and a large variety of crepes. They also have an amazing selection of fresh-squeezed juices. The fruit sorbets are excellent as are their pastries. Chef Marc Penvenne and Evelyne have a knack for keeping this a happy Greenwich favorite. The breakfast menu features delicious omelets. Rosanna and Clifford rave about it. This is where Holly met Tod.
Hours: Breakfast, Weekdays 7am-11am, Saturday & Sunday 8am -12pm; Full course menu, Weekdays 7am-10pm, Saturday & Sunday 8am-10pm. No reservations.
Prices: Crepes & sandwiches $8-$16, salads $6-$14, dessert crepes $3-$11.   Size: seats 60.

RESTAURANTS

Meetinghouse (American)

Route 22 (next to the Bedford Playhouse), Bedford Village NY, 914.234.5656

www.BedfordMeetingHouse.com

With sweet service and cheerful, arty decor, this a fun spot for a meal timed to the movie next door (Bedford Playhouse Cinema 914.234.3315). Burgers and salads are popular.

Hours: Lunch, Wednesday-Saturday 11:30am-3pm; Brunch, Sunday 11:30am-3pm; Dinner, Tuesday 5:30pm-10pm, Wednesday & Thursday 5pm-10:30pm, Sunday 3pm-9pm.

Prices: Lunch $13-23; Dinner, 16-34; Kids' menu $11; glass of wine, $9-$14.   Size: seats 40, reservations only for parties of 6 or more.

(The) Melting Pot (Swiss, Fondue)

14 Grove Street, Darien CT, 203.656.4774

www.MeltingPot.com

Don't expect to dash in and have a quick fondue. This restaurant chain, with its 138 locations scattered across the US, is for "an experience," a date or a party. The "experience" will take, at least, two hours. The menu offers an extensive array of choices, great for some, daunting for others. A long, dark hall leads to a variety of private alcoves. Our friends in Switzerland surely could not imagine what has happened to the traditional fondues we savored in the Alps. A whole new genre of fondues is on the menu in this entertaining, if not traditional, restaurant. After trying some of the unusual combinations we settled on the traditional Emmenthaler cheese fondue and one of the chocolate fondues (original or pure chocolate or flaming turtle) as our favorites.

Hours: Lunch, Friday & Saturday 11:30am-2:30pm; Dinner, Monday-Thursday 5pm-10pm, Friday & Saturday 4pm-11pm, Sunday 4pm-9pm.

Prices: Entrees $20-$29, Four-course dinner for two $42 each; glass of wine $5-$14.

Size: seats 136; two private rooms, seats 12-16 and 26-36.

Moderne Barn (American)

430 Bedford Rd, Armonk NY, 914.730.0001

www.ModerneBarn.com

A large, swish, noisy, crowd-pleasing place. Wear your designer jeans and have a good time. The only sign of animals in this barn are the pretty horse murals on the walls. Whether you choose scallops or a pizza, you can count on the food being fresh and well-prepared. On Sundays they have fixed menu featuring a different area of the world each month.

Hours: Sunday Brunch, 11am-2:30pm; Lunch, Weekdays 12pm-2:30pm; Dinner, Monday-Thursday 5pm-10pm, Friday & Saturday 5pm-10:30pm, Sunday 5pm-9pm.

Prices: Lunch Sandwiches $12-$15, entrees $16-$29; Dinner entrees $15-$32; Sunday 3- course menu, $25; glass of wine $8-$22. Size: seats 200.

Morello Bistro (Italian)

253 Greenwich Avenue, Greenwich CT, 203.661.3443

www.MorelloBistro.com

Bernard's, Dome, Gaia-this architectural gem of a restaurant has given us many happy memories. Morello now presents Chef Mark Medina-Rios interpretation of Italian cuisine. Expect the same exciting domed interior, a meeting place-style bar, pleasant service and relaxed dining.

Hours: Lunch, Weekdays 12pm-4pm; Brunch, Saturday 12pm-4pm, Sunday 11:30am-4pm; Dinner, Sunday-Thursday 4pm-9pm, Friday & Saturday 4pm-10pm.

Prices: Sunday, prix fixe Brunch $29; Lunch, pasta entrees $20-$21, meat & fish entrees $24-$26, Paninis $12-$16, prix fixe weekday lunch $22; Dinner, Pasta entrees $20-$21, Meat and Fish entrees $24-$32; Glass of wine $10-$15; Kid's Menu $10 for children 12 and under.

Size: seats 120 (second-floor private dining rooms for 30+).

TIP: DINING IN RECIPES

Moffly Media, publishers of Greenwich Magazine, have collected popular recipes from area chefs and organized them by contributor and category for your dining pleasure. It's well worth a look when deciding to eat in. www.ilovefc.com/Food-and-Drink/Dining-In

RESTAURANTS

Morgans Fish House (Seafood)
22 Elm Place (bet. Purchase & Theodore Fremd), Rye NY, 914.921.8190
www.morgansFishHouse.net
Morgans is part of the Pearl Restaurant group which also owns the Rye Grill, 1020 Post and Elm Street Oyster House. When in Rye this is a good choice. The service is cheerful and the fish is reliable. The soft-contemporary decor is attractive and comfortable. The chefs preparing food are clearly on view. For less noise request a booth or a seat in the back.
Hours: Sunday Brunch, 11:30am-3pm; Lunch, Monday-Saturday 11:30am-4pm; Dinner, Monday 4pm-9pm, Tuesday-Thursday 4pm-10pm, Friday & Saturday 4pm-11pm, Sunday 3pm-9pm.
Prices: Sunday Brunch $12-$25; one menu for Lunch & Dinner: entrees $20-$32; glass of wine $9-$15.
Size: seats 150, plus a private room which seats 50.

(The) Mumbai Times (Indian)
140 East Putnam Avenue, Cos Cob CT, 203.625.5500
www.MumbaiTimesCT.com
We eat often at this small, charming Cos Cob restaurant which has an extensive menu. The decor is simple, the service is kind and the food is very good. We suggest the Goan Fish Curry, Chicken Basil Tikka Kabab and Malai Kofte along with the Peshawari Naan and Sweet Lassi.
Hours: Open everyday; Lunch, Weekdays 11:30am-2:30pm, Saturday & Sunday 12pm-3pm; Dinner 5pm-10pm Prices: Lunch Specials Weekdays, $9-$12; Dinner entrees $11-$24. Size: 12.

Napa & Company (New American)
75 Broad Street (in Marriott Courtyard), Stamford CT, 203.353.3319
www.NapaAndCompany.com
This restaurant has not only good food, but is fun too. It is like an upscale "gastro bar." There are over 40 wines by the glass. Diners get an iPad to peruse the wines. The walls in this somewhat dimly-lit restaurant are decorated with bottles of wine. It is California-informal with waiters in jeans and white dress shirts. The food goes well with the wine. We like starting with the superb artisanal cheese plate followed by the wagu burger. Parking is easy in the hotel's parking garage.
Hours: Breakfast, Weekdays 6:30am-10am, Weekends 7:30am-10:30am; Lunch Weekdays 11:30am-2:30pm;Dinner Monday-Saturday 5:30pm-10pm.
Prices: Lunch, (salads, sandwiches, small plates, entrees) $10-$25; Dinner entrees $26-$34; glass of wine $7-$26. Size: seats 70.

Navaratna (Indian, vegetarian)

133 Atlantic Street, Stamford CT, 203.348.1070 www.navaratana.com
Low key, simply decorated with an open kitchen. The menu is completely
vegetarian. The staff is glad to explain the numerous choices on the
menu. We like the lentil doughnuts and the Malaki Kofta.
Hours: Open Sunday-Thursday 11:30am-10pm, Friday & Saturday
11:30am-10:30pm.
Prices: Lunch & Dinner, entrees $8-$10   Size: seats 44.

Nessa (Italian)

325 North Main Street, Port Chester NY, 914.939.0119
www.NessaRestaurant.com
Try this charming enotecca, named after co-owner Marc Tessitore's wife,
Vanessa. Intimate, with glowing candles and low light. The main part of
the restaurant is lively and noisy. For a quieter space, request the room
at the back of the restaurant or seating in the pretty garden. The restaurant seems understaffed and consequently the service is slow and the
waiters stressed. We are fond of starting with the prosciutto & fig
bruschetta or a ½ portion of cavatelli sausage pasta or the linguine con
vongole followed by the monkfish picatta. Be sure to reserve on weekends.
Hours: Sunday Brunch, 11am-3pm; Dinner, Tuesday-Thursday 5:30pm-
10pm, Friday & Saturday 5:30pm-11pm, Sunday & Monday 5:30pm-
9:30pm.
Prices: Brunch $11-$14; Dinner entrees $20-$27, Wine by the quartino
(about a glass & ½) $9-$21.   Size: seats 86 inside and 36 outside.

Old Mill Saloon and Smokehouse (Southwestern)

2 Wilton Avenue, Norwalk CT, 203.847.7500
http://www.oldmillsaloon.com/
We are lamenting the loss of Ash Creek. No more chicken fried steak on
this menu. We find the food OK, but there are better BBQ places closer to
Greenwich. The service is kind and accommodating and the atmosphere
still has an old west feel. It is an easy place to dine with children. They
opened in November 2013, perhaps with time the food will improve.
Hours: Dinner, Sunday-Thursday 11am-10pm, Friday & Saturday 11am-
11pm; Bar open until 1 or 2 am.
Prices: burgers and sandwiches $10-$11, entrees $12-$25; kids' menu
$5-$10; glass of wine $7-$9.   Size: seats 160.

Olio (New American)
934 Hope Street, (Springdale) Stamford CT, 203.817.0303
www.OlioStamford.com
Moria Hyland and Chef Steve Costanzo have combined their passion for fine food, service and design in creating Olio. The black and white decor is crisply modern. The service is warm and welcoming. The limited menu is filled with creative dishes-we love the scallops and pork chops. Reservations for parties of 6 or more.
Hours: Sunday Brunch, 11am-2pm; Dinner, Tuesday-Thursday 5:30pm-10pm, Friday 5:30pm-11pm.
Prices: Brunch $12-$18, Kids $7; Dinner $18-$28; glass of wine $6-$11.
Size: seats 38.

Opus 465
(aka Wild Westchester BBQ), (aka Three Little Pigs BBQ)
465 Main Street, Armonk NY, 914.273.4676, 4995
www.Wildwestchesterbbq.com
www.threelittlepigsofwestchester.com
www.opus465.com
With all the colorful advertisements about the "Three Little Pigs" BBQ, we had to give it a try. We have been there, so you don't need to try it.

Oriental Gourmet (Chinese)
214 Sound Beach Avenue, Old Greenwich, 203.637.1010
For years Olivia and her family have been traveling across town to eat in their favorite Chinese restaurant, where they always order Szechuan dumplings and sesame chicken. Old Greenwich residents have long been in the know about the very good food in this modest restaurant. Eat-in or takeout, this is a real find. This restaurant was the launching place for the owners of Penang and Asiana.
Hours: Lunch, Monday-Saturday 11am-3pm; Dinner, Monday-Thursday 3pm-10pm, Friday & Saturday 3pm-11pm, Sunday 12pm-10pm.
Prices: Lunch specials, $7; Dinner entrees $10-$15.   Size: seats 27.

RESTAURANTS

Outback (Steak)

60 South Broadway, White Plains NY, 914.684.1397 www.Outback.com
Outback is a casual chain based in Florida. It was founded in 1988 and
has 900 locations. Despite its Australian theme, Outback serves American cuisine, with Creole influences. The Bloomin' Onion is the signature
Outback item. Most Outbacks serve Foster's Lager, an Australian brand
of beer largely sold outside of Australia. We like having the calories listed
on the menu, but sometimes the calorie count is a little frightening.
Hours: Lunch, Saturday & Sunday 11am-4pm; Dinner, Monday-Thursday 4pm-10pm, Friday & Saturday 4pm-11pm, Sunday 4pm-9pm.
Prices: Weekend Lunch, (burgers & sandwiches) $7-$11, entrees $12-
$18; Dinner, (burgers & sandwiches) $10-$12, entrees $14-$26; kids (un-
der 10) $2-$8. Size: seats 60, 30 on each side.

P.F. Chang's China Bistro (Chinese)

- Stamford Town Center, 230 Tresser Blvd, Stamford CT, 203.363.0434
- Westchester Mall, 125 Westchester Avenue, White Plains NY
  914.997.6100

www.PFChangs.com
This chain of 133 restaurants manages to keep their large, elaborately-
decorated dining rooms filled with adults and children, clearly having a
good time. If you have enjoyed delicacies from the different regions of
China, you will discover this is not Chinese food as you know it, but it is
still good. It comes from that mystical Chinese region "P.F. Chang", where
the cuisine is intended to please the American palate. (Actually the ini-
tials stand for the founder Paul Fleming.) Enjoy it for what it is. Try their
orange peel chicken and lettuce wraps. This is family fare for mall shoppers. If the restaurant is busy, ask for a pager, then shop until your table
is ready.
Hours: Lunch, Everyday 11am-4pm; Dinner, Sunday-Thursday 4pm-10pm,
Friday & Saturday 4pm-11:30pm.
Prices: Lunch entrees $10-$14; Dinner entrees $13-$25. Size: seats 360.

RESTAURANTS

(La) Paella (Spanish)

44 Main Street, Norwalk CT, 203.831.8636
www.LaPaellaRestaurant.com
On a mostly commercial street, you will discover a cheerful, bright, attractive restaurant. There is something about this restaurant that makes you expect the kitchen to turn out top quality Paellas and tapas. You won't be disappointed. On the dinner menu there are 7 paella choices; we recommend the seafood paella and the white sangria. Right next to the restaurant they have a small parking lot.
Hours: Lunch, Thursday-Saturday 12pm-4pm; Dinner, Sunday-Thursday 4pm-10pm, Friday & Saturday 4pm-11pm.
Prices: Lunch, paellas $9-$15, tapas $4-$8; Dinner, paellas $18-$30, tapas $8-$30; glass of wine $7-$15.   Size: seats 70.

(Le) Pain Quotidien (Bakery, American)

382 Greenwich Avenue, Greenwich CT, 203.404.7533
www.LePainQuotidien.com
Le Pain Quotidien has 151 locations and is decorated in rustic, farmhouse style with long wooden communal tables. There are some individual tables for the less gregarious. This is a popular meeting place for mothers after the morning school drop-off. Fresh food and friendly service. Susan recommends the Tuscan white bean salad. The desserts and breads, like their famous Challah bread, are worth the calories.
Hours: Open Weekdays 7am-7pm, Saturday & Sunday 8am-7pm
Prices: Breakfast $6-$14; Lunch/Dinner $11-$16.
Size: seats 100 (2 large tables, each seats 24; 26 tables for 2).

Paloma (Nuevo Latino)

15 Harbor Point Road (Waterfront Square), Stamford CT, 203.998.7500
(If your GPS can't find it, use 100 Washington Street)
www.palomaGrill.com
Celebrity chef Aaron Sanchez wanted to make this his "dream restaurant." The design is creative modern, with yucca branches on the ceiling. Many windows have views of the harbor. In the season, there is a large outside eating area. His contemporary Latin dishes are good, unique and very tasty. It's a menu where we want to try everything, from the cactus fritters to the chorizo empanadas. The experienced staff are pleasant.
Hours: Open Sunday-Thursday 11:30am-10pm,
Friday & Saturday 11:30am-11pm.
Prices: Dinner: entrees $18-$25, small plates $8-$15;
glass of wine $8-$14.   Size: seats 240 (inside, outside, second floor).

RESTAURANTS

Panda Pavilion 3 (Chinese)
420 West Putnam Avenue, Greenwich CT, 203.869.1111, 203.869.1931
www.Panda3gw.com
We always feel relaxed at this established Chinese restaurant. This is a good place for little ones to learn to use chopsticks. Try one of our favorites: orange beef, ginger beef or General Tso's chicken, which scored at the top of our tasting contest.
Hours: Lunch, Weekdays 11:30am-3pm, Saturday & Sunday 12pm-3pm; Dinner, Sunday-Thursday 3pm-9:30pm, Friday & Saturday 3pm-10:30pm.
Prices: Lunch specials $8-$9; Dinner entrees $11-$30, sushi $5-$12; Glass of wine, $4; check their website under "special" for coupons.
Size: seats about 60.

(La) Panètiere (French)
530 Milton Road, Rye NY, 914.967.8140   www.lapanetiere.com
For over 24 years, one of Westchester County's best, only fifteen minutes away, serving classic French food in an attractive Provençal-style dining room. Relatively quiet, you can have a conversation. For that special evening, the decor, attentive, kind service and delightful food make this restaurant a perfect choice. We recommend the July 14 (Bastille Day) tasting menu. Jackets expected, ties preferred.
Hours: Lunch, Tuesday-Friday & Sunday 12pm-2:30pm; Dinner, Tuesday-Saturday 6pm-9:30pm, Sunday 6pm-8pm. Advance reservations strongly recommended.
Prices: Lunch, entrees $24-30, Pre Fix menu $32; Dinner, entrees $28-$48, Tasting menus $85 & $130 (with wine); glass of wine $13-14.
Size: seats 50, (private rooms upstairs for 20 or 50).

Pasquale Ristorante (Italian)
2 Putnam Avenue (border of Greenwich), Port Chester NY, 914.934.7770
www.pasqualeristorante.com
For 15 years the same owner, staff and chef have been serving traditional southern Italian food in this friendly, comfortable spot. The setting is unpretentious and a little dowdy. The white table cloths and tapestries give it an old-world feeling. Many diners are regulars, coming for years at a certain time and ordering the same dish. We like the Pollo alla Francese, Pollo alla Scarpariello and the Salmone ala Dijonese.
Hours: Lunch, Tuesday-Thursday 12pm-3pm; Dinner, Tuesday-Thursday 3pm-10pm, Friday & Saturday 3pm-11pm, Sunday 1pm-9pm.
Prices: Lunch, $11-$16; Dinner, $13-$33; glass of wine $8.
Size: Main dining room seats 58, party room for 60.

RESTAURANTS

Pasta Nostra (Italian)

116 Washington Street, Norwalk CT, 203.854.9700

www.PastaNostra.com

You must dine at this restaurant. Restaurants come and go, this one has been in business 28 years. The Spartan, simple decor sends a clear message: this place is about food and service. Its inventive, continually-changing menu is brilliant. If it says the best stuffed pepper you will ever eat, it is. If they have seafood on the menu, devour it. Their fish comes from the Bon Ton Fish market in Greenwich. Beware: reservations are usually necessary but owner Chef Bruno often requires a $25 credit card deposit in case you don't show or don't cancel by 3 pm. American Express cards are not accepted.

Hours: Dinner, Wednesday 6pm-10pm, Thursday-Saturday 5:30pm-10pm. Closed Sunday-Tuesday

Prices: Entrees, $27-$35; wine by 1/4 bottle $8-$17.   Size: seats 40.

Pasta Vera (Italian)

48 Greenwich Avenue, Greenwich CT, 203.661.9705 www.pastavera.com

If you have grown up in Greenwich you have most likely eaten a number of meals in this popular, casual restaurant or dined on their take-outs at home. First opened on the Avenue in 1986, it has consistently served good food. At the front is a large deli-style counter filled with prepared foods ready to go. Take home fresh pasta (drop in your own pot of boiling water), good sauce, seafood salad, a loaf of bread and ricotta cheesecake. Your family will love you. If you choose to dine at one of the tables in the back, relax and enjoy their homemade ravioli or a seafood special.

Hours: Open Monday-Saturday 8am-10pm, Sunday 4pm-9pm.

Prices: Lunch entrees, $12-$17; Dinner entrees, $18-$24.

Size: seats 58; reservations are accepted for parties of six or more.

Penang Grill (Asian)

55 Lewis Street, Greenwich CT, 203.861.1988

www.culinarymenus.com/penanggrill.htm

Casual dining with very good Pan-Asian food. When you want something flavorful and unique, head to this small, established restaurant. The service is friendly and attentive. The refreshing mango chicken is our favorite. Popular for takeout.

Hours: Open Monday-Thursday 11am-9:30pm, Friday & Saturday 11am-10:30pm, Sunday 12pm-9:30pm.

Prices: Lunch specials $8-$11; Dinner entrees, $12-$23.

Size: seats 24. No reservations accepted. Bring your own wine.

(Le) Penguin (French)

61 Lewis Street, Greenwich CT, 203.717.1200

www.LePenguinBistro.com

Like the other noticeably happy diners, the dancing drinking penguin has us charmed. The contrasting orange and blue decor dominated by a drawing of the penguin gives the restaurant a light-hearted vibe. The attentive wait staff dress in black and white (penguin style?) and the very good food make this place a hit. Typical bistro items are on the menu. But Fish, like the black bass, is a forte. Arrive early to avoid the high-level, late evening, noise.

Hours: Lunch, Weekdays 10am-3pm; Dinner, Weekdays 5:30pm-10pm; Brunch, Saturday & Sunday 11:30am-2pm.

Prices: Lunch entrees, $14-$27; Dinner entrees $22-$36; glass of wine $8-$15.   Size: seats 60.

Piero's (Italian)

44 South Regent Street, Port Chester NY, 914.937.2904

www.PierosNY.com

Casual, off-the-beaten-path Italian. This little restaurant, with decor that doesn't seem to change, has a loyal and happy following. They like being greeted by the owner and being treated like family by the waiters. The food is first rate. Children are always welcome-you may want to ask to be served by Rafael the "Magic Man." Reservations are needed for most nights, but on the weekends reservations are mandatory.

Hours: Lunch, Tuesday-Friday 12pm-2pm; Dinner, Tuesday-Thursday & Sunday 5pm-9pm, Friday & Saturday 5pm-10pm.

Prices: Lunch $12-$18; Dinner $17-$26; glass of wine $9. Visa and Mastercard only.   Size: seats 48.

Plan B Burger Bar (American)

230 Tresser Boulevard @ The Stamford Mall, Stamford CT, 203.964.8353

Stamford is the fifth location for this upscale "old El Paso" style burger place. Our energetic, friendly waiter immediately wanted us to understand the "B" stands for "burgers, beer & bourbon." With over 20 different burgers, it's hard to think of a combination they missed. Give it a try and be sure to order the sweet potato fries.

Hours: Kitchen open: Sunday-Thursday 11:30am-midnight, Friday & Saturday 11:30am-1am; Bar open to about 1am.

Prices: Burgers $11-$16, Glass of wine $6-$10, Beers $5-$18. Size: seats 100.

RESTAURANTS

Plaza Restaurant (American)

87 Railroad Avenue (across from train station), Greenwich CT, 203.622.9260

www.plazarestaurantgreenwich.com

Since 1970 Plaza Restaurant has made a lot of pancakes for Greenwich youngsters. This lunch and breakfast spot just keeps satisfying. A great place to have a chat or get a quick bite before hopping on the train. If you are stopping for lunch, try their turkey club.

Hours: Open Weekdays 6am-5pm, Saturday 6am-4pm, Sunday 6am-3pm.

Prices: Breakfast $4-$14; Lunch (sandwiches, burgers, wraps) $5-$9, entrees $10-$17; glass of wine $4.25. Size: seats 28+14 at the counter.

Polpo (Italian)

554 Old Post Road #3, Greenwich CT, 203.629.1999

www.polporestaurant.com

This out-of-the-way Italian Restaurant, in a charming 100 year-old stone house, serves pleasing Tuscan cuisine. It is a popular Greenwich destination, with good vibes. The ambiance is warm, the service is attentive. The diners always seem to be in a festive, noisy mood. Quieter tables are upstairs. The lively piano music is downstairs. Allow time for making decisions- the menu is filled with appealing choices. We applaud having the specials on a blackboard with prices. We don't applaud the $4 suggested tip for the valet parking or to have a tip for the captain and the server suggested on the bill.

Hours: Lunch, Monday-Saturday 11:30am-4pm; Dinner, Monday-Saturday 4pm-11pm, Sunday 1pm-11pm.

Prices: Lunch prix-fixe $26, Dinner entrees, $25-$48; glass of wine $11-$14. Size: seats 53 inside, 34 on the terrace.

Pomodoro (Italian)

1247 East Putnam Avenue (Riverside Shop Cntr), Riverside CT, 203.698.7779   www.pomodoroRiverside.com

Friendly, casual, family dining. A popular spot with youngsters. If there were a contest for the largest portions, this small, charmingly-decorated restaurant might win. Pizzas are popular, but they also have sandwiches, paninis, pastas and wraps. We like their Greenwich Salad and Chicken Francese. They sell sauces by the pint.

Hours: Lunch everyday, 11am-4pm; Dinner every night, 5pm-10pm (11pm on weekends).

Prices: Lunch $7-$21; Dinner $15-$22; glass of wine $7. Size: seats 40.

RESTAURANTS

Port Chester Hall (Gastropub)

3 Broad Street, @ the Train Station, Port Chester NY, 914.305.8383
www.portChesterHall.com
This is an amazing transformation of a 5,600 sf 1890 train station into an attractive pub, restaurant, hot spot-and it is still an active train station. Tickets can be purchased inside until 2:30. Kudos to John Bloostein, owner of Heartland Brewing, for the renovation. Bloostein owns 7 other brew pubs in NYC. Everyone enjoys the warm, giant pretzels and good pub fare. Hours: Open Monday-Thursday 5pm-10pm, Friday 5pm-midnight, Saturday 12pm-midnight, Sunday 12pm-10pm.
Prices: Lunch & Dinner, burgers and sandwiches $13-$15, entrees $16-$23; glass of wine $7-$15; beer (16 0z) $8; Children's menu $9.
Size: 100 inside and 140 outside.

Purdy's Farmer & The Fish (American, Seafood)

100 Titicus Road, North Salem, NY, 914.617.8380
www.FarmerAndTheFish.com
A casual, unique, circa 1775 farmhouse restaurant. It is surrounded by verdant gardens, where during the season, vegetables are picked daily. True to its title, there are many seafood choices. This is a winning combo. The place is buzzing. The bar is very active, a good place to have a drink and throw your peanut shells on the floor. Plan to have a relaxed evening, the kitchen is often slow. Arrive by 5:30 for a quiet dinner.
Hours: Brunch, Sunday 12pm-3pm; Lunch, Monday-Saturday 12pm-3pm; Bar menu every day, 3pm-5pm; Dinner, Sunday-Thursday 5pm-10pm, Friday & Saturday 5pm-11pm.
Prices: Lunch $20 -$29; Dinner $24-$32; glass of wine $8-$15 (priced to make the bottle price attractive). Size: Seats 60 (25 cramped tables).

Putnam Restaurant (American)

373 Greenwich Avenue, Greenwich CT, 203.869.4683
Few restaurants have been in business since 1955. We hope this inexpensive informal hometown restaurant stays. This is what the Avenue was like in the 1950s. The menu has lots of selections, many Italian. Their specials are handwritten and a good choice. We like the Gorgonzola salad and Fettuccine Alfredo. Very good cakes are displayed on the counter. Stop here for a traditional breakfast, morning, noon and night.
Hours: Open Monday-Thursday 7am-10pm, Friday & Saturday 7am-10:30pm, Sunday 7am-9pm. Open most holidays.
Prices: Burgers & sandwiches, $6-$8; entrees $14-$18, glass of wine $5.
Size: seats 32 in the front booths & 32 at tables in the back.

Q (Barbeque)

112 North Main Street, Port Chester NY, 914.933.7427

www.QrestaurantAndBar.com

We are grateful to Jeffrey and Jennifer Kohn, owners of the terrific Kneaded Bread, for opening another top-notch place. They went on a 25-restaurant barbecue tasting journey before opening Q, a slightly Spartan barbecue restaurant. Order at the counter and they bring the food to your table. Thank heavens they took this journey and now we can satisfy our cravings for authentic pulled pork and beef brisket. For sides, order collard greens and baked beans.

Hours: Monday-Saturday, 11:30am-9:30pm (Friday and Saturday to 10:30); Sunday 12pm-9 pm.

Prices: Plates $13-$18, Kids' menu $7-$8.   Size: seats 75.

Quattro Pazzi (Italian)

269 Bedford Street, Stamford CT, 203.324.7000 www.QuattroPazzi.com

Informal and bright, located right across from the Avon theater, this place hits the spot when we want to have a hearty bowl of pasta with friends. Try the fettuccine a la Mitty.

Hours: Lunch, Monday-Saturday 11am-3:30pm, Sunday 11:30am-3:30pm; Dinner, Sunday-Thursday 3:30pm-10pm, Friday & Saturday 3:30pm-11pm.

Prices: Lunch $8-$20, Dinner $17-$27; glass of wine $7-$12.

Size: Downstairs seats 22, upstairs seats 40, private rooms for 30 & 90.

Rebecca's (New American)

265 Glenville Road, Glenville CT, 203.532.9270

www.RebeccasGreenwich.com

This Manhattan-chic restaurant is tucked in southwestern Greenwich. It serves modern American cuisine with a French flair. Rebecca Kirhoffer has assembled a sophisticated wine list to match her husband Chef Reza Khorshidi's awesome food. No wonder he was awarded CT Magazine's best contemporary chef. The restaurant has a sleek minimalist-modern look, complete with a large window that allows you to see the kitchen. There is some sound proofing,but it can get noisy.

Hours: Lunch, Tuesday-Friday 11:30am-2:30pm; Dinner, Tuesday-Thursday 5pm-9:30pm, Friday & Saturday 5pm-10:30pm.

(Make a reservation, but you can sometimes drop in and eat at the bar.)

Prices: Lunch entrees about the same as dinner; Dinner entrees $40-$145 (most entrees are in the $40s); glass of wine $10-$60 (most $10-$20).   Size: seats 74.

Restaurant North (New American)

386 Main Street, Armonk NY, 914.273.8686

www.RestaurantNorth.com

This attractive, stark white restaurant with minimalist decor, unobtrusively located in a small shopping center, has a chef recognized as a rising star. The menu features farm-fresh local produce and changes almost every day. We always choose to eat upstairs; downstairs is much too noisy. We like the perky wait staff, but when you order only an entree, the staff may suggest you order an appetizer because you will need to wait 20 minutes for your entree. With appetizers almost the same price as entrees, we suggest you munch on their delicious pumpernickel bread and wait.

Hours: Lunch, Tuesday-Sunday 12pm-2:30pm; Dinner, Tuesday-Thursday 5pm-9:30pm, Friday & Saturday 5pm-10:30pm, Sunday 5pm-8:30pm.

Prices: Dinner entrees $28-$35, glass of wine $10-$28.

Size: downstairs seats 40, upstairs seats 35, 20 people can sit outside and look at the parking lot.

Rio Border (Mexican/Tex Mex)

330 Connecticut Avenue, Norwalk CT, 203.855.9577

When CT Magazine awarded their best Mexican in Fairfield County to Rio Border we were surprised. Rio is a tacky restaurant in a unpretentious shopping center, serving large portions of mediocre food. Many of the friendly servers have been there since Rio opened 13 years ago.

Hours: Lunch, Monday-Saturday 11:30am-2:30pm; Dinner, Monday-Thursday 5pm-9:30pm, Friday & Saturday 5pm-10:30pm, Sunday 11:30am-9pm.

Prices: Lunch, entrees $8-$11; Dinner, entrees $14-$17. Size: seats 100.

Rizzuto's (Italian)

1980 West Main Street (East Putnam), Stamford CT, 203.324.5900

www.Rizzutos.com

Bill Rizzuto, a former general manager of the Greenwich Hyatt, has opened his fourth casual Italian restaurant just across the Greenwich border in the ShopRite Shopping Center. The wood-fired Neapolitan pizzas and home-style pastas are not the only draw. It was named as the Best Happy Hour by Greenwich Magazine's readers.

Hours: Lunch, Everyday 11:30am-4pm; Dinner, Monday-Thursday 4pm-9:30pm, Friday & Saturday 4pm-10pm, Sunday 4pm-9pm.

Prices: Lunch (pizzas & sandwiches) $9-$16; Dinner, (pizzas & entrees) $15-$26. Size: seats 160.

RESTAURANTS

Rowayton Seafood Company (Seafood)

89 Rowayton Avenue, Rowayton CT, 203.866.4488
www.rowaytonseafood.com
Located in a charming town, this popular, informal and relaxed restaurant is just right for summer dining. A good place to bring landlocked visitors for lobster and a view of the water. Consistently good food and our favorite place for New England clam chowder and fried oysters. The service is kind and accommodating.
Hours: Open Sunday-Thursday 11:30am-10pm, Friday & Saturday 11:30am-11pm. On weekends, make reservations well in advance.
Prices: Lunch, (sandwiches & entrees) $14-$32; Dinner, entrees $25-$34; glass of wine, $8-$12. Size: seats 65.

Ruby's Oyster Bar and Bistro (Seafood)

45 Purchase Street, Rye NY, 914.921.4166   www.rubysoysterbar.com
No need to redesign a bistro like this one. It has been popular for more than 10 years. We like the style and vibe of this friendly place. And, we like the oysters too. Ruby's is part of the Pearl Restaurant Group which includes the Rye Grill, Morgan's Fish House and the Elm Street Oyster House.
Hours: Breakfast, Monday-Saturday 8am-11:30am; Brunch, Sunday 11:30am-3:30pm; Lunch, Monday-Saturday 11:30am-3:30pm; Dinner, Monday-Thursday 5pm-10pm, Friday & Saturday 5pm-11pm, Sunday 4pm-10pm.
Prices: The menu is the same for Lunch and Dinner, only the specials change. Salads and lighter fare $9-$23, entrees $22- $36; wine by glass $9-$16.
Size: seats 100 downstairs and 26 upstairs (where it is lonely but quiet)

Rye Grill & Bar (American)

1 Station Plaza, Rye NY, 914.967.0332   www.RyeGrill.com
"Lets meet at the Rye Grill"-this fun, attractive, high-energy place is a great location to meet and greet your NY friends. The bar is large, noisy and an evening hot spot. In the main dining area, tables are filled with families. The service is swift and friendly. The food is well-prepared. The un-fussy menu has something to please everyone. This place is popular, always reserve on weekends.
Hours: Open Monday-Thursday 11:30am-10pm, Friday & Saturday 11:30am-11pm, Sunday 11am-9pm.
Prices: Lunch & Dinner menu, sandwiches/sliders $9-$17, entrees $2 1-$30; glass of wine $9-$15.   Size: seats 300, party room seats 45.

Rye House (Gastropub)

126 North Main Street, Port Chester NY, 914.481.3771
www.ryehousenpc.com

Rye House, a Manhattan gastropub which specializes in craft cocktails, has complately renovated a two-story 5,000 sf space in Port Chester. The upper level has mostly low tables for 2 to 4 people. Windows wrap around on two sides with distressed wood beams above, brick walls and wood flooring. The lower level is a lounge outfitted with low tables, banquet seating and an area for acoustic music. Michael Ganetta, a co-owner, says "We're not just trying to be a bar, we want to be all things to all people–families, couples, the bar crowd..."

Hours: Lunch weekdays 12pm-5pm; Brunch weekends 11am-4pm; Dinner Sunday-Thursday 5pm-10pm; Friday & Saturday 5pm-11pm.

Prices: Dinner, large plates $14-24; small plates and sandwiches $9-!4; wine by the glass $9-$14. Size Seats 160+ bar; 80 on first floor; 80 on lower level. Reservations for parties of 6 or more.

(The) Rye Roadhouse (Cajun)

12 High Street, Rye NY, 914.925.2668   www.RyeRoadHouse.com

When you arrive, you may say "where am I?" This hidden restaurant is on a residential street, some distance from the center of Rye. It has roadhouse charm, with wood and stone walls. The casual food is a mix of Southern and New Orleans food, such as: Creole gumbo, southern fried chicken and Crawfish Etouffee. The restaurant has been featured on the Cooking Channel's Road Trip, where they served blackened gator nuggets & bacon explosion sliders.

Hours: Open every day 11:30am-11pm; Brunch, Sunday 11:30am-3pm. Reservations on the weekend for 4 or more.

Prices: Sandwiches, Po' Boys, & burgers $11-$17; entrees $18-$30; glass of wine $7-$9.

Size: seats 46 on the dining side, the bar area seats 14, outside seats 12.

RESTAURANTS

School House Restaurant (New American)
34 Cannon Road, Cannondale section of Wilton CT, 203.834.9816
www.SchoolhouseatCannondale.com
It is rated one of the top 50 restaurants in the USA by www.opentable.com and after eating in this quaint, attractive restaurant we know why. The menu is limited (usually only 5 entrees), but you should expect each one to be superb. The servers want the diners to have a pleasant evening. Don't even think about going without a reservation.
Hours: Sunday Brunch, 10am-2pm; Lunch, Friday & Saturday 11:30am-2pm; Dinner, Wednesday-Saturday 5:30pm-9:30pm. Closed Monday & Tuesday.
Prices: Brunch $12-$23, Lunch & Dinner entrees $28-$30, 4-course prix-fixe dinner menu Thursday evenings $40; glass of wine $9-$14.
Size: seats 36.

Siena (Italian)
519 Summer Street, Stamford CT, 203.351.0898 www.sienastamford.com
When you enter this cozy, charming Tuscan restaurant, you feel a connection with Italy. The owner and wait staff are welcoming. Their homemade pastas are our choice. Try the duck ragu. For quiet dining, you may want to skip the weekends. It can be noisy. Be sure to reserve.
Hours: Lunch, Weekdays 12pm-2:30pm; Dinner, Monday-Saturday 5:30pm-10pm.
Prices: Lunch, entrees $14-$22, Dinner, entrees $20-$34, 3-course menu $28; glass of wine $9-$14.   Size: seats 60.

Sign of the Whale (Gastropub)
6 Harbor Point Road (Waterfront Square), Stamford CT, 203.883.8282
(If your GPS can't find it, use 100 Washington Boulevard.)
www.signofthewhalect.com
Modern industrial design with lots of windows, a huge bar, and big screen TVs tuned to sports, line all of the walls. It is the perfect setting for the 20 something crowd to meet friends and watch a game. The mediocre food and slow service, due to lack of staff, may make you wish you had partied at home.
Hours: Open Sunday-Thursday 11:30am-1am;
Friday & Saturday 11am-2am.
Prices: Burgers & pizzas $13-$16, entrees $18-$29, Beer $6-$7, wine by glass $8-$10
Size: seats 100 on first floor, 5000 sq ft rooftop with 25 tables and a large bar.

RESTAURANTS

SoNo Seaport Seafood (Seafood)
100 Water Street, South Norwalk CT, 203.854.9483
www.sonoseaportseafood.com
A very, very, informal spot on the water to have lobster or fish and chips.
We like being here. The service is friendly and equally informal. Nice
outside deck with picnic tables. Bring your family and have a good time.
Hours: Open Sunday-Thursday 11am-9pm; Friday & Saturday 11am-
10pm.
Prices: sandwiches & entrees $10-$20; glass of wine $6-$7;
children's menu $4-$8.   Size: seats 46 inside and 220 outside.

Sonora (Nuevo Latino)
179 Rectory Street, Port Chester NY, 914.933.0200
www.sonorarestaurant.net
We continue to sing the praises of this popular, out-of-the-way restaurant, although it can be ultra noisy. The unique decor, cheerful service,
and "Latin American food with a flair" make us happy. Start with the
fresh guacamole (one order is more than enough for two) and it is sooo
good. The country of origin is listed by each entree. You are bound to find
one that fits your mood. Be sure to save room for passion fruit flan.
Hours: Lunch, Friday & Saturday 11:30am-3pm;
Dinner, Sunday-Thursday 5pm-10pm, Friday & Saturday 5pm-11pm.
Prices: Lunch entrees $17-$19; Dinner entrees $20-$30;
glass of wine $9.   Size: seats 87 downstairs, 60 upstairs.

South End (New American)
36 Pine Street, New Canaan CT, 203.966.5200
www.southendNewCanaan.com
Good, casual comfort food in an attractive, informal setting. We particularly like the Tagliatelle Bolognese. It's close to the train station and
parking is easy. When the restaurant is filled, it can be noisy and the
service is rather slow.
Hours: Lunch, Monday-Saturday 11:30am-2:30pm; Brunch, Sunday
11:30am-3pm; Dinner Monday & Tuesday 5pm-9pm, Wednesday & Thursday 5pm-9:30pm, Friday & Saturday 5pm-10pm, Sunday 3pm-9pm.
Prices: Brunch $15-$26; Lunch $14-$26; Dinner entrees $23-$36;
children $8-$10; glass of wine $10-$20.   Size: seats 114.

RESTAURANTS

(The) Spread (New American)

70 North Main Street, Norwalk CT, 203.939.1111

www.TheSpreadSono.com

The talented chef changes menus with the season and perhaps on a whim. The decoration is playful, funky and informal-cement floors, a variety of wood table tops and miscellaneous china and tableware. The friendly servers fit into this theme perfectly. When you are in the mood to relax and enjoy inventive dishes, the Spread is a good choice.

Hours: Sunday Brunch, 11am-4pm; Dinner, Sunday-Thursday 5pm-10pm, Friday & Saturday 5pm-11pm

Prices: Brunch $10-$17, Dinner entree $12-$22 (wine bottles 1/2 off Sunday & Monday); glass of wine $8-$15.

Size: Seats 90 in the main area & 20 in the bar area.

Strada 18 (Italian, Pizza)

122 Washington Street, (South) Norwalk CT, 203.853.4546

www.strada18.com

Just around the corner from the aquarium is our go-to-place. They have an extensive wine list and tons of thin-crust pizza possibilities. They are good. Equally good are the desserts. They make all their desserts, including the gelatos and sorbets. The decor and the service are very informal, as are the guests. If you are in a hurry you should tell them; service can be slow.

Hours: Open Sunday-Thursday 11am-10pm, Friday & Saturday 11am-11pm. Prices: Entrees $15-$25, pizzas $10-$20; glass of wine $6-$13.

Size: seats 54.

Sundown Saloon (Casual American)

403 Greenwich Avenue, Greenwich CT, 203.629.8212

www.sundownsaloon.com

In the Anderson Hamburger Contest, Sundown's slider and saloon burger came in as top choices. There are seven different burgers. An interesting combination of adult bar and informal, cute casual western-style restaurant. With a special menu for "little dudes," friendly staff, and crayons for writing on the paper tablecloths, it's a good choice for the whole family. The large bar is a popular after-work meeting place and later a hot spot for the 20-something crowd.

Hours: Kitchen open everyday 11:30am-10 or 11pm. The bar is open to midnight on weekdays & 1:30am weekends. No reservations.

Prices: Entrees, $16-$22 (burgers $10-$12); Glass of wine $7-$9.

Size: seats 60 in the dining area.

RESTAURANTS

Sushi Nanase (Japanese)
522 Mamaroneck (corner of DeKalb Ave), White Plains NY, 914.285.5351
Eating in this minuscule sushi place is a very special treat. Step inside and you are in Japan. This unique restaurant serves only sushi and sashimi, but this is served to perfection. If you have never had Omakase (chef's choice), treat yourself here, but be sure to order it in advance. Never expect to eat here without a reservation. It is important to be on time; the restaurant is tiny and seatings are scheduled carefully.
Hours: Open Thursday-Tuesday 6pm-10pm;
Closed Wednesday and holidays.
Prices: Minimum per person is $35; Omakase, $80, $125, $150 and must be ordered a week in advance.
Size: 5 tables for 2, plus 6 seats at the bar.

Sushi Soba (Japanese)
1345 East Putnam Avenue, Old Greenwich CT, 203.990.0888
www.oldGreenwichKikuSushi.com
A handy spot for residents on the Eastern side of town. This small place has a large menu, serving mostly Japanese with a smattering of Thai. Is it our favorite Japanese place? No. But it's OK. The owners have a much larger restaurant, Kiku Shusi at 1074 Hope Street, Stamford CT.
Hours: Monday -Saturday 11am-10pm, Sunday 12pm-10pm.
Prices: Lunch, $10-$16 (Lunch ends at 3pm, the lunch menu is not available on weekends); Dinner, special rolls $12-$14, entrees $14-$38.
Size: seats 14. Most of their business is take-out; delivery is free.

Tabouli Grill (Middle Eastern)
59 High Ridge Road (Bull's Head Plaza), Stamford CT, 203.504.8888
www.TabouliGrill.com
In the middle of a shopping strip, this small, simple but attractive eatery serves Middle Eastern food with an Israeli twist. The food is prepared by Culinary Institute graduate Judith Roll. A wonderful place to enjoy chicken Shawarma (thinly-sliced marinated meat) or spinach and Feta in Phyllo. The baklava is excellent.
Hours: Open Monday-Thursday 11:30am-9pm, Friday & Saturday 11:30am-10pm, Sunday 12pm-9pm.
Prices: Entrees $9-$21, Children $7, wine the glass $7-9.   Size: seats 30.

RESTAURANTS

Tandoori (Indian)
163 North Main Street, Port Chester NY, 914.937.2727
www.Tandooritasteofindia.com
For many people, this is their "tried and true" Indian restaurant. The decor and menu haven't changed for a long time. The service is casual and friendly. And, we like it. We usually order chicken tikka masala, shrimp malabar and Kandahari Naan. We always order sweet lassi.
Hours: Lunch buffet everyday 12pm-2:30 pm;
Dinner, every day 5 pm-10 pm.
Prices: Lunch buffet $11 (Sunday $13); Dinner entrees $16-$25; glass of wine $7.   Size: seats 50.

Tarry Lodge (Italian)
18 Mill Street, Port Chester NY, 914.939.3111   www.tarrylodge.com
Everyone who grew up in Greenwich knows the Tarry Lodge. It has been at this same location for over 100 years. Once a Speakeasy, it is now a totally restored restaurant. The bold yellow walls and separate dining areas give it a refined old world charm. It is owned by superstars Mario Batali and Joe Bastianich, proprietors of Babbo in Greenwich Village, so it is not a surprise that they have very good food, exceptional service and an extensive wine list. The black fettuccini is brilliant. Be sure to make a reservation.
Prices: Brunch $15-$18; Lunch specials $12-$18, 2-course lunch $20, entrees, $19-$29; pizzas $12-$19; glass of wine $10-$25.
Hours: Open Sunday-Monday 12pm-9pm, Tuesday & Wednesday 12pm-10pm, Thursday-Saturday 12pm-11pm.   Size: seats 180.

Tawa (Indian)
211 Summer Street, Stamford CT, 203.359.8977, 8978
www.TawaOnLine.com
Reviews of this upscale Indian restaurant often tout their breads and we certainly agree. Be sure to order the Nan stuffed with dry fruits and nuts. They also have top-notch Indian cuisine. We love the Baingan Bharta (eggplant) and chicken Chettinad. We suggest you don't take their challenge, like we did, to eat "Five Alarm Curry." Save your taste buds for their other delightful choices.
Prices: Entrees $12-$30; glass of wine $8-$10.
Hours: Lunch, Monday-Saturday 12pm-2:30pm; Dinner, Weekdays 5pm-10:30pm, Saturday 5pm-11pm, Sunday 12pm-9pm.
Size: seats 60 (almost all of the seating is upstairs).

Tengda Asian Bistro (Asian/Japanese)

- 21 Field Point Road, Greenwich CT, 203.625.5338
- 235 Bedford Street, Stamford CT, 203.353.8005

www.tengdaasianbistro.com

When Tengda Greenwich opened in 2004, our review was "The decor is hip factory, with lots of metal, noise, and chic clientele in a festive mood." This description still holds true, but something now strikes us as dated and dark. Sushi is a favorite here and we can't resist the coconut creams. It seems the take-out crowd is as large as the dining-in one. Tengda Tuesdays, coined by a Greenwich dad, is now the "in thing." Tengda Tuesday means Chilean sea bass for the parents plus sushi and chicken sate for the kids-all happy. We like the cheerful, fast-paced service. Tengda now has restaurants in Stamford, Westport, Katonah, Darien and Milford.

Greenwich Hours: Lunch, Weekdays 11am-3pm, Saturday 11:30am-3pm, Sunday 12pm-3pm; Dinner, Sunday-Friday 4:30pm-10pm, Saturday 4:30pm-11pm.

Greenwich Prices: Lunch, lunch boxes $9-$14, sushi rolls $5-$16, special rolls, $13-$20, entrees $12-$30; Dinner, sushi rolls $5-$16, special rolls $15-$22, entrees $20-$32; Glass of wine $8-$16.

Size: Greenwich seats 100, Stamford 40.

Tequila Mockingbird (Mexican)

8 Forest Street, New Canaan CT, 203.966.2222

www.culinarymenus.com/tequilamockingbird.htm

A fun restaurant with colorful decorations surrounding the booths. A place to go when you are in the mood for chips and salsa or a Margarita. This is not a gourmet Mexican restaurant, but it is popular with families and adults of all ages. On weekends you will need a reservation.

Hours: Open Sunday-Thursday 5pm-9:30pm, Friday & Saturday 5pm-10pm; bar may be open to midnight or later.

Prices: Dinner, $13-$23; Children's menu $5-$8; Margaritas $9 -$11.

Size: seats 100.

Terra Ristorante Italiano (Italian)

156 Greenwich Avenue, Greenwich CT, 203.629.5222
www.TerraOfGreenwich.com

Walking along Greenwich Avenue, wonderful smells come from their wood-burning ovens. Don't let this mislead you, the pizzas are good but they also serve up terrific Northern Italian food. A popular, lively, dressy, slightly dark trattoria, with attentive service. If you want to escape the noise, dine on the terrace.

Hours: Open every day 12pm-10pm.

Prices: Lunch Pasta and Pizza $14-$23, entrees $17-34; Dinner, pasta & pizza entrees, $15-$23, entrees $26-$38; Glass of wine $8-$16.

Size: seats 62 inside, small outside terrace.

Thai Basil (Thai)

95 Railroad Avenue, Greenwich CT, 203.618.9888
www.thaibasilofgreenwich.com

Just across from the train station and movie theater is a simply-decorated, "authentic" Thai restaurant that we love. Expect friendly greetings and good service. If you are not familiar with Thai food, they will be happy to guide you. The drunken noodles and green curry we often order are not for the faint of heart. Many milder dishes-curries and wok-stirred dishes- are on the menu. The coconut sticky rice is listed as a side, but we like it as a dessert. The owner of Penang and Asiana also owns this restaurant.

Prices: Lunch, Bangkok bowl $9-$12; Lunch & Dinner, entrees $11-$22.

Hours: Lunch, Everyday 11am-3:30pm; Dinner, Sunday-Thursday 3:30pm-10pm, Friday & Saturday 3:30pm-11pm.

Size: seats 38.

TIP: FOOD + WINE FESTIVAL

Top chefs from the area plus local vineyards show their stuff at Roger Sherman Baldwin Park. This event is organized by Serendipity and is held in early October. This is fun and we hope it keeps on going. For information contact Serendipity Magazine at 203.588.1363 or visit www.GreenwichFoodAndWine.com

RESTAURANTS

Thali (Indian)

87 Main Street, New Canaan CT, 203.972.8332   www.thali.com
This is not just another Indian restaurant. A waterfall rolls across the ceiling of what was formerly a bank. Expect delightful and unusual flavors. Many of the dishes seem to be a fusion of French and southern Indian with a touch of whimsy. The ragda patties, jalapeno nan and the Navrattan Korma are wonderful. Yes, their chicken tikka masala is also very good. David Rosengarten says this is the best Indian restaurant in the U.S. We haven't tried them all, but he could be right.
Hours: Lunch, Monday-Saturday 10:30am-2:30pm; Dinner, Monday-Thursday 4:30pm-10pm, Friday & Saturday 4:30pm-11pm, Sunday 4pm-9pm.
Prices: Lunch $9-$16, price fixed $14; Dinner entrees $18-$34; glass of wine $9-$10.   Size: seats over 100 + private room for 40.

Thomas Henkelmann (French)

420 Field Point Road (@ Homestead Inn), Greenwich CT, 203.869.7500
www.ThomasHenkelmann.com
Nestled in Belle Haven, in a lovely, formal inn with antiques and a garden setting is a restaurant with delicious contemporary French food. Diners feel pampered here in the rustic, refined, elegant dining room. The owner and chef, Thomas Henkelmann, is regarded as one of the premier chefs in the US. The wait staff is attentive, polite and informed. Men should wear a jacket and tie.
Hours: Breakfast only for the inn guests; Lunch, Tuesday-Friday 12pm-1:45pm; Dinner, Tuesday-Saturday 6pm-8:30pm. Usually closed the first two weeks in March. Make reservations in advance.
Prices: Lunch entrees, $23-$30; Dinner entrees, $38-46; glass of wine $14-$20+ (by glass is not on the menu so you have to ask).
Size: seats 120; two private dining rooms, 10-14 & 20-30.

Tigin (Irish Pub)

175 Bedford Street, Stamford CT, 203.353.8444
www.TiginIrishPub.com
An enjoyable Irish pub, with lots of cozy nooks, where you can find shepherd's pie, fish & chips, corned beef & cabbage or simply a burger and a pint of one of their 30 beers.
Hours: Open Sunday-Thursday 11am-midnight,
Friday & Saturday 11am-2:30am.
Prices: One menu $9-$15; glass of wine, $9-$8.   Size: seats 80.

RESTAURANTS

Two Door (American)
176 Hamilton Ave, Greenwich CT, 203.622.9079
Since 1920, this Chickahominy tavern has been a local favorite. If you don't like change, this is your place. When you enter this slightly dark, but very friendly place, it is easy to imagine it may have always been this way. Several Greenwich attorneys meet here often for lunch. Reserve Thursday for chicken parm night or Friday for their fish & chips night.
Hours: Lunch, Weekdays 12pm-2pm; Dinner, Tuesday-Friday 6pm until they run out of food; Sunday open for football.
Prices: $8-$10.   Size: seats 18.

Trattoria632 (Italian)
632 Anderson Hill Road, Purchase NY, 914.481.5811
www.trattoria632.com
The portions are large, the wait staff is nice and there is plenty of parking. However, there are many better Italian restaurants in the Greenwich area. If you find yourself here, order a pizzette with a whole wheat crust. On Saturday nights they often have jazz, which draws a crowd.
Hours: Open everyday 11:30am-10pm.
Prices: pizzettes $12-$17; entrees $14-$32; kids menu $8;
glass of wine $10-$14.   Size: seats 60.

Truck (Southwestern)
391 Old Post Road, Bedford NY, 914.234.8900
www.truckRestaurant.com
When we discovered Nancy Allen Roper, the former chef at Boxcar, had opened her own restaurant, we were keen to try it. Truck is located in a stand-alone house with easy parking. Inside is a large room decorated in a snappy, informal style with blue chairs and barn wood siding. This chef has always believed in farm-fresh ingredients and her menu lists her local farms. The service is informal and friendly. We like the tortilla soup and the enchiladas. On weekends you may need a reservation.
Hours: Lunch, Tuesday-Friday 11:30am-3:30pm; Dinner, Tuesday-Thursday 5:30pm-9:30pm, Friday 5:30pm-10:30pm, Saturday 5pm-10:30pm, Sunday 4:30pm-9pm.
Prices: Lunch combos $12-$17;
Dinner Plates $14-$19; wine on tap $8 glass.   Size: seats 67.

RESTAURANTS

Valbella (Italian)
1309 East Putnam Avenue, Riverside CT, 203.637.1155
http://www.valbellact.com
Excellent Italian food in a dressy decor. Everyone gets good service, just like the celebrities who dine here frequently. There is something wonderful on the menu for everyone. Top off your meal with a napoleon or chocolate souffle by their outstanding pastry chef Raphael Dequeker. The wine cellar has 850 wines to choose from. A town favorite and our vote as the best Italian restaurant in town. Reservations required.
Hours: Lunch, Weekdays 9am-3pm; Dinner, Monday-Thursday 3pm-10pm, Friday 3pm-11pm, Saturday 5pm-11pm. Closed Sunday.
Prices: Lunch entrees, $25-$45; Dinner entrees, $29-$45, glass of wine $12.   Size: seats 120.

Valencia Luncheria (Latin American)
164 Main Street, Norwalk CT, 203.846.8009 www.ValenciaLuncheria.com
The food was so popular in this funky, very casual Venezuelan restaurant, they doubled the space and still the tables are filled. The service, like the restaurant, is cheerful. Despite the "out-of-the-way" location, we can't resist their interesting fare. Be sure to start out with ceviche.
Hours: Breakfast, Weekdays 6am-11:30am, Saturday & Sunday 8am-11:30am; Lunch, Everyday 11:30am-4pm; Dinner, Monday-Thursday 4pm-9pm, Friday & Saturday 4pm-10pm, Sunday 4pm-8pm.
Prices: Lunch $8-$15; Dinner $14-$22; glass of wine $7-$10.
Size: seats 50.

Versailles (French Bistro & Patisserie)
339 Greenwich Avenue, Greenwich CT, 203.661.6634
www.VersaillesGreenwich.com
The new owners (Marc and Evelyne Penvenne of Meli Melo) have made one of our favorite restaurants even better. As always, a front counter full of rich pastries greets you as you enter. Exposed brick, large French posters and wooden tables create a casual, attractive setting. We love their quiche, onion soup and salmon. With their good food and pleasant service, it's a perfect place to meet a friend for lunch or dinner.
Hours: Breakfast, Weekdays 7am-11:30am, Saturday & Sunday 8am-11am; Lunch, Weekdays 11:30am-3:30pm; Brunch, Saturday & Sunday 11am-3:30pm; Midday menu, Everyday 3:30pm-5:30pm; Dinner, Monday-Thursday 5:30pm-9pm, Friday-Sunday 5:30pm-10pm.
Prices: Breakfast $5-$10, Weekend Brunch $13-$14, Lunch, prefix $17.50, $12-$22, Dinner, $18-$26; glass of wine $7-$10.   Size: seats 58.

RESTAURANTS

Villa Italia (Italian)

26 Mill River Street (@ Hampton Inn), Stamford CT, 203.348.7742
www.VillaItaliaStamford.com
This little family restaurant, long a favorite of ours, is now in a hotel and
has gone from seating 56 to 190. The staff is still adjusting to their new
size. The restaurant is bright and spacious with lots of windows. Fortu-
nately the menu is the same. Bob's favorite is still manicotti. George
only orders the chicken parmigiana. Carolyn really likes the lasagne. Sue's
favorite is the Bronzini. What will your favorite be? They accept reservations, but to avoid waiting arrive before 7pm or after 8pm. Despite being
in a hotel, parking is tight.
Hours: Lunch, Weekdays 11:30am-3pm; Dinner, Sunday-Thursday
4:30pm-9:30pm, Friday & Saturday 4:30pm-10:30pm.
Prices: Lunch, entrees $10-$14; Dinner, entrees $16-$24; glass of wine
$8-$10.   Size: seats 130 in the main room and 60 in the lounge.

Washington Prime (New American, Steak)

141 Washington Street, (South) Norwalk CT, 203.857.1314
www.WashingtonPrimeCT.com
Without exception everyone greeted us as if we were celebrity guests.
Our good mood continued to elevate as we tasted the food. We will return to this industrial chic restaurant for the Burrata, lobster bisque and
perfectly-prepared steak. Steak portions are generous enough for two,
unless you are a NY Giants lineman. The lunch menu is more like a
brunch, with eggs Benedict and other classic dishes.
Hours: Lunch, Wednesday-Sunday 11:30am-2:30pm; Dinner, everyday
4pm- 10pm.
Prices: Lunch, $14-$22; Dinner, entrees $21-$27, steaks $41-$78 (sides
extra); glass of wine $7-16.
Size: seats 90 inside plus 30 outside during warm weather.

RESTAURANTS

Westchester Burger Company (American)

- 106 Westchester Avenue, White Plains NY, 914.358.9399
- 275 South Ridge Street, Rye Brook NY, 914.305.6095

www.westchesterburger.com

The menu is designed to make you smile. Who would think of Ruben Spring Rolls (they are great) or crispy pickle chips? Several entrees are on the menu, but we can't resist choosing one of the 20 huge and tasty burgers. If you don't want one of their 30 beers, have one of their 8 milk shakes. Our favorite is the Nutella shake. If you are at the Westchester Mall, WBC is right across the street, otherwise we prefer the spacious Rye Brook location. Servers are young and enthusiastic. Reservations are only for parties of 8 and over, so come early on weekends to avoid a wait.

Rye Hours: Open Sunday-Wednesday 11am-9pm; Thursday 11am-9:30pm; Friday & Saturday 11am-11pm.

Rye Prices: Burgers $13-$16; Entrees $16-$26; 30 beers $4-$6.

Size: White Plains seats 90; Rye Brook seats 100 in the main dining room, plus several smaller room seating 20-30 plus a terrace seating 20.

Winfields @ The Hyatt (American, Brunch)

Hyatt Regency, 1800 East Putnam Avenue, Old Greenwich CT, 203.637.1234 (hotel) / 203.409.4400 (dining reservations)

www.greenwich.hyatt.com

Set in a beautifully-converted publishing building, this is not a typical hotel restaurant, nor do they serve typical hotel fare. The Hyatt demonstrates what good hotel dining can be. Winfields is located in the atrium. The atrium's indoor garden, with water, flowers and very high ceilings, gives one the feeling of dining outdoors, even in the middle of the winter. The Sunday brunch, a large buffet with many choices, should not be missed.

Hours: Breakfast, Weekdays 6:30am-10:30am; Lunch, Monday-Thursday 11am-3pm, Friday & Saturday 11am-5pm, Dinner, Friday & Saturday 5pm-10pm; Sunday Brunch 12pm-1:30pm. (Sunday-Thursday, dinner is in the Gazebo lounge); Reservations are a good idea, especially for Sunday brunch.

Prices: Brunch, adults $55, Children 6-12, $28, Children under five are free; Dinner, entrees $25-$34, Children's menu $6-$11; glass of wine $10-$13.   Size: seats 120.

RESTAURANTS

World of Beer

18 Harbor Point Road (waterfront Square), Stamford CT, 203.290.4317
(If your GPS can't find it, use 100 Washington Street.)
www.worldofbeer.com/locations/stamford
The World of Beer is a chain with 55 locations. The 4,220 sf Stamford location has more than 500 beers including about 50 on tap. Despite some bad press, we find the food and service to be fine. This is not a place for an upscale dinner, but it is a good place to relax, have a drink and snack on the Margherita flatbread. Inside is dimly lit with TVs completely surrounding the bar and with lots of live or piped-in music. For a conversation, you should choose the outside area.
Hours: Open Monday-Thursday 3pm-1:00am; Friday 1pm-2am; Saturday 11am-2am; Sunday 11am-1am.
Prices: flatbreads and sandwiches $12-$16; draft beers (mixed & regular) $7-$12; glass of wine (9 oz) $10-$12.
Size: Seats 150, including a large outside seating area.

Xaviar's (New American)

506 Piermont Avenue, Piermont NY, 845.359.7007
www.xaviars.com
Rockland County's best. Just twenty-five minutes from Greenwich across the Tappan Zee Bridge. This intimate, romantic restaurant serves contemporary cuisine. It is the Hudson Valley's most celebrated restaurant. Piermont has a number of good art galleries, so arrive in time to visit them. Don't even consider going without making reservations well in advance.
Hours: Lunch, Friday & Sunday 12pm-2pm; Dinner, Wednesday-Friday 6pm-9pm, Saturday seatings at 5:30pm-6pm and 8:30pm-9pm, Sunday 5pm-8pm. Closed Monday and Tuesday.
Prices: Lunch, price fixed at $35; Dinner, price-fixed menus $100 or $90, entrees $33-$39; glass of wine $10-$26.
Size: seats 40.

X20 (New American)

71 Water Grant Street, Yonkers NY, 914.965.1111

www.xaviars.com/restaurants/xaviars-x20-on-the-hudson

About 40 minutes from Greenwich, this is a special occasion restaurant-impeccable food and service. As you drive through Yonkers, the city can look pretty scruffy, but the area by the water is quite nice. Just under the railroad bridge is the restaurant with valet parking. Although most tables have water views, ask for a table next to the window.

Hours: Sunday Brunch, 12pm-2 pm; Lunch, Tuesday-Friday 12pm-2 pm; Dinner, Tuesday-Friday 5:30pm-10pm, Saturday 5pm-10pm, Sunday 5pm-9pm.

Prices: Brunch, price fix $38; Lunch, prix-fixe $25; Dinner entrees $28-$35; glass of wine $9-$20.

Size: seats 100 downstairs and about 80 upstairs. You will want to be seated downstairs.

Zanni @ Mark Mariani's Garden Center (Napa-inspired Italian)

45 Bedford Road, Armonk NY, 914.273.6700

www.zannirestaurant.com

This stylish greenhouse garden center with rare trees, shrubs, and decorative pottery has an equally stylish restaurant. It's no surprise that the Marianis would want only the best. Dining in this serene restaurant with excellent service and unique, seasonal food is a treat.

Hours: Breakfast every day 8am-3pm; Lunch everyday 11am-3pm; Dinner Tuesday-Sunday 5pm-10pm (11pm Friday & Saturday, 9pm Sunday)

Prices: Breakfast $7-$12; Lunch $14-$25; Dinner entrees $25-$37.

Size: seats 72 inside, 24 outside in the summer.

ZAZA Gastrobar (Gastrobar)
122 Broad Street, Stamford CT, 203.348.2300
www.zazaGastrobar.com
What is a gastrobar? It is an upscale bar with trendy food. This place with its black tables and red leather seats is vibrant and fun. We like the old movies with sub-titles and the friendly servers in their white shirts and jeans. Relax, order a variety of tapas or the balsamico pizza, and have a good time. Reservations are not accepted.
Hours: Lunch, Everyday 11:30am-4pm; Dinner, Sunday-Thursday 4pm-10pm, Friday & Saturday 4pm-11pm.
Prices: Lunch, tapas, pasta & pizza same as dinner, entrees $14-$16; Dinner, tapas $7-$13, pizza $11-$15, entrees $16- $22; glass of wine $7-$15.
Size: seats 58 in the front and 44 in the rear terrace. We prefer the front.

TIP: DIGITAL FOOD DELIVERY

Seamless Web, now called Seamless, www.seamless.com was launched in 1999 to allow companies to order food on-line. In 2005 it was opened to anyone wanting to order food for delivery. It has agreements with over 7,000 restaurants. It serves about 3,500 companies and 1,000,000 individuals. Enter your address on the website or on their app and Seamless will list the restaurants that will deliver to your address, together with reviews of each. Seamless charges the restaurant 12-18 percent of the order. A competing service is www.GrubHub.com . It was founded in 2004. It has about 250,000 restaurants, but is more concentrated in larger cities like New York. If you order regularly from a restaurant, I am sure they would appreciate a direct call.

SCHOOLS

For early childcare and after school programs, see CHILDREN.
For enrichment opportunities, including language schools, see CHILD EN-
RICHMENT.
For local Colleges see CONTINUING EDUCATION.

SECTIONS
• Pre-Schools
• Private/Parochial Schools
• Public School Information
• Public Elementary Schools
• Public Middle Schools
• Public High Schools
• Magnet Schools
• Tutors and SAT Preparation

PRE-SCHOOLS
Pre-school programs are usually very popular. You should contact the school well in advance to make sure you have reserved a place. Usually programs are half-day until the child is four years old.

Bridges
26 Valley Road, Cos Cob CT, 203.637.0204
Children, ages 2 - 4. Morning and afternoon sessions. Full day program available.

Brunswick Pre-school
www.brunswickschool.org
Pettengill Campus, 116 Maple Avenue, Greenwich CT, 203.625.5800
Boys pre-K (age 4) and Kindergarten, admission to pre-K often ensures admission to the school.

Children's Day School
Glenville Civic Center, 449 Pemberwick Road, Glenville CT, 203.532.1190
8 Riverside Avenue, 203.637.1122
http://www.childrensdayschool.net/
Children, ages 6 weeks to 6 years. All-day, year-round childcare and pre-school. Emphasizes cooperation and integration of projects.

SCHOOLS

Christ Church Nursery School
254 East Putnam Avenue, Greenwich CT, 203.869.5334
http://www.ccnsgreenwich.org/
Children, ages 2 - 5. Blend of enrichment and free play. Kindergarten alternative, 9am - 2:00pm.

Clover Hill Early Childhood Learning
Office: The Clover Hill School, P.O. Box 206, Riverside CT 06878-0206
Christ Episcopal Church, 2 Emerson Street, East Norwalk CT, 203.661.6484
www.cloverhillschool.org
A Waldorf-based school for children, ages 3 to 6.

Convent of the Sacred Heart Early Learning Program
1177 King Street, Greenwich CT, 203.531.6500
www.cshgreenwich.org
Girls, ages 3 - 4; Half-day program for 3-year-olds optional; 4-year-olds, full day. Grounded in the Roman Catholic tradition, although 35% of students are not Catholic.

Family Center
40 Arch Street, Greenwich CT, 203.869.4848
www.familycenters.org
Children, ages 3 - 4. An all-day, year-round childcare and pre-school. 5:30 pm pickup available. Learn-through-discovery approach.

Giant Steps Head Start at Wilbur Peck Court
203.869.2730 Ages: 3 - 4.

Kids' Corner Head Start at Armstrong Court
203.869.2730 Ages: 3 - 4.

First Church Pre-School
108 Sound Beach Avenue, Old Greenwich CT, 203.637.5430
www.firstchurchpreschool.org
Children, ages 3 - 4. Hours: 9am - 11:30am or 12:30pm - 3pm. Extended day program for 4 year olds: 9am - 2pm. Some preference is given to church members. Summer camp program for ages 3 - 4.

SCHOOLS

First Presbyterian Church Pre-School
37 Lafayette Place, Greenwich CT, 203.869.7782
www.fpcg.org
Children, ages 2 - 4. Morning and afternoon classes.
Also 2 x 2 program, 2 days per week. Enrichment programs change every
6 - 8 weeks. Art Scampers summer camp for ages 3 - 6.

Greenwich Academy
200 North Maple Avenue, Greenwich CT, 203.625.8900
www.greenwichacademy.org
Girls, ages 4 - 5. Morning and afternoon sessions. Admission to pre-K
usually ensures admission to the school.

Greenwich Catholic School
471 North Street, Greenwich CT, 203.869.4000
www.greenwichcatholicschool.org
Children, ages 4 - pre-K. Pre-K is a structured program with academics
for 4 year olds. Little Angels is a play group for younger children. Admission to these programs does not ensure admission to the school.

Greenwich Country Day
401 Old Church Road, Greenwich CT, 203.863.5600
www.greenwichcds.org
Starting at age 3. Admission to pre-K often ensures admission to the
school. Summer camp for children ages 4 - 5.

Greenwich Kokusai Gakuen
Worldwide Children's Corner, 521 East Putnam Avenue, Greenwich CT,
203.629.5567
http://www.greenwichkokusai.org
Children, ages 2 - 5 years. Full-day program.

Greenwich Public Pre-Schools
Office: 290 Greenwich Avenue, Greenwich, CT, 203.698.7796
www.greenwichschools.org/page.cfm?p=76
Held at a number of locations around the community on a lottery basis.
Their integrated model includes children with special needs.

Just Wee Two
800.404.2204
www.JustWeeTwo.com
Fun-filled programs for children 8 months to 3½ years and their mommy (daddy, nanny or grandparents). Programs are held at Western Greenwich Civic Center, 449 Pemberwick Road, Glenville CT and other locations around town.

Mead School
1095 Riverbank Road, Stamford CT, 203.595.9500
www.meadschool.org
Co-ed ages 2 - 5. Warm learning environment where families work in partnership with educators. Children work with specialists in Spanish, music, drama and movement.

Mencius Mandarin Preschool
First United Methodist Church, 2nd Floor, 59 East Putnam Avenue, Greenwich CT, 203.540.5770
www.menciusmandarin.com
English-Mandarin Chinese bilingual preschool for children ages 2 to 5 years old. No prior knowledge of Mandarin Chinese is required.

Pre-School at Second Congregational Church
Second Congregational Church, 139 East Putnam Ave, Greenwich CT, 203.869.8388
www.ThePreSchoolGreenwich.com
Established in 1996, it is an independent, non-sectarian preschool for children ages 2 to 5 years. Flexible 3, 4 or 5 day a week programs. Half-day programs with extended-day options. Summer camp program.

Preschool at St. Barnabas Church
(formerly Banksville Nursery School)
954 Lake Avenue, Greenwich CT, 203.661.9715
http://www.preschoolatstbarnabaschurch.org
Children, ages 3 - 4. Creative movement classes. Morning and afternoon sessions available. Closed during the summer.

Putnam Indian Field School
101 Indian Field Road, Greenwich CT, 203.661.4629
www.pifs.net
Co-ed pre-school, children, ages 2 - 5.
Summer camp program for ages 2 - 6.

SCHOOLS

Round Hill Nursery School
466 Round Hill Road, Greenwich CT, 203.869.4910
www.roundhillnurseryschool.com
Children, ages 2 - 4. Fifty years of giving children a love of going to school. Computer training and special teachers for music and art.

St. Paul's Day School
200 Riverside Avenue, Riverside CT, 203.637.3503
http://www.stpaulsriverside.org
Children, ages 2 - 5. Non-sectarian, with enrichment program for older children. Summer camp program for ages 3 - 6.

St. Savior's Nursery School
350 Sound Beach Avenue, Old Greenwich CT, 203.698.1303
Children, ages 2 yrs 5 mos - 5 years old. Non-denominational. Summer camp program for ages 3- 5.

Selma Maisel Nursery School
Temple Sholom, 300 East Putnam Avenue, Greenwich CT, 203.622.8121
http://www.templesholom.com/smns
Children, ages 2 - 5. "Mommy & Me" program for 2 and under. Programs with Judaic content.

Stanwich School Pre-Kindergarten
257 Stanwich Road, Greenwich CT, 203.542.0032
www.stanwichschool.org
Character-based education.

Tiny Tots
97 Riverside Avenue, Riverside CT, 203.637.1398
Children, ages 3 - 5. Residential setting. One of the oldest nursery schools in town. Summer camp program for ages 2 years 9 months - 6 years.

Whitby School
969 Lake Avenue, Greenwich CT, 203.869.8464
www.whitbyschool.org
Children, ages 1 - 5 years. One of the oldest American Montessori schools. Summer camp program for ages 3 - 5.

SCHOOLS

YMCA Child Care Center
2 St. Roch Avenue, Greenwich CT, 203.869.3381
www.gwymca.org/childcare.php
Children, ages 2 years & 9 months - 5 years, 9am - 1pm. Follows public school calendar. Offers enrichment curriculum.

YWCA 123 Grow/Beginnings
259 East Putnam Avenue, 203.869.6501 x 221
www.ywcagreenwich.org
Children, ages 15 months - 3 years; toddlers, 9am - 11:30am; age 2, 9am - 11:30am or 12pm - 3pm.

YWCA Tinker Tots
259 East Putnam Avenue, Greenwich CT, 203.869.6501 x 241
www.ywcagreenwich.org
Children, ages 3 - 5. Half-day program for age 2; ages 3 - 5, full-day, 7:30am - 6pm. Enrichment programs. Summer camp.

PRIVATE/PAROCHIAL SCHOOLS

Greenwich has an abundance of excellent private schools. Annual tuition ranges from $11,000 to $39,000 and can go as high as $63,000, depending upon the school and the grade. Most schools have financial assistance programs. Private schools typically have more applicants than they have spaces. It is prudent to apply early. Private schools often have one or more open houses for parents of prospective attendees. Many offer extended-day programs or early drop off for their pre-schoolers.

Brunswick School
www.brunswickschool.org
203.625.5800
Brunswick is a boys school with three locations on 121 acres.
• Pettengill Campus, 116 Maple Avenue, pre-K (age 4) and Kindergarten
• Edwards Campus, 1252 King Street, Lower and Middle School
• Maher Campus, 100 Maher Avenue, Upper School
Brunswick's sister school is Greenwich Academy, which is located two blocks from Brunswick's Upper School campus. The two schools share classes with each other.

SCHOOLS

Carmel Academy
270 Lake Avenue, Greenwich CT, 203.863.9663
www.CarmelAcademy.com
Private co-ed Jewish/secular education program for K-8th grade. 17-acre campus (former Rosemary Hall School campus). They also provide programs for children with learning disabilities (PALS).

Chabad Lubavitch of Greenwich (Hebrew School)
75 Mason Street, Greenwich CT, 203.629.9059
www.ganofgreenwich.org
www.chabadgreenwich.org
First Taste program for ages 4-8. Hebrew School ages 9-11. Discovery ages 11-13, Hebrew High ages 13-16.

Convent of the Sacred Heart
1177 King Street, Greenwich CT, 203.531.6500
www.cshgreenwich.org
Girls, pre-K (age 4) through 12th grade, located on a 118-acre campus. It is privately operated within the Roman Catholic Diocese of Bridgeport. It strives to be a 21st century school with emphases on digital learning.

Eagle Hill
45 Glenville Road, Greenwich CT, 203.622.9240
www.eaglehillschool.org
Coed, ages 6 - 16. A school for bright children with learning disabilities. Day and 5-day boarding. Student faculty ratio is 4:1.

French-American School
Admissions Office, 914.250.0400
www.fasny.org
The pre-school is in Scarsdale, the elementary in Larchmont and the secondary in Mamaroneck.

German School
50 Partridge Road, White Plains NY, 914.948.6513
www.dsny.org
The German School is an independent bilingual (German/English) international school which teaches classes according to German as well as American standards. The elementary school includes grade K (for five-year-olds) through grade 4 and the secondary school includes grade 5 through 12.

SCHOOLS

Greenwich Academy
200 North Maple Avenue, Greenwich CT, 203.625.8900
www.greenwichacademy.org
Girls, pre-K (age 4) through 12th grade, set on a 39 acre campus. The Academy's sister school is Brunswick, which is located two blocks from The Academy. The two schools share classes with each other.

Greenwich Country Day
401 Old Church Road, Greenwich CT, 203.863.5600
www.greenwichcds.org
Co-ed, pre-K (age 3) through 9th grade, set on an 88-acre campus. The school was founded in 1926 and is one of the largest independent elementary and middle schools in the country.

Greenwich Catholic School
471 North Street, Greenwich CT, 203.869.4000
www.greenwichcatholicschool.org
Co-ed, pre-K (age 4) through 8th grade on a 38-acre campus. The school was founded in 1970 and strives to have a low student to teacher ratio. It admits students of any religious preference.

Greenwich Japanese School
15 Ridgeway (270 Lake Avenue), Greenwich CT, 203.629.9039
www.gwjs.org
Co-ed, grades 1 - 9. Relocated from Queens in 1992, this co-ed day school provides a standard Japanese grade-school curriculum for children, with English taught as a second language. The campus is shared with the Carmel Academy, listed separately.

Mead School
1095 Riverbank Road, Stamford CT, 203.595.9500
www.meadschool.org
An innovative, progressive school founded in 1969. Co-ed, pre-school through 8th grade.

Stanwich School
257 Stanwich Road, Greenwich CT, 203.542.0032
www.stanwichschool.org
A thriving co-educational independent day school, founded in 1998 by the former head of the lower school at Greenwich Academy. It serves students in grades Pre-K through 12th grade on its 41-acre campus.

SCHOOLS

Westchester Fairfield Hebrew Academy
270 Lake Avenue, Greenwich CT, 203.863.9663
www.WFHA.org
Co-ed, grades K - 8. Founded in 1997, Westchester Fairfield Hebrew Academy serves 110 students. It is a Jewish community day school with a curriculum in general and Judaic studies. It includes children from all branches of Judaism.

Whitby School
969 Lake Avenue, Greenwich CT, 203.869.8464
www.whitbyschool.org
Co-ed, grades pre-K - 8. Founded in 1958, it is one of the oldest Montessori schools in the country. During the summer Whitby conducts a drama day camp for ages 8 - 16.

PUBLIC SCHOOL INFORMATION

www.greenwichschools.org
Greenwich public schools rank among the best in the nation and are consistently ranked among the best in Fairfield County. In addition to their other fine programs, Greenwich schools have outstanding ESL (English as a second language) programs for all grades K through 12.

The Greenwich School System
Greenwich has 11 elementary, 3 middle, 1 high school and alternative high schools, Arch School and CLP (Community Learning Program). 40% of the graduates go to the "Most Competitive Colleges." The school budget is more than $125 million. The average cost per student is $17,728. The average class size is 20 and 91 percent of the teachers have masters' degrees. There are over 9,000 students in the public school system. To attend you must be a Greenwich resident.

The elementary schools serve students in grades K - 5, the middle schools serve students in grades 6 - 8, Hamilton Avenue, Julian Curtiss, New Lebanon and Dundee are Magnet schools. The high school has 2,745 students and serves grades 9 - 12. Schools open for students around Labor Day and close in the middle of June.

SCHOOLS

Alternative High Schools
- Arch School
6 Riverside Avenue, Riverside CT, 203.990.0441
An alternative branch of Greenwich High School for students with special needs.

- Community Learning Program (CLP)
6 Riverside Avenue, Riverside CT, 203.990.0441, 0442
An alternative education option for Greenwich High School students. It focus on academics, community service and adventure education.

Board of Education
290 Greenwich Avenue, Havemeyer Building
Weekdays, 8am - 4pm, 203.625.7400
www.greenwichct.org/BoardOfEd/BoardOfEd.asp
Call 203.625.7400 for school district information.
Call 203.625.7447/6 for brochures and pamphlets.
Superintendent, Dr. William S. McKersie

Public School Before and After School Child Care Programs
Ten of the elementary schools offer before and after-school programs for enrolled students. These programs are paid for by the parents. Children can usually be dropped off at 7:30 am and must be picked up by 6 pm. There is often a waiting list, so apply early. Some of the schools also offer enrichment programs where children can take computer or other classes. Call your elementary school to see what programs they sponsor. For other programs, see CHILDREN, Childcare or Pre-schools.

Public School Kindergarten
To register for kindergarten, your child must have reached the age of five on or before January 1 of his or her kindergarten year. Parents must provide a birth certificate and proof of residence. Your child must also have a complete physical examination and a record of immunizations.

Public School Closings
www.greenwichschools.org
If schools are closed for snow, or if opening is delayed, listen to Greenwich Radio WGCH (1490). Announcements begin at 6:30 am. You may also find information on cable channel 12.

SCHOOLS

Public School Bus Information
203.625.7446
Call for information on school bus pickup times and locations. If your child is young and other children are not nearby, you can often get the school bus to stop in front of or near your home. Bus service is provided for students who live beyond these distances:
- Grades K - 5, one mile from the school;
- Grades 6 - 8, one and a half miles from school;
- Grades 9 - 12, two miles from school.

PTA Council (PTAC)
PTA Council is the umbrella organization formed by the 15 PTAs of the Greenwich Public Schools. Their main roles are to coordinate PTA efforts, to advocate with a unified voice, to be the liaison for state and national PTA, and to provide training and support.
www.greenwichschools.org/page.cfm?p=91#

PUBLIC ELEMENTARY SCHOOLS

Cos Cob Elementary School
300 East Putnam Avenue, Cos Cob CT, 203.869.4670
http://www.greenwichschools.org/ccs

Glenville Elementary School
33 Riversville Road, Glenville CT, 203.531.9287
http://www.greenwichschools.org/gs

Hamilton Avenue Elementary School
184 Hamilton Avenue, Greenwich CT, 203.869.1685
http://www.greenwichschools.org/has

International School at Dundee
55 Florence Road, Riverside CT, 203.637.3800
http://www.greenwichschools.org/isd

Julian Curtiss Elementary School
180 East Elm Street, Greenwich CT, 203.869.1896
http://www.greenwichschools.org/jcs

SCHOOLS

New Lebanon Elementary School
25 Mead Avenue, Byram CT, 203.531.9139
http://www.greenwichschools.org/nls

North Mianus Elementary School
309 Palmer Hill Road, Riverside CT, 203.637.9730
http://www.greenwichschools.org/nms

North Street Elementary School
381 North Street, Greenwich CT, 203.869.6756
http://www.greenwichschools.org/nss

Old Greenwich Elementary School
285 Sound Beach Avenue, Old Greenwich CT, 203.637.0150
http://www.greenwichschools.org/ogs

Parkway Elementary School
141 Lower Cross Road, Greenwich CT, 203.869.7466
http://www.greenwichschools.org/ps

Riverside Elementary School
90 Hendrie Avenue, Riverside CT, 203.637.1440
http://www.greenwichschools.org/rs

PUBLIC MIDDLE SCHOOLS

Central Middle School
9 Indian Rock Lane, Greenwich CT, 203.661.8500
http://www.greenwichschools.org/cms

Eastern Middle School
51 Hendrie Avenue, Riverside CT, 203.637.1744
http://www.greenwichschools.org/ems

Western Middle School
Western Junior Highway, Greenwich CT, 203.531.5700
http://www.greenwichschools.org/wms

SCHOOLS

PUBLIC HIGH SCHOOLS

Arch School
6 Riverside Avenue, Greenwich CT, 203.990.0441
The Arch School is an alternative high school for students who need special attention.

Greenwich High School
10 Hillside Road, Greenwich CT, 203.625.8000

MAGNET SCHOOLS

International School at Dundee,
International Baccalaureate School

Renaissance School at Hamilton Avenue,
International Baccalaureate School

Julian Curtiss School,
French or Spanish is offered in grades K-5

New Lebanon School,
International Baccalaureate School

Western Middle School,
International Baccalaureate School

TUTORS & SAT PREPARATION COURSES

Community Answers
www.communityanswers.org/tutors-notebook
Community Answers lists Tutors by subject as well as SAT preparation courses.

Greenwich Public School Tutor List
Greenwich Public Schools has a tutor listing of certified teachers and staff members. This book exists in all the Public School offices and is available upon request.

SENIORS

Seniors in Greenwich typically stay actively involved in the community, often serving on town boards, the RTM, and philanthropic organizations. Many of our volunteer organizations are run by the retired presidents and leaders of major companies. This wealth of talent of our senior leaders is a significant reason Greenwich is America's number one town. Most senior citizens continue living in their own homes by utilizing the many services the town has available.

Senior Activities
Friendly Connections
Greenwich Adult Day Care
Senior Center
Weekend Lunch Bunch
YMCA Exercise Programs
YWCA Exercise Programs

Senior Clubs and Organizations
Greenwich Old Timers Athletic Association
Greenwich Seniors Club
Red Hat Society
Retired Men's Association of Greenwich

Senior Education
Diane McKeever (Computer Training)
Lifetime Learners Institute
Senior Net

Senior Home Services
At Home in Greenwich
Comfort Keepers
Friendly Connections
Greenwich Adult Day Care
Life Alert
Life Line
Meals on Wheels
Medical Equipment Loan Closet
Premier Home Health Care of CT
Supermarketing for Seniors

SENIORS

Senior Housing (Independent & Assisted Living)
Atria
Brighton Gardens
Edgehill
(The) Greens At Greenwich
Greenwich Woods Rehabilitation and Health Care Center
Hill House
Mews
Nathaniel Witherell and Friends of Nathaniel Witherell
Osborn
Parsonage Cottage
Waveny Life Care

Senior Information and Referral
For information on medical resources, see the HEALTH section.
Commission on Aging
Elder Care Service Locator
Greenwich Senior Services Information (Community Answers)
Infoline
Medicare Ratings for Nursing Homes
Senior Health Fair

Senior Resources
AARP Income Tax Assistance
AARP 55 Alive Driving Course
Burke Rehabilitation Center
Friendly Connections
Greenwich Adult Day Care
Greenwich Department of Social Services
Greenwich Hospital (Healthy Living and Aging)
Health Insurance Counseling
USE Utilize Senior Energy

Senior Transportation
Call-A-Ride
TAG

AARP 55 Alive Driving Course
Greenwich Hospital, 5 Perryridge Road, Greenwich CT, 203.863.4277
www.aarp.org
www.benefitscheckup.org
A 4-hour course offered every other month. A good review of current rules of the road and safe driving habits.

AARP Income Tax Assistance
The Commission on Aging, 203.862.6710
Income tax assistance for older adults and low income taxpayers is given by persons qualified and trained in income tax preparation. Available from early February until April 14. Located in Town Hall.

At Home in Greenwich
139 East Putnam Avenue, Greenwich CT, 203.422.2342
www.AtHomeInGreenwich.org
For Greenwich Residents 50 and over who enjoy living in their own home and want to stay in their own home as they grow older. They provide a broad range of services such as problem-solving information, vetted commercial services and social activities. It is a form of assisted living in your own home. The annual fee is $500 per individual ($650 per household).

Atria
Rye Brook NY, 914.939.2900
www.AtriaSeniorliving.com
http://www.atriaseniorliving.com/community.aspx?id=1472
Independent living in an attractive setting, with a dining room that makes your family and friends want to visit. Atria Senior Living Group is a privately-held, for-profit seniors company based in Louisville, Kentucky. It operates 121 facilities in 27 states. Atria is one of the largest assisted living companies in the United States, with the capacity to house and provide services to as many as 14,000 residents. The company serves a moderate-to-upscale assisted living niche, primarily in suburban markets.

Brighton Gardens
59 Roxbury Road, Stamford CT, 203.322.2100
www.sunriseseniorliving.com
Sunrise owns Brighton Gardens. Sunrise is a senior living company based in McLean Virginia, which operates over 440 Sunrise locations worldwide. Sunrise Senior Living is a provider of senior care services, including independent and assisted living, short-term stays, Alzheimer's and hospice care, and rehabilitation and nursing services.

Burke Rehabilitation Center
785 Mamaroneck Avenue, White Plains, 914.948.0050
www.burke.org
Burke is known for its extensive rehabilitation services, it also offers geriatric evaluations, memory evaluations and treatment services.

Call-A-Ride
37 Lafayette Place, Collyer Center, 203.661.6633
Non-profit volunteer organization. Five days a week, residents 60 years or older can call for a ride anywhere in Greenwich for any purpose. Please give them 48 hours' notice.
Hours: weekdays 9am-3pm.

Center for Healthy Aging
Greenwich Hospital, 5 Perryridge Road, 203.863.4373
www.greenhosp.org/center_for_healthy_aging
The Center offers comprehensive aging assessments, geriatric psychiatry services and support groups.

Comfort Keepers
17 Heronvue Road, Greenwich, 203.629.5029, 203.899.0465;
cell: 203.461.1013
www.comfortkeepers.com
A national franchise that offers non-medical services to those who might not otherwise be able to live independently. They provide services such as in-home meal preparation, grocery shopping, transportation, housekeeping and companionship. Dennis and Marian Patouhas decided to buy the franchise for this much-needed business in Greenwich. They maintain a library of information at www.thehealthyagingshow.com.

SENIORS

Commission on Aging

Senior Center, 299 Greenwich Avenue, 203.862.6710, 203.622.3992
www.greenwichct.org/CommissionOnAging/CommissionOnAging.asp
Located in the Senior Center, the Commission on Aging is a town department dedicated to the needs of the elderly. They provide information, referral services and written materials on a variety of issues of interest to seniors. They have compiled the most amazing, helpful guide to services in Greenwich-The Directory of Aging and Disability Services for Greenwich. This 84 page guide has all kinds of programs and services listed. Kudos to our Commission on Aging!
Office Hours: Monday-Friday 8 am-4 pm.

Diane McKeever, CPP (Computer Training)

www.dianemckeever.com
www.linkedin.com/pub/diane-mckeever/5/b9/923
Diane gives private lessons for students of all levels-she is a CPP (Certified Patient Person). Diane's book, 100 Amazing Computer Tips, is available on Amazon.

Edgehill

122 Palmers Hill Road, Stamford CT, 203.323.2323
www.EdgehillCommunity.com
Independent, almost condo style living, in an attractive setting. Skilled nursing and rehabilitation services in the same facility.

Elder Care Service Locator

800.677.1116
www.eldercare.gov
A public service of the U.S. Administration on Aging. The Eldercare Locator helps you find local agencies anywhere in the US, to help older persons and their families access home and community-based services like transportation, meals, home care, and caregiver support services.

Friendly Connections
20 Bridge Street, 203.629.2822
www.familycenters.org
Family Centers, 40 Arch Street, 203.869.4848 provides three Friendly Connections programs:

• Telephone Groups

This program brings seniors (or those who have difficulty getting out) together on the telephone for a variety of recreational, support and discussion groups. All groups are conducted over the phone and are facilitated by a moderator. There are more than 50 groups scheduled each month. They are a great way to meet new friends and stay connected.

• Friendly Callers

Professionally trained volunteers make daily calls to elderly, homebound or isolated individuals. Telephone Reassurance provides an opportunity to have a friendly chat, stay in touch and feel safer at home. They can also provide medication reminders and a "safety check," when requested. Calls are made every day from 9am-9pm.

• Friendly Visitors

This program provides volunteers to visit seniors.

(The) Greens At Greenwich
1155 King Street, Greenwich, 203.531.5500
www.TheGreensAtGreenwich.com
28 apartments and assistance with daily living for residents with memory impairment. The Greens is affiliated with Greenwich Woods which provides priority admission for its specialized Alzheimer's Unit.

Greenwich Adult Day Care (GADC)
125 River Road Extension, Cos Cob, 203.622.0079
www.gadc.org
Day programs designed to give home caregivers a day off and participants a day filled with socialization, activity and fun. GADC has completely renovated a wonderful center at the historic 1927 Railroad Pump House on the Mianus River in Cos Cob. The renovation creates a facility designed specifically for adult day care. With more than 8,000 square feet of space, the facility has capacity for 75 clients a day.

Greenwich Department of Social Services
Town hall, 101 Field Point Road, 203.622.3800
www.greenwichct.org/Government/Departments/Social_Services/
Social Services helps seniors with a broad range of their needs. They offer temporary (emergency) financial assistance, help with applications for benefit and entitlement programs, give assistance with employment and job training, provide homemaker services, and they offer protective service for seniors who may be experiencing neglect, abuse or financial exploitation.

Greenwich Hospital
5 Perryridge Road, Greenwich, 203.863.3000
(Healthy Aging 203.863.4373)
www.greenhosp.org
Provides community outreach by offering support groups, health screenings and community health education. They have very strong programs for Healthy Living and Healthy Aging.

Greenwich Old Timers Athletic Association
www.greenwicholdtimers.org
A large social club for men interested in sports. They provide scholarship help and support youth sports in Greenwich.

Greenwich Seniors Club
A social club for area residents over 55. Meetings are held once a month at Saint Mary's Parish on Greenwich Avenue.

Greenwich Senior Center for Computer Learning
Greenwich Senior Center 299 Greenwich Avenue, 203.862.6700
www.Computerlrngsrctr.com
Their mission is to provide education and computer access to older adults. Classes for seniors, 50 and older and an open lab on Friday mornings.

Greenwich Senior Services Information
Community Answers: 203.622.7979
www.CommunityAnswers.org
A valuable point of contact for all local services for seniors can be found on the Community Answers home page or by calling 203.622.7979. Gathering this information was the joint initiative of the United Way of Greenwich, Commission on Aging and Community Answers.

Greenwich Woods Rehabilitation and Health Care Center

1165 King Street, Greenwich, 203.531.1335
www.GreenwichWoods.com
A privately owned 217-bed rehabilitation and nursing facility. They have a 33-bed secured dementia unit.

Health Insurance Counseling Program

Commission on Aging, 203.862.6710
Volunteer counselors review your supplementary health insurance options and/or Medicare Prescription options.

Hill House

10 Riverside Avenue, 203.637.3177
37 one-bedroom apartments with kitchen and bath for the healthy elderly. Residence is open to any able-bodied person over age 62 who meets income guidelines.

Infoline

In Connecticut dial 211 (outside CT 800.203.1234)
www.infoline.org
Immediate telephone counseling and suicide intervention provided 24/7. A 24-hour confidential information, referral, advocacy and crisis help line supported by The United Way and the State of Connecticut. Caseworkers have information about hundreds of services, including health, transportation, housing, safety, employment, support services, counseling, financial/legal services and activities.

Life Alert

New York City Office, 350 5th Ave. Ste 929, Ny NY, 800.920.3410
www.LifeAlert.com, www.seniorprotection.com
Life Alert is a nationwide company which provides a service that helps the elderly contact emergency services. The company's system uses a base unit connected to the telephone line and a small wireless help button that is worn by the user at all times. Help buttons can be a pendant or built into a watch.

Life Line Connecticut

9 Mott Avenue, Norwalk CT, 203.831.2900, 800.390.3111
Lifeline Systems, 111 Lawrence Street, Framingham MA, 877.221.8756
www.LifeLineSystems.com, www.familyandchildrensagency.org
The Life Line help button can be worn as a neckless or a bracelet or on a Tempo Watch. The button connects wirelessly to a base station connected to the telephone line.

Lifetime Learners Institute

Norwalk Community College, 188 Richards Avenue, Norwalk CT, 203.857.7316, 203.857.3330

www.LifeTimeLearners.org email: info@LifeTimeLearners.org

A fabulous organization, affiliated with the Elderhostel Institute Network. It is an independent continuing education program within NCC. To join you must be over 50 and want to continue learning. Dues are $50 per academic year. Members can choose from over 40 courses for $30 per course. Members also have free use of the well-equipped college fitness center.

Meals on Wheels

89 Maple Avenue, Greenwich CT, 203.869.1312

www.Mealsonwheelsofgreenwich.org

Non-profit organization prepares, packages and delivers meals to homes of anyone in need. There are no income restrictions and no medical referrals are required. One delicious dinner and a tasty lunch for $7. In this past year, this wonderful group- Meals-On-Wheels delivered over 30,000 meals to Greenwich residents. Drivers deliver meals Monday-Friday, 10:30am-noon.

Medical Equipment Loan Closet

The American Red Cross, 99 Indian Field Rd, Greenwich CT, 203.869.8444 When you have a temporary need for a wheel chair or walker, this is a good resource.

Medicare Ratings for Nursing Homes

www.Medicare.gov

On Medicare.gov's home page is a link to addresses and ratings for nursing homes in the USA. There are 23 nursing homes listed within 10-miles of the Greenwich zip code 06830. The top rating is 5 stars. Nathaniel Witherell has a five-star rating.

(The) Mews

½ Bolling Place, Greenwich CT, 203.869.9448

Assisted living for seniors 65 and over. The Mews is a managed-care residential community in the heart of downtown Greenwich, very close to the town's Senior Center. 88 rooms and suites are available at affordable rates.

Nathaniel Witherell
70 Parsonage Road, 203.618.4200, 4232, 4227
www.thenathanielwitherell.org/
Newly renovated, our Town-owned nursing home has a 5-star Medicare Rating. Two programs are offered: long term care and inpatient short-term rehab care. Physical, occupational and speech therapy is available. They have a large Alzheimer program. Admission preference is given to Greenwich residents, but because the facility is almost always 100% occupied, it is wise to call for an application well in advance of expected need.

Friends of Nathaniel Witherell
70 Parsonage Road, 203.618.4227
www.friendsofwitherell.org
A nonprofit group supporting the Town-owned nursing and rehabilitation center.

(The) Osborn
101 Theall Road, Rye NY, 914.967.4100, 914.921.2200
www.theosborn.org
Independent and assisted living and skilled nursing in a landscaped 56-acre setting in Rye. A luxurious, popular choice.

Parsonage Cottage
88 Parsonage Road, 203.869.6226
www.Parsonagecottage.org
A charming residence for 40 seniors (32 private rooms and 4 semi-private rooms). It is funded by low income tax credits, the Town of Greenwich, CDBG (Community Development Block Grant) and private donations. It is on land leased from Nathaniel Witherell, but it is a separate operation.

Premier Home Health Care of CT
Stamford CT Office: 777 Summer Street, Suite 401, 203.323.3000
www.PremierHealthCare.com
Live-in and hourly home health aides, homemakers and companions to assist the elderly to live in their own home.

Red Hat Society

Fullerton, CA, 714.738.0001, 866.386.1850

www.RedHatSociety.com

The Red Hat Society began as a result of a few women deciding to greet middle age with verve, humor and elan. To contact one of the local chapters use the website.

Local Greenwich Chapters:
- All Ahead Reds
- Red Hot Babes of Greenwich
- Scarlet Harlots of Greenwich
- The Chickahominy Chicks

Retired Men's Association of Greenwich

37 Lafayette Place, Greenwich CT

www.greenwichrma.org

This active group of retirees holds weekly meetings-open to the public-with interesting speakers. Celebrating 60 years in our town, this amazing group, each year provides Greenwich non-profit organizations with between 40,000 and 50,000 volunteer hours of service. They also have special interest activities and trips. You may want to join their opera club or walking group. Membership is for retired men in the Greenwich area, 55 and older.

Senior Center

299 Greenwich Avenue, 203.862.6720

www.greenwichct.org/CommissionOnAging/caSeniorCenter.asp

Their motto is "Excite Your Life." Their monthly calendar includes exercise, games, language classes, art, health forums, and much more, plus weekend trips and daily luncheons. The nutritious meal is $3.00. For Greenwich seniors 55 and older, there are a lot of activities going on! Check out their calendar of events, newsletter and menus on their web site.

Hours: weekdays 9am-4pm.

Senior Health Fair

Contact Greenwich Commission on Aging, 203.862.6710, for details.

The Commission on Aging, Department of Health and Greenwich Hospital join together once a year in October to provide free tests and helpful information.

SENIORS

Supermarketing for Seniors
One Holly Hill Lane, 203.622.1881
www.jfsgreenwich.org
A free service of the Jewish Family Services of Greenwich. They provide home-bound Greenwich residents over 60 (any denomination) with grocery shopping. They will come to your home, pick up the list and shop for or with you. They provide this wonderful service for many grateful homebound elderly Greenwich residents annually.

TAG (Transportation Association of Greenwich)
13 Riverside Avenue, Riverside CT, 203.637.4345
www.ridetag.org
Non-profit organization provides transportation for elderly and disabled people of all ages to health, social and educational organizations in Greenwich and neighboring communities. Fees are charged to the referring agency or to the individual.
Hours: TAG operates Monday-Friday 6:30am-7pm, Saturday 8:30am-6pm.

USE Utilize Senior Energy
Greenwich Senior Center, 299 Greenwich Avenue, 203.629.8032
This non-profit "employment agency" is run by volunteers from the basement of the Senior Center. This brilliant organization founded in 1977 by Viola Caldwell allows retired seniors to continue working and provides an excellent resource for the community. It is a good place to find all manner of help: receptionists, business consultants, painters, baby sitters, etc.
Hours: Weekday, 9:30 am to 12:30 pm.

Waveny Life Care
3 Farm Road, New Canaan CT, 203.594.5200
www.Waveny.org
Waveny offers several options, independent living at the very attractive New Canaan Inn, Assisted Living for Alzheimer's at the Village and skilled nursing at Waveny Care Center. They also have adult day care and geriatric evaluations.

Weekend Lunch Bunch

Greenwich Hospital, 203.863.3690

Anyone age 55 or older can enjoy a $6.50, four-course meal in the cafeteria. Call to find out the menu for the weekend. Once you have your Lunch Bunch ID (obtained at Greenwich Hospital), you can use it in the hospital cafeteria and receive a 30% discount on many items.

Hours: Saturday & Sunday noon-2 pm.

YMCA Exercise Programs

50 East Putnam Avenue, 203.869.1630

www.gwymca.org

The Y offers a number of programs tailored to the needs of seniors, including volleyball, stretching, healthy back, resistance training and swimming.

YWCA Exercise Programs

259 East Putnam Avenue, 203.869.6501

www.ywcagreenwich.org

The Y has senior aqua toning, Encore (a post-mastectomy program), swimming and adapted aquatics for handicapped persons.

TIP: EMERGENCY REGISTRY

The Department of Health has a registry of people with disabilities and special needs. The Office of Emergency Management, The Department of Social Services and the Department of Health use this database and encourage seniors to register. In the event of a storm or other emergency the Town will use the registry to evacuate or help seniors and other people with special needs.

SERVICES INDEX

For Wildlife and Animal Rescue see PETS.
For Home Delivery also see FOOD, RESTAURANTS and SENIORS.
For Sports Training see FITNESS.
For Car and Truck Rentals and Auto Services see AUTOMOBILES.
For Travel Agents see TRAVEL.
For Ticket Agencies see CULTURE.
For Baby Sitting and language training see CHILDREN, CHILD ENRICH-MENT.
For Art Shops and Framing see STORES.
For Barbers, Hairdressers Spas and Nail Salons see, GROOMING.
For Senior Services see SENIORS.
For Photographers see PHOTOGRAPHY.
For Eyeglasses see STORES.
For Medical Services see HEALTH.
For Home Food Delivery see FARMS and HOME DELIVERY.

Alarm Systems (Also see Security)
Advanced Electronic Systems
PI Security

Appliance Repair
Action Appliance Services (Large Appliance Repair)
Appliance Service Center of Stamford
Aerus (Electrolux Vacuums)
Bills Refrigeration (Commercial Refrigerators)
David A Sabini Company (Large Appliance Repair)
Panza Appliance Service (Large Appliance Repair)
Sears Home Services
Willett Vacuum

Art
Art Shops and Farmers are reviewed in STORES.
Lending Art Program of the Greenwich Library
John Vitagliane (Fine Art Conservation)
Miranda Arts (Frame Repair)
New York Fine Art Appraisers
Textile Conservation Workshop (Fabric Restoration)
Trimaxion Fine Arts (Fine Art - Storage, Crating, Shipping)

SERVICES INDEX

Audio Visual / Home Theater
Everett Hall (Sale and Rental of AV Equipment)
Performance Imaging (Home Theater)
Cos Cob TV (Home Theater)
See also, Contractors.
See also, Television.
See Computer for repair and software help,
The following AV stores are reviewed in STORES,
• Best Buy, 330 Connecticut Avenue, Norwalk CT, 203.857.4543
• Computer Super Center, 103 Mason Street, Greenwich CT, 203.661.1700
• Cos Cob TV, 5 Strickland Road, Cos Cob CT, 203.869.2277

Banking
Greenwich has been invaded by banks, 30 at last count. Many Greenwich residents still prefer to work with in-town banks. Friendly hellos and loans from bankers who know and work in the community are a much more civilized way to bank than dealing anonymously with a big, inflexible institution. Greenwich is fortunate to have two locally owned hometown banks. Drop in and say hello.
• First Bank of Greenwich
• Greenwich Bank & Trust

Building Resources
See Contractors

Environmental and Water Remediation Services
Connecticut Basement Systems (Water)
Connecticut Basement Systems Radon
Enviro Shield
Home Guard Environmental (Envirotech)
Normal Aquatics
Service Master

Child Safety
For Babysitting See CHILDREN.
Baby Pro (Internet Directory)
Children Car Seat Help (Greenwich Fire Department), 203.622.8087
Child Pool Fencing (Internet Directory)
Safety Mom

SERVICES INDEX

Chimney Cleaning
You should have your chimneys cleaned every three years. This business seems to attract con men, so be sure you know who is coming into your home. We recommend the following cleaning services:
Bill Ingraham, Cos Cob
Chimney Swifts, Steve Oldham, Cos Cob

Closets
Closet & Storage Concepts
Connecticut Closet and Shelf
Custom Closets
Royal Closet

Cleaning
Health First Home Cleaning
Superior Home Services
Safe Wash Exterior Cleaning
See, Chimney Cleaning.
See, Dry Cleaning.
See, Duct Cleaning.
For Carpet Cleaning and repair see Rugs and Carpets.
For Trash removal see Refuse Collection.

Computer (Donations)
See Recycling

Computer (Repair, Training, Services & Networking)
Canaan Technology
Computer Super Center
Diane McKeever
Fast Teks
Geek Squad
MacInspires (See review in Stores.)
PC Repair and Sales
Vernon Computer Rentals

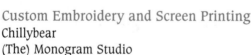

Custom Embroidery and Screen Printing
Chillybear
(The) Monogram Studio

SERVICES INDEX

Deer, Tick & Mosquito Control
Connecticut Tick Control
Deer Tech by SaveATree
Round Hill Tree Service

Delivery Services (Including Home Delivery)
ASAP Messenger Services
Berman Newspaper Delivery
Deliver Ease
Kinko's / FedEx
Mail Boxes Etc
Packages PlusNMore
UPS (The UPS Store)
For US Postal Services see POST OFFICES.
For Food Deliveries see FARMS & HOME DELIVERY.

Dressmakers
See Tailors

Dry Cleaning and Laundry
Brighton Cleaners
Commuter Cleaners
Sung Yun Cleaners
Thomas Dry Cleaning & Chinese Laundry
Triple S Carpet and Drapery Cleaners

Drains
All American Sewer & Drain Services
All County Sewer and Drain
Connecticut Basement Systems
Hupal Septic and Excavating

Duct Cleaning
Duct-Clean
Duct & Vent Cleaning of America
Health First Cleaning
Service Master

Dump Runs
See Refuse Collectors.

SERVICES INDEX

Dumpster
City Carting & Recycling
Mark Longo and Sons
Santaguida Sanitation

Estate Sales
See Tag Sales.

Exterminators
Aavon Pest Control
All About Bats
Honey Bees (Bee Expert Relocates Bees)

Firewood
A cord is a stack of wood 4 feet high x 4 feet wide x 8 feet long
Augustine's Farm
Firewood by Gus
Glenville Hardware
Vermont Good Wood

Framers
Miranda Arts (Repair Frames)
See STORES for framers.

Furniture Repairs
Patti's Portico
Raphael's Furniture Restoration
Wood Den

Garbage
Refuse Collectors
Recycling

Generators
Cannondale Generators

Glass, Mirrors and Acrylic
Associated Glass
Mr. Shower Door (in STORES)
Select Plastics (Custom Acrylic and Plastics)

SERVICES INDEX

Handyman and Painters
AG Williams Painting Company (Wallpapering)
Detail Painting & Home Improvement (Painting, Minor Repairs)
Jason, The Handyman, Inc.
Joseph Williamson (Wallpapering)

Home Delivery Services
See Delivery Services.

Home and Office Services (also see Delivery Services)
Greenwich Blueprint Company
Judith Heft & Associates
Kinko's / FedEx
Landmark Document Services (Printing)
MBA graphics (Printing)

Home Theater (also See Audio/Visual)
Performance Imaging (Home Theater)
Cos Cob TV (Home Theater)

Information
Angie's List (Internet Service)
Better Business Bureau
Bright Home
Community Answers
CT Energy Information
Franklin Report (Internet Service)
Greenwich Chamber of Commerce
Greenwich Library Online
Home Advisor (Internet Service)

Installers
Detail Painting and Home Improvement (Hardwood floors)
Joe Piro (Tile Mason)
John Calorossi (Carpet / Laminate Flooring)

Insurance
Greenwich Independent Insurance (aka Elkanah Mead)
Rand Insurance

SERVICES INDEX

Landscaping (Sprinklers and Tree Services)
County Wide Sprinklers
Round Hill Tree Service

Locksmiths
Greenwich Lock and Door
(Charles) Stuttig

Money
See Banking.

Moving and Storage
Your move depends on the people assigned to your job. We sure hope you get the best. Perhaps it will help if you tell them you will be reporting both good and bad news to us. To check on a moving company and any complaints that have been filed, call the Department of Transportation at 860.594.2870. They are very helpful.
Callahan Brothers
Easy Going Home
Morgan Manhattan Moving & Storage
Navis Pack & Ship
Packages PlusNMore
PODS
(the) Settler
Westy Self Storage

Painting
See Handyman & Painters.

Pests
See Exterminators.

Photographic Services
See the Section PHOTOGRAPHY.
For passport Photos also see, TRAVEL.

Piano (Lessons and Tuning)
Robert Marullo (Lessons, Repair & Tuning)
Piano Service (Tuning and Consulting)
Pyrianos Collection (Steinway Pianos)

SERVICES INDEX

Printing & Copying
Greenwich Blueprint Company
Kinko's / FedEx
Landmark Document Services (Printing)
MBA graphics (Printing)

Property Management
Also see Security
Home Solutions
York Residential Management

Public Speaking
Gilda Bonanno (Public Speaking and Presentation Coach)

Radon (See, Environmental and Water Remediation Services)
Connecticut Basement Systems Radon

Rentals
Coppola Tailors Tux Rentals
Cort Furniture Rental
Longo's Rent-a-Tool
Sophia's Great Dames Costume Rentals
United Rentals
Vernon Computer Rentals
For Car and Truck Rentals see, AUTOMOBILES.
For Boat Rentals see, STORES.

TIP: HAVING A TAG SALE
No Town permit is required. The best days for sales are Saturday and Sunday 9am - 4pm. The best seasons are Fall and Spring. Avoid sales on or near a holiday. Advertise one week before and the weekend of the sale in The Greenwich Time (203.629.2204) in the Friday Tag Sale section. If you are planning a large sale, off-duty Greenwich Police can help you manage crowds. Call the traffic division (203.622.8016). Professional Tag Sale managers typically charge from 20% to 30% commission, depending on the services rendered. For more information on tag sale companies see SERVICES.

SERVICES INDEX

Recycling

The Public Works department of the Town has a good description of your options: http://greenwichct.org/PublicWorks/pwWARecycling.asp
Recycling is now mandated by the state, but it is interesting to note that thanks to the active Greenwich Recycling Advisory Board of community volunteers, Greenwich recycling has been organized for over twenty-five years. Our recycling program saves the Town money and protects the environment.

Got-Junk
Holly Hill Recycling Facility (aka The Dump)
Junk Luggers
Leaf Collection
Recycling Cell Phones
Recycling Christmas Trees
Recycling Single Stream, Garbage and Hazardous Waste
Refuse Collection
Recycling Computers
• Cristina Foundation
• Goodwill
• Salvation Army
• www.YouRenew.Com (Recycling Electronics and Computers)

Repairs and Services (Misc)

American Typewriter Repair
Atelier Constantin Popescu (Musical Instrument Rental & Repair)
Betteridge Jewelers (Fine Jewelry Repair and Appraisal)
Ed's Garage Doors
Greenwich Metal Finishing
Glenville Hardware (Screen Repair)
Homegrown Harvest
Hupal Masonry
Hupal Septic and Excavation
Mr. Mailbox (see review in, STORES.)
Mr. Shower Door (see review in, STORES.)
New York Steel Window
Nimble Thimble
Post Road Iron Works
ProGas (Gas Equipment Servicing)
Seekircher Steel Window Repair

SERVICES INDEX

Architects and General Contractors
There are many good architects, general contractors and trade contractors. We have opted not to try to list them. To find a reliable contractor (service provider), try these Internet Rating services. They are usually reliable. However, most contractors charge more when they are busy and less when they are not, so be sure to get at least two estimates. It would also be a good idea to check the service providers with the Better Business Bureau and call their references.

• Angie's List www.AngiesList.com is a website that rates these and other service providers. You pay to use the site. Service providers do not pay but they can advertise for a fee.

• Franklin Report www.FranklinReport.com The Franklin Report rates service providers by price and quality.

• Home Advisor, www.HomeAdvisor.com This website tries to match you with service providers. It's free to users. Service providers pay.

Replace or Repair China or Crystal (Oops, I broke it!)
China & Glass Restoration
Lakeside Pottery
Tabletop Designs
Thomas Libby
If for some reason these resources can't help you, try these out-of-the-area replacement services:
Pattern Finders, 631.928.5158, www.StacysFinds.com
Replacements Ltd, 800.737.5223, www.replacements.com

Rugs and Carpets (Repair and Cleaning)
Carpet Ron
Golden Horn
John Calorossi (Carpet / Laminate Laying)
Personal Touch
Triple S Carpet and Drapery Cleaners

Security and Safety (Also see, Alarm Systems.)
Dark House Service (Greenwich Police)
Estate Watch
Greenwich Dark House
Executive Services
Interstate Fire and Safety (Fire Extinguishers)
Kennedy Security Services
Metroguard
Off-Duty Policemen

SERVICES INDEX

Shoe & Handbag Repair
Greenwich Shoe Repair
Occhicone
Tony's Alteration and Shoe Repair

Shipping
See Moving or Delivery Services.

Snow Plowing
Most landscapers and refuse collectors also plow.

Student Employment Services
QuadJobs
Student Employment Service (Greenwich High School)

Tag Sales (aka Garage Sales, Estate Sales)
For book sales see LIBRARIES AND BOOKS.
Stacey Cross
Consign It Tag Sales *(Also see review in STORES.)*

Tailors & Dressmakers
Charles Custom Tailor
Coppola Tailors
Greenwich Furs
Nibia Stezano, Master Seamstress
Ted The Tailor

Telephone
Greenwich is on the border between Verizon (formerly Bell Atlantic, formerly Nynex) and AT&T (formerly SNET, formerly SBC) coverage areas. Old Greenwich exchanges (637 & 698) are covered by AT&T. The rest of Greenwich is controlled by Verizon. All customers must dial the area code for all calls, including local calls. The following continue to require only 3 digits: 911 (emergency), 411 (information), 811 (Call before you Dig) and 611 (phone repair.) New numbers given out in the 203 area code have a new area codes like: 475 or 860.
Note: Telephone company shops are described in STORES.

SERVICES INDEX

Television (also see Audio Visual & Home Theater)
Cablevision of Connecticut (aka Optimum)
Computer Super Center
Satellite TV Networks
- Direct TV, 888.777.2454
- Dish Network, 888.825.2557
Ultrawiz Electronics Repair
Verizon FIOS

Termites
See Exterminators.

Tux Rentals
Coppola Tailors

Trash Removal
See Refuse Collectors.

Upholstery
Tiger Lily's
Triple S Carpet and Drapery Cleaners
Upholstery by Paul

Utilities
Aquarion (Water Company), 203.869.5200
Connecticut Natural Gas, 203.869.6900
CT Energy Information, www.CTEnergyInfo.com
Suburban Propane, 203.869.4226
Northeast Utilities / Connecticut Light & Power, 800.286.2000
See also, Telephones, Television and Generators,
A more complete list is in NUMBERS YOU SHOULD KNOW.

Wallpapering
See Handyman & Painters.

Web Sites
See also Computers
Web Weavers

Wine Storage
Horse Ridge Cellars, 860.763.5380

SERVICES

Aavon Pest Control (Exterminator)
49 Ryan Street, Stamford CT, 203.329.2600
www.aavonpestcontrol.com
They will get rid of almost any kind of unwelcome pest: termites, ants and even bats and yellow jackets. Call Dave Curtis and he will be able to help you.

Action Appliance Services (Appliance Repair)
569 Old Stamford Road, New Canaan CT, 203.698.0211
If you have washers, dryers, dishwashers, ranges or refrigerators that aren't working, call Bill Miles. For 16 years Bill has rescued many a home owner.

Advanced Electronic Systems (Alarm Systems)
16 Brookfield Street, Norwalk CT, 203.846.0700
www.AdvancedElectronicSystems.net
They have been helping Greenwich residents with alarm systems for over 30 years. Howard Friedman can be counted on to help you choose the right system.

Aerus (Electrolux Sales and Repair)
78 East Putnam Avenue, Cos Cob CT, 203.869.5362
www.aerushome.com
They are a dealer and an authorized provider of parts and services for all Electrolux vacuums. They have over 500 locations.

AG Williams Painting Company (Painting and Wallpapering)
26 Arcadia Road, Old Greenwich CT, 800.227.1906
www.AGWilliamsPainting.com
Doug Kitchen is active in ASID and is a graduate of the US School of Professional Paper Hanging. When you need something done to the highest standards, contact Doug.

All about Bats and Wildlife (Pest Removal)
30 Esquire Road, Norwalk CT, 203.323.0468 www.aabats.com
They carefully remove wildlife from your home and relocate it, so you won't have unwanted pets. They can also help prevent furry intrusions.

All American Sewer & Drain Services (Drain Repair)
52 Larkin Street, Stamford CT, 203.661.6199
www.allamericansd.com
They can fix just about any drain problem.

All County Sewer and Drain (Drain Repair)
128 Old Barn Road North, Stamford CT, 203.667.1846
Ask for Jimmy or Henry, they are very helpful.

American Typewriter (Repair)
Route 202, New Milford CT, 860.354.6903
David Morrill repairs typewriters and sells refurbished ones. One of the last places around to do this work.

Angie's List (Information)
www.AngiesList.com
A website that rates service providers. You pay to use the site. Service providers do not pay.

Appliance Service Center of Stamford (Repair)
15 Cedar Heights Road (off High Ridge Road), Stamford CT, 203.322.7656
If you can carry it, they can probably repair it. They are authorized to service most vacuum cleaners, they will repair and rewire lamps.

Aquarion (formerly Connecticut-American Water Company)
www.aquarion.com 203.869.5200 (Main Number),
800.732.9678 (Customer Service).
Our local water company.

ASAP Messenger Services (Delivery Service)
914.769.2727   www.asapmessenger.com
An affiliate of Leros Limousines, they deliver small packages in the tri-state area.

Associated Glass (Glass and Mirror Repair)
71 Cottage Street, Port Chester NY, 914.937.7300 www.associatedglass.net
This is a helpful, cost-effective resource for shower doors, glass and mirror replacement. They do a lot of work for contractors. They would prefer you to measure, but will come out if you need them to.

Atelier Constantin Popescu (Musical Instrument Rental & Repair)
403 East Putnam Avenue (Cos Cob Plaza), Cos Cob CT, 203.661.9500
www.atelierconstantinpopescu.com
Sells, repairs and rents string instruments. The Riverside School of Music is located next to his store at 401 East Putnam Avenue (203.661.9501).

SERVICES

AT&T/SNET/SBC: (Telephone)
From AT&T coverage area, dial 811 for repairs; from out-of-state, 800.453.7638 (Customer Service); 203.420.3131 (repairs) or 611 from cell phone. www.snet.com, www.sbc.com, www.att.com
They service Old Greenwich exchanges 637 & 698. Verizon services the rest of Greenwich.

Augustine's Farm (Firewood)
1332 King Street, Greenwich CT, 203.532.9611
Kathy and John Augustin sell firewood at their farm.

Baby Pro (Child Safety)
www.babypro.com, www.babypro.com/childproofing-directory.aspx
Child-proofing products and a directory of child proofers in CT.

Berman Newspaper Delivery (Home Delivery)
203.323.5955
www.bermannews.com
Depending upon where you live, Berman will deliver to your home between 5 and 6 am, where you want it, all of the major papers including: The New York Times, Financial Times and USA Today. The local papers come out too late for this delivery, so unless you want these papers a day late, you should contact them directly: Greenwich Time, 203.625.4400;

Better Business Bureau (Information)
94 South Turnpike Road, Wallingford CT, 203.269.2700
www.bbb.org/connecticut

Betteridge Jewelers (Jewelry Repair and Appraisal)
117 Greenwich Avenue, Greenwich CT, 203.869.0124
www.betteridge.com
A third-generation family-owned business. Totally trustworthy with excellent service and repair, as well as appraisal services.

Bill Ingraham (Chimney Cleaning)
105 River Road, Cos Cob CT, 203.869.5242
Bill is a very reliable chimney/fireplace cleaner.

SERVICES

Bill's Refrigeration
237 West Avenue, Stamford CT, 203.324.0030
www.refrigeratorsfairfieldcounty.com
They repair commercial-size refrigerators. We like this company.

Bright Home (Energy Solutions)
5 Westchester Plaza, Elmsford NY, 914.909.5300
www.BrightHome.com
Energy assessments, air sealing, insulation.

Brighton Cleaners (Dry Cleaners)
25 Glenville Street, Glenville CT, 203.531.5679
146 Sound Beach Avenue, Old Greenwich CT, 203.698.1135
Reliable dry-cleaning on their premises. Drop off between 7:30am and 9am and pick up your cleaning the same day after 4pm.

Cablevision of Connecticut/Optimum (Television, Internet, IP Phone)
28 Cross Street, Norwalk CT, 203.348.9211, 203.531.1166
www.cablevision.com www.optimum.com
Internet, phone service and, of course, cable TV. They are in a price war with Verizon Fios which competes in all three of these areas, www22.verizon.com/Residential/fiostv/ and with Satellite TV networks (www.directTv.com or www.dishnetwork.com)

Callahan Brothers (Movers)
133 Post Road, Cos Cob CT, 203.869.2239
www.callahanbrothers.net
They are the local agent for Joyce Van Lines and have been a fixture in Greenwich for many years. When you need to move across the country or across the world, give them a call.

Canaan Technology (Computer/Internet Support)
194 Main Street, Norwalk CT, 203.847.2444
www.Canaantechnology.com
Canaan Technology specializes in services to individuals and small e-businesses needing help with technology (design, repair, installation, support, home automation, surveillance cameras, and more). If you are installing or servicing a network be sure to call David Felton.

SERVICES

Cannondale Generators (Generators)
390 Danbury Road, Wilton CT, 203.762.2608
www.cannondalegenerators.com
A complete and reliable generator installation and maintenance company. They carry Generac, Kohler, Cummins and Briggs & Stratton generators.

Carpet Ron (Rug Cleaning)
Ron Laroche, 52 Toms Rd, Stamford CT, 203.359.4285, cell 203.326.0758
Recommended by our friends as a good rug cleaner. We recommend him too! He also cleans upholstery.

Charles Custom Tailor
Charles Park, 36 Glenville Street, Glenville CT, 203.531.7640
Recommended by friends as an excellent tailor with good prices.

Children Car Seat Help (Child Safety)
Children under the age of one need to be in a rear-facing car seat. Children between the ages of one and seven need to be in car seats. The Greenwich Fire Department, 203.618.8338, will help you install or inspect your seat. Call for an appointment. Requirements change frequently, be sure to check.

Child Pool Fencing (Child Safety)
800.992.2206
www.protectachild.com
A list of local distributors of "Baby Safe" permanent and removable pool fencing.

Chillybear (Custom Embroidery)
180 Sound Beach Avenue, Old Greenwich CT, 203.622.7115
www.chillybear.com
A great resource for custom printing, embroidery and silk screening on shirts, hats, bags and all kinds of clothing, as well a store for the hip young adolescent. Very nice customer service. See STORES.

Chimney Swifts (Chimney Cleaning)
Steve Oldham, Cos Cob CT, 203.661.7243
They will inspect and clean your chimney. They have been operating in Greenwich since 1979 and are very reliable and honest.

SERVICES

China & Glass Restoration (Repair)
324 Guinevere Ridge, Cheshire CT, 203.271.3659
www.chinaandcrystalrepair.com/crystal-repair.html
Send them a photo of your broken or chipped piece and they will give you an estimate for repair.

City Carting & Recycling (Dumpsters and Trash Removal)
8 Viaduct Road, Stamford CT, 203.324.4090, 0646
www.CityCarting.net
Residential waste removal and dumpsters from 2 yards to 30 yards. City Carting will provide weekly curbside trash pickup. City Carting has little open-top dumpsters for small repair jobs.

Closet & Storage Concepts (Closets)
356 Ely Avenue, Norwalk CT, 203.957.3304
www.ClosetandStorageconcepts.com
Closets, garage, office, pantry, entertainment and utility rooms.

Commuter Cleaners (Dry Cleaners)
121 East Putnam Avenue, Cos Cob CT, 203.861.7121
www.commutercleaners.com
Same day-dry cleaning, shirt laundry, tailoring and alterations, drapery / curtain and leather cleaning - even Shoe Repair. If you want home delivery, they will pick-up on Monday and deliver back to your home on Thursday. Prices are on their website.

Computer Super Center (Computer & HDTV Repair)
103 Mason Street, Greenwich CT, 203.661.1700
www.ComputerSuperCenter.com
A helpful, friendly store that sells and services PC & Apple computers as well as HDTV and Audio equipment, such as Apple - Sony - BOSE - Shure - HP - Lenovo (IBM) - Fujitsu and OKI.

Community Answers (Information)
101 West Putnam Avenue in the Greenwich Library, 203.622.7979
www.communityAnswers.org
A good source of information.They maintain an extensive database on Greenwich activities and resources as well as specialized files on local groups - computer training, tutors and other cottage industries such as dog sitting. If you can't find an answer on their website. Call and ask them just about any question about Greenwich.

SERVICES

Connecticut Natural Gas (Utility)
16 Old Track Road, Greenwich CT (drive behind Equinox, enter at the fenced gate, it's really there).
203.869.6900 (customer service)   203.869.6913 (repair & emergency)
www.cngcorp.com

Connecticut Basement Systems (Wet Basement Mitigation)
60 Silvermine Road, Seymour CT, 800.541.0487
www.connecticutbasementsystems.com
They specialize in curing wet basements and have been fixing Greenwich basements for many years.

Connecticut Basement Systems Radon (Radon Mitigation)
720 Woodend Road, Stratford CT, 203.381.9633
www.connecticutradon.com
A separate company from the one above, they specialize in mitigating Radon. The EPA recommends that Radon at or above 4.0 pCi/L should be mitigated.

Connecticut Closet and Shelf
26 Fitch Street (showroom), Norwalk CT, 203.838.9089
www.CTcloset.com
They design, manufacture and install closets. Ask for Melissa.

Connecticut Tick Control
Richard Whitman, 1 Testa Place, Norwalk CT, 203.855.7849
A privately-owned, 15 year old company exclusively devoted to eliminating ticks in your yard. They operate franchises in Connecticut, New Jersey, New York and Rhode Island. They do low dose sprays and use a tick management system developed by the Center for Disease Control and Prevention.

Consign It Tag Sales
115 Mason Street, Greenwich CT, 203.869.9836   www.Consignitinc.com
Antiques and fine furnishings are their specialty, but they will help you sell everything from the basement to the attic. See their review in STORES.

SERVICES

County Wide Sprinkler (Lawn Sprinklers)
Mamaroneck NY, 914.698.5112
You can depend on Rudy Amatuzzo to set up a good sprinkler system and keep it running. Very nice to deal with. During the winter months they are closed and Rudy is in Florida.

Coppola Tailors (Tailor and Tux Sales / Rental)
347 Greenwich Avenue, 203.869.2883
Just the right place for suit alterations. Greenwich residents have been renting and buying their tuxes here for years. See STORES.

Cort Furniture Rental
417 Shippan Avenue, Stamford CT, 203.353.0400   www.Cort.com
A Berkshire Hathaway company. They claim to have the world's largest inventory of rental furniture.

Cos Cob TV (Home Theater)
5 Strickland Road, Cos Cob CT, 203.869.2277   www.coscobtv.com
This local store, run by second-generation owner Sean Mecsery, will design and install a dedicated home theater or transform your media room. See their complete review in STORES.

Cristina Foundation (Recycle Computers)
203.863.9100   www.cristina.org
Donate your used computers, printers, peripherals and software. National Cristina Foundation (NCF) is a not-for-profit organization that provides computer technology to people with disabilities and economically disadvantaged persons. They only accept more recent computers under 5 years old. Systems must have a hard drive, monitor, keyboard, & mouse.

CT Energy Information
www.CTEnergyInfo.com, 877.947.3873
If you have ever wanted to know your options for alternate, clean energy, this is the first place to go. The site was developed by the Connecticut Department of Public Utility Control to help consumers navigate the ever increasing number of energy-related resources.

Custom Closets (aka Transform)
20 Jones Street (showroom), New Rochelle NY, 203.349.2280
www.Transformhome.com
Garages, closets, home offices, laundry rooms and more.

SERVICES

Dark House Service (Home Security)
Greenwich Police, 203.622.8000 (main number)
If residents notify the police that they will be away for an extended period of time, Greenwich police will patrol the area with an extra-cautious eye. You can also hire an off-duty police officer to personally check your home when you are away.

David A Sabini Company (Large Appliance Repair)
Darien CT, 203.324.6109
David specializes in repairing dishwashers, dryers, washers and refrigerators.

Deer Tech Deer Deterrent by SavATree
34 Smith Street, Norwalk CT, 203.853.9526
www.deertechusa.com   www.NatureTechnologies.com
The company was founded in 2003. They operate throughout the tristate area and have a number of happy customers, but very few happy deer.

Deliver Ease of Greenwich (Delivery)
203.532.0370   www.deliverease.com
For $10 for every 15 minutes of travel time, this reliable service will pamper your every need. They promptly deliver to or pick up from your door just about anything you can imagine: aspirin from your drugstore, poster board for a project, food from your favorite restaurant, forgotten dry cleaning, a late video, or just a cup of Dunkin' Donuts' coffee. Why not send a gift to cheer up someone at the hospital? Open daily from 8am- 9pm.

Detail Painting & Home Improvement (Painting, Handyman)
Norwalk CT, Marcos Souza, 203.846.1157, Cell 203.515.8256
If you need an expert interior or exterior paint job, if you need your gutters cleaned, hardwood floors installed or minor carpentry, you will not find a nicer person to work with and you will be pleased with the results.

Diane McKeever, CPP (Software Training & Social Media Marketing)
www.linkedin.com/pub/diane-mckeever/5/b9/923
www.dianemckeever.com,
If you want to learn a Microsoft program, you should enroll in one of Diane's classes. But if you don't have the time to attend a class, she gives private lessons for students of all levels - she is a CPP (Certified Patient Person) as well as a good teacher. Send Diane an email to set up an appointment diane@dianemckeever.com

Duct & Vent Cleaning of America (Duct Cleaning)
Stamford CT, 203.327.5655   www.ductandvent.com
A large company with 21 offices. All calls go to the national office for scheduling.

Duct-Clean (Duct Cleaning)
20 Stagg Street, Stratford CT, 203.380.0191   www.ctductcleaning.com
A small local company with a good reputation.

Easy Going Home (Movers)
212.535-3511   www.easygoinghome.com
Recently a client hired this relocation consultant and moving coordinator to help her move from her Greenwich home to an apartment in a senior residence. As our client said, they were not inexpensive but they were enormously helpful. They took care of everything, even the selection of the movers, the careful labeling of her items and when she arrived at her new home the pictures were hung and the books were in the same order as before.

Ed's Garage Doors (Garage Door Repair)
136 Water Street, Norwalk CT, 203.847.1284   www.edsgaragedoors.com
Whether you are looking for a new overhead door, a new garage door opener or just a repair, Ed's is very dependable and an excellent resource. For hours see entry in STORES.

Enviro Shield (Environmental Remediation)
Stratford CT, 203.380.5644   www.enviroshield.com
A trustworthy group to call if you have any concerns about mold abatement, testing, removal or installation of oil tanks or remediation of areas contaminated by petroleum or other chemicals.

SERVICES

Estate Watch (Home Security)
Randy Stone, 203.609.4560   www.EstateWatch.net
Randy Stone, who we highly recommend, provides protection services, including key holder response, electronic security, cameras and video monitoring.

Everett Hall (Audio/Visual Equipment)
76 Progress Drive, Stamford CT, 203.325.4328   www.EverettHall.com
They rent & sell AV equipment and stage shows.

Executive Services (Home Security)
7 Adrienne Court, Smithtown NY, (Cell) 203.496.0216, (O) 631.863.1117
www.VanCoExec.com
Bodyguards, chauffeurs, property management, protection for parties and other special events. Run by ex-law enforcement professionals.

Fast Teks (Computer Help)
286 North Ridge Street, Rye Brook NY, 203.674.9181 www.FastTeks.com
On-site computer troubleshooting, virus removal and software training. Fast Teks is a computer franchise serving over 200 cities. Gus Carmona is the area director, his cell is 914.393.8783.

Firewood by Gus aka CT Demolition (Firewood)
2 Apple Tree Lane, Riverside CT, 203.637.5804
www.firewoodbygus.com
$220 per cord, they charge $40 extra for stacking.

(The) First Bank of Greenwich (Banking)
www.TheFirstBankOfGreenwich.com
444 East Putnam Avenue, Cos Cob CT, 203.629.8400
This local bank was founded by Greenwich residents, who care about our community.
Hours: Monday, Tuesday, Wednesday & Friday 8:30am-4pm,Thursday 8:30am-6pm, Saturday 9am-12pm.

Franklin Report (Information)
www.FranklinReport.com
The Franklin Report rates service providers (aka contractors) by price and quality. We have found their ratings to be reliable. However, most contractors charge more when they are busy and less when they are not, so be sure to get at least two estimates.

SERVICES

Gilda Bonanno (Public Speaking Coach)
25 Old Kings Highway North, Darien CT, 203.979.5117
www.gildabonanno.com
We are lucky to have a top-notch public speaking and presentation coach in our area. Check out her helpful newsletter.

Geek Squad (Computer Help)
www.geeksquad.com
A Best Buy Computer Service that will work on items whether or not they were purchased from Best Buy. For an on-site appointment call 800.433.5778 or call Best Buy in Norwalk at 203.857.4543. Besides computers, they handle Audio/Visual equipment, mobile phones, GPS and just about anything electronic.

Glenville Hardware (Firewood, Propane, Screen Repair)
1 Riversville Road, Glenville Center, Greenwich CT, 203.531.5599
www.glenvillehardware.com
A good old-fashioned hardware store with most everything you would need. They repair screens and sell propane for your barbecue. Firewood is $275 a cord delivered, but unstacked. They don't stack.
Hours: Weekdays 8am-7pm, Saturday 8am-6pm, Sunday 9am-3pm.

Golden Horn (Carpet Repair)
464 North Main Street, Port Chester NY, 914.670.6666
www.RugRestoration.com
They specialize in restoration, cleaning and sale of fine oriental and European carpets. They can repair almost any woven art including tapestries. They are open Monday-Saturday 8:30am-6pm.

Got Junk (Trash Removal)
Chris Kirk, 456 Seymour Street, Stratford CT, 800.468.5865, 203.992.7526
www.1800gotjunk.com/fairfieldcounty
1-800-Got-Junk is a Canadian company with more than 220 franchised locations throughout the United States and Canada. They will remove just about anything from old furniture to used appliances to yard waste to concrete, bricks and electronics.

Greenwich Blueprint Company (Blueprints)
255 Greenwich Avenue, 2nd floor, Greenwich, CT, 203.869.0305
Friendly, quick service. This upstairs blueprint company is known to architects and builders. It is the perfect source for homeowners to get copies of their plans.

SERVICES

(The) Greenwich Bank & Trust Company (Banking)
A Division of Connecticut Community Bank
- 115 East Putnam Avenue, 203.618.8900 (main branch)
- 22 Railroad Avenue, 203.983.3370
- 1103 East Putnam, Riverside, 203.698.4030
- 273 Glenville Road, Glenville 203.532.4784

www.ccbankonline.com
A local bank with operations in Stamford, Darien, Norwalk and Westport. It's great to walk into a bank where everyone knows you and says hello. Hours: Monday-Thursday, 8:30am-4p;Friday,8:30am-5pm; Saturday 9am-12pm. The Glenville branch is not open on Saturday.

Greenwich Chamber of Commerce (Information)
45 East Putnam Avenue, 203.869.3500
www.GreenwichChamber.com

Greenwich Dark House (Vacant House Management)
Tim Hilderbrand (Greenwich Police Sergeant), 203.561.1661
www.GreenwichDarkHouse.com
Ten to twelve off duty police officers will watch over your home while you are away, make visits to pick up mail, turn on lights, move cars in the driveway and make your home appear occupied. If requested, they will even stay in your home. All officers live in Greenwich and if your alarm is activated they will respond immediately and using your key check your home. They also provide transportation to airports and the city.

Greenwich Furs (Fur Storage, Alteration, Repair, Cleaning)
1076 East Putnam Avenue, Riverside CT, 203.869.1421
www.greenwichfursct.com
Since 1948 residents have been storing their furs here. They will repair or alter or restyle your fur, and clean it. If you want a new garment, they will design one for you.

Greenwich Harbor Cruises
See ENTERTAINING.

Greenwich Independent Insurance aka Elkanah Mead (Insurance)
87 Greenwich Avenue, 203.869.0302   www.greenwichinsurance.com
They have been serving Greenwich since 1891. Call them, reach them on Facebook or do your insurance online.

SERVICES

Greenwich Library ONLINE
(Databases, Digital Books and Web Catalog)
101 West Putnam Avenue, Greenwich CT, 203.622.7900
www.GreenwichLibrary.org
To search the library catalog on-line, https://pac.greenwichlibrary.org
The Library has a huge number of databases you can search for free with
a library card. Most of the databases can be accessed on-line.
www.greenwichlibrary.org/Research%20and%20Resources/Databases
The Connecticut digital library has over 2,300 audiobooks and ebooks
you can download for free, using your Greenwich Library card. To check
the Connecticut Digital Library go to www.iConn.org

Greenwich Lock and Door (Locksmith)
280 Railroad Avenue, Greenwich CT, 203.622.1095
A reliable local source for architectural hardware, doors, security products and lock-smithing. Good customer service.
Hours: See their hours in STORES.

Greenwich Metal Finishing (Metal Polishing)
300 West Main Street, Stamford CT, 203.977.0494
www.GreenwichMetalFinishing.com
If you have an ailing silver piece, andirons that need to look like new,
outdoor furniture that needs protection or a chandelier in need of repair,
you may want to visit these metal artisans. They polish, re-plate, refinish and even fabricate metal items. They will completely refinish and
rewire your chandelier.

Greenwich Shoe Repair (Shoe Repair)
15 East Elm Street #4, Greenwich CT, 203.869.2288
Greenwich's oldest shoe repair shop is hidden in an alley off of East Elm.
George Togridis has been making Greenwich residents happy for over 20
years. Hours: Monday-Saturday 8am-5pm.

Health First Cleaning (House Cleaning)
20 Palace Place, Port Chester NY, 914.690.9294
www.HealthFirstCleaning.com
George Botticelli uses hepa-filters and non-toxic cleaning products to clean
homes, including ducts, carpets, upholstery and even post-construction
clean up.

SERVICES

Holly Hill Recycling Facility aka The Dump (Recycling)
Holly Hill Lane, Greenwich CT, 203.622.0550
Greenwich has one of the world's best dumps. You have to see it to believe it. On any given day, you may see BMWs and Mercedes dropping off items. The "in" decal for your car is a dump permit. Permit applications are available at the Holly Hill entry gate or on line at www.GreenwichCT.org. Go to Public Works or search for "Vehicle Dumping Permit." To get one of these valuable permits, you must show proof of residency, as well as valid vehicle registration and insurance.
Hours: The Dump is open weekdays 7am-3pm & Saturday 7am-12pm.

Home Advisor (Information)
www.HomeAdvisor.com
This website tries to match you with service providers. It's free to users. Service providers pay.

Homegrown Harvest (Garden Design & Maintenance)
24 East Avenue, New Canaan CT, 203.966.1623
www.homegrownharvest.com
Mark and Christine will come to your home to meet with you to discuss your gardening goals and to evaluate potential sites for your new garden.They will plant and maintain your garden as well as clean up the beds. They offer "garden sitting" while you are on vacation.

Home Guard Environmental aka Envirotech (Environmental Remediation)
48 Union Street, Stamford CT, 203.323.8000   www.environmental.net
Asbestos, lead and mold abatement, decontamination, hazardous waste, oil tank services - removal, soil remediation, and more. For years we have enjoyed working with Gary Stone. They do quality work.

Home Solutions of Greenwich (Property Management)
19 Ivanhoe Lane, Greenwich CT, 203.340.2289
www.HomeSolutionsOfGreenwich.com
Home maintenance, property management and home watching by John Duffy, a Greenwich resident and builder of many Greenwich homes.

Honey Bees (Bee Removal and Bee Keeping)
Ray DuBois, Greenwich CT, 203.249.2733   www.BeeLove.org
If honey bees have inappropriately chosen your home as their home, Ray will remove and relocate the swarm. The fee for extractions is based on the degree of difficulty. If you are interested in keeping bees you should also contact Ray. He is extraordinarily nice to work with and a great local resource. See a you tube video of Ray at work on a swarm of bees www.youtube.com/watch?v=wYldyShwxaM

Horse Ridge Cellars (Wine Storage)
11 South Road, Somers CT, 860.763.5380   www.HorseRidgeCellars.com
Where serious collectors store their wine. They are about a 2 hour drive from Greenwich, but they will pick-up and deliver.

Hupal Masonry (Stone Mason)
242 Weaver Street, Greenwich CT, 203.531.5245
Tim Hupal is not only an excellent stone mason, he can be very helpful with the project's design.

Hupal Septic and Excavation (Septic Systems and Excavation)
244 Weaver Street, Greenwich CT, 203.532.1401
Problems with your present septic system, need a new one, need a foundation dug? You will be in good hands with our friend Mike Hupal.

Interstate Fire and Safety (Fire Extinguisher Servicing)
404 Willett Avenue, Port Chester NY, 203.531.1333, 914.937.6100
www.interstatefireandsfty.net
If you have ever wondered where to get your fire extinguisher refilled, you can't beat this place. Serving Greenwich residential and commercial needs since 1951, they sell new extinguishers and even kitchen stove hoods. Hours: Weekdays 8 am-4 pm.

Jason, The Handyman, Inc.
17 Cognewaugh Road, Cos Cob CT, 203.625.0411
www.jasonthehandyman.com
If you need a mirror hung, gutters installed or cleaned, walls painted, tile re-grouted, or an electrical outlet installed, call Jason Wahlberg. Reasonably priced and offers senior discounts. If he can't do it, he'll recommend someone who can.

SERVICES

John Calarossi (Carpet, Vinyl and Wood Laminate Flooring)
Call John on his cell phone 203.249.1721.
John installs flooring. We have had the pleasure of working with him on several occasions. We like him and his work.

Joe Piro (Tile Mason)
104 Hamilton Avenue, Greenwich CT, 203.661.2266
Joe is reputed to be the best tile mason in the area. We believe it.

John Vitagliano (Fine Art Conservation)
31 Mamaroneck Avenue, Studio 810, White Plains NY, 646.239.2806
www.JohnVitagliano.com
John specializes in the cleaning and restoration of fine paintings.

Joseph Williamson (Wallpapering)
2 Kent place, Cos Cob CT, 203.629.7911
A graduate of the US School of Professional Paperhanging in Rutland VT, he does decorative painting and faux finishes as well.

Judith Heft & Associates (Financial Concierge)
15 East Putnam Avenue #122, Greenwich CT, 203.978.1858
http://judithheft.com
A professional financial organizer, bookkeeper, bill payer and personal organizer.

Junk Luggers (Trash Removal)
168 Irving Avenue, Suite 500F, Port Chester NY, 888.584.5865
www.JunkLuggers.com
Call Kevin Phillips. He will take away just about anything from yard waste, to used appliances, to electronics and renovation debris. The prices are in writing and include labor and dump fees. They sort for recyclables and give you a tax-deductible receipt.

Kennedy Security Services (Security)
58 East Elm Street, Greenwich CT, 203.661.6814
www.KennedySecurity.com
For extra security while you are away from home, Kennedy Security has been serving Greenwich residents for over 40 years.

SERVICES

Kinko's / FedEx (Office Services)
- 48 West Putnam Avenue, Greenwich CT, 203.863.0099
- 980 High Ridge Road, Stamford CT, 203.968.8100

www.kinkos.com, www.FedEx.com
FedEx / Kinko's offers a wide variety of production and finishing services, as well as FedEx shipping. Their target clients are small business and home offices. You can place an online print order using the FedEx web site.
Greenwich Hours: weekdays 7:30am - 9pm, Saturday 10am - 6pm.
Stamford Hours: Open 24 hours

Lakeside Pottery (Ceramic and China Repair)
543 Newfield Avenue, Stamford CT, 203.323.2222
www.lakesidepottery.com
They provide professional ceramic, porcelain, china, stone (or plaster) sculpture and pottery repair and restoration services for individuals, antique dealers & museums.

Landmark Print (Office Services)
375 Fairfield Avenue, Building 3, Stamford CT, 203.325.4300
www.landmarkprint.com
A good place for large volume printing - mailing & fulfilment, web to print and wide format for posters, signs and banners.
Hours: Weekdays 8am-5:30pm.

Leaf Collection
Town leaf collection is limited to all properties on PUBLIC STREETS ONLY in building zones R20 (half-acre) and below. Many residents with one or more acres compost on their own property. For a schedule of leaf collection, call 203.622.7718, 203.618.7698 or watch for the schedule printed by the Greenwich Time in the fall.

Lending Art Program of the Greenwich Library
Greenwich Library, 101 West Putnam Avenue, Greenwich CT, 203.622.7900
www.greenwichlibrary.org
The Lending Art Program of the Library has an extensive collection of artworks acquired by the Friends of the Library. It is available to all patrons and can be checked out on a short-term or long-term basis.

Longo's Rent-a-Tool (Tool Rentals)
134 Jefferson Street, Stamford CT, 203.629.9151
A family-owned company renting just about any power tool. A do-it-yourselfer's paradise.

Mail Boxes Etc / UPS Store (Packing and Shipping)
www.TheUPSStore.com
• (Store # 0822) 15 East Putnam Avenue, Greenwich CT, 203.622.1114
Weekdays, 8am-6pm, Saturday & Sunday, 10am-3pm.
• (Store # 0217) 1117 East Putnam Avenue, Riverside CT, 203.698.1333
Weekdays 8am-6pm, Saturday 8am-4pm.
Mail box rentals, packing, crating and shipping, even Notary services.

Mark Longo and Sons (Dumpsters)
203.629.9209, 203.496.2891
They have dumpsters of all sizes to keep as long as you need.

MBA Graphics (Printing)
76 Progress Drive, Suite 230G, Stamford CT, 203.658.3967
www.MBAgraphics.com
Digital & offset printing, mailing services, graphic design, signage, trade show displays and binding services. Free pickup and delivery.

Metroguard Inc (Home Security)
Fairfield CT, 203.226.3638, 800.495.0400
www.MetroGuardInc.com
A CT firm which will watch your house while you are away, hold your key, and perform other private security services.

Miranda Arts (Museum Quality Framing, Restoration and Gilding)
6 North Pearl Street, Suite 404E, Port Chester NY, 914.318.7178
www.MirandaFineArts.com
Art gallery featuring local artists. Patricia Miranda teaches painting and gilding techniques to adults and youth. She does museum-quality framing and frame repair.

Monogram Studio (Custom Embroidery)
222 Pemberwick Road, Greenwich CT, 203.428.5700
http://themonogramstudio.com
The Monogram Studio offers full-service monogramming and embroidery to individuals, schools and businesses. Hours by appointment.

SERVICES

Morgan Manhattan Moving & Storage (Movers)
16 Bruce Park Avenue, Greenwich CT, 203.869.8700
www.morganmanhattan.com
A regional moving company with corporate headquarters in Greenwich.

NAVIS Pack & Ship (Movers)
Patrick Ryan, 540 Grant Street, Bridgeport CT, 203.335.7447,
  800.344.3528   www.gonavis.com
NAVIS specializes in small shipments, ones that are too big for a mail
and parcel center (UPS, Fed Ex), but too small for a traditional mover.
They pick up items from your home or business, like a chandelier, a
computer, a painting or a dining table, and deliver them to your destination across town or around the world.

New York Fine Art Appraisers
410 Park Avenue, Suite 1530, New York NY, 212.772.0319
www.NYFAA.com
An independent appraisal firm which does not buy or sell and is not
affiliated with any auction house or gallery. Founded in 1980 by Jason
Rahm, they appraise private collections throughout the country.

New York Steel Window (Steel Window Repair)
12G White Street, Buchanan NY, 914.736.5208
Denis Rooney makes storm windows for leaded-glass steel windows. See
Seekircher Steel Windows for repairs to steel casement windows.

Nibia Stezano (Master Seamstress)
203.629.5474
Nibia works out of her attic studio in Cos Cob. She is an extremely skilled
dressmaker capable of designs from scratch. She is also willing to do
small alterations for both men and women.

Nimble Thimble (Sewing Machine Repair)
21 Putnam Avenue, Port Chester NY, 914.934.2934
www.thenimblethimble.us
The resource for home sewing needs. Lots of fabrics, notions, quilting
supplies and sewing machines. This is a good place to have your sewing
machine repaired.
Hours: Weekdays 10am-5pm, Saturday 10am-1pm.

SERVICES

Normal Aquatics (Pond Maintenance)
15 East Putnam Avenue #347, Greenwich CT, 203.292.5922
http://normalaquatics.com
Aquarium and pond design, installation and repair.

Northeast Utilities / Eversource (Utility)
Customer Care Walk-in Center, 107 Selden Street, Berlin CT,
800.286.2000 (Customer Service, Emergencies), 800.286.5000 (Corporate Headquarters) www.nu.com
Our local power company.

Occhicone (Leather Repair)
42 North Main Street, Port Chester NY, 914.937.6327
Expert repairs, by Italian craftsmen, for high-quality leather items, such as handbags, briefcases, leather apparel, suitcases and shoes. They can make just about anything look new.
Hours: Tuesday-Saturday 8:30am-5pm.

Off-Duty Policeman
To hire an off-duty officer for services such as directing traffic at a party, call 203.622.8016 or call the main number 203.622.8000 and select the extension.

Packages PlusNMore (Shipping & Notary Services)
Mill Pond Center, 215 East Putnam Avenue, Cos Cob CT, 203.625.8130
www.packagesplusnmore.com
An up-scale packing and shipping company that we highly recommend. If requested, they will pick up a package from your home or office. They are authorized shippers for FedEx, DHL and UPS. Use them to ship your luggage, golf clubs and skis directly to your hotel without having to check and lose them during air travel. They are particularly good with fragile objects. Hours: Weekdays 7am-7pm, Saturday 9am-4pm, Sunday (Christmas Season Only).

Panza Appliance Service (Large Appliance Repair)
203.494.5795
Joe Panza services all makes and models of major appliances, central air conditioners and hot water heaters. Joe could even fix our South Bend gas stove.

Patti's Portico (Outdoor Furniture Repair)
140 Highland Street, Port Chester NY, 203.869.6227
My garden chair needed re-strapping and Patti did a great job. She repairs just about any outdoor furniture, powder coating, sandblasting, welding, re-strapping and sling repair. Hours: Weekdays 8 am-4 pm.

PODS (Portable On Demand Storage)
95 Leggett Street, East Hartford CT, 866.229.4120   www.pods.com
PODS allow you to load at your own pace. Move local, cross country, or store in their storage center.

Post Road Iron Works (Metal Work and Welding)
345 West Putnam Avenue, Greenwich CT, 203.869.6322
Serving Greenwich since 1927, they do a lot of ordinary iron work, but their specialty is structural and ornamental welding. A good place to find a pair of andirons.
Hours: weekdays 8am-5:30pm, Saturday 8am-noon.

PC Repair and Sales (Computer Repair & Custom Computers)
502 Glenbrook Road, Stamford CT, 203.359.4732
www.pcrepairandsales.com
They repair and recover data. They will also build a computer for you to your specifications.

Performance Imaging (Home Theater)
550 West Avenue, Stamford, 203.862.9600 or 203.504.5200
www.performanceimaging.net
They are a terrific source for system integration, home theater design and installation.

Personal Touch Cleaning (Rug Cleaning)
124 Pilgrim Drive, Greenwich CT, 203.531.7431
Scott Nastahowski cleans carpets, rugs, upholstery and draperies. Hopefully you will never need it, but he also does flood restoration, water and septic clean ups. Shayne says "We've seen him work miracles on rugs we were sure would have to be ripped up."

PI Security (Home Fire & Security Systems)
81 Ridge Brook Drive, Stamford CT, 203.862.9300
A high-end, completely trustworthy, alarm system distributor/installer that can meet anyone's needs.

SERVICES

Piano Service (Piano Tuning and Consulting)
1127 High Ridge Road, Stamford CT, 203.359.2231
Ken Svec tunes pianos and is a good consultant if you wish to buy or sell a piano.

Pro Gas (Gas Equipment Servicing)
Greg Moore, 336 Hamilton Avenue, Greenwich CT, 203.625.4751, 877.776.4275
www.ProGas5.com
Greg Moore services natural and propane gas equipment (stoves and other household appliances, boilers, swimming pool heaters). He will provide 24/7 emergency service.

Pyrianos Collection (Steinway Piano Restoration)
90 Linden Street, New Haven CT, 203.661.2566
www.pyrianos.com
Maureen Walsh specializes in the acquisition, restoration, and sales of vintage Steinway pianos.

QuadJobs (Student Job Service)
30 East Elm Street, Greenwich CT, mail@quadJobs.com
www.QuadJobs.com
Online service connecting local college and graduate students with jobs in the area.

Rand Insurance (Insurance)
1100 East Putnam Avenue, Riverside CT, 203.637.1006
www.randinsurance.com
A local, very knowledgeable insurance agency that handles it all. They have great service.

Raphael's Furniture Restoration (Furniture Repair)
652 Glenbrook Road (Glenbrook Industrial Park), Stamford CT,
 203.348.3079   www.raphaelsfurniture.com
They will repair and restore just about any piece of furniture, but they specialize in the restoration of antiques.
Directions: When you enter the Glenbrook Industrial Park, drive around the building clockwise. You will pass a brick smokestack. An auto detail shop is on the left. Raphael's is on the right side. Look for the sign. Raphael's is not easy to find, but you will be glad you did.
Hours: Monday - Thursday 8am-5pm, Friday 8am-3pm,
Saturday 8am- 12 pm. Call for an appointment before you go.

SERVICES

Recycling Cell Phones

Collection boxes are located all over town for old cell phones, PDAs, pagers and chargers. Check the Public Works site www.greenwichct.org/ParksAndRec/ParksandRec.asp for their location or call the Greenwich Recycling Advisory Board, at 203.629.2876. This equipment is refurbished and used for 911 phones for women in crisis. Older equipment is sent to countries where the technology is less advanced. Support this program. Collection boxes are available to put in your own workplace.

Recycling Christmas Trees

Between December 26 and January 5, you can bring your un-decorated tree to Bruce Park, Byram Beach or Greenwich Point and the tree will be chipped and transported by the town. Of course, you can bring your tree at any time to the Holly Hill recycling facility. The idea that the tree will be recycled back to nature lifts our spirits.

Recycling Single Stream, Garbage, Hazardous Waste

In the same recycling bin you can throw away clean paper, newspapers, magazines, phone books, plastics, glass bottles, mirrors, plates, tin cans and empty aerosol cans. Be careful not to throw in food, fabric, used paper towels and other contaminated items. That is garbage. Hazardous waste is anything that is flammable, corrosive, toxic or reactive. These substances should not be put in garbage and are not accepted at the Holly Hill Resource Recovery Facility. Oil-based paint is hazardous waste. Dried latex paint is trash. Check the town website or call the Waste Disposal Division of the Town at 203.869.6910 for the date of Hazardous Waste Day in the spring.

Refuse Collectors

Garbage collection is done by independent contractors. New residents may call the Greenwich Independent Refuse Collector's Association at 203.622.0050 to find out which collector services their home. When you move to a home be sure to ask the former owner or a neighbor who is servicing their home.

SERVICES

Robert Marullo (Piano Lessons, Repair and Tuning)
203.869.4943
This popular, talented piano teacher at Greenwich Academy also gives private lessons. We strongly recommend him for lessons as well as piano repairs, tuning and reliable advice about purchases.

Round Hill Tree Service (Tree Service)
1 Armonk Street, Greenwich, 203.531.5759
www.roundhilltreeservice.com
Rick Masi will make sure your dead trees are cut down, your limbs are trimmed back and your yard sprayed for mosquitoes.

Royal Closet (Closets)
6-B Muller Park, Norwalk CT, 203.847.4179
www.RoyalCloset.com
Custom-designed clothing closets, as well as home offices, pantries and garage systems.

Safe Wash (Exterior Cleaning)
James Jagodzinski, 203.536.2400   www.FCSafeWash.com
Low-pressure washing of roofs and home exteriors (siding, decking, fencing and concrete surfaces) using biodegradable chemicals.

Safety Mom Enterprises (Child Safety)
267 Thayer Pond Road, Wilton CT, 203.594.7452
Www.safetymomsolutions.com
Alison Rhodes or her partner will come out to consult with new parents. Alison is a well-known safety expert.

Santaguida Sanitation (Dumpsters)
65 Valley Road, Greenwich CT, 203.869.6987
www.SantaguidaSanitation.com
A family-owned business for four generations. They have 12, 20 and 30 yard dumpsters.

Satellite TV Networks
- Direct TV, 888.777.2454, www.directTv.com
- Dish Network, 888.825.2557, www.dishnetwork.com

SERVICES

Seekircher Steel Window Repair (Steel Window/Door Repair)
423 Central Avenue, Peekskill NY, 914.734.8004
www.SeekircherSteelWindow.com
John Seekircher repairs leaded-glass steel casement windows. New York
Steel Window makes interior storm/screen windows for steel windows.

Select Plastics (Custom Acrylic and Plastics)
219 Liberty Square, Norwalk CT, 203.866.3767   www,selectplastics.com
They craft all sorts of things from marine hatches and windshields to
simple counter top displays.

Service Master (Home Services)
Steven Wills, Stamford CT, 203.327.3477
www.servicemasterclean.com
Their core service is disaster cleaning and disaster restoration. They also
do carpet, floor and upholstery cleaning. Service Master has more than
5,500 company-owned and franchise locations around the country. It
employs 32,000 people.

Sears Home Services (Appliance Repair)
Bridgeport CT, 800.349.5075, 800.424.2047
www.searshomeservices.com
A nation-wide network of service people servicing just about anything.
Service live www.servicelive.com is a Sears auction system which allows
users to name their own price for services such as home and appliance
repair. The Service Live site also allows consumers to rate and review
contractors, as well as forums and guides on home improvement and
repair topics. Service live screens contractors for licenses and criminal
records.

(The) Settler (Moving Service)
25-13 Old Kings Highway North, Darien CT, 203.810.4873
www.TheSettlersUSA.com
Pinny Randal helps you take the stress out of moving. She helps hire
movers and manage them. Helps you dispose of unneeded furnishings,
helps pack, unpack, and organize utilities.

SERVICES

Sophia's Great Dames (Costumes - Women and Children)
1 Liberty Way, Greenwich CT, 203.869.5990
www.SophiasCostumes.com
Wonderful shop for vintage clothing, antiques, collectibles, gifts and costumes. A large selection of costumes (for all occasions) for sale or rent. Fun to visit. Hours: Tuesday-Saturday 10am-5:30pm.

Stacey Cross / Cross Pond Antiques (Appraisals & Estate Sales)
203.570.5372 (Cell), Staceycross9@aol.com
Stacey, a Greenwich resident, offers an alternative to tag sales. She will go to your home, photograph and appraise the items you want to sell, contact the appropriate dealers or auction houses and coordinate the sale.

Student Employment Service
Greenwich High School, 203.625.8008
www.ghs-ses.org
An online job listing and referral service. Employers list their part-time or full-time jobs (office or party event assistance, childcare, tutoring, moving help, computer installation and more) and students log in to see what is needed.

(Charles) Stuttig (Locksmith)
158 Greenwich Avenue, Greenwich CT, 203.869.6260
www.stuttiglocksmith.com
A fixture in Greenwich for many years, they provide a wide variety of locks and safes. Whether you have an emergency or just need a key replaced, they can be counted on and trusted.
Hours: Weekdays 8am-3pm.

Suburban Propane
55 Old Field Point Road, Greenwich CT, 203.869.4226
www.Suburbanpropane.com
Suburban is a nation-wide propane supplier. Many Greenwich residents use them for their gas stoves, pool heaters and generators.

Sung Yun Cleaners (Dry Cleaners)
282 Mason Street, Greenwich CT, 203.869.7650
A good choice for your curtains and draperies.
Hours: Weekdays 7am-6:30pm, Saturday 7:30am-4:30pm.

SERVICES

Superior Home Services (Cleaning)
31 Parker Avenue, Stamford CT, 203.359.3861
www.shscleaning.com
A reliable, very accommodating, residential and commercial cleaning service that can do just about anything, thorough house cleaning, windows and even post construction clean up.

Table Top Designs (Replace Missing China or Silver)
57 Vista Terrace, Cheshire CT, 800.801.4084
www.tabletopdesigns.com
Formerly called Tablescraps, if you are missing a piece of china, crystal or silver from your collection, this is a good place to find a replacement. Call, visit their website or email them.

Ted The Tailor (Tailor)
2 Church Street, Greenwich CT, 203.869.5699
They have been tailoring in Greenwich since 1948. Mr. Puglia and his staff can do everything from alterations to custom suits. They also work on leather.

Textile Conservation Workshop (Fabric Restoration)
3 Main Street, South Salem NY, 914.763.5805
www.textileconservationworkshop.org
Patsy Orlofsky specializes in treating, preserving and restoring historic textiles.

Thomas Dry Cleaning and Chinese Hand Laundry
68 Lewis Street, Greenwich CT, 203.869.9420
A good choice for fine linens and tablecloths. Cash or check only.

Thomas Libby (Crystal/Ceramic Repair)
50 John Street, Stamford CT, 203.602.0500
www.TKLibby.com
An excellent source for ceramic and glass repairs. He also sells Japanese and Chinese 19th & 20th century ceramics.

Tiger Lily's (Upholstery)
154 Prospect Street, Greenwich CT, 203.629.6510
www.tigerlilysgreenwich.com
Custom upholstery and window treatments. They have been doing custom work for more than 20 years.

SERVICES

Tony's Alteration and Shoe Repair
70 Lewis Street, Greenwich CT, 203.769.1916
Women and men's shoe repair.

Trimaxion Fine Arts (Fine Art - Storage, Crating, Shipping)
29-76 Northern Boulevard, Long Island City NY, 718.784.5070
www.trimaxion.com
A company specializing in fine art services such as crating, packaging on site, storage and transportation.

Triple S Carpet and Drapery Cleaners (Carpet Cleaning)
400 West Main Street (Post Road), Stamford CT, 203.327.7471
www.triplesclean.com
They clean draperies and upholstery and will come to the house to clean rugs and upholstery. They do a great job of cleaning and/or repairing rugs. They will clean and store boat and patio cushions for the winter.

Ultrawiz Electronics (TV Repair)
242 Mill Street, Byram CT, 203.532.0175   www.UltraWiz.com
Have you ever wondered how to get a plasma or projection television repaired? Greenwich residents are lucky to have Ultrawiz, a factory-authorized service center for most plasma TVs. They also repair VCRs, camcorders and hi-fi equipment.
Hours: Weekdays 9am-5pm, Saturday 9:30am-1pm.

United Rentals
224 Selleck Street, Stamford CT, 203.327.0090 www.UnitedRentals.com
They are the largest equipment rental company in the world, with over 800 rental locations. They rent construction and industrial equipment as well as homeowner equipment and tools.

Upholstery by Paul
244 Columbus Avenue, Port Chester NY, 914.939.3902
www.Upholsterybypaul.com
Paul will re-glue, restyle or just re-upholster furniture as well as make draperies and curtains.

SERVICES

UPS
www.ups.com/tracking/tracking.html
Self-Serve Drop Boxes
• 100 Field Point Rd, Greenwich
• 100 Mason Street, Greenwich
The UPS Store, 65 High Ridge Road, Stamford CT, 203.356.0022
The UPS Store, 15 East Putnam Avenue, Greenwich CT, 203.622.1114
www.theupsstore.com
See STORES for details on UPS Stores.

Verizon (Telephone)
800.837.4966 (Customer Service & Repairs)
www22.verizon.com, www.verizon.com
They service Greenwich, Byram, Cos Cob, Glenville & Riverside.
AT&T services Old Greenwich.

Vermont Good Wood (Fire Wood)
17 Binney Lane, Old Greenwich CT, 203.637.5200
www.VermontGoodWood.com
Home delivery and stacking of kiln-dried oak and white birch. Not your ordinary wood nor your ordinary price. Check their website for details.

Vernon Computer Source (Computer Rentals)
77 Selleck Street, Stamford CT, 800.827.0352
www.vernoncomputersource.com
Daily, weekly or monthly computer equipment rentals. Delivery and on-site business installation services are also available.

Westy Self Storage (Storage)
• 80 Brownhouse Road, Stamford CT, 203.961.8000
• 351 North Main Street, Port Chester NY, 914.937.2222
www.westy.com
Convenient, clean, secure, private storage rooms. They will recommend a mover or loan you a truck for self-storage moving.

Willett Vacuum (Vacuum Repair)
440 Willett Avenue, Port Chester NY, 914.937.5948
www.WillettVacuumNY.com
They repair many types of vacuum cleaners.

Wood Den (Furniture Repair, Stripping, Refinishing)
266 Selleck Street, Stamford CT, 203.324.6957
www.TheWoodDen.com
Wood and metal furniture stripping, chair caning and furniture repairs, sandblasting and powder coating.
Hours: Tuesday, Wednesday & Friday 9am-5pm, Thursday 8am-8pm, Saturday 9am-3:30pm.

www.YouRenew.Com (Electronics Recycling)
129 Church Street, New Haven CT, 815.431.8576
www.YouRenew.com
Greenwich resident David Walker helped develop a company that pays you to recycle your old electronic devices. You Renew is part of the Yale Entrepreneurial Institute.

York Residential Management (Property Management)
210 Sound Beach Avenue, Old Greenwich CT, 203.698.3460
www.YorkResmgmt.com
Nick Barile has been building and renovating homes in Greenwich for many years. You can trust him to manage your property. He will tailor his services to your needs.

TIP: FINDING TAG SALES
Tag sales, aka. estate sales or garage sales, are a popular Greenwich weekend pastime. The Friday and weekend Greenwich Time newspaper lists tag sale locations.

SPORTS INDEX

Fans and players of almost every imaginable sport live in Greenwich. Paddle tennis was even invented in Greenwich. Best of all, whether you are a professional or an amateur, finding a place to fish, skate, golf, sail or play ball is easy in our town. This section is primarily sports for Adults and Juniors.

Children's sports and child focused activities are listed in CHILDREN.
See FITNESS for exercise classes, yoga, personal trainers and gyms.
Uniforms and Equipment listed in STORES.
Children's Summer Camps are listed in CHILDREN.
If you need to recover from an excess of activity see HEALTH.
To exercise your mind see CONTINUING EDUCATION, CULTURE or BOOKS AND LIBRARIES.

Archery
Cos Cob Archers

Auto Racing
See also, Go Karts.
Lime Rock Park
Overland Experts
Skip Barber Racing School
Sports Car Driving Association

Badminton
YWCA
See also, Tennis and Squash.

Baseball (including Softball)
For T-Ball See, CHILDREN SPORTS.
Blue Fish Professional Baseball
Blue Fish Professional Baseball is also listed in CHILDREN under FAMILY OUTINGS.
(Greenwich) Department of Parks and Recreation Programs
Sports Center of Connecticut

Basketball
Eastern Greenwich Civic Center
Men's Basketball League
Nike Adult Sports Schools
Western Greenwich Civic Center (aka Bendheim Civic Center)
YMCA
YWCA

SPORTS INDEX

Biking
For Spinning see FITNESS.
Appalachian Mountain Club
(The) Bicycle Tour Company
Connecticut Bicycle and Trail Map
East Coast Greenway
Greenwich Safe Cycling
Sound Cyclists

Boating
(including Sailing, Rowing, Rafting, Canoeing and Kayaking)
Appalachian Mountain Club
Clarke Outdoors
Downunder Kayaking
Greenwich Community Sailing
Greenwich Marine Facilities
Greenwich Sail and Power Squadron
Greenwich Rowing Club
Greenwich Water Club (see CLUBS)
Indian Harbor Yacht Club Sailing
Kayak Adventure
Kayak/Canoe Guide
Kittatinny Canoes
Longshore Sailing School
Mianus River
New York Sailing School
Norwalk Rowing Association
North American Outdoor Adventure
Old Greenwich Yacht Club (see CLUBS)
Rex Marine Center
Sound Environmental Associates (Safe Boating & Jet Ski Courses)
Small Boat Shop (Kayak Instruction)
Sound Sailing Center
Stamford Kayak Meetup Group
Yachting Magazine

Bowling
(including lawn bowling)
AMF Bowling Centers
Greenwich Lawn Bowling Club
Sports Center of Connecticut

SPORTS INDEX

Bridge
Lest you wonder why bridge is in this section, we regard it as fitness for the brain.
YWCA

Camping
See, CHILDREN for summer camps.
Camping on Greenwich Islands
Camping with RVs
Northcamp (Wildness Survival Skills)

Canoeing
See Boating.
The Mianus River in Greenwich is a good place to practice canoeing. There is no need to worry if you fall in because the water is very clean. For the more adventurous, the Housatonic River has class I and II rapids, and is a center for trips and instruction.

Cheerleading
See CHILDREN.

Chiropractors
For chiropractors and other therapies see, HEALTH.

Climbing
See also, Hiking.
Appalachian Mountain Club
(The) Cliffs
Club Get Away
YWCA Climbing Wall

Croquet
Greenwich Croquet Club

Curling
Nutmeg Curling Club

Driving
See Auto Racing.

Fencing
Stamford Fencing Center
Western Greenwich Civic Center

Field Hockey
See CHILDREN.

Fishing
Greenwich is ideally located on the Long Island Sound for excellent salt-water fishing from May to December. Going east or west at different times of the year provides a multispecies catch including Striped Bass, Blue-fish, Fluke, Porgies and Blackfish. Light spin, fly or bait tackle is the most fun. Freshwater fishing for Trout and Bass is good in the Mianus River. Fishing in reservoirs is prohibited. Blue ribbon trout streams in CT and NY are within a 90-minute drive. The resources below can help you. Also see Fishing Stores, such as Orvis or the Sportsman's Den, under STORES for more than just equipment. The fishing season for trout runs from April to February. Fishermen 16-years and older must have a valid state fishing license. Bedford Sportsman
Compleat Angler (See STORES)
Connecticut Outdoor Recreation
DEEP Family Fishing Classes
Licenses and Permits
Magic Touch Fishing Charters
North East Saltwater Fishing Magazine
Shell Fishing
Sportsman's Den (also see STORES.)
Trout Unlimited
Also see, Sportsman's Den and Rudy's Tackle Barn in STORES.

Salt Water Fishing Charters
Sound Fishing Charters (Snow Goose), 203.255.4522; sails from Byram
Sparky Charters, 914.747.5825; sails from Cos Cob.

Flying (including: Soaring, Skydiving & Ballooning)
Fighter Pilot for a Day
Flight Safety
K & L Soaring
Performance Flight School
Soaring Adventures of America
Westchester Flying Club

Football
See CHILDREN.

Golf

There are a number of nearby courses open to non-residents. Some of these have limited times for non-residents. Many facilities have discounts for seniors, juniors, early morning or late afternoon play, or for 9-hole rounds. If you like the course, check out their policy on season passes. Be sure to book before you go. Check out the following sites www.ctgolfer.com & www.co.westchester.ny.us/parks   If you need a little practice before playing, use the golf range at Griffith Harris Memorial Golf Course or one of these.

Doral Golf Club
Eastern Greenwich Civic Center (indoors)
Gaynor Brennan Municipal Golf Course
Griffith Harris Memorial Golf Course
Lake of Isles Golf Course and Golf Academy
Maple Moor Golf Course
Nike Golf Schools and Junior Camps
Oak Hills Golf Course
Richter Park Golf Course
Ridgefield Golf Course
Saxon Woods
Sports Center of Connecticut
Sterling Farms
Westchester Golf Range

Go Karts

Checkered Flag Raceway
Grand Prix New York
Norwalk Karting Association
On Track Karting

Gymnastics
See CHILDREN.

Hiking (including Walking)
See also Climbing.
See also Running.
Appalachian Mountain Club
Audubon Center
Babcock Preserve
Connecticut Walking Books
Mianus River Park
Montgomery Pinetum Park
Outward Bound

Hockey (Ice)
See also Field Hockey.
Chelsea Piers
Dorothy Hamill Skating Rink
Greenwich Blues Youth Ice Hockey Association (See CHILDREN.)
Stamford Twin Rinks

Horseback Riding (Including Polo)
Picture fall leaves, stone walls and a rider on a handsome horse on a scenic woodland trail. Yes, this is Greenwich, where we have over 150 miles of riding trails which connect to the 100 miles of trails in Stamford. For insurance reasons, most stables will not rent horses for unaccompanied trail rides unless you have been taking a series of lessons and they have determined your skill level.
Back Barn Farm
Coker Farm
Getner Farm
Greenwich Polo Club
Greenwich Riding and Trails Association
Kelsey Farm
Lionshare Farm
Mead Farm
Ox Ridge Hunt Club
Pegasus Therapeutic Riding
Red Barn Stables
Stratford Stables

SPORTS INDEX

Hunting
Connecticut Outdoor Recreation
Hunting & Trapping (Guide and Maps)
State Forest Camping Areas
See also Shooting & Archery.

Karate (and other Martial Arts)
Calasanz Physical Arts
Cho's Tae Kwon Do
Citizens' Police Academy
Devita Karate
Dynamic Martial Arts Family Center
Kang Tae-kwon-do & Hapkido
Kimpo Academy of Martial Arts
Old Greenwich School of Karate
Shaolin Studios
Shidogakuin
Tiger Schulmann's Mixed Martial Arts
White Tiger Tae Kwon Do
Women's Self Defense

Kayaking
See Boating.

Lacrosse
Bridgeport Barrage major League Lacrosse is listed in CHILDREN, FAMILY OUTINGS.
(Greenwich) Department of Parks and Recreation Programs
See CHILDREN.

Laser Tag
See CHILDREN, Parties Away from Home.

Paddle Ball
See Tennis.

Paintball
For paintball equipment try Chili Bears in Old Greenwich, listed in STORES.
Liberty Paintball

Pickleball
Pickleball

SPORTS INDEX

Platform Tennis
See Tennis

Riding
See Horseback Riding

Rock Climbing
See Climbing.

Rowing
See Boating

Running
See also Hiking
For Orthotics see Stride Custom Orthotics or Foot Solutions in HEALTH.
Greenwich Kids Triathlon (See CHILDREN.)
Greenwich Point
Jim Fixx Memorial Day Race
Running Events in Greenwich

Sailing
See Boating

Skating (Ice and Roller Skating)
See also Hockey (for Ice Hockey)
See also Skateboarding and Skating in CHILDREN
Binney Pond
Dorothy Hamill Skating Rink
Eastern Greenwich Civic Center (Roller Skating)
Greenwich Skating Club (see CLUBS)
Mianus River
Western Greenwich Civic Center
Windy Hill Figure Skating Club

Skateboarding
For skate boards and inline skates, try Chili Bears or Rink & Racquet.
Greenwich Skateboard Park

Squash
See Tennis

Soccer
See CHILDREN

SPORTS INDEX

Shooting
See also Archery
Cos Cob Revolver & Rifle Club
Licenses and Permits (Hunting)

Skiing (Snow)

LOCAL FAMILY SKI RESORTS
Hunter Mountain
Mohawk Mountain
Mount Southington
Powder Ridge
Windham Mountain
Winding Trails Cross Country Ski Center

LARGE REGIONAL SKI AREAS
These areas have extensive summer family activities. Check their websites for details.
Killington Resort
Mount Snow Resort
Mount Tom / Suicide 6
Okemo Mountain
Stowe Mountain Resort
Stratton Mountain Resort
Sugarloaf
Whiteface Mountain

Skydiving
See Flying.

Swimming (Including Water Polo and Scuba)
For Greenwich Beaches see PARKS & BEACHES.
Greenwich Point
Licenses and Permits (Beach Pass)
Nike Sports Schools
Rex Dive Center
Ski & Scuba Connection
YMCA
YWCA

SPORTS INDEX

SPORTS

(This section is primarily sports for Adults and Juniors)
Children's Sports are listed in CHILDREN
Uniforms and Equipment are listed in STORES
Children's Summer Camps are listed in CHILDREN
Exercise classes are listed in FITNESS

AMF Bowlmor Bowling Centers (Bowling)
Bowlmor Lanes, 701 Connecticut Avenue, Norwalk CT, 203.838.7501
47 Tarrytown Road, White Plains NY, 914.948.2677
www.amfcenters.com, www.bowlmor.com
Multi-lane ten-pin bowling for all ages. Bowlmor AMF is the largest operator of bowling centers in the world with 7,500 employees and 272 bowling centers. Bowlmor is an upscale bowling spot.

Appalachian Mountain Club (Outdoor Sports)
Fairfield County Group, 7 Vera Drive, Bethel CT, 203.762.0216
www.ct-amc.org
The Fairfield County group sponsors or participates in a variety of outdoor activities, such as hiking, mountain and road biking, rock climbing, canoeing and kayaking and cross-country skiing. You can opt-in to the newsletter on their website.

Armonk Tennis Club
546 Bedford Road, Armonk NY, 914.273.8124
www.ArmonkTennis.com
Situated on 14-acres, they have 14 courts-10 outdoor (5 red clay & 5 Har-Tru) and 4 Har-Tru indoor courts. Adult and Junior programs, summer camps and tournaments.

Audubon Center (Hiking)
613 Riversville Road, 203.869.5272
Greenwich Audubon Society, PO Box 7487, Greenwich CT 06831.
www.greenwich.center.audubon.org
• A 63-page guide to 26 area walking trails is available.
• 280 acres of well-kept trails, a delightful place to walk. The entrance is on the corner of Riversville Road and John Street.

Babcock Preserve (Running, Hiking)
North Street, 203.622.7814
The Preserve has 297 acres of well-marked running trails from 1 to 3.5 miles. Open to the public sunrise to sunset. The entrance is on the left, about 5 miles North of the Merritt Parkway and just past the reservoir.

Back Barn Farm aka New England Farm (Riding)
203 Greenwich Road, Bedford NY, 914.234.6692
www.backbarnfarm.com
Boarding as well as lessons both indoor and outdoor. They have an equestrian consignment shop, usually including saddles.

Bedford Sportsman (Fly Fishing Instruction & Guide Services)
25 Adams Street, Bedford Hills NY, 914.666.8091
www.bedfordsportsman.com
Specializes in freshwater fly and spin fishing equipment. A good resource for New York watershed streams & guide services. They teach fly fishing during the summer.

Binney Pond (Ice Skating)
Sound Beach Avenue, Old Greenwich
This is the prettiest pond for skating and it is town-tested for safety.

(The) Bicycle Tour Company
9 Bridge Street, Kent CT, 888.711.5368
www.BicycleTours.com
Bicycle explorations give you a whole new perspective. Tour Greenwich and many other interesting sites on the Eastern Seaboard. Bicycle Tour Company routes are generally 25-30 miles per day. They rent bicycles & construct routes for all ability levels. Owner Sal Lilienthal grew up in Greenwich.

Blue Fish Professional Baseball (Baseball)
Harbor Yard, Bridgeport, CT 203.345.4800
www.bridgeportbluefish.com

Calasanz Physical Arts (Karate)
507 Westport Ave (Rt. 1) in Norwalk CT, 203.847.6528
www.Calasanz.com
Self defense using a number of techniques from kickboxing to kung fu.

Camping on Greenwich Islands (Family Camping)

www.greenwichct.org/Government/Departments/Parks_and_Recreation/
Overnight_Camping

You can camp on Island Beach & Great Captain's Island between June 10 and September 16. Families find this lots of fun. Reservations must be made in person at the Department of Parks and Recreation, 2nd floor, at least 2 weeks prior to date. We suggest reserving much earlier. Many people make their reservation requests in January. Proof of residency is required. Camping reservations are limited to one night per family per season.

Camping with RVs

www.campConn.com

This is the site of the Connecticut Campground Owner's Association. They list sites throughout CT.

Checkered Flag Raceway (Go-Karts)

http://www.gokartrides.com/
1762 Berlin Turnpike, Berlin CT, 860.829.5278

The Checkered Flag Raceway offers three different go-karts: two seaters for an adult and a child. Fast karts for drivers 16 years-old and above.

Chelsea Piers
(Tennis, Squash, Triathlon, Masters Swimming & More)

One Blachley Road, Stamford CT, 203.989.1801

Wendy Gardiner is Adult Tennis Director. You don't have to be a member to play on their tennis courts. They have a separate Squash membership. See review of adult sports in FITNESS and youth activities in CHILDREN.

Cho's Tae Kwon Do (Karate)

5 Oak Street, Greenwich CT, 203.661.8611
www.chos-taekwondo.com

Besides teaching the Korean martial art of Tae Kwon Do, master Cho teaches Kum Ye Do and weapons to teens and adults.

Citizens' Police Academy

Greenwich Police Department, Community Impact Section, 203.618.8308

Taught by the Greenwich Police Department, the Academy meets for seven weeks, two nights a week. Each session is about 2.5 hours. The academy teaches the inner workings of the Department.

Clarke Outdoors (Canoeing)
163 Route 7, West Cornwall CT, 860.672.6365
www.clarkeoutdoors.com
Canoeing and kayaking rentals, lessons, and white water rafting on the Housatonic River.

(The) Cliffs (Indoor Climbing)
1 Commerce Park, Valhalla NY, 914.328.7625
www.thecliffsClimbing.com
Indoor climbing practice on over 200 climbs set by a full-time professional staff. Climbers can start at age 9. Training programs for beginners and advanced climbers.

Club Getaway (Adventure Weekends)
P.O. Box 737, Kent CT, 800.643.8292, 860.927.3664
http://www.clubgetaway.com
About an hour away, the Club is a 300 acre resort in the foothills of the Berkshire Mountains, with just about every activity available: trapeze school, tennis, volleyball, rock climbing, yoga and more.

Coker Farm / Benchmark Farm (Riding)
69 Stone Hill Road, Bedford, (North Salem) NY, 914.234.3954
http://www.justhorses.com/ind/C53.html
http://www.benchmarkfarmny.net
Set on 100 acres with indoor and outdoor riding areas, they give lessons from beginner to advanced. Judy Richter specializes in hunters and jumping.

Connecticut Outdoor Recreation (Fishing, Hunting, Trapping and More)
Connecticut Department of Environmental Protection, 860.424.3474
http://www.ct.gov/deep/site/default.asp (Click on Outdoor Recreation)
The Angler's Guide should come with your fishing license. It provides a summary of the rules and regulations governing sport fishing in Connecticut, descriptions of places to fish, the kinds of fish found there, and license information.

Connecticut Bicycle and Trail Maps
Information: 860.594.2000
2800 Berlin Turnpike, PO Box 317564, Newington, CT 06131-7564
www.traillink.com www.ctbikemap.org www.mapmyride.com/us/ct

Connecticut Walking Books (Hiking & Walking)
For information call 860.346.2372
www.ctwoodlands.org or www.walkct.org
The books (Eastern and Western Connecticut) are published by the Connecticut Forest and Park Association. They are available on their website. The Association is a non-profit group of hikers and conservationists. The Walk Books are complete guides to day trips, with fold-out maps.

Cos Cob Archers
205 Bible Street, Greenwich CT, Clubhouse: 203.625.9421
www.CosCobArchers.com
Twenty-four regular targets. Members must have their own equipment and be over 18. Members have a key to the range and can practice any time. To join, visit the range Saturday or Sunday or attend the meeting on the second Wednesday of each month at 7 pm.

Cos Cob Revolver & Rifle Club
Physical Address: 451 Steamboat Road, Greenwich CT, 203.769.5002
Mailing Address: PO Box 44, Cos Cob, CT 06807   www.ccrrc.com
A safe way to practice target shooting, this Greenwich club (despite its Cos Cob name), just across from the train station, has terrific facilities and a very helpful membership (including the Greenwich Police, many of whom practice here). To join, send them an email from their website. Usually, all you have to do is attend a meeting (the second Wednesday of each month at 8 pm). To transport a gun to and from the club you need a Connecticut handgun license, which they can help you obtain.

DEEP Family Fishing Classes
www.CT.Gov/DEEP
Deep (the State Department of Energy & Environmental Protection) teaches classes about fish and fishing, including safety tips and casting practice to parents and children ages 9 and older.

(Greenwich) Department of Parks and Recreation Programs
2nd floor, Town Hall, 101 Field Point Road, Greenwich CT, 203.622.7814
www.greenwichct.org/ParksAndRec/ParksandRec.asp
The Department sponsors a multitude of sports programs. Always go to their website to see what they are currently sponsoring. The Department publishes a number of valuable publications such as the Town's Bicycle Master Plan, measured running and walking routes (created as an Eagle Scout Project).   Office Hours: Weekdays 8am-4pm.

Devita Karate (Tang Soo Do Karate)
37 West Putnam Avenue, Greenwich CT, 203.629.2467
www.devitakarate.com
Tang-soo-do Karate, Tai Chi Classes and kickboxing. Joseph Devita is a 6th degree Black Belt and has been teaching in Greenwich since 1981.

Doral Arrowwood (Tennis, Racquet Ball, Squash)
975 Anderson Hill Road, Rye Brook NY, 914.935.6688
Main Hotel Desk: 844.214.5500
www.ProformTennis.com www.doralarrowwood.com/proform_tennis.asp
www.doralarrowwood.com/health_racquetballandsquash.asp
4 hard courts (2 indoor and 2 outdoor), with ATP professionals to provide junior and adult programs. Two racquetball courts and one squash court are located in their fitness center.

Doral Golf Club (Golf)
975 Anderson Hill Road, Rye Brook NY, 914.323.4478
www.doralarrowwood.com
Nine holes, par 35. 5,689 yards, pro shop, driving range, putting green and restaurant.
Hours: Monday-Thursday 7am-6pm.

Dorothy Hamill Skating Rink (Skating, Hockey)
Sue Merz Way off Sherman Avenue, Greenwich CT, 203.531.8560;
Off Season: 203.622.7830.
www.greenwichct.org/ParksAndRec/prSkating.asp
An excellent municipal skating facility for Greenwich residents and their guests. You will need proof of residency such as a beach card. The Rink offers a full schedule of skating & figure skating lessons and ice hockey programs for children, teens, and adults.
Directions: US-1 W, L on Western Junior Highway, R on Henry, R on Sherman Avenue.

Downunder (Kayaking & Paddle Boarding)
157 Rowayton Avenue, Rowayton CT, 203.642.3660
575 Riverside Avenue, Westport CT, 203.956.6217
www.DownUnderCT.com
Located on the Five Mile River, they provide instruction and guided tours of Long Island Sound. They have instruction and rentals for kayaking and stand-up paddle boarding. Rowayton is seasonal from Mother's Day to Labor Day; Westport is open year round.

Dynamic Martial Arts Family Center (Kempo Karate & Tai Chi)
202 Field Point Road, Greenwich CT, 203.629.4666
www.GreenwichKarate.com
They have many children's classes and kempo karate, cardio kickboxing and Tai Chi classes for adults.

East Coast Greenway (Bicycle Routes)
Headquarters: 5315 Highgate Drive, Suite 105, Durham NC, 919.797.0619
www.greenway.org
The East Coast Greenway Alliance has created bicycle routes along the East Coast, part of which is between Greenwich and New Haven. A map of this route, championed by local resident Franklin Bloomer, is available by calling the headquarters. If you want an adventure, try the 2,900 mile route from Maine to Florida.

Eastern Greenwich Civic Center
aka Old Greenwich-Riverside Community Center
90 Harding Road, Old Greenwich, 203.637.3659
www.greenwichct.org/ParksAndRec/prFacilityPrograms.asp#eastern
Old Greenwich-Riverside Community Center, 203.637.3659, www.myogrcc.org
Together they sponsor a variety of basketball, baseball and softball teams and instruction programs for girls and boys from kindergarten through 8th grade. Among their activities are indoor golf, indoor soccer, adult pick-up basketball for 18 and over, roller skating and yoga. OGCC sponsors basketball programs for young children through adults: youth basketball for children in the 3rd and 4th grades; boys' basketball and girls' basketball for 5th to 8th graders and summer tennis, baseball and soccer camps. The Old Greenwich-Riverside Soccer Association has a program for over 700 youngsters who play for fun, as well as those who compete. The Van Williams Academy of Martial Arts teaches here.

Fighter Pilot for a Day (Flying)
800.522.7590, www.aircombat.com
Since 1988 they have been giving civilians the experience of being a fighter pilot. Guest pilots fly real military fighters with licensed fighter pilots in the cockpit with them. Aircraft are outfitted with high-end digital multi-camera systems to capture your fighter pilot experience. No pilot's license is required. Course begins with pilot training, then a real dogfight experience, then a briefing on your performance (or lack thereof). They travel around the country, but fly out of Montgomery, New York in April & October. It is great fun. Carolyn beat Jerry 4 out 5 times.

Flight Safety (Flying)
Vero Beach Florida, 772.564.7600 or 800.800.1411
www.flightsafetyacademy.com
The premier flight training school. Started by Greenwich resident Al Ueltschi and now a Berkshire Hathaway Company. It is directed toward teaching people who want to be professional pilots, but there is no better place for a private pilot to begin their training. The weather is great so you will be able to fly every day.

Gaynor Brennan Municipal Golf Course (Golf)
451 Stillwater Road, Stamford CT, 203.324.4185
www.brennangolf.com
Par 71. You can reserve seven days in advance.

Getner Farm (Riding)
22 Richards Avenue, Norwalk CT, 203.524.3275
www.GetnerBarn.com, www.wishesforhorses.com/GetnerBarn2/
English riding in a relaxed atmosphere for ages 6 and up. Blue jeans are the norm. The website has several contact numbers.

Grand Prix New York (Go-Karting and Bowling)
333 North Bedford Road, Mount Kisco NY, 914.241.3131
http://www.gpny.com/
120,000 square foot indoor go-kart racing for 8 years and above. Special adult races.

Grand Slam (Tennis)
1 Bedford-Banksville Road, Bedford NY, 914.234.9206
www.grandslamtennisclub.com
Five HarTru courts, five DecoTurf II (hard surface) courts. During the winter, eight are indoor, during the summer, five are outside. Excellent junior and adult programs including USTA League Play.

Greenwich Community Sailing
PO Box 195, Old Greenwich CT, 203.698.0599
www.GreenwichSailing.com
CT approved safe boating certificate courses. They have a variety of junior and adult programs open only to Greenwich residents. The Junior programs are for ages 9-16. Learn to sail, keelboat or kayak in group or private lessons.

Greenwich Croquet Club
www.facebook.com/GreenwichCroquetClub
Founded by Greenwich residents Bill and Marjorie Campbell in 1986, this private club is open to everyone. It plays on the Bruce Park Green. Besides providing instruction, the Club holds the Greenwich Invitational Tournament every July 4th, and in August, hosts the Connecticut State Championship. To join, stop by the lawns at Bruce Park on Thursday evenings in the summer.

Greenwich Lawn Bowling Club (Lawn Bowling)
www.bowlsusa.us/divisions.php
Call Rose Claus, 203.629.9211, about membership.
This 25-member club welcomes men and women of all ages. The group has fun bowling on the course, built in 1940 in Bruce Park. The club is affiliated with the Northeast Division of the U.S. Lawn Bowl Association.

Greenwich Marine Facilities (Boat Moorings)
Location: Town Hall, Second Floor
Hours: Open from 8:15am to 3:45pm.
www.greenwichct.org/ParksAndRec/prBoating.asp
They assign boat moorings for the town. To apply for a slip (as always, bring in a utility bill as proof of residency and a photo ID) you must own a boat and know the vessel's length, draft and beam. Boats are categorized as sail or power and over or under 20 feet; 20 feet and over receive deepwater moorings. After registering, you are put on a waiting list. The list is never short, but the amount of time varies with the vessel's type and size, as well as the location you request. The town has moorings at Greenwich Point, Cos Cob, Grass Island and Byram. They will also provide storage of kayaks and canoes.

Greenwich Point / Tod's Point (Swimming, Bicycling, Running)
Shore Road, Old Greenwich
www.greenwichct.org/government/departments/parks_and_recreation/beaches/
147 acres at the end of Sound Beach Avenue and Shore Road. Greenwich Point is a popular spot for water sports, as well as walking, bicycle riding, roller blading and running. A network of trails leads along the changing coastline and through the woods. A trail guide is available at the Seaside Center of the Bruce Museum. During the summer a beach pass is required. See PARKS & BEACHES.

SPORTS

Greenwich Polo Club

Field Location: 1 Hurlingham Drive (Upper North Street at Conyers Farm)
Office: 80 Field Point Road, Greenwich CT, 203.561.5821
www.GreenwichPoloClub.com
Greenwich has a world-class polo facility. Most summer Sundays you can watch a good polo match in a beautiful setting. Matches begin at 3pm, the gates open at 1 pm. General admission is $40 per car. Attire is "Garden Party Chic." The Greenwich Polo Club also offers individual and group polo lessons. Lessons include the use of a polo pony, all tack, polo mallets and balls. Call their office to get a copy of their magazine "Greenwich Polo."

Greenwich Racquet Club (Tennis)

1 River Road, Cos Cob CT, 203.661.0606
www.leontennis.net
4 indoor DecoTurf hard-surface courts. They have an excellent junior development program, as well as adult clinics taught by USPTA certified pros. You can play in round robins for men and women or rent a court for the season. During the summer they operate the Wire Mill Racquet Club.

Greenwich Riding and Trails Association (Riding)

PO Box 1403, Greenwich CT, 06836, 203.661.3062
www.thegrta.org
Greenwich has an extensive trail network. This 100 year-old organization maintains 150 miles of horse trails in town and devotes its resources to conservation and open space. For information and help, call them. A great organization to join.

Greenwich Rowing Club (Rowing)

The Greenwich Water Club, (Mianus River) at 67 River Road, Cos Cob CT, 203.661.4033
www.GreenwichWaterClub.com
The Club staff is ready to help you learn, train, and push the limits to meet your every goal, whether you are a competitive crew team or a new trainee. The club has 35 rowing machines and a training staff available to accommodate your needs, whether you are a novice, intermediate, or highly advanced rower. Membership is open to men and women of all ages and juniors 12-18. Stop by the Club to see their facilities and meet the coaches. You don't have to join the club to participate in rowing.

Greenwich Safe Cycling (Bicycle)

PO Box 117, Cos Cob CT 06807-0117

www.greenwichsafecycling.org

The mission of this organization of Town residents, both serious cyclists and recreational riders, is to make Greenwich a bicycle and pedestrian friendly community. They helped develop the Town's Master Bicycle Plan. They are responsible for the 7.5-mile bicycle trail from Grass Island to Greenwich Point.

Greenwich Sail and Power Squadron (Boating)

PO Box 307, Greenwich CT 06830

For information or to join email them through their website.

http://greenwichsps.wordpress.com

The Power Squadron is an all-volunteer civic organization with 200 Greenwich members. The Squadron's primary goal is education and boating safety—both sailing and powerboating. The Squadron teaches two Safe Boating courses at the Greenwich High School through the Continuing Education program (203.830.8144) and depending upon demand, runs additional courses throughout the year. All boaters (even jet skiers) must have a Connecticut Boating License. The Power Squadron course qualifies you for your Connecticut license. This course is the first step for anyone who wants to enjoy the miles of coastline available to Greenwich residents.

Greenwich Tennis Headquarters

54 Bible Street, Cos Cob CT, 203.618.7613

There are 36 all-weather courts available throughout Greenwich, as well as a paddle tennis court location. The town runs junior and adult clinics for all levels (including tots) and provides private lessons. It also sponsors a junior and adult town tennis tournament which attracts some very good players. Call 203.618.7613 for information, a map of the courts and tennis permit information. For more information call Contact Greenwich Parks & Recreation, 203.622.7821.

- Directions to Town Tennis Courts

  www.greenwichct.org/ParksAndRec/prDirectionsTennis.asp

Courts are available at:

Binney Park, Bruce Park, Byram Shore Park, Central Middle School, Christiano Park, Eastern Greenwich Civic Center, Eastern Middle School, Greenwich High School, Loughlin Ave. Park, Western Middle School, Pemberwick Park. The lights at the Eastern Greenwich Civic Center are usually on until 10 pm.

- Tennis Passes

www.greenwichct.org/ParksAndRec/prTennis.asp
Resident's tennis card is $31 for the season. Guest cards are $60. Cards are available at Town Hall Lobby, Park Pass Office, Monday-Thursday.

- Tennis Court Reservations

Tennis reservations must be by phone. Call 203.622.2210 starting in May.

- Platform Tennis

www.greenwichct.org/Search/?q=platform+tennis
The town has two Platform Tennis courts, located at Loughlin Avenue in Cos Cob. This 6-acre park has the only public paddle tennis courts in Greenwich. The courts are lighted and can be used by Greenwich residents and their guests. Courts are open October to April. Seasonal permits amazingly cost $325 for residents. Lights are on Tuesday-Thursday, dusk to 9pm. When you purchase a permit you should register for two 1-hr time slots per week. For information or cancellations call 203.618.7650 or 203.622.7830.

Griffith Harris Memorial Golf Course

1300 King Street, Greenwich CT, 203.531.7200, for reservations 203.531.8253 www.greenwichct.org/ParksAndRec/prGolfCourse.asp
Open only to Greenwich residents (including tenants). This par 71, 18-hole golf course designed by Robert Trent Jones has a clubhouse, pro shop, putting green and driving range. Call about obtaining a membership card. You must complete the application form from the golf course office. You will need to bring proof of Greenwich residency (such as a current phone bill) and a photo ID such as a driver's license. Membership is $165 for an adult permanent resident.

Hunter Mountain (Skiing)

Route 23A, Hunter NY, 800.486.8376
www.huntermtn.com
Difficulty: Beginner, Intermediate, Advanced.
Size: 12 lifts, 53 trails, snowmaking, snow tubing.
Distance: 2.5 hrs from Greenwich.

Hunting and Trapping (Guide and Maps)

Guide and Wildlife area maps can be obtained from the Town Clerk's office, 203.622.7894 or online at:
http://dep.state.ct.us/burnatr/wildlife/fguide/fgindex.htm, click on Outdoor Recreation.

Indian Harbor Yacht Club Sailing
710 Steamboat Road, Greenwich CT, 203.869.2484
Ask for the Sailing Office. One of the few private clubs with a sailing program open to the public. The program has such a good reputation that it is usually filled by February.

Jim Fixx Memorial Day Race
Greenwich Recreation Office, 203.622.7830 or
Threads and Treads, 17 East Putnam Avenue, Greenwich, 203.661.0142
www.Threadsandtreads.com
The Jim Fixx Memorial 5-mile race starts and ends on Greenwich Avenue. It is usually in May and begins the running season. If you run in no other event, you should consider it. It is always well-attended and attracts a great variety of talented and not-so-talented runners.

K & L Soaring
5996 State Route 224, Cayuta NY, 607.594.3329 www.klsoaring.com
A good place to purchase the Schweizer Soaring School Manual before you go for a glider lesson. They are about 4 hours from Greenwich.

Kang Tae-Kwon-Do & Hapkido (Karate)
263 Sound Beach Ave, Old Greenwich CT, 203.637.7867
www.kangtaekwandohapkido.com
One of several locations run by Grand Master Ik Jo Kang.

Kayak Adventure
24 Poplar Street, Norwalk CT, Cell: 203.247.1390
www.kayak-adventure.net
Instruction & day trips on the Long Island Sound.

Kayak/Canoe Guide
SWRPA (South Western Regional Planning Agency) publishes a full-color laminated guide to help you find your way around Norwalk's 23-island archipelago. SWRPA is located at 888 Washington Blvd in Stamford. Call 203.316.5190 for a copy.

Kelsey Farm (Horseback Riding)
1016 Lake Avenue, Greenwich CT 203.869.5595 www.kelseyfarm.com
Kelsey Farm, a family business, has been teaching kids to ride and compete since 1949. They have an excellent reputation. They run a terrific summer camp where they teach their students to groom, tack up, care for and learn all about their mounts. They pride themselves on making "horsemen and women" not just riders.

Kempo Academy of Martial Arts (Shaolin & Kung Fu Karate)
450 East Putnam Avenue, Cos Cob CT, 203.769.1444
www.KempoKarateCT.com
They teach Shaolin Kempo Karate, Kung Fu and cardio kickboxing for children and adults. They have classes the whole family can try together.

Killington Resort (Skiing)
4763 Killington Road, Killington VT, 800.621.6867, 802.422.6200
www.killington.com
One of the areas largest and most popular ski resorts. Spread out over six mountains, it has 141 trails and has a very extensive snowmaking system.

Kittatinny Canoes (Canoeing, Kayaking , Rafting)
Dingmans Ferry PA, 800.356.2852, 570.828.2338
www.kittatinny.com
Canoeing, kayaking or rafting the Delaware. Calm water for families or beginners, white water for experts. Paintball and dual racing ziplines. They are about 2 hours from Greenwich.

Lake of Isles Golf Course
1 Clubhouse Drive, North Stonington CT (Near Foxwoods Casino), 888.475.3746
www.lakeofisles.com
36-hole top-rated golf course and golf academy.

Liberty Paintball
(Thunder Ridge Ski Area) 1 Thunder Ridge Road, Patterson NY, 845.878.6300
www.libertypaintball-ny.com
350 acres of varied terrain just North and West of Danbury, CT and about an hour north of Greenwich. Friends tell us they rate it 5 stars. They suggest beginners bring their own group of about 20-participants and rent equipment there. Kids' parties require a group of 15. Don't forget to wear protective clothing. Laser Tag locations are described in CHILDREN.

SPORTS

Licenses and Permits
• Fishing Licenses can be purchased in our Town Clerk's office, 203.622.7897. They are good for the calendar year.
There is usually good trout fishing at the Mianus River Park, Merrybrook Road (Cognewaugh Road), 203.622.7814. Be sure you have your license, they do check. See section on PARKS & BEACHES for directions.
• Hunting Licenses are issued by the Connecticut Department of Environmental Protection, (DEP License and Revenue Unit, 79 Elm Street, Hartford, CT 06106-5127). License applications can be obtained from the Town Clerk's office, 203.622.7897.
• Landowner Deer Permit can be obtained from the Town Clerk's office, 203.622.7897. It is required to hunt deer on your own property.
• Parking Permits
Parking permits are available through the Department of Parking Services, contact Christina Gorbal, 203.622.7730.
www.greenwichct.org/Parking/psParkingPermits.asp
• Park/Beach/Daily Passes
Day passes are available at Town Hall, 101 Field Point Road. The Park Pass Office is open Monday through Friday, 8:00am to 3:45pm or at the Eastern and Western Civic Centers. Passes are required from May 1 through October 31. Leashed dogs are only allowed from December 1 through March 31. New residents can get an application from the Park Pass Office at Town Hall or on line at: www.greenwichct.org/government/departments/parks_and_recreation/park_beach_tennis_passes.
• See Greenwich Tennis Headquarters above for information on Tennis and Paddle Tennis passes.

Lifetime Adult and Junior Tennis
Lifetime Fitness. See review in FITNESS.

Lime Rock Park (Auto Racing)
60 White Hollow Road, Lakeville CT, 800.435.5000
www.limerock.com
About two hours north of Greenwich is the Lime Rock Race Track. The track is closed on Sundays, but most Saturdays (from early April to November) there are formula and sports car races. Lime Rock has no grandstands. You can get tickets online or at the gate. Call to find out about the race schedule or to get a copy of their free newspaper, Track Record. The biggest race days are usually Memorial Day and Labor Day.

Lionshare Farm (Riding)
404 Taconic Road, Greenwich CT, 203.869.4649
www.lionsharefarm.com
An excellent riding academy with programs for children and adults. The farm, owned by Peter Leone, an Olympic silver medalist, has two indoor rings and an outdoor ring, as well as access to the Greenwich trails. It is the premier show jumping stable in the Greenwich area. This is a good place to go if you want to buy a jumper.

Longshore Sailing School
260 Compo Road South, Westport CT, 203.226.4646
www.longshoresailingschool.com
If you or your children (ages 9-16) want to learn to sail and can't get into one of the Greenwich programs, try this school in Westport. It provides instruction from basic sailing to racing techniques. Register in February for two-week sessions blending fun and substance.

Magic Touch Fishing Charters
www.MagicTouchCharters.com
Captain Andrew Fox, 914.563.2743
The 30-foot Stormy Gale II is moored in Byram behind Rudy's Tackle Barn (242 South Water Street). Captain Fox runs a fishing charter for one to six passengers.

Maple Moor Golf Course
1128 North Street, White Plains NY, 914.995.9200
Automated reservations: 914.995.4653
http://golf.westchestergov.com/maple-moor-golf-course
Par 71, You can reserve seven days in advance.

Mead Farm (Riding)
107 June Road, Stamford CT, 203.322.4984
www.meadfarm.com
They give outdoor riding lessons for boys and girls 5-17. No previous riding experience is required. Located at the Greenwich/Stamford border, the stable has access to 150 miles of Greenwich trails. Their June through August pony summer camp is extremely popular. Sign up early. Campers have fun riding, learning horse etiquette and how to tack and clean their horses.

SPORTS

Men's Basketball Leagues (Basketball)
Call Department of Parks & Recreation 203.622.7821 for information.
A recreation program from January through March at the Eastern Greenwich Civic Center, Central and Eastern Middle School. Programs for Town resident teams, B and C corporate teams.

Mianus River (Ice Skating, Canoeing)
Park off of Valley Road, bring your skates and hockey sticks (a snow shovel, too).

Mianus River Park (Walking)
Cognewaugh Road, Cos Cob, 203.622.7814
www.greenwichct.org/ParksAndRec/prFacilitiesIndex.asp
220 acres stretching from Greenwich into Stamford. The entrance is ½ mile east of Stanwich Road on Cognewaugh Road. The two trails we think are of most interest are the Pond Trail and the Oak Trail.

Mohawk Mountain (Skiing)
46 Great Hollow Road, Cornwall, CT, 860.672.6100, 800.895.5222
www.mohawkmtn.com
Difficulty: Beginner & Intermediate.
Size: 5 lifts, 24 trails, snowmaking, night skiing.
Distance: 1.5 hrs, I-95 N to Rte 8 N to exit 44.

Montgomery Pinetum Park (Walking)
Bible Street, Cos Cob, 203.622.7814
www.greenwichct.org/ParksAndRec/prFacilitiesIndex.asp
91 acres, just off of Bible Street in Cos Cob. The entrance is on the west side directly opposite Clover Place. Obtain a map and tree guide from the Garden Center office, then enjoy the extraordinary diversity of trees and plantings. One path leads to the 22-acre Greenwich Audubon Society's Mildred Bedard Caldwell Wildlife Sanctuary.

Mount Snow Ski Resort
12 Pisgah Road, West Dover VT, 800.451.4211, 800.245.7669
www.mountsnow.com
A large and very popular ski resort about 3 hours North of Greenwich.

SPORTS

Mount Southington (Skiing)

396 Mount Vernon Road, Plainsville CT, 860.628.0954, 800.982.6828
www.mountsouthington.com
Difficulty: Beginner & Intermediate.
Size: 7 lifts, 14 trails, snowmaking, night skiing.
2 hours north of Greenwich, I-84 N exit 30.

Mount Tom / Suicide 6 (Skiing, Hiking, Fishing)

Woodstock VT, Information: 802.457.6661, Snow Phone: 802.457.6666
www.suicide6.com
www.woodstockvt.com/hiking.php
A great place to learn to ski in the winter, wonderful hiking in the summer -all in a town beautified by Laurance Rockefeller. The Woodstock Inn is the place to stay. (www.woodstockinn.com, 800.448.7900). It's about 4 hours north of Greenwich.

New York Sailing School (Sailing)

22 Pelham Road, New Rochelle NY, 914.235.6052
www.nyss.com
Sailing programs for all skill levels. Take their course and then rent a boat to practice your sailing.

Nike Adult Sports Schools and Junior Camps

800.645.3226
www.ussportscamps.com
Nike sponsors a great number of adult and junior sports camps: tennis, golf, volleyball, hockey, soccer, lacrosse, softball, baseball, rugby, water polo and more.

Northcamp (Wilderness Survival Skills)

www.NorthCampSurvival.com
Steve Lancia (203.496.1102) teaches a 3 hour class on basic survival as well as a wilderness weekend class learning survival skills and how to survive hardships.

Norwalk Rowing Association (Rowing)

1 Moodys Lane, Norwalk CT, 203.866.0080
www.NorwalkRiverRowing.org
Adult and youth programs range from learn-to-row to racing. Youth programs start in the 6th grade.

North American Outdoor Adventure
(White Water Rafting, Snowmobiling)
West Forks ME, 800.727.4379, 207.663.4472
www.nawhitewater.com
Whitewater rafting from Maine to Connecticut, as well as kayaking, canoeing,
snowmobiling and hunting primarily in Maine.

Northeast Saltwater Fishing Magazine
www.noreast.com
A publication devoted to Northeast Sportfishing.

Norwalk Karting Association
124 Spring Hill Avenue, Norwalk CT, 203.246.3386
http://www.norwalkkartingassociation.net/
NKA is a go kart racing club located in Norwalk Connecticut. They race at
Calf Pasture Beach on the weekend.

Nutmeg Curling Club
123 Blenwood Avenue, Bridgeport CT, 203.615.0077
www.NutmegCurling.com
Open October to late March.

Oak Hills Golf Course (Golf)
165 Fillow Street, Norwalk CT, 203.838.0303   www.oakhillsgc.com
Par 71; you can reserve seven days ahead for weekdays only. They have
an automated tee time reservation system.

Okemo Mountain (Skiing)
77 Okemo Ridge Road, Ludlow VT, 800.786.5366; Snow reports
800.228.5222
www.Okemo.com
A family ski place with lodging right on the slopes, about 4 hours north
of Greenwich. 5 mountain areas serviced by 19 lifts. Great training programs for the younger skier, starting at age 2.

Old Greenwich School of Karate (Karate)
242 Sound Beach Avenue (Action Arts), Old Greenwich CT, 203.637.2685
www.ogkarate.com
Japanese Isshinryu Karate and Filipino Jitsu taught by 6th dan Sensei
Rick Zimmerman.

SPORTS

Old Greenwich-Riverside Community Center
See Eastern Greenwich Civic Center above.

Old Greenwich Tennis Academy
151 Sound Beach Avenue, Old Greenwich CT, 203.637.3398
www.OldGreenwichTennisacademy.com
5 indoor HarTru courts. Often used by groups who contract for court time. Open September to May, they have Junior and Adult programs for all levels.

On Track Karting
984 North Colony Road (Rt 5), Wallingford CT, 203.626.0464
www.Ontrackkarting.com
Adult and Junior racing in a 63,000 sf indoor karting facility.

Outward Bound (Adventure Trips)
910 Jackson Street, Golden CO, 866.467.7651   www.outwardbound.org
It was founded in Greenwich in 1961 and offers adventure-based learning to develop personal growth through experience and challenge. One of its five core programs is climbing.

Overland Experts (Auto Racing)
112 Hemlock Valley Road, East Haddam CT, 860.873.9640
www.overlandexperts.com
4WD on and off-road driving instruction as well as international expeditions.

Ox Ridge Hunt Club (Riding)
512 Middlesex Road, Darien CT, 203.655.2559   www.oxridge.com
There are many places to learn to ride, but serious riders will like Ox Ridge. This private hunt club gives public riding lessons and summer camps for fun and experienced riders. You will find good horses, indoor and outdoor facilities and top instructors.

Pegasus Therapeutic Riding Inc (Riding)
845.669.8235   www.pegasustr.org
Non-profit organization provides riding as therapy for disabled children and adults.

Performance Flight (Flying Training, Aircraft Rental)
136 Tower Lane, Hanger M, Westchester County Airport, 914.397.1444
They train, charter planes with pilots, rent planes and manage owner's planes.

Personal Pro Services (Tennis)
May-October, Greenwich, 203.962.2673;
November-April, Scottsdale Arizona, 480.575.9702.
Tim Richardson is a USPTA Pro 1 tennis instructor. During the playing season, Tim will help you perfect your tennis game in the privacy of your own court and on your own schedule. Tim has been teaching on private Greenwich courts for almost 20 years.

Pickleball
Christiano Park Courts, 25 Lyon Avenue (off Holly Hill Lane) Greenwich
www.usapa.org
For information call Greenwich Parks and Recreation Department, 203.622.7814. It's played on a small court with a light racket and a wiffle-like ball. No permit is required.

Powder Ridge (Skiing, Snowboarding, Tubing, Mountain Biking)
99 Powder Hill Road, Middlefield CT, 860.349.3454
www.powderridgepark.com
Difficulty: Beginner & Intermediate.
Size: 7 lifts (2 for tubing), 5 wide runs, 14 trails, night skiing.
Distance: 45 minutes, Merritt Pkw N exit 67.

Red Barn Stables (Riding)
43 Bangall Road, Stamford CT, 203.223.3358
Family run, affordable facility with 200'x100' lighted indoor riding arena, indoor riding stables, boarding, horses for sale and lighted working pens, private lessons and birthday parties. Nearby access to Greenwich trails.

Rex Dive Center (Diving Instruction)
144 Water Street, South Norwalk CT, 203.853.4148
www.rexdivecenter.com
A good place to go for your scuba equipment. You will be greeted by a friendly, knowledgeable staff. They provide lessons for beginners. See review in STORES.

Rex Marine Center (Boating)
144 Water Street, South Norwalk CT, 203.866.5555
50 Calf Pasture Beach Road, East Norwalk CT, 203.604.1295
www.rexmarine.com
You can charter a boat with a captain. The Rex Boating Club provides training and rental boats. See review in STORES.

Richter Park Golf Course (Golf)
100 Aunt Hack Road, Danbury CT, 203.792.2550
www.richterpark.com
Considered to be the top public course in Connecticut. 18 holes, weekday starting times can be reserved 3 days in advance; slots start at 9 am.

Ridgefield Golf Course (Golf)
545 Ridgebury Road, Ridgefield CT, 203.748.7008
www.RidgeFieldGC.com
Par 71; you can reserve up to 3 days ahead for weekends.

Running Events in Greenwich
For Information contact: Threads and Treads
17 East Putnam Avenue, Greenwich, 203.661.0142
www.Threadsandtreads.com
This fine outfitting store has sponsored and created all kinds of running events for our town. Stop in to find out about running events all over Fairfield County. Typical events are the Greenwich Cup Biathlon, Greenwich Cup Triathlon, The Tour De Greenwich, Beach Front Bushwack and Jingle Bell Jog. The Jim Fixx Memorial 5-mile race starts and ends on Greenwich Avenue. It is usually in May and begins the running season. If you run in no other event, you should consider it. It is always well-attended and attracts a great variety of talented and not-so-talented runners.

Saxon Woods (Golf)
315 Mamaroneck Road, Scarsdale NY, 914.231.3461
Automated reservations: 914.995.4653
http://golf.westchestergov.com/saxon-woods-golf-course-
18 hole, Par 69 and driving range.

Shaolin Studios (Kempo Karate)
397 East Putnam Avenue, Cos Cob CT, 203.661.5501
www.sdsskungfu.com
Private and group lessons for adults (16+), teens (12-15) and kids (4-6 & 7-11) in martial arts and self defense. An interesting place to hold a birthday party.

SPORTS

Shell Fishing

Due to the efforts of our wonderful Shellfish Commission (which is working to restore the oyster beds in Greenwich waters), residents can have the fun of digging for shellfish (clams and oysters) in the sand at Greenwich Point. A season permit is required and can be obtained from the Town Clerk's office. The season starts about mid-October, but call 203.622.7777 first to learn which beds are open.

Shidogakuin (Iaido)

Shidogakuni Dojo, 100 Research Drive, Stamford CT, 630.414.6644
Send mail to 38 Mary Lane, Riverside, CT 06878.
www.kendoka.org

Shippan Racquet Club

45 Harbor Drive, Stamford, 203.323.3129
www.shippanracquet.com
Junior, adult clinics & ATP program on their 6 hard courts.

(The) Ski & Scuba Connection (Scuba Lessons)

26 Saint Roch Avenue, Byram CT, 203.629.4766
www.SkiAndScubaConnection.com
Scuba lessons and equipment for scuba or snorkeling. See review in STORES.

Skip Barber Racing School (Auto Racing)

Lime Rock Park, 60 White Hollow Road, Salisbury CT, 860.435.1300
www.skipbarber.com, http://skipbarber.com/track/lime-rock-race-track
Skip Barber is the largest racing school in the country. If you have always wanted to learn to race, this is the place to go. Two basic driving courses are offered, with a lot of variations for each course: Advanced Driving School (one and two-day courses driving three different cars supplied by the school); Racing School (three hours to eight days). The school supplies the formula cars.

Small Boat Shop (Kayak Instruction)

144 Water Street (in Rex Marine), Norwalk CT, 203.854.5223
www.thesmallboatshop.com
A shop offering tours, instruction and rentals. See Review in STORES.

SPORTS

Soaring Adventures of America
800.762.7464, 203.762.9583   www.800soaring.com
They have 200 locations in the US for hot air balloons, soaring and skydiving. Call them to arrange for a fun adventure for you or your family.

Solaris Indoor Tennis Club
23 Radio Place, Stamford CT, 203.359.0601
www.stamford.solarisclubs.com
6 courts and excellent instruction. On most Friday nights from 8pm, Hank Silverston (203.324.3397) runs a terrific late-night doubles party for players who love the sport.

Sound Cyclists (Bicycling)
PO Box 1144, Darien CT   www.SoundCyclists.com
This social cycling club offers, at no cost, rides for all levels of ability led by experienced cyclists. Routes are along scenic coastlines and country roads and vary from 12 miles to 60+ miles. To join, contact them by email through their website.

Sound Environmental Associates (Boating Courses)
800.510.9995   www.seadolphin.com
One-day Safe Boating and PWC Jet Ski courses to meet Connecticut requirements. Courses are held around the state and are usually held Saturday or Sunday 9am-5pm.

Sound Fishing Charters
Byram Dock, Captain Kevin Reynolds
1-11 Willett Avenue, Port Chester NY, 203.255.4522
www.snowgoose2.com
Starting in April, they sail 7 days a week. Join a group or rent the boat for a private party.

Sound Sailing Center (Sailing Instruction)
54A Calf Pasture Beach Road, Norwalk CT, 203.838.1110, After hours, call 203.454.4394.   www.SoundsailingCenter.com
US Sailing Certified Instruction as well as sailboat rentals & charters on 23 foot-44 foot sailboats. Selected to manage the Old Greenwich Yacht Club sailing program, SSC focuses on adult education at its Norwalk Harbor facility.

SPORTS

Sound Shore Tennis
303 Post Road, Port Chester NY, 914.939.1300
www.SoundShoreIndoorTennis.com
Twelve indoor hard surface courts. Open September to May and rain-only weekends after May.

Sparky Charters (Fishing)
Riverscape Marina on the Mianus, Cos Cob CT, Captain Hank Weis, 914.769.1447   www.sparkycharters.com
An experienced fisherman will lead you to the fish in his 28-foot boat "Sparky."

Sports Car Driving Association (Auto Racing)
23 Belmont Avenue, Deep River CT, 516.500.7232
www.scda1.com
SCDA provides drivers of all skills the opportunity to experience high-performance driving. Events are strictly educational and non-competitive. They operate out of Watkins Glen NY, Thompson Speedway CT, Lime Rock CT, Monticello NY and other locations.

Sportsman's Den (Fishing)
33 River Road, Cos Cob, 203.869.3234
Supplies and classes on angling and fly fishing. Get your fishing license here. See Review in STORES.

Sports Center of Connecticut
784 River Road (Route 110) Shelton CT, 203.929.6500
www.sportscenterct.com
About 50 minutes north of Greenwich, they have a golf driving range, 18 hole mini-golf course, jungle-themed laser tag arena, bowling, game zone arcade, baseball/softball batting cages and ice skating.

Stamford Fencing Center (Saber, Foil, Epee)
425 Fairfield Avenue, Stamford CT, 203.989.0080
www.StamfordFencingCenter.com
Private and group classes for adults and children. They will work with kids as young as 5 years old.

SPORTS

Stamford Kayak Meetup Group
www.meetup.com/stamfordKayakgroup
The Stamford Kayak Group is a local group of paddling enthusiasts looking to meet up with others who share the same interest. This group is for people of all skill levels. They meet in the Stamford, Greenwich and Rowayton areas. They were founded in 2007 and have over 400 members. Email them through the website to join.

Stamford Twin Rinks (Ice Skating and Ice Hockey)
1063 Hope Street, Stamford CT, 203.968.9000
www.StamfordTwinRinks.com
They have a wide variety of programs for all levels and interests.

Sterling Farms (Golf)
1349 Newfield Avenue, Stamford CT, 203.461.9090
www.sterlingfarmsgc.com
Par 72, 18 hole golf course and driving range. On weekends, non-residents can play after 2:30pm. You can reserve up to seven days in advance.

Sterling Farms Tennis Center (Tennis)
1349 Newfield Avenue, Stamford CT, 203.561.7713
www.sterlingfarmsgc.com
Located on the grounds of Sterling Farms Golf Course, the tennis facility has 6 outdoor courts. Spring session begins May 1; Summer session begins June 26; Junior Camp begins about June 12.

Stowe Mountain Resort (Skiing)
5781 Mountain Road, Stowe VT, 802.253.3000
www.stowe.com
The premier ski mountain on the East Coast has every activity from Dog Sledding to a wellness center. Like all of the major ski resorts they also have a variety of summer programs, such as: horseback riding, hiking, tennis, inflatable obstacle course and Alpine slides.

Stratford Stables (Riding)
120 Cottage Avenue, Purchase NY, 914.939.9294
www.StratfordStables.net
Seven acre boarding and training facility, which includes an 80' X 200' indoor arena. Lessons for beginners through advanced ages 6 and up, with a specialty in training for show.

SPORTS

Stratton Mountain Resort (Ski & Golf)
Stratton Mountain (South Londonderry) VT, 802.297.4000
www.stratton.com
Stratton is another major ski destination. During the summer it is the home of the David Leadbetter Golf Academy, 800.787.2886

State Forest Camping Areas
(Camping, Trap Shooting, Fishing & Hunting)
Campsites are usually available May-September.
www.ct.gov/deep/site/default.asp and click on Outdoor Recreation.
There are 11 Connecticut State Park camping areas and 2 State Forest camping areas. The State Forests also have equestrian campgrounds.

Sugarloaf (Skiing)
5092 Access Road, Carrabassett Valley Maine, 207.237.2000
www.sugarloaf.com (See website for lodging and other information.)
Sugarloaf is the only above-the-timberline ski area in the East. Sugarloaf has excellent beginner and intermediate trails as well as a Nordic ski area and even double black diamond trails for the adventurous. Sugarloaf has 1,400 skiable acres and 138 trails. It usually has great snow, but can be very cold. Sugarloaf is about 7 hours from Greenwich. During the summer they have an adult golf school and a Nike Junior Golf School.

Tiger Schulmann's (Karate)
2770 Summer Street, Stamford CT, 203.969.0352, 203.388.1091
www.tsk.com
The largest Mixed Martial Arts training school in the United States, with over 45 schools in five states. They teach self-defense skills combining karate, Thai kickboxing and submission grappling.

Trout Unlimited, Mianus Chapter (Fishing)
Mianus TU, P.O. Box 475, Wilton, CT 06897
www.mianustu.org
Non-profit organization dedicated to preserving water quality. The Mianus Chapter has over 500 members living in the Greenwich, Stamford, Darien, Norwalk, New Canaan, Ridgefield and Wilton communities. Classes in fly fishing and fly tying.

United States Tennis Association
70 West Red Oak Lane, White Plains NY, 914.696.7000
Membership services: 800.990.8782   www.usta.com
National governing body for the sport of tennis. Join and play in a league.

Westchester Flying Club (Flying)
Westchester County Airport
www.wfc-hpn.org Click on Contact for numbers or email.
Westchester Flying Club provides economical flying for its members.

Westchester Golf Range
701 Dobbs Ferry Road, White Plains NY, 914.592.6553
www.westchester-golfrange.com
Professional instruction available. Privately owned.

Western Greenwich Civic Center
a.k.a. Bendheim Greenwich Civic Center
449 Pemberwick Road, Glenville CT, 203.532.1259
www.greenwichct.org/ParksAndRec/prFacilityPrograms.asp
The Center has programs for a variety of activities such as weight lifting, fitness and exercise, roller skating, basketball, indoor soccer, youth and adult ballet, indoor field hockey, fencing (See Greenwich Fencing), Tennis for Tots, kendo, guitar lessons, theater and dance classes, karate classes, coed volleyball, little language league, chess club, boot camp and sports clinics for children. They are also the site of a child care/ children's day school.

Whiteface Mountain
(Skiing, Skating, Bobsled, Cross Country, Jumping)
Lake Placid, Route 86, Wilmington NY, 518.946.2223
www.Whiteface.com
Site of the 1980 Winter Olympics, besides great skiing, the Olympic Sports Complex has bobsledding, cross country, ski jumping and skating. The Olympic Center runs a variety of programs for figure skaters training for regional, national and international competitions. For more information on training, visit www.lakeplacidskating.com

White Tiger Tae Kwon Do (Karate)
181 Greenwich Avenue (second Floor), 203.661.6054
www.wttkd.com
Master Kwan Ji, 5th Degree Black Belt, teaches adult and junior classes.

TIP: OX RIDGE HORSE SHOW
Enjoy the nationally-acclaimed hunter-jumper competition in June at the Ox Ridge Hunt Club in Darien, CT. Olympic as well as local riders compete in this Grand Prix event. Call 203.655.2559 for details or visit www.oxridge.com .

Wiffle Ball

www.GreenwichWiffle.com

www.facebook.com/greenwichwiffle.bal

Wiffle Ball has taken hold in Greenwich. The Boys and Girls Club http://bgcg.org/imagineadventures has a wiffle Ball travel team. The United Way gave the town a gift of $25,625 to build a removable Wiffle Ball field at Byram Shore Park. No town license is required to play.

Windham Mountain (Skiing and Golf)

Windham NY, 518.734.4300, Snow report hotline 800.729.4766

www.skiwindham.com

Difficulty: Beginner, Intermediate & Expert.

Size: 33 trails, 7 lifts, snowmaking. Distance: 2.5 hrs

Winding Trails Cross Country Ski Center

50 Winding Trails Drive, Farmington CT, 860.677.8458

www.windingtrails.com

Difficulty: Beginner, Intermediate.

Size: 20 Kilometers of trails in 350 acres of woodland, lakes and wildlife. Distance: 2.5 hrs.

Windy Hill Figure Skating Club

www.windyhillsc.com

Non-profit skating club affiliated with the US Figure Skating Association. Membership is open to all figure skaters who have progressed beyond "Basic 6." Home ice is the Dorothy Hamill Rink.

Wire Mill Racquet Club

578 Wire Mill Road, Stamford, 203.329.9221

www.leontennis.net

Just off exit 35 of the Merritt Parkway, Wire Mill (four outdoor red clay courts) is owned by the pros who teach in the winter at the Greenwich Racquet Club. Excellent junior and adult programs. The season is May to September. There is no membership fee.

Women's Self Defense

Greenwich Police Department, Community Impact Section, 203.618.8308

Taught by the Greenwich Police Department, the Self Defense Course runs 5 weeks, two nights a week. Each session is about two hours.

Yachting Magazine

www.yachtingmagazine.com
Published in Norwalk, this is the magazine for sailors. Subscribe from the website.

YMCA (a.k.a. Greenwich Family Y)

50 East Putnam Avenue, Greenwich CT, 203.869.1630
www.gwymca.org, www.greenwichymca.org
The Y is open to men and women. You should consider joining, but you don't have to be a member to use their facilities. The Y spent $6,000,000 to build an Olympic size pool. As you might expect they have some terrific swimming programs for adults and children of all ages. The YMCA is the home of the Marlins youth swim and diving teams, ages 6-18. The Y has an impressive weight room and programs for a variety of activities such as aerobics, studio cycling (spinning), baseball, basketball and yoga, Pilates, Zumba, indoor tennis, cardio dance, boot camp and many others. There is a flag football league and informal, co-ed volleyball games for adults. The Y has gymnastics programs for ages 12 months to 12 years. Experienced babysitters are usually available to watch children while you work out.

YWCA

259 East Putnam Avenue, Greenwich, 203.869.6501
Adrianne Singer, President and CEO
www.YWCAGreenwich.org
The Y provides supervised round-robin youth badminton for all skill levels and hosts tournaments sanctioned by the USA Badminton Association. The Y has a good indoor pool and many swimming programs. The YWCA is the home of the Dolphins swim team, a major competitor of the YMCA's swim team. In addition the Y hosts a great variety of programs, including bridge lessons from beginner to advanced, tournament bridge, Zumba, youth & adult ballet, fitness classes, belly dancing, mat Pilates, spinning, climbing wall, basketball clinics, soccer, gymnastics, SCUBA certification, tennis, weight room, personal training, yoga, tai chi and many more classes. The Y has gymnastics programs for ages 16 months to 12 years. Experienced babysitters are available to watch children while you work out.

STORE INDEX

Store Hours: *Stores change their hours frequently; the hours given should only be used as a guide. Stores often move in and out of town, not surprising with rents running $85 to $150 a square foot. At these prices it's hard for a local store to survive unless it is supported by town residents. Shopping at these stores keeps our cherished stores in business.*

FOOD STORES: *Grocery stores, ethnic food markets, fruit & vegetables, cheese shops, butchers, seafood and spices are described in GROCERY AND SPECIALTY FOOD STORES. Bakeries, Delicatessens and Wine each have their own section. Ice Cream and Chocolates are in their own section.*

Pharmacies, vitamins, exercise equipment, health products and services are reviewed under the section HEALTH.
Pet Services are reviewed under the section PETS.
Video Rentals are described in the section CULTURE, under Movies: Video & DVD.
Spas are reviewed in the section GROOMING.

Accessories
Accessories for Men & Women are listed under Shoes & Accessories.
Home Accessories are listed under Home Decorating & Accessories.
Linens are listed under Bedding.

Antiques
Antique Area of Stamford
   Greenwich Antique and Artisan
      Center
   Greenwich Living Antiques
   Hamptons Antique Galleries
   Harbor View Center for Antiques
   Hiden Galleries
   John Street Antiques
Braswell Galleries (antiques & auctions)
Greenwich Oriental Art
Rue Faubourg St. Honore
United House Wrecking
Vallin Galleries
(A) Woodhouse & Sons

Aquariums
Aquariums are listed under, Fish.

Appliances, Kitchen Equipment and Cookware
Bath and Kitchen fixtures are listed under Fixtures
Aitoro Appliances
Bed Bath & Beyond
Cook and Craft
Crate & Barrel
Globe Kitchen Equipment
Harris Restaurant Supply
PC Richard
Vinci's Home Products (Miele)
Williams-Sonoma

STORE INDEX

Art
(Galleries, Supplies, Framing)
Abby M Taylor
Bendheim Gallery
Cavalier Galleries
Colonial Framing
Flinn Gallery
(A.I.) Friedman
Galerie Greenwich
Images
J Pocker & Son
Michaels
Miranda Arts Project Space
(C.) Parker Gallery
Samuel Owen Galleries
Silvermine Arts Center
Weber Fine Art
Zorya Fine Art

Auto Part Stores
Automobile and Motorcycle Dealers are listed under the section AUTO-MOBILES.
Advance Auto Parts
Auto Zone
Delta Auto Parts / CarQuest

Babies/Toddlers
(Clothing, Furniture, Equipment for Babies and Toddlers)
Anna Banana
Babies "R" Us
Bellini Juvenile Designer Furniture
Buy Buy Baby
Carter's
Gap Kids
Giggle
Jacadi
Janie and Jack
Maclaren Showroom

Bathroom and Kitchen
Tile is listed under Flooring.
Bath and Kitchen fixtures are listed under Fixtures.

Bedding
(Mattresses and Linens)
Bed Bath & Beyond
(The) Clean Bedroom
Duxiana Beds
Hastens
Home Boutique of Greenwich
Lexington Clothing Co.
Linen Press
Lynnens
Norwalk Mattress Company
Sleepy's

Bicycles
Dave's Cycle and Fitness
Greenwich Bicycles
River Bicycles
Signature Cycles

Blinds
Blinds and Shutters are listed under Windows.
Draperies, Curtains, Fabric & Upholstery are listed under Fabric .

Boating
See section SPORTS for boating instruction and information.
Landfall Navigation
Rex Marine Center (Small Boat Shop)

STORE INDEX

Book Stores

See Section BOOKS & LIBRARIES for donations, stores and book sales. The following bookstores are listed in that section.

- Barnes & Noble, 203.323.1248
- Diane's Books, 203.869.1515
- (A) Timeless Journey, 203.353.1720

Cameras

Cameras are listed under Photography.

Carpets

Carpets are listed under Flooring.

Cell Phones

Cells phones are listed under Wireless.

Children

Baby & Toddler Clothing, Furniture, Equipment are listed under Babies. Children's furniture in listed under Furniture.
Toys and outdoor play items are listed under Toys.
Clothing & Shoes for Children and Youth are listed under Clothing-Shoes.

Clothing - Children and Youth

Sportswear, including athletic shoes, is listed under Sporting Goods.
Equestrian wear is listed under Riding.
Scouting and Team Uniforms are listed under Clothing - Children Uniforms.

Anna Banana
Brandy USA
Beam & Barre (dance wear)
Boast
Carter's
Children's Cottage
Claire's
Darien Sport Shop
Everything But Water
Gap
Gap Kids
Janie and Jack
Lacoste Boutique
Lilly Pulitzer
Sound Beach Sportswear
Splendid
Steven Alan
Vineyard Vines
Vilebrequin
Wishlist

Clothing - Children and Youth Uniforms

Scout Uniforms
Darien Sport Shop
Team Uniforms
Bruce Park Sports
Lacrosse Unlimited
Rink and Racquet

STORE INDEX

Clothing - Men
Shoes & Accessories and Department Stores are listed separately. Men's Sporting wear is listed under Sporting Goods.
See SERVICES for tailors.
Banana Republic
Boast
Brooks Brothers
Casablanca
Club Monaco
Coppola Tailors (Tuxedos)
Darien Sport Shop
Everything But Water
Gap
J Crew
Jack Wills
JoS A Bank
Lacoste Boutique
Lands' End
Lucky Jeans
Rag & Bone
Ralph Lauren
Richards of Greenwich
Scoop
Steven Alan
Vilebrequin
Vince
Vineyard Vines

Clothing - Women
(including maternity clothing)
See SERVICES for tailors.
Shoes & Accessories are listed under Clothing - Shoes, handbags and Accessories.
Department Stores are listed separately.
Lingerie is listed under Clothing-Lingerie
Women's Sporting wear is listed under Sporting Goods.
Women's Exercise wear is listed under Clothing - Women's Exercise.
Albe Furs & Outerwear
Alease Fisher
Alice + Olivia
Amina Rubinacci
Ann Taylor
Ann Taylor LOFT
Anne Fontaine
Anthropologie
Banana Republic
BCBG Max Azria
Beach Box
Boast
Brooks Brothers
Calypso St. Barth
Carlisle
Club Monaco
Cochni
Comptoir Des Cotonniers
Courage.b
Crave
Darien Sport Shop
Eres
Everything But Water
Fontana
Fred

Free People
Gabby
Gap
Great Stuff
Greenwich Diva
Greenwich Furs
Helen Ainson
Hermes
Intermix
Irresistibles
J Crew
J McLaughlin
Jack Wills
Joie
Lacoste Boutique
Lands' End
Letarte
LF Stores
Lilly Pulitzer
Lucky Jeans
Madewell
Magashschoni
Maje
Marietta
Michael Kors
OGGI 5
Olivine Gabbro
Out of the Box
Pastiche
Pinky
Rag & Bone
Ralph Lauren
Reflection
Richards of Greenwich
Roam
Roberta Roller Rabbit
Sandro
Scoop

Simple
Sophia's Great Dames
Sound Beach Sportswear
Splendid
Steilmann
Steven Alan
Theory
Tory Burch
Vince
Vineyard Vines
Zara

Clothing - Women's Exercise
lululemon athletica
Sweaty Betty
Yogasmoga

Clothing - Women's Lingerie
Patricia Gourlay
Petticoat Lane

Clothing - Shoes, Handbags &
Accessories for Men & Women
& Children
*Athletic Shoes are listed under
Sporting Goods.*
Coach
Cochni
Diane B.
DSW
Hermes
Kate Spade
Little Eric
Petticoat Lane
Pinky
Shoes N More
Stuart Weitzman
Timeless Gallery

STORE INDEX

Christmas Shops
Christmas Tree Shops
(The) Historical Christmas Barn
Pier I Imports

Cookware
Cookware is listed under Appliances and Cookware.

Consignment/Resale (Furniture, Silver, Jewelry & Clothing)
Thrift Shops are listed separately under Thrift.
Children's Cottage
Consign It
Consigned Couture
Consigned Designs
Elle Encore
Estate Treasures of Greenwich
Roundabout
Second Time Around
Severed Ties
Silk Purse
United House Wrecking

Construction
See Hardware.

Cosmetics
L'Occitane
Sephora
Whole Body @ Whole Foods

Curtains
Draperies & Curtains are listed under Fabric.

Department Stores
Discount stores and Outlets are listed under Outlets.
Bloomingdale's
Burlington Coat Factory
Costco
Kmart
Kohl's
Lord and Taylor
Macy's
Marshalls
Neiman Marcus
Nordstrom
Old Navy
Saks Fifth Avenue
Sears
Target
T J Maxx
Walmart

Discount and Off-Price Stores
Discount, off price stores and Outlets are listed under Outlets.

Doors (including Garage Doors)
See Hardware for Decorative Hardware
Ed's Garage Doors
Interstate / Lakeland Lumber
Ring's End Lumber
Greenwich Lock and Door
(Charles) Stuttig Locksmith

Draperies
Draperies, Curtains, Fabric are listed under Fabric.

STORE INDEX

Electronics (Audio/Visual, Computer & Electronics)
Appliances are listed under Appliances and Cookware.
Cell Phones Stores are listed under Wireless, Land Phones are under Telephones.
Apple Store
Best Buy
Computer Super Center
Cos Cob TV
Costco
MacInspires
P C Richard
Walmart

Eyewear
20/20 Optical
20/20 Kids
Copeland Optometrists
Greenwich Optics
LensCrafters
Optical Options
Optyx
Pearle Vision
Sunglass Hut
Trapp Optical
Vision Consultants

Fabric (Draperies, Curtains, Upholstery, Home Sewing)
Blinds & shutters are listed under Windows.
(The) Barn
Curtain Works of Greenwich
Fabric House
Home Works
Marcia Jean
Nimble Thimble
Village Ewe

Firearms
For instruction, see the section SPORTS.
Griffin & Howe
Galazan Gunmakers
Hansen & Hansen

Fish & Aquariums
(Greenwich) Aquaria
House of Fins

Fixtures (Bathroom & Kitchen)
Best Plumbing
Klaff's
Mr. Shower Door
Porcelanosa
Plimpton & Hills
Waterworks

TIP: EYE HEALTH: WHO TO SEE

Doctors of Optometry (O.D.) hold a degree from a college of optometry. Optometrists are considered the general practitioners of eye health care. They prescribe eyeglasses and contact lenses to correct nearsightedness, farsightedness and astigmatism. Opticians make the lenses. Ophthalmologists are medical doctors (M.D.) or Doctors of Ophthalmology (D.O.) who have completed a college degree, medical school, and additional years of post-graduate training in ophthalmology.

STORE INDEX

Flooring (Carpets, Rugs, Tiles, Wood)

Installers are listed in SERVICES.

ABC Carpet Warehouse Outlet
Apadana
A T Proudian
Floor Covering Warehouse
Golden Horn
Historic Floors by Stephen Gamble
PID Floors
Riverside Floor Covering
Rye Ridge Tile
Safavieh
Stark Carpet Outlet

Florists (including Flower Shops, Nurseries & Garden Accessories)

Blanchet
Cos Cob Farms
Greenwich Hospital Gift Shop Flowers
Greenwich Orchids
Kenneth Lynch & Sons
Mark Mariani's Garden Center
McArdle-MacMillen Florist & Garden Center
Sam Bridge Nursery & Greenhouses
Shanti Bithi Bonsai Nursery
Tulips Greenwich

Framing

Framing is listed under Art.

Furniture (Indoor and Outdoor)

Office Furniture is listed under Office.

Antique Furniture is listed under Antiques.

Children's outdoor play sets are listed under Toys.

Bellini Juvenile Designer Furniture
Classic Sofa
Cocoon
Consign It
Crate & Barrel
Design Within Reach
Estate Treasures of Greenwich
Ethan Allen
Federalist
HB Home
Housewarmings
IKEA
Lillian August
Mitchell Gold + Bob Williams
Oriental Furniture Warehouse
Patio.com
Patti's Portico (outdoor)
Pottery Barn
Relax the Back
Restoration Hardware
Rinfret Home and Garden
Safavieh
Stickley
Trovare Home
Walpole Woodworkers (outdoor)

Garden

Nurseries, plants and garden accessories are listed under Florists.

STORE INDEX

Gifts and Gift Shops (including Dishes & Crystal)

Abigail Fox Designs
Baccarat
Back 40 Mercantile
Bed Bath & Beyond
CM Almy (religious gifts)
(The) Connecticut Store
Gift Shop at Audubon Center
Gift Shop at Bruce Museum
Gift Shop at Greenwich Hospital
Gift Shop at Hyatt Regency
Greenwich Exchange for Women's Work
Hoagland's of Greenwich
Image
J Papers
Juliska
Michelangelo of Greenwich
Splurge
Tiffany & Co

Glasses

See Eyewear.

Golf

Golf courses are listed in the section SPORTS.
Golf equipment is listed under Sporting Goods.

Guns

See Firearms.

Hardware (Decorative & Fireplace Hardware & Lumber Yards)

Ben Romeo
Cos Cob Hardware
Feinsod
Fence Factory
Glenville Hardware
Grainger
Greenwich Hardware
Greenwich Lock and Door
Home Depot
Interstate Fire and Safety (fire extinguishers)
Interstate / Lakeland Lumber
Klaff's (decorative hardware)
MakerBot
Mr. Mail Box
Mr. Shower Door
(the) Nanz Company (decorative hardware)
Nordic Stove and Fireplace Center (fireplace hardware)
Post Road Iron Works (fireplace hardware)
Restoration Hardware (decorative hardware)
Ring's End Lumber
Rue Faubourg St. Honore (decorative hardware)
(Charles) Stuttig Locksmith
Super Handy Hardware

STORE INDEX

Health (Equipment, Furniture & Products)

Pharmacies, vitamins, exercise equipment, glasses, hearing aids, physical therapy and medical equipment are reviewed in a the separate section - HEALTH.
Spas are reviewed in the separate section - GROOMING.

Home Needs

See Lighting and Accessories.
See Appliances and Cookware.
See Paint and Wall Paper.
Antique Furniture and accessories are listed under Antiques.
See Furniture .
Floor covering including wood, rugs, carpets and tile are listed under Flooring.
Mattresses and Linens are listed under Bedding.
Draperies, Curtains, Fabric are listed under Fabric.
Blinds, Shades, Shutters, Replacement Windows are listed under Windows.
Lumber Yards, Window and Door hardware are listed under Hardware.
Door replacements are listed under Doors.
Bathroom and Kitchen Fixtures are listed under Fixtures.
Closet companies are reviewed in SERVICES.

Home Decorating and Accessories

Accessory Store
Bed Bath & Beyond
Cocoon
(The) Container Store
Crate & Barrel
Ethan Allen
Federalist
HB Home
Hoagland's of Greenwich
Home Goods
Housewarmings
Jonathan Adler
Juliska
Oriental Furniture Warehouse
Pier 1 Imports
Pottery Barn
Restoration Hardware
Rinfret Home and Garden
Simon Pearce
SM Home
United House Wrecking

Horseback Riding

For riding attire and equipment see Riding.
For instruction see the section SPORTS.

Hunting

See Firearms.

STORE INDEX

Jewelry
Alexis Bittar
Bennett Jewlers
Betteridge Jewelers
Lux Bond & Green
Manfredi
Penny Weights
R Simantov
Shreve, Crump & Low
Simon Teakle
Sorab & Roshi
Steven B. Fox
Sunray Jewlers
Tiffany & Co
Viggi

Kitchen
Appliances & Cookware are listed under Appliances.
Kitchen and Bath tile are listed under Flooring.
Kitchen & Bath Fixtures are listed under Fixtures.

Lighting (Lighting, Shades and Accessories)
Accessory Store
Fashion Light Center
Just Shades
Klaff's
Remains Lighting
Restoration Hardware
Rue Faubourg St. Honore

Linens
Linens are listed under Bedding.

Luggage
Innovation Luggage
Tumi

Magazines & Newspapers
East Putnam Variety
Zyns News

Mall
See Shopping Center or Outlets.

Music (Instruments)
Alegro Pianos
Atelier Constantin Popescu
Greenwich Music
Steinway Piano Gallery

Office (Furniture, Supplies, Service & Equipment)
Stamford Office Furniture
Staples
SWC Furniture Outlet
UPS Store

Outlets, Discount, Off-Price Stores
ABC Carpet Warehouse Outlet
(The) Barn
Burlington Coat Factory
Carter's
Clinton Crossing Outlet Mall
Costco
Jones New York discount store
Liberty Village Outlet Mall
Lillian August Outlet Store
Orvis Outlet
Stark Carpet Outlet
Tanger Outlet Center
T J Maxx (Off-price)
Walmart
Woodbury Commons Outlet Mall

Paint and Wallpaper
Farrow & Ball
McDermott Paint & Wallpaper

475

STORE INDEX

Party Goods
See ENTERTAINING for Caterers.
East Putnam Variety
Packages Plus-N-More
Party City
Party Paper and Things

Pets
Services and information are listed in PETS.
Choice Pet Supply
Pet Pantry

Pharmacies
Pharmacies are listed in HEALTH.

Phones
Phone stores are listed under the sections Telephones or Wireless.

Picture Framing
Picture Framers are listed under Art.

Photography
PHOTOGRAPHERS have their own section.
Framing is listed under Art.
Camera Wholesalers
Images

Resale
Resale shops are listed under Consignment.

Riding (Equestrian wear and equipment)
For riding instruction see SPORTS.
Beval Saddlery
Children's Cottage

Rugs
Rugs are listed under Flooring.

Sewing (including Knitting & Needlework)
Nimble Thimble
String
Village Ewe

Shooting
See Firearms.

Shopping Centers (Malls)
Outlets are listed under Outlets and Discount Stores.
Galleria
Ridgeway Shopping Center
Stamford Town Center
(The) Westchester Mall

Skis and Skating
Skis and Skating are listed in this section under Sporting Goods.

STORE INDEX

Sporting Goods (Equipment, Shoes & Clothing)
Boating is listed under Boating.
Bicycles are listed under Bicycles.
All Sports Apparel
Bedford Sportsman
Bruce Park Sports
Chilly Bear
Compleat Angler
De Mane Golf
Eastern Mountain Sports
EuroChasse
Galazan Gunmakers
Greenwich Golf Fitting Studio
Gut Reaction
Gym Source
Harrow
Hickory & Tweed
Instant Replay
Lacrosse Unlimited
lululemon athletica
Marmot
Modell's
(Greenwich) Running Company
Orvis
Outdoor Traders
Recreation Equipment (REI)
Rex Dive Center
Rink and Racquet
Rudy's Tackle Barn
Skaters Landing
(The) Ski & Scuba Connection
Soccer and Rugby
Sportman's Den
Sports Authority
Sweaty Betty
Treads and Threads
Utopia
Yogasmoga

Stationery, Invitations & Greeting Cards
j papers
Packages Plus-N-More
Papyrus
Saint Clair

Telephones
Also see Wireless.
Radio Shack
Staples

Tennis
Tennis Equipment and Clothing is listed under Sporting Goods.
Tennis Instruction is in SPORTS.

Thrift
See THRIFT SHOPS.

Tile
Kitchen and Bath tile are listed under Flooring.
Tile masons are in SERVICES.

Toys (including Children's Playhouses & Outdoor Play Equipment)
Amish Land (playhouses)
Creative Playthings
Graham's Toys
(The) Great Outdoor Toy Company (outdoor)
Hobby Center
Smart Kids Company
Toys "R" Us
Walmart
Walpole Woodworkers (outdoor)
Whimsies Dollhouse & Miniature Shop
Patio.com (pool & ping pong tables)

STORE INDEX

Wall Paper
See Paint and Wall Paper.

Windows (Blinds, Shades, Shutters, Replacement Windows)
See Fabric for upholstery & window draperies and curtains.
See Hardware for decorative hardware.
Blinds To Go
Greenwich Window Treatments
Interstate / Lakeland Lumber
JSJ Window Treatments
Ring's End Lumber

Wireless
A T & T Wireless
Radio Shack
Sprint Nextel
T-Mobile
Verizon Wireless

TIP: SIDEWALK SALES

Greenwich residents eagerly await summer sidewalk sales. Expect a good time with bargains galore. Don't forget to go inside the stores; they are also full of incredible buys during these sales. Sidewalk sales are In mid-July (on a Thursday, Friday and Saturday) in Central Greenwich and Old Greenwich. Call the Chamber of Commerce, 203.869.3500. www.greenwichchamber.com and www.oldgreenwich.org

20/20 Optical
20/20 Kids
15 Arcadia Road, Old Greenwich CT, 203.698.2255
The optician has a specialty working with children. Youngsters love to go there to pick out glasses.
Hours: Weekdays 9:30am-5:30pm, Saturday 9am-4:30pm.

ABC Warehouse Outlet (Home Decorating Outlet)
1055 Bronx River Avenue (@ Bruckner Boulevard), Bronx NY, 718.842.8772
www.ABCHome.com
A wonderland of rugs and carpets. ABC has been selling off-price rugs at its huge Bronx warehouse for over five years. The company has expanded the space and filled it with bed linens, furniture and accessories. Bargain hunters can buy ABC's merchandise for 20 to 70 percent off downtown NYC prices. You can park in a secure parking lot attached to the building.
Hours: Weekdays 10am-7pm, Saturday 9am-7pm, Sunday 11am-6pm.

Abigail Fox Designs (Gift Shop)
187 Sound Beach Avenue, Old Greenwich CT, 203.344.1707
www.abigailfox.com
Home decor and gift shop, many items with a nautical theme.
Hours: Monday-Tuesday 10am-5pm, Wednesday-Saturday 10am-6pm.

Abby M Taylor (Art)
43 Greenwich Avenue, Greenwich CT, 203.622.0906
www.amtFineArt.com
At the top of the Avenue, this gallery focuses on 19th and 20th century American and European paintings and sculpture by known artists. Prices range from $15,000 to $500,000.
Hours: Weekdays 10am-5pm, Saturday 11am-5pm.

Accessory Store (Lamps & Accessories)
69 Jefferson Street, Stamford CT, 203.327.7128
www.StamfordShades.com
Dealers and decorators use this store and you should, too. They have a large selection of lamp shades and chandelier parts. They also have many lamps, display stands and more, all at great prices.
Hours: Monday-Saturday 10:30am-5:30pm, Sunday 12pm-5pm.

STORES

Advance Auto Parts (Auto Parts)
305 West Avenue, Stamford CT, 203.406.0126
www.AdvanceAutoParts.com
With 3,300 stores, Advance is slightly smaller than AutoZone.
Hours: Monday-Saturday 8am -10pm, Sunday 8am-9pm.

Aitoro Appliances (Appliances)
401 Westport Avenue, Norwalk CT, 203.847.2471 For Service
203.846.1629. www.aitoro.com
Most top brands of kitchen, laundry appliances and BBQ grills, as well
as televisions and home theater electronics. A good website to help you
decide before you visit. Be sure to read the store policies on their website
before you buy your Flat Screen TV here.
Hours: Weekdays 9am-6pm (Thursday to 8pm), Saturday 9am-5pm, Sunday 11am-5pm.

Albe Furs & Outerwear (Furrier)
1212 E Putnam Avenue, Riverside CT, 203.637.3883
www.albefurs.com
They have stores in Westport and in Greenwich. In addition to their attractive designs, they store, clean, restyle, repair and appraise furs.
Hours: Monday-Saturday 10am-5pm (during the winter they may be open
Sunday).

Alease Fisher (Clothing-Women)
60 Lewis Street, Greenwich CT, 203.340.2771   www.AleaseFisher.com
Alease Fisher Tallman, one of our stylish Greenwich residents, has a
boutique featuring her made-to-order designs. She also carries some ready-
made resort wear from other designers. Her designs have been carried by
Saks for many years.
Hours: Tuesday-Friday, 10am-5pm, Saturday 11am-5pm.

Alexis Bittar (Jewelry)
371 Greenwich Avenue, Greenwich CT, 203.340.2599
www.AlexisBittar.com
Using a mixture of semi-precious stones, Lucite and metals, Alexis Bittar
has created a unique and notable line of costume jewelry. He sells his
jewelry in more than 34 countries.
Hours: Monday-Saturday 10am-6pm, Sunday 12pm-5pm.

STORES

Alice + Olivia (Clothing-Women)
335 Greenwich Avenue, Greenwich CT, 203.826.8540
www.aliceandolivia.com
Contemporary women's clothing designed by founder Stacey Bendet. Her designs are worn by many celebrities and are sold in over 800 stores, such as Neiman Marcus. There are only a few free-standing stores.
Hours: Monday-Saturday 10am-7pm, Sunday 12pm-5pm.

All Sports Apparel (Sporting Goods & Clothing)
146 Sound Beach Avenue, Old Greenwich CT, 203.698.3055
www.allsportsapparel.com
Pat Cecio's store has apparel for most sports, even yoga. Team licensed products including hats and jerseys. They carry field hockey and lacrosse equipment. Custom embroidery and screen printing.
Hours: Weekdays 10am-5pm, Saturday 9am-3pm, Sunday 11am-4pm.

Allegro Pianos
1086 Long Ridge Road, Stamford CT, 203.968.8888
www.AllegroPianos.com
A large attractive store, with locations in NYC and CT, selling used and new pianos, such as: Bosendorfer, Bluthner, Steingraeber, Estonia, August Forster, Haessler, Yamaha, Steinway and Kawai. They also sell digital pianos and do piano restoration / rebuilding. Piano prices can range from $2,000 to $150,000. Unless you are just browsing, you should make an appointment with Ori Bukai to help you make a selection.
Hours: Showroom hours are flexible, so you should call ahead. You can generally expect the showroom to be open from 10am-6pm.

Amina Rubinacci (Clothing- Women)
71 Lewis Street, Greenwich CT, 203.340.2794   www.AminaRubinacci.it
An Italian company based in Naples with only 11 stores, known for classic woolen clothing for women of all ages.
Hours: Monday-Saturday 10am-6pm.

Amishland (Playhouses)
66 Sugar Hollow Road (Route 7), Danbury CT, 203.205.0204
www.AmishlandSheds.com, www.amishlandofCT.com
Wonderfully detailed children's playhouses, as well as attractive sheds. Don't buy a playhouse until you have been here.
Hours: Open most days 9am-5pm, be sure to call before you go.

STORES

Ann Taylor (Clothing-Women)
100 Greyrock (Stamford Town Center), Stamford CT, 203.359.1616
125 Westchester Ave (The Westchester), White Plains NY, 914.644.8380
www.anntaylor.com
High-end casual and classic professional clothing plus shoes. Their clothing is targeted at the more affluent career woman.
Hours: Monday-Saturday 10am-9pm, Sunday 11am-6pm.

Ann Taylor LOFT
100 Greyrock (Stamford Town Center) Stamford CT, 203.406.9544
125 Westchester Ave (The Westchester), White Plains NY, 914.644.8380
www.anntaylor.com
The Loft was established in 1996 as an extension of the original Ann Taylor brand. It offers more relaxed fashions for work and home, in the "upper moderate" price category. Although the selection is different from Ann Taylor stores, the styles at the Loft stores are similar and the prices lower.
Hours: Monday-Saturday 10am-9pm, Sunday 11am-6pm.

Anam Cara Gallery (Art)
18 Greenwich Avenue, Greenwich CT, 203.869.2824
www.AnamCaraGallery.com
Abstract and contemporary paintings and sculpture priced in the $1,000 to $25,000 range. The owner, Patty Kane Maguire, also sells jewelry, some of which she designed.
Hours: Thursday-Saturday 10:30am-5:30pm, Sunday 12pm-5pm.

Anna Banana (Clothing-Children)
248 Sound Beach Avenue, Old Greenwich CT, 203.637.0128
Kathy O'Malley of Hoaglands, has gifted Greenwich with the most cheerful, adorable clothing shop for babies and young children imaginable. Fashions are by designers such as: Ralph Lauren, Lili Gaufrette, Charlie Rocket, Hartstrings and E-Land.
Hours: Monday-Saturday 9:30am-5:30pm.

Anne Fontaine (Clothing-Women)
234 Greenwich Avenue, Greenwich CT, 203.422.2433
www.annefontaine.com
Originally from Paris, with stores on Madison Avenue and in SoHo, this boutique specializes in black and white. You will find an assortment of sophisticated, trendy and top-of-the-line blouses for all occasions.
Hours: Monday-Saturday 10am-6pm, Sunday 12pm-5pm.

Anthropologie (Clothing-Women)

480 West Putnam Avenue, Greenwich CT, 203.422.5421
www.anthropologie.com
A retailer of high-end casual clothing designed to appeal to the 30- to 40-something affluent professional woman. Though mainly clothing and accessories, the store also sells furniture and home furnishings. The company prides itself on its one-of-a-kind items. There are approximately 90 stores in the US. They are owned by Urban Outfitters parent, URBN Inc. Hours: Monday-Saturday 10am -7pm (open to 8pm on Thursday), Sunday 12pm-6pm.

Antique Area of Stamford (Antiques)

Tucked away in converted manufacturing buildings are collections of antique dealers with collectibles and antiques to suit just about anyone. With antiques from hundreds of dealers, it's hard to imagine anyone not finding something they want. A great outing for the antique enthusiast. When you are in the area, visit the many restaurants in Harbor Point. Don't forget to also look at Braswell Galleries in Norwalk.
Hours for Galleries in the Antique Area: Monday to Saturday 10:30am-5:30 or 6pm, Sunday 12pm-about 5 or 6pm.

- Antique and Artisan Center, 69 Jefferson Street, 203.327.6022
www.antiqueandartisancenter.com www.StamfordAntiques.com
55 dealers in 20,000 square fee.
- Greenwich Antique & Auction Center, 83 Harvard Avenue, 203.355.9335
www.connecticutStyle.com, www.GreenwichAcution.net
96 dealers in 13,000 square feet. They have auctions every 3 weeks.
- Greenwich Living Antiques, 481 Canal Street, 203.274.5130
www.GreenwichLivingAntiques.com
63 dealers in 30,000 square feet.
- Hamptons Antique Galleries, 441 Canal Street, Stamford, 203.325.4019
www.hamptonsantiquegalleries.com
95 dealers in 26,000 square feet.
- Harbor View Center for Antiques, 101 Jefferson Street, 203.325.8070
www.HarborViewAntiques.com
70 dealers in 22,000 square feet.
- Hiden Galleries, 47 John Street, 203.363.0003
www.hidengalleries.net
250 dealers in 47,000 square feet.
- John Street Antiques, 50 John Street, 203.324.4677
www.JohnStreetAntiques.com
20 dealers in about 15,000 square feet.

STORES

Apadana (Rugs)
539 East Putnam Avenue, Cos Cob CT, 203.422.0700
31-35 South Main Street, Norwalk CT, 203.299.1760
www.ApadanaInc.com
Apadana has been in Greenwich for several years, but New Yorkers have known them for over 20 years. They have antique and reproduction rugs in modern and traditional patterns.
Greenwich Hours: Monday-Saturday 10am-6pm.

Apple Store
356 Greenwich Avenue, Greenwich CT, 203.203.6691
www.apple.com/greenwichavenue
An attractive, large, sleek store with every conceivable Apple product, a Genius bar and lots of workshops. Just the kind of store Steve Jobs wanted.
Hours: Monday-Saturday 10am-7pm, Sunday 11am-6pm.

(Greenwich) Aquaria (Fish)
1064 East Putnam Avenue, Riverside CT, 203.344.1572
www.GreenwichAquaria.com
The store is divided into fresh water and saltwater sections, they specialize in large tanks. The filtration systems can be run to the home's basement. Hours: Tuesday-Friday 10am-6pm, Saturday 11am-5pm.

Atelier Constantin Popescu (String Instruments)
403 East Putnam Avenue (Cos Cob Plaza), Cos Cob CT, 203.661.9500
www.atelierconstantinpopescu.com
Sells, repairs and rents string instruments. Professionals and amateurs alike count on his repair services. Constantin Popescu is a graduate of both the Bucharest Conservatory in Romania and of Juilliard School of Music. Constantin is the Principal Bassist of the Greenwich Symphony. The Riverside School of Music is located next to his store at 401 East Putnam Avenue. (203.661-9501).
Hours: Weekdays 10am-6pm, Saturday 10am-2pm.

AT Proudian (Oriental Rugs)
120 East Putnam Avenue, Greenwich CT, 203.622.1200
www.atproudian.com
A family-owned and operated Oriental rug business. They sell new and old rugs. They have been in Greenwich since 1974 and have a good reputation. A source for cleaning, repair and appraisal. They also sell broadloom on the lower level.
Hours: Monday-Saturday 10am-5pm.

AT&T Wireless (Wireless)
42 Greenwich Avenue, Greenwich CT, 203.629.8008
www.wireless.att.com/cell-phone-service/welcome
The wireless subsidiary of AT&T Inc, with 80 million subscribers, is the second-largest mobile phone company in the United States, behind Verizon Wireless. It provides GSM and UMTS voice communications.
Hours: Weekdays 10am-7pm, Saturday 10am-6pm, Sunday 11am-5pm.

AutoZone (Auto Parts)
799 East Main Street, Stamford CT, 203.406.1327
www.AutoZone.com
With over 4,000 stores, it is one of the largest auto stores in the world. Its major competitors are Advance, CarQuest and NAPA.
Hours: Monday-Saturday 7am-11pm, Sunday 8am-9pm.

Babies "R" Us (Babies)
2700 Central Park Avenue, Yonkers NY, 914.722.4500
www.babiesrus.com
Mega baby store specializing in clothing, furniture, bedding, toys and other accessories for babies. This is just one of the baby stores on Central Park Avenue in Yonkers. Central Park Avenue is approximately 20 minutes from Greenwich. It runs through Yonkers and Scarsdale.
Hours: Weekdays 10am-9:30pm, Saturday 9am-10pm, Sunday 10am-8pm.

Baccarat (Gifts-Crystal)
236 Greenwich Avenue, Greenwich CT, 203.618.0900
www.baccarat-us.com
A table set with their French luxury crystal is very special. They also have a selection of pretty vases, giftware and jewelry.
Hours: Monday-Saturday 10am-5:30pm.

Back 40 Mercantile (Gift Shop & Farm Products)
264 Sound Beach Avenue, Old Greenwich CT, 203.637.0240
www.Back40Mercantile.com
This small store carries artisan products and sustainably-produced home goods, including locally made honey and jam. Their sister business is the Organic Planet restaurant. They have a family farm in Washington, CT and sell their produce at the Old Greenwich Farmer's Market. The owners Lesley and Bill King are founders of this farmer's market.
www.OldGreenwichFarmersMarket.com
Hours: Everyday 10am-6pm.

STORES

Banana Republic (Clothing-Men & Women)
- 100 Greyrock (Stamford Town Center) Stamford CT, 203.324.6323
- 125 Westchester Ave (The Westchester), White Plains NY, 914.644.8640

www.bananarepublic.com

They sell the Gap's higher end casual career clothing. Most of the clothes are rather trendy. In the US there are over 500 Banana Republic stores.
Hours: Monday-Saturday 10am-9pm, Sunday 11am-6pm.

Banchet Flowers (Flowers)
40 East Putnam Avenue, Greenwich CT, 203.622.5939

www.BanchetFlowers.com

A high-end flower shop with locations in Manhattan and Greenwich. Seven variations of orchid (from Lady Slippers to Phalaenopsis) are this shop's primary stock and trade. Of course, they also have cut flowers.
Hours: Weekdays, 9am-6pm, Saturday 10am-5pm.

Back Barn Farm aka New England Farm (Equestrian Consignment)
203 Greenwich Road, Bedford NY, 914.234.6692

www.backbarnfarm.com

Boarding and lessons both indoor and outdoor. They have an equestrian consignment shop, usually including saddles.

(The) Barn (Fabrics, Home Decorating Accessories)
50 Hurd Avenue, Bridgeport CT, 203.334.3396

www.thebarn-bridgeport.com

If you want to see a wide variety of fabrics, visit this old barn with 20,000 square feet of well priced bolts: silks, linens, velvets, cottons. You can also get upholstered headboards and throw pillows.
Hours: Monday-Saturday 10am-5pm.

Barnes & Noble (Books)
100 Greyrock Place (Stamford Town Center), Stamford CT, 203.323.1248

www.bn.com

See Review in BOOKS.

Hours: Monday-Saturday 9am-10pm (Friday & Saturday to 11pm), Sunday 9am-9pm.

STORES

BCBG Max Azria (Clothing-Women)
200 Greenwich Avenue, Greenwich CT, 203.861.7303
www.bcbg.com
Bon Chic Bon Genre caters to modern women who want trendy, chic, unique fashions at mid-scale prices. The company's newest line of clothing is for college students. Their upscale garments are in the Max Azria Collection. Max Azria's boutiques have a very restrictive return policy.
Hours: Monday-Saturday 10 am-6 pm, Sunday 12pm- 5 pm.

Beach Box (Clothing-Women)
73 Greenwich Avenue (upstairs), Greenwich CT, 203.625.9696
www.outoftheboxclothes.com
During the summer, Out of The Box opens this shop selling swim suits, tunics, sun dresses, cover-ups, pool party dresses and accessories.
Summer Hours: Monday-Saturday 10am-5:30pm, Sunday 12pm-5pm.

Beam & Barre (Children's Dance Wear)
352 Greenwich Avenue, Greenwich CT, 203.622.0591
www.beamAndbarre.com
Dance wear to suit even the most discriminating ballerina's tastes. Plus exercise wear, skating attire and costumes.
Hours: Weekdays 10am-5:30pm, Saturday 10am-5pm.

Bed Bath & Beyond (Home Decorating-Accessories, Appliances)
• 2275 Summer Street (Ridgeway Shopping Cntr), Stamford CT, 203.323.7714
• 25 Waterfront Place, Port Chester NY, 914.937.9098
www.bedbathandbeyond.com
A huge store with medium-to-high quality items for the bedroom, bathroom, breakfast room and kitchen. They operate 819 stores across the US. Their main competitor, Linens n' Things, liquidated its 570 stores.
Stamford Hours: Monday-Saturday 9am-9pm, Sunday 9:30am-6pm.
Port Chester Hours: Monday-Saturday 9am-9:30pm, Sunday 10am-7pm.

Bedford Sportsman (Fly & Spin Fishing Equipment)
25 Adams Street, Bedford Hills NY, 914.666.8091
www.bedfordsportsman.com
Specializes in freshwater fly and spin fishing equipment. A good resource for New York watershed streams & guide services. They teach fly fishing during the summer.
Hours: Closed Monday, Tuesday-Friday 10am-6pm (Thursday until 7pm), Saturday 10am-6pm, Sunday 10am-3pm.

Bellini (Children & Baby Furniture)
40 West Putnam Avenue, Greenwich CT, 203.869.9170
www.Bellini.com
Well-made baby and children designer furniture and furnishings. This is one of 18 stores worldwide.
Hours: Monday-Saturday 10am-6pm, Sunday 12pm-5pm.

Ben Romeo (Contractor Supplies)
1 Edgewood Ave (@ West Putnam Avenue), Greenwich CT, 203.869.4108
The most-needed items for contractors and landscapers. They have safety cones and Child Safety signs. They also sharpen tools.
Hours: Weekdays, 8am-4:30pm.

Bendheim Gallery (Art)
299 Greenwich Avenue, Greenwich CT, 203.622.3998
www.greenwichartscouncil.org
Inside the Art Center, the Arts Council Gallery has interesting exhibits you will not want to miss.
Hours: Weekdays 10am-5pm, Saturday 12pm-4pm.

Bennett Jewelers (Jewelry)
254 Sound Beach Avenue, Old Greenwich CT, 203.637.0217
www.bennettjewelersoldgreenwich.com
Bennett was started in 1945. Sisters Alyson and Laurie Bennett are the fourth generation to run this store. They have long been known for their clock watch and jewelry repairs.
Hours: Tuesday-Saturday 9:30am-5pm.

Best Buy (Electronics)
330 Connecticut Avenue, Norwalk CT, 203.857.4543   www.bestbuy.com
Best Buy is the biggest electronics retailer in the US, with 1,400 stores. The Norwalk store is 45,000 square feet. Their arch rival, Circuit City, has liquidated all 576 of its stores. Their new rival is Walmart, who saw the opportunity and is working hard to fill the gap.
Hours: Monday-Saturday 10am-9pm, Sunday 10am-8pm.

Best Plumbing (Tile, Bath & Kitchen Fixtures)
1989 West Main Street, Stamford CT, 203.975.9448
www.bestplg.com www.bestplg.com/Blog
Just across the Greenwich border on US 1, they represent a myriad of manufactures including Kohler. A nice showroom, worth the visit.
Hours: Monday-Saturday 9am-5pm.

STORES

Betteridge Jewelers (Jewelry)
239 Greenwich Avenue, Greenwich CT, 203.869.0124
www.betteridge.com
A third-generation family-owned business; buying, selling and collecting some of the finest jewelry. The shop specializes in fine timepieces, rare and exceptional stones, estate jewelry and pearls, plus a broad collection of classic and contemporary jewelry and silver to suit a diverse clientele. They carry many renowned brands, such as Cartier and Van Cleef & Arpels. Totally trustworthy with excellent service and repair, as well as appraisal services.
Hours: Closed Monday, Tuesday-Saturday 9am-5pm.

Beval Saddlery (Riding Attire & Saddles)
50 Pine Street, New Canaan CT, 203.966.7828
www.beval.com
A small chain with English saddlery and clothing. They do a good job fitting a saddle to you and your horse.
Hours: Monday-Saturday 9am-5pm (Thursday until 7pm).

Blinds To Go (Windows)
411 Westport Avenue, Norwalk CT, 203.840.1357
www.Blindstogo.com
One of 120 superstores providing blinds and shades of all descriptions. They claim to be the largest retailer of these items in the world.
Hours: Monday-Saturday 10am-7pm, Sunday 12pm-5pm.

Bloomingdale's (Department Store)
175 Bloomingdale Road, White Plains NY, 914.684.6300
www.Bloomingdales.com
A large stand-alone store, with lots of parking. Bloomingdale's is a chain of upscale American department stores owned by Federated Department Stores, which is also the parent company of Macy's. Bloomingdale's has 36 stores nationwide. It competes on an average price level with Nordstrom and slightly below that of Saks Fifth Avenue and Neiman Marcus.
Hours: Monday-Saturday 10am-8pm (Thursday & Friday until 9pm), Sunday 11am-6pm.

STORES

Burlington Coat Factory (Department Store)
74 Broad Street, Stamford CT, 203.363.0450
www.Coat.com
An off-price store with a traditional department store layout, this national chain has 360 stores. They have branched out since their founding in 1924 and now sell women's apparel, including suits, shoes and accessories. They even have a baby department and sell linens. Its principal competitor is TJ Maxx.
Hours: Everyday 9:30am-9:30pm.

Buy Buy Baby (Babies)
441 Boston Post Road, Port Chester NY, 914.937.3473
1019 Central Park Avenue, Scarsdale NY, 914.725.9220
www.buybuybaby.com
The Scarsdale store is one of many baby stores about 20 minutes away on Central Park Avenue (see Babies R Us). Here, everything is for children ages 0-3. It's a large store so wear comfortable shoes!
Hours: Monday-Saturday 9:30am-9:30pm, Sunday 10am-7pm.

BOAST (Clothing-Men, Women, Children)
10 Greenwich Avenue, Greenwich CT, 203.861.1973
www.BoastUSA.com
An American brand, despite sporting a maple leaf logo. It was started by Bill St. John, a Greenwich resident and Field Club Pro. They sell preppy men's, women's and kid's casual and sports clothing.
Hours: Tuesday-Saturday 10am-6pm, Sunday 11am-5pm.

Brandy USA (Clothing- Girls)
375 Greenwich Avenue, Greenwich CT, 203.661.6122
www.BrandyMelvilleUSA.com
Clothing targeted at girls 14 to about 24.
Hours: Friday & Saturday, 10am-9pm, Sunday-Thursday 10am-7pm.

Braswell Galleries (Antiques & Auctions)

1 Muller Avenue (entrance on Sniffin Street), Norwalk CT, 203.847.1234
www.braswellgalleries.com   www.antiquesofgreenwich.com
Occupying an old lace factory, this 40,000 sf place is crammed with furniture, paintings and just about everything else. The Gallery typically has mid-level antiques. The Estate Center specializes in higher level antiques. Buyers can have fun taking part in their auctions, which are held once or twice a month. Leave a silent bid or attend the auction and you may be able to purchase the item you want at a very competitive price. Remember all prices in the Gallery are negotiable, so don't just buy at the listed price. See Antiques Area of Stamford for more antique galleries.
Norwalk Gallery Hours: Monday-Saturday 10:30am-6pm, Sunday 12pm-6pm. Auctions are held at different times and on different days, see their website.

Brooks Brothers (Clothing-Men & Women)

181 Greenwich Avenue, Greenwich CT, 203.863.9288
www.brooksbrothers.com
This 12,000 sf store carries classic men's, women's and boy's clothing. Brooks has 240 stores and is the oldest men's clothier in the US.
Hours: Weekdays 10am-7pm, Saturday 9am-6pm, Sunday 11am-6pm.

Bruce Park Sports (Sporting Goods, Team Uniforms)

104 Mason Street, Greenwich CT, 203.869.1382
www.bruceparksports.com
A family-owned sports store carrying team uniforms and equipment for most sports. When I am not sure where to get something, they are always a good bet and they have excellent customer service.
Hours: Monday-Saturday 8am-5:30pm, Sunday 11am-3pm.

Calypso St. Barth (Clothing-Women's Resort Wear)

254 Greenwich Avenue, Greenwich CT, 203.625.3332
www.calypsostbarth.com
A retailer of Caribbean-accented ladies casual and resort-wear clothing. Most of the apparel is private label. Calypso is owned by Solera Capital and has over 35 stores, including 13 in Manhattan and 4 in Paris.
Hours: Monday-Saturday 10am-7pm, Sunday 11am-5pm.

STORES

Camera Wholesalers (Photography)
1034 High Ridge Road, Stamford CT, 203.357.0467
www.CameraWholesalers.com
A family-owned store that has been in business since 1978. They are authorized dealers for most makes of cameras and many are in stock. They are one of the few area camera stores left. They have a knowledgeable staff to help you make selections. They have a photo lab for photo cards, enlargement and even film development. Yes, film.
Hours: Sunday-Friday 10am to 6pm (Thursday to 8pm), Closed Saturday.

Carter's (Clothing-Babies, Toddlers, Children)
2329 Summer Street (Ridgeway Shopping Cntr), Stamford CT, 203.975.9725   www.carters.com
Founded in 1865, Carter's is a major American manufacturer of children's clothing. It owns OshKosh B'Gosh and many other children's brands. Mothers love this store for good buys for newborns, toddlers and kids (through size 7). This is where you will find all of the basics.
Hours: Monday-Saturday 9am-9 pm, Sunday 10 am-6 pm.

Casablanca (Men's Polo Clothing)
113 Greenwich Avenue, Greenwich CT, 203.661.0930
www.casablancepolo.com
Casablanca has two stores in Buenos Aires, one in Houston and one in London, in addition to its Greenwich store. Its specialty is men's polo clothing and equipment, however its casual clothing would complement any fashion conscious man. They placed their store here because of the 7 polo clubs within 100 miles of Greenwich.
Hours: Monday-Saturday, 9:30am -5:30pm, Sunday 12pm-5pm.

Carlisle (Women's Clothing)
40 Greenwich Avenue (Second Floor), Greenwich CT, 203.422.2464
www.carlislecollection.com
Traditionally doing trunk shows, the Connaught Group has opened a showroom showing their fashionable lines. Lots of custom possibilities.
Hours: Weekdays 9am-5pm, Saturday 10am-3 pm (or by appointment).

Cavalier Galleries (Art)
405 Greenwich Avenue, Greenwich CT, 203.869.3664
www.cavaliergalleries.com
Ronald Cavalier specializes in painting and sculpture by contemporary artists working in a representational style. You may already have smiled at one of the gallery's lifelike sculptures on a sidewalk in Greenwich or Stamford. Prices range from $100 to $100,000.
Hours: Monday-Saturday 10:30am-6pm; Open Sundays in the winter, 12pm- 5pm.

Children's Cottage (Consignment-Children)
23 Catoonah Street, Ridgefield CT, 203.438.3933
www.Childrenscottageonline.com
Children's designer clothing, infant to size 16. They usually have equestrian wear.   Hours: Monday-Saturday 9:30am-4:30pm.

Chilly Bear (Clothing & Sports Equipment- Youth)
180 Sound Beach Avenue, Old Greenwich CT, 203.622.7115 or 888.463.2707   www.chillybear.com
Richard Fulton's shop is a great resource for customized shirts and hats, as well a store for the hip young adolescent. It is filled with the latest teenage garb as well as skateboards, inline skates, paint ball guns and accessories. Very nice customer service.
Hours: Monday-Saturday 10am-6pm, Sunday 12pm-5pm.

Choice Pet Supply (Pets)
80 East Putnam Avenue (Whole Foods Plaza), Greenwich CT, 203.869.4999
www.ChoicePet.com
One of nine Connecticut locations, they specialize in natural, organic and holistic foods for pets (dogs, cats, companion birds, small animals, fish and reptiles).
Hours: Monday-Saturday 10am-9pm, Sunday 9am-7pm.

Christmas Tree Shops
393 North Central Avenue, Hartsdale NY, 914.948.3721
www.christmastreeshops.com
Christmas Tree Shops are bargain stores, selling everything from food to toys to household furnishings to, of course, Christmas decorations and wrapping paper. The chain has over 70 stores and is owned by Bed Bath and Beyond.
Hours: Monday-Saturday 9am-9pm, Sunday 10am-7pm.
(extended hours during the Christmas season)

STORES

Claire's (Clothing-Children)
344 Greenwich Avenue, Greenwich CT, 203.618.4461
www.claires.com
Greenwich once had the title "Preppy Capital of The World." If Claire's is successful, does this mean Greenwich will lose this title? Claire's has 3,000 locations worldwide. It caters to girls, pre-teen through teenager. Claire's sells perfumes, as well as accessory products such as jewelry, make-up, hair and belt accessories. The store offers a wide variety of styles from punk, gothic, emo, and rock chick to pink, glittery, girly and flowery items. Claire's offers free ear piercing with the purchase of piercing studs and ear care antiseptic. Claire's owns "Icing by Claire's," which caters to girls 17-27.
Hours: Monday-Saturday 10am-7pm, Sunday 11am-5pm.

Classic Sofa (Furniture)
28 Bruce Park Avenue, Greenwich CT, 203.863.0005
www.classicSofa.com
This is a custom sofa store: any size, any shape, any fabric. Select a model from the many samples in the showroom or show them a picture, choose your fabric and size. Within 3-4 weeks after the fabric arrives, the sofa will be in your home.
Hours: Monday-Saturday 10am-5pm.

(The) Clean Bedroom (Bedding)
79 East Putnam Avenue, Greenwich CT, 203.292.9275
www.TheCleanBedroom.com
One of 7 US stores selling mattresses and bedding made from organic and natural materials. They also sell air purifiers, non-toxic bedroom furniture, towels, robes and shower curtains.
Hours: Monday-Saturday 10am-6pm, Sunday 12pm-5pm.

Clinton Crossing (Outlet Mall)
20-A Killingworth Turnpike (@Route 81), Clinton CT, 860.664.0700
www.premiumoutlets.com
The largest outlet center in Connecticut (see also Tanger Outlet), they have seventy upscale stores. If you have time, you could always go to exit 92 and visit Foxwoods Casino.
Regular Hours: Monday-Saturday 10am-9pm, Sunday 10am-6pm.
Directions: I-95 N exit 63.

STORES

Club Monaco (Clothing-Men and Women)
171 Greenwich Avenue, Greenwich CT,   www.ClubMonaco.com
A high-end, trendy clothing store with more than 140 locations. Its parent is Ralph Lauren, however it seeks to have more affordable selections than are found at the Ralph Lauren stores. Collections alternate between casual and formal.

CM Almy (Religious Gifts & Books)
228 Sound Beach Avenue, Old Greenwich CT, 203.637.2739
www.Almy.com
A supplier of high-end clerical attire. The front of this shop is filled with Christian books and gifts, including devotional gifts, keepsakes and First Communion gifts.
Hours: Weekdays 10am-5pm, Saturday 10am-2pm.

Coach (Accessories-Women)
100 Greyrock (Stamford Town Cntr) Stamford CT, 203.965.0666,
125 Westchester Ave (Westchester Mall) White Plains NY, 914.644.8244
www.coach.com
For 65 years, this company has been a leading handbag designer. It is also known for its leather items such as briefcases and wallets. One of the hallmarks of the Coach company is their policy which states that any Coach product may be repaired for the life of the product by simply shipping it back to the home office for a nominal fee, with a note or letter stating the problem. Its main competitors are Louis Vuitton (Westchester Mall) and Kate Spade (Greenwich Avenue). This is one of 730 coach stores.
Hours: Monday-Saturday 10am-9pm, Sunday 11am-6pm.

Cochni (Clothing, Shoes & Accessories -Women)
50 Greenwich Avenue, Greenwich CT, 203.422.0970
www.cochni.com
A boutique with fun items such as unbelievable belt buckles, jeweled slippers, cashmere sweaters with embroidery & trim, and a selection of silk scarves. All at reasonable prices.
Hours: Monday-Saturday 10am-6pm.

STORES

Cocoon (Furniture and Home Accessories)
34 East Putnam Avenue, Greenwich CT, 203.717.1500
www.cocoonGreenwich.com
This shop is filled with unusual art objects and furniture, designed by Mitchell, the owner, and made in his Filipino factory. These one-of-a-kind objects are made from exotic woods, stones, plants and shells.
Hours: Monday-Saturday 10am-6pm, Sunday 12pm-4pm.

Colonial Framing (Framing)
135 Mason Street, Greenwich CT, 203.869.4384
This independent framing store has been serving Greenwich since 1951.
Hours: Monday 11am-4pm, Tuesday-Friday, 9am-5pm,
Saturday 10am-5pm.

Compleat Angler (Fishing Equipment & Clothing)
555 Post Road, Darien CT, 203.655.9400
www.compleat-angler.com
A large selection of fly fishing and light tackle spin fishing equipment as well as outdoor clothing. Ask about their lessons and guide service.
Hours: Monday-Saturday 9:30am-5pm, Sunday 11am-4pm.

Comptoir Des Cotonniers (Clothing-Women)
271 Greenwich Avenue, Greenwich CT, 203.869.0640
www.comptoirdescotonniers.com
This Paris-based (Counter of Cottons) has 374 stores. Their clothes are intended to appeal to modern, active women. Lots of comfortable and youthful styles.
Hours: Monday-Saturday 10am-6pm (Thursday until 7pm),
Sunday 12pm-5 pm.

Computer Super Center (Electronics-Computer & AV)
103 Mason Street, Greenwich CT, 203.661.1700
www.computersupercenter.com
For friendly help and expert advice on PCs and Apples try the Super Center. A good selection of hardware and software and a very active repair business. They also sell and service Sony LCD home theater equipment. We highly recommend this store. They will have what you need and they care. Hours: Weekdays 9am-6pm, Saturday 10am-5pm.

(The) Connecticut Store (Gift Shops, Clothing)
116 Bank Street, Waterbury CT, 800.474.6728
www.theconnecticutstore.com
This store specializes in items made in Connecticut. This is a great resource if you are looking for a unique gift. Best of all, you can buy almost everything from their website without making a trip. We especially like the blazer buttons from the Waterbury Button Company, their selection is amazing.
Hours: Tuesday-Friday 10am-3pm. Directions: I-84 East to exit 22.

Consign It (Consigned Furniture and Accessories)
115 Mason Street (Village Square), Greenwich CT, 203.869-9836
www.consignitinc.com
This shop is a good place to consign and a good place to buy pre-owned furniture, jewelry, silver and china. They do high-level tag sales.
Hours: Monday-Saturday 10am-5pm.

Consigned Couture (Consignment Clothing)
24 East Elm Street, Greenwich CT, 203.869.7795
Lots of designer clothing. Consigned clothing is less than two years old (except vintage items). The split between store and consigner is 50/50.
Shop Hours: Monday-Saturday 10am-5pm.
Consignment Hours: Weekdays 11am-3pm (with appointment).

Consigned Designs by Ellen (Consignment Clothing)
115 Mason Street (Village Square) Greenwich CT, 203.869.2165
www.ConsignedDesigns.com
2 floors of consigned clothing for women and children. Reduced price items are on the second floor. Consigned designer clothing such as: Hermes, Pucci, Prada, Armani is sold in her next door shop, Elle Encore (listed separately). Prices downstairs are generally 30% off retail, upstairs is usually 65% off retail. The split between store and consigner is 50/50.   Hours: Monday-Saturday 10am-5pm.

(The) Container Store (Home Decorating)
145 Westchester Avenue (next to the Westchester Mall), White Plains NY, 914.946.4767   www.containerStore.com
A 25,000 sf store designed to help you organize your life and hopefully the life of your college student. This is one of 60 stores.
Hours: Monday-Saturday 9am-9pm, Sunday 10am-6pm.

Cook and Craft (Cookware)
27 Arcadia Road, Old Greenwich CT, 203.637.2755
www.cookandcraft.com
This shop has high quality essentials and attractive items. The cookware, knives, utensils, gadgets, cookbooks and gourmet pantry items are selected by the owner, a local resident who cares about our town.
Hours: Monday-Saturday 10am-5pm.

Copeland Optometrists (Eyewear)
203 South Ridge Street, Rye Brook NY, 914.939.0830
For years, they were just over the border in Port Chester, but now they are 5 minutes away in Rye Brook. We followed them because of their reliable, caring service. Owned and operated by the Copeland Family, you can count on a good eye examination, the correct prescription and a set of fashionable glasses or contact lens at a reasonable price.
Hours: Weekdays 9am-6pm (closed Wednesday, Thursday to 8pm), Saturday 9am-4pm.

Coppola Tailors (Men's Formal Clothing)
347 Greenwich Avenue, Greenwich CT, 203.869.2883
A long time Greenwich store specializing in Tux sales and rental. They also do alterations.
Hours: Monday-Tuesday & Thursday-Friday 9:30am-5:30pm, Saturday 9am-5pm, closed Wednesday & Sunday.

Cos Cob Farms (Flowers)
6163 East Putnam Avenue, Cos Cob CT, 203.629.2267
A local store with fresh fruit, vegetables and flowers at reasonable prices.
Hours: Monday-Saturday 8am-7pm, Sunday 9am-6pm.

Cos Cob Hardware (Hardware)
136 East Putnam Avenue, Cos Cob CT, 203.869.9254
www.coscob.doitbest.com
This convenient, small hardware store has been helping residents for over 70 years. As you can imagine, after this length of time, they are likely to have what you need. They have a good website where you can order most items and pick them up at the store.
Hours: Monday-Saturday 8am-6pm, Sunday 9am-5pm.

STORES

Cos Cob TV (AV Sales & Services)
5 Strickland Road, Cos Cob CT, 203.869.2277
www.coscobtv.com
Whether you are looking for a small TV or large Flat screen, an Apple iPod or iMac, this local store, run by second generation owner Sean Mecsery, has been offering good prices and good service for more than 60 years. They will design and install a dedicated home theater or transform your media room.
Hours: Weekdays 9:30am-5:30pm, Saturday 9:30pm-5pm

Costco (Grocery & Department Store)
1 Westchester Avenue, Port Chester NY, 914.935.3103
www.costco.com
You have to buy a membership to shop at this international chain, but that hasn't kept this megastore, a.k.a. warehouse, from being a Greenwich hit. From pesto in their grocery section to a DVD player to a refrigerator, this huge store tries to give good value. If you want an expensive electronic item or a large quantity of a staple, this could be your best bet. If you want to run in quickly to get something, forget it.
Hours: Weekdays 10am-8:30pm, Saturday, 9:30am-6 pm, Sunday 10am-6pm.

Courage.b (Clothing-Women)
85 Greenwich Avenue, Greenwich CT, 203.422.5660
www.courageb.com
One of 4 locations, the other 3 stores are located in Scarsdale, Englewood and New York City. Scarves and colorful clothing, some reminiscent of the popular fashions in the '60s. The name comes form the courage it takes to open a store.
Hours: Monday-Saturday 10am-6pm, Sunday 12pm-5 pm.

Crate & Barrel (Home Decorating, Furniture & Cookware)
125 Westchester Avenue (Westchester Mall), White Plains NY, 914.682.0900   www.CrateAndBarrel.com
A chain specializing in housewares, indoor and outdoor furniture and home accessories. Much of the merchandise is direct from Europe. Their major competitors are Pottery Barn and Williams-Sonoma.
Hours: Monday-Saturday 10am-9pm, Sunday 11am-6pm.

Crave (Clothing-Women)
39 Lewis Street, Greenwich CT, 203.769.1966
Crave, owned by local resident and mother of four, Sonia Hedvat targets customers 14 to 50, who want the latest fashions. She has stores in Manhattan's upper east side and one in Port Chester. She carries clothing, shoes and jewelry from California and up-and-coming designers.
Hours: Monday-Tuesday, 10am-6pm, Wednesday 10am-7pm, Thursday-Saturday 10am-8pm, Sunday 11am-5pm.

Creative Playthings (Children's Play Equipment)
65 Harvard Avenue, Stamford CT, 203.359.9702
www.creativeplaythings.com
They manufacture and sell wooden play sets for homes and playgrounds.
Hours: Monday-Saturday 10am -6pm, Sunday 12pm-5pm.

Curtain Works of Greenwich (Windows-Curtains)
30 East Putnam Avenue, Greenwich CT, 203.622.2354
www.CurtainWorksofGreenwich.com
The perfect place to find ready-made curtains that have the designer look at reasonable prices. There are over 100 fabrics to choose from. Many of the silks are from India. They provide measuring services and hardware.
Hours: Weekdays 10am-5:30pm, Saturday 10am-3pm.

Darien Sport Shop (Clothing-Men, Women, Children)
1127 Post Road, Darien CT, 203.655.2575
www.DarienSport.com
Good-looking casual and sports attire as well a ski and skateboard shop. They also carry Boy and Girl Scout uniforms.
Hours: Monday-Saturday 9am-5:30pm, (Thursday until 7pm).

Dave's Cycle (Bicycles)
78 Valley Road, Cos Cob CT, 203.661.7736, 7803
www.davecycle.com
Slightly off the beaten path, this shop provides friendly, knowledgeable help for cyclists at all levels. A good place to select a bicycle or clothing. They can repair just about any type of bike. They sell used bikes and will accept trade-ins for many bikes. They carry Giant and Special brands.
Hours: Weekdays 11am-6pm, (Thursday until 8pm), Saturday 9am-5pm, Sunday 11am-4pm.

De Mane Golf (Golf)
35 Chapel Street, Byram CT, 203.531.9126
www.demanegolf.com
Golfers in the know visit Rick's shop for custom clubs and repairs. Their state-of-the-art demo room allows you to compare clubs from different manufacturers and determine which would be best for you. The demo room costs $150 per hour.
Hours: Tuesday-Saturday 10am-5pm.

Delta Auto Parts /Carquest (Auto Parts)
315 West Putnam Avenue, 203.869.6550
www.CarQuest.com
Carquest has 3,400 stores throughout the US. It competes with Advance Auto Parts and Autozone.
Hours: Weekdays 8am-5:30pm, Saturday 8am-2pm.

Design Within Reach (Furniture)
711 Canal Street at Harbor Point, Stamford CT, 203.422.2013
www.dwr.com
A small chain dedicated to classic, modern furniture, most from known designers. Their goal is to provide furniture traditionally found only in design showrooms.
Hours: Monday-Saturday 10am-6pm (Thursday to 7pm),
Sunday 12pm-5pm.

Diane B. (Shoes-Women)
346 Greenwich Avenue, Greenwich CT, 203.629.8090
www.DianeBShoes.com
A store filled with pretty shoes and handbags. Cell phone conversations are not permitted in the store.
Hours: Monday-Saturday 10am-6pm (Thursday until 7pm),
Sunday 12pm -5pm.

Diane's Books (Books)
8A Grigg Street, Greenwich CT, 203.869.1515
See Review of Greenwich's favorite bookstore in BOOKS AND LIBRARIES.
Hours: Monday-Saturday 9am-5pm.

STORES

DSW (Shoes-Men & Women)
429 Boston Post Road (Kohls Shop Cntr), Port Chester NY, 914.908.5999
www.DSWshoes.com
The Designer Shoe Warehouse has 300 stores in 37 states. This location
carries more than 30,000 pairs of adult men's and women's shoes in an
amazing variety of styles.
Hours: Monday-Saturday 10am-9pm, Sunday 11am-7pm.

Duxiana Beds (Bedding)
15 West Putnam Avenue, Greenwich CT, 203.661.7162
www.DuxBed.com
Made in Sweden with several layers of springs, Dux beds are guaranteed
for 20 years and cost, depending upon the model, between $7,000 and
$13,000 for a king-size bed and between $3,600 and $6,000 for a single.
They have 28 stores in North America and over 80 locations worldwide.
Owners of these beds tell us they are worth the price.
Hours: Monday-Saturday 10am-6pm, Sunday 12pm-5pm.

East Putnam Variety (Magazines & Newspapers)
26 Greenwich Avenue, Greenwich CT, 203.869.8789
This conveniently located shop has magazines, cards, newspapers, and
a myriad of party goods, including a fabulous balloon selection. Great
customer service.
Hours: Monday-Saturday about 8am-9pm, Sunday about 8am-2pm.

Eastern Mountain Sports (Sporting Goods & Clothing)
2235 Summer Street (Ridgeway Shop Cntr), Stamford CT, 203.461.9865
www.ems.com
A general purpose chain sports store with an emphasis on camping, climbing and kayaking. A good place to find out about climbing and kayaking
instruction.
Hours: Monday-Saturday 10am-8pm, Sunday 11am-5pm.

Ed's Garage Doors (Overhead Doors)
136 Water Street, Norwalk CT, 203.847.1284
www.edsgaragedoors.com
If you are looking for a new overhead door they have a large store making selections easy. They will repair or provide garage door openers for
any door.
They are a very reliable resource.
Hours: Weekdays 8am-5pm, Saturday 9am-3pm.

Elle Encore (Consigned Designer Clothing)
115 Mason Street (Vilage Square), Greenwich CT, 203.912.1148
www.consigneddesigns.com/elle-encore
A sister store to Consigned Designs (listed separately). They carry consigned designer clothing such as: Hermes, Pucci, Prada and Armani.
Hours: Monday-Saturday 10am-5pm.

Eres (Clothing-Women's Swimwear)
372 Greenwich Avenue, Greenwich CT, 203.340.9500
www.eresct.com
One of 4 USA stores. They are owned by Channel, but carry their own branded swimsuits and lingerie.
Hours: Open every day 10am-6pm.

Estate Treasures of Greenwich
(Consignment-Furniture, Jewelry, Silver)
1162 East Putnam Avenue, Riverside CT, 203.637.4200
www.EstateTreasures.com
An antique consignment shop which has a wide selection of jewelry and china. A good source for silver services and serving pieces. A large number of tables and desks, although some are high-quality reproductions (always marked as reproductions).
Hours: Monday-Saturday 10am-5:30pm, Sunday 12pm-5:30pm.
Closed on Sunday in August.

Ethan Allen (Furniture, Home Decorating)
2046 West Main, Stamford CT, 203.352.2888
www.EthanAllen.com
This 30,000 square-foot store just on the border of Greenwich is the company's largest store. Its collections are divided between informal and classic. They carry just about everything for a home, including a large selection of furniture, window treatments, area rugs and accessories.
Hours: Monday-Saturday 10am-6pm, Sunday 12pm-5pm.

EuroChasse (Fishing & Hunting)
398 Greenwich Avenue, Greenwich CT, 203.625.9501
www.eurochasse.com
Two floors of fascinating gifts and fashionable men's and women's sporting apparel. If you plan to hunt in Europe, this is a must. They also have serious fly fishing equipment and gifts just right for your sporting friends. A good place to get your hunting license.
Hours: Monday-Saturday 10am-5pm.

STORES

Everything But Water (Clothing -Women, Men, Children)
84 Greenwich Avenue, Greenwich CT, 203.622.1878
www.EverythingButWater.com
One of over 75 stores carrying designer swimsuits and resort wear. They have just about everything you need for a day at the pool or a beach trip. Swimsuits are arranged by color.
Hours: Monday-Saturday 10am-6pm, Sunday 12pm-5pm.

Fabric House (Drapery & Upholstery Fabric)
20 Henry Street, Byram CT, 914.948.5198
www.TheFabricHouse.com
High-end fabrics and trims at wholesale prices from items in stock or ordered from major mills or designer showrooms. They will design and make custom draperies and do custom re-upholstery.
Hours: Tuesday-Saturday 11am-5pm, (closed Saturday in the summer)

Farrow & Ball (Wallpaper & Paint)
32 East Putnam Avenue, Greenwich CT, 203.422.0990
www.Farrow-Ball.com
A favorite of designers, this shop is open to everyone. The soft and classic patterns of the wallpaper are color coordinated with their paints. Paints are available in many colors and finishes. This British paint manufacturer can match just about any historic color pallet. They offer in-home color consultation.
Hours: Weekdays 9am-5:30pm, Saturday 10am-3pm.

Fashion Light Center (Lighting)
168 West Putnam Avenue, Greenwich CT, 203.869.3098
www.lighttrends.com
A handy, helpful local resource for bulbs, lamp shades, lamps, chandeliers and repairs. This 3,500 square-foot showroom has more than 23,000 indoor and outdoor light fixtures and carries all of the top brands. The owner, Archie Russell, can help you with just about any lighting project. They have a good website.
Hours: Monday-Saturday 9am-5:30pm.

Federalist (Home Decorating, Furniture)
95 East Putnam Avenue, Greenwich CT, 203.625.4727
www.thefederalistonline.com
Not antiques, but only experts would know it. The shop is filled with fine reproductions of 18th century American furniture and accessories.
Hours: Weekdays 10am-6pm.

STORES

Feinsod True Value Hardware (Hardware)
268 Sound Beach Avenue, Old Greenwich CT, 203.637.3641
43 N Main Street, Port Chester NY 914.939.3872
www.feinsodhardware.com
Friendly, well-stocked hardware store run by people who take customer service that extra step. They even repair storm windows and screens.
Hours:Old Greenwich: Monday-Saturday 8am-5:30pm, Sunday 10am-3pm. Port Chester: Weekdays 7:30am-6pm, Saturday 8am-6pm, Sunday 9am-1pm.

Fence Factory (Fence)
22 Dyke Lane, Stamford CT, 203.324.3654   www.fence-factory.com
Owned and operated by the Bellissimo family since 1979. They manufacture and install fences for just about any need.
Showroom Hours: Weekdays 9am-5pm, Saturday 9am-1pm.

Flinn Gallery (Art)
101 West Putnam Avenue (@ Greenwich Library), Greenwich CT, 203.622.7947   www.flinngallery.com
This attractive gallery on the second floor is sponsored by the Friends of Greenwich Library. It has rotating exhibits selected by a jury. The Gallery also hosts the annual juried exhibition of the Greenwich Art Society.
Hours: Monday, Tuesday, Wednesday, Friday 10am-5pm, Thursday 10am-8pm, Saturday 10am-5pm.

Floor Covering Warehouse (Carpets & Rugs)
112 Orchard Street, Stamford CT, 203.323.3113
www.floorcoveringwarehouse.org
Tucked away, yet close to Greenwich, this family-owned rug and carpet store has good prices and good service.
Hours: Tuesday-Thursday 8am-5pm, Friday 8am-4pm, Saturday 8:30am-12:30pm.

Fontana (Bridal Salon-Eveningwear)
51 East Putnam Avenue, Greenwich CT, 203.204.8600
www.FontanaBridalSalon.com
A bridal and evening wear dress shop, with dresses from over 40 designers. We haven't used the shop but reviews on the internet are a mix of very positive and very negative.
Hours: Closed Wednesday, Monday & Thursday 11am-7pm, Tuesday & Friday 11am-6pm, Saturday 10am-5pm, Sunday 11am-4pm.

STORES

Fred (Clothing-Women)

236 Sound Beach Avenue, Old Greenwich CT, 203.344.9533
www.OGFred.com
Owner Kelly Frey named the shop after her young daughter's nickname.
Stylish clothing for young adults.
Hours: Monday-Saturday 10am-6pm, Saturday 12am-5pm.

Free People (Clothing- Women)

351 Greenwich Avenue, Greenwich CT, 203.622.0127
www.freepeople.com
Free People is a women's clothing store operated by Urban Outfitters,
which also operates Anthropologie. This small chain has colorful, creative and somewhat quirky designs. They also carry women's accessories and lingerie.
Hours: Monday-Saturday 10am-6pm (Friday & Saturday 7pm),
Sunday 12pm-5 pm.

(A I)Friedman (Art Supplies and Framing)

495 Boston Post Road (Kohls Shop Cntr), Port Chester NY, 914.937.7351
www.aifriedman.com
Discount art and craft supply store frequented by many local artists. Large
selection of quality pre-made frames and mats.
Hours: Monday-Saturday 9am-9pm, Sunday 10am-7pm.

Gabby (Clothing-Women)

70 Greenwich Avenue, Greenwich CT, 203.661.5044
This woman's boutique carries good quality and stylish sweaters, jack-
ets, blouses and pants. The service is friendly and the atmosphere is
appealing. If you quickly need to find something to wear for dinner on
Friday night, you should give this place a try.
Hours: Monday-Saturday 10am-5:30pm, Sunday 1am-5pm.

Galazan Gunmakers (Shotguns and Clothing)

24 Sound View Drive, Greenwich CT, 203.661.1701
www.ConnecticutShotgun.com
Most of their guns are made by the Connecticut Shotgun Manufacturing
Company in New Britain, CT. This showroom is like a museum of fine
quality, beautifully engraved shotguns. They also carry Holland and
Holland shotguns and apparel.
Hours: Thursday, Friday, Saturday 11am-5pm.

STORES

Galerie Greenwich aka Glen Aber Contemporary Art (Art)
5 West Putnam Avenue, Greenwich CT, 203.717.1111
www.GalerieGreenwich.com
Contemporary art. Prices range from about $4,000 to $40,000.
Hours: Tuesday-Saturday 10am-5pm.

Galleria (Shopping Center)
100 Main Street, White Plains NY, 914.682.0111
www.simon.com/mall/the-galleria
The anchor stores are Sears (914.644.1400), Macys (914.946.5015), Old
Navy (914.682.0482) and H&M (914.422.3777). Sears bought Lands End
in 2002 and has a Lands End store at this location.
Hours: Monday-Saturday 10am-9:30pm, Sunday 11am-7pm.

Gap (Clothing-Men & Women)
100 Greyrock Place (Stamford Town Center), Stamford CT, 203.327.3448
www.Gap.com
The Gap targets teenagers to 40s. Its merchandise is divided between
career clothing and trendy attire and includes maternity. Its lower price
line is sold at Old Navy (an anchor store in the Ridgeway Shopping Center
and in the Galleria). Banana Republic carries their higher-end casual
career clothing.
Hours: Monday-Saturday 10am-9pm, Sunday 11am-6pm.

Gap Kids (Clothing- Babies, Youth)
100 Greyrock Place (Stamford Town Center), Stamford CT, 203.327.3448
www.gapkids.com
Casual clothes for babies and children to age 8. They are also a uniform
center. Hours: Monday-Saturday 9am-8pm, Sunday 11pm-7pm.

Gift Shop at Audubon Center (Gifts)
613 Riversville Road, Greenwich CT, 203.869.5272
The perfect place to find nature objects, field guides and books. Many
unique gifts for children and adults.
Hours: Tuesday-Friday 10am-4pm, Saturday 9am-5pm,
Sunday 12pm-5pm.

STORES

Gift Shop at Bruce Museum (Gifts)
1 Museum Drive, Greenwich CT, 203.869.0376
www.brucemuseum.org
This attractive, high-quality store is filled with unique gifts from around the world, including many with educational value and an excellent selection of books. Merchandise complements the Museum's current exhibits. Be sure to attend their holiday gift bazaar.
Hours: Tuesday-Saturday 10am-4:30pm, Sunday 1pm-4:30pm.

Gift Shop at Hyatt Regency (Gifts)
1800 East Putnam Avenue, Old Greenwich CT, 203.409.4599
Hotel guests find this shop convenient, but we also dash there when we need a gift with "Greenwich" on it.
Hours: Monday-Saturday 7am-11pm, Sunday 8am-8pm.

Gift Shop at Greenwich Hospital (Gifts)
5 Perryridge Road, Greenwich CT, 203.863.3371
www.greenhosp.org
They have a wide array of gifts for patients, including pretty planters and beautiful nightgowns. The items selected by the volunteer staff have made this shop a place to go whether or not you are visiting in the hospital. Selections are well-priced and tax-free. All profits go the hospital.
Hours: Monday, Wednesday & Friday 9:30am-7pm, Saturday 10am-5pm, Sunday 12pm-5pm.

Gift Shop at Greenwich Hospital Flowers (Florist)
5 Perryridge Road, Greenwich CT, 203.863.3371
www.greenhosp.org
The gift shop keeps a selection of fresh flowers in vases, get well balloons and a number of Baby and Mom items for the new moms. Call or buy online and they will deliver to your favorite patient.
Hours: Monday, Wednesday & Friday 9:30am-7pm, Saturday 10am-5pm, Sunday 12pm-5pm.

Giggle (Baby-Clothing & Furniture)
102 Greenwich Avenue, Greenwich CT, 203.622.6775 www.Giggle.com
A store for new parents, ready to help you stock your nursery with the best of everything. Their collection includes baby items selected to be healthy, stylish and fun, from strollers, car seats, bedding and furniture to toys, baby care and cleaning products. Giggle is a small chain with 5 stores. Hours: Monday-Saturday 10am to 6pm, Sunday 11am-5 pm.

STORES

Globe Kitchen Equipment
(Kitchen Equipment, Appliances & Cookware)
300 Dewey Street, Bridgeport CT, 203.367.6611, 866.604.5623
www.GlobeEquipment.com
Just about everything for the commercial kitchen or a special home kitchen.
Hours: Weekdays 8:30am-5pm, Saturday 9am-2pm.

Golden Horn (Oriental Rugs- Sale and Restoration)
464 N Main Street, Port Chester NY, 914.670.6666
www.RugRestoration.com
They specialize in restoration, cleaning and sale of fine oriental and European carpets. They can repair most woven art including tapestries. In addition to repairs, they have more than 2,000 new and antique rugs for sale in their 5,000 sf space.
Hours: Monday-Saturday 8:30am-6pm.

Glenville Hardware (Hardware)
12 Riversville Road, Glenville Center, Glenville CT, 203.531.5599
www.GlenvilleHardware.com
A good old-fashioned hardware store with most everything you would need for light and heavy-duty home projects, barbecue grills and more. It's wonderful, you can stop in, tell one of the sales people what you want and they will find it for you immediately. From firewood to screen repair, they do it all.
Hours: Monday-Saturday 8:30am-5pm, Sunday 9am-3pm (hours somewhat flexible).

Graham's Toys (Toys)
60 Greenwich Avenue, Greenwich CT, 203.983.6800
www.landbridgetoys.com www.GrahamsToys.com
A unique toy store, with toys you won't find anywhere else. We love their interesting children's books. They have a children's barber shop in the back; call for appointments.
Hours: Monday-Saturday 10am-5pm, Sunday 12pm-5pm.

STORES

Grainger (Industrial Supplies)
339 West Avenue, Stamford CT, 203.323.0005
www.Grainger.com
350,000 items including supplies, such as material handling, safety and security, cleaning and maintenance, pumps and plumbing, electrical, lighting, ventilation, tools, metal working, fluid power, heating and air-conditioning products, motors, and power transmissions. A paradise for the do-it-yourselfer.
Hours: Weekdays 7am-5pm.

(The) Great Outdoor Toy Company (Children's Play Equipment)
9 Kings Highway, Westport CT, 203.222.3818
www.thegreatoutdoortoycompany.com
Playhouses, hoops, trampolines and redwood swing sets with interchangeable parts, allowing you to make your own fun designs.
Hours: Monday-Saturday 9:30am-5:30pm, sometimes open Sunday 12pm-5pm.

Great Stuff (Clothing-Women)
321 Greenwich Avenue, Greenwich CT, 203.861.6872
Eclectic selections with a flair-informal and formal, with lots of possibilities for evening wear.
Hours: Monday-Saturday 10am-6pm, Sunday 12pm-5pm.

Greenwich Bicycles (Bicycles)
35 Amogerone Crossway, Greenwich CT, 203.869.4141
www.greenwichbikes.com
Road bikes, mountain bikes, this large store has all the right equipment and a very helpful website to review before you shop for a bike. They carry Trek, Cannondale, Pinarello, Cervelo, Devinci & Electra.
Hours: Weekdays 10am-6pm (8pm Thursday), Saturday 9:30am-5:30pm; (April-September, open Sunday 11am-4pm). Check for winter hours.

Greenwich Diva (Clothing-Women)
177 Sound Beach Avenue, Greenwich CT, 203.536.3607
www.GreenwichDivaStore.com
Claudette Rothman is a Greenwich resident and a graduate of FIT. Her shop is filled with bright, colorful, easy-to-wear clothing for teens and adults. Hours: Monday-Saturday 10am-6pm.

STORES

Greenwich Exchange for Women's Work (Gifts)
28 Sherwood Place, Greenwich CT, 203.869.0229
www.greenwichexchange.org
This small shop's mission is to help others help themselves. It has reasonably priced, handmade items. If you want to give a gift to a newborn or young child, you will adore their hand-knit sweaters and smocked dresses. Hours: Weekdays 10am-4pm; Saturday 10am-1pm.

Greenwich Furs (Furrier)
1076 East Putnam Avenue, Riverside CT, 203.869.1421
Since 1948 this furrier has been helping Greenwich residents select, repair, remodel and store their furs.
Hours: Monday-Saturday 10am-5pm. (Check for summer hours).

Greenwich Golf Fitting Studio (Golf)
222 Mill Street, Byram CT, 203.532.4810   www.Greenwichgolf.com
Jacques Intriere repairs your clubs or analyzes your swing to fit custom golf clubs to make you a better golfer.
Hours: Check their website for store hours.

Greenwich Hardware (Hardware)
195 Greenwich Avenue & Liberty Way Parking Area, Greenwich CT, 203.869.6750
www.GreenwichHardwareAndHome.com
Anyone moving into town will find this a valuable resource. A helpful place to call when you have forgotten something: they will deliver it to you. Ask them about renting tools.
Hours: Monday-Saturday 8am-5:30pm, Sunday 9:00am-4pm.

Greenwich Lock and Door (Locksmith)
280 Railroad Avenue, Greenwich CT, 203.622.1095
www.greenwichLockandDoor.com
A reliable local source for architectural hardware, doors, security products and lock-smithing. Good customer service.
Hours: Weekdays 10am-4pm.

STORES

Greenwich Music (Music)
1200 East Putnam Avenue, Riverside CT, 203.637.1119
www.greenwichmusic.com
Their store is filled with sheet music and instruments. They have a large selection of guitars & drums and a helpful staff. A full line of instruments is available for rent: a great way to discover if that instrument is right for you or your child. They have a music school (Fraioli School of Music) next door where they give lessons for the instruments they carry. See their website for details.
Hours: Weekdays 11am-6pm, Saturday 10am-5pm.

Greenwich Optics (Eyewear)
9 West Putnam Avenue, Greenwich CT, 203.552.6830
Dr. Leland Bass, OD, has a nice selection of eyeglasses.
Hours: Tuesday-Thursday 10am-5pm, Friday & Saturday 10am-4pm.

Greenwich Orchids (Florist)
106 Mason Street, Greenwich CT, 203.661.5544
www.GreenwichOrchids.com
Grown in their 56,000 square foot greenhouse, the orchids are exquisite. They have many varieties, some with unusual colors. They also make lovely flower arrangements.
Hours: Monday-Saturday 9am-6pm.

Greenwich Oriental Art (Antiques)
7 East Putnam Avenue, Greenwich CT, 203.629.0500
www.greenwichorientalart.com
A mixture of old and modern oriental art. Their website gives a good sampling of what they carry.
Hours: Monday-Saturday 10:30am-5:30pm.

Greenwich Window Treatments (Windows)
79 East Putnam Avenue, Greenwich CT, 203.992.1000
www.GreenwichWindowTreatments.com
Blinds, shades, sheers, shutters and Hunter Douglas motorized systems. They measure and install.
Hours: Weekdays 10am-5pm, Saturday 10am-2pm.
Summer hours may vary.

STORES

Griffin & Howe (Shotguns, clothing, accessories)
340 West Putnam Avenue, Greenwich CT, 203.618.0270
www.griffinhowe.com
Excellent sporting firearms, clothing and accessories. This is the place where serious skeet and trap shooters buy their shotguns. They also have shooting schools and an excellent selection of rifles.
Hours: Weekdays 10am-6pm, Saturday 9am-4 pm. Be sure to call, hours may vary.

Gut Reaction (Racquet Sport Equipment)
16 Lewis Street, Greenwich CT, 203.769.5329
www.GutReactionTennis.net
Tennis racquets, stringing, shoes, apparel, and accessories for men, women and children.
Hours: Weekdays 10am-6pm, Saturday 9am-5pm.

Gym Source (Exercise Equipment)
20 Railroad Avenue, Greenwich CT, 203.622.5069.
www.GymSource.com
With 31 stores, they are the largest US distributor of fitness equipment. They seem to carry everything from sophisticated equipment to TheraBands.
Hours: Monday-Saturday 10am-6pm or 7pm (Thursday until 8pm), Sunday 11am-5pm.

Hansen & Hansen (Antique Guns)
244 Old Post Road, Southport CT, 203.259.7337
www.hansenguns.com
They buy, sell and appraise antique firearms, swords, knives and related collectibles.
Hours: Tuesday-Friday 12pm-5pm (Wednesday & Thursday 6pm), Saturday 10am-4pm.

Harris Restaurant Supply (Cookware)
25 Abendroth Avenue, Port Chester NY, 914.937.0404
www.hrs-foodservice.com
Commercial restaurant supplier which also allows the general public to buy. Cooks go crazy here.
Hours: Weekdays 9am-4pm.

513

Harrow (Sporting Goods)

Liberty Way, Greenwich CT, 203.742.6060

www.HarrowSports.com

Harrow designs and manufactures a variety of equipment for sports, such as: squash, field hockey, lacrosse, ice hockey, badminton, pickleball, platform tennis and court tennis. The store sells only products made by Harrow. Squash racquets, clothing and accessories are their top sellers.
Greenwich Hours: Weekdays 10am-6pm, Saturday 10am-2pm.

Hästens (Bedding)

23 East Putnam Avenue, Greenwich CT, 203.629.8022

www.hastens.com

A family-owned business since 1852. The Beds are handmade in Sweden with natural materials like cotton, horse hair, wool and flax, rather than foam. They are sold in over 22 countries. King size beds sell for $6,000 to $37,000.
Hours: Monday-Saturday 10am-6pm.

HB Home (Home Fabrics and Furniture)

23 Lewis Street, Greenwich CT, 203.629.4999

www.hbhomedesign.com

HB stands for the name of the designers Patricia Healing and Dan Barsanti. Their furniture is a mix of stylish period and country designs.
Hours: Weekdays 9am-4pm, Saturday 10am-3:30pm.

Helen Ainson (Clothing-Women)

1078 Post Road, Darien CT, 203.655.9841

www.HelenAinson.com

For over 25 years Helen Ainson has helped ladies in our area look their best at special occasions. When you discover you are soon to be "mother of the bride," you will like their friendly, knowledgeable advice and fashions from over 150 manufacturers.
Hours: Monday-Saturday 9:30am-5:30pm (Tuesday & Thursday 7 pm).

STORES

Hermes (Clothing-Men & Women)
289 Greenwich Avenue, Greenwich CT, 203.622.3007
www.hermes.com
Established in 1837, this public company has more than 100 company-owned stores and about 299 franchises. Although they have 14 product lines, the majority of their sales are leather goods, clothes, scarves, ties and tableware. In 2012, Hermes changed its return policy. Consumers may only exchange items within ten days of purchase, and only for another color variant of the original purchase. No other post-purchase exchanges are permitted and refunds are never offered, regardless of the consumer having a receipt. Hours: Monday-Saturday 10am-6pm.

Hickory & Tweed (Skiing Equipment & Clothing)
410 Main Street, Armonk NY, 914.273.3397
www.hickoryandtweed.com
A wide selection of skis, boots and clothing. Good technical help. When you are planning to buy equipment, this store is definitely worth the trip. It was voted the number one ski shop in America by Ski Magazine.
Hours: Weekdays 10am-5:30pm (Thursdays 8pm), Saturday 9:30am-5:30pm, Sunday (except July & August) 12pm-4pm.

(The) Historical Christmas Barn
146 Danbury Road, Wilton CT, 203.761.8777
www.historicalChristmasbarn.com
Yes, this Christmas store closes at 5 pm. They are in a residential zone and this seems to be a town rule. But what wonderful ornaments and figurines! This is like no other Christmas store you are likely to find.
Hours: Monday-Saturday 10am-5pm, Sunday 11am-5pm. From January-August it's closed on Mondays.

Historic Floors by Stephen Gamble
5 Lewis Street, Greenwich CT, 203.866.0892
www.HistoricFloorsInc.com
Custom floors from new and reclaimed wood, with just about any finish. Stephen will also do custom staining.
Hours: Weekdays 8am-4pm.

Hoagland's of Greenwich (Home Accessories & Gifts)
175 Greenwich Avenue, Greenwich CT, 203.869.2127
www.Hoaglands.com
A first-class gift shop owned for years by a Greenwich resident with exquisite taste. This is THE place for brides and grooms to register. In addition to their crystal, china and silver, they have charming baby gifts.
Hours: Monday-Saturday 9am-5pm.

(Ann's) Hobby Center (Toys)
405 East Putnam Avenue (Cos Cob Plaza), Cos Cob CT, 203.869.0969
www.AnnsHobby.com
For years, kids in Greenwich have been rewarded for cleaning their room or finishing their homework with a trip to Ann's Hobby Center. Rockets and radio-controlled boats are favorites. No matter what your hobby, they are likely to have what you need.
Hours: Monday-Saturday 9:30am-5:30pm (Saturday until 5pm).

Home Boutique of Greenwich (Linens)
14 Lewis Street, Greenwich CT, 203.869.2550
www.HomeBoutique.com
When you feel like treating yourself or want to create a picture-perfect bedroom, visit this shop filled with pretty bed, bath & table linens.
Hours: Monday-Saturday 10am-5:30pm.

Home Depot (Hardware)
www.homedepot.com
They have 40,000 brand names to choose from.
• 600 Connecticut Avenue, Norwalk CT, 203.854.9111
Hours: Monday-Saturday 6am-10pm, Sunday 7am-9pm.
• 150 Midland Avenue, Port Chester NY, 914.690.9745
Hours: Monday-Saturday 7am-10 pm, Sunday 9am-6pm.

Home Goods (Home Decorating- Accessories)
• 27 High Ridge Road (@ Cold Spring Road), Stamford CT, 203.964.9416
• 423 Boston Post Road (Kohl's Shop Cntr), Port Chester NY, 914.939.0937
www.homegoods.com
When you are ready to accessorize a room, this store is a must. Casual, fun items at good prices.
Stamford Hours: Monday-Saturday 8am-10pm, Sunday 11am-8pm.

Home Works (Windows & Fabric)
509 North Main Street, Port Chester NY, 914.934.0907
www.HomeWorksNY.com
When you want to redo your window draperies or upholster a chair, they are a good resource for your fabric. Hours: Weekdays 10am-5pm.

House of Fins (Fish)
99 Bruce Park Avenue, Greenwich CT, 203.661.8131
www.houseoffins.com
Owned by Greenwich resident Robert Bray, House of Fins has a huge inventory of everything you need to make a successful aquarium or stock a pond. Good advice as well. Complete service and many exotic fish to choose from. Hours: Monday-Saturday 10am-7pm, Sunday 12pm-5pm.

Housewarmings (Home Decorating -Furniture & Gifts)
264 Sound Beach Avenue, Old Greenwich CT, 203.637.5106
Home furnishings and decorative accessories. Comfortable furniture with a choice of fabrics. Hours: Monday-Saturday 10am-5:30pm.

IKEA (Furniture)
www.Ikea.com/us
A huge store and a huge chain (296 stores), with moderate prices and several grades of Scandinavian-designed furniture and housewares. Popular with Europeans. There is a supervised children's play area. A good place to go when you are on a limited budget and need to furnish a home or dorm room quickly.
• 1000 IKEA (Center) Drive, Elizabeth, NJ, 908.289.4488 (44 miles)
Hours: Monday-Saturday 10am-9pm, Sunday 10am-8pm.
• 450 Sargent Drive, New Haven CT, 203.865.4532 (51 miles)
Hours: Every day 10am-9pm.

Images (Framing, Gifts & Photography)
202 Sound Beach Avenue, Old Greenwich CT, 203.637.4193
www.imagescenter.com
For years this shop has been the go-to place for framing photographs. They restore damaged photographs by removing scratches, tears and stains, enhance photographs to reduce redeye or correct color and brightness, and, of course, enlarge, crop or add a border. No negative is required. It is also an art gallery and gift shop with unique items.
Hours: Tuesday-Saturday 10am-5pm, Sunday 11am-3pm (photograph and framing help only on weekdays).

Innovation Luggage (Luggage)
86 Greenwich Avenue, Greenwich CT, 203.869.5322
www.InnovationLuggage.com
A national chain carrying medium-priced luggage, casual bags, business cases and travel accessories. Nice selection and helpful service.
Hours: Monday-Saturday 10am-6pm, Sunday 12pm-5pm.

Instant Replay (Hockey Equipment)
1074 Hope Street, Stamford CT, 203.322.7502
Located across from the Stamford Twin Rinks is a shop where parents in the know can save money outfitting their family with everything they will need for playing hockey or baseball. They have a wide selection of new and used equipment.
Hours: Weekdays 10am-6pm, Saturday 9am-5pm, Sunday 11am-4pm.

Intermix (Clothing-Women)
325 Greenwich Avenue, Greenwich CT, 203.302.3200
www.intermixonline.com
Upscale casual clothing from a variety of fashion designers. This is one of 35 plus boutiques in the USA.
Hours: Monday-Saturday 10am-6pm, Sunday 11am-5pm.

Interstate Fire and Safety (Fire Extinguishers)
404 Willett Avenue, Port Chester NY, 914.937.6100
www.interstatefireandsfty.net
Fire extinguishers for home or business.
Hours: Weekdays 8am-5pm.

Interstate / Lakeland Lumber (Hardware-Building Materials)
184 South Water Street, Greenwich CT, 203.531.8050
www.InterstateLumber.com
A convenient place to look for doors, windows and trim. A good window design showroom.
Hours: Weekdays 7:30am-5pm, Saturday 8am-12pm.

Irresistibles (Clothing-Women)
104 Main Street, New Canaan CT, 203.966.0608
www.Irresistibles.com
A small 13 store chain with contemporary sportswear for women. At a holiday luncheon, many of the ladies had purchased their pretty decorated sweaters at this shop.
Hours: Monday-Saturday 9:30am-6pm, Sunday 12pm-5pm.

STORES

J Crew (Clothing-Men & Women)
126 Greenwich Avenue, Greenwich CT, 203.661.5181
www.jcrew.com
A large store with classic, preppy-casual men's and women's clothing.
Check out "Crew Cuts" for children ages 2-12. The high-end adult clothes
are in the J Crew Collection. Michelle Obama wears J Crew clothes.
Hours: Monday-Saturday 10am-6pm, Sunday 12pm-5pm.

J McLaughlin (Clothing-Women)
55 East Putnam Avenue, Greenwich CT, 203.862.9777
www.jmclaughlin.com
Primarily women's informal, quality, preppy clothing-"stylish, but not
stuffy."
Hours: Monday-Saturday 9:30am-5:30pm, Sunday 11am-4pm.

Jones New York (Discount Women's Clothing)
517 Westport Avenue, Norwalk CT, 203.847.3794
A company-owned store, co-located with Nine West shoe outlet, some
merchandise is slightly discounted some is dramatically discounted. A
good resource.
Hours: Monday-Saturday 10am-9pm, Sunday 11am-6pm.

JoS A Bank (Clothing-Men)
Cos Cob Plaza (409 East Putnam Avenue), Cos Cob CT, 203.869.6087
www.josbank.com
With over 400 retail stores, its clothing is targeted at male professionals.
They have several different lines: the basic business express, executive
collections, the mid-range signature collection and the high-quality signature gold collection. The Greenwich store is 4,000 square feet. Customer service is a priority.
Hours: Monday-Saturday 10am-9pm, Sunday 10am-6pm.

j papers (Stationery & Gifts)
100 Bruce Park Avenue, Greenwich CT, 203.769.5104
www.jpapers.biz, https://www.facebook.com/jpapersandco
This is a wonderful place to find out-of-the-ordinary invitations, greeting cards, or unique gifts. When you need a special design or help with
an invitation, make an appointment with Jill, the owner, or one of her
talented staff. You will be delighted with the result.
Hours: Monday-Sunday 10am-5pm (during July & August,
closed Sunday & Monday).

J Pocker & Son (Framing)

175 West Putnam Avenue, Greenwich CT, 203.629.0811
www.JPocker.com
A family business since 1926. Good suggestions for appropriate frames and mats. They have a large portfolio of limited-edition prints.
Hours: Tuesday-Saturday 10am-5:30pm.

jacadi (Clothing-Baby & Toddler)

22 Greenwich Avenue, Greenwich CT, 203.422.2202
www.jacadiusa.com
This Paris-based company has 400 boutiques worldwide and 27 US locations. Although the company has a wide selection of nursery furniture and accessories, the Greenwich shop features their very fashionable, ultra-simple, elegant, newborn through toddler clothing.
Hours: Monday-Saturday 10am-6pm, Sunday 12pm-5pm.

Jack Wills (Clothing-Men & Women)

252 Greenwich Avenue, Greenwich CT, 203.422.5950
www.JackWills.com
A British clothing brand aimed at university students, from 18-25, which is not to say that 40-somethings won't like them as well. There are 13 stores in the USA and 54 in the UK.
Hours: Monday-Saturday 10am-6pm, Sunday 11am-6pm.

Janie and Jack (Baby to Children's Clothing)

107 Greenwich Avenue, Greenwich CT, 203.422.5080
www.Janieandjack.com
Owned by the Gymboree company, there are over 100 Janie and Jack stores. They carry adorable clothing for children-babies to age 6.
Hours: Monday-Saturday 10am-6pm, Sunday 12pm-5pm.

Joie (Clothing-Women)

163 Greenwich Avenue, Greenwich CT, 203.413.1330
www.joie.com
California-inspired, contemporary, casual clothing for women. Created by Joie Rucker in 2001, the brand was initially purchased from her in 2007 by the Dutch Group which is now controlled by TA Associates. Joie has 9 boutique stores and is sold in 75 countries, mainly through department stores such as Nordstrom, Neiman Marcus, and Saks.
Hours: Monday-Saturday 10am-6pm (Thursday to 7pm),
Sunday 12pm-5pm.

STORES

Jonathan Adler (Home Furnishings)
88 Greenwich Avenue, Greenwich CT, 203.622.1476
www.Jonathanadler.com
Jonathan Adler is a potter, designer, author. He has 26 stores worldwide. Known for his whimsical pottery, he has expanded into home furnishings and accessories. It is hard to go into his store without wanting to buy something.
Hours: Monday-Saturday 10am-6pm, Sunday 12pm-5 pm.

JSJ Window Treatments (Windows)
3 Strickland Road, Cos Cob CT, 203.661.5123
www.JSJwindowtreatments.com
A locally-owned, reliable source for blinds, shades and shutters. They carry Hunter Douglas and fabrics for curtains. Shades can be cut on the premises.
Hours: Weekdays 9am-5pm, Saturday 10am-2pm.

Juliska (Glassware)
465 Canal Street, Stamford CT, 203.316.9118
www.Juliska.com
Stores all over the USA, like Saks, Neiman Marcus and Michael C Fina, carry this distinctive glassware. This flagship store has scrumptious table settings and dramatic pieces. Juliska's outlet store is located in Lillian August's outlet store at 85 Water Street in Norwalk.
Hours: Monday-Saturday 9am-5pm, Sunday 12pm-5pm.

Just Shades (Lampshades)
154 Prospect Street, Greenwich CT, 203.681.2757
www.JustShadesCT.com
A good resources for custom and ready-made lampshades. Returns are for store credit or exchange only.
Hours: Monday-Saturday 10am-6pm.

Kate Spade (Accessories- Women and Home)
271 Greenwich Avenue, Greenwich CT, 203.622.4260
www.KateSpade.com
Women's specialty shop selling chic handbags, shoes, and home accessories. Kate Spade has over 200 stores in 20 countries.
Hours: Monday-Saturday 10am-6pm (Thursday 7pm), Sunday 12pm-6pm.

Kenneth Lynch & Sons (Garden Accessories)
114 Willenbrook Road, Oxford CT, 203.264.2831
www.klynchandsons.com
If you are looking for an elaborate fountain, pretty garden bench, statuary, topiary, weathervane or sundial, this will be paradise for you. The Lynch family has been crafting garden ornaments for over sixty years. Ornaments are made to order. Their extensive catalog is available for about $15. Hours: Weekdays 8:30am-5pm.

Klaff's (Lighting, Hardware, Fixtures)
28 Washington Street, South Norwalk CT, 800.552.3371 or 203.866.1603
www.klaffs.com
A tremendous selection of indoor and outdoor lighting fixtures, door hardware, bathroom fixtures. They even have kitchen cabinets, tile and mirrors. Hours: Monday-Saturday 9am-5:30pm.

Kmart (Department Store)
399 Tarrytown Rd, White Plains NY, 914.684.1184
www.Kmart.com
Discount store, owned by Sears, which competes with Wal-Mart and Target. They carry clothing, footwear, bedding, furniture, jewelry, electronics and housewares. Kmart is a primary source for Martha Stewart & Jaclyn Smith brands. Hours: Monday-Sunday 8am-10pm.

Kohl's (Department Store)
431 Post Road (Shopping Center), Port Chester NY, 914.690.0107
www.Kohls.com
Similar to JC Penney, they sell men's and women's clothing and accessories, as well as some household items at discounted prices.
Hours: Weekdays 9am-10pm, Saturday 8am-11pm, Sunday 9am-9pm.

L'Occitane (Cosmetics)
236 Greenwich Avenue, Greenwich CT, 203.422.0234
www.loccitane.com
Fragrances, candles and body care products with the soft scents of southern France. L'Occitane has more than 700 stores worldwide. The company does no animal testing and no animal product or by-product is used, except for beehive products.
Hours: Monday-Saturday 10am-6pm, Sunday 12pm-5pm.

STORES

Lacoste Boutique (Clothing-Men, Women & Youth)
98 Greenwich Avenue, Greenwich CT, 203.422.0180
www.Lacoste.com
A French apparel company founded in 1933 that sells preppie, high-end clothing. It is famous for its tennis shirts and the company's logo, a green crocodile. I couldn't resist their white tennis sweater. The collections are divided between active sports wear, casual sportswear (green crocodile) and club wear (grey crocodile). The founder, René Lacoste, was a famous French tennis player who achieved fame in tennis as well as in fashion. The family still owns control of the company.
Hours: Monday-Saturday 10am-6pm, Sunday 12pm-5pm.

Lacrosse Unlimited (Sporting Goods)
1239 East Putnam Avenue, Riverside CT, 203.344.9402
www.LacrosseUnlimited.com
One of 44 stores, they sell equipment, clothes, team uniforms and custom apparel. They are a good source for sports camps.
Hours: Monday-Saturday 10am-8pm, Sunday 11am-5pm.

Landfall Navigation (Boating)
151 Harvard Avenue, Stamford CT, 203.487.0775
www.landfallnavigation.com
Captain Henry Marx, the owner, is very knowledgeable and helpful. If you have a boat, he has what you need: charts, supplies or just information. Be sure to get a copy of his catalog. They have excellent nautical gifts.
Hours: (June 1-August 15) Weekdays 9am-7pm, Saturday 9am-2pm; (August 20-December 24 & March 1-June 1) Weekdays 9am-5pm, Saturday 9am-2pm; (January 1-March 1) Weekdays 9am-5pm.

Lands' End at Sears (Clothing-Men & Women)
100 Main Street (Galleria Shopping Center), White Plains NY, 914.644.1400
www.landsend.com
Attractive casual clothing for women, men and youth. Lands' End, an internet retailer, was purchased by Sears and has opened shops in a number of Sears stores.
Hours: Monday-Saturday 9am-9pm, Sunday, 10:30am-7pm.

LensCrafters (Eyewear)

100 Greyrock Place (Stamford Town Cntr), Stamford CT, 203.348.2080
www.lenscrafters.com
LensCrafters started in 1983 and has expanded to over 850 stores. They sell prescription eyewear and non-prescription sunglasses. They have the same parent as Pearle Vision. You can usually get a prescription before 6 pm and glasses within one hour.
Hours: Monday-Saturday 10am-9pm, Sunday 11am-6pm.

Letarte (Clothing-Women's Resort Wear)

369b Greenwich Avenue, Greenwich CT, 203.992.4377
www.LetarteSwimwear.com
This Maui-based chain was created by sisters Lisa Letarte Cabrinha and Michele Letarte in 2000. It now has stores in Maui, Nantucket, Southampton, Newport Beach and Palm Beach as well as Greenwich. In addition, over 400 retailers carry their clothing. Lisa, who lives in Maui, does the designing. Her colorful trademarked prints are used to create swimwear, sportswear, tunics and beach accessories, including tropical-weight cashmere.
Hours: Monday-Saturday 10am-6pm, Sunday 12pm-5pm.

Lexington Clothing Co. (Bedding, Clothing-Men & Women)

73 Greenwich Avenue, Greenwich CT, 203.489.3355
www.lexingtoncompany.com
Known for their upscale, colorful home furnishings (sheets, blankets, bathrobes, table linens, etc.) They also carry casual, cottage-style apparel for men and women. Despite their name and American flag emblem, they are a Swedish company, with only 3 of their 900 locations in the USA. Their designs are, theoretically, inspired by New England. This is one of their 55 concept stores.
Hours: Monday-Saturday 10am-6pm, Sunday 12pm-5pm. Closed on Sunday in the Summer.

LF Stores (Clothing-Women)

319 Greenwich Avenue, Greenwich CT, 203.629.6193
www.lfstores.com
LF wants to be an alternative to mainstream brands. With their California ultra-hip merchandise, we think they have met their goal.
Hours: Monday-Saturday 10am-6pm, Sunday, 11am-5pm.

STORES

Liberty Village (Outlet Mall)
1 Church Street, Flemington NJ, 908.782.8550
www.premiumoutlets.com/libertyvillage
Shop until you drop. About 2 hours away, there are more than 120 outlet stores in a number of outlet centers in Flemington. Forty of the shops are in Liberty Village.
Hours: Sunday-Wednesday 10am-6pm, Thursday-Saturday 10am-9pm.

Lillian August (Furniture)
• 28 Putnam Avenue, Greenwich CT, 203.629.1539
• 32 Knight Street, Norwalk CT, 203.847.3314
www.lillianaugust.com
Sofas, chairs and desks designed by Lillian August. The Norwalk store, their flagship store, is housed in a converted factory. It has 60,000 sf of selling space, double the size of the next largest store.
Greenwich Hours: Monday-Saturday 10am-6pm.
Norwalk Hours: Monday-Saturday 10am-7pm, Sunday 11am-6pm.

Lillian August Outlet Store (Furniture)
85 Water Street (SoNo Square), South Norwalk CT, 203.838.0153
www.lillianaugust.com
Sofas, chairs and desks designed by Lillian August.
Hours: Monday-Saturday 10am-6pm, Sunday 12pm-6pm.

Lilly Pulitzer (Clothing-Women & Children)
92 Greenwich Avenue, Greenwich CT, 203.661.3136
www.LillyPulitzer.com
Popular since the 1960's. Lots of pink and green and pretty colors for upscale casual women and children. Totally charming mother-daughter dress alikes.
Hours: Monday-Saturday 10am-6pm, Sunday 12pm-5pm.

Linen Press (Linen)
16 Arcadia Road, Old Greenwich CT, 203.637.0200
Unique luxury items for bed, bath and table. Much of the inventory is imported from France, Italy and Switzerland.
Hours: Monday-Saturday 10am-5pm.

STORES

Little Eric (Children-Shoes)
15 East Elm Street, Greenwich CT, 203.622.1600
www.littleEricGreenwich.com
A children's shoe store with high quality dress and play shoes. A helpful sales staff eliminates the usual shoe-shopping hassles.
Hours: Monday-Saturday 10am-6pm, Sunday 11am-5pm.

Lord and Taylor (Department Store)
110 High Ridge Road, Stamford, 203.327.6600
www.LordAndTaylor.com
A large full-service, stand-alone store, with easy parking and attractive, up-scale fashions for men and women 35 and up. Father and son, Robert and Richard Baker of Greenwich, purchased the 50 store chain in 2006. Lord & Taylor's merchandise is on a par with Barneys New York, Saks Fifth Avenue, Neiman Marcus and Bergdorf Goodman and slightly above Bloomingdale's and Nordstrom.
Hours: Weekdays 10am-9:30pm, Saturday 10am-9pm,
Sunday 11am-7pm.

Lucky Brand Jeans (Clothing-Men & Women)
244 Greenwich Avenue, Greenwich CT, 203.861.4039
www.LuckyBrandJeans.com
This large retro-shop is filled with garments reminiscent of the Jack Kerouac era. Everything from the shop's decor to the music is designed to make the 50's and 60's ooze from the clothing. Denim makes up most of their business. Lucky Brand Jeans first became popular due to the words, "LUCKY YOU" being stitched into the fly of every pair. They try to have the right pair of jeans for every body type. Jeans cost about $100. From their start in 1990 they have expanded to more than 110 stores.
Hours: Monday-Saturday 10am-6pm, Sunday 11am-6pm.

lululemon athletica (Exercise Clothing-Men and Women)
151 Greenwich Avenue, Greenwich CT, 203.622.5046
www.lululemon.com
Often referred to as "lulu," this yoga-inspired athletic apparel company has 100 stores which not only sell athletic attire but encourage a healthy lifestyle. On Sunday they convert their store into a yoga studio. Join them for a free yoga class.
Hours: Monday-Saturday 10am-6pm, Sunday 11am-6pm.

STORES

Lux Bond & Green (Jewelry)
169 Greenwich Avenue, Greenwich CT, 203.629.0900
www.LBGreen.com
They carry David Yurman jewelry and Steuben gifts.
Hours: Tuesday-Saturday 9:30am-5pm.

Lynnens (Linen)
278 Greenwich Avenue, Greenwich CT, 203.629.3659
www.lynnens.com
Since 1980 this high-end bed, bath, linen and nightwear store has been a real favorite of Greenwich residents. Lynne Jenkins has stocked her store with luxury products from around the world. Their specialties are service and customizing linens. Located in her shop is Sferra's high-end linen boutique. Hours: Monday-Saturday 9:30am-5:30pm.

MacInspires (Computers)
53 Greenwich Avenue, Greenwich CT, 203.531.5720
Their mission is to answer all Apple computer questions- simple and complex. They have a major concentration on education and out-of-warranty repair. They don't sell hardware but they do sell accessories. Hours: Monday-Saturday, 10am-7pm, Sunday 11am-5pm.

Maclaren Showroom (Baby Buggies)
10 Marshall Street, Norwalk CT, 203.354.4437
www.MaclarenBaby.com
This is a US factory store for the British company's fashionable, lightweight buggies (a.k.a. strollers), baby carriers and rockers. Maclaren products are sold in over 50 countries. The Techno XLR and the Techno MX3 models can be fitted with a car seat to become travel systems. Their repair center is also located in Norwalk at 25 Van Zant Street, 203.354.4439. Giggle, on Greenwich Avenue, sells their strollers. Hours: Call for an appointment.

Macy's (Department Store)
100 Greyrock Pl (Stamford Town Center), Stamford CT, 203.964.1500
www.macys.com
Macy's holds a special place in many people's hearts. Macy's opened in 1858 and has 850 department stores. The company competes on an average price level above Kohl's, JCPenney, and Sears, and below Nordstrom and sister chain Bloomingdale's. Hours: Weekdays 10am-9pm, Saturday 9am-10pm, Sunday 11am-8pm.

Madewell (Clothing -Women's Jeans & T-shirts)

256 Greenwich, Avenue, Greenwich CT, 203.661.1591
www.madewell1937.com
Launched in 2006 by J. Crew, the name of this 14-store chain's name was taken from a former Massachusetts workwear company. The workers in that 1937 company would be amazed at the edgy, ripped-up, ex-boyfriend jeans sold here for about $125 to $140 a pair.
Hours: Monday-Saturday 10am -6pm, Sunday 12pm-5 pm.

Magaschoni by Ellen (Clothing-Women)

115 Mason Street (Village Square), Greenwich CT, 203.869.2119
www.magaschoni.com
Stylish designs for jackets, sweaters and blouses that can be worn together or as separates. Magaschoni has 4 free-standing boutiques and 800 stores carry their designs. This shop is owned by Ellen Atkinson, who owns Consigned Designs and Elle Encore, also at the Village Square.
Hours: Monday-Saturday 10am-5pm.

Maje (Clothing-Women)

200 Greenwich Avenue, Greenwich CT, 203.622.7483
www.Maje.com
Maje founder Judith Milgrom opened two shops in Paris 10 years ago. Like her older sister's stores, Sandro, they are part of the Groupe SMCP which was acquired in 2013 by KKR. In addition to the Greenwich Store, Maje has 10 stores in NYC and many outside of the USA. Their trendy Parisian fashions are targeted at stylish young women. Her clothes are slightly more classic than Sandro's. Prices are mid-market. Both Maje and Sandro are located at 200 Greenwich Avenue.
Hours: Monday-Saturday 10am-6pm, Sunday 12pm-5pm.

MakerBot

200 Greenwich Avenue, Greenwich CT, 203.297.6175
www.makerbot.com
MakerBot was named one of Time Magazine's best inventions in 2012. Everyone is curious about the new frontier in desktop 3D printing. You can attend workshops and make 3D designs from their Photo Booth or use designs developed by their online community, www.Thingiverse.com. Their president, is Jenny Lawton, a Greenwich resident. She owned and managed Just Books and Arcadia.
Hours: Monday-Saturday 10am-6pm, Sunday 11am-5pm.

STORES

Manfredi (Jewelry)
121 Greenwich Avenue, Greenwich CT, 203.622.1414
www.manfredijewels.com
Roberto Chiappeloni's store focuses on current fashion and cutting-edge pieces. A good place to have your watch repaired.
Hours: Tuesday-Friday 10am-5pm, Saturday 10am-5:30pm (closed Mondays in the summer).

Marcia Jean (Sewing & Fabrics)
177 Sound Beach Avenue, Old Greenwich CT, 203.990.0688
www.MarciaJeanFabricAndCraft.com
Marcia Davis's small shop is full of yarns and pretty fabrics to buy by the yard. She teaches classes in knitting and crocheting. The handmade dolls are darling.
Hours: Tuesday-Saturday 10am-5pm.

Marietta (Clothing-Womens)
436 East Putnam Avenue, Cos Cob CT, 203.661.2171
www.Marietta.com
Marietta Contadino designs all the clothing in her store. In addition to daytime wear, she designs many dresses for brides and their mothers.
Hours: Tuesday-Saturday 10am-4pm.

Mark Mariani's Garden Center (Plants and Shrubs)
45 Bedford Road, Armonk NY, 914.273.3083
www.MarianiGardens.com
This stylish, unusual greenhouse and garden center is filled with shrubs, rare trees and decorative pottery. They also have a stylish restaurant, Zanni, reviewed in the RESTAURANT section.
Garden Cntr Hours: Weekdays 8:30am-5pm,
Saturday & Sunday 9am-4pm.

Marmot (Sports Clothing-Men & Women)
165 Greenwich Avenue, Greenwich CT, 203.869.0162
www.marmot.com
Good-looking, quality outdoor clothing and accessories for the well-dressed adventurer or sportsman. The Greenwich store is one of 7 flagship stores.
Hours: Monday-Saturday 10am-6pm, Sunday 11pm-5pm.

STORES

Marshalls (Department Store)

- 2235 Summer Street (Ridgeway Shop Cnter), Stamford CT, 203.356.9667
- 20 Waterfront Plaza, Port Chester NY, 914.690.9380

http://www.marshallsonline.com/off_price.asp

Marshalls and T J Maxx have the same parent company and have similar product assortments. Marshalls sells brand name and designer clothing at off-prices. They carry clothing for men, women, kids, and teens. They also carry footwear, bedding, furniture, jewelry and housewares.

Hours: Monday-Saturday 9:30am-9:30pm, Sunday 11am-8pm.

McArdle-MacMillen Florist & Garden Center (Florist)

48 Arch Street, Greenwich CT, 203.661.5600

www.mcardles.com

Many pretty dinner tables are adorned with their arrangements. A good place to buy flowers (they have a large selection), corsages and plants. Come early on weekends during the garden season, as it is always busy or place an order on their website. They have a newsletter filled with helpful gardening tips. If you are busy, they will come to your home and "deck your halls." Be sure to get on their mailing list.

Hours: Monday-Saturday 8am-5:30pm.

McDermott Paint & Wallpaper (Paint & Wallpaper)

35 Spring Street, Greenwich CT, 203.622.0699

(We often use the back door on Old Track Road.)

www.McdermottPaintWallpaper.com

If you are planning to do any of your own home painting, you can count on good advice and Benjamin Moore paints from this longtime Greenwich shop. If you are trying to match a color, take a sample and they can duplicate it with their computer. A good selection of wallpaper as well as wallpaper and painting supplies.

Hours: Monday-Saturday 7am-5pm.

TIP: BABY STORES ON CENTRAL PARK AVENUE

It's worth the drive to visit these baby stores which you will find along both sides of the street. Central Park Avenue is approximately 20 minutes away in Scarsdale, NY (Westchester County). You'll find everything you need for your children. Bring a lot of energy–it's going to be an exhausting day!

Directions: I-95 S to 287 W to exit 4 (RT-100A), L off Ramp towards Hartsdale. At 3rd main intersection R on Central Park Avenue.

STORES

Michaels (Craft Supplies)
• 2233 Summer Street (Ridgeway Shop Cntr), Stamford CT, 203.978.0026
• 27 Waterfront Plaza, Port Chester NY, 914.937.3060
www.michaels.com
Michaels has over 1,000 stores. A favorite source for scrapbook makers, the average store contains over 40,000 different products for crafts, framing, beading, knitting, floral, and wall décor, as well as seasonal merchandise. Michaels provides custom framing and custom floral service, as well as classes and demonstrations-featuring skills such as cake decorating, beading and knitting. Michaels has children's birthday parties, where a craft is made.
Hours: Monday-Saturday 9am-9pm, Sunday 9am-7pm.

Michael Kors (Clothing-Women)
279 Greenwich Avenue, Greenwich CT, 203.618.1200
www.michaelkors.com
Michael Kors is renowned for his classic, chic but sensible American sportswear and other clothing styles. His designs are worn by many celebrities. This store is one of about 20 USA Lifestyle Stores.
Hours: Monday-Saturday 10am-7pm, Sunday 11am-5pm.

Michelangelo of Greenwich (Gifts)
353 Greenwich Avenue, Greenwich CT, 203.661.8540, 800.677.4490
www.mikegifts.com
Wide selection of clocks, crystal, pewter, brass and silver which they will engrave for personal or corporate gifts. They have produced awards for the Super Bowl and the Pebble Beach Golf Tournament.
Hours: Tuesday-Friday 10:15am-5:30pm, Saturday 10:15am-5pm.

Miranda Arts Project Space (Art & Framing)
6 North Pearl Street, Suite 404E, Port Chester NY, 914.318.7178
www.MirandaArtsProjectSpace.com
Art Gallery featuring local artists. Patricia Miranda teaches painting and gilding techniques to adults and youth. She does museum-quality framing and frame repair.
Exhibition Hours: usually Wednesday-Saturday 12pm-5pm, call to confirm.

Mitchell Gold + Bob Williams (Furniture)

45 East Putnam Avenue, Greenwich CT, 203.661.4480

Www.mgandbw.com

A residential furniture manufacturer founded in 1989 by Gold and Williams. Mitchell Gold + Bob Williams products are sold through furniture stores such as Crate & Barrel, Restoration Hardware, Pottery Barn, ABC Carpet & Home and Lillian August. The have 24 signature stores, including this Greenwich location. Their product line offers relaxed design slipcovered and tailored upholstery, leather, sectionals, beds, ottomans, recliners, and dining chairs.

Hours: Monday-Saturday 9:30am-6pm (Thursday until 8pm), Sunday 12pm-5pm.

Modell's (Sporting Goods)

- 2113 Summer Street (Ridgeway Shop Cntr) Stamford CT, 203.353.0700
- 427 Boston Post Road (Kohls Shop Cntr), Port Chester NY, 914.934.1500

www.modells.com

They have 144 locations in the Northeast carrying sporting goods and related apparel. They have a wide selection of licensed professional sports team items.

Hours: Monday-Thursday 9:30am-9pm, Friday & Saturday 9am-9pm, Sunday 10am-6pm.

Mr. Mail Box

7 Cross Street, Norwalk CT, 203.849.1144

www.mrmailbox.com

It would be hard to find a better mail box. They have lots of options, their prices are reasonable and they will install.

Hours: Weekdays 8am-5pm, Saturday 9am-3pm.

Mr. Shower Door

651 Connecticut Avenue, Norwalk CT, 800.633.3667

www.mrshowerdoor.com

A large number of options, they will help you design exactly what you need. A good website and store. They will come out to measure and install. Hours: Monday-Saturday 9am-5pm.

(The) Nanz Company (Decorative Hardware)
44 West Putnam Avenue, 203.987.4403
www.Nanz.com
Nanz has their own plant in Brooklyn, where they turn out beautiful, high-end hardware as well as custom designs.
Hours: Weekdays 9:00am-5pm. Best to make an appointment.

Neiman Marcus (Department Store)
125 Westchester Avenue (Westchester Mall), White Plains NY, 914.428.2000
www.NeimanMarcus.com
An upscale, specialty, retail department store which competes with Bloomingdale's, Nordstrom, and Saks Fifth Avenue.
Hours: Monday-Saturday 10am-8pm, Sunday 11am-6pm.

Nimble Thimble (Sewing & Quilting)
21 Putnam Avenue, Port Chester NY, 914.934.2934
The resource for home sewing needs. Lots of fabrics, notions, quilting supplies and sewing machines. This is the place to have your sewing machine repaired.
Hours: Tuesday-Friday 10am-5pm, Saturday 10am-1pm.

Nordic Stove & Fireplace Center (Fireplace Accessories)
220 Harvard Avenue, Stamford CT, 203.406.9881
www.nordicstoveandfireplace.com
Everything you might want for your fireplace. Good customer service.
Hours: Tuesday-Friday 10am-5pm, Saturday 9am-4pm.

Nordstrom (Department Store)
125 Westchester Ave (Westchester Mall), White Plains NY, 914.946.1122
www.Nordstrom.com
An upscale department store with clothing, footwear, accessories, handbags, jewelry, cosmetics and home furnishings. The company competes at an average price level above J. C. Penney, Macy's, and Sears, on par with Bloomingdale's, but below that of Neiman Marcus and Saks Fifth Avenue.
Hours: Monday-Saturday 10am-9pm, Sunday 11am-6pm.

Norwalk Mattress Company (Bedding)
145 West Cedar Street, Norwalk CT, 203.866.6913
www.NorwalkMattress.com
Near Greenwich is a mattress company that will custom make any size, any level of comfort or type of mattress, including space-age memory foam. Within 10 days you will have the mattress on your bed, all at very competitive prices.   Hours: Monday-Saturday 9am-5pm.

OGGI 5 (Clothing-Women)
365 Greenwich Avenue, Greenwich CT, 203.717.115
www.oggi5.com
Designer brands from Milan and Paris. Olivier Goureau's shop carries Louisa Spagnoli, Toupy as well as his own label, OG.
Hours: Monday Saturday 10am-6pm, Sunday 12am-5pm.

Old Navy (Department Store)
• 2175 Summer Street (Ridgeway Shop Cntr) Stamford CT, 203.325.4088
• 100 Main Street (Galleria Shop Cntr), White Plains NY, 914.682.0469
www.oldNavy.com
Owned by the Gap which also owns Banana Republic. Their clothing is trendy and more affordable than the Gap or Banana Republic or competitors such as American Eagle (Stamford Center). They have specialized sections for infants, boys, girls, men and women, including a collection of business clothes for women.
Stamford Store Hours: Monday-Saturday 9am-about 9:30pm,
Sunday 10am-8pm.

Olivine Gabbro (Clothing-Women)
243 Greenwich Avenue, Greenwich CT, 203.493.3526
www.OlivineGabbro.com
www.facebook.com/pages/Olivine-Gabbro/219109504791308
Grace Kang designs lovely, sophisticated women's wear and evening dresses. Choose something in her showroom or have something custom-designed just for you.   Hours: Monday-Saturday 10am-6pm.

Optical Options (Eyewear)
18 Greenwich Avenue, Greenwich CT, 203.661.2020
http://opticaloptions.net/
Call in advance to schedule an eye exam. They sell contact lenses and high-fashion eyewear.
Hours: Weekdays 9:30am-6:00pm, Saturday 10am-5pm.

Optyx by Gruen (Eyewear)
229 Greenwich Avenue, Greenwich CT, 203.862.9441
www.grueneyes.com
High-fashion eyewear, call ahead to schedule an eye exam.
Hours: Tuesday-Friday 9:30am-5:30pm, Saturday 10am-6pm.

Oriental Furniture Warehouse (Furniture & Home Accessories)
602 West Avenue, Norwalk CT, 203.853.7553
www.orientalfurnishings.com
A large selection of oriental furniture and accessories from Japan, Korea, China and Tibet.   Hours: Tuesday-Saturday 10am-6pm.

Orvis Company Store (Fishing Equipment & Clothing)
432 Boston Post Road, Darien CT, 203.662.0844
www.orvis.com
Orvis is the world's largest manufacturer of high-quality fly rods and reels. They carry high-end fishing equipment, as well as clothes and luggage for the well-attired fisherman. They also have a large book and video selection. Ask them about their guide service.
Hours: Monday-Saturday 10am-6 pm, Sunday 12pm-5pm.

Orvis Outlet Store (Clothing-Men & Women)
56 Westport Avenue, Norwalk CT, 203.846.5901
A store filled with quality, casual wear at good prices.
Hours: Monday- Saturday 10am-6pm, Sunday 11am-5pm.

Out of the Box (Clothing-Women)
73 Greenwich Avenue, Greenwich CT, 203.625.9696
www.outoftheboxclothes.com
You will be happy you stopped by this out-of-the-ordinary clothing store. Jill duPont's name for the store is just right. You will find pretty jackets and dresses. She has a workshop for alterations and custom work. If she doesn't have your size, she can usually get it. Upstairs Jill has shows, special events and seasonal offerings such as Beach Box during the summer (listed separately).
Hours: Monday-Saturday 10am-6pm, Sunday 12pm-5pm.

Outdoor Traders (Sporting Goods & Clothing)
55 Arch Street, Greenwich CT, 203.862.9696
www.OutdoorTraders.com
Outfitters for just about any outdoor sport, trip or trek. Easy to park.
Hours: Monday-Saturday 10am-6pm, Sunday 11am-5pm.

Packages Plus-N-More (Office Services & Cards)

215 East Putnam Ave (Mill Pond Shopping Cntr), Cos Cob CT, 203.625.8130
www.PackagesPlusNMore.com
Pretty wrapping paper and supplies. One of the few places that carries Greenwich gift items including postcards with local scenes. A dependable up-scale packing and shipping company, that will not only ship packages for you, but will pick up a package from your home or office upon request.
Hours: Weekdays 8am-6pm, Saturday 9am-4pm
(open Sunday during holiday season).

Papyrus (Stationery)

268 Greenwich Avenue, Greenwich CT, 203.869.1888
www.PapyrusOnline.com
Papyrus has more than 170 stores nationwide selling fine custom social stationery and invitations. If you want a traditional or an out-of-the ordinary invitation, you will have fun here. You will be sending more greetings to your friends when you see their large selection of high-end greeting cards.
Hours: Monday-Wednesday 9:30am-6pm,
Thursday & Friday 9:30am -7pm,
Saturday 10am-7pm, Sunday 12pm-5pm.

(C) Parker Gallery (Art)

17 East Putnam Avenue, Greenwich CT, 203.253.0934
www.CParkerGallery.com
With locations in Newport and New York as well as Greenwich, they have a group of about 50 contemporary artists as well as works by established artists such as Andy Warhol. Most of the art in the gallery is in the $2,000 to $3,000 range.
Hours: Open everyday 10am-4:30pm.

TIP: ONLY GEESE HONK IN GREENWICH

Residents know that Greenwich is a place to relax, unwind and enjoy life. Yes, we still need to get to places on time, but we drive with consideration. Honking – except in dangerous situations – is taboo. If someone is honking inappropriately, it is probably a car with an out-of-town license plate. We like to say "in Greenwich only the geese honk."

STORES

Party City (Party Supplies)

- 2255 Summer Street (Ridgeway Shop Cntr), Stamford CT, 203.964.4961
- 435 Boston Post Road, Port Chester NY, 914.939.6900

www.PartyCity.com

Party City is the largest retailer of party supplies. They operate 249 company-owned stores and 258 franchised stores and as a result stores often have different merchandise. These stores sell decorations, wrapping paper, helium balloons and custom-made balloon bouquets, plastic eating utensils, tableware, paper plates, party music CDs, small toys, candy, and other items of a similar nature themed for birthday parties, weddings, baby showers, graduation, communion, confirmation, christenings and holidays. Many stores print invitations and party banners right on site. At Halloween there are always lots of costumes.

Hours: Monday-Saturday 9:30am-8:30pm (9pm Thursday & Friday), Sunday 10am-6pm.

Party Paper and Things (Party Supplies)

410 East Putnam Avenue, Cos Cob CT, 203.661.1355

An excellent selection of high-quality party paper goods, wrapping paper, disposable serving dishes and lots of balloons. They will deliver for a very modest fee.

Hours: Monday-Saturday 10am-5:30pm, Saturday 8:30am-4:30pm (shorter hours during the summer.)

Pastiche (Clothing-Women)

250 Sound Beach Avenue, Old Greenwich, 203.637.4444

Designer casual clothing with a fashionable, dressy flair.

Hours: Monday-Saturday 10am-5pm.

Patio.Com (Furniture)

600 East Putnam Avenue, Cos Cob CT, 203.869.3084

(Office 800-340-4710)

www.Patio.com

One of 11 stores, this independently-owned, CT-based store sells a wide variety of outdoor furniture, as well as indoor sports equipment such as pool tables and ping pong tables. They are a major retailer of Brunswick pool tables.

Hours: Monday-Saturday 10am-7pm, Sunday 10am-6pm.

STORES

Patricia Gourlay (Clothing-Women)
45 East Putnam Avenue, Greenwich CT, 203.869.0977
Brides-to-be love this fine lingerie shop. This is also a good place to find the right bra. Wonderful customer service! They are more conservative than their advertisements would indicate. You will enjoy shopping here.
Hours: Monday-Saturday 9:30am-5:30pm.

P C Richard (Electronics & Appliances)
444 Connecticut Avenue, Norwalk CT, 203.604.1104
www.PCRichard.com
PC Richard is a 100+ year old privately-owned electronics store. The Chain has 52 stores in the NY area. They compete by providing better service and more knowledgeable staff than giants like Best Buy. This 33,000 square-foot store sells appliances as well as TVs and other electronics. Delivery, installation and service are all done by PC Richard employees. If you need something in a hurry they can usually accommodate. Hours: Monday-Saturday 9am-9pm, Sunday 10am-7pm.

Patti's Portico (Outdoor Furniture)
140 Highland Street, Port Chester NY, 203.869-6227
Is it possible Patti's Portico has been there over 12 years and I am just now discovering it? My garden chair needed re-strapping and Patti DeFelice did a great job. Her showroom is filled with refurbished outdoor furniture to buy. This shop is easy to find: just off Main Street in Port Chester.
Hours: Weekdays 8am-3pm.

Pearle Vision (Eyewear)
111 Broad Street, Stamford CT, 203.348.3200   www.pearlevision.com
With more than 1,000 stores, Pearle is one of the largest retailers of eyewear. They have the same parent as LensCrafters. Call for an eye exam appointment. Most glasses can be made within one hour. It's one of the few places that carries anti-fog spray.
Store Hours: Weekdays 9am-6pm (Thursday 7 pm), Saturday 9am-5pm. Call for optometrist hours.

Penny Weights (Jewelry)
124 Elm Street, New Canaan CT, 203.966.7739 www.pennyweights.com
This is a great place to find an inexpensive piece of jewelry for a teenager. Most of the jewelry is silver. The sales staff is friendly and helpful.
Hours: Monday-Saturday 10am-6pm (Thursday 8 pm),
Sunday 12pm-5pm.

Pet Pantry (Pets)
290 Railroad Avenue, Greenwich CT, 203.869.6444
www.PetPantryCT.com
Large store with a gigantic inventory. Friendly, helpful service. Our dogs love going here to pick their own dog food and meet new friends.
Hours: Weekdays 8am-8pm, Saturday 8am-6pm, Sunday 9am-6pm.

Petticoat Lane (Handbags and Lingerie)
347 Greenwich Avenue, Greenwich CT, 203.863.0045
www.BagShop.com
One of our familiar shops that has been on the Avenue a long time. This 6-store chain has a large selection of handbags and lingerie.
Hours: Monday-Saturday 10am-6pm, Sunday 12pm-5pm.

PID Floors of Greenwich
38 West Putnam Avenue, Greenwich CT, 203.622.4394
www.Pidfloors.com
PID makes custom, pre-finished hardwood floors in their Brooklyn factory. They have two showrooms in NYC.   Hours: Weekdays 9am-5pm.

Pier 1 Imports (Home Accessories)
• 777 Connecticut Avenue, Norwalk CT, 203.852.1718
• 427 Boston Post Road (Kohls Shop Cntr), Port Chester NY, 914.937.2189
www.pier1.com
Affordable 1,000 store chain carrying everything for the home, from table linens to wicker furniture and throw pillows. The Port Chester store is one of their largest stores.
Port Chester Hours: Monday-Saturday 10am-9pm, Sunday 11am-7pm.

Pinky (Clothing and Accessories-Women)
58A William Street, Greenwich CT, 203.504.8737
www.PinkyOfGreenwich.com
Nancy Wasche has a shop full of colorful, fun dresses, jackets, tops and baubles. We enjoy shopping here.   Hours: Monday-Saturday 10am-5pm.

Plimpton & Hills Waterware (Bath Fixtures)
92 Research Drive, Stamford CT, 203.965.5959
www.CTshowrooms.com
A lovely showroom and a separate plumbing supply house in Stamford's industrial section. This is the source for most of the high-end plumbers in our area. You can't go wrong with their knowledgeable sales people.
Showroom Hours: Weekdays 9am-5pm, Saturday 9am-4pm.

STORES

Porcelanosa (Tile & Bath Fixtures)
1063 East Putnam Avenue, Riverside CT, 203.698.7618
www.porcelanosa-usa.com
A Spanish factory store. The company has over 8,000 stores worldwide. All the tile and fixtures are their own design and are available only in their stores. A must-see for anyone interested in contemporary designs. Hours: Monday-Saturday 10am-6pm.

Pottery Barn (Home Accessories & Furniture)
• 100 Greyrock Place (Stamford Town Center), Stamford CT, 203.323.0007
• 125 Westchester Avenue (Westchester Mall), White Plains NY 914.328.2434
www.PotteryBarn.com   www.PotteryBarnKids.com
This fresh, appealing furniture is very popular in Greenwich. They have a strong emphasis on bed, bath, dining as well as adorable furniture for children. The Pottery Barn is a subsidiary of Williams-Sonoma and operates 200 US stores.
Hours: Monday-Saturday 10am-9pm, Sunday 11am-6pm.

Post Road Iron Works (Fireplace Accessories)
345 West Putnam Avenue, Greenwich CT, 203.869.6322
www.priw.com
Serving Greenwich since 1927, although they do a lot of ordinary iron work, they are the local resource for ornamental welding. They also sell a good selection of fireplace accessories and can order weathervanes.
Hours: Weekdays 8am-5:30pm, Saturday 8am-12pm.

R. Simantov (Jewelry)
276 Greenwich Avenue, Greenwich CT, 203.661.6717
www.Rsimantov.com
Accessed through the door to Lynnens, this is one of two stores, the other is in Nantucket. Their contemporary jewelry is in some permanent museum collections. Hours: Monday-Saturday 10:30am-5:30pm.

STORES

Rag & Bone NY (Clothing-Men & Women)
195 Greenwich Avenue, Greenwich CT, 203.622.6222
www.Rag-bone.com
Their clothes sell in more than 700 stores around the world. Greenwich is one of their 17 retail stores where you can buy a pair of distressed skinny jeans for about $187. Rag & Bone designers David Neville and Marcus Wainwright specialize in modern classic clothing, much of which is in black and white. Hours: Monday-Wednesday 10am-6pm, Thursday-Saturday 10am-7pm, Sunday 11am -5pm.

Ralph Lauren (Clothing-Men & Women)
265 Greenwich Avenue, Greenwich CT, 203.869.2054
www.ralphlauren.com
Ralph Lauren has over 35 boutiques in the United States. Whether or not you are interested in buying something from Ralph Lauren, you have to tour this extraordinary shop. The store is breathtaking-as are the prices.
Hours: Monday-Saturday 10am-6pm (Thursday to 7pm),
Sunday 12pm-5pm.

REI-Recreation Equipment Inc (Sporting Equipment)
189 Connecticut Avenue, Norwalk CT, 203.838.1938   www.REI.com
Founded in Seattle and with over 110 stores, REI sells a great variety of outdoor equipment for sports such as camping, climbing, cycling, fitness, hiking, paddling, and snow sports. REI operates as a cooperative with a lifetime fee of $20 to join. REI Adventures offers vacations for active travelers all over the world. Offerings range from a 2 day weekend getaway in Yosemite to a 14 day trek to Everest Base Camp. REI's Outdoor School teaches a series of one day outings in the local area and in store classes. Offerings include mountain biking, road biking, kayaking, backpacking, rock climbing, outdoor photography, family hiking, snowshoeing and others. The Norwalk store is 18,000 sq. ft.
Hours: Monday-Saturday 10am-9pm, Sunday 10am-6pm.

STORES

Relax the Back (Health, Furniture)
367 Greenwich Avenue, Greenwich CT, 203.629.2225
www.relaxtheback.com
For people seeking relief and prevention of back and neck pain, they offer attractive posture and back support products and self-care solutions. Many products are exclusive to the store. Started in 1984 by an osteopath, there are now 121 stores.
Hours: Monday-Saturday 10am-6pm, Sunday 12pm-4:30pm.

Remains Lighting (Lighting Fixtures)
44 West Putnam Avenue, Greenwich CT, 203.629.1000
www.Remains.com
Sharing a showroom with one of our favorite stores: Nanz, which makes high-end hardware. Remains sells antique lighting but also has its own factory, where they produce high quality lighting fixtures both original and based on classic designs.
Hours: Weekdays 9am-5:30pm (in the summer 9am-3pm on Friday).

Restoration Hardware (Home Accessories & Furniture)
310 Greenwich Avenue, Greenwich CT, 203.552.1040
www.restorationhardware.com
An American chain with more than 133 stores. A very upscale, trendy store with a combination of decorative hardware and furniture based on period designs. Their renovation of the 1917 post office is spectacular. It is a treat to stroll through this 23,000 sf store.
Hours: Monday-Saturday 10am-7pm, Sunday 12am-5pm.

Rex Dive Center / Oceanblue (Sporting Equipment-Diving)
144 Water Street (at Rex Marine Cntr), South Norwalk CT, 203.853.4148
www.RexDiveCenter.com , www.oceanbluedivers.com
A good place to go for your scuba equipment. You will be greeted by a friendly, knowledgeable staff. They provide lessons for beginners in NYC. Owner Michael Feld has been promoting a social group, Ocean Blue, catering to divers.
Hours: Tuesday-Friday 11am-7pm, Saturday 9am -5pm,
Sunday 12pm-5pm.

Rex Marine Center (Boating)
144 Water Street, South Norwalk CT, 203.831.5236
Small Boat Shop, 203.854.5223
50 Calf Pasture Beach Road, East Norwalk CT, 203.604.1295
www.rexmarine.com   www.TheSmallBoatShop.com
If you are looking for a yacht or a small boat or boating paraphernalia, they are worth a visit. You can even charter a boat with a captain. The Rex Boating Club provides training and rental boats. The small boat shop carries sea and recreational kayaks, canoes, dinghies, row boats, rowing shells, small sail boats and paddle boats. Their services include tours, instruction, rentals, small boat storage and repair.
Hours Weekdays 8am-5:30pm.

Richards of Greenwich (Clothing-Men & Women)
359 Greenwich Avenue, Greenwich CT, 203.622.0551
www.mitchellsonline.com
A Greenwich classic carrying fine-quality men's and women's clothing from the world's leading designers. Nowhere will you find better customer service or parking.
Hours: Monday-Wednesday & Friday 10am-6pm, Thursday 10am-8pm, Saturday 9am-6pm.

Ridgeway Shopping Center (Mall)
2235 Summer Street, Stamford CT, 203.325.2629
The anchor stores in this updated 400,000 square foot center are Marshall's, Old Navy and Michaels. It has a very large Bed Bath & Beyond as well as a huge Super Stop & Shop.
Hours: Monday-Saturday 9:30am-9pm (Bed Bath & Beyond is open Sunday 9:30am-6pm).

Rinfret Home and Garden (Furniture & Accessories)
354 Greenwich Avenue, Greenwich CT, 203.622.0000, 0204
www.rinfretltd.com
Classic English antique and reproduction furniture and accessories. If you are wondering what is "Classic Greenwich Style," you will want to visit this store and buy a copy of Cindy Rinfret's book.
Hours: Weekdays 10am-6pm, Saturday 10am-5pm, Sunday 12pm-5pm.

Ring's End Lumber (Hardware-Building Materials)

181 West Avenue, Darien CT, 203.655.2525   www.ringsend.com
A large supplier of lumber, hardware and building materials. They cater to both builders and home do-it-yourselfers. Good displays of kitchens and windows. If possible, shop on weekdays; they can be very busy on Saturday.
Hours: Monday-Saturday 7am-5pm
(Thursday 9pm except in winter months).

Rink and Racquet (Sporting Equipment, Team Uniforms)

24 Railroad Avenue, Greenwich CT, 203.622.9180
www.RinkAndRacquet.com
Hockey (field & ice), figure skating, baseball, softball, tennis, lacrosse, roller blades, team uniforms. If they don't have what you need for ice hockey, it is probably not made.
Hours: Weekdays 9am-5:30pm, Saturday 9am-5pm.

River Bicycles (Bicycles)

17 Glenville Street, Glenville CT, 203.532.1718
www.RiverBicycles.com
A full-service sales and service store. They sell Felt Bicycles, Litespeed, Ciocc (Zarbikes), Bria, Scott and Raleigh.
Hours: Monday-Saturday 10am-7pm (closed Wednesday),
Sunday 11am-4pm.

Riverside Floor Covering (Carpeting)

5 Riverside Lane, Riverside CT, 203.637.3777
www.RiversideFloorCovering.com
A small showroom brimming with carpet choices from many manufacturers. They have been helping Greenwich residents for years.
Hours: Weekdays 9:30am-5pm, Saturday 9am-12pm.

ROAM (Clothing-Women)

19 West Elm, Greenwich CT, 203.625.0200
www.WhenInRoam.com
Babe Rizzuto and her daughter, Sophia Wojezak, have selected a collection of designer clothing for hip young people that ranges from elegant to edgy in their stylish boutique.
Hours: Monday-Saturday 10am-7pm, Sunday 11am-5pm.

Roberta Roller Rabbitt (Clothing-Women & Children)
103 Greenwich Avenue, Greenwich CT, 203.869.1969
www.RobertaRollerRabbitt.com
One of 13 stores by Roberta Feyman, whose colorful, eclectic designs are hand-blocked by artisans in India. Her cotton prints are perfect for resort or casual wear. Her pajamas and bedding are fun.
Hours: Monday-Saturday 10am-6pm, Sunday 11am-5pm.

Roundabout (Consignment/Resale Clothing-Women)
48 West Putnam Avenue, Greenwich CT, 203.552.0787
Clothes must be from a well-known designer, in perfect condition, and less than 2 years old to be consigned. The store also buys show and end-of-season stock from designers.
Hours: Monday- Saturday 10am-5pm, Sunday 12pm-5pm (seasonally).

Ruby & Jenna (Clothing-Women)
348 Greenwich Avenue, Greenwich CT, 203.622.7016
www.RubyAndJenna.com
Youthful, casual, trendy clothing. Greenwich is one of 9 locations.
Hours: Monday-Saturday 10am-7pm, Sunday 11am-7pm.

Rudy's Tackle Barn (Fishing & Archery)
242 South Water Street, Byram CT, 203.531.3168
Dan Ortiz has all your archery, freshwater and saltwater supplies.
Summer Hours: Monday-Saturday 6am-7pm, Saturday 6am-6 pm, Sunday 6am-4pm.

Rue Faubourg St. Honore (Home Accessories & Antiques)
44 West Putnam Avenue, Greenwich CT, 203.869.7139
For over 30 years this small shop has supplied antique lighting fixtures and fireplace accessories to Greenwich estates and vintage homes.
Hours: Weekdays 9:30am-5pm (closed 1pm-2pm).

(Greenwich) Running Company
(Running Shoes, Clothing & Accessories)
2 Greenwich Avenue, Greenwich CT, 203.861.7800
www.TheRunningCompany.net
One of 12 stores devoted to helping everyone enjoy running and look good while they are doing it. The Running Company started in Princeton, New Jersey in 1998. They carry most major running, walking and cross training shoes, as well as spikes, classy apparel and accessories.
Hours: Weekdays 10am-7pm, Saturday 10am-6pm, Sunday 12pm-5 pm.

Rye Ridge Tile (Bath & Kitchen Tile)

520 North Main Street, Port Chester NY, 914.939.1100

www.RyeRidgeTile.com

The 6,000 sf showroom is covered with a great variety of tile patterns from 75 different manufacturers, making it easy to visualize choices. They also have the Villeroy & Boch line of very modern plumbing fixtures.

Hours: Weekdays 9am-5pm (Wednesday to 7pm by appointment), Saturday 9am-4pm.

(Therese) Saint Clair (Stationery)

96 Greenwich Avenue, Greenwich CT, 203.661.2927

www.theresesaintclair.com

Going to Cartier's for fine stationery is not necessary if you live in Greenwich. For many years Greenwich residents have shopped here for their invitations and elegant stationery. Stop in and see the range of things they can do.

Hours: Monday-Saturday 9:30am-5:30pm, Saturday 10am-5pm.

Saks Fifth Avenue (Department Store)

205 Greenwich Avenue, Greenwich CT, 203.862.5300

www.saks.com

An upscale clothing store that competes on a price level with Neiman Marcus, Bergdorf Goodman and Lord and Taylor and above Bloomingdale's and Nordstrom.

Hours: Monday-Thursday 10am-6pm, Friday & Saturday 10am-7pm, Sunday 12pm-5pm.

Sam Bridge Nursery & Greenhouses (Plants & Shrubs)

437 North Street, Greenwich CT, 203.869.3418

www.sambridge.com

A family-run operation that has been welcoming Greenwich residents to their greenhouses since 1930. Many of the more than 100,000 plants available are grown in their own greenhouses. They offer classes on topics such as perennial gardening and pruning. You can select live or cut Christmas trees, which they will deliver to you when you are ready.

Hours: Monday-Saturday 8:30am-5pm.

STORES

Samuel Owen Galleries (Art)

382 Greenwich Avenue, Greenwich CT, 203.325.1924

www.SamuelOwen.com

The Gallery, with a collection of contemporary art, was started in 2005 by Lee and Cindy Milazzo as an expansion of Pacific Street Framing. They have a variety of unique frames. Their art selections include Andy Warhol and Damien Hirst. Paintings cost from several hundred dollars to more than $10,000.

Hours: Monday-Saturday 10:30am-6pm, Sunday 11am-3pm.

Sandro (Clothing-Women)

200 Greenwich Avenue, Greenwich CT, 203.863.0923

www.Sandro-Paris.com

Evelyne Chetrite is the founder/designer. Her stores compete with her younger sister's Maje. Both are located at 200 Greenwich Avenue. Both are owned by SMCP. Sandro has more than 200 stores. Their stylish Parisian clothing is geared to young women and is positioned to be between luxury labels and stores like Zara. Her clothes are slightly edgier than Maje's.   Hours: Monday-Saturday 10am-6pm, Sunday 12pm-5pm.

Safavieh (Furniture & Rugs)

248 Atlantic Street, Stamford CT, 203.327.4800

www.safaviehhome.com

This family-owned 11-store chain has been in Stamford for 25 years. It has oriental rugs galore and lots of quality English, French and American reproduction furniture from firms such as Kindel, Baker, Widdicomb, Henredon and others. They have parking behind the store.

Hours: Monday-Saturday 10am-5:30pm (Thursday 8pm), Sunday 11am-5:30pm.

Sears (Department Store)

100 Main Street (Galleria Shopping Center), White Plains NY, 914.644.1400   www.Sears.com

Home furnishings, home improvement, appliances, electronics, clothing, including a Lands' End Store. They own the brands: Kenmore, Craftsman & DieHard. Sears competes with Macy's, pricing below Bloomingdale's, Nordstrom and Saks and above JC Penney and Kohl's.

Hours: Monday-Saturday 9am-9pm, Sunday 10:30am-7pm.

STORES

Scoop (Clothing-Men & Women)

283 Greenwich Avenue, Greenwich CT, 203.422.2251 www.scoopnyc.com
One of 12 stores, from Manhattan to Greenwich Avenue, this clothing store has trendy and fun pieces designed to attract men and women of all ages, but perhaps the 12 to 25 year-olds are happiest here. You'll find everything from shirts, shoes, jewelry, hats, t-shirts and handbags.
Hours: Monday-Saturday 10am-6:30pm, Sunday 12pm-5pm.

Second Time Around (Consignment Clothing)

6 Greenwich Avenue, Greenwich CT, 203.422.2808
www.SecondTimeAround.net
At the top of the Avenue, almost on sidewalk level, is a large boutique with clothing so nicely displayed you might not realize it is all resale and designer over-runs. The Greenwich store is one of about 20; anything consigned must be less than 2 years old. Items are priced 1/3rd to 1/4th of their original retail price.
Hours: Monday-Saturday 10am-6pm, Sunday 12pm-5pm.

Sephora (Cosmetics)

75 Greenwich Avenue, Greenwich CT, 203.422.2191 www.sephora.com
This French 750 store chain has a vast selection of men's and women's beauty products including makeup, skin care, fragrance, bath, hair products, hair tools, and beauty accessories. There are eight make-up stations, with consultants to help you bring out your inner self.
Hours: Monday-Saturday 10am-6pm, Sunday 12pm-5pm.

Severed Ties (Consignment)

111 Cherry Street, New Canaan CT, 203.972.0788
www.SeveredTiesAntiques.com
A large showroom of consigned mid-century modern and traditional furniture as well as jewelry. They will do custom upholstery.
Hours: Monday-Saturday 10am-5pm, Sunday 1pm-5pm.

Shanti Bithi Nursery (Bonsai Greenhouse)

3047 High Ridge Road, Stamford CT, 203.329.0768 www.shantibithi.com
Wonderful greenhouse of bonsai trees as well as supplies and instructions to create your own bonsai. They also have a nice selection of Asian garden ornaments.   Hours: Thursday-Saturday 9am-5pm.

STORES

Shoes N More (Shoes)
251 Greenwich Avenue, Greenwich CT, 203.629.2323
www.ShoesNMore.com
A fun assortment of boy's and girl's clothing, sizes 2T-16. They have an excellent shoe selection including Astor, Elefanter, Nike and Merrell. They carry some western boots and accessories. Twice a year they have a very good shoe sale (summer & after Christmas). They have 6 more locations in the NYC Metropolitan area.
Hours: Monday-Saturday 9am-6:30pm, Sunday 11am-6pm.

Shreve, Crump & Low (Jewelry)
125 Greenwich Avenue, Greenwich CT, 203.622.6205
www.ShreveCrumpAndLow.com
They were founded in 1796 and are the oldest jeweler in North America. They are responsible for trophies such as the Davis Cup. This is their third location. They are known for high-end jewelry and luxury time-pieces.

Signature Cycles (Bicycles)
14 Railroad Ave, Greenwich CT, 203.485.0500
www.signaturecycles.com http://blog.signaturecycles.com
Not your ordinary bicycle shop. Besides excellent customer service, bikes can be customized to meet your needs. They will fit your existing bike (and tune it up or overhaul it to like-new condition), fit you for a new stock bike by Specialized or fit you to a new custom bike. They record your measurements and uses, so that you get the bike that would be best for you. All this comes at only a slight premium over an equal, un-customized, bike. Check with them about weekly bike rides. They also have very nice selection of apparel and accessories.
Hours: Tuesday, Wednesday, Friday 10am-6pm, Thursday 10am-8pm, Saturday 11am-4pm, (on Sunday, they ride).

(The) Silk Purse (Consignment Furniture)
118 Main Street, New Canaan CT, 203.972.0898
www.TheSilkPurse.com
For 35 years this shop, which features formal polished furniture, has been a good resource for Greenwich residents. They also have paintings, decorative items and jewelry. This shop is worth the visit.
Hours: Monday-Saturday 10am-5pm, Sunday 12pm-5pm.

STORES

Silvermine Arts Center (Art)
1037 Silvermine Road, New Canaan CT, 203.966.9700
www.silvermineart.org
The Silvermine Arts Center has been a gathering place for artists and art lovers for almost 100 years. The Silvermine galleries have 20 shows each year in addition to the juried annual Art of The Northeast, held late in April. Silvermine offers many lectures, workshops and art classes. During the summer they run Art Day Camps for children ages 4 and up. Gallery Hours: Wednesday-Saturday 12pm-5pm, Sunday 1pm-5pm.

Simon Pearce (Home-Accessories)
125 East Putnam Avenue, Greenwich CT, 203.861.0780
www.simonpearce.com
Simon Pearce started his first factory in Quechee, Vermont in 1981. He is considered to be the prominent US designer of glassware. Be sure to visit this large store to see his beautiful hand blown glass, pottery, tableware and lamps. Hours: Monday-Saturday 10am-6pm, Sunday 12pm-5 pm.

Simon Teakle (Jewelry)
4 Grigg Street, Greenwich CT, 203.769.5888
www.simonTeakle.com
Simon Teakle, a Greenwich resident, has a shop full of interesting jewelry and objets d'art. He represents jewelry designers such as James de Givency. Hours: Tuesday-Saturday 10am-6pm.

Simple (Clothing-Women)
22 West Putnam Avenue, Greenwich CT, 203.622.7575
Edgy & casual but fashionable clothing. Their other store is in California. Hours: Monday-Saturday 10am-6pm.

Skaters Landing (Skating Equipment, Sharpening and Clothing)
242 Mill Street, Byram CT, 203.542.0555
www.Skaterslanding.com
When you buy your skating equipment from a skating instructor like Mark Magliola, you know you are getting expert advice. This shop has everything you need for figure skating; skates, costumes, blades and sharpening. Make appointments for fittings and while-u-wait sharpening. There are two other stores, one in Boston and Hamden.
Hours: Monday-Wednesday & Friday 12am-5 or 6pm, Thursday & Saturday 11am-5:30pm. Call before going.

STORES

(The) Ski & Scuba Connection (Scuba)
26 Saint Roch Avenue, Byram CT, 203.629.4766
www.SkiAndScubaConnection.com
Scuba lessons and equipment for scuba or snorkeling. Friendly, knowledgeable service. Sign on for one of their scuba trips with Don Brown, Master Instructor.
Hours: Weekdays 11am-6pm (Thursday 7pm), Saturday 10am-6pm.

Sleepy's (Bedding)
- 159 West Putnam Avenue, Greenwich CT, 203.869.5255
- 2000 West Main Street, Stamford CT, 203.356.3576
www.sleepys.com
A chain of over 700 mattress and bedding shops, carrying most major brands as well as some exclusive to them. It is the largest specialty mattress retailer and the largest bedding retailer in the United States.
Greenwich Hours: Weekdays 10am-9pm, Saturday 10am-8pm, Sunday 11am-7pm.

SM Home (Art, Antiques, Home Furnishings)
70 Arch Street, Greenwich CT, 203.629.8121
www.SandraMorganInteriors.com
Sandra Morgan's retail boutique has unique pieces personally selected by her–furniture, Swedish antiques & accessories, that will cheer up any room. She also carries art from contemporary and emerging artists.
Hours: Tuesday-Friday, 10am-5:30pm, Saturday (Fall & Winter) 1pm-5pm.

Smart Kids Toys (Toys)
17 East Elm Street, Greenwich CT, 203.869.0022
www.SKToys.com
The toys in this shop may look like a lot of fun, but most have been selected to help in your child's growth and educational development through play. This local shop has a global clientele from the website and is very popular for party presents. If your child receives two of the same gift, they are very gracious with returns.
Hours: Monday-Saturday 9am-6pm, Sunday 11am-5pm.

Soccer and Rugby (Sporting Goods)
42 West Putnam Avenue, Greenwich CT, 203.661.7622
www.SoccerAndRugby.com
Everything you need for soccer and rugby, attractively displayed.
Hours: Weekdays 10am-6pm, Saturday 10am-5pm, Sunday 11am-4pm (in season).

STORES

Sophia's Great Dames (Clothing-Costumes Women and Children)
1 Liberty Way, Greenwich CT, 203.869.5990
www.SophiasCostumes.com
Wonderful shop for vintage clothing, antiques, collectibles, gifts and costumes. A large selection of costumes (for all occasions) for sale or rent. Fun to visit. Where else could you get a Venetian mask?
Hours: Tuesday-Saturday 10am-5:30pm.

Sorab & Roshi (Jewelry)
30 West Putnam Avenue, Greenwich CT, 203.869.5800
www.SorabAndRoshi.com
Handcrafted jewelry designed by husband and wife team Sorab Bouzarjomehri and Roshi Ameri. They are best known for their bold signature pin designs.
Hours: Tuesday-Saturday, 10:30am-5:30pm.

Sound Beach Sportswear (Clothing-Women & Children)
239 Sound Beach Avenue, Old Greenwich CT, 203.637.5557
The sportswear is an interesting mix. Expect a friendly reception in this family-owned business.
Hours: Monday-Saturday 10am-5:30pm.

Splendid (Clothing-Men, Women, Children)
343 Greenwich Avenue, Greenwich CT, 203.622.5027
www.Splendid.com
One of 18 USA stores. Casual, comfortable, colorful knits & tees. They believe every woman should have a romper in their wardrobe and every man should have a chambray shirt.
Hours: Monday-Saturday 10am-6pm, Sunday 12pm-5pm.

Sports Authority (Athletic/Sports Equipment)
295 Tarrytown Road (East 295 Main Street), Elmsford NY, 914.347.2989
444 Connecticut Avenue, Norwalk CT, 203.838.2583
The Sports Authority is one of the largest sporting goods retailers in the US and has more than 460 stores. They sell many different brands as well as products under their own labels. The Elmsford Store is 60,000 sf and is about 20 minutes west of Greenwich. The Norwalk store is 44,000 sf and is about the same distance in the opposite direction.
Hours: Monday-Saturday 9am-10pm, Sunday 9am-9pm.

Sportsman's Den (Fishing)
33 River Road, Cos Cob CT, 203.869.3234
www.sportsmansdenct.com
Supplies and classes on angling and fly fishing. One visit and you will be hooked! Get your fishing license here. They carry kayaks, kayaking accessories, paddle boards and all kinds of of fishing & clothing accessories. Billy Ingraham is a licensed captain and leads fishing charters.
Hours: Weekdays 9am-5 pm (Friday until 8pm),
Saturday & Sunday 6am-5 pm.

Splurge (Gift Shop)
39 Lewis Street, Greenwich CT, 203.869.7600
www.splurgegifts.com
We are delighted with this gift shop filled with artisan crafts, jewelry & glassware. Select from a great variety of unique gifts, including gifts for hostess, teacher, bride & groom, new baby, children and gourmet cooks. Sonia Malloy has exquisite taste. The prices, which range from $15 to $350, make it easy for you to splurge. We always find the "just right" gift here. Good parking behind the store.
Hours: Monday-Saturday 10am-6pm.

Sprint Nextel (Wireless)
170A North Main Street, Port Chester NY, 914.937.6900
Sprint Solutions Center, 53 High Ridge Road, Stamford CT, 203.363.3655
www.sprint.com
The third-largest wireless telecommunications network in United States, with 48.8 million customers, behind Verizon Wireless and AT&T Mobility. Sprint operates DCSNet, the U.S. Federal Government's private surveillance network. In 2009, Sprint turned over operations management to the Sweden-based Ericsson. Sprint operates a combination 2G & 3G wireless network using CDMA and iDEN.
Port Chester Hours: Weekdays 10am-8pm, Saturday 10am-5pm.
Stamford Hours: Weekdays 9am-8pm, Saturday 9:30am-7pm,
Sunday 11am-5pm.

Stamford Office Furniture (Office Furniture)
328 Selleck Street, Stamford, 203.348.2657
www.StamfordOfficeFurniture.com
New (& some used) furniture. They represent over 200 manufacturers. They sell, lease or rent.
Hours: Weekdays 9am-5pm.

STORES

Stamford Town Center (Shopping Center)
100 Greyrock Place & Tresser Blvd, Stamford CT, 203.324.0935
www.ShopStamfordTownCenter.com
A 850,000 sf, attractive mall with 130 stores, including shops such as: Ann Taylor, Pottery Barn, Banana Republic, The Limited, Talbots, Brookstone and Williams-Sonoma. Macy's (203.964.1500) and H&M (203.357.0417) are the anchor stores. There is a 40,000 sf Barnes and Noble and more than 5 stand-alone restaurants.
Hours: Monday-Saturday 10am-9pm, Sunday 11am-6pm.

Staples (Office Furniture and Supplies)
1297 East Putnam Avenue, Old Greenwich CT, 203.698.9011
www.staples.com
Office supplies of every sort. This store also carries electronics and office furniture. They are the world's largest office supply retail store chain, with over 2,000 stores. The major competitors Office Max and Office Depot merged in 2013, and now Staples has agreed to buy Office Depot.
Hours: Weekdays 8am-9pm, Saturday 9am-9pm, Sunday 10am-6pm.

Stark Carpet Outlet (Carpet Outlet)
375 Fairfield Avenue, Stamford CT, 203.899.1771
www.starksale.com
Good selection of carpets from the famous New York Designer Source. Some wallpaper, fabric & furniture. Check their website for clearance sales.
Hours: Weekdays 9am-6pm, Saturday 10am-6pm, Sunday 11am-5pm.

Steilmann (Clothing-Women)
354 North Main Street, Port Chester NY, 914.939.1500
www.steilmann.de
This is a huge warehouse of classic European-style clothing. Steilmann is a German Company.
Hours: Open everyday 11am-6pm (Thursday usually 7pm).

Steinway Piano Gallery (Music)
501 Post Road East, Westport CT, 203.227.8222
www.steinway.com www.spgwestport.com
The Steinway Piano Gallery, owned by the Steinway & Sons company, sells, rents and finances their pianos. They have floor-patterns to help you position a piano in your home.
Hours: Weekdays 10am-6pm, Saturday 10am-5pm.

STORES

Steven Alan (Clothing-Men, Women, Children)
82 Greenwich Avenue, Greenwich CT, 203.714.8062
www.StevenAlan.com
Alan's designs are carried in over 300 stores. His Greenwich location is one of 22 Steven Alan boutiques. A store for hip consumers, his reinterpretation of the classics has been described as "edgier versions of traditional garb."
Hours: Monday-Wednesday, 10am-6pm, Thursday-Saturday 10am -7pm, Sunday 12pm-5pm.

Steven B. Fox (Jewelry)
8 Lewis Street, Greenwich CT, 203.629.3303
A full-service family-owned jewelry store specializing in precious jewels, pearls, watches, estate jewelry and objets d'art. Repairs are done on the premises. They make estate purchases.
Hours: Monday-Saturday 9am-5:30pm
(Sunday 12pm-5 pm, from Thanksgiving to Christmas).

Stickley (Furniture)
50 Tarrytown Road, White Plains NY, 914.948.6333
www.stickley.com
Stickley mission furniture and fine English reproduction furniture.
Hours: Monday-Saturday 10am-6pm (Thursday 8 pm),
Sunday 12pm-5pm.

Stuart Weitzman (Women's Shoes & Accessories)
120 Greenwich Avenue, Greenwich CT, 203.622.5036
www.StuartWeitzman.com
Weitzman's trademark is using unique materials to make beautifully-crafted, expensive shoes. His shoes, which are made in his Spanish factory, are sold in over 70 countries and through his more than 100 stores. Greenwich is proud to have him as a resident.
Hours: Monday-Saturday 10am-6pm, Sunday 12pm-5pm.

(Charles) Stuttig Locksmith (Hardware)
158 Greenwich Avenue, Greenwich CT, 203.869.6260
www.stuttiglocksmith.com
A fixture in Greenwich for many years, they provide a wide variety of locks and safes. Whether you have an emergency or just need a key copied, they can be counted on and trusted.
Hours: Weekdays 8am-3pm.

STORES

Sunglass Hut (Eyewear)
260 Greenwich Avenue, Greenwich CT, 203.629.7907
www.SunglassHut.com
Sunglass Hut International is North America's largest retailer of sunglasses. The company operates over 1,800 stores. They sell non-prescription, high-fashion sunglasses.
Hours: Monday-Saturday 10am-7pm, Sunday 11am-6pm.

Sunray Jewelers (Jewelry)
133 Mason Street, Greenwich CT, 203.861.4080
Jay and Sandra Sunray have been in Greenwich for 9 years. They will re-create jewelry, custom design jewelry, or repair jewelry or watches.
Hours: Monday, Tuesday, Thursday & Friday, 11am-5pm.

SWC Furniture Outlet (Office Furniture)
375 Fairfield Ave, Stamford CT, 203.967.8367
www.SWCoffice.com
Their 50,000 sf showroom is a great resource for new and used office furniture at good prices. To sell furniture, call 888.404.3375 (it must be less than 10 years old and in good shape)
Hours: Weekdays 8:30am-5:30pm, Saturday 10am-4:30pm.

Sweaty Betty (Clothing-Women's Activewear)
200 Greenwich Avenue, Greenwich CT, 203.717.1095
www.SweatyBetty.com
A British-based brand specializing in women's activewear (yoga, Pilates, running, exercising, etc.). There are 32 Sweaty Betty stores in the UK, as well as this one in Greenwich. The store hosts instructors for exercise classes such as yoga and cardio boxing.
Hours: Monday-Saturday 10am-6pm, Sunday 12pm-5pm.

T-Mobile (Wireless)
100 Greyrock (Stamford Mall), Stamford CT, 203.425.9600
T-Mobile is a holding company for Deutsche Telekom's various subsidiaries outside of Germany. It is the 4th largest wireless company in the US. T-Mobile is rapidly deploying Voice Over LTE (VoLTE) and HD voice.
Hours: Monday-Saturday 10am-9pm, Sunday 11am-6pm.

STORES

Tanger Outlet Center (Mall-Outlet)
I-95 Exit 65, Westbrook CT, 866.665.8685
www.TangerOutlet.com
With 65 stores, it is just barely smaller than Clinton Crossing and only one exit away. If you are in the area, you should stop by.
Hours: Monday Saturday 10am-9pm, Sunday 10am-6/8pm.

Target (Department Store)
21 Broad Street, Stamford CT, 203.388.0006
www.Target.com
This discount department store is the 6th largest retailer in the US with 1,494 stores. They are the 3rd largest seller of music in the US. Target competes with Wal-Mart and Kmart. Since its founding in 1962, it has differentiated its stores from its competitors by offering what it believes is more upscale, trend-forward merchandise at low cost.
Hours: Monday-Saturday 8am-11pm, Sunday 8am-11pm.

Theory (Clothing-Women)
396 Greenwich Avenue, Greenwich CT, 203.422.0020
www.theory.com
You can't go wrong with the high-quality clothes from Theory, known for their contemporary fashions. The simple, quiet, "uncomplicated and un-assuming" (almost nondescript) fashions are perfect for business and social attire, as well sports wear. This store has wonderful suits and blouses for women, as well as dresses, sweaters, slacks, shoes and bags. There is also a small men's section. The Greenwich store is one of 16 signature US stores.
Hours: Monday-Saturday 10am-6pm (Thursday 7pm), Sunday 12pm-5pm.

Timeless Gallery (Accessories-Women)
112 Mason Street, Greenwich CT, 203.769.1300
www.timelessgallery.com
Mint condition, pre-owned designer handbags (Birkin, Hermes, Chanel, Vuitton), jewelry and luxury watches (Rolex, Patek Phillipe, Piguet, Cartier). They also provide estate appraisals for jewelry and timepieces as well as watch repair.
Hours: Tuesday-Saturday 10am-6pm, Sunday 11am-5pm.

STORES

TJ Maxx (Department Store)
330 Connecticut Avenue, Norwalk CT, 203.854.9890
www.TJMaxx.com
The largest off-price apparel retailer in the US with over 700 stores. Merchandise is normally 20-50% below regular department store prices. In this 25,000 sf store, they sell just about everything, from clothing and footwear to bedding, furniture, jewelry and housewares.
Hours: Monday-Saturday 8am-10pm, Sunday 10am-8pm.

Threads and Treads (Sport Clothing)
17 East Putnam Avenue, Greenwich CT, 203.661.0142
www.threadsandtreads.com
A Greenwich fixture since 1979, this locally-owned store is our favorite source for biking, swimming and running attire. They have entry forms for the latest races. They sponsor the Road Hogs which conducts classes for runners, cyclers and swimmers of all ages and abilities.
Hours: Weekdays 9:30am-6pm, Saturday 9:30am-5:30pm,
Sunday 12pm-4pm.

Tiffany & Co (Jewelry, Gifts)
140 Greenwich Avenue, Greenwich CT, 203.661.7847
www.tiffany.com
This famous store has a nice collection of jewelry, silverware and giftware, as well as helpful sales people. It is one of more than 64 US stores.
Hours: Monday-Saturday 10am-6pm, Sunday 12pm-5pm.

Tory Burch (Clothing-Women)
255 Greenwich Avenue, Greenwich CT, 203.622.5023
www.ToryBurch.com
Sportswear, swimwear, shoes, bags and jewelry by a New York designer. This store is one of 15 in the US. Her style has been described as Preppy-hobo and is popular with the fans of Gossip Girl. Tory Burch has won many fashion awards.
Hours: Monday-Saturday 10am-6pm, Sunday 12pm-5pm.

Toys "R" Us & Babies "R" Us (Toys)
59 Connecticut Avenue, Norwalk CT, 203.852.6988   www.Toysrus.com
A typical mega toy store. The company currently operates 585 stores in the United States and 716 stores in 34 other countries. Its main competitors are Wal-Mart and Target. Babies "R" Us has supplies for infants and toddlers.   Hours: Weekdays 10am-9:30pm, Saturday 9am-9:30pm, Sunday 10am-8pm.

STORES

Trapp Optical
87 Greenwich Avenue, Greenwich CT, 203.552.1072
www.TrappOptical.com
High-fashion eyewear with a myriad of brands.
Hours: Weekdays 9:30am-5:30pm, Saturday 9:30am-5pm; Call for a doctor appointment.

Trovare Home (Vintage Furniture)
245 East Putnam Avenue, Cos Cob CT, 203.869.5512
www.trovareathome.com
Pamela Frisoll specializes in vintage furniture. Some of the vintage furniture is left untouched and some is modernized.
Hours: Monday-Saturday 10:30am-5pm.

Tulips Greenwich (Florist)
91 Lake Avenue (at the Lake Avenue Circle), Greenwich CT, 203.661.3154
www.tulipsofGreenwich.com
European floral design shop known for its creative and innovative bouquets of Dutch and French flowers.
Hours: Weekdays 9am-5pm, Saturday 10am-4pm.

Tumi (Luggage)
289 Greenwich Avenue, Greenwich CT, 203.861.2920   www.tumi.com
Traveling is a hassle. Why not, at least, go in style! Attractive and distinctive luggage, wallets, business cases, even some sportswear. The company is named for a Peruvian ceremonial knife used for sacrifices.
Hours: Monday-Saturday 10am-6pm, Sunday 12pm-5pm.

United House Wrecking (Home Accessories & Furniture)
535 Hope Street, Stamford CT, 203.348.5371
www.unitedhousewrecking.com
An unusual source for the unusual. 30,000 sf of inventory with everything from collectibles to antiques to architectural items to junk. Don't miss it. Hours: Monday-Saturday 9:30am-5:30pm, Sunday 12pm-5pm.

STORES

UPS Store
(For packaging/shipping see SERVICES, Delivery Services.)
15 East Putnam Avenue, Greenwich CT, 203.622.1114
http://greenwich-ct-0822.theupsstorelocal.com/about-our-store
1117 East Putnam Avenue, Riverside CT, 203.698.0141
http://riverside-ct-1217.theupsstorelocal.com/
Besides their shipping and mailbox services they carry some office and
mailing supplies.   Hours: Weekdays 8am-6pm, Saturday 11am-2pm.

Utopia (Skateboards)
150 Connecticut Avenue, Norwalk CT, 203.838.8782
www.10topiact.com
One of the largest skateboard shops in the area.
Hours: Monday-Saturday 10am-8pm, Sunday 12pm-6pm.

Vallin Galleries (Asian Antiques)
516 Danbury Road (Route 7), Wilton CT, 203.762.7441
www.vallinGalleries.com
Located far from the source of these antiques is a quaint saltbox filled
with a collection of Asian art, some rare, all beautifully displayed.
Hours: Call to make an appointment.

Verizon (Wireless)
• 315 Greenwich Avenue, Greenwich CT, 203.340.9046
• Wireless One, 1269 East Putnam, Riverside CT, 203.637.5441
www.verizonwireless.com , www.yourWirelessInc.com
Verizon has 88 million subscribers and is the largest US network. The
company is a joint venture of Verizon Communications and Vodafone
Group. They can provide GSM/CDMA dual-mode phones. Verizon has been
criticized for making transfers of MP3s and ring tones difficult and re-
stricting EV-DO use. Don't expect customer service to be the highest priority at the Greenwich Avenue Store.
Greenwich Ave Hours: Monday-Saturday 10am-7pm, Sunday 11am-5pm.
Riverside Hours: Monday-Saturday 10am-8am, Sunday 11am-5pm.

STORES

Walmart (Department Store)
680 Connecticut Avenue, Norwalk CT, 203.854.5236
www.Walmart.com
Founded in 1962, it is the largest retailer in the world. They are also the largest grocery retailer and the largest toy retailer in the US with an estimated 22% of the toy business. With the demise of Circuit City, they are hoping to also become the largest retailer of electronics. Walmart has been attempting to upgrade its merchandise to compete with Target.
Hours: Everyday 7am-10pm.

Walpole Woodworkers (Outdoor Furniture)
1835 Post Road East, Westport CT, 203.255.9010
www.walpolewoodworkers.com
Outdoor furniture, some play sets, bridges, gazebos and more.
Hours: Monday-Saturday 8:30am-5pm, Sunday 10am-5pm.

(The) Westchester Mall (Mall)
125 Westchester White Plains NY, 914.683.8600
www.simon.com/mall/the-westchester/stores
An even larger mall than the Stamford Town Center boasting over 150 fine upscale stores including: Crate & Barrel, Pottery Barn Kids, Louis Vuitton, Gucci, Apple, Brooks Brothers, Tumi, Sony Style and P.F. Chang's China Bistro. Neiman Marcus (914.428.2000) and Nordstrom (914.946.1122) are the anchor stores.
Hours: Monday-Saturday 10am-9pm, Sunday 11am-6pm
(store hours may vary).

Whole Body @ Whole Foods (Cosmetics, Vitamins and More)
90 East Putnam Avenue, Greenwich CT, 203.661.0631
www.wholefoodsmarket.com/stores/greenwich
Products to promote health and wellness, such as: vitamins, herbal teas, cosmetics, hair care and homeopathic remedies.
Hours: Open daily 7am-10 pm.

Williams-Sonoma (Cookware)
• 100 Greyrock Place (Town Center), Stamford CT, 203.961.0977
• 125 Westchester Avenue (Westchester Mall), White Plains NY, 914.644.8360
www.Williams-Sonoma.com
Speciality cookware and housewares as well as a variety of gourmet foods that are difficult to find elsewhere. They teach cooking classes as well. Hours: Monday-Saturday 10am-9pm, Sunday 11am-6pm.

Viggi (Jewelry)

40 Greenwich Avenue, Greenwich CT, 203.622.2900
www.JewelsByViggi.com
Named for Danny Arbusman's wife, Viggi, this store specializes in diamonds from 3 to 20 carats. Hours: Monday-Saturday 10am-5pm.

Vilebrequin (Swimwear-Men & Boys)

200 Greenwich Avenue, Greenwich CT, 203.869.6989
www.vilebrequin.com
One of about 15 US stores, this Saint-Tropez based company has over 100 stores worldwide. They specialize in colorful, matching Father and Son swimwear and have been called the "Hermes ties of beachwear" A great item is their waterproof wallet. You may have to go to Youtube to see how to pronounce their name.
Hours: Monday-Saturday 10am-6pm, Sunday 12pm-5pm.

Village Ewe (Needlepoint)

244 Sound Beach Avenue, Old Greenwich CT, 203.637.3953
www.thevillageewe.com
Beware of stopping here unless you are ready to get hooked on needlepoint. Individual lessons for beginners can be arranged. Group classes are offered in the fall and spring. They are a full-service needlepoint studio with over 1,500 hand-painted canvases.
Hours: Tuesday-Friday 10am-5pm, Saturday 10am-4pm.

Vince (Clothing-Men & Women)

161 Greenwich Avenue, Greenwich CT, 203.742.5858 www.vince.com
One of about 20 stores. They have comfortable, casual, contemporary clothing for the 40-something crowd. Vince's CEO is Jill Granoff, a Greenwich resident. Hours: Monday-Saturday 10am-6pm, Sunday 12pm-5pm.

Vinci's Home Products (Miele Showroom)

37 East Elm Street, Greenwich CT, 203.869.1114
www.vincishomeproducts.com
An exclusive dealer of Miele products including vacuum cleaners, dishwashers, laundry systems, ovens, cooktops and wine coolers.
Hours: Weekdays 10am-6pm (Thursday 7pm), Saturday 10am-5pm.

STORES

Vineyard Vines (Clothing-Men, Women, Children)
145 Greenwich Avenue, Greenwich CT, 203.661.1803
www.VineyardVinesByRichards.com   www.VineyardVines.com
Greenwich residents are proud of this 5,000 square foot shop filled with colorful, informal, delightful clothing. Shep and Ian Murray of Greenwich began their company a few years ago by creating unique ties-worn by presidents, celebrities and many Greenwichites. You will love this shop.
Hours: Monday-Saturday 10am-6pm (Thursday 7 pm),
Sunday 11am-5pm.

Vision Consultants (Eyewear)
79 East Putnam Avenue, Greenwich CT, 203.661.7711
Stylish frames in a convenient location. A nice choice of prescription ski and diving goggles.
Store Hours: Tuesday-Friday 10am-6pm, Saturday 10am-4pm.
Call for the optometrist's hours.

Waterworks (Bath & Kitchen Fixtures)
23 West Putnam Avenue, Greenwich CT, 203.869.7766
www.waterworks.com
High-end bathroom and kitchen fixtures as well as a very nice selection of tiles. Excellent customer service.
Hours: Weekdays 9am-5pm, Saturday 10am-4pm.

Weber Fine Art (Art)
24 West Putnam Avenue, Greenwich CT, 203.422.5375
www.weberfineart.com
Modern post-war and contemporary art. Prices range from about $15,000 to $50,000
Hours: Tuesday-Saturday 11am-5pm (usually closed in August).

Whimsies Dollhouse & Miniature Shop (Toys)
39 Lewis Street (entrance on Liberty Way), Greenwich CT, 203.629.8024
www.whimsiesdollhouseshop.com
The ultimate dollhouse store.
Hours: Tuesday-Saturday 10am-5pm.

STORES

Wishlist (Clothing-Youth)
350 Greenwich Avenue, Greenwich CT, 203.629.4600
www.ShopWishList.com
Stylish clothing, nicely displayed, for sophisticated teens and pre-teens.
Hours: Monday-Saturday 10am-6pm, Sunday 12pm-5pm.

Woodbury Commons (Mall, Outlet)
498 Red Apple Court, Central Valley (@Harriman) NY, 845.928.4000
www.premiumoutlets.com
A huge outlet location with over 220 stores, occupying more than 800,000 sq. ft. It is one of the largest outlet centers in the world. Definitely worth the 60-minute drive. If you go to the website first and sign up for a coupon book, it can really pay off. It is part of the Simon Property Group, the largest real estate company in the US.
Hours: Everyday 10am-9pm.

(A) Woodhouse & Son (Antique Silver & Jewelry)
7 West Putnam Avenue, Greenwich CT, 203.422.2500
www.awoodhouse.com
Founded in 1690 in London, this shop specializes in antique jewelry and sterling silver items such as: tea sets, candlesticks and serving pieces.
Hours: Tuesday-Saturday 10am-5pm.

Yogasmoga (Yoga Clothing-Men & Women)
68 Greenwich Avenue, Greenwich CT, 203.861.9642
www.yogasmoga.com
Yogasmoga is a New York-based manufacturer of high-quality yoga wear made in the US. They pride themselves on having fabrics that have superior wicking and are made with Eco-friendly colors that won't bleed. This is their first retail store. It is located in a two floor building; the top floor is a communal area. They are promoting the fashion trend that yoga garments are the new casual.
Hours: Monday-Saturday 10am-6pm, Sunday 11am-6pm.

STORES

ZARA (Clothing-Women, Children to size 13)
221-225 Greenwich Avenue, Greenwich CT, 203.861.7411
www.Zara.com
Zara, the flagship chain store of Inditex Group owned by Spanish tycoon Amancio Ortega, launches around 10,000 new designs each year. The company has 200 designers and can turn out a new design and have it in the stores within 5 weeks, from start to finish. If a design doesn't sell well within a week, it is withdrawn from shops. They have a zero advertising policy, a very liberal return policy and over 1,500 stores worldwide. New designs usually arrive Monday and Thursday.
Hours: Monday-Saturday 10am-7pm, Sunday 11am-6pm.

Zorya Fine Art (Art)
38 East Putnam Avenue, Greenwich CT, 203.869.9898
www.ZoryaFineArt.com
Emerging and established Ukrainian artists. Price range $3,000-$100,000.
Hours: Tuesday-Saturday 11am-7pm.

Zyns News (Magazines & Newspapers)
345 Greenwich Avenue, Greenwich CT, 203.661.5168
This store has the largest selection of magazines and newspapers in Fairfield County. For many years, Greenwich residents have loved finding all of their favorite publications here.
Hours: Monday-Saturday 6am-8pm, Sunday 6am-6pm.

TIP: COMMUNITY CALENDARS
- Community Events Calendar
    If you want to know the coming Town events, you will love the Community Answers "Planning Ahead Community Calendar." Call Community Answers, 203.622.7979 and ask to be on their list or check out their calendar www.greenwichlibrary.org/commanswers.htm Click on Events Calendar.
- Event Calendar
    Greenwich Magazine publishes an event Calendar for Fairfield County. It can be found on-line at
    www.greenwichmag.com/g/Countywide-Calendar
- Town Committee Meeting Calendar
    The Town committee and department calendar can be found at www.greenwichct.org/calendar

TEENS and YOUNG ADULTS

See also the sections CHILDREN and CHILD ENRICHMENT.
See also FITNESS & SPORTS for year-around activities.

Arch Street Teen Center

100 Arch Street, Greenwich CT, 203.629.5744   www.ArchStreet.org
Founded in 1993, Arch Street (also known as the Greenwich Teen Center, Inc.) is a refurbished warehouse right on the harbor. Whether at the dance floor and bandstand or the upstairs snack shop with booths, Arch Street gives teens the opportunity to be together in a healthy environment. Arch Street is more than a place to hang out; the Center provides everything from college application advice and counseling help, to opportunities for teens to participate in community service projects or to learn leadership skills. Although there is an adult board, the teens run Arch Street through the teen board. The board has sixty members, from 9th to 12th grades, and has representatives from private and public schools. Arch Street is open to Greenwich students from 7th through 12th grade.

Babysitting Training

Red Cross, 99 Indian Field Road, Greenwich CT, 203.869.8444.
www.redcross.org/ct/greenwich
The Red Cross sponsors a comprehensive all-day babysitting course which is open to 11-15 year olds and offered 2 to 3 times a month. Call 1-800-Red-Cross for details on when courses are offered in Greenwich.

Boys and Girls Club

4 Horseneck Lane, Greenwich CT, 203.869.3224   www.bgcg.org
This club is awesome. The totally-renovated facility has a gymnasium, game room, library, swimming pool, and skating rink used for ice skating in winter, and roller skating/street hockey or basketball during other seasons. Members must be Greenwich residents or have a parent working in town. Transportation by bus or van is provided to and from several areas around town including Central and Western Middle Schools. The Club also has a 77-acre preserve, Camp Simmons, for summer teen activities.

Boy Scouts

63 Mason Street, Greenwich CT, 203.869.8424
www.GreenwichScouting.org
Cub Scouts are boys 1st grade through 5th grade. Boy Scouts are for boys in 6th grade until their 17th birthday. Venturing and Exploring are co-ed programs for high school students, ages 14-20.

TEENS and YOUNG ADULTS

Department of Parks and Recreation
www.greenwichct.org/ParksAndRec/ParksandRec.asp
The Department has a great many athletic programs for teens. For instance, the Skate Park described in PARKS is a good place for teens to meet. *Also see all of the sports activities in FITNESS AND SPORTS.*

Girl Scouts
203.762.5557, 800.882.5561   www.greenwichgirlscouts.com
They offer a broad range of activities for girls. Greenwich is part of the Girl Scouts of Connecticut www.gsofct.org. Girl Scouts has programs for girls in grades K through 12.

Greenwich Student Employment Service
203.625.8008   www.ghs-ses.org
GHS Student Employment Service helps employers who want to fill jobs find students looking for work. Jobs are not restricted to high school students. Graduates are also using the service.
Hours: Office is open School days 11:45pm-2pm.

Greenwich Teen Connections
The United Way has developed a 40-page resource directory for teenagers in the Greenwich community. It contains information and contact numbers of teen services offered in the area.
www.unitedway-greenwich.com/greenwich-teen-connections

YMCA Teen Programs
YMCA, 50 East Putnam Avenue, Greenwich CT, 203.869.1630
www.gwymca.org
In addition to the Y's many traditional programs they offer a number of programs for teens.
See FITNESS & SPORTS for more information on the Y.

YWCA Teen Programs
259 East Putnam Avenue, Greenwich CT, 203.869.6501 x 225
www.ywcagreenwich.org
In addition to the Y's many traditional programs they offer a number of programs for teens.
See FITNESS & SPORTS for more information on the Y.

THRIFT SHOPS

Proceeds from these shops, which are often run by volunteers, go to helping others. Thrift Shops are "win-win" for everyone! Donating your unwanted possessions to thrift shops is a practical way to help our neighbors in need.

See STORES for Consignment Shops.
See BOOKS for Book donations.
See SERVICES for Computer and Cell Phone donations.

Act II Consignment Shop (Clothing)

48 Maple Avenue, Greenwich CT, 203.869.6359
In a lovely old stone house behind the Second Congregational Church there are five rooms of gently worn women's, men's and children's clothing. Also bric-a-brac and small household items.
Store Hours: Wednesday 10am-2pm, Thursday 10am-1pm.
Consignment Hours: Wednesday 12pm-3pm, Thursday 10am-1pm.
Closed June through September.

Goodwill Industries of Western CT (Clothing, Home)

Greenwich Recycling Center, Holly Hill Lane, Greenwich CT, 203.661.5520
www.goodwillwct.com
A large trailer with a friendly person ready to receive your donations is conveniently parked just inside our town "dump." Goodwill needs clothing, shoes, toys, tools, kitchenware, linens and small appliances in "saleable" condition. This is recycling in the true sense of the word.
Hours: Every day 7am-3pm, Saturday 7am-12pm.

Greenwich Hospital Auxiliary Thrift Shop (Clothing, Furniture)

199 Hamilton Avenue, Greenwich CT, 203.869.6124
This thrift shop is an experience in itself. You are unlikely to find a nicer thrift shop anywhere. Large furniture items plus clothing and books are welcome here. Our finds: an old steamer trunk and a lovely white Laura Ashley graduation dress for $45! One of our friends found a chesterfield coat! A holiday sale had so many people, the customers were waiting in line to get inside for embroidered sweaters and evening gowns.
Shopping Hours: Monday-Saturday 9am-4:30pm.
Donation Hours: Monday-Saturday 9am-2pm.

THRIFT SHOPS

Laurel House Thrift Shop (Clothing, Furniture)
501 Summer Street, Stamford CT, 203.327.7334
http://www.treasurehuntersthriftstore.com/
They will pick up items or you can drop them off.
Proceeds from their sales help educate, house and clothe people with mental illness.   Hours: Every day 10am-4pm, Saturday 10am-3pm.

Rummage Room (Clothing)
191 Sound Beach Avenue, Old Greenwich CT, 203.637.1875
Notice the artistic window displays of this gem of a shop manned by cheerful volunteers. The shop is filled with clothing for young and old and interesting bric-a-brac.
Shop Hours: weekdays 10am-5pm, Saturdays 10am-1pm.
Donation Hours: Monday-Thursday 9am-4:30pm, Friday & Saturday 9:30am-1pm. Closed in August.

Salvation Army (Clothing, Furniture)
Truck pickup: 800.958.7825
www.salvationarmy.com
A marvelous service is available for picking up furniture for donation. Every time we have called, a courteous, strong man has arrived promptly to take items destined to help people serviced by this most worthy organization. 2 to 4 days' notice is appreciated for pickups. A bin for donations (clothing only) is located inside our Recycling Center on Holly Hill Lane.   Dispatcher Hours: Monday-Saturday, 7 am-3 pm.

Neighbor to Neighbor (Clothing, Food)
Christ Church Annex, 248 East Putnam Avenue, Greenwich CT, 203.622.9208
http://www.ntngreenwich.org/
This volunteer organization is greatly respected and appreciated in our Greenwich community. They have helped many people in a sensitive way. Donations of food, warm coats and clothing (in good condition) are always needed. The shop is restricted to people identified by our social service agencies as "in need" and the selections made in the nicely-organized shop are free.   Hours: Everyday 8:30am-2pm.

TRAVEL

For Car and Truck Rentals see AUTOMOBILES.
For Hotels and Inns worth a trip see HOTELS AND INNS.
For an International Driver's License see AUTOMOBILES.
For Commuting information see AUTOMOBILES.
For Parking see AUTOMOBILES; for Permits at the Greenwich Station go
to http://www.greenwichct.org/Parking/psParkingPermits.asp

Sections
- Airports
- Flight Delay Information
- Airport Parking
- Airport and Local Transportation
- Passports
- Passport Photos
- Travel Agencies
- Public Transportation (Bus & Train)
- Private Jets

AIRPORTS

Kennedy Airport (JFK)
Queens NY, 718.244.4444
www.panynj.gov

La Guardia Airport (LGA)
Queens NY, 718.533.3400
www.panynj.gov

Newark Airport (EWR)
Newark, NJ, 973.961.6000
www.panynj.gov
Of the major New York City airports, Newark in New Jersey takes the longest to get to (80 minutes). Newark Airport is somewhat less congested than the other two. In addition, flights out of Newark are sometimes less expensive, especially for United Airlines, who uses it as a hub.

Westchester County Airport (HPN)

240 Airport Road, White Plains NY, 914.995.4860

www.co.westchester.ny.us/airport

This airport is located on upper King Street. It has good parking facilities. Commercial flights are limited and somewhat more expensive than those from the major NYC airports, but nothing could be easier or more convenient. Some of the airlines that fly out of Westchester are American Airlines, Cape Air, Delta, Jet Blue, United (Chicago), & US Airways. Directions: Glenville Road to King Street; R on King; L at light to Rye Lake Rd.

AIRPORT FLIGHT DELAY INFORMATION

FAA Flight Delay Information

www.fly.faa.gov/flyfaa/usmap.jsp

A good source of independent information for airports around the country. Even if NY airports are clear, if the hub of the airline you are using is experiencing delays, your flight is likely to be delayed.

USA Today

www.usatoday.com/travel/flights/front.htm

This site provides real-time flight information.

AIRPORT PARKING

Parking long-term or overnight at short-term airport parking lots is not recommended for new or late model cars. To be sure, use a private lot. The cost seems to be about the same, the service better and your car is safe.

The Parking Spot (formerly Avistar)

LGA: 90-01 23rd Avenue, East Elmhurst NY, 718.507.8162

JFK: 130-24 South Conduit Avenue, Jamaica NY, 718.322.2221

EWR: 176-192 McClellan street, Newark NJ, 973.242.2100

www.TheParkingSpot.com

The Parking Spot operates valet off-airport parking for Kennedy, La Guardia and Newark. A secure parking lot with quick transportation to and from your airline. Their website has good instructions to each of their airport locations. You must make a reservation in advance.

AIRPORT AND LOCAL TRANSPORTATION

CT Limousine Shuttle Service
800.472.5466   www.CTlimo.com
Shared transportation to La Guardia & Kennedy. Pick up is just about every hour at the Greenwich Hyatt.

Greenwich Dark House (Vacant House Management)
Tim Hilderbrand (Greenwich Police Sergeant), 203.561.1661
www.GreenwichDarkHouse.com
Ten to twelve off duty police officers will watch over your home while you are away, make visits to pick up mail, turn on lights, move cars in the driveway and make your home appear occupied. They also provide transportation to airports and the city.

Greenwich Off-Duty Police
A Greenwich off-duty policeman will drive you to any of the NY-area airports and pick you up in your own car. This is often less expensive than a limousine service. To hire an off-duty officer, call 203.622.8016 or call the main number 203.622.8000 and select the extension.

Greenwich Taxi
At Greenwich RR Station, 203.869.6000   www.GreenwichTaxi.com
An old stand-by for getting around town or to the train station. Call ahead and make a reservation to be picked up. This is a good way to get to Westchester and NY airports. Their website has rates for just about any trip. More companies should do this.

Leros Point to Point Connecticut (Limo Service)
6 Skyline Drive, Hawthorne NY, 203.329.1301, 800.365.3767
www.leroslimo.com
They provide travel to and from US and international airports. Leros has over 500 national and international locations. They could be your best bet when traveling abroad.

Red Dot Airport Shuttle
800.673.3368   www.rideTheDot.com
Shared transportation to and from Kennedy and La Guardia airports from the Hyatt Regency in Greenwich. Their website has times and fares.

Rudy's Limousine Service

203.609.8000, Curbside Pickup 866.678.3700   www.RudyLimo.com
A comfortable, reliable service. When several people travel together, this is a good choice. Their drivers are very professional and pleasant.
Hours: 24 hours a day every day.

Uber Taxi

www.Uber.com
Uber is a Google and Goldman Sachs funded venture. Uber relies on a network of independent drivers who use their own unmarked vehicles. No need to tip. Flat rates apply to direct trips between specified locations. Request a ride and pay via your mobile phone. Uber uses your phone's GPS to detect your location and connect you with the nearest available driver. So you can be picked up just about anywhere even if you don't know your exact address.

PASSPORTS

Passport Information

Automated Appointment Number: 877.487.2778
www.Travel.state.gov
You can use this site to download renewal forms (DS-82).

Connecticut Passport Agency

850 Canal Street, Stamford CT, 877.487.2778
http://www.uspassporthelpguide.com/connecticut-passport-agency
The Connecticut Passport Agency is a US State Department location which serves only customers who are traveling within 2 weeks (14 days), or who need foreign visas for travel. An appointment is required.
Hours: Every day 9am-4pm, excluding Federal holidays.

Ferguson Library

One Public Library Plaza, Bedford & Broad, Stamford CT, 203.964.1000
www.fergusonlibrary.org
You can apply for a passport but they can no longer renew adult passports. Hours: Monday-Thursday & Saturday 10am-5pm, Friday 10am-6pm; Sunday 1pm-5pm.

Passport Renewals

You can apply for a passport renewal through the Greenwich Post Office; the wait time may be as long as 6 weeks.

TRAVEL

Travel Immunizations
The Department of Infectious Diseases at Greenwich Hospital offers many types of immunizations required for foreign travel to less-developed countries. Call 203.863.3270 for an appointment between 8am & 4pm. It is best to schedule an immunization, at least, 6 weeks before your departure.

PASSPORT PHOTOS
Many places will take your picture for a passport or visa, but if you want a good picture properly sized, consider using one of the following. *See their reviews in PHOTOGRAPHY.*

Action Arts Photography
242 Sound Beach Ave, Old Greenwich CT, 203.637.2685

Glenville Photo and Image Center
25 Glen Ridge Road (next to Stop and Shop), Greenwich CT, 203.532.1211

Images
202 Sound Beach Avenue, Old Greenwich CT, 203.637.4193

TRAVEL AGENCIES

Liberty Travel
2367 Summer Street, Stamford CT, 203.357.1300
www.libertytravel.com
Liberty is a large operation with over 189 stores; they have big buying power for packages in the Caribbean and Florida. They are a good place to go to get a cruise or packaged tour.

Valerie Wilson Travel
1455 East Putnam Avenue, Old Greenwich, 203.637.5436
www.vwti.com
With 14 locations, Valerie Wilson Travel is large enough to get you good rates and small enough to give you good service.
Hours: weekdays 9 am-5 pm.

TRAVEL

PUBLIC TRANSPORTATION (BUS AND RAIL)
See SENIORS for free Transportation Sources.
For more Commuting information see AUTOMOBILES.

Connecticut Transit (CTtransit)
203.327.7433
www.cttransit.com
CT Transit provides frequent bus service from Greenwich and Old Greenwich to Port Chester, Stamford and Norwalk. They also operate one route in Greenwich.
• I-Bus is an express connecting Greenwich and White Plains RR stations.

Greenwich Commuter Connection
800.982.8420
www.NorwalkTransit.com
Norwalk Transit provides commuter bus routes linking the Greenwich Railroad station and the central business district. Service is during the morning and late afternoon rush hours.

Amtrak (National Railroad Passenger Service)
800.872.7245
www.amtrak.com
Operates from Stamford Station and connects to cities throughout the US and Canada.

Metro-North Commuter Railroad
www.MTA.info/mnr
Offers frequent service to Grand Central Station, New York City, on weekdays. Check the schedule for weekend and holiday times. Greenwich has four stations.
• Cos Cob Station, Sound Shore Drive, off Exit 4 of I-95
• Greenwich Station, Railroad Ave, off Exit 3 of I-95
• Old Greenwich Station, Sound Beach Ave, off Exit 5 of I-95
• Riverside Station, Between exits 4 & 5 off I-95

TRAVEL

PRIVATE JETS

Net Jets

38 Loop Road, Westchester County Airport, White Plains NY, 914.287.6760
www.NetJets.com, 877.356.5823
If you are thinking how convenient it would be to have your own private jet, this is the company to use. It's a Berkshire Hathaway company that provides charter services, maintenance and fractional ownership. You can purchase 25 and 50-hour jet cards in the aircraft of your choice or have as little as a 1/16 fractional interest.

TIP: TOUR GREENWICH HOMES

Each year in December, Antiquarius (The Greenwich Historical Society, www.hstg.org) organizes a fabulous tour of some of Greenwich's most beautiful homes. The annual fundraiser costs about $100. You can also buy a ticket for lunch, held at one of the Country Clubs. Call 203.869.6899 for details.

Fairway Wine Shop (Wine & Beer)
699 Canal Street, Stamford CT, 203.388.1292
www.FairwayWines.com/stamford
Next door to the huge grocery is a wine store with over 2,500 wines and 100 brands of beer. Their staff know the wines and are helpful if you need advice. *See Fairway Grocery review in GROCERY AND SPECIALTY FOOD STORES.*
Hours: Monday-Saturday 9am-9pm, Sunday 10am-5pm.

Greenwich Wine Society (Wine)
Greenwich CT, 203.629.1261   www.GreenwichWineSociety.com
They taste wine, visit wineries and meet monthly for tastings at a local restaurant. There are no age parameters. Married couples as well as singles are welcome.

Horseneck Liquors (Wine)
25 East Putnam Avenue, Greenwich CT, 203.869.8944
www.horseneckwinesandliquors.com
Established in 1934, this shop was purchased by Terry Rogers in 1989. Always known as the premier wine store in Greenwich, Terry has continued to make it a favorite destination for wine lovers. Horseneck has a large inventory of Bordeaux, Burgundy and Italian wines, plus an excellent selection of wines from California and all over the world. You can count on their friendly, good advice. They will deliver and, if needed, gift wrap for you. Terry supports a multitude of charitable events.
Hours: Monday -Saturday 9am-7pm, Sunday 12pm-5pm.

Le Wine Shop (Wine)
39 East Elm Street, Greenwich CT, 203.869.6008
www.leWineShop.com
A small shop, run by Etienne Touzot, with a good selection of well-priced wines. Hours: Monday -Saturday 10am-7pm.

Var Max Liquor Pantry (Wine)
16 Putnam Avenue, Port Chester NY, 914.937.4930   www.VarMax.com
A large store with a great variety of wines. Nice descriptions of their wines make browsing easy. The knowledgeable staff is always ready to help. Buy a green bag and get a discount every time.
Hours: Monday -Thursday 9am -9pm, Friday -Saturday 9am -10pm, Sunday 12pm -6pm.

Connecticut Vineyards

There are 28 vineyards in two viticultural areas: Southeastern New England and the Western CT Highlands. If you want to tour the vineyards, try the CT Wine Trail, but more than 3 wineries a day may be a stretch. The trail starts in Litchfield. To learn more about CT wineries, CT vineyards and the CT Wine Trail, contact the CT Winery Association 860.2166439 or www.CTwine.com

Favorite CT wineries:

Many of the vineyards, like Sharp Hill and Chamard, have good restaurants. Vineyards are also popular wedding spots. The hours for tastings and meals vary with the season, so always check first and reserve before going. Be sure to check on prices for tastings.

Chamard Vineyards

115 Cow Hill Road, Clinton CT, 860.664.0299
www.chamard.com
Try their bistro and Wine Bar. Their French-American meals get rave reviews.

Hopkins Vineyard

25 Hopkins Road, New Preston CT, 860.868.7954
www.HopkinsVineyard.com
CT Magazine's tasting competition winner -Westwind (white).

Priam Vineyards

11 Shailor Hill Road, Colchester CT, 860.267.8520
www.PriamVineyards.com
CT Magazine's tasting competition winners -Late Harvest Riesling, Late Harvest Gewurztraminer.

Saltwater Farm Vineyard

349 Elm Street, Stonington CT, 860.415.9072
www.SaltWaterFarmVineyard.com
CT Magazine's tasting competition winners -Estate Chardonnay and Estate Cabernet Franc.

WINE

Sharpe Hill Vineyards
108 Wade Road, Pomfret CT, 860.974.3549
www.SharpeHill.com
CT Magazine's tasting competition winners -Reserve Chardonnay, Ballet of Angels (white), Angelica Rose and Dry Summer Rose, Select Late Harvest (white).

Stonington Vineyards
523 Taugwonk Road, Stonington CT, 860.535.1222
www.StoningtonVineyards.com
CT Magazine's tasting competition winner -Cabernet Franc.

TIP: HOW TO PRICE YOUR GREENWICH HOME
How much your home is worth is determined not by Realtors, but by supply and demand at the time you list. Buyers are comparison shoppers. They look at what has sold and what is for sale. Then they decide value. It is the job of your Realtor to educate you about the local real estate market and how your home fits into it. It is your job to set an informed price for your home.

When you list your home it will be competing with similar homes on the market—as well as those that have recently sold. Your Realtor should provide you with a complete analysis of the real estate market, the sales in your neighborhood and comparable homes presently for sale. You should consider driving by these homes and let your Realtor explain how they compare, and why they sold or were priced the way they were. Don't confuse pricing your property with choosing your Realtor. Choose the Realtor you like and trust first. Then work with them to price your home.

INDEX

INDEX

INDEX

INDEX

INDEX

INDEX

INDEX

INDEX

INDEX

INDEX

INDEX

INDEX

INDEX

INDEX

INDEX

INDEX

600

INDEX

INDEX

INDEX

INDEX

INDEX

INDEX

INDEX

INDEX

INDEX

INDEX

INDEX

INDEX